Grounded Phonology

Current Studies in Linguistics
Samuel Jay Keyser, general editor

Grounded Phonology

Diana Archangeli and
Douglas Pulleyblank

The MIT Press
Cambridge, Massachusetts
London, England

This book was set in Times Roman by Asco Trade Typesetting Ltd., Hong Kong and was printed and bound in the United States of America.

Library of Congress Cataloging-in-Publication Data

Archangeli, Diana B.
   Grounded phonology / Diana Archangeli and Douglas Pulleyblank.
      p.   cm.—(Current studies in linguistics; 25)
   Includes bibliographical references and index.
   ISBN 0-262-01137-9
      1. Grammar, Comparative and general—Phonology. I. Pulleyblank, Douglas George.
II. Title. III. Series: Current studies in linguistics series; 25.
P217.A78   1994
414—dc20   93-8873
                                                                              CIP

to Anne-Marie and Dante

Contents

Acknowledgments

Ten years of dreams in the forest!
Now on the lake's edge laughing,
Laughing a new laugh.
Isshū Miura and Ruth Fuller Sasaki, *The Zen Koan*

This book began as a short paper on Tiv ablaut in 1983. By 1986, the paper had grown into a book manuscript, *The Content and Structure of Phonological Representations*, Tiv ablaut having at some point slipped through the cracks. In the seven years since then, the book has evolved to the extent that its relation to earlier incarnations seems more historical than conceptual—with the optimal analysis of Tiv ablaut yet to be revealed.

During the decade-long process, the ideas that we explored were shaped and buffeted by colleagues and friends. Among the most persistent of these are Mike Hammond and Larry Hyman, colleagues and friends to both of us. Others whose advice, curiosity, challenges, and enthusiasm were influential are given below (we apologize to those we have inadvertently omitted here, notably to K. P. Mohanan, with whom we have had many long and extremely stimulating discussions): Akinbiyi Akinlabi, Jean Ann, Nick Clements, Jennifer Cole, Megan Crowhurst, Chip Gerfen, Morris Halle, S.-H. Hong, Michel Jackson, John Jensen, Darlene LaCharité, John McCarthy, Ian MacKay, Diane Meador, N. M. Mutaka, James Myers, Moussa Ndiaye, Long Peng, Edwin G. Pulleyblank, Debbie Schlindwein Schmidt, Pat Shaw, Paul Smolensky, Cari Spring, Donca Steriade, Margaret Stong-Jensen, Moira Yip.

We particularly want to thank the linguistics communities in and around the University of Arizona, the University of Southern California, the University of Ottawa, the University of British Columbia, the 1989 LSA Summer Institute, and the 1990 and 1992 Girona International Summer Schools in Linguistics, as well as numerous others who have given us feedback at various conferences and talks where we have presented portions of this work: Steve Anderson, Andy Barss, David Basilico, Mary

Beckman, Janet Benger, Nicola Bessell, Janet Bing, Juliette Blevins, Eulàlia Bonet, Mike Broe, Mike Cahill, Guy Carden, Prathima Christdas, John Coleman, Ewa Czaykowska-Higgins, Robert Davis, Dick Demers, Seipati Dichabe, Osamu Fujimura, Kazuhiko Fukushima, John Goldsmith, Bruce Hayes, Andrea Heiberg, Peter Hendriks, José Hualde, Marie Huffman, Harry van der Hulst, Masahide Ishihara, Junko Itô, Ping Jiang-King, Omar Ka, Pat Keating, Michael Kenstowicz, Paul Kiparsky, Phil LeSourd, Marcy Macken, Fernando Martínez-Gil, Joan Mascaró, Janice Melville, Armin Mester, Tara Mohanan, Shaun O'Connor, Richard T. Oehrle, Diane Ohala, Nikẹ Ọla, Blanca Palmada, Carole Paradis, Pat Pérez, David Perlmutter, Janet Pierrehumbert, Glyne Piggott, Pilar Prieto, Alan Prince, Jean-François Prunet, Curt Rice, Keren Rice, Anne Rochette, Sharon Rose, Linda Rousos, Kofi Saah, Betsy Sagey, Sanford Schane, Jim Scobbie, Pep Serra, Mark Steedman, Susan Steele, Joseph Stemberger, C.-K. Suh, Bernard Tranel, Jane Tsay, Akihiko Uechi, Robert Vago, Jeroen van de Weijer, Wendy Wiswall.

Research on this book has been funded in part by the following organizations: For Diana Archangeli, the Social and Behavioral Sciences Research Institute, the Program in Cognitive Science, the Department of Linguistics, and the Provost' s Author Support Fund at the University of Arizona; National Endowment for the Humanities Summer Stipend FT-27533; and National Science Foundation grant no: BNS-9023323. For Douglas Pulleyblank, Faculty Research and Innovation Fund, University of Southern California; Sumitomo Electric; Research Grant, University of Ottawa; UBC Research Development Fund; Social Sciences and Humanities Research Council of Canada grant no: 410-91-0204.

We take this opportunity to note that the authors' names appear in this book in alphabetical order for reasons of convention; otherwise, we would have determined the order by chance.

On behalf of our readers, we thank Anne Mark for her copyediting magic and Chip Gerfen for creating the index.

For their support (sometimes bewildered but always enthusiastic) we thank Arlene Zastera Bennett, Robert Bowen Bennett, Frank Brown Bennett, Dorothy Frickelton Pulleyblank, and Robert Willoughby Pulleyblank. And we sincerely appreciate the opportunity to restore Doug's reason provided somewhere each summer (and now more frequently) by Robyn, John, Bryna, Jonas, and Nathan McKay.

Throughout the writing of this book, we have depended, individually and jointly, on the support of Dante Archangeli and Anne-Marie Comte. Their belief that one day a book would materialize has turned out to be more than just fevered optimism. We thank them for patience, for encouragement, and for the occasional reminder that finished manuscripts are nice too. Special thanks go to Catherine, Ingrid, and Victor: to Victor for sharing his room, to Ingrid for sharing CorelDraw, to Catherine for sharing her skis and her skates—and to all of them for checking for an email connection before using the phone.

Finally, we express our appreciation for Joshua Tree, Yosemite, the Chiricahuas, La Gatineau, Rideau Canal, Agua Caliente, Cheakamus Lake. If we have learned anything, it is that when inspiration, energy, or spirit fails, take a hike.

Grounded Phonology

Chapter 1
A Modular Phonological Theory

Human language is an intricate crystal defined by tight sets of intertwining constraints ...
Paul Smolensky, "On the Proper Treatment of Connectionism"

1.1 Introduction

The world's languages exhibit a sometimes bewildering array of phonological inventories and phenomena. To account for the wide range of variation, phonological theory must reconcile the occurrence of differences with the repeated appearance of robust and pervasive phonological patterns and subpatterns. Even if a narrowly defined class of phonological phenomena is considered, one observes what might at first appear to be a highly unconstrained degree of variation. Take, for example, the position of the tongue in the eight vowels of Igbo, illustrated in (1). Ladefoged (1968) demonstrates that these eight vowels fall into four pairs: *i/e; ɛ/a; u/ʊ; o/ɔ*. Although the tongue body features are relatively constant for both members of each pair, for the first vowel of each pair the tongue root is relatively advanced while for the second vowel of each pair it is retracted.

(1) *Igbo* (Ladefoged 1968)

Tracings from single frames in a cineradiology film showing the tongue position in the two sets of Igbo vowels. From Ladefoged 1968:38.

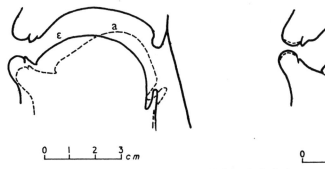

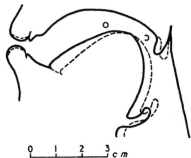

N.N.D. Okonkwo (Igbo, Onitsha):
óbi, ọ̀bé, ḿbɛ̀, ḿbà, ḿbɔ̀, ɛ́bó, ɔbɔ̀, íbu
'heart, poverty, tortoise, boast, effort,
*person, it is, weight'   23 May 62

Data such as those in (1) serve to establish a particular phonetic relationship between various pairs of vowels. The phonological interest of this property of Igbo derives from the way that these vowels interact. It has been observed in research such as that of Stewart (1967) that in certain languages, the tongue root maintains a relatively advanced position throughout the production of one class of words, while it maintains a relatively retracted position during the production of others.[1] Igbo falls into this set: within particular morphologically defined domains, all vowels of Igbo must share a single value for the tongue root feature. That is, all vowels must be produced with an advanced tongue root, as in the left-hand column of (2), or with a retracted tongue root, as in the right-hand column.[2]

(2) *Advanced tongue root: [+ATR]*   *Retracted tongue root: [−ATR]*

a.	ó-[rì]-rì	'he ate'	e.	ɔ́-[pè]-rè	'he carved'
b.	ó-[mɛ̀]-rɛ̀	'he did'	f.	ɔ́-[sà]-rà	'he washed'
c.	ó-[zò]-rò	'he did'	g.	ɔ́-[dɔ̀]-rɔ̀	'he pulled'
d.	ó-[gbù]-rù	'he killed'	h.	ɔ́-[zɔ̀]-rɔ̀	'he bought'

The vowels of the four verb roots in (2a–d), enclosed in square brackets for purposes of exposition, have advanced root position and therefore condition advanced variants of the prefix, [o], and advanced variants of the suffix, [ri/rɛ/ro/ru];[3] the vowels of the four verb roots in (2e–h) are retracted and therefore condition retracted variants of the prefix, [ɔ], and retracted variants of the suffix, [re/ra/rɔ/rɔ].

Such agreement between a sequence of vowels with respect to tongue root values characterizes the canonical tongue root harmony system. As illustrated in (3), root vowels are specified for a tongue root value; after affixation, the domain of the root value extends to include both prefixes and suffixes.

(3) *Canonical [ATR] harmony*

In order to express the systematicity of the distribution of tongue root advancement or retraction in Igbo, a rule or convention with the effect of (3) is necessary; a set of abstract representations related by this rule completes the picture. But are things truly as simple as this?

Such a "canonical" pattern is rarely, perhaps never, entirely sufficient as an actual description of a natural language harmony pattern. When a tongue root harmony system is studied in any detail, numerous complexities arise that obscure such straightforward symmetrical harmony: for instance, harmony may apply between roots and affixes, but leave compounds unaffected; harmony may affect only nonlow vowels; harmony may affect vowels to the left of the trigger, but not those to the right; and so on. The central problem in the study of such systems (see Comrie 1981b) is to determine the extent to which representations and processes are regulated by constraints of a universal nature, and the extent to which each is open to language-specific variation.

Phrased in terms specific to a single pattern such as tongue root harmony, however, the problem as presented constitutes but one facet of the complex interwoven fabric of natural phonology. A more general sampling of phenomena reveals that natural language exhibits an astonishingly rich array of phonological behavior. The types of sounds found in different languages vary immensely, as do the types of combinations of sounds allowed by different languages' phonotactics. Similarly, the range of ways in which one phonological representation may be related systematically to another exhibits considerable variation cross-linguistically. Yet despite the abundant variation found in the sound patterns of languages, such systems are also highly constrained. For example, although certain sounds are quite rare, many occur in virtually all languages (see Greenberg 1963, Chomsky and Halle 1968, Kean 1975, Maddieson 1984), and some conceivable sounds do not occur at all. In like fashion, although the details may vary, many rule-governed processes are found in many, if not most, phonological systems (see Stampe 1979, Mohanan, to appear).

The challenge faced by a theory of phonology is to express the core similarities of different phonological patterns while allowing for the wealth of variation that accompanies the core. Phonological theory must provide an explicit characterization of the full range of attested representations and rules, but at the same time should be incapable of characterizing many of the imaginable patterns that are not attested in natural language.[4] The success of a particular theory can then be measured by the tightness of the fit between the theory and the range of attested phonological patterns.

This book argues that this challenge is best met with a modular approach. Under this view, a "theory" is composed of several modules, or subtheories, each responsible for a particular aspect of phonological systems. Each subtheory is independently motivated, supported by a class of robustly attested phenomena. The role of each module is to constrain the range of possibilities—that is, the range of *well-formedness*—in its particular domain.

Under the modular view, differences between languages arise in two ways. Variation may arise when languages make different selections *within a module*. More dramatic perhaps, *interaction between modules* produces the complex—and sometimes surprising—patterns that are observed in different languages.

Our goal in the first part of this introductory chapter is to elucidate the modular approach to the study of phonology and to present some preliminary reasons for considering this a viable direction for research. In the second part of the chapter, we lay out the properties of certain specific phonological modules that constitute important background for the discussion of later chapters.

1.2 Modularity in Linguistics

Modularity is not a new idea in the study of language. Indeed, it reflects the most pervasive general approach to linguistics, where the field divides into the subfields, or modules, of morphology, phonetics, phonology, semantics, and syntax (see (4)), with research focusing both on properties of individual components and on the interaction between them. A modular approach to grammar is vividly illustrated in work within the Government and Binding school of syntactic theory (Chomsky 1981, 1982, 1986, etc.). Research shows that complex patterns for which fairly meager input is available to the language learner (e.g., parasitic gaps) may be explained in terms of the interaction of subpatterns for which the available data are strong and robust. With regard to phonology, the modularity hypothesis predicts a class of interactions between the phonological module and other linguistic modules.[5]

(4)

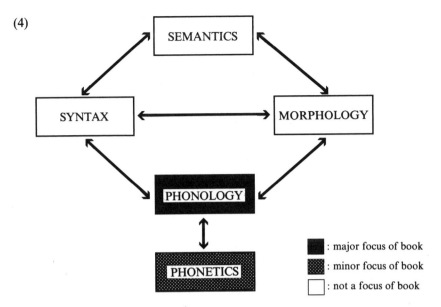

Returning for illustration to our example of tongue root harmony, consider in this light the fact that such systems differ cross-linguistically with respect to the morphological or syntactic domain within which harmony is applicable. In some cases, harmony may apply between a root and suffixes, in others, between a root and prefixes, in still others, between a root and both prefixes and suffixes; harmony may be restricted so as to apply or not apply between the different members of a compound; harmony may distinguish between different classes of morphemes, be applicable to some prefixes but not others; and so on. Languages may also differ with respect to which morphological classes may underlyingly bear harmonic values. In certain cases, only roots may bear tongue root features, with all affixes receiving their values by virtue of harmony ("root control" systems); in other cases, both roots and affixes may initiate harmony ("dominant/recessive" harmony). At a syntactic level, harmony may be completely inapplicable between words, be applicable in certain classes of configurations, depend on factors such as speech rate, register, and so on. The modular approach to such variation involves the interaction of the phonological component with the morphological and syntactic components of the grammar.

In addition to morphosyntactic limitations, [ATR] harmony rules suffer *featural* restrictions on the source and/or target of harmony. For example, a rule may allow the spreading of the advanced tongue root feature, [+ATR], only from high vowels (5a) or only from high front vowels (5b); another system may allow high vowels to be the sole recipients of [+ATR] (5c,d). Some systems disallow the targeting of low vowels by [+ATR] generally (5e), while still others disallow such targeting but only in specific configurations.

(5)   +ATR   +ATR   +ATR
         |⸜⸜ |⸜⸜ |⸜⸜
   a.   V C V   b.   V C V   c.   V C V
         | | |
        +HI   +HI   +HI
                          −BK

        +ATR   +ATR
         |⸜⸜ |⸜⸜
   d.   V C V   e.   V C V   etc.
             | |
            +HI   −LO
            −BK

In addition, one finds essentially the converse of such conditions functioning within systems that involve the spreading of the retracted tongue root feature, [−ATR] (6a–e).

(6)   −ATR   −ATR   −ATR
         |⸜⸜ |⸜⸜ |⸜⸜
   a.   V C V   b.   V C V   c.   V C V
         | | |
        −HI   −HI   −HI
                          +BK

        −ATR   −ATR
         |⸜⸜ |⸜⸜
   d.   V C V   e.   V C V   etc.
             | |
            −HI   +LO
            +BK

Such spreading of retraction may be restricted to nonhigh vowels and may assign special status to low triggers, for example. With systems employing both [+ATR] and [−ATR], such featural constraints may play an important role in the general determination of the composition of the vowel inventory.

With such a plethora of feature-based variation, the question naturally arises whether such substantive restrictions are purely random, or whether there are principles governing the phonological interaction of features. In this regard, consider certain substantive properties involved in tongue root movements. From an articulatory perspective, tongue root movement interacts closely with tongue body movement, particularly with tongue body raising and lowering. Such articulatory interaction is reinforced acoustically. The primary acoustic correlate of tongue root advancement is a lowering of the first formant frequency, while tongue root retraction correlates with a raising of the same formant; such lowering and raising of the first formant is also the primary indication of tongue body raising and lowering, respectively.

Perhaps unsurprisingly, such phonetically based conditions turn out to play a significant role in the ways in which some phonologies deviate from the canonical tongue root harmony pattern seen in (3); these conditions are reflected in the featural constraints that limit how rules apply. Our basic proposal for such cases of substantive featural interaction is modular (see (4)): the phonological imposition of such featural interdependencies interacts with the phonetics to define the class of well-formed conditions, an interaction referred to as the *Grounding Conditions* (discussed extensively in chapter 3).

Let us turn now to a type of deviation from the canonical [ATR] harmony rule of (3) that is related in one sense to the types of substantive conditions just seen, but which is rather different in another sense. We refer to a class of deviations that fall under the general rubric of *neutrality*, discussed in chapters 3 and 4. Neutral elements do not undergo harmony. In many cases, the neutral element is *transparent*; in others, the neutral element is *opaque*. Transparent elements are ignored by the harmony process: harmony proceeds right across the transparent elements and has no perceptible effect on them. In (3), [ATR] values spread from vowel to vowel regardless of the number or nature of intervening consonants: all intervening consonants are transparent. In some systems, certain classes of vowels exhibit comparable behavior, acting transparent to the harmony process (the V_j class in (7a)).[6]

(7) *Neutrality in [ATR] harmony*

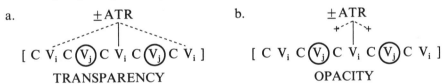

a. $\pm$ATR

$[\ C\ V_i\ C\ \textcircled{V}_j\ C\ V_i\ C\ \textcircled{V}_j\ C\ V_i\ ]$

TRANSPARENCY

b. $\pm$ATR

$[\ C\ V_i\ C\ \textcircled{V}_j\ C\ V_i\ C\ \textcircled{V}_j\ C\ V_i\ ]$

OPACITY

Neutral elements may also be *opaque*, preventing the harmonic process from propagating over them and, typically, failing to undergo the harmonic process themselves. It is not uncommon for a specific class of vowels to be opaque in a harmony process (the V_j class in (7b)). Yet more variation is possible in languages in which the harmonic value is a property of both consonants and vowels. For example, where [ATR] is a property of both vowels and consonants, harmony may take place from a vowel to adjacent consonants—or from a consonant to an adjacent vowel, sometimes with subsequent application from vowel to vowel, skipping consonants after the initial consonant/vowel effect. And the variation continues—for example, harmony may take place across at most one consonant but not across two.

Such patterns of neutrality raise various questions. Substantively, one must identify the classes of segments that may function neutrally in languages exhibiting such behavior. As with the substantive issues illustrated in (5)–(6), we propose to account for this aspect of neutrality in terms of the Grounding Conditions. At a more formal level, if vowels and/or consonants can be skipped during the application of harmony, then we must determine how many such segments can be skipped. Are there any constraints on just how close the trigger of a harmonic process must be with respect to the target? More generally, we can ask what constitutes sufficient "closeness" between two phonological elements involved in some systematic phonologically defined relation.

Bearing on such formal questions, consider a typical pattern found when consonants assimilate to each other, a pattern that contrasts markedly with the neutrality outlined schematically for vowel harmony. For instance, the juxtaposition of the morphemes *in-* and *possible* in English results in the nasal consonant of the prefix being assigned bilabial place features by a regular rule of place assimilation: *i[m]possible*. In such an example, where rule application is licensed, the consonants in question are immediately next to each other, unlike the vowels in typical cases of vowel harmony (cf. (3)). Were a vowel to intervene, the consonants would be too far apart and application of the rule would be suspended.[7] In (8), compare the allowable application in *i[m]possible* with the impossibility of application in *i[n]applicable* (**i[m]applicable*) and *i[n]urbane* (**i[m]urbane*).

(8)

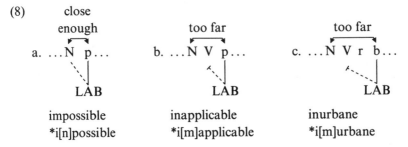

In marked contrast to the pattern just described for English, recall that canonical harmony (3), as illustrated in Igbo, applies from vowel to vowel over a consonant. In general, it can be observed that string-adjacent consonants, vowels in adjacent syllables, and the heads of adjacent feet constitute elements that are sufficiently "close" for rules to define relations between them, while numerous other configurations do not qualify. In line with most current work in phonological theory, we conclude that a principle of *Locality* is required to appropriately restrict the allowable class of rule-governed relations. Locality establishes that some relations are formally close enough for a phonological relation to be well defined, while other relations are not.

Locality is only one of many restrictions obtained by imposing general constraints on representations. Along with Locality, two additional constraints, *Well-formedness* and the *Obligatory Contour Principle*, are addressed later in this chapter. Well-formedness encodes the requirement that no representation may be allowed, even temporarily, to violate conditions. One effect of this, directly applicable for various cases of harmony, is that any condition on representations at level *n* holds necessarily of any rule producing output at level *n*. That is, any condition on representations is automatically a condition on rules. For instance, the Obligatory Contour Principle, relevant, among other cases, in determining the types of representations that can constitute the input and output of harmony rules, imposes restrictions on the cooccurrence of sets of feature specifications that are identical.

In addition to the conditions mentioned so far, two constraints on feature selection, *Simplicity* and *Recoverability*, are proposed and examined in chapter 2. Both conditions govern the inclusion of phonological information in representations, but with somewhat opposing goals. Whereas Simplicity assigns value to the *exclusion* of any derivable feature specification, Recoverability assigns value to the *inclusion* of any feature that contributes to the establishment of a contrast. Phonological representations, we suggest, exhibit evidence for a trade-off relation between these different constraints. Finally, chapter 3 is devoted to an examination of the many implications of the Grounding Conditions, a class of constraints derived from the modular interaction of the phonetics with the phonology. These conditions and constraints are summarized in (9).[8]

(9)

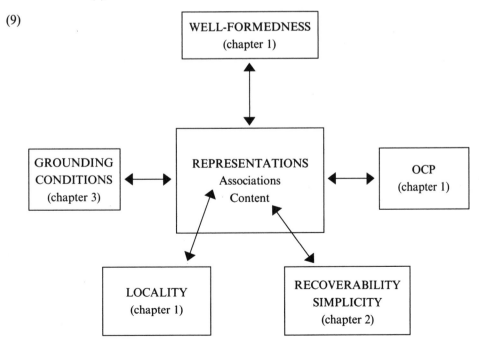

Additional divergences from the canonical harmony pattern may be of a purely formal type—in combination, of course, with any of the variations already noted above. Depending on the environment, harmony may apply strictly from left to right, strictly from right to left, or bidirectionally. Harmony may extend from a triggering vowel to an unlimited number of targets within the relevant domain; conversely, harmony may only apply to a vowel immediately abutting the harmonic source. To account for this class of diversity, we argue in chapter 4 that rule theory allows the limited set of formal parameters shown in (10): *Function, Type, Direction, Iteration.*

(10)

> PARAMETRIC RULES
> Function
> Type
> Direction
> Iteration

These formal parameters produce surface diversity in two ways. First, different combinations of parameter settings produce different formal effects. Second, some particular cluster of parameter settings may produce varying effects in combination with Grounding Theory and the various principles defining formal well-formedness, such as Locality. The general claim is that natural language grammars impose only a very narrowly constrained set of phonological rules, rules derived from the interaction of the four formal parameters with conditions determined by other phonological modules and principles.

To round out this introduction to the notion of phonological modularity, we close with a discussion of two rather different issues that affect the characterization of processes such as [ATR] harmony, namely, *underspecification* and *association conventions*. Consider again the characterization of canonical harmony given in (3). There, both "plus" and "minus" values of the tongue root feature are affected; that is, the rule spreads [±ATR]. To the extent that such a characterization is correct, one would expect the behavior of [+ATR] and [−ATR] values to be largely symmetrical. In fact, however, it is often observed that harmony applies in a highly asymmetrical fashion. To encode such asymmetries, among other things, various theories of *underspecification* have been proposed. In addition to such questions of feature content, a wide range of issues have been raised in the phonological literature concerning the manner in which feature content is associated to prosodic units. For example, do the elements involved in tongue root harmony link and spread automatically, by universal convention, or is their distribution determined by language-specific rules? Since both of these issues figure prominently in the autosegmental literature, and since both issues figure prominently in this book, we introduce them here, relating each to the central theme of modularity. As we explore these issues, it will become clear that the specific components of the theory we present differ in a number of regards from much earlier phonological work; the result is that our model allocates rather different properties to Universal Grammar and to specific languages than do many earlier theories.

1.2.1 Underspecification

Various theories of underspecification have been proposed, each balancing in a different way considerations of *quantitative* specification (how much to specify, which values to specify), *structural* underspecification (encoding asymmetries between feature values), and *markedness* (the structural expression of cross-linguistic patterns). In general, the conditions on the ways in which segments are created from features are intrinsically built into the theories in question. In some approaches, notably those referred to as "contrastive (under)specification," certain types of feature combinations must be present, while other types of feature combinations must be absent (Steriade 1987a, Clements 1987, Mester and Itô 1989). In alternative approaches such as "radical underspecification," a more extensive range of combinations is prohibited (Kiparsky 1982, 1985, Archangeli 1984, Pulleyblank 1986a, Archangeli and Pulleyblank 1989). Such theories share the property of encoding constraints on whether features are or are not representationally present into the structure of the theory itself. With the implementation of the various proposals depending on the role of markedness, the claim in such theories is that the built-in restrictions are part of Universal Grammar and so subject to only very limited language-particular variation.

Chomsky and Halle (1968; hereafter *SPE*) propose representations that are fully specified for all features, but supplement this with a theory of markedness and linking rules whose effect is to weight both derived and underived representations in the direction of unmarked systems. A number of subsequent proposals argue that well-formed representations are, at least initially, only partially specified, although there is abundant disagreement on the type and motivation for what is or is not specified. Kiparsky (1982), Grignon (1984), and Pulleyblank (1986a) accept the centrality of markedness theory and suggest that asymmetrical phonological behavior results from representing unmarked feature values as phonologically absent from underlying representations, deriving a configuration where only marked values are phonologically "active." Archangeli (1984), Itô and Mester (1986), Abaglo and Archangeli (1989), and Archangeli and Pulleyblank (1989) abandon any necessary connection between markedness and formal representations, opting for representations defined in terms of phonological alternations: any feature specification may be specified or unspecified as the language facts demand (although these proposals also limit features to a single value in well-formed underlying representations). Clements (1987), Steriade (1987a), Christdas (1988), and Mester and Itô (1989) abandon both markedness and phonological patterning to focus on the contrastive function of distinct segments, proposing to specify both values of any feature used to distinguish segments, and only on the segments that are so distinguished. More recently, Mohanan (1991) and Myers (1991) have advocated a return to full specification and the *SPE*-style linking rules in an effort to once again encode markedness in the formal model of feature specification. Crosscutting such proposals is research suggesting that at least certain features intrinsically involve underspecification in that feature theory provides a monovalent feature only (Anderson and Ewen 1987, Ewen and van der Hulst 1987, van der Hulst 1988, 1989, Avery and Rice 1989), the sole expression possible for an affected opposition being the presence of the monovalent feature ("specification") or its absence ("intrinsic underspecification").

In contrast, the approach argued for here focuses on modularity. Phonological representations are posited that freely select appropriate sets from the universally designated featural primitives. The extent to which a representation appears *fully specified, partially specified,* or *underspecified* depends on the particular paradigmatic combinations of featural primitives in the language in question. Without incorporating special constraints into the actual theory of feature specification, we propose that free combinatorial possibilities define the attested range of featural possibilities (chapter 2). Constraints on combination derive not from intrinsic properties of a theory of "underspecification," but from the interaction of feature theory with other phonological modules. In this regard, choice of a particular set of selected feature values is evaluated in terms of an independent theory of feature markedness (chapter 3). Allowable feature combinations are regulated to a large extent by their interaction with an independently motivated module governing feature cooccurrence (also chapter 3). This interaction, in turn, is affected by the interplay of the phonology with morphosyntactic representations. An important, though somewhat unexpected, result is that the most important effects of both "radical" and "contrastive" underspecification theories are derivative, not part of a universal theory of specification per se.

1.2.2 Association Conventions

Classifying effects in terms of whether they are universal or language-specific is not an isolated challenge, nor does it arise only with respect to representations: the same type of concern emerges when considering relations between representations. The notion of "association conventions" provides a relevant example.

A significant body of recent research has focused on the characterization of a well-formed representation, with a concomitant attempt to derive a variety of phonological phenomena (harmony, dissimilation, assimilation, stability, polarity, etc.) directly from properties of the input representation (Goldsmith 1976, McCarthy 1981, 1984b, 1986a, Clements 1985a, Sagey 1986, Hayes 1986, 1989, Schein and Steriade 1986, Steriade 1990, 1991, Paradis and Prunet 1991, etc.). In characterizing the input and output representations necessary to express such relations, a pervasive assumption has been that once the input representation is established, the appropriate output representation is determined automatically, the result of a convention. For example, under the autosegmental hypothesis, where features are independent elements each assigned to a semi-independent level of representation (Goldsmith 1976, Clements 1981, 1985a, etc.), universal well-formedness conditions govern association, spreading, the behavior of geminates, and so on.

In this regard, it is instructive to explore the problem of defining the relation between (i) a representation that includes free features and (ii) the corresponding representation where the free features have been associated to appropriate anchors. Over the past twenty years, a wide range of proposals have been offered to characterize this relation. The shared assumption in all of these proposals is that the relation itself is to some extent an automatic, universal consequence of correctly expressing the input representation.

What is problematic, however, is that the "universal and automatic" conventions proposed have tended to vary from language to language and from case to case. Different proposals have had strikingly different empirical effects, with a series of innovations, each proposed to account for a previously unexplained array of facts. An idea of the range of proposals is given here (the list is not intended to be comprehensive).

Williams (1976: Margi and Igbo tone) and Clements and Ford (1979: Kikuyu tone) propose essentially that autosegments associate to anchors in a left-to-right fashion, initially linking in a one-to-one relation and then automatically spreading a linked autosegment onto remaining free anchors, if any. Leben (1973: Tiv, Mende tone, etc.) and Goldsmith (1976: Tiv, Mende tone, etc.) propose a well-formedness condition whose effect is not only to link and spread autosegments to available free anchors, but also to automatically create contour segments in cases where there are more autosegments than available anchors. Goldsmith (1976: Ganda and Tonga tone) and Haraguchi (1977: Japanese tone) also make provision for initial association to take place between "accented" melodic elements and "accented" anchors. Halle and Vergnaud (1982: Tonga tone) restrict the automatic application of spreading to autosegments that are initially free; that is, free autosegments link and spread automatically, prelinked autosegments spread only by rule. Pulleyblank (1986a: Tiv,

Yoruba tone, etc.) argues that the universal and automatic aspects of association are nothing more than the one-to-one relation, applying from left to right. Archangeli and Pulleyblank (1989: Yoruba [−ATR] harmony) argue that direction of "automatic" association varies, left to right in some cases, right to left in others. Yip (1988a: templatic effects) and Mutaka (1990: Kinande tone) propose that the association of free elements proceeds from the edges inward. Mester and Itô (1989: Japanese mimetics) argue that association applies directionally to a preferred subset of autosegmental anchors (coronals for the palatalization feature they examine) with default docking at the edge of the span if no preferred anchor is available.

In each case, the unifying assumption is that some automatic universal convention of association takes an independently motivated representation with floating features and creates a well-formed mapping between those features and the appropriate anchors. The problem, of course, is that the myriad association effects noted above cannot all result in any straightforward way from the interaction between a single automatic universal convention and independently motivated representations. Given an input representation of a particular type, a *convention* predicts a single related output representation: to assume multiple "conventions" becomes euphemistic, concealing the language-particular nature of the association process. To the extent that the behavior of the association process cannot be determined through reference to the input representation, its particular properties must be stipulated for each case. Despite considerable success in understanding the nature of well-formed representations, the apparently inescapable result is that certain properties of representations cannot automatically be the result of universally defined well-formedness conventions.

Our proposal here again involves modularity. We propose in chapter 4 that the various association effects attested in different languages derive from the modular interaction of a set of phonological principles with a highly constrained set of rule parameters. The choices within each module allow for cross-linguistic variation; at the same time, the restrictions placed by each module reflect the notion of universality focused on by convention-based models.

1.3   An Overview

This book as a whole constitutes an argument in favor of phonological modularity: we demonstrate that significant phonological insights are captured by focusing on the modular interaction of a small number of phonological subtheories. To the extent that this work succeeds in accounting for a complex array of cases, the basic modular hypothesis is supported. This same success provides support for our substantive proposals about specific modules. We narrow our exploration of phonological modules to those addressing specific issues with respect to featural relations and/or representations, Combinatorial Specification, Grounding Conditions, and Parametric Rules.[9] The result is a small number of robustly motivated modular principles specific to the phonological component, whose interaction (schematized in (12)) produces the richer set of attested cross-linguistic patterns.

Combinatorial Specification (chapter 2) takes as its starting point that representations are composed of sets of features, and that these features may or may not be associated to prosodic structure. With regard to the question of which features are necessarily present in representations, the phenomena considered argue for a fairly impoverished formal model: the primitives are *features* and *associations*; representations composed of these primitives are governed by considerations of *simplicity* and *recoverability*. Substantively, this approach must make concrete assumptions concerning the set of distinctive features adopted. As defined in works like Jakobson, Fant, and Halle 1963 and *SPE*, we assume such features to be formal objects that have substantive correlates, acoustic and articulatory.[10]

(11)

> **CHAPTER 2**
>
> **FEATURE SPECIFICATION**
>
> featural primitives
>
> **CONSTRAINTS**
>
> Recoverability
> Simplicity

The Grounding Conditions (chapter 3; see (12)) provide a theory of the restrictions on well-formed paradigmatic combinations of features. Formally, the theory consists of *implicational statements* governing feature cooccurrence; substantively, the model proposes that languages make use only of implicational relations that are *grounded in their phonetic correlates* (articulatory or acoustic). We argue that such grounded implications define well-formed feature combinations for specific languages; further, we show that in languages where the implicational relations do not hold of representations as a whole, these implications may still play a role in restricting the application of specific rules. Chapter 3 also introduces a theory of Feature Markedness; the interaction of Feature Markedness with the Grounding Conditions accounts for a variety of patterns attested cross-linguistically.

(12)

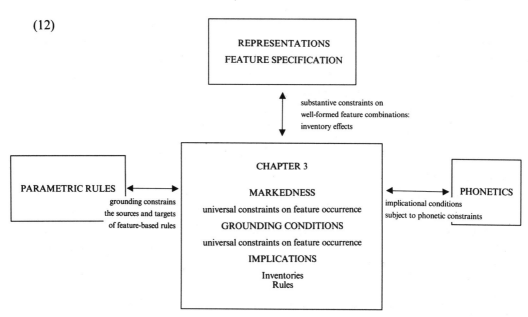

Parametric Rule Theory (chapter 4; see (13)) addresses the problem of defining well-formed relations between different levels of representation. Formally, we propose that such relations are expressed by rules consisting of a cluster of values for an extremely small set of binary parameters, namely, the four parameters *Function*, *Type*, *Direction*, and *Iteration*. We argue that combinations of the values for these parameters identify a wide range of formal relations between representations, including the various "association convention" effects discussed above.

(13)

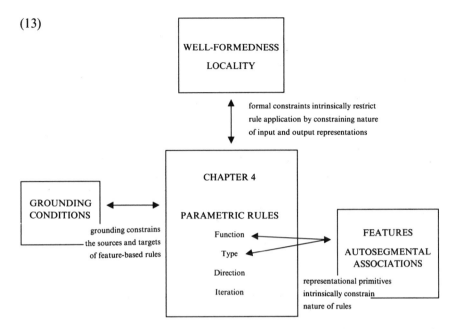

In each chapter, we motivate the relevant subtheory independently and then explore the phenomena predicted by each subtheory and by the interaction of the subtheories with each other. Support for the modular approach comes from the range of attested phenomena that are successfully accounted for through the interaction of the various phonological modules. We discuss a number of such predictions: the interaction of Grounding Theory with Combinatorial Specification predicts certain types of "segment" inventories, Structure Preservation effects, and possible/impossible effects of rule application, while the interaction of Grounding Theory with Parametric Rules predicts specific classes of redundancy rules and association rules, of conditions on source or target of a rule, and of neutrality effects.

Central to this work is the Grounding Hypothesis, an attempt to define well-formedness of feature combinations and to explore the effects in phonological systems of imposing phonetically based conditions on well-formedness. Our entire discussion of such substantive well-formedness, however, relies on certain assumptions about structural, or formal, well-formedness. Making these assumptions explicit is the focus of the remainder of this chapter.

1.4   The Phonological Component

It is impossible to give a constrained account of feature combination and rule interaction without first establishing the primitives of the system. In this regard, we adopt a fairly standard picture.

The actual content of a phonological representation is a set of features (to be expanded upon below), where features are assembled into paradigmatic sets by associative linkings—the basic autosegmental hypothesis of Goldsmith (1976). We assume in addition that such sets of features are grouped into phonological constituents: mora, syllable, foot, phonological word, and so on (Hyman 1985, McCarthy and Prince 1986, 1990, Selkirk 1984, Nespor and Vogel 1982, 1986, Hayes 1989, etc.). Autosegmental features and linkings in conjunction with constituency relations define the basic content of the phonological component. Additional issues involve the interaction of the phonology with other components: the morphology, the syntax, the phonetics, and so on. In this work, we focus on the actual feature content of the phonological component. Interactions with nonphonological modules will figure in certain places, but the central concern throughout is autosegmental feature structure.

Before developing the hypothesis that we propose concerning feature organization, we address three types of basic assumptions. First, we outline properties of the primitives of feature theory. Second, we clarify background assumptions concerning prosodic organization. Finally, we discuss certain well-motivated constraints on phonological organization that will be assumed throughout this work.

1.4.1   Featural Content: Hierarchical Organization

Following a well-trodden path, we assume that the primitives of phonological representations are distinctive features (Jakobson, Fant, and Halle 1963, *SPE*, etc.). Individually, features serve to identify classes of segments that either trigger or undergo rules (assimilation, deletion, morpheme structure constraints, etc.): the [+back] segments, the [−continuant] segments, the [+voiced] segments, and so on. In addition, classes of segments that trigger or undergo rules may be defined by sets of features. In this case, we follow research such as that of Clements (1985a), Sagey (1986), and McCarthy (1988) in assuming that the class of such feature sets is narrowly constrained, limited to perhaps fewer than ten feature sets such as the Place features, the Laryngeal features, and so on.

Representationally, we follow Clements (1985a) in expressing feature sets by a hierarchically organized tree structure, as shown schematically in (14).

(14) *Schematic feature geometry*

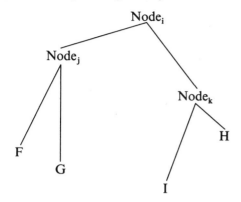

Nodes in such a structure identify sets of features that can function in a phonologically unified fashion, for example with respect to a spreading or delinking process, as shown by the schematic rules in (15).

(15) *Schematic rules*

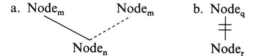

In (14), features F and G may function together as a unit by identifying $Node_j$ in a particular rule (e.g., *spread Node$_j$* (15a) or *delink Node$_j$* (15b)). Similarly a rule identifying $Node_k$ would treat features H and I as a single set, while a rule identifying $Node_i$ would affect the entire set of features, F, G, H, I.

As schematized in (14), the hypothesis that features are classed in such sets is a purely formal proposal. Determining specific values for the various nodes and the features dominated by particular nodes is an area of much interesting work, including McCarthy 1988, Clements 1989, 1991a,b, Odden 1989, Wiswall 1991b, Peng 1992. Research exploring features and their organization in signed languages makes use of the same formal hypothesis, though the substance is dramatically different due to the differing modalities. See, for example, Corina and Sagey 1988, Corina 1990, Sandler 1990, Brentari 1990, and Ann 1991.

Much of the substantive detail regarding how features are hierarchically organized does not affect the central claims of this book. Important, however, is Sagey's (1986) proposal that the Place node is defined by articulator nodes, although we incorporate the suggestion by Steriade (1986b) and Cole (1987) that there are four articulator nodes, not the three originally proposed by Sagey. For the sake of concreteness, we give in (16) the complete structure that we assume throughout this work.

(16) *Feature geometry* (after Sagey 1986)

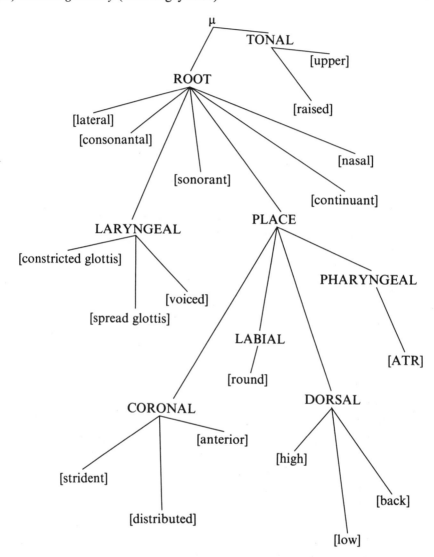

The organization in (16) allows rules that affect all nontonal features (by targeting the Root node) as well as rules that affect some smaller subset of the features (by targeting a particular node, such as the Place node). Additionally, since binary features are individual terminal elements in this model, processes affecting single features can also be readily expressed.

   Unlike theories such as that of *SPE*, which are strictly binary, Sagey's proposal effectively posits both binary and unary features (cf. Trubetzkoy 1969). Features like [±ATR] and [±continuant] are binary in the traditional sense; class nodes such as

Labial, Coronal, Dorsal, and Pharyngeal, however, have no negative counterpart, although they, like the binary features, are associated with definable phonetic content (corresponding to constrictions ranging from the lips (Labial) to the pharynx (Pharyngeal)). The claim intrinsic to this proposal is that both the class defined by a positive feature value like [+ATR] and the class defined by its negative counterpart, [−ATR] in this example, are natural classes, occurring in rules of natural language; with a feature like Coronal, on the other hand, the class defined as Coronal is a natural class, while the class not defined by Coronal is not.

We follow Sagey in allowing such unary class nodes to be terminal. That is, representations may be well formed even if such a class node does not dominate any daughter features. Unlike Sagey (1986) and Avery and Rice (1989), we postulate that all terminal nodes must correspond to phonetic content. Strictly organizational nodes, such as the Place and Laryngeal nodes, may not occur terminally since they have no phonetic content. For example, the Laryngeal node, which dominates features like [±voiced] and [±constricted glottis] that define the laryngeal configuration, cannot appear terminally since it does not define a particular configuration in and of itself.

Formally, therefore, purely structural nodes like Laryngeal and Place must dominate featural content, while content-bearing class nodes like Labial and Coronal may occur terminally or may dominate daughter features. Thus, a representation containing a structural node bearing no content is ill formed. Compare the ill-formed (17c) with the well-formed (17a,b).

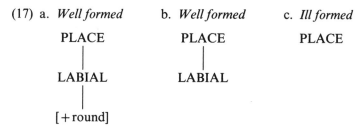

(17) a. *Well formed*　　　b. *Well formed*　　　c. *Ill formed*

　　　PLACE　　　　　　　PLACE　　　　　　　PLACE
　　　　|　　　　　　　　　|
　　　LABIAL　　　　　　LABIAL
　　　　|
　　　[+round]

1.4.2　The Association of Features: Node Generation

Within an autosegmental theory along the lines of the one sketched above, each feature appears on its own independent tier.[11] It is therefore necessary to provide a mechanism for correctly aligning the various feature specifications. Since Goldsmith 1976, the mechanism employed is autosegmental *association*. The relation of association may hold between nodes and features, other nodes, and/or prosodic structure. The domain *path* extends over a particular type of such associations.[12]

(18) *Path (informal)*

　　　Any set of associated nodes, features, or prosodic categories such that no more than one token of any node, feature, or prosodic category is included in the set.

In this section, we focus on the well-formedness and ill-formedness of imaginable paths.

Not all nodes and not all features need to be present in the representation of any single sound. However, if a feature or node is present and is associated, then the dominating nodes represented in (16) must also be present. For example, the association of [+round] in (19a) is well formed, while that in (19b) is ill formed, because no Labial node is present.

(19) a. *Well formed*   b. *Ill formed*

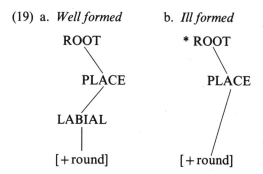

The rationale for this type of ill-formedness derives from the basic claims of the feature hierarchy. If a segment involves a daughter feature, then by definition, the segment involves the dominating feature: [+round] cannot be implemented without constituting a value for Labial; a segment cannot have Dorsal or Coronal specifications without being specified for Place; and so on. A rule could not, for example, spread all Place specifications *except Dorsal* by allowing Dorsal to bypass the Place node by associating it directly to the Root node as shown in (20b). Such a possibility would invalidate the basic claims of the feature hierarchy concerning the sets of features that can function in a unitary fashion.

(20) a. *Well formed*   b. *Ill formed*

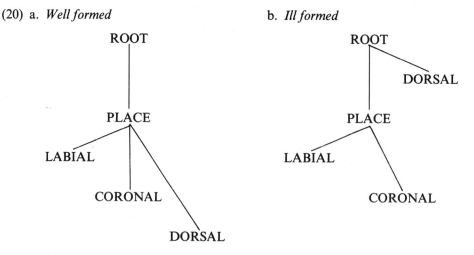

To associate a feature like [+ back] therefore entails the specification of nodes like Dorsal, Place, and Root. That is, some target specified for [+ back] will have nonnull Dorsal, Place, and Root specifications. In terms of graphic representations, spreading of such a daughter node must automatically generate any dominating hierarchical set structure (see Clements 1985a).

(21) *Node Generation*

   A rule or convention assigning some F-element α to some anchor β creates a path from α to β.

It is possible to imagine that since a representation without the appropriate dominating nodes is ill formed, a rule spreading a feature like [+ back] could not apply to a structure that has no Dorsal node (see Avery and Rice 1989).[13] We argue in this work, however, that such rules do apply, with intervening nodes spontaneously generated by the convention of Node Generation.

In summary, the feature hierarchy in (16) makes both a formal and a substantive claim about the sets of features that constitute natural classes for the purposes of phonological rules in natural languages. The formal hierarchical structure plays a central role in numerous case studies examined here, as do certain aspects of the substantive instantiation of such structure. Other substantive aspects of the feature structure in (16), however, are not crucial here; somewhat different proposals for feature organization could be consistent with the evidence of this book.

1.4.3   Anchors and Prosodic Structure

In the preceding sections, we have given background concerning the basic content of the autosegmental component of the phonology. Although our focus throughout this study is on such autosegmental structure, it is nevertheless important to make certain assumptions concerning syllabic constituency relations, especially with respect to the way in which features associate to prosodic structure: given the *Prosodic Licensing* hypothesis of Itô (1986), features can only be realized on the surface if they are incorporated into prosodic structure; we take such "incorporation" to be association.

The proposals made here are consistent with a variety of different prosodic structures, provided that such structures distinguish certain standard prosodic configurations, long and short vowels, syllable heads, codas. We assume a prosodic model along the lines proposed by Hyman (1985), McCarthy and Prince (1986, 1990), Hayes (1989), and Itô (1986, 1989): nodes dock into prosodic structure (directly or indirectly, depending on their position in the feature hierarchy), either into moras (μ) or into syllables (σ). As illustrated in (22), moras are dominated by syllables, and vowels anchor into moras; a long vowel is represented with two moras.

(22) a. *Short vowel*   b. *Long vowel*

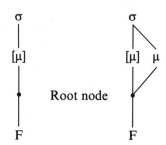

Root node

Vowel features are not the only ones that may dock into moras: coda consonants may be moraic as well (see Hayes 1989). Finally, in some cases, it is necessary to isolate the *syllable head* (see Shaw 1991b). The syllable head appears to be derivative from properties of position, typically the leftmost mora in a syllable, and from properties of sonority, typically the most sonorous mora in a syllable. Where relevant, we indicate headship by square brackets, as in (22).

Crucial for the work presented here is the role of prosodic structure in identifying the relevant *anchor* for each feature. An anchor is the highest significant level of structure, either organizational or prosodic.

Both consonants and vowels have *organizational anchors*, the Root node. This level of structure coordinates and orders the various feature specifications that go together to constitute a particular consonant or vowel. Appropriate features may also have prosodically defined anchors. For example, some features dock only to moras that are syllable heads, the "syllabic/vocalic" features. Other features dock to moras that are not syllable heads: in one language, these might be restricted to the vowel features (which can also constitute syllable heads) while in another language, some—or all—nonhead features ("consonants") may also be moraic.[14] Depending on the language and feature in question, the *prosodic anchor* is defined as (i) a nonhead mora, (ii) a mora that is the syllable head, or (iii) any mora, head or nonhead.

(23) *Anchors*

    a. Organizational anchors   Root nodes

    b. Prosodic anchors   moras
                                    syllable-head moras
                                    nonhead moras

Whatever the appropriate prosodic anchor, a representation is invariably ill formed if a feature is linked in a path with an illicit prosodic anchor.

Note that nonmoraic consonants such as onsets must be adjoined to prosodic structure to be prosodically licensed (Itô 1986). In such cases, however, the syllable is not a prosodic anchor for such nonmoraic features. To take the syllable as a prosodic anchor means being anchored to the *head* of a syllable. That is, defining a prosodic anchor for some feature as the *syllable* is equivalent to defining the prosodic anchor as the *syllable-head mora*. As a consequence, nonmoraic consonants have only organizational anchors and not prosodic ones.

In various places below (e.g., in the discussion of Precedence (55) in section 1.5.2), we refer to the class of paths including an anchor as *a(nchor)-paths*. Features in a-paths contrast with floating "unanchored" specifications.

1.4.4 Summary

In this section, we have laid out the basic building blocks of the phonological component: features, set structure, associations, constituency relations. In each domain, we have identified conditions for distinguishing between well-formed and ill-formed representations, both with respect to the organization of features and with respect to their mapping to prosodic structure. The central aim of this study is to develop a typology of feature interactions within such a constrained autosegmental theory.

Our proposals build on a number of constraints that have been well documented in the autosegmental literature, constraints to which we turn in the following section. We consider a variety of structural representations, arguing that certain ones are well formed and others are not—and so are ruled out. In particular, we propose a formal account of *Locality*, arguing that locality depends on both a tier-internal notion of *Adjacency* and a cross-tier notion of *Precedence*. Locality governs constraints like the Obligatory Contour Principle (OCP) and derives constraints like the No Crossing Constraint.

1.5 Well-formedness: Locality and Structural Relations

Following Liberman and Prince (1977), Kiparsky (1985), and Itô (1986), we assume that the following principle governs the phonological component:

(24) *Well-formedness Principle*

   Representations and relations between representations are well formed.

Although at first glance a fairly straightforward proposal, it becomes clear upon closer consideration that this principle has far-reaching, nontrivial consequences. The Well-formedness Principle governs all representations, whether derived or underived. Consequently, rules cannot create representations of types that are not independently motivated. This consequence is not respected in numerous published analyses, for example, in many analyses of harmony systems exhibiting transparent vowels (see McCarthy 1984a, Archangeli and Pulleyblank 1987, Cole 1987, Schlindwein 1987, Steriade 1987a, Ringen 1988, Vago 1988, etc.). Discussion in this chapter of the "gapped configuration" bears on such analyses. Additionally, the Well-formedness

Principle governs rules, both in their effect (they cannot create ill-formed representations) and in their expression (only well-formed rules are possible).[15]

Given the Well-formedness Principle, it is crucial to establish and to make explicit the precise composition of the class of well-formed expressions. We suggest that well-formedness in phonology is determined by criteria from the different phonological submodules. For instance, the feature hierarchy discussed in section 1.4.1 establishes a variety of well-formed and ill-formed relations between features and nodes. The phonological components focused on in this book each contribute to well-formedness. In chapter 3, a restrictive set of substantive implicational conditions governs rules and representations, a set whose basis lies in phonetic patterns; in chapter 4, a highly restricted set of parameters governs allowable relations between representations (i.e., rules).

Additionally, we propose that relations within representations, both tier-internal and cross-tier, are governed by a general Locality Condition. In the immediately following discussion, we deal with the effect of Locality on representations, a prerequisite to understanding the effect of Locality on rule application.

One of the central results of autosegmental theory concerns Locality. Although there has been widespread agreement that rules involve elements that must in some sense be close to each other, linear theories such as that of *SPE* have encountered significant difficulties in defining exactly what "being close" means. (See, for example, the literature on the Relevancy Condition: Jensen 1974, Jensen and Stong-Jensen 1979, and Odden 1977, 1980.) Within a linear framework, long-distance phonological effects require the use of powerful devices such as variable notations whose effects go considerably beyond the class of cases motivating their postulation. Autosegmental theory takes a large step toward resolving these problems by allowing the elimination of such powerful variables in favor of multitiered analyses of long-distance effects (see Poser 1982).

Allowing multiple tiers can, of course, overgenerate in a manner quite reminiscent of the overgeneration encountered in linear frameworks. To prevent such a negative result, some condition of locality must be imposed. We suggest here that the appropriate condition must have two separate effects. On the one hand, a condition of *Adjacency* is imposed on *tier-internal* rules, representations, and conditions; on the other hand, a condition of *Precedence* is imposed on *cross-tier* rules, representations, and conditions.

(25) *Locality Condition*

Phonological relations respect Adjacency and Precedence.

In the following sections, we focus first on the tier-internal representations, motivating Adjacency, and then go on to the cross-tier cases, motivating Precedence.

1.5.1   Tier-internal Effects: Adjacency and the OCP

When addressing the issue of locality as it governs tier-internal representations, the "negative" condition of the Obligatory Contour Principle (OCP; McCarthy 1986a) provides a strong diagnostic.[16]

(26) *Obligatory Contour Principle*

A sequence of identical elements within a tier is prohibited.

In McCarthy's (1986a) formulation of the OCP, on which (26) is based, it is explicitly required that the prohibition on identity apply to *adjacent* elements. Given the Locality Condition in (25), this restriction need not be stipulated in the actual formulation of the OCP. Since tier-internal phonological relations are subject to Adjacency, and since the OCP expresses a tier-internal relation, the OCP is of necessity applicable only to adjacent elements. As we demonstrate below, an examination of the types of configurations that are either subject to, or not subject to, the OCP provides a clear indication of whether or not adjacency holds (see Myers 1987).

With Myers (1987) and Hewitt and Prince (1989), we note that it is important when defining adjacency to distinguish between *free* and *linked* features/nodes. With regard to both structural possibilities, it is well established that floating features, depicted in (27a), and linked features, (27b), constitute well-formed representations. Even if (27b) is preferred to (27a) in typical situations (see Goldsmith 1976 and much subsequent work), the persistence of floating tones in downstepping languages provides abundant evidence for (27a) as a possible configuration (see Clements and Ford 1979, 1981, Clements and Goldsmith 1984, Pulleyblank 1986a, etc.).[17]

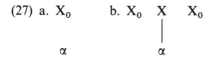

$$(27) \text{ a. } X_0 \qquad \text{b. } X_0 \quad X \quad X_0$$

OCP effects involving sequences of floating elements are widely attested in the autosegmental literature (McCarthy 1986a, Mester 1986, Myers 1987, etc.). Numerous examples will be seen in this book as well—for example, in the discussions of Yoruba, Ngbaka, and Tiv (chapter 2). We do not dwell on these arguments here, and adopt the following relatively uncontroversial version of *Adjacency* as it affects floating specifications (Myers 1987:154):[18]

(28) *Adjacency of free specifications*

An element α is structurally adjacent to an element β iff at least one of the two is unassociated, both are on the same tier, and no element intervenes between the two on that tier.

The situation becomes both more complex and more interesting when linked specifications are involved. Consider a trimoraic form such as the Yoruba word for 'card-
board', *páálí*, where a sequence of H-toned vowels surfaces. This sequence involves
both contiguous vowels (as in the first two moras) and noncontiguous vowels (as with
the second and third moras). As noted since early work such as Leben 1973, various
structural analyses are logically possible in a case where there is a superficial sequence
of vowels on the same tone. First, it might be assumed as in (29) that each mora bears
its own tone.[19]

(29)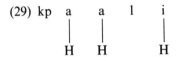

Second, it might be assumed as in (30) that contiguous vowels share a single tone,
while noncontiguous vowels have distinct tones.

(30)

Third, it might be assumed that all three vowels share a single tone, as in (31). In the
ensuing discussion, we refer to a representation involving a multiply linked autosegmental representation (the long vowel in (30) and the entire tonal representation
in (31)) as a *plateau*.

(31) *Plateau representation*

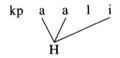

The plateau representation in (31) is, of course, the only representation of the three
that is consistent with the OCP. In this simple case, sequences of identical tones on
adjacent moras must therefore count as adjacent for purposes of the OCP.

But while the plateau representation in (31) is the standard autosegmental treatment for a monomorphemic surface HHH sequence, there are other configurations
where it is not so clear that the multiply linked representation is appropriate. Consider cases where two linked prosodic anchors (moras in this tonal example) are
separated by a third free prosodic anchor. Such a configuration is possible in Yoruba
since in this language there is evidence that surface M(id) tones are underlyingly
unspecified for tone (Pulleyblank 1986a, 1988b, Akinlabi 1984). Thus, a form such as

kátabá 'strong tobacco' with a HMH tonal pattern could be specified either with two individual H-tones (32a), a "twin peaks" representation, or with a single multiply linked H-tone (32b), a "gapped" representation.[20]

(32) a. *Twin peaks representation*   b. *Gapped representation*

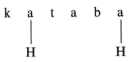   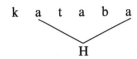

Although the OCP might be thought to favor the gapped representation, we argue below that it is actually the twin peaks representation that is correct for such a case. We suggest that cases such as *kátabá* exhibit a tension between tier-internal Adjacency and its implications for the OCP on the one hand (constituting pressure for a gapped representation), and a cross-tier principle of Precedence constituting pressure for the twin peaks representation. In the following section, we first review the type of evidence adduced in favor of the OCP, then turn to the evidence in favor of the cross-tier aspect of the Locality Condition.

1.5.1.1   Kukuya H-Tone Lowering   In Kukuya, there is a rule of H-Tone Lowering that changes a phrase-final H-tone to a M-tone (Paulian 1974, Hyman 1987). This rule provides strong evidence for the plateau representation, the representation of a tonal sequence that is compatible with the OCP. Consider the rule's effect on the single (stem) H-tone of a form like *bá* 'oil palm' (33a).

(33) *Phrase-medial and prepausal H-tones*

a.	mà + bá…	LH…	'oil palms …'
	mà + ba	LM #	'oil palms'
b.	má + bá…	HH…	'they are oil palms …'
	má + ba	HM #	'they are oil palms'
	*ma + ba	*MM #	

First, when the H of *bá* is phrase-medial, it remains high; but when it is final, it lowers to mid. Second, when the morpheme *bá* is preceded by another H-tone from a different morpheme, such as the copular marker (33b), it is still only the final H-tone that is affected by the rule. (See section 4.6.4 for more on tone patterns in Kukuya.)

Note in particular that Lowering does not iterate across the domain; lowering of a final H-tone does not subsequently induce lowering of a preceding H-tone. We represent Lowering here by a rule deleting a phrase-final H-tone, supplemented by a default M-tone, but this aspect of the discussion is not crucial.[21]

(34) *Kukuya H-Tone Lowering*

    a. H → ∅ / _____]_phrase

    b. ma ba → ma ba → [má ba] 'they are oil palms'
         | | |
         H H   H

Such rules provide a diagnostic for the appropriate autosegmental association patterns to be assigned to monomorphemic forms involving sequences of like tones. Consider forms such as the following, all involving sequences of phonetic H-tones:

(35) *Kukuya H-tone sequences in nonprepausal position*

        mà + báá...   'cheeks'
        mà + bágá...   'show knives'
        lì + báámá... 'liana'
        lì + bálágá... 'fence'

In principle, such forms could exhibit any of the associations shown (29)–(31). In practice, two types of considerations, conceptual and empirical, serve to choose among the various possibilities.

At a conceptual level, the OCP requires a multiply linked single H-tone comparable to that of (31). Representations like (36a) and (36b) would thus be ruled out, leaving the multiply linked plateau in (36c) as the only viable representation.

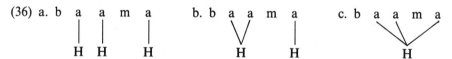

(36) a. b a a m a   b. b a a m a   c. b a a m a

Moreover, Hyman (1987), building on observations by Paulian (1974), demonstrates that all morphemes of Kukuya select a tonal melody from the following set: H, L, HL, LH, LHL. (See section 4.6.4 for a review of these tone patterns.) All the forms in (35) reflect the melody with a single underlying H-tone.

What is particularly interesting about the Kukuya case is that the rule of H-Tone Lowering provides an empirical test for confirming or disconfirming the predictions about stem tones made by considerations of the OCP and melodic distribution. Since, as seen in (33), the rule affects only a single H-tone that occurs in phrase-final position (recall that the rule does *not* iterate), the surface tonal form predicted for stems involving multiple surface H-tones will vary depending on the tonal representation postulated. If tones are individually assigned to vowels, then only the final vowel should be affected by Lowering. If, on the other hand, like surface tones result from a single multiply linked tone, then Lowering should affect the entire string. The correct prediction is made by the multiple-linking hypothesis, the hypothesis preferred anyway for conceptual reasons.

Compare the phrase-medial forms in (35) with the prepausal forms in (37).

(37) *Polymoraic prepausal forms*

mà + baa	'cheeks'	*...báa
mà + baga	'show knives'	*...bága
lì + baama	'liana'	*...bááma
lì + balaga	'fence'	*...bálága
cf.		
mà + ba	'oil palms'	

The Kukuya plateau effect provides a strong argument for a single feature being multiply linked. A rule that affects a single feature causes a contiguous string of prosodic anchors to undergo a single change.[22] If the rule is demonstrably not applying in an iterative fashion (as is the case here), then for a string of anchors to be affected, the entire string must be associated to a single autosegment, not to a sequence of identical autosegments.

We began this discussion by introducing three formal configurations: plateau, twin peaks, and gapped representations. Noting that the OCP requires plateau configurations in certain situations, we have provided empirical support from Kukuya for this theoretical position. Our interim conclusion is that the plateau configuration is necessary, and so it must be well formed. Before making concrete our proposal for Adjacency involving linked features, we turn to the issue of whether the two remaining configurations under consideration, twin peaks and gapped representations, are similarly motivated.

1.5.1.2 Twin Peaks and OCP Violations An initial consideration of the configurations in (38) might lead one to exclude both representations as OCP violations, since in both cases two tokens of α appear in sequence on the α-tier. Supporting similar arguments in work such as Archangeli (1986), Myers (1987), and Pulleyblank (1988b), we argue in this section that the twin peaks representation (38a) is necessary and so must be well formed, while only the representation involving identical adjacent F-elements linked to adjacent prosodic anchors (38b) is a true OCP violation and therefore ill formed.

(38) a. X   X   X   b. *   X   X
        | | | | |
        α   α   α   α

Our evidence comes from the distribution of H-tone in object clitics in Yoruba
(Pulleyblank 1988b).[23] Object clitics in Yoruba follow the verbal host. Following a
M-toned or L-toned verb, an object clitic is H-toned (39a,b). Following a H-toned
verb, however, it is M-toned (39c), a distribution known as *tonal polarity*.[24]

(39) *Polarity with object clitics in Yoruba*

a. rà	á	'buy it'	lù	mí	'beat me'
b. jẹ	ẹ́	'eat it'	pa	mí	'kill me'
c. rí	i (*rí í)	'see it'	rí	mi (*rí mí)	'see me'

The complete predictability of tone across all object clitics is expressed by inserting
tone by rule. The forms in (39a,b) demonstrate in this regard that a H-tone is inserted
on the final vowel. The pattern cannot be derived by H-tone spread because there is
no H-tone present in the input representation in such cases. In (40), we illustrate the
effect of H-Tone Insertion on each of the forms in (39).

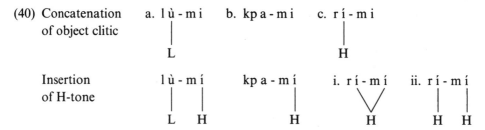

The insertion of a H-tone creates the desired results in two of the forms, (40a,b),[25]
but derives the wrong form in the third case, (40c). Note that H-Tone Insertion
derives an incorrect result in (40c) whether the original H-tone ends up multiply
associated (40c-i) or whether a new token of the H-tone is inserted (40c-ii). Since a
H-tone cannot be inserted, the object clitic surfaces with a default M-tone in exactly
this case.

Before providing further confirmation of this analysis, we comment briefly on the
reason for discussing this case, namely to observe the formal configurations that are
allowed or disallowed in such a derived environment. First, the derived representation in (40c-i) is a perfectly well formed plateau—a comparable structure has just
been motivated for Kukuya. Since *rí mí is *not* the correct surface form, the rule of
H-Tone Insertion cannot have the formal properties that would produce the effect of
plateau creation.[26] The alternative derived representation is that of (40c-ii), a pseudoplateau. With the pseudoplateau, adjacent prosodic anchors, the two vowels, are
associated to adjacent identical F-elements, the H-tones. Since H-Tone Insertion

takes place in (40a,b) but is blocked from applying in (40c), we conclude that the pseudoplateau of (40c-ii) must be ill formed. This is schematized in (41).

(41) *Ill-formed representation: Pseudoplateau*

Recall that the central aim of the current discussion is to determine whether a twin peaks representation or a gapped representation is appropriate for a form such as Yoruba *kátabá* 'strong tobacco' (32).

(42) a. *Plateau*   b. *Gapped*   c. *Twin peaks*

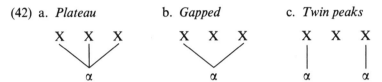

The ill-formedness of (41), combined with the well-formedness of the plateau representation in (42a), might suggest on this count that the gapped representation (42b), involving a multiply linked F-element, is to be preferred over the twin peaks representation (42c), involving a sequence of tokens of identical F-elements. Interestingly, however, Yoruba object clitics provide evidence of exactly the opposite type.

In the above discussion, we demonstrated that Yoruba object clitics involve the insertion of a H-tone, and that this insertion is blocked when there is a preceding H-tone: *rí mi, *rí mí* 'see me'. Consider what would happen with forms containing a third mora, where the H-tone of the verb root would be separated from the vowel targeted for H-Tone Insertion by an intervening mora as in (43). Assuming that the correct representation for a HMH sequence to be a twin peaks representation versus assuming it to be a gapped representation would make opposite predictions for such a bimoraic object clitic.

(43) μ   +   μ   μ
      |
      H

Consider first the possibility that a gapped formal structure is well formed, and that a twin peaks structure is universally ill formed (e.g., ruled out by the OCP). Under such an account, the representation that would correspond to a surface HMH sequence (potentially created by H-Tone Insertion) would be as in (44a) since (44b) would be ill formed.

(44) a. *Gapped*   b. *Twin peaks*

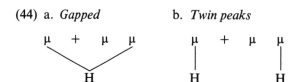

We have already seen, however, that H-Tone Insertion on clitics in Yoruba does *not* create the type of multiple linking that characterizes a plateau, ruling out the possibility that this particular rule results in a gapped configuration. Since under this hypothesis a twin peaks structure is invariably bad, H-Tone Insertion could not apply. As a result, a surface HMM pattern should result, analogous to the HM pattern of a verb + clitic sequence like *rí mi* 'see me' (39c).

Consider next the possibility that a twin peaks structure is well formed (44b), and that a gapped formal structure is universally ill formed (44a). Allowing H-Tone Insertion to derive a gapped structure from an input like (43) would now be ruled out on two counts. First, a multiply linked structure is not the appropriate result for H-Tone Insertion; second, even if it were, multiple linking would not be allowed to involve gaps. Turning to the twin peaks structure, the result of H-Tone Insertion would be completely well formed. As shown above, the rule affecting clitics inserts a H-tone on the final mora. The extra mora in (43) would act as a buffer to prevent the type of violation that blocks tonal insertion in a form like *rí mi* (*rí mi*) 'see me' (39c). The result would therefore be a HMH pattern.

The second person plural clitic, *-Vyín* 'you-PL', provides a test case in Yoruba.[27] The disyllabic clitic creates exactly the type of trimoraic sequence seen schematically in (43), the configuration needed to distinguish between gapped and twin peaks representations. The attested surface form is as predicted by the twin peaks structure, with a H-tone on the final vowel of the clitic, even when following a H-toned verb root.

(45) a. búuyín   'abuse you-PL'   *búuyin

    b. *After concatenation*

        b   u   –   V   y   ĩ

            |

           H

    c. *After H-Tone Insertion*

        b   u   –   V   y   ĩ

            | |

           H   H

The behavior of clitics provides clear evidence for the well-formedness of a twin peaks structure. The cases with monomoraic clitics in (39) demonstrate that the tonal patterns of clitics are accounted for by a rule that inserts a H-tone autosegment; the data in (45) demonstrate that such tonal insertion is not blocked when it creates a twin peaks structure, a structure where the medial anchor provides a buffer protecting against a potential OCP violation involving the two peripheral anchors.

1.5.1.3 Linked Adjacency We conclude that the representations in (46) are well formed.

(46) *Well-formed representations*

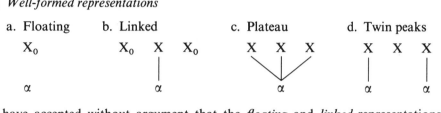

We have accepted without argument that the *floating* and *linked* representations (46a,b) are well formed; these configurations constitute the essential, defining properties of autosegmental representations. The discussions of Kukuya in section 1.5.1.1 and Yoruba in section 1.5.1.2 establish the plateau representation (46c) and the twin peaks structure (46d) as well formed.

In contrast, representations such as (47a,b) are ill formed.

(47) *Ill-formed representations*

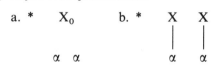

In (47a), two identical free autosegments are adjacent; in (47b), two identical autosegments are associated to adjacent prosodic anchors.

These configurations are precisely those defined as adjacent by Myers's (1987) definition of Adjacency. In (28), we gave the part of the definition that is relevant for free specifications; in (48), we give the complete definition.[28]

(48) *Adjacency*

   α is structurally adjacent to β iff:

   a. at least one of the two is unassociated, both are on the same tier, and no element intervenes between the two on that tier; or,

   b. both α and β are associated to the same anchor tier and no anchor intervenes on that tier between the anchors to which α and β are associated.

Given this definition of Adjacency, the OCP rules out both of the ill-formed configurations in (47). It does not rule out the twin peaks configuration: even though this structure contains identical autosegments on the same tier, they are not formally adjacent because they are not linked to adjacent anchors. The structure is therefore not subject to the OCP, and is therefore well formed.

In the next section, we turn to a rather different type of well-formedness issue, investigating configurations that involve either gaps or crossed lines. We demonstrate that such configurations are ruled out by a principle of Precedence.

1.5.2   Precedence and Formal Well-formedness

Within a tier, it is trivial that featural elements (features and hierarchical class nodes) occur in some order.[29] The left-to-right ordering of elements corresponds to real-time sequencing, with order playing an important contrastive role. One example is the distinctions in English based on the order of the root specifications [a], [p], and [t] in words like [pat] 'pot', [apt] 'opt', and [tap] 'top'. A second is the distinction caused by the two orders possible for the tonal features [L] and [H] in Igala, a language distinguishing between low, mid, and high tones: LH [àwó] 'a slap'; HL [áwò] 'hole (in a tree)'. (Welmers (1973) provides these as two members of a six-way minimal set whose members differ only in their tones.)

Such phonological order can be referred to in phonological processes. Contextual conditions may specifically define either a left-hand or a right-hand context for rule application to be appropriate. For example, Wolof and Akan provide cases of a left-hand context and a right-hand context, respectively (see chapter 3).

Of perhaps more interest is the issue of order when featural elements are found on different tiers. How do we talk about linear order relations when the items whose order we are trying to establish are not directly aligned? For example, in the configuration in (49), does [+round] precede [+high] or vice versa?

(49)

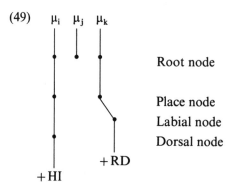

Root node

Place node
Labial node
Dorsal node

There is a clear sense in which [+high] precedes [+round]: [+high] is associated to μ_i, [+round] is associated to μ_k, and on the moraic tier, μ_i precedes μ_k. By appealing to the association to moraic anchors for the features in question, we indirectly establish the order between [+high] and [+round]: [+high] and [+round] inherit the order of the moras that they are associated to. In general terms, cross-tier precedence relations are determined by the transitive order relation established by phonological paths.

For the case in (49), it can be established on the moraic tier that μ_i precedes μ_j, which in turn precedes μ_k:

(50) $\mu_i < \mu_j < \mu_k$

Since μ_i is on a path to [+high], and since [+round] is on a path to μ_k, this means that [+high] precedes [+round]:

(51) $\mu_i/[+high] < \mu_j < \mu_k/[+round]$

Several points should be noted about such cases of derived order.

First, we propose that only a-paths are relevant for the establishment of cross-tier ordering relations. That is, derived order is established either at the root level or at the level of prosodic structure.

(52) *Anchor Hypothesis*

Anchor-paths establish cross-tier ordering.

For the present, we simply assert this restriction, motivating it in section 4.7.

Second, an element neither precedes nor follows itself; nor can an element precede or follow an element with which it is on a path (see Coleman and Local 1991). Consider, for example, a simple plateau representation such as (53).

(53) *Plateau representation*

In such a representation, μ_i precedes μ_j, which in turn precedes μ_k. Since μ_i is on an a-path to α, and since μ_k is on an a-path to α, it might be thought that one could derive the following contradictory statement:

(54) $\mu_i/\alpha < \mu_j < \mu_k/\alpha$

The problem with such a statement is that it formally asserts that α both precedes and follows μ_j—an apparent contradiction.

The implicit assumption that allows (54) to appear as a problem is that α is ordered with respect to μ_j. But since α is on an a-path with μ_j, it overlaps with μ_j (Sagey 1986, 1988, Hammond 1988); formally, α does not precede or follow μ_j.

Given this preamble, we propose the following *Precedence Principle*:

(55) *Precedence Principle*

Precedence relations cannot be contradictory.

In the remainder of this section, we discuss some perhaps surprising results obtained by this principle. We demonstrate that the Precedence Principle rules out gapped configurations, and we show that it derives the generally accepted prohibition against crossed association lines.

1.5.2.1 The Ill-formedness of the Gapped Configuration The gapped configuration, repeated in (56), has received virtually no motivation, although it has frequently appeared in the autosegmental literature (see McCarthy 1984a, Archangeli and Pulleyblank 1987, Cole 1987, Schlindwein 1987, Steriade 1987a, Ringen 1988, Vago 1988, etc.).

(56) *Gapped configuration*

Unlike plateaus without gaps, there has been a virtually complete absence of cases where nonadjacent anchors are simultaneously affected by a process affecting α.[30]

There are two ways of interpreting such a lacuna. On the one hand, it might be thought that this is simply an accident of the languages that have so far been examined in autosegmental terms. While this may conceivably be the case, we take the stronger position here that the gap is nonaccidental, that such gapped configurations are universally ruled out. Note that if gapped configurations are not attested underlyingly, then the Well-formedness Principle (24) requires that they not occur in derived configurations.

How then is the gapped configuration ruled out? Very simply, such a configuration creates a contradiction in terms of Precedence. In (56), consider the order on the moraic tier (the anchor tier for α):

(57) $\mu_i < \mu_j < \mu_k$

Via association, this can be filled out to the following:

(58) $\mu_i/\alpha < \mu_j < \mu_k/\alpha$

As can be seen, α both precedes and follows μ_j, a contradiction.[31] Hence, the Precedence Principle rules out gapped configurations.

There is, however, a class of well-formed representations that might at first glance appear to involve the gapped configuration, namely, cases where a feature is associated to syllable heads across intervening consonant(s). The configuration in (59) is motivated for Tiv in chapter 2, and comparable structures appear in various examples throughout the book. See especially section 4.7 for related discussion.

(59)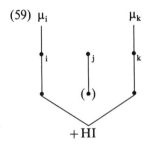

Representations like that in (59) are well formed under the Precedence Principle because the anchors for [+high] are moras, not Root nodes. At the moraic level, no element intervenes between μ_i and μ_k; hence, no anchor is available to create an ordering contradiction with respect to [+high]. A similar configuration involving a nonmoraic feature, where the anchors were Root nodes (not moras), would be ill formed. In chapter 4, we discuss some of the important implications of Precedence for various types of harmony systems.

1.5.2.2 The No Crossing Constraint   The No Crossing Constraint has enjoyed a lively formal existence, from Goldsmith's original (1976) proposal through Sagey's (1988) and Hammond's (1988) attempts at deriving (or not deriving) it from general principles, from Bagemihl's (1987) arguments that it can be temporarily violated to Coleman and Local's (1991) effort to demonstrate its incoherence in a three-dimensional model of phonology.

In this section, we demonstrate that the No Crossing Constraint follows from the Precedence Principle (55). Consider a typical No Crossing Constraint violation like the one shown schematically in (60).

(60) *No Crossing Constraint violation*

Precedence relations in (60) are incoherent. On the one hand, μ_i precedes μ_j on the mora tier, and α precedes β on their tier.

(61) a. $\mu_i < \mu_j$

   b. $\alpha < \beta$

In addition, since α is associated to μ_j, and since β is associated to μ_i, the following derived order is present:

(62) $\mu_i/\beta < \mu_j/\alpha$

This produces a contradiction: according to (61), α *precedes* β; according to (62), α *follows* β. Since the two orders contradict each other, the configuration in (60) is ruled out by Precedence. Thus, the No Crossing Constraint results automatically from assuming that the Precedence Principle governs phonological representations.

1.5.3 Summary

In this section, we have argued for a general Locality Condition governing phonological systems. Locality has two effects, Adjacency and Precedence. The combined effect of these principles is a phonology that allows free and linked specifications to occur in certain configurations but not others. In conjunction with the OCP, a condition on the cooccurrence of identical specifications, Locality allows plateau configurations and twin peak configurations, but disallows gapped configurations and crossing violations.

1.6 Conclusion

In this introduction, we have attempted to lay out the background necessary for the remainder of this work. The remaining chapters focus on the interactions between features; here, then, we have focused on the structure organizing the features, with particular attention to the feature hierarchy and to anchors.

Two themes that were introduced here will continue throughout the work. First, representations at all stages (derived or underived) must be *well formed*. In this chapter, well-formedness is the driving force behind Node Generation and the Locality Condition, along with the subparts of Locality, Adjacency and Precedence. Subsequent chapters explore well-formedness as it pertains to feature representations (chapter 2), combinations of features in paths (chapter 3), and rules and their application (chapter 4).

The second theme is *modularity*. The demonstration that structural ill-formedness results either from the OCP or from Precedence is one instance of the partitioning of phonological theory into several subtheories. A second example is the separation between substantive and formal proposals. For instance, the generic feature hierarchy is a formal proposal; assigning specific features and nodes in a hierarchy constitutes a substantive proposal. The separation of structural relations as discussed in this chapter from the feature relations on which the remainder of this book will focus is a further example of modularity within the phonological component.

The chapters to come reflect modularity in a more profound way: the three main chapters each motivate formal and substantive aspects of a separate subtheory, as well as demonstrating how each subtheory interacts with other aspects of the overall theory. Combinatorial Specification in chapter 2 proposes a formal model of feature combination; specific features provide a substantive instantiation of this theory. The Grounding Hypothesis of chapter 3 is a formal theory of implicational relations between features and the role of such implications in languages; values for features in specific implications constitute the substantive side of this proposal. The Grounding Hypothesis interacts with Combinatorial Specification to constrain the formally possible feature combinations and feature systems. The Parametric Rule Theory of chapter 4 proposes that rules are formally expressed by values for a limited set of parameters; the substantive contribution is to specify values for those parameters. Again the Grounding Hypothesis provides constraints on formally possible rules through its interaction with Parametric Rule Theory. The question we are left with at the end of the core chapters is "What serves to constrain formally possible *rule systems*?" In the concluding chapter, we sketch the outline of a possible answer.

Chapter 2
Combinatorial Specification

Only a few easily frightened souls have been ready to do without the phoneme.
Morris Halle, "On the Bases of Phonology"

2.1 Introduction

It has long been recognized that phonological segments are composed of subsegmental elements. Phonetic work has studied the various articulatory gestures that go together to derive speech sounds, and phonological work has recognized the relevance of such gestures in determining the patterning of speech sounds. The importance of such subsegmental elements has been particularly clear since work on distinctive feature theory such as Jakobson, Fant, and Halle 1963 and Chomsky and Halle 1968 (henceforth, *SPE*). But even where distinctive features have been posited as important components of phonological representations, *segments* have continued to play a central role in phonological descriptions.

Following in the well-established structuralist tradition (see, for example, Bloomfield 1933, Hockett 1958), generative phonology has tended to assume that one aspect of phonological description consists of determining the correct class of *segmental* phonemes for a language. Levels of description differ in their accounts of the precise composition of the segmental inventory, for example, whether a particular segment is a "phoneme," whether it is an allophonic variant, even whether it represents some kind of morphophonemic archiphoneme. Whatever levels are recognized, segmental representations typically play a central role. In *SPE*, for example, it was assumed that lexical formatives were composed of consonant and vowel *segments* (linearly arranged columns of distinctive feature specifications, as in (1)), and a clear task of phonological description necessarily consisted of identifying and describing such classes.

(1) *The* SPE *segment*

$$\begin{bmatrix} +\text{nasal} \\ +\text{coronal} \\ +\text{voiced} \\ \vdots \end{bmatrix}$$

In the highly influential chapter of *SPE* that discussed the *phonetic framework* of phonological theory, it was assumed that languages exhibited certain sets of consonants and vowels, some subsets of which would form natural classes. The essential role of subsegmental features was to describe such sets and to make it possible to characterize natural classes in a straightforward fashion. Hence, in generative phonological descriptions, as in earlier structuralist descriptions, it has been standard practice to begin a description by (i) identifying the consonant and vowel segments of a language and (ii) providing a description of these segments in distinctive features or in other terms.

With the arrival of autosegmental theory (particularly Goldsmith 1976), the situation changed in a radical way. Goldsmith pointed out that phonetic representations consist of "orchestrations" where articulatory gestures of various kinds overlap in a highly nonsegmental fashion. As work in this area has developed (see, in particular Clements 1985a and Sagey 1986), it has become clear that the foundation of feature representation involves a constrained but complex array of partially overlapping articulatory gestures. Consider, for example, the partial representations in (2) of [±voiced], [±nasal], and Coronal in an English word like *slam*.

(2) *The disintegration of the segment*

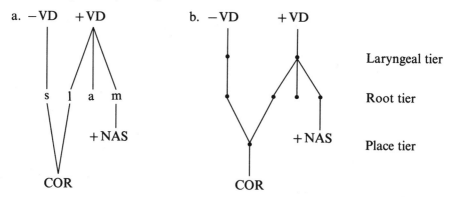

The forms in (2a) and (2b) represent the same word, but in (2a), the hierarchical node structure is suppressed and the Root nodes are replaced by orthographic symbols to make the overlap in feature values more apparent. In such representations the only serious candidate for "segmenthood" is the "root" level, the level of hierarchical structure that dominates all feature information.

But even the "root" does not correspond in a very exact way to the traditional notion "segment." Although a large class of segment types do have exactly one Root node, several classes may not. Some types of "contour segments" (3a) (affricates, prenasalized stops, diphthongs, etc.) may be appropriately analyzed as having more than one Root node (see Clements 1985a, Selkirk 1988), and various configurations appear to involve multiple "prosodic segments" associated to a single Root node (3b) (e.g., long vowels and geminate consonants; see Hayes 1986, Schein and Steriade 1986).

(3) *Roots versus segments*

    a. Contour segments   b. Multiple associations

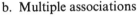

                                           Root tier

        x   x   x   Prosody or Nodes

The conclusion appears to be that there is no unit of feature content that strictly corresponds to the notion of segment.

Although the focus of this book is feature content, we note at this juncture that a similar conclusion is plausible with respect to any attempt at defining the notion of segment in prosodic terms. Although works such as McCarthy 1979, Clements and Keyser 1983, Kaye and Lowenstamm 1984, and Levin 1985 have posited a prosodic level of structure including segment-sized units such as CV-slots or X-slots, more recent studies such as Hyman 1985, McCarthy and Prince 1986, 1990, Itô 1989, Hayes 1989, and Archangeli 1991 argue in favor of a theory *without* a prosodic equivalent of the segment: Root nodes are directly gathered into mora and syllable constituents.

If segment-sized groupings are to be found neither at the level of featural units nor at the level of prosodic constituency, then there would appear to be no clear use for the traditional notion of segment.

In addition to the arguments briefly reviewed above, the notion of segment has come under attack for a very different kind of reason. Developing work such as that of Williams (1976) and Leben (1973), Goldsmith (1976) demonstrated that the underlying representations of lexical formatives may contain "floating" features that are completely unaffiliated with *segmental* material. This proposal, related in interesting ways to aspects of the theories of *prosodic analysis* (Firth 1948, Palmer 1970) and *long components* (Harris 1951), took a significant step toward weakening motivation for the notion of segment in underlying representation.[1] If individual features and sets of features enter the phonology unlinked to any type of segmental anchor, then one can no longer think of morphemes as composed solely or perhaps even predominantly of sets of alphabetic segments selected from some language-particular inventory. Although early work in the autosegmental literature tended to focus on tone (see Williams 1976, Leben 1973, Goldsmith 1976), even from the very early stages of the theory it was clear that tone was not isolated in its ability to "float."[2] For example, free nasal autosegments have been proposed for languages like Guarani (Goldsmith 1976) and Gokana (Hyman 1982); free [continuant] features have been proposed for languages like Classical Yucatec (Lombardi 1990) and Shona (LaCharité, in preparation); free [ATR] features have been proposed for a variety of languages (for a sample of such cases, see chapter 3); free glottal features have been proposed for languages like Yawelmani (Archangeli 1983, 1991; see section 4.6.5) and Coeur d'Alene (Cole 1987); free features of palatalization have been proposed for languages like Chaha (McCarthy 1983; see section 4.4.1) and Japanese (Mester and Itô 1989; see also section 4.6.1). This list could easily be extended both in terms of the types of features exhibiting the property of "floating" and in terms of the analyses motivating this property. The conclusion to be drawn is that neither underlying representations nor surface representations consist of discrete ordered sets of consonant and vowel segments.[3]

There is of course no requirement that a formal notion of segment needs to correspond directly to some traditional notion. One might simply define "segment" as being, for example, "the set of feature values dominated by a single Root node." The point to stress is that such a formally defined segment is not a primitive unit, and its role in natural phonologies cannot be assumed a priori. The role of the segment in phonological theory can therefore be framed as follows: phonological theory includes primitive notions of (i) features and (ii) associations between features; in addition, it may be the case that sets of associated features of a defined type may be assigned the theoretical status of "segments." Given these three notions, two primitive and one derivative, one may examine a variety of phenomena (such as the characterization of morpheme structure) to determine whether the underlying phonological representations of morphemes are established through direct reference to the primitive notions of features and associations, or whether they are established through necessary reference to the derivative notion of segment.

What is perhaps surprising in this connection is the importance that the derivative notion of segment has continued to play in spite of work on the central importance of subsegmental feature-sized units. It has continued to be normal practice, for example, to speak of *segmental inventories*, to identify a set of segments as appropriate for some language, and to view the characterization of these segments' properties as an important task for phonological analysis. Theories of underspecification, for example, essentially posit segments and then seek to determine the degree of feature specification necessary to underlyingly characterize such segments. Theories of *radical* underspecification (Kiparsky 1982, Archangeli 1984,1988, Pulleyblank 1986c, Itô and Mester 1986, Archangeli and Pulleyblank 1989, etc.) identify segments, and then argue that such segments should be specified with the minimal possible number of feature values. *Contrastive* underspecification (Clements 1987, Steriade 1987a, Mester and Itô 1989, etc.), on the other hand, retains feature specifications specifically where they serve to contrast *segments* but removes them if they serve no contrastive function. In a different vein, Mohanan and Mohanan (1984) and Mohanan (1986) propose that an understanding of lexical/postlexical distinctions cross-linguistically involves in part the correct identification of the *alphabets* that correspond to different levels of representation: underlying, lexical, and perhaps postlexical (if a distinction is made between postlexical and phonetic levels of representation; see Liberman and Pierrehumbert 1984, Kaisse 1985, Pulleyblank 1986a, Bagemihl 1988). The crucial aspect to note about such work is its reliance on the notion of segment as a point of departure in spite of (i) the derivative nature of this notion, and (ii) the frequently noted problems in motivating a featurally defined characterization of the segmental unit.

In this chapter, we argue for reference to the primitive notions of features and associations, directly deriving lexical formatives through reference to such primitives. Apparent reference to "segmental" units, we suggest, is reference to the constituent "Root node" in the feature hierarchy, comparable to reference to the "Place node," the "Laryngeal node," and so on.[4]

To summarize the above introduction, the proposal developed here, referred to as *Combinatorial Specification*, depends on two primitive notions of featural representation that have been central to all work on autosegmental theory:

(4) *Combinatorial Specification*

    a. F-elements

    b. Association status

The second property of (4), association status, refers to whether a particular F-element is *free* (unassociated) or *linked* (associated), familiar concepts from the autosegmental literature.

Regarding the first point, we propose that the primitives of a formal model of phonological feature content are *F-elements*, that is, positive and negative feature specifications ([+F], [−F], etc.) and the class nodes that group them into larger sets:

(5) *F-elements*

    a. Positive and negative feature specifications

    b. Class nodes

We follow Sagey (1986) in assuming a version of feature theory that combines binary features such as [±high], [±nasal], and [±voiced] with unary class nodes such as Place, Labial, and Coronal. If a theory with strictly monovalent features were assumed (see Anderson and Ewen 1987, Ewen and van der Hulst 1987, van der Hulst 1988, 1989, Avery and Rice 1989), the class of F-elements would be substantively changed but the formal properties of F-element combination would in principle be largely unaffected. In the approach to feature structure developed by Sagey (1986), certain class nodes bear intrinsic content (e.g., the articulator nodes *Coronal* and *Dorsal*) while other class nodes correspond to sets of features but do not in themselves bear any intrinsic feature content (e.g., the *Place* node and the *Laryngeal* node). As noted in chapter 1, we assume that only F-elements bearing intrinsic content may be terminal. This means that a class node such as Place cannot appear in a representation without dominating some content-bearing node such as Coronal, although Coronal itself, being content-bearing, may or may not dominate an additional feature such as [±anterior]. For some further discussion, see section 2.4.3.

F-elements and association status form the primitives of Combinatorial Specification; representations are constructed from *combinations* of these primitives. As background to the notion of combination, consider work such as Stanley 1967 and *SPE*: once the marking conventions applied, all segments in such models were specified for all features. As a result, all features were combined with all others at virtually all levels of representation. Formally, this minimized the importance of combination, since for all intents and purposes all features were always combined. Compare this with an autosegmental model. Particularly with phonological representations that are incompletely specified and/or involve the postulation of single-valued features, both formal and substantive notions of *combination* figure centrally. Formally, features may be unassociated at one stage of a derivation and become associated at another; substantively, not all feature values begin or end up linked with all others. Determining the types of nonrandom feature combinations that occur therefore becomes a nontrivial matter.

The formal aspects of combination involve the interplay of F-elements, both *free* and *linked*. In this chapter, we address the types of properties attributable to each formal type, examining the patterns resulting from sets of free F-elements, sets of linked F-elements, and sets of F-elements involving both the free and linked tokens. Note that free F-elements may combine with other F-elements during the course of a derivation, thereby creating paradigmatic combinations, or *paths* of F-elements. We turn now to explore the notion of path.

Consider again the partial feature representation for English *slam* seen in (2), reproduced here in (6).

(6) *Features and paths*

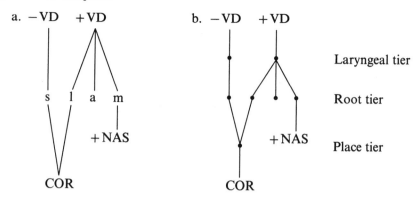

From (6b), it is evident that the [−voiced] specification is connected through association lines to the Coronal feature (as well as to the intervening Laryngeal, Root, and Place nodes); that is, [−voiced] is on a path with Coronal. The adjacent [+voiced] F-element is on three paths, one of which includes the F-element [+nasal].

It is important to clarify several issues concerning the notion of path. First, why is it necessary to invoke such a notion at all? As will be argued extensively in chapter 3, not all combinations of F-elements are allowable. We suggest that a large class of cooccurrence restrictions prohibit or require particular combinations of F-elements *on paths with each other*.[5] For example, in English, the values [+nasal] and [−voiced] do not combine, all nasals being redundantly voiced: *[+nasal, −voiced]. Although the path between [+voiced] and [+nasal] in (6) is perfectly well formed, this condition would rule out a configuration such as that in (7).

(7) −VD

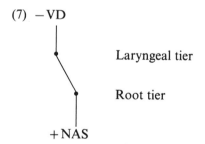

A *path*, therefore, characterizes the domain of paradigmatic linkings of F-elements that occur either underlyingly or as a result of association or spreading.

The domain defined by a path must exclude complex long-distance sets of associations; the prohibition against *[+nasal, −voiced], for example, cannot be used to rule out the cooccurrence of the [+nasal] value of the [m] in *slam* with the [−voiced] value present on the initial consonant [s] (6b). Note, however, that there is an unbroken set of associations connecting the two feature values, shown by the double lines in (8).

(8) *Associations, not paths*

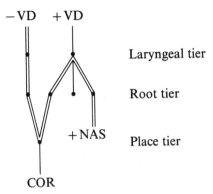

It is necessary to exclude "long-distance" sets of associations from the scope of such cooccurrence conditions, while continuing to include the relevant paradigmatic sets of associations as subject to such constraints. We exclude such linkings from the effect of paradigmatic conditions by restricting their domain to that of a path, defined in (9).[6]

(9) *Path*

There is a *path* between α and β iff

a. α and β belong to a linked set Σ of nodes or features or prosodic categories, and

b. in the set Σ, there is no more than one instance of each node or feature or prosodic category.

Only linked features can be on paths with other features; floating tones, and the like, are not on paths. This is the result of clause (9a).

   The effect of clause (9b) is to restrict the scope of path-related feature cooccurrence constraints such as the long-distance sets of associations discussed above with respect to [+nasal] and [−voice] in (6)/(8): the linked set of nodes and features including [+nasal] and [−voiced] also includes three tokens of the Root node and two tokens of the Laryngeal node, contrary to (9b) (shown in (8)). Thus, [+nasal] and [−voiced] are not in a single path in (6)/(8).

   In discussing the notion of path, it should be clear that there is a definite relation between this notion and the intuitive notion of segment. Often the types of features that would have been considered to characterize a segment are precisely the set of features on a single path with a given Root node. Two points are crucial in this regard. First, the correspondence between the two notions breaks down in the case of multiple linkings and melodic contours as noted above. Second, the notion of path does not suggest the assignment of any primitive status to the domain involved. As discussed above in relation to the general concept of the segment, the notion of path is completely derivative, determined by inspecting the arrangement of F-elements in any given representation.

Finally, paths serve to delimit the scope of various well-formedness conditions to be discussed in detail below; but paths themselves do not constitute well-formedness conditions. There is no general requirement that F-elements obligatorily occur on paths with other F-elements; the notion of path simply defines a particular type of F-element relation that occurs and that constitutes the domain of various implicational relations.

Rather than couch phonological analyses in terms of sets of segment-like entities that may exist underlyingly or in derived representations, we suggest that the phonological properties of featural representations involve in large measure the determination of (i) the correct set of F-elements, (ii) the free or linked status of those F-elements, (iii) the formal properties governing paths resulting from the association of F-elements, and (iv) the substantive constraints governing such paths.

Regarding the last point, since not all logically possible combinations of F-elements actually occur in paths in languages, a theory restricting path combinations is needed. In chapter 3, we consider two types of *implicational relations* between F-elements (sympathetic and antagonistic), proposing a restrictive theory of "grounding" to govern such relations. The presence of an element α may *preclude* an association with an element β. For example, the presence of the F-element [+nasal] typically precludes the presence of the F-element [−voiced]; the presence of the F-element [+high] typically precludes the presence of the F-element [+low].[7] In other cases the presence of an element α may be *contingent* on the presence of an F-element β. For example, the F-element [+nasal] may be possible only for the class that is [+sonorant]; the F-element [−ATR] may require the specification [−high].

The overall picture, therefore, is one in which the lexical formatives of a language are comprised of sets of F-elements, some linked, some free, that form paths governed by positive and negative implicational conditions. In this chapter, we concentrate on the basic properties of *combination*; in chapter 3, we concentrate on the substantive properties of *implications*; and in chapter 4, we examine the formal mechanisms by which differing representations may be related.

The first languages that we discuss are Tiv and Barrow Inupiaq. The data considered illustrate two extremes of a continuum between underlyingly free and underlyingly linked F-elements. In each case, the central role of F-elements as opposed to segments is illustrated; in Tiv, the purely derivative nature of the segment is also apparent. We go on to argue that a wide array of phonological patterns in other languages result from the simple notion of F-elements being *free* or *linked*. We contrast F-elements that play *active* roles with those that are *inert*, suggesting that both unpredictable, lexically specified F-elements as well as completely predictable F-elements may play either active or inert roles in the phonologies of different languages. Our argument is that notions of contrast, predictability, and compatibility can only be properly understood through reference to the F-element, not to the segment, and that the notion of segment is both inadequate and superfluous. In short, phonology is *nonsegmental*.

2.2 Combinatorial Specification

In this section, we discuss the range of phenomena that are possible within a model of Combinatorial Specification. We begin with discussion of the formal properties of combination, followed by substantive discussions of the vowel systems of Tiv and Barrow Inupiaq.[8]

The central proposal is that morphological formatives result from combining sets of F-elements paradigmatically and syntagmatically. Particular languages select particular sets of F-elements, with markedness theory assigning varying degrees of naturalness to the sets chosen (see Christdas 1988 and chapter 3). F-elements may constitute independent aspects of a particular formative, comprising in that case a *free* morpheme-level F-element that will associate to particular anchors during the course of the phonology. Alternatively, F-elements may be underlyingly assigned to an anchor, constituting a member of some *linked* set of F-elements.

Formally, if the phonology of a language contains n F-elements, then the maximum number of combinations of these F-elements possible is 2^n.[9] We illustrate this with vowel features in (10).[10]

(10) a. 1 F-element $2^1 = 2$ combinations:

	1	2
	+HI	∅

b. 2 F-elements $2^2 = 4$ combinations:

	1	2	3	4
	+HI	+HI		∅
	+RD		+RD	

c. 3 F-elements $2^3 = 8$ combinations:

	1	2	3	4	5	6	7	8
	+HI	+HI	+HI	+HI				∅
	+RD	+RD			+RD	+RD		
	+LO		+LO		+LO		+LO	

d. 4 F-elements $2^4 = 16$ combinations, etc.

The maximum number of logically possible representations that can be distinguished with three F-elements is eight (2^3). These eight combinations may manifest themselves in one of two ways: (i) within paths (i.e., where F-elements are linked) or (ii) within morphemes (i.e., where F-elements are free). In the case of paths, a particular selection of F-elements may result in a path combination like [+high, +low] or [+low, +round] that is incompatible either in general or for a particular language. In such a case, the number of combinations that are exploited by the language would be smaller than the number of logically possible combinations, because of substantive (not purely formal) restrictions on path combinations. In the case of morpheme-level F-elements, such combinations are still predicted to be possible if the specifications concerned are not linked in a single path. That is, all logically possible combinations of F-elements could occur as morpheme combinations (i.e., where F-elements are free) even in a language prohibiting specific path combinations. The relevance of this possibility will be demonstrated in our discussion of Tiv, where we argue that the underlying representations of vowels in Tiv verbs have exactly the eight combinations shown in (10c), in spite of the incompatibility in that language of [+high] and [+low]: in Tiv, this is possible because in underlying representations, all vowel F-elements are free.

It is possible, particularly where F-elements are underlyingly linked, that a language does not make full use of the range of combinations available to it in principle. As mentioned, for instance, it might be the case that a language does not allow [+low] and [+round] to combine, removing two of the eight combinations in (10c). The limit in this direction is to allow no combinations at all. We argue that Barrow Inupiaq is just such a language: in underlying representation, vowel F-elements are linked and no path combinations are licensed. If no combinations are allowed, a language with n linked F-elements can make $n + 1$ distinctions, illustrated in (11) with the same F-elements used in (10). We argue that the array in (11c) accounts for the vowel alternations in Barrow Inupiaq.

(11) a. 1 F-element $1 + 1 = 2$ distinctions:

	1	2
	+HI	$\emptyset$

b. 2 F-elements $2 + 1 = 3$ distinctions:

	1	2	3
	+HI	+RD	$\emptyset$

c. 3 F-elements $3 + 1 = 4$ distinctions:

	1	2	3	4
	+HI	+RD	+LO	$\emptyset$

d. 4 F-elements $4 + 1 = 5$ distinctions, etc.

Thus, given n F-elements, we know that m distinctions are feasible, where $n + 1 \leq m \leq 2^n$.

The two types of feature combination illustrated in (10) and (11) constitute two extremes in the possible interplay between the number of F-elements and the number of contrasts achieved. Free combination of the type seen in (10) makes maximal use of the smallest number of F-elements possible to achieve a particular set of contrasts; linked F-elements with restricted combination, as in (11), require a maximally large number of F-elements for a particular set of contrasts.

With this brief introduction to manipulating combinations, we are in a position to consider a "*2ⁿ* language," Tiv, and an "*n + 1* language," Barrow Inupiaq. After concluding the discussion of these two languages, we present the beginnings of a typology of the ways in which F-elements may combine cross-linguistically, going beyond the *2ⁿ* and *n + 1* patterns. The remainder of the chapter is devoted to exploring some of the other types of patterns predicted.

2.2.1 Unrestricted F-Element Combinations: Vowels in Tiv Verbs

The distribution of vowels in monomorphemic Tiv verbs provides an interesting starting point for our discussion of Combinatorial Specification because of a particularly flexible set of underlying combinatorial possibilities.[11] Morphemes of Tiv exhibit combinations of the three F-elements [+high], [+low], and [+round]. These F-elements combine to produce six distinct vowels on the surface, as shown in (12). (The symbol [ɔ] is used here for a [+low, +round] vowel.)

(12) *Surface realizations of Tiv vowels*

i	u
e	o
a	ɔ

These six vowels do not combine freely in verb stems. Of the 36 logically possible patterns for bimoraic stems, only 13 are robustly attested; of the 216 logically possible patterns for trimoraic stems, only 12 are robustly attested.[12] The problem raised by the vowels in Tiv verbs is to explain their restricted distribution.

Our account of the attested distributional patterns rests crucially on the hypothesis that the three vocalic F-elements are unassociated in underlying representation, verbs being lexically assigned one of the eight logically possible combinations seen in (10c). How these free F-elements associate and spread accounts for the limited possibilities of vowel combination.[13] The existence of more than eight surface patterns (one each corresponding to the underlying sets of F-elements) is the result of the interaction of four rules, High Spread, Round Spread, High Lowering, and Place Spread, interacting with representations that may differ prosodically, and that may or may not exhibit an Invisible ("extrametrical" or "extraprosodic") final mora.

This analysis motivates the central claims of Combinatorial Specification. Tiv strongly supports the analysis of morphemes in terms of sets of F-elements rather than in terms of sets of segments. This is transparently the case in Tiv because of the number of underlyingly free F-elements. Surface vowel patterns derive from one of eight underlying combinations of F-elements: the notion of vocalic "segment" is entirely derivative.

2.2.1.1 The Tiv Vowel System   Following Pulleyblank (1988a), we take [+high], [+low], and [+round] to be the F-elements present in underlying representations in Tiv, as given in (13a). We also assume that these F-elements are free in underlying representation. The appropriateness of assuming these particular F-elements will become apparent as the analysis is developed. Apart from the evidence of phonological patternings that is presented below, [+high] and [+low] are selected because these values are assumed to be active in the unmarked case.[14] The feature [+round] is selected, rather than [+back] or [−back], because of the presence in Tiv of two low vowels that contrast for rounding but not for backness, [a] versus [ɔ].

The reason for assuming underlyingly free F-elements is that *all* linkings of the underlying values of [high], [low], and [round] are predictable. Since linkings are predictable, they are not necessary underlyingly. In general, when morphemes exhibit a contrast involving some feature [±F], at least one value of [F] must be included in lexical representations to encode this contrast. The values of [F] that are so included may be either (i) predictable in their distribution or (ii) unpredictable. Where the distribution is unpredictable, values of [F] must be associated underlyingly; that is, they must be predistributed. On the other hand, where the distribution of a feature [F] within a string is completely predictable, such distribution may be accomplished by rules or conventions and the feature need not be linked underlyingly; that is, values of [F] may be underlyingly free.

For Tiv, it is important to note that all surface specifications of the features [high], [low], and [round] can be predicted from the presence or absence of a single specification for each feature within a verb root. We assume that single specifications are the automatic result of (i) the vowel F-elements' being free and (ii) their being governed by the OCP (see McCarthy 1986a; see also chapter 1): sequences of identical F-elements are disallowed.

Under these hypotheses, monomorphemic verb stems can be distinguished underlyingly by the eight combinations of F-elements given in (13c) (see also (10c)). The linking of these initially free F-elements is constrained by the incompatibility of [+high] and [+low], stated in (13b).

(13) *Tiv vowel representation*

   a. F-elements

b. Conditions

    HI/LO Condition: If [+high] then not [+low].
    LO/HI Condition: If [+low] then not [+high].

c.

e	i	a	o	ɔ	u	?₁	?₂
+HI					+HI	+HI	+HI
	+LO		+LO			+LO	+LO
		+RD	+RD	+RD	+RD		

In the type of representation given in (13a), a circle around a feature indicates that it is free in underlying representation. The eight combinations in (13c) are exactly those found in (10c). The constraints in (13b) are formulated as implicational conditions, rather than as *[+high, +low], for reasons that are discussed in chapter 3.

The Use of Vowel Symbols

It is important to recognize that the symbols heading each column of vowel (or consonant) specifications stand for path combinations of F-elements: what has theoretical significance is the F-elements themselves, not the symbols. The symbols are used simply as a convenience in presenting representations: for example, it is much easier expositionally to make sense of the Yoruba form for 'oil' if it is symbolized as *ekpo* rather than as *[−high]kp[−high, +round]*, yet the former is merely a shorthand notation for the latter. Other symbols could be used as well, but again, the traditional vowel symbols are easier to process than using numbers (e.g., "*4kp3*") or some other set of arbitrary symbols (e.g., "*#kp$*"). For further discussion of this issue, see section 2.8.1.

In the case of Tiv, two combinations of free F-elements that occur underlyingly do not correspond to surface vowels in any obvious way since they involve incompatible F-elements, namely, [+high] and [+low] (symbolized as *?₁* and *?₂* in (13)). This underscores the necessity of thinking in terms of F-elements, not in terms of segments/symbols.

To give a brief overview of our analysis of Tiv verbs, we run through the central aspects of how the representations in (13) are mapped onto surface realizations (see Pulleyblank 1988a). The specification [+high] links from left to right and spreads throughout a verb (High Link/Spread), subject to lexically determined final Invisibility. The specification [+round] links and spreads between vowels with identical specifications for [high] (Round Spread). [Round] is unaffected by Invisibility; hence, Round Spread must apply after the loss of Invisibility. The F-element [+low] links from left to right and is not individually subject to any rule of spreading.

Before beginning our proposed account of F-element combination, we digress briefly to discuss a process, Place Spread, that slightly obscures the general surface patterns.

2.2.1.2 Place Spread The specification of a vowel V_2 is identical to that of a preceding vowel V_1 in the following contexts: (i) when V_2 immediately follows V_1 with no intervening consonant, (ii) when V_2 follows V_1 with an intervening [h], the sole laryngeal consonant of Tiv.[15]

In the following examples, we illustrate Place Spread with all six surface vowels of Tiv.[16] Only the VV and VhV sequences in the following data are of importance in this regard; all other aspects of the examples given are the result of other distributional properties and are discussed in subsequent sections.[17] To be noted in these forms is the identity of V_1 and V_2 in the sequences V_1V_2 and V_1hV_2.

(14) [i]

(C)VV	ìi	'bury'
(C)VhV	víhi	'spoil'
(C)VVCV	nyìishi	'change one's mind'
(C)VVC∅	tíil	'press with force on a thing' ($<$ *tíili*)
(C)VhVC∅	ndìhil	'become lost' ($<$ *ndìhili*; $=$ *ndìil*)

(15) [e]

(C)VV	tsèe	'mock'
(C)VhV	téhe	'cough'
(C)VVCV	péese	'be or become light in weight'
(C)VVC∅	pèel	'winnow by shaking winnowing-mat up and down' ($<$ *pèele*)
(C)VhVC∅	féher	'sweep out of X; sweep X along'

(16) [a]

(C)VV	tsàa	'sift on a winnowing-mat'
(C)VhV	tsáha	'punish'
(C)VVCV	tsáase	'beat a knife with a hammer to sharpen it'
(C)VVC∅	dàal	'play the fool' ($<$ *dàale*)
(C)VhVC∅	ndáhar	'be small' ($<$ *ndáhare*)

(17) [ɔ]

(C)VV	kɔ̀ɔ	'rub thing on to another (as soot)'
(C)VhV	kɔ̀hɔ	'dig out with a pointed tool, etc., a thing embedded in an orifice'
(C)VVCV	yɔ́ɔso	'chat'
(C)VVC∅	mɔ̀ɔr	'transplant (tobacco, mangoes)' ($<$ *mɔ̀ɔro*)
(C)VhVC∅	ndɔ́hɔr	'become wet (from rain, river, etc.)' ($<$ *ndɔ́hɔro*)

(18) [o]

(C)VV	òo	'slough skin'
(C)VhV	gòho	'dart away'
(C)VVCV	nyóoso	'be fully grown'
(C)VVC∅	kòom	'turn' (< *kòomo*)
(C)VhVC∅	yóhor	'what has to be borne is too much for person'
		(< *yóhoro*)

(19) [u]

(C)VV	pùu	'despise, think of no importance'
(C)VVCV	gbúusu	'be abundant'
(C)VVC∅	vùur	'root up soil' (< *vùuru*)
(C)VhVC∅	njùhur	'pucker up thing' (< *njùhuru*)

Following Pulleyblank (1988a), we analyze these cases as involving a rule of Place Spread (20), a rule that spreads Place specifications from mora to mora and is blocked by Place-bearing elements, that is, any consonant specified for supralaryngeal F-elements (see Steriade 1987b, Wiswall 1991a,b).

(20) *Tiv Place Spread and derivations*

    a. Place Spread

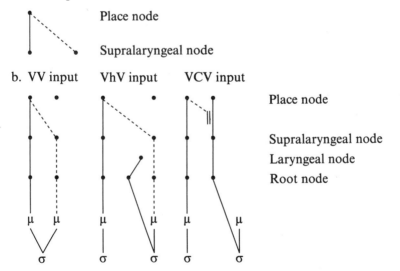

    b. VV input   VhV input   VCV input

Of crucial importance for the discussion here is simply that the surface realization of V_2 in these cases is entirely predictable. As a consequence, there is no reason to assign it some underlying specification for vowel F-elements.

> **The Parametric Formalization of Rules**
>
> In chapter 4, we argue for a parametric theory of phonological rules. All rules motivated in this work can be reformulated in terms of the parametric model; the few cases that raise problems are footnoted. It is such parametric rule expressions that would constitute the formal expression for each rule. Graphic expressions of rules included in the text are for expositional purposes only.

2.2.1.3 No Spread Rules We now move beyond the process of Place Spread to examine the sorts of specifications that are needed to derive the various vowel patterns found in Tiv verbs. First, we discuss a class of forms in which no spread rules apply, forms with no underlying F-elements. Next, we discuss forms in which no rule other than Place Spread is potentially applicable, the forms involving [+low] only. Finally, we work through the forms involving rules spreading the individual F-elements [+high] and [+round].

No F-Elements: 172 Examples—18% of Total Sample In a large class of cases in Tiv, illustrated in (21), all vowels of a verb stem surface as [e], regardless of the length of the stem. We analyze this class as being entirely devoid of F-elements underlyingly (see Pulleyblank 1988a).

(21) *No F-elements*

(C)V	dè	'leave'
(C)VCV	bènde	'touch'
(C)VV	tsèe	'mock'
(C)VCØ	gér	'be in excess' (< *gére*)
(C)VCVCV	yévese	'flee'
(C)VCVCØ	kéver	'catch thing thrown to one' (< *kévere*)
(C)VVCV	péese	'be or become light in weight'
(C)VVCØ	pèel	'winnow by shaking winnowing-mat up and down' (< *pèele*)

The strongest reason for considering [e] as phonologically unspecified is the occurrence of a left-to-right distributional asymmetry. All vowel contrasts are found on the first mora of a verb. Abstracting from certain bimoraic forms involving [+low] on the second mora, noninitial moras of a verb are of two types: (i) they share features with the preceding mora; (ii) they are [e]. It is clear that in Tiv, the realization [e] corresponds to the default case, the realization that occurs when no other feature is assigned.[18] Since such morphemes have no F-elements in underlying representation, their derivation involves no phonological process of linking or of spreading.

(22) *No F-elements; no rules*

    b μ n d μ → [bènde]

Following the convention established in the "Default Values" box, we do not include rules inserting [−high], [−low], and [−round] in (22) because we have no evidence that these values are ever inserted phonologically. Surface results here are completely consistent with having default values inserted either phonologically or phonetically; they are equally compatible with having no default values inserted, but instead invoking a default phonetic interpretation mechanism.

"Default" Values

The question arises whether absent values are ever filled in. For instance, do the vowels of the Tiv verbs in (21) exit the phonological component specified as [−high, −low, −round] or do they exit the phonological component with no such F-elements?

    The evidence on this issue suggests that in some cases absent F-elements are inserted and in other cases they are not. Examples of the former type, where certain absent F-elements are inserted, include Yoruba (section 2.4), Pulaar, and Eastern Javanese (section 2.6). Phonetic evidence from Japanese tone interpolation (Pierrehumbert and Beckman 1988), from interpolation of [back] (and the lack thereof) across Russian consonants (Keating 1985, 1988), and from interpolation of nasality in Sundanese (Cohn 1989) argues that the same set of F-elements may be absent phonetically as well as phonologically, in some cases at least.

    At this point, we know of no criteria determining which way a particular F-element will behave. For our purposes here, rules inserting absent F-elements will be included only if there is evidence that the F-element *must* be inserted for purposes of the phonology proper. In the ambiguous cases, we do not include rules phonologically inserting the F-elements.

[+ Low] Only: 184 Examples—20% of Total Sample In the second class of forms to be considered, the specification of [+low] is sufficient to allow a complete derivation of surface values. All members of this class have the low vowel [a] in the initial syllable (e.g., *dzà* 'go to'), accounted for by having a morpheme-level F-element link up from left to right.[19]

(23) *Tiv Low Link*

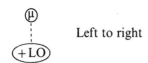

                    Left to right

Except for vowel sequences affected by Place Spread (e.g., *tsàa* 'sift on a winnowing-mat', *tsáha* 'punish') (see section 2.2.1.2), all noninitial vowels in this class surface as [e] (e.g., *kpámbese* 'nonplus').

(24) *[+LO] F-element*

(C)V	dzà	'go to'
(C)VCV	màse	'somewhat later than first verb, person did subsequent action'
(C)VCØ	wàm	'to conciliate by a gift a person who bears one rancor' (< *wàme*)
(C)VCVCV	kpámbese	'nonplus'
(C)VCVCØ	áser	'wrench off; break off' (< *ásere*)
(C)VV	tsàa	'sift on a winnowing-mat'
(C)VhV	tsáha	'punish'
(C)VVCV	tsáase	'beat a knife with a hammer to sharpen it'
(C)VVCØ	dàal	'play the fool' (< *dàale*)
(C)VhVCØ	ndáhar	'be small' (< *ndáhare*)

The sample derivation of *áser* in (25) illustrates this pattern. Place Spread is inapplicable in this example because of the supralaryngeal specifications of [s]. (The surface realization also shows the effect of final vowel deletion. See point (iv) in note 17.)

(25) *[+LO] Link*

$$\mu \quad s \quad \mu \quad r \quad \mu \quad \rightarrow \quad \mu \quad s \quad \mu \quad r \quad \mu \quad \rightarrow \quad [áser]$$

$$+LO \qquad\qquad\qquad +LO$$

We turn now to the cases involving rules of single F-element assimilation, beginning with the process of High Spread.

2.2.1.4 High Link/Spread In a fairly large class of verbs (71 examples—8% of total sample), all vowels surface as [i] as the result of a lexical specification of a [+high] F-element that links and spreads. Examples illustrating this pattern are given in (26).

(26) *[+HI] F-element*

(C)V	shí	'remain all day or a great part of the day doing something'
(C)VCV	tíndi	'send'

(C)VCØ	gbìl	'put a thing down' (< gbìli)
(C)VCVCØ	víngil	'knead into a ball' (< víngili)
(C)VV	ìi	'bury'
(C)VhV	víhi	'spoil'
(C)VVCV	nyiishi	'change one's mind'
(C)VVCØ	tíil	'press with force on a thing' (< tíili)
(C)VhVCØ	ndìhil	'become lost' (< ndìhili; = ndìil)

Place Spread is relevant in a subclass of such cases. However, a supplementary rule is needed to account for the full range of this pattern. We posit a rule, High Link/Spread (27), that links the [+high] specification and spreads it rightward.

(27) *Tiv High Link/Spread*

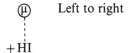

Left to right

Unlike Low Link (23), which links a free autosegment only, we analyze High Link/Spread as both linking a free autosegment and linking an associated autosegment—each to a free anchor. Graphically, the distinction between these rule types is encoded by circling autosegments or anchors that are necessarily *free* (e.g., Low Link). In chapter 4, a formal account of these structural possibilities is presented.

A sample derivation, that of *tíndi* 'send', is given in (28); we postpone discussion of why linking and spreading are accomplished by a single iterative process until the rest of the rules have been presented.

(28) *[+HI] Link/Spread*

t μ nd μ → t μ nd μ → [tíndi]

+HI   +HI

In cases not affected by Place Spread,[20] we have seen that morphemes involving a morpheme-level F-element [+high] (26) differ systematically from morphemes involving a morpheme-level F-element [+low] (24): while the [+high] specification links and spreads, the [+low] specification links and does not spread. There is a subset of cases involving a morpheme-level specification [+high], however, where spreading does not the place (34 examples—4% of total sample). These are illustrated in (29).

(29) *[+ HI]: Linking without spreading*

(C)VCV	pìne	'ask'
	kíne	'groan'
	hímbe	'become warped'
(C)VVCV	nyìise	'change one's mind'

Following Pulleyblank (1988a), we propose that as a lexically marked property of these forms, the final vowel is *Invisible* (extrametrical) when High Link/Spread applies (see Hayes 1982, Kiparsky 1985, Poser 1984, Inkelas 1989, etc.).[21] As such, when the rule tries to apply, it can only associate [+ high] to the initial vowel since the final vowel is not visible; the final (unspecified) vowel surfaces as [e]. A sample derivation is given in (30), where Invisibility is represented with angled brackets ("⟨...⟩").

(30) *[+ HI] Link & Invisibility: No Spread*

$$p \quad \mu \quad n \quad \langle\mu\rangle \quad \rightarrow \quad p \quad \mu \quad n \quad \langle\mu\rangle \quad \rightarrow \quad [\text{pìne}]$$

$$+\text{HI} \qquad\qquad\qquad +\text{HI}$$

It should be noted that virtually all morphemes of this type are disyllabic, a point we return to in the discussion of patterns involving the combination of a [+high] F-element with other F-elements.[22]

To summarize, our sample contains 105 examples of regular forms that require the postulation of a single [+high] F-element underlyingly. This number constitutes 11% of the total sample of verbs. Within this group, 68% exhibit spreading of the [+high] specification throughout the form (whether due to High Link/Spread or to Place Spread), while 32% (restricted to disyllables) exhibit Invisibility of the final vowel.

2.2.1.5 Round Link and Round Spread   We have shown so far the surface result of positing the single F-elements [+low] or [+high] for a morpheme. The remaining case of a single F-element concerns the F-element [+round]. In our sample, there are 86 verbs with the pattern ...*o*...(*o*)...(*o*) (9% of the total). These verbs, we argue, are the [+round] class.

(31) *[+ RD] F-element*

(C)VCV	dóndo	'adjoin, be the neighbor of'
(C)VC∅	dzòr	'assemble component parts of machinery, cycle, etc.'
		(< *dzòro*)
(C)VCVC∅	yòghor	'to shake thing in its socket to loosen it' (< *yòghoro*)
(C)VV	òo	'slough skin'
(C)VhV	gòho	'dart away'

(C)VVCV	nyóoso	'be fully grown'
(C)VVCØ	kòom	'turn' (< kòomo)
(C)VhVCØ	yóhor	'what has to be borne is too much for person'
		(< yóhoro)

The F-element [+round] by itself results in a surface manifestation of [o]. If a morpheme-level [+round] were to link from left to right and not spread (as seen in Tiv with [+low]), then the surface patterns ...o...e and ...o...e...e would be expected; if, however, [+round] were to link and spread (as with [+high]), then the patterns ...o...o and ...o...o...o would be predicted. The many examples of the latter patterns, as in (31), in conjunction with a complete absence of examples of the former ones, argues for postulating a rule of spreading, as illustrated in the derivation of *dóndo* 'adjoin, be the neighbor of' (32).

(32) *[+RD] Link and Spread*

d μ nd μ   →   d μ nd μ   →   d μ nd μ   →   [dóndo]
                    | ∕
 +RD   +RD   +RD

In this derivation, the linking of [+round] requires two steps: (i) Round Link: a free [+round] F-element links from left to right, (ii) Round Spread: the linked [+round] F-element resulting from (i) spreads from left to right. The motivation for this distinction becomes clear when we consider the behavior of the F-element [+round] in combination with [+high] and/or [+low]. We therefore postpone schematizing the rule that spreads [+round] until those combinations are discussed. The rule that links a free specification of [+round] is shown in (33).

(33) *Tiv Round Link*

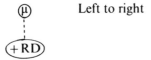

Left to right

Before we leave this class of cases, however, it is important to note that unlike High Link/Spread, there are no examples involving Round Spread that exhibit Invisibility effects. The pattern exhibiting the spreading of [+round] is not only the most common pattern, it is the *only* one. Unless Invisibility could be made specific to a particular F-element (e.g., [+high] but not [+round] in Tiv), Round Spread must apply after the loss of Invisibility to ensure that no stems are immune to spreading. Note in this regard that selective Invisibility (applicable to one F-element but not another) is impossible in the restrictive approach to this property taken by Inkelas (1989), although resolution of this issue is orthogonal to present concerns.

We now turn to the morphemes that combine F-elements in their underlying representations. The first case we consider is the one where [+high] cooccurs with [+round], that is, the two F-elements that have just been discussed.

2.2.1.6 Combinations of F-Elements The combination of [+high] with [+round] results in the surface manifestation [u]. Hence, if these two F-elements are the only F-elements of a verb, and given the rules discussed above that spread both [+high] and [+round], all vowels of such a verb are straightforwardly predicted to be [u]. In our sample, there were 84 such examples (9% of the total sample).

(34) *[+ HI] and [+ RD] F-elements*

(C)V	lù	'remain, stay (etc.)'
(C)VCV	úndu	'leave person or thing behind'
(C)VCØ	dúgh	'take out' (< *dúghu*)
(C)VCVCØ	gúvul	'hem, make selvedge' (< *gúvulu*)
(C)VV	pùu	'despise, think of no importance'
(C)VVCV	gbúusu	'be abundant'
(C)VVCØ	vùur	'root up soil' (< *vùuru*)
(C)VhVCØ	njùhur	'pucker up thing' (< *njùhuru*)

This pattern exhibits behavior of [+high] that is entirely comparable to the examples in (26) that involved [+high] only; it exhibits behavior of [+round] that is entirely comparable to the examples in (31) that involved only [+round]. This combination of effects is illustrated by the derivation in (35), which shows the application of High Link/Spread, Round Link, and Round Spread.[23]

(35) *[+ HI] Link/Spread; [+ RD] Link and Spread*

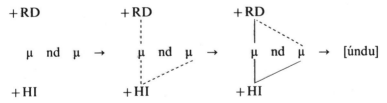

Since the spreading of [+high] is blocked in certain cases by final Invisibility, one would expect the cases in (34) to be supplemented by a class where spreading of [+high] is blocked. There were 47 examples of this type (5% of the total sample), illustrated in (36): as with the forms involving [+high] only, cases exhibiting Invisibility are almost exclusively disyllabic. The number of forms itself appears significant since cases exhibiting Invisibility constitute 36% of the examples with the F-elements [+high] and [+round], and 32% of the examples with the F-element [+high] alone;

that is, independently of the presence or absence of a floating [+round] F-element,
Invisibility affects roughly one-third of the [+high] verb stems.[24]

(36) *[+HI] and [+RD] F-elements with Invisibility (No Spread)*

    (C)VCV   únde   'mount'
                  hùre   'drive away'
                  búme   'be foolish'

It is immediately noteworthy that Round Spread is blocked in these cases. There
are two obvious ways to account for this fact. First, it could be assumed that Invisibility blocks the spreading of [+round] in a manner analogous to that observed with
[+high]. As seen in the last section, however, such an analysis makes incorrect predictions for the cases involving [+round] only. That is, such an analysis would predict the occurrence of the unattested pattern *CoCe*. We therefore adopt the analysis
proposed by Pulleyblank (1988a) that Round Spread has a vowel height condition:
spreading takes place only between vowels that agree in their value for [high]. Independently of Invisibility, such a condition accounts for the applicability of Round
Spread in (31) and (34), and its inapplicability in (36). And as we will show, the
condition correctly blocks round harmony in a *u...a* sequence as well.[25]

(37) *Tiv Round Spread*

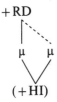

To summarize, the derivation of the forms in (36) is comparable in all essential
respects to the derivation of *pine* in (30). The one property that causes the forms to
differ is the F-element [+round]; this F-element links from left to right but does not
spread because of the height difference between the first and second vowels. The
derivation of the forms in (34) provides a contrast: there is no Invisibility, so both
[+high] and [+round] spread. The total class of cases with [+high] and [+round]
in their underlying representation comprises 14% of our sample (131 examples).

Having considered the results of combining [+round] with [+high], we now turn
to the results of combining [+round] and [+low]. We showed in the discussion of
(24) that [+low] does not spread rightward individually, although it may be affected
by Place Spread. We therefore expect an initial low round vowel [ɔ]. If Place Spread
is applicable, the low value may spread; otherwise, the initial low vowel is followed

by mid vowels. Note that since low and mid vowels share the same value for [high], Round Spread is never blocked. Hence, surface forms of either the type ɔ(h)ɔ...(o) or the type ɔCo...(o) are derived. In our sample, 107 examples (11% of total) exhibited precisely this array of patterns.

(38) *[+RD] and [+LO] F-elements*

(C)VCV	nɔ́ndo	'drip'
(C)VCØ	ɔ́v	'cut into strips' (< ɔ́vo)
(C)VCVCV	nyɔ́ngoso	'run'
(C)VCVCØ	sɔ́som	'approach' (< sɔ́somo)
(C)VV	kɔ́ɔ	'rub thing on to another (as soot)'
(C)VhV	kɔ́hɔ	'dig out with a pointed tool, etc., a thing embedded in an orifice'
(C)VVCV	yɔ́ɔso	'chat'
(C)VVCØ	mɔ́ɔr	'transplant (tobacco, mangoes)' (< mɔ́ɔro)
(C)VhVCØ	ndɔ́hɔr	'become wet (from rain, river, etc.)' (< ndɔ́hɔro)

Note that Invisibility is not relevant here: (i) [+low] does not spread and so would not be affected by final Invisibility, (ii) as noted above, Invisibility does not affect the application of Round Spread. The fact that there is no more than a single exceptional case of the type ɔ...e supports this characterization of the relation between Round Spread and Invisibility (see (1) in the Appendix).

A derivation of forms involving [+low] and [+round] would be comparable to that given for a [+round] case in (32), differing only by the presence of [+low] that links to the leftmost vowel.

We have now exhausted the combinations that involve compatible F-elements. Two combinations remain: (i) [+high] and [+low], (ii) [+high], [+low], and [+round]. These two cases exhibit special properties because of the impossibility of combining [+high] and [+low] on a single path.

2.2.1.7 [+High] and [+Low] Together If the F-elements [+high] and [+low] are underlyingly free, then their combination within the same morpheme is logically possible in underlying representations. At the same time, their association to a single anchor is blocked by the cooccurrence conditions in (13c) prohibiting [+high] and [+low] in a single path. To resolve this discrepancy, there are essentially three possibilities for the linking of such incompatible free F-elements. On the one hand, if neither F-element were assigned priority, then linking would be impossible (see Pulleyblank 1988a). On the other hand, priority could be assigned to the linking of [+high] (39a), or to the linking of [+low] (39b).

(39) a. *Priority to [+ High] Link*

```
C  μ  C  μ   →   C  μ  C  μ   →   C  μ  C  μ
                    |                 |
   + HI            + HI            + HI  |
      + LO            + LO            + LO
```

b. *Priority to [+ Low] Link*

```
C  μ  C  μ   →   C  μ  C  μ   →   C  μ  C  μ
                       |             |    |
   + HI            |+ HI         |    + HI
      + LO            + LO         + LO
```

In Tiv, only the option illustrated in (39a) is employed, where [+ high] links first.[26]

First, consider cases involving the combination of [+ round], [+ high], and [+ low]. In our sample, we found 60 examples of this type, 6% of the total.

(40) *[+ RD], [+ HI], and [+ LO] F-elements*

(C)VCV	búsa	'break fragment off'
	kùma	'suffice'
	tsúmba	'abrade, scratch'
(C)VV	wùa	'grind dry substance'
(C)VhV	wùha	'adorn'
(C)VVC∅	húan	'be or become silent' (< *húane*)

As mentioned above, priority is assigned to linking the [+ high] F-element, which therefore surfaces on the leftmost vowel, as in (41); the [+ low] specification finds a place on the final vowel. As for [+ round], it links to the initial vowel but does not spread because of the height condition on Round Spread.

(41) *[+ High], [+ Low], and [+ Round] Link*

```
+ RD                + RD
                      |
b  μ  s  μ   →   b  μ  s  μ   →   [búsa]
                    |     |
   + HI            + HI   |
      + LO            + LO
```

Two apparently unrelated problems present themselves. Assuming that some mechanism causes the [+ high] to link, not [+ low], as already discussed, the first issue is how to resolve the technical problem of preventing [+high] from spreading. The second is how to account for an interesting distributional property governing the class of morphemes in (40): all members of the {[+high], [+low], [+round]} class are disyllabic.

We suggest that the two problems are related and that a single proposal resolves both—namely, final Invisibility, already motivated to account for [C_0iCe] and [C_0uCe] roots. There are, of course, alternatives to the Invisibility account, for example, assigning priority to the association of [+high]. This can be formally accomplished by simply ordering the rule of High Link/Spread *before* the rule of Low Link.[27] However, this order produces a perhaps surprising result. It has already been discussed that High Link/Spread both associates and spreads the F-element [+high]. At least until this point, there has been no reason to differentiate the association of [+high] from its spreading. But if this is so, then High Link/Spread and Low Link would apply to a form with both [+high] and [+low] as shown in (42).

(42)   +HI   +HI

    C μ C μ   →   C μ C μ

    +LO   +LO

Priority to association/spreading of [+high] means that the F-element [+low] would have no place to associate: the [+high] specification would have already occupied all available anchors. Given this analysis, a representation with [+high] and [+low] would be highly marked from the perspective of learnability: there could be no morpheme-internal evidence to cause the language learner to posit a [+low] specification.

However, the situation changes in exactly one class of cases. As illustrated in (43), in those disyllabic stems that exhibit final Invisibility, High Link/Spread does not assign [+high] to the final vowel.

(43)   +HI   +HI

    C μ C ⟨μ⟩   →   C μ C ⟨μ⟩

    +LO   +LO

We know from the *i...e* and *u...e* patterns ((29) and (36), respectively) that High Link/Spread does not apply after the removal of Invisibility. By simply assuming that Low Link *does* apply after loss of Invisibility, correct results are now obtained. A suitably revised derivation of *búsa* (cf. (41)) is given in (44).

(44) +RD   +RD   +RD
                              | |
   b μ s ⟨μ⟩ →   b μ s ⟨μ⟩ →   b μ s μ →   [búsa]
            | | | |
   +HI   +HI   +HI |
      +LO   +LO   +LO

Given this analysis, the restriction of the *u...a* pattern to disyllabic stems is explained: as noted above, only disyllabic forms exhibit Invisibility. Moreover, this
account provides an explanation for the relatively small number of *u...a* forms,
numbers more aptly corresponding to the Invisible class of other patterns than to the
overall class.[28]

The final combination to consider is {[+high], [+low]}, without [+round]. In our
sample, there are roughly the same number of cases of this type (58 examples, or
6% of total) as of the comparable cases including [+round]. As in the cases with
[+round], we propose that the association of [+high] takes priority over the association of [+low], and that the failure of [+high] to spread throughout a form should
be attributed to Invisibility. A complication arises in the surface realizations of the
{[+high], [+low]} class, however: two patterns surface, rather than one. The first
pattern is as expected: the first vowel is [i] and the second [a].

(45) *[+HI] and [+LO] F-elements*

    (C)VV   vía   'become ripe'
                hía   'burn up'
                cía   'be afraid that'
    (C)VVC∅   pìam   'place one thing on another' (< *pìame*)

The deviant pattern results in a surface *e ... a* sequence.[29]

(46) *[+HI] and [+LO] F-elements*

    (C)VCV   témba   'thread' (< *tímba*)
                dzènda   'drive away' (< *dzìnda*)
                tsèva   'curse' (< *tsìva*)

Comparing the two patterns, we note a systematic prosodic difference between the
two classes. The examples in (45) all involve adjacent vowels, while those in (46)
involve vowels with an intervening consonant. On the assumption that the vowel
sequences of (45) are tautosyllabic while the *VCV* sequences of (46) are heterosyllabic, the distinction between the two sets of forms can be straightforwardly
derived as follows. First, association of [+high] and [+low] takes place as in the [ia]

class. Next, a rule of High Lowering causes a heterosyllabic *iCa* sequence to change into *eCa*.[30]

We conclude from this discussion of [+high] and [+low] that it is possible for incompatible free F-elements to cooccur in underlying representation, but that they do not occur linked on a path with each other (whether in a derived or an underlying representation). In Tiv, such incompatible specifications can receive a surface interpretation only when an affected stem exhibits final Invisibility.

2.2.1.8 Conclusion   The analysis presented above accounts for 96% of the Tiv data sample. The percentage breakdown of types of verbs is given in (47), recapitulating figures given throughout the text. In this table, vowel patterns are illustrated by schematic representations of bisyllabic patterns; percentages, however, refer to the total number of cases involving a particular set of F-elements (i.e., monomoraic, bimoraic, and trimoraic). The first column gives forms that result with long vowels and *VhV* sequences; the second column gives forms resulting from a *VCV* sequence ($C \neq h$), where all vowels are visible; the third column illustrates forms involving final Invisibility, including the possibility of Invisibility with *V(h)V* sequences. Braces in the table indicate patterns of a somewhat special nature. They represent what would result if the relevant combination occurred; in each such case, however, there is a simpler representation that would derive the same result. For example, unless the final vowel is Invisible, the [+low] specification of a [+high], [+low] combination cannot surface. The double specification [+high], [+low] would therefore be logically possible in a form without final Invisibility, but there would be no reason to choose it over the simpler [+high] representation that would derive the same result.

(47)

	V(h)V	VCV	V(C)⟨V⟩	No. of cases	%
No F-element	e...e	e...e	{e...e}	172	18
[+RD]	o...o	o...o	{o...o}	86	9
[+HI]	i...i	i...i	i...e	105	11
[+HI] & [+RD]	u...u	u...u	u...e	131	14
[+LO]	a...a	a...e	{a...e}	184	20
[+LO] & [+RD]	ɔ...ɔ	ɔ...o	{ɔ...o}	107	11
[+HI] & [+LO]	{i...i}	{i...i}	ia/eCa	58	6
[+HI] & [+LO] & [+RD]	{u...u}	{u...u}	u...a	60	6

The 4% of cases that are exceptions for this analysis (34 forms from the 937-verb sample) are listed in the Appendix.

There are two central points to this section. First, Tiv presents a rather dramatic introduction to the theory of Combinatorial Specification. As outlined in the introduction, Combinatorial Specification has two formal components, (i) F-elements and (ii) their association status, components already familiar from distinctive feature theory and autosegmental theory, respectively. Because the association status of all the underlying vocalic F-elements in Tiv verbs is *free*, morphemes exhibit all eight of the logically possible combinations of [+ high], [+ low], and [+ round]. Beyond these basic components of Combinatorial Specification, all that is needed to account for the Tiv patterns is a fairly generic autosegmental analysis: rules may link and/or spread F-elements.

A particularly interesting property of the analysis motivated here is that underlying representations may include incompatible F-elements, a type of inclusion that is possible only (i) if the F-elements involved are on different paths, or (ii) if at least one of the F-elements is free. In Tiv, underlying representations of verbs with incompatible F-elements are sanctioned because *all* the vocalic F-elements are free; derived representations are sanctioned because the relevant F-elements ([+ high] and [+ low]) associate to different moras. Other examples discussed in this book share the property of containing incompatible F-elements: in this chapter, the discussion of Ngbaka (section 2.5) and the discussion of Yoruba, Maasai, and Nupe (section 2.7) present additional cases of such free incompatibilities.

This section has also stressed the importance of the subsegmental unit, the F-element. We have explored a language with no underlying vocalic "segments": rather, underlying representations of vowel quality consist solely of free F-elements. This runs counter to much research into representations, which has in some way or other focused on the "segment" as crucial: within a "segment"-based (or "alphabet"-based) theory, the normal expectation would be that underlying vowels are drawn from the members of the surface inventory of segments. However, as shown here, the distribution of vowels in Tiv verbs does not exhibit any behavior identifiable as "segmental."

To show this, we briefly consider an alternative to the feature-based account of Tiv presented here: to build up Tiv verbs from an alphabetic inventory of segments. Such an account would have two components. First, all vowels would be assigned some underlying quality. Second, morpheme structure conditions would govern the sequence of such vocalic segments.

The assignment of some quality to every underlying vowel raises a serious problem of arbitrariness: given the large number of spreading rules necessary for an analysis of Tiv, how can the underlying "segmental" identity of a vowel be determined, when its quality is invariably determined by the application of some spreading rule?

As for the attempt to account for the distribution of vowels in Tiv verbs in terms of morpheme structure conditions, there are numerous complications. The basic core of such morpheme structure conditions would be to capture the same generalizations concerning shared features as those captured here by High Link/Spread, Round

Spread, and Place Spread. In addition, a segmental approach would have to explain why low segments must be initial when paired with a mid vowel (the $a \ldots e$ and $ɔ \ldots o$ patterns) while low segments must be final when following a high vowel in a disyllabic stem (the $i \ldots a/u \ldots a$ pattern) and impossible when following a high vowel in a trisyllabic stem.

If segments were assumed underlyingly, but the observed patterns were derived by the application of feature-changing rules rather than governed by Morpheme Structure Conditions, then the individual rules posited would require complications. Instead of referring solely to [+high], for example, High Spread would have to spread both [+high] and [−high] to prevent patterns like $*e \ldots i$ and $*o \ldots u$. Because such an account would require such spreading rules to be feature-changing, this would raise the problem of preventing feature-changing spreading rules from applying in the cases involving noninitial low vowels ($i \ldots a/u \ldots a$). In sum, phrased in terms of segmental specifications rather than featural specifications, even a descriptive account of Tiv verbs becomes much more difficult to achieve, let alone an explanatory account.

In the remainder of this chapter, we examine implications of the nonsegmental approach that we advocate. We argue that not only are segments derivative, not primitive, but they are also inadequate for an understanding of a variety of phenomena. We suggest that notions of contrast, notions of "active" element, and notions of absolute neutralization all require reference to the F-element, not to the segment, in an adequate theory.

In the next case we examine, vowel assimilation in Barrow Inupiaq, we argue for representations that are essentially the antithesis of those in Tiv. In Tiv, F-elements are free in underlying representation; in Barrow Inupiaq, F-elements are linked. In Tiv, certain F-elements may combine with each other, even when linked; in Barrow Inupiaq, no combinations are licensed. Despite these stark formal differences, Barrow Inupiaq and Tiv make the same point with respect to F-elements and the segment: F-elements and association status are necessary and sufficient primitives, while the segment is inadequate and misleading.

2.2.2 Restricted F-Element Combinations: Barrow Inupiaq Vowel Assimilation

In Barrow Inupiaq, there are three types of interaction between vowels and consonants: Coronal Palatalization, Dorsal Assimilation, and Labial Assimilation.[31] On the surface, there are three distinct vowels [i, u, a], one each involved in the three processes just mentioned. One might conclude that a simple mapping holds between surface segments and rule processes. As Kaplan (1981) argues, however, the situation is rather more complex because *four* vocalic classes must be distinguished underlyingly, not just the three that appear on the surface. The problem is the following. Two classes of morphemes containing a vowel designated here as $/i_1/$ and $/i_2/$ exhibit the vowel [i] on the surface in contexts where no rule of assimilation has applied. The properties of these two classes are essentially disjoint: $/i_1/$ triggers Coronal Palatalization but does not undergo either Dorsal Assimilation or Labial Assimilation; $/i_2/$, in contrast, does *not* trigger Coronal Palatalization, but is subject to both Dorsal and Labial Assimilation.

A segment-based analysis of such data has essentially two options: (i) to posit four vowels underlyingly in conjunction with a rule of feature-changing absolute neutralization, or (ii) to assume that $/i_2/$ is an epenthetic vowel, inserted after Coronal Palatalization and before the other two rules. There are problems with the epenthesis account, leaving only the feature-changing absolute neutralization analysis, which Kaplan (1981) therefore adopts.[32]

We argue here that the problems inherent in such work derive directly from the *segmental* hypothesis. By adopting the nonsegmental approach of Combinatorial Specification, a system like that of Barrow Inupiaq is predicted to be possible.[33] The core of our analysis is as follows. The three processes mentioned above require reference to three F-elements: (i) Coronal Palatalization: [−back],[34] (ii) Dorsal Assimilation: [+low], (iii) Labial Assimilation: [+round]. In Barrow Inupiaq, conditions rule out the combination of any of these F-elements: front vowels cannot be low or round, nor can a low vowel be round. Since combinations of F-elements are not possible, exactly four underlying representations are predicted given this particular set of F-elements—precisely the desired result. That is, Barrow Inupiaq is an "*n + 1* language."

In the following discussion, we motivate the three rules that have been mentioned, which in turn motivate the particular F-elements that we propose. We demonstrate that the fourth vowel of Barrow Inupiaq exhibits precisely the properties expected of a vowel underlyingly devoid of F-elements.

2.2.2.1 The Barrow Inupiaq Alternations As mentioned, the three alternations of interest in Barrow Inupiaq are Coronal Palatalization, Dorsal Assimilation, and Labial Assimilation. These are illustrated below.

First, Coronal Palatalization results in the palatalization of a coronal stop; this occurs when the appropriate consonant follows a particular subset of morphemes exhibiting the vowel [i].

(48) *Coronal Palatalization*

    t → s/č (onset/coda, respectively)
    n → ñ
    l → λ

In (49a), suffixes following $[i_1]$ undergo palatalization, while in (49b), the same suffixes following the three vowels $[a, u, i_2]$ do not: compare the underlined coronal liquids in *tiṇiḻḻa* 'be able to take flight' with those in *niRiλλa* 'be able to eat'. The cases in (49c,d) show the same contrast with different suffixes (the (c) cases triggering the rule and the (d) cases not triggering it). Finally, (49e) provides a few further examples of the palatalization process. Of interest in the forms in (49e) is that palatalization ignores intervening noncoronal consonants (e.g., the [g] in *puqigñiaq* 'be smart-FUTURE').[35,36]

(49) *Coronal Palatalization*

	Stem	*-lla* 'be able'	*-niaq* 'FUTURE'	*-vluni* '3SG REALIS'	
a. /i₁/	niġi	niġilḷa	niġiñiaq	niġivl̥uni	'eat'
	[niRi]	[niRiλλa]	[niRiñiaq]	[niRivλuni]	
b. /a/	iga	igalla	iganiaq	igavluni	'cook'
	[iɣa]	[iɣalla]	[iɣaniaq]	[iɣavluni]	
/u/	sisu	sisulla	sisuniaq	sisuvluni	'slide'
/i₂/	tiŋi	tiŋilla	tiŋiniaq	tiŋivluni	'take flight'

		-lu 'and X'	*-nik* 'PLURAL'	*-tun* 'like a X'	
c. /i₁/	iki	ikilu	ikiñik	ikisun	'wound'
		[ikiλu]			
	savik	saviglu	savigñik	saviksun	'knife'
		[savigλu]		[savixsun]	
d. /u/	iglu	iglulu	iglunik	iglutun	'house'
/i₂/	kamik	kamiglu	kamignik	kamiktun	'boot'
	aivik	aiviġlu	aiviġnik	aiviqtun	'walrus'
		[aiviRlu]	[aiviNnik]		
	ini	inilu	ininik	initun	'place'

		-tuq '3SG INT'	*-niaq* 'FUTURE'	*-luni* '3SG IRREALIS'	
e. /i₁/	isiq	isiqsuq	isiġñiaq	isiġl̥uni	'be smoky'
		[isiχsuq]	[isiRñiaq]	[isiRλuni]	
	puqik	puqiksuq	puqigñiaq	puqigḷuni	'be smart'
		[puqixsuq]		[puqigλuni]	
	tikiṭ	tikitṭuq	tikiññiaq	tikilḷuni	'arrive'
		[tikič]	[tikitčuq]		[tikiλλuni]	

Coronal Palatalization is a rule whereby specifically the vowel /i₁/ (but not /i₂/) affects consonants; Dorsal and Labial Assimilation, on the other hand, are rules whereby certain consonants and vowels affect specifically the vowel /i₂/ (but not /i₁/). We begin a consideration of the two latter rules by looking at Dorsal Assimilation. In (50), the velar consonant [k], the uvular consonant [q], and the low vowel [a] trigger Dorsal Assimilation: the rule has no effect on the vowels /u, a, i₁/ (50a,c,e); it does, however, affect instances of /i₂/, causing them to alternate with [a] (50b,d,f).[37]

(50) *Dorsal Assimilation*

		Stem	-*k* 'DUAL'	
a.	/a/	nuna	nunnak ~ nunak	'land'
	/u/	nanuq	nannuk	'polar bear'
	/i₁/	savik	savvik	'knife'
		amiq	ammik	'skin'
		gargi [ɣarɣi]	gargik [ɣařɣik]	'men's house'
b.	/i₂/	ini	inik ~ innak	'place, room'
		kamik	kammak	'boot'
		punniq	punnak	'loaf of bread'

		Stem	-*q* 'NOMINALIZER'	
c.	/a/	sana	sannaq	'to carve'
	/u/	saluk	salluq	'to be thin'
	/i₁/	niġi [niRi]	niġġiq [niRRiq]	'to eat'
d.	/i₂/	qupi	quppaq	'to cleave'
		titiq	tittaq	'to make a mark'

		Stem	-*a* '3SG POSSESSIVE'	
e.	/a/	pana	panaa	'spear'
	/u/	ulu	ulua	'woman's knife'
	/i₁/	panik	pania	'daughter'
f.	/i₂/	ini	inaa	'place'

The correlation between the behavior of /i₁/ and /i₂/ in (49) and (50) is that /i₁/, which triggers Coronal Palatalization, does not undergo Dorsal Assimilation, while /i₂/, which does undergo Dorsal Assimilation, does not trigger Coronal Palatalization. For example, the final [i] of *kamik* 'boot' undergoes Dorsal Assimilation (*kammak* 'boot-DUAL') and does *not* trigger Coronal Palatalization (*kamignik* 'boot-PL', *kamigñik). In contrast, the final [i] of *savik* 'knife' triggers Coronal Palatalization (*savigñik* 'knife-PL') but does not undergo Dorsal Assimilation (*savvik* 'knife-DUAL', *savvak).

The same correlation holds with a rule that inserts Dorsal F-elements, illustrated in (51). Vowel-initial suffixes like -*uruq* typically cause the appearance of an [a], the result of a rule that applies only to replace a stem-final /i₂/. We have little to say about this pattern, beyond including it to demonstrate how entrenched the distinction between /i₁/ and /i₂/ is in Barrow Inupiaq. The contrast between the two forms with [i] is important here: note that the /i₂/ form surfaces as *in̩uruq* 'is a place, etc.' (*iniuruq) while the /i₁/ form surfaces as *amịuruq* 'is a skin, etc.' (*amauruq).

(51) *Dorsal Insertion*

	Stem	*-uruq* 'is a X; has many Xs; there are many Xs'	
/a/	pana	panauruq [panaův̌uq]	'spear'
/u/	ulu	uluuruq [uluův̌uq]	'woman's semilunar knife'
/i₁/	amiq	amiuruq [amiův̌uq]	'skin'
/i₂/	ini	inauruq [inaův̌uq]	'place, room'

Turning to Labial Assimilation, we find exactly the same distinction between /i₁/ and /i₂/: Labial Assimilation turns /i₂/ into [u] when adjacent to the relativizer *-m*; /i₁/ in a similar context is unaffected. In (52a), vowels are unaffected while in (52b), the vowel alternates: compare for instance *amiq/ammim* 'skin' (*ammum*) with *kamik/kamŋum* 'boot' (*kamŋim*).

(52) *Labial Assimilation*

		Stem	*-m* 'RELATIVIZER'	
a.	/a/	qayaq	qayyam	'kayak'
	/u/	ulu	ulum	'woman's knife'
	/i₁/	amiq	ammim	'skin'
b.	/i₂/	kamik	kamŋum	'boot'
		aiviq	aivġum [aivRum]	'walrus'
		tupiq	tupqum	'tent'

As already noted, the same stems that undergo Labial Assimilation also undergo Dorsal Assimilation. For example, *kamik* 'boot' undergoes Labial Assimilation in (52) and Dorsal Assimilation in (50b): *kamŋum, *kamŋim; kammak, *kammik*. In contrast, a form like *amiq* 'skin' does not undergo Labial Assimilation (52), and similarly does not undergo Dorsal Assimilation (50b): *ammim, *ammum; ammik, *ammak*.

To summarize, /i₁/ triggers Coronal Palatalization; no other vowel triggers this rule. By contrast, /i₂/ undergoes Dorsal Assimilation (and Dorsal Insertion) and Labial Assimilation; no other vowels are targeted by these rules. It is this systematic dual behavior of the underlying representations which typically surface as [i] that leads to the conclusion that four vowels are distinguished underlyingly in Barrow Inupiaq, despite surface appearances.

2.2.2.2 The Underlying Representation of Barrow Inupiaq Vowels Adapting the analysis of F-element representations of Bourgeois (1988), we take the F-elements [+round], [+low], and [−back] to be those relevant for Barrow Inupiaq vowels, one F-element involved in each of Round, Dorsal, and Palatal Assimilation.[38] The combinatorial possibilities of these F-elements are given in (53).

(53) *Barrow Inupiaq vowel representation*

    a. F-elements

       +RD, +LO, −BK

    b. Conditions

LO/RD Condition:	If [+low] then not [+round].
LO/BK Condition:	If [+low] then not [−back].
RD/LO Condition:	If [+round] then not [+low].
RD/BK Condition:	If [+round] then not [−back].
FR/LO Condition:	If [−back] then not [+low].
FR/RD Condition:	If [−back] then not [+round].

    c.

*	*	a	*	u	*	i_2	i_1
+LO	+LO	+LO	+LO				
+RD	+RD				+RD	+RD	
	−BK		−BK			−BK	−BK

The constraints in (53b) render it impossible for any of the F-elements of Barrow Inupiaq to combine. Consequently, exactly four combinations are predicted to occur, as indicated in (53c).

The three processes of Barrow Inupiaq that have been discussed here can now be straightforwardly accounted for. We briefly discuss the formal properties of each rule, noting that formal properties only are presented here.[39]

Palatal Assimilation   With regard to Palatal Assimilation (54), [−back] is spread from [i_1] to a following coronal consonant.[40] The rule takes [i_1] as a trigger because it alone has the specification [−back] that is affected by the rule (55a); the vowels [a] and [u] are not front, while the vowel [i_2] has no specifications at all (55b). With regard to the targets of assimilation, only consonants are eligible since only consonants bear the Coronal feature required by the rule. The rule cannot, therefore, spread a [−back] feature from a consonant that has undergone assimilation onto a subsequent vowel.

(54) *Barrow Inupiaq Palatal Assimilation*

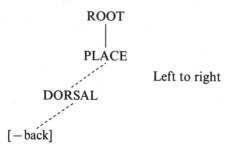

(55a) and (55b) illustrate the applicability of Palatal Assimilation with [i_1] ([savigλu] 'and knife' (49c)), and its inapplicability with [i_2] ([kamiglu] 'and boot' (49d)). Only articulator nodes and vowel specifications are indicated.[41]

(55) a.

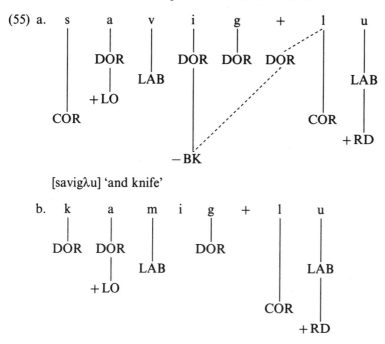

[savigλu] 'and knife'

b.

[kamiglu] 'and boot'

Dorsal Assimilation   The rule of Dorsal Assimilation (56) targets vowels, spreading from right to left the Dorsal node of a velar or uvular stop, as well as the Dorsal node of a low vowel. To make this analysis possible, we follow Cole (1987), Czaykowska-Higgins (1987), McCarthy (1989b), and Bessell (1990) in assuming that uvulars are represented with a complex articulation that includes a dorsal component.[42] In addition, we assume that a Dorsal vowel receives the F-element [+low] redundantly.[43] If a potential vowel target is specified as [−back] or as [+round], Dorsal Assimilation is blocked by the conditions in (53c), which rule out the combination of [+low] with either of these F-elements.[44]

(56) *Barrow Inupiaq Dorsal Assimilation*

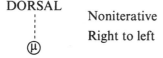

DORSAL   Noniterative

             Right to left

The application of this rule is illustrated in (57).

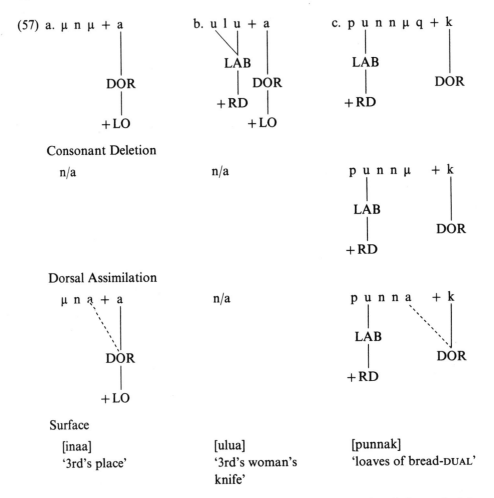

(57) a. μ n μ + a   b. u l u + a   c. p u n n μ q + k

Consonant Deletion

n/a   n/a   p u n n μ   + k

Dorsal Assimilation

μ n a + a   n/a   p u n n a   + k

Surface

[inaa]   [ulua]   [punnak]
'3rd's place'   '3rd's woman's   'loaves of bread-DUAL'
                           knife'

The first stage of these derivations gives relevant aspects only of the underlying representations of [inaa], [ulua], and [punnak]. In the second stage, a rule of Consonant Deletion (not discussed here) deletes the final consonant of the root /punnVq/. The third stage illustrates the application of Dorsal Assimilation, inapplicable in (57b) because of the [+round] specification of the vowel preceding the Dorsal node trigger.[45]

Labial Assimilation   Labial Assimilation applies in a manner entirely comparable to Dorsal Assimilation. Vowels are targeted; the Labial node is spread. As with the relation between Dorsal and [+low], we assume that [+round] is assigned redundantly to a Labial vowel.

(58) *Barrow Inupiaq Labial Assimilation*

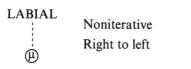

LABIAL   Noniterative

         Right to left

2.2.2.3 Conclusion We have argued that Barrow Inupiaq vowels are distinguished underlyingly by specifications for the three F-elements [−back], [+low], and [+round]. Three of the vowels correspond to the specification of a unique F-element while the fourth is represented by the absence of any F-elements whatsoever. That is, we propose that the four logical possibilities involving three incompatible F-elements are formally instantiated. Allowing the absence of any F-elements whatsoever in the representation of one vowel resolves the issue of how to represent the "abstract" vowel, Kaplan's (1981) *i* and our i_2. Since a vowel with no F-elements is compatible with the representation of any of the other vowels, malleable surface representations result: adding Labial/[+round] renders i_2 identical with *u*; adding Dorsal/[+low] renders it identical with *a*. Where [i_2] is not subject to any rule of assimilation, it surfaces as [i]. This last effect can be obtained either by assuming a late default rule assigning the value [−back] or by assuming that [i] is the phonetic result (in Inupiaq) of interpreting a vowel with no phonologically represented F-elements: see the "default values" box in section 2.2.1.3 for further discussion of default values that apparently have no role in phonological processes. Note that either the phonetic interpretation of a featureless vowel as [i] or the redundant assignment of [−back] to a featureless vowel has the effect of neutralizing the underlying contrast between /i_1/ and /i_2/. We return to the issue of such neutralization in section 2.4.2.[46]

The analysis offered here of the Barrow Inupiaq alternations focuses again on the phonological role of F-elements, not segments. As shown here, F-elements are necessary in accounting for the vowel and consonant interactions; furthermore, nothing beyond the linked F-elements is required—F-elements are sufficient to account for the attested interactions. This supports the conclusion of section 2.2.1, that F-elements are the pivotal phonological primitives and that the notion of segment is derivative. That both Tiv and Barrow Inupiaq support the same result is particularly striking since the formal nature of underlying representations in the two languages is so different: in Tiv, F-elements are free and combine readily (though subject to certain restrictions) while in Barrow Inupiaq, the F-elements are linked and cannot be combined at all.

It might be asked whether a "segmental" analysis of Barrow Inupiaq (i.e., involving fully, or at least more fully specified, combinations of F-elements) would actually be desirable, even if not strictly required. There are essentially two ways in which this could be done, each showing that more complete specification is undesirable.

First, a fourth segment (e.g., Kaplan's *i*) could be assumed, accompanied by a rule of feature-changing absolute neutralization that turns all remaining instances of the abstract segment into [i] after the application of the assimilation rules. Specifying the fourth vowel as [−low, +back, −round] (with or without a value for [high]) loses the unified account of why the two spreading rules affect precisely the vowel that does not trigger Palatal Assimilation. A fully—or even partially—specified fourth vowel would require that the rules targeting vowels, Dorsal Assimilation and Labial Assimilation, necessarily have the effect of changing feature values (eliminating [−low] and [−round], respectively), contrary to the rules proposed here for Inupiaq that assign values in a feature-filling fashion. Further, since feature changing would be necessary, it would also be necessary to identify the targets of change. For example, Dorsal Assimilation could not be stated as in (56), since under partial/full specification, no mora is featureless and so no mora would be an eligible target. The same would hold true for Labial Assimilation (58). The combined result is that both of the rules that spread features to moras would identify the target mora by specifying certain features in the rule itself. As a result, it becomes arbitrary that the two rules target a single vowel. Equally arbitrary is the fact that this vowel is exactly the vowel that does not trigger Palatal Assimilation. The unified explanation of such behavior is lost.

Importantly, the motivation for including these features is solely theoretical: the specifications are not empirically motivated since no rules need refer to them.[47] As shown here, a highly explanatory account of the Barrow Inupiaq vowels is possible without reference to features beyond the three specified in (53), and without invoking feature-changing rules. By identifying the "fourth" vowel of Inupiaq by its absence of specifications, both empirical and conceptual results of a desirable type are obtained. Empirically, the unified account of vowel behavior just described is obtained. Conceptually, such an account places an upward bound on the number of possible "abstract" vowels at *one*. The logic of the combinatorial approach to feature specification allows a single vowel to be devoid of specifications; hence, "abstractness" is a possibility for no more than one vowel per system. In contrast, a theory that allows partially or fully specified "abstract" vowels places no limit on the potential number of such vowels. Just as *one* vowel can be considered abstract in Inupiaq, so *two* or more vowels could be similarly targeted for neutralization (cf. Okpẹ and Chukchi, section 3.3.1). As a final but crucial point, the full or partial specification analysis would require a powerful class of absolute neutralization rules that are otherwise unmotivated, and impossible to express in the theory of rules presented in chapter 4. (For related discussion, see sections 2.4.2, 2.7, and 3.3.1.)

Second, a theory might posit fully specified "segments" for /i$_1$, a, u/ but maintain the fully unspecified analysis of /i$_2$/. Such an analysis would be empirically equivalent to the account given here but would suffer from two conceptual drawbacks. For one thing, more complex formal representations would be posited where the simpler representations proposed in the account here are perfectly adequate. In addition, the motivation for positing precisely the four representations necessary for Barrow Inupiaq would be lost. In the Combinatorial Specification analysis, the four vowel representations that occur are predicted by the range of combinations possible given the F-elements actually required in the assimilation rules of the language: the effects of Palatal Assimilation require [−back]; the effects of Dorsal Assimilation require [+low]; the effects of Labial Assimilation require [+round]. Without such a theory of combination, the selection of /i, u, a/ as specified vowels appears to be much less clearly motivated.

2.2.3 Typology of F-Element Combinations

In the preceding sections, we have introduced an approach to feature specification that takes as its cornerstones two traditional properties of autosegmental phonology: (i) F-elements and (ii) association status. We examined two cases: Tiv, where all lexical F-elements are underlyingly free, becoming linked during the course of a derivation; and Barrow Inupiaq, where lexical F-elements are underlyingly linked.

From the examination of such cases, we can isolate four potential parameters of variation, assuming some set of F-elements Φ active in a particular language.

(59) *Parameters of variation*

    a. The identity of the specific set of F-elements comprising Φ

    b. Compatibility vs. incompatibility of the F-elements in Φ

    c. Linked vs. free status of F-elements in Φ

    d. Derived vs. underlying status of F-elements in Φ

With regard to (59a), the identity of F-elements in Φ, languages may differ in the particular F-elements that are active, where by "active" we mean those F-elements that play a role in making morphological distinctions, and those F-elements that function in the operation of phonological processes. For example, a language like Tiv does not appear to include the F-element [+ATR] in its set Φ, although it does include the F-elements [+high], [+low], [+round]. With regard to compatibility/ incompatibility (59b), some members of a language's set Φ may cooccur on a path, while others may not. For example, Tiv does not allow [+high] and [+low] to cooccur on a path, but it does allow [+round] to cooccur with either [+high] or [+low]. As for F-elements being linked or free (59c), Tiv and Inupiaq provide a clear example of how languages may differ on this count. Finally, we will show that languages may differ with respect to underlying or derived status of the F-elements that make up Φ (59d): while any F-element involved in establishing a morphological distinction (distinguishing between different morphemes) is by definition an "active" member of the class Φ, languages differ with respect to whether active F-elements are restricted to that class. In some languages, it appears that all members of Φ are involved in morphological contrasts; in other languages, additional F-elements are introduced into Φ whose role is solely phonological.

In the following sections, we explore the types of possibilities just outlined, sketching the foundations of a typology of F-element combination. As different languages are presented, it will become clear that the 2^n pattern illustrated by Tiv and the $n + 1$ pattern illustrated by Barrow Inupiaq constitute only two of a variety of ways in which Combinatorial Specification provides for the interaction of F-elements.

2.3 Simplicity in F-Element Combinations

Any two given F-elements may be either compatible or incompatible with each other (59b). Compatible F-elements may occur on a path with each other; incompatible F-elements may not. In the following sections, we begin by considering a range of combinations of *compatible* F-elements. In particular, we address the representation of cases where the presence of some F-element β is predictable on the surface as a result of the presence of a second F-element α. For example, low vowels in Yoruba (α = [+low]) are predictably produced with a retracted tongue root (β = [−ATR]).

We demonstrate that the array of possible patterns exhibited by such cases is in essence that predicted by Combinatorial Specification: (i) α may occur without β in underlying representation, but β is inserted onto a path with α during the course of the phonology (Yoruba); (ii) α may occur without β in underlying representation, and α may function phonologically without β (Haya); (iii) morphemes may contrast the specification α with the specification α, β (Ainu). One case appears to be missing, namely, a situation where α, β occurs to the systematic exclusion of α underlyingly. We propose that the explanation for this gap lies in a principle of Representational Simplicity (96).

2.3.1 Yoruba Vowel Harmony

The [ATR] harmony pattern of Standard Yoruba, a Niger-Congo language spoken in Nigeria, involves the spreading of [−ATR] from both mid and low vowels.[48] In particular, all low vowels serve as harmonic triggers. In spite of this, however, the vocalic patterns in the language appear to indicate that low vowels are not assigned [−ATR] in underlying representation, but rather have this F-element inserted prior to application of the harmony rule.

This analysis is of importance in developing the typology just discussed. Even though the phonology of Yoruba requires the assignment of [−ATR] to all low vowels prior to application of vowel harmony, properties of vowel distribution provide empirical evidence that the simpler representation of low vowels—[+low] *without* [−ATR]—is necessary in underlying representation. That is, at a fairly early stage of the derivation, [+low] vowels appear systematically combined with the F-element [−ATR]; in underlying representation, however, these entirely compatible F-elements, which ultimately are obligatorily combined, do not cooccur.

Our discussion of Yoruba vowel harmony closely follows that of Archangeli and Pulleyblank (1989).[49] But before turning to the harmony pattern itself, we give an overview of the vowels of Yoruba and how they are derived.

2.3.1.1 Yoruba Vowels On the surface, Standard Yoruba distinguishes seven oral vowels.

(60) *Surface oral vowels in Yoruba* (ẹ = [ɛ]; ọ = [ɔ])

i		u
e		o
ẹ		ọ
	a	

Following Pulleyblank (1988c), we take the active F-elements in underlying representation to be [−high], [+low], [+back], and [−ATR], as shown in (61a).[50] The harmonic [−ATR] is free in underlying representation, except in the limited class of loanwords; arguments for this are sketched-below. (See Archangeli and Pulleyblank 1989 for more detailed argumentation.) The association of [−ATR] (and its linked presence in unassimilated loanwords) is governed by the condition on representations given in (61b) that limits the presence of [−ATR] to [−high] vowels. (Recall that the circle around the [−ATR] specification indicates that it is floating in underlying representation; the F-elements [−high], [+low], and [+back] are linked underlyingly.)[51]

(61) *Yoruba vowel representation*

a. F-elements

−HI, +LO, +BK; (−ATR)

b. Condition

RTR/HI Condition: If [−ATR] then [−high]. (If [−ATR] then not [+high].)

The three linked F-elements give rise to eight logically possible combinations.

(62)

i	u	e	o	a_1	a_2	a_3	a_4
		−HI	−HI			−HI	−HI
				+LO	+LO	+LO	+LO
	+BK		+BK		+BK		+BK

Given the common situation where low vowels are redundantly back and nonhigh, the surface results of the four last columns in (62) would all be [a]. Although we do not discuss evidence pertaining to the correct specification of [−high] and [+back] in

relation to the [+low] of low vowels, we demonstrate below that with respect to
[ATR], there are arguments for adopting the simplest representation, the representation of [+low] *without* [−ATR]. At the end of this section, we propose a principle of
Representational Simplicity (96) to obtain this effect. To be consistent with Representational Simplicity, we adopt here the representation a_l for the low vowel of Yoruba
without further discussion.

The focus of this section is the interaction of the morpheme-level specification
[−ATR] with low vowels in Yoruba. We begin, however, by briefly illustrating the
general pattern of [ATR] harmony found in Yoruba,[52] arguing that a_l is selected as
the underlying representation of the low vowel in Yoruba, but that distributional
evidence forces the positing of a rule that assigns [−ATR] to low vowels prior to
harmony.

2.3.1.2 Triggers for Harmony Include /a/ Systematically In the harmony system of
Yoruba, low vowels have a special status in that they systematically trigger harmony
on mid vowels to their left, but have no effect on mid vowels to their right. This
pattern is accounted for (i) by ensuring that low vowels are specified for the harmonic
value [−ATR] at least by the point at which harmony takes place, and (ii) by positing
a rule of harmony that is directional, applying from right to left.

The general pattern of harmony in Yoruba is as follows. Mid vowels exhibit both
[+ATR] and [−ATR] possibilities, and sequences of mid vowels in native vocabulary agree in their value for [ATR].

(63) *Agreement for [ATR]: Mid vowels*

	a.	ebè	'heap for yams'	epo	'oil'
		olè	'thief'	owó	'money'
	b.	ẹsẹ̀	'foot'	ẹkọ	'pap'
		ọbẹ̀	'soup'	ọkọ̀	'vehicle'

All high vowels are [+ATR] in Yoruba, and high vowels have no harmonic effect on
Yoruba stems with a single span of mid vowels; such a mid vowel span in conjunction with high vowels continues to exhibit both [+ATR] and [−ATR] possibilities,
whether to the left or to the right of a high vowel.[53]

(64) *Symmetry: Nonlow vowels*

	a.	ilé	'house'	ìgò	'bottle'
		ebi	'hunger'	orí	'head'
		eku	'bush rat'	ojú	'eye'
	b.	ilẹ̀	'land'	itọ́	'saliva'
		ẹbi	'guilt'	òkín	'egret'
		ẹwu	'clothing'	òrun	'heaven'

With low vowels, the symmetrical pattern seen so far breaks down. As can be seen in (65), mid vowels *to the right of* a low vowel exhibit the same [+ATR] and [−ATR] varieties seen with mid vowels following a high vowel.

(65) *Asymmetry: Low vowels on the left*

    a. ate   'hat'
         àwo   'plate'

    b. àjè̩   'paddle'
         as̩o̩   'cloth'

In contrast to this pattern, however, mid vowels to the left of a low vowel are invariably [−ATR].

(66) *Asymmetry: Low vowels on the right*

    a. è̩pà   'groundnut'
         o̩jà   'market'

    b. *èpà
         *ojà
         etc.

The asymmetry of this harmonic behavior is derived by ensuring that low vowels are specified as [−ATR] by (67) at least by the point where harmony takes place.

(67) *Yoruba [−ATR] Insertion*

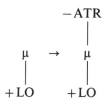

As with morpheme-level specifications of [−ATR], the [−ATR] value of a low vowel spreads from right to left as in (68), making any preceding mid vowel [−ATR]. In this regard, it is important to recall that high vowels do not have a comparable "[+ATR]" effect on mid vowels either to their left or to their right; this is part of a larger set of arguments for positing [−ATR], not [+ATR], as the active harmonic value of Yoruba.

(68) *Yoruba [−ATR] Spread*

    −ATR   Iterative

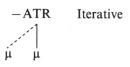

Having established both the direction of [ATR] harmony in Yoruba and the systematic triggering effect of low vowels, we are now in a position to demonstrate the importance of representing low vowels as underlyingly unspecified for the F-element [−ATR]. There are essentially three possibilities for the representation of morphemes with a low vowel as far as [ATR] is concerned: in (69a), /a/ is underlyingly *linked* to [−ATR]; in (69b), a *free* [−ATR] is necessarily present underlyingly in morphemes with /a/; in (69c), [−ATR] is *inserted* on low vowels by a rule that precedes the harmony rule. Only (69c) is consistent with the attested patterns of Yoruba.[54]

(69) *Possible representations with [+LO] vowels*

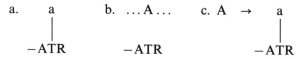

As will be demonstrated below, possibility (69a) necessitates a variety of ad hoc stipulations in order to account for the distribution of [−ATR] in words with mid and low vowels. Possibility (69b) makes false empirical predictions. Possibility (69c), on the other hand, accounts for the data without any stipulations beyond ordering the rule assigning [−ATR] to [+low] vowels prior to the application of [−ATR] harmony.

2.3.1.3 [−ATR] Linked to /a/ in Underlying Representation   To argue against prelinking low vowels with the value [−ATR], we consider three sequences of vowel types. We demonstrate that only by assuming a rule of [−ATR] Insertion for low vowels can the full range of distributional properties be straightforwardly accounted for.

Mid-Low   It has been observed in (66) that a mid vowel preceding a low vowel is systematically [−ATR]. The account that has been proposed involves (i) ensuring that all low vowels have a [−ATR] specification, and (ii) having [−ATR] spread from right to left. This account is essentially equivalent for approaches that posit the prelinking of [−ATR] to low vowels and for approaches that assign [−ATR] to low vowels by rule. In the former approach, it must be stipulated that all low vowels are underlyingly [−ATR]; in the latter, it must be stipulated that all low vowels undergo [−ATR] Insertion. Note moreover that the presence or absence of a morpheme-level [−ATR] specification has no effect on the surface output since all vowels in a mid-low sequence surface as [−ATR].

Low-Mid   Unlike the case of a mid-low sequence, when the order is inverted, conceptual problems result. Consider again the representative forms given in (65). There is no morpheme-level [ATR] specification for forms like (65a); hence, only the low vowel surfaces as [−ATR]. Whether this result is achieved by the prelinking of [−ATR] to low vowels, or by the effect of [−ATR] Insertion, surface forms are straightforward. Complications would arise for forms where a morpheme-level [ATR] specification is posited, however, if low vowels were underlyingly linked to a [−ATR] value. Compare the schematic derivations of forms like *ate* 'hat' and *àjè* 'paddle', which illustrate the patterns for forms with and without a morpheme-level [−ATR] specification.

(70) *[+low, −ATR] vowels in underlying representation*

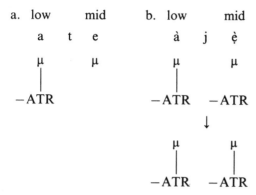

In (70a), [ATR] harmony is inapplicable (since [−ATR] spreads only from right to left); hence, the [−ATR] ... [+ATR] pattern of forms like *ate* is derived. In (70b), although harmony is inapplicable, the free morpheme-level [−ATR] specification links to the final vowel, deriving the [−ATR] ... [−ATR] pattern of a form like *àjè*.

Although able to derive correct surface forms, the representations in (70) pose conceptual problems because the underlying representation postulated in (70b) violates the OCP (McCarthy 1986a, Yip 1988b, etc.; see discussion in chapter 1). Important in this regard, the OCP violation is a direct result of positing an underlyingly linked, non-morpheme-level [ATR] specification.[55] Moreover, abandoning the OCP would be problematical empirically as well as conceptually. Patterns such as (71) are systematically absent in Yoruba.

(71) mid high mid   mid high mid

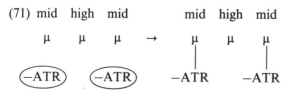

Allowing a single floating [−ATR] specification correctly derives forms like *èlùbọ́* 'yam flour' and *odídẹ* 'Grey Parrot' with a single [−ATR] mid vowel to the right of the medial high vowel; allowing two such specifications would derive unattested forms like **ẹ̀lùbọ́* and **ọdídẹ* with two [−ATR] mid vowels flanking a medial high vowel. (Trisyllabic words with a medial high vowel but without a floating [−ATR] specification are also possible—for example, *òyìbó* 'any European', *orúpò* 'mud-bench serving as bed', *èsúró* 'Redflanked Duiker'.) In an approach to Yoruba harmony that assumes the OCP, such unattested forms are correctly excluded without stipulation: given the formulation of Adjacency in conjunction with the OCP as in chapter 1, there is no choice but to exclude such a sequence. But in an approach that allows representations like (70b), forms like **ẹ̀lùbọ́* can be excluded only by an ad hoc stipulation such as the following: "Underlying representations may contain at most one *floating* specification of [−ATR]."

Compare the problematical account in (70) with the alternative in (72) of positing a rule inserting [−ATR] on low vowels prior to harmony. Because [−ATR] is inserted by a redundancy rule, a form like *àjẹ̀* contains only a floating, morpheme-level specification underlyingly.

(72)   A   j   E

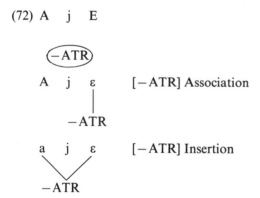

The morpheme-level [−ATR] specification links from right to left to the final vowel, and the initial low vowel receives [−ATR] by the redundancy rule assigning that value to all low vowels. It is crucial to assume that the rule of insertion produces a multiply linked representation if the OCP is not to be violated by its application. Note in this regard that little evidence has been presented in the autosegmental literature in favor of either inserting individual redundant values on segments (73a) or inserting multiply linked segments (73b). In the absence of evidence to the contrary, it is therefore preferable to assume that the OCP is respected (73b). This contrasts with the assumption concerning redundant values made, for example, in Pulleyblank 1986a, namely, that redundant values were assigned one per anchor, creating massive derived violations of the OCP.

(73) *Mode of redundant feature assignment*

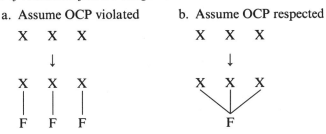

a. Assume OCP violated   b. Assume OCP respected

To summarize, the decision to represent the redundant [−ATR] specification of a low vowel in underlying representation forces a weakening or rejection of the OCP. If, on the other hand, the redundancy is expressed by a rule of insertion, no violation of the OCP need result.

Mid-High-Low The final configuration that we consider here is one where a mid vowel span precedes a tautomorphemic sequence of high and low vowels. In such a configuration, the mid vowel invariably surfaces as [+ATR].

(74) a. yorùbá   'Yoruba'   *yọruba

     b. òjiyá   'Daniellia Ogea'   *ọjiya

In an account of Yoruba that posits low vowels underlyingly linked to a [−ATR] value, this pattern can be derived only by stipulation, requiring a condition such as the following:[56] "Underlying representations may contain at most one *floating* specification of [−ATR], which occurs *to the right of* a linked [−ATR] specification (on a low vowel), if any." Given this stipulation, a representation like that of (75a) is allowed, while a representation like that of (75b) is disallowed. It is important to keep in mind that sequences of [−ATR] specifications could not be ruled out in general under the prelinking approach because of low-mid examples like àjè 'paddle' and low-high-mid examples like àkùrò 'a type of farmland', both of which would require a floating [−ATR] specification *to the right of* the linked specification (75c).

(75) a. mid   high   low   b. mid   high   low   c. low   high   mid

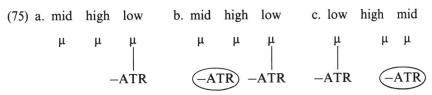

The representation in (75b) would result in an unattested pattern involving a [−ATR] initial mid vowel. Note in this regard that the association of a free [−ATR] specification may take place across high vowels in Yoruba, as witnessed in forms like èbi 'guilt' and ègúsi 'a food made from seeds of melon'.[57]

The type of stipulation required to rule out (75b) is entirely an artifact of prelinking low vowels with [−ATR]. In an account where low vowels receive their tongue root specification by the rule of [−ATR] Insertion, no such stipulation is needed. If low vowels, like mid and high vowels, are unspecified underlyingly for [ATR], then there are two possible underlying representations for a mid-high-low sequence, the first corresponding to a morpheme without a lexical [−ATR] specification (76a), the second corresponding to a formative specified for a morpheme-level [−ATR] specification (76b).

(76) a. mid   high   low   b. mid   high   low

     μ   μ   μ   μ   μ   μ

$$\boxed{-\text{ATR}}$$ (circled)

Although different underlying, both (76a,b) would derive identical surface [ATR] patterns. The representation in (76a) would be converted into the intermediate representation given in (77) as a result of [−ATR] Insertion; the representation in (76b) would similarly be converted into the intermediate (77), though by [−ATR] Association rather than [−ATR] Insertion.

(77) mid   high   low

    μ   μ   μ
                |
        −ATR

Spreading is blocked by the presence of the opaque high vowel, and a surface form like *yorùbá* 'Yoruba' correctly results.[58]

In (76b), the free [−ATR] specification links to the final low vowel through the right-to-left application of [−ATR] Association.[59,60] Consequently, the result of association is again the configuration in (77): spreading is blocked and the surface pattern [+ATR] ... [high] ... [−ATR] is derived.

To summarize, the prelinking approach requires a stipulation concerning the linear ordering of free and linked [ATR] specifications, while the approach employing [−ATR] Insertion requires no such stipulation.

In conclusion, both prelinking and rule-based approaches require at least one stipulation: prelinking must stipulate that *all* low vowels are prelinked to a [−ATR] specification; the rule-based account must posit a rule assigning *all* low vowels the value [−ATR]. For the insertion account, no additional stipulation is necessary. Morphemes may or may not include in their lexical representation a free morpheme-level specification of [−ATR], and such specifications associate and spread according to general rules. No special reference needs to be made to low vowels except for the rule inserting [−ATR] onto that class. By contrast, the prelinking approach produces two undesirable results. First, the OCP must be weakened or abandoned, with some of its effects retained by ad hoc conditions. Second, a stipulation must be introduced to order morpheme-level specifications with respect to linked ones.

2.3.1.4   Free [−ATR] and /a/ in Underlying Representation   In (69), we presented three options for expressing the relation between low vowels and the [ATR] feature. In the last section, we argued that prelinking [−ATR] to low vowels (69a) is problematical, while assuming that underlying unspecified low vowels receive their [−ATR] value by a rule of insertion (69c) straightforwardly accounts for these features' distributional properties. In this final section, we reject the third possibility, that any morpheme with an /a/ be required to include a free [−ATR] specification (69b).

At a conceptual level, the hypothesis is problematical and perhaps incoherent. Consider the following autosegmental representations:

(78) a. α   b. α
                   |
     β   β

In (78a), α and β are not linked to each other; in (78b), they are. In the linked case (78b), it is entirely straightforward to qualify the association of α and β as either well formed or ill formed: in Yoruba, for example, if α is [−ATR], then the path in (78b) is well formed if β is [−high] but ill formed if β is [+high].

If the two F-elements are not linked to each other, however, standard theory does not allow the expression of any interdependency (positive or negative) between the two features. That is, the presence of some feature α may not be required/precluded on the basis of some feature β to which it is not associated. Consider the alternative to the standard assumption. Imagine a condition requiring the presence of a high vowel in any morpheme including a floating [+ATR] specification.[61] Such a condition would license any of the following representations (where capital letters indicate vowels unspecified for [ATR]):

(79) a. I   b. ICE   c. ICECE   d. ICECECE   e. ICECECECE

     +A   +A   +A   +A   +A

Postulating right-to-left association, such representations would be converted into the following by the linking process:

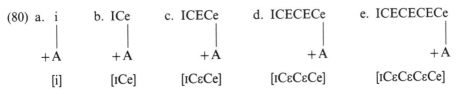

(80) a. i   b. ICe   c. ICECe   d. ICECECe   e. ICECECECe
     | | | | |
     +A   +A   +A   +A   +A

     [i]   [ICe]   [ICεCe]   [ICεCεCe]   [ICεCεCεCe]   .

Under such conditions, the presence of [+ATR] would be licensed by a potentially distant vowel that bears no formal relation to the [+ATR] specification.

To summarize, the net effect would be to establish a licenser/licensee relation between two completely unrelated elements in (79) and between two nonlocal elements in (80c–e). Since such patterns do not seem to be attested, we retain the standard assumption that feature-dependent interrelations between F-elements are defined over sets of linked features.

In the model presented in this book, such restrictions on linkings are expressed by *path conditions* (see chapter 3). Hence, if features are not connected by some set of associations, implicational relations between them cannot be expressed. As a concrete example, we showed in section 2.2.1 that two conditions govern the cooccurrence of [+low] and [+high] in Tiv: the HI/LO Condition *(If [+HI] then not [+LO])* and the LO/HI Condition *(If [+LO] then not [+HI])*. These conditions prevent the assignment of both [+high] and [+low] to a single path, but have no effect on the cooccurrence of floating specifications of [+high] and [+low] within the same morpheme.

With regard to the representation (69b) under consideration for Yoruba, this means that it would be impossible to ensure that all morphemes with a low vowel have a [−ATR] specification *unless the [−ATR] specification were actually linked to the low vowel*—effectively ruling out (69b) as an expression of this restriction.

Let us ignore this conceptual problem for a moment, however, and consider the result of allowing such an implicational condition between F-elements not linked to each other. First, forms like *ate* 'hat' and *àwo* 'plate' would be underivable. Archangeli and Pulleyblank (1989) present considerable evidence that the association of [−ATR] in Yoruba takes place from right to left. Because forms like *ate* contain a low vowel, the hypothesis under consideration would require that they include a [−ATR] specification; right-to-left association would therefore incorrectly derive **ate̩*. In contrast with the free [−ATR] specification of a form like *àjè̩* 'paddle' (a morpheme-level specification that has nothing to do with the initial low vowel), the [−ATR] specification of a word like *ate* is specifically a property of the initial low vowel, and this property must be encoded in some way.

A similar problem can be observed in forms with the pattern *low...high...mid*. Because of the initial low vowel, a floating [−ATR] would have to be postulated; via right-to-left association such a [−ATR] specification would link to the rightmost vowel, deriving a form like *àkùrò̩* 'a type of farmland'. Under such an approach, however, there would be no obvious account for a form like *àbúrò* 'younger sibling', where the rightmost vowel is not [−ATR] despite the presence of a low vowel. Forms like *àkùrò̩* are additionally problematical in that there is no obvious source for the [−ATR] value that the initial low vowel exhibits on the surface: if a free [−ATR] value links to the final mid vowel, and since high vowels are opaque to the spread of [−ATR] (e.g., *yorùbá* 'Yoruba'), how then does the initial vowel receive its [ATR] specification? Presumably a rule inserting [−ATR] on low vowels could be invoked, but this would remove any need or desirability for positing floating specifications in low vowel morphemes.

Since the conceptual undesirability of the account in (69b) is immediately matched by empirical shortcomings, we conclude that it is not a viable possibility.

2.3.1.5 Conclusion Two points of central importance emerge from the above discussion of Yoruba: (i) low vowels are unspecified for [−ATR] underlyingly, and (ii) low vowels are specified for [−ATR] at the point where [−ATR] Spread applies. The required ordering of processes is therefore as given in (81).[62]

(81) *Yoruba rule order*

    1. Associate morpheme-level [−ATR] from right to left.

    2. [−ATR] Insertion: Insert [−ATR] onto [+low] vowels.

    3. [−ATR] Spread: [−ATR] spreads leftward.

The general conclusion to be drawn from specifying low vowels as [+low] only, not as [+low, −ATR], is that the formally simpler representation is necessary in underlying representations in this language. Underlying representations of Yoruba morphemes contain sufficient information to distinguish their phonological properties but do not contain extraneous information, even when that information is necessary for the correct application of phonological rules.

Prior to beginning the discussion of Yoruba, we briefly laid out a typology of F-element combinations. The Yoruba case illustrates a situation where two compatible F-elements are involved, [+low] and [−ATR], and where the presence of one can be predicted on the basis of the other: all low vowels have retracted tongue root. Of interest in the Yoruba pattern is the evidence that in such a case of predictability, the simpler representation holds initially, being replaced by the more complex one during the course of the derivation. In the next section, we discuss a case in Haya that involves similar predictability, but where there is evidence only for the simpler representation.

2.3.2 Simpler Representations and Simpler Rules: Haya Post-Root Harmony

The behavior of low vowels in Yoruba harmony demonstrates the empirical necessity of selecting the simpler of competing underlying representations, that is, the one with fewer F-elements. In this section, we consider a particular prediction made by this proposal, arguing that selection of the simplest representation leads to formulation of the simplest rule in a language like Haya, a Bantu language spoken in Tanzania.

In Haya (Byarushengo 1975), high suffix vowels are lowered to mid vowels following roots with mid vowels. Formally, this harmony can be accounted for by spreading [−high] rightward. Interestingly, only mid vowels trigger the harmony: the low vowel /a/ does not function as a trigger even though low vowels are certainly nonhigh vowels. We show here that representing Haya /a/ as [+low], rather than the more complex [+low, −high], derives the correct results.[63]

Haya has five vowels on the surface, [i, e, a, o, u]. The forms in (82) illustrate the rule lowering high suffix vowels when they follow a root with a mid vowel: in this context, the high vowels of the causative -is and applicative -il lower to mid vowels, producing -es and -el, respectively (82a). This change does not take place if the root has either a high vowel (82b) or a low vowel (82c).[64]

(82) *Haya post-root harmony* (Byarushengo 1975)

			Root	Causative	Applicative	
a. Mid	[e]		-teg-	teg-es-a	teg-el-a	'set up a trap'
	[o]		-kom-	kom-es-a	kom-el-a	'tie up'
b. High	[i]		-sib-	sib-is-a	sib-il-a	'pleat'
	[u]		-kub-	kub-is-a	kub-il-a	'fold'
c. Low	[a]		-gab-	gab-is-a	gab-il-a	'offer'

The rule of harmony spreads [−high] from left to right. In its simplest expression, the rule would therefore impose no additional stipulations, allowing the informal formulation "Spread [−high] rightward."

(83) −HI
       ⌐‾‾⌐
       │   ╲
       μ   μ

Whether this is an adequate characterization of the rule depends essentially on which vowels are specified for the feature [−high]. What is striking about the Haya rule is that it is triggered only by the root vowels whose value for [high] is contrastive (Clements 1987, Steriade 1987a). That is, the value for [high] cannot be determined based on other F-elements (or on other phonological properties of the stems). By contrast, the low vowel /a/ is predictably [−high] and does not trigger the rule.

In order to distinguish morphemes in Haya, five F-element combinations must be differentiated phonologically; this can be achieved with the representations in (84). Three F-elements are posited, since this is sufficient to differentiate the five surface vowels of Haya.[65]

(84) *Haya vowel representation*

    a. F-elements

      −HI, +LO, +BK

  b. a_1 a_2 o   e a_3 a_4 u   i

a_1	a_2	o	e	a_3	a_4	u	i
−HI	−HI	−HI	−HI				
+LO	+LO			+LO	+LO		
+BK		+BK		+BK		+BK	

The combinations of F-elements in (84) unambiguously define the four vowels [o, e, u, i]. With respect to [a], however, there are several possibilities. Consider first the analysis of Haya if /a_4/, the simplest representation, is the one selected for underlying representations. Post-Root Harmony spreads [−high] rightward from mid vowels: /a/ does not trigger the rule because it has no [−high] specification. Derivations of *tegesa* and *gabisa* in (85) illustrate this.

(85) *Derivations with mid and low vowels*

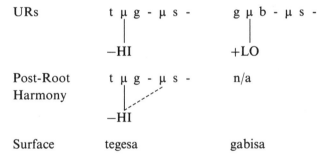

URs	t μ g - μ s -	g μ b - μ s -
	−HI	+LO
Post-Root Harmony	t μ g - μ s -	n/a
	−HI	
Surface	tegesa	gabisa

Now consider the analysis of Haya if the underlying representation for surface [a] is /a_1/ or /a_2/, that is, one of the representations where a low vowel is specified with both [+low] and [−high] underlyingly. If the rule is formulated along the lines of (83), /a/ would incorrectly trigger Post-Root Harmony, by virtue of its representation: [−high, +low]. If we do not simplify the representation for /a/, then it is necessary to complicate the rule: the trigger must be only the [−low] vowels. This will prevent /a/ from triggering the harmony rule, but it also necessitates the otherwise unmotivated insertion of [−low] on the mid vowels (either in underlying representation or by rule).

The above demonstrates that the more F-elements are used to represent /a/, the more complex the grammar becomes, both in terms of more complex rules and in terms of more complex derived or underived representations elsewhere. In contrast, the simpler representation for /a/ correlates with the maximally simple formalization of the Haya rule, as well as with simpler representations for the mid vowels.

2.3.3 Ainu Melodic Dissimilation

For F-elements, to be compatible means that they can cooccur. Free combination of such compatible F-elements therefore creates the possibility of a four-way distinction using two F-elements.

(86)

1	2	3	4
α	α	—	—
β	—	β	—

There is a class of straightforward cases where all four such combinations are distinguished both underlyingly and at the surface. For example, the vowels [o, e, u, i] of Haya can be distinguished by the two F-elements [−high] and [+back] (as seen in (87)).

(87)

o	e	u	i
−HI	−HI	—	—
+BK	—	+BK	—

In this section, we demonstrate that the combinatorial possibility of (86) can be attested even in cases where there is a redundant surface relation between α and β. That is, even where there is not a four-way surface contrast, there can be a four-way underlying contrast. The language to be considered is Ainu, a linguistic isolate spoken in northern Japan (Patrie 1982, Itô 1984). We demonstrate that Ainu, like Barrow Inupiaq, has more combinations underlyingly (six) than are realized at the surface (five: [i, e, a, o, u]). The "extra" representation is one that is predicted by a model that allows F-elements to combine freely.[66]

In Ainu, the transitivizing verbal suffix has one of two forms: either it is identical to the root vowel or it is a high vowel that disagrees in backing with the root vowel. The second case is the one of interest here: it is represented in (88). (See Itô 1984 for discussion of the first case, complete identity between the root and suffix vowel, as well as for a slightly different approach to the dissimilation cases.) In (88a), the stem vowel is [+back], either [u] or [o]: the suffix vowel surfaces as [i]. In (88b), the stem vowel is front, either [i] or [e]: the suffix surfaces as [u].

(88) *Dissimilation: Nonlow vowel roots*

a.	CuC+i	hum-i	'to chop up'	mus-i	'to choke'
	CoC+i	pok-i	'to lower'	hop-i	'to leave behind'
b.	CiC+u	pir-u	'to wipe'	kir-u	'to alter'
	CeC+u	ket-u	'to rub'	rek-u	'to ring'

We follow the essence of Itô's analysis and assume that the high vowel in the transitive form is represented simply as [+high] in underlying representation: the value for [back] is specified by a rule of Ainu Melodic Dissimilation (89). Assuming that [+back] is the value of [back] that is phonologically active, Melodic Dissimilation assigns the value [+back] to the transitivizing suffix, but is blocked from applying by the OCP if the stem is already [+back].[67]

(89) *Ainu Melodic Dissimilation*

> Conditions
> Phonological: right to left
>   noniterative
>   subject to the OCP
> Morphological: transitivizing suffix

The rule is free to apply in a word like *pir-u* 'to wipe', but is blocked from applying to one like *hum-i* 'to chop up'.

(90) a. pir + μ   b. hum + μ
                                            |
                                           +BK

    pir + μ   n/a   Ainu Melodic Dissimilation
          |
         +BK

                            hum + μ
                               | |
                      * +BK   +BK

    [piru]   [humi]

Of interest here is the additional fact that this rule applies after some stems with [a], but not after others. We designate a_1 as the [a] after which [+back] is inserted (91a) and a_2 as the [a] after which [+back] is not inserted (91b).

(91) *Dissimilation: Low vowel roots*

> a. $Ca_1C + u$ ram-u 'to think'   rap-u 'to flutter'
> b. $Ca_2C + i$ kar-i 'to rotate'   sar-i 'to look back'

In the face of these data, Itô (1984:509) concludes that there is no principled explanation for the behavior of [a]: "This analysis cannot be extended to the *a*-roots in (4)

[=(91)], since they may occur with either back or front suffixes." However, under Combinatorial Specification, these patterns are not unexpected. Free combination of the F-elements [+high], [+low], and [+back] gives rise to eight logically possible combinations, two of which are ruled out by the prohibition against [+high, +low]. This is represented in (92).

(92) *Ainu vowel representation*

    a. Active F-elements

      +HI, +LO, +BK

    b. Conditions

      HI/LO Condition: If [+high] then not [+low].
      LO/HI Condition: If [+low] then not [+high].

    c.

*	*	i	u	a_1	a_2	e	o
+HI	+HI	+HI	+HI				
+LO	+LO			+LO	+LO		
	+BK		+BK		+BK		+BK

Consider the two logically possible combinations with [+low] that are not ruled out by the conditions in (92b), the combinations given in the columns headed by a_1 and a_2. The vowel a_1 is simply [+low], while a_2 is [+low, +back]. Since Ainu Melodic Dissimilation does not apply if the feature [+back] is present, the two representations for [a] will respond differently to this rule. The rule applies if a stem includes a_1, which has no [back] specification: the suffix is realized as [u]. By contrast, the rule is blocked in stems with a_2, which is [+back]: the suffix is realized as [i] (see (91a,b), respectively).

(93) a. ra_1m + μ   b. ka_2r + μ
                                  |
                                  +BK

  ra_1m + μ   n/a   Ainu Melodic Dissimilation
          |
        +BK

                        ka_2r + μ
                         | |
                 * +BK   +BK

  [ramu]   [kari]

Although the behavior of [a] in Ainu seems anomalous if considered in terms of the set of surface vocalic segments, we have shown here that it is an expected type of pattern under Combinatorial Specification: the active F-elements combine freely, subject to constraints on certain combinations, creating two representations for [a]. The two different representations create different effects when Ainu Melodic Dissimilation applies since the rule is blocked from applying if [+back] is present. The unusual property of Ainu is that [+low] and [+low, +back] are realized identically, a point we discuss further in sections 2.8.1 and 3.3. Barrow Inupiaq presents another case with this same property: in Barrow Inupiaq, however, no F-element combinations are permitted.[68] As a result, vowels represented both by [−back] and by no F-elements at all receive identical surface realizations.

2.4 Representational Simplicity

In early work in generative phonology, Halle (1962:55) proposed the following evaluation metric:

(94) Given two alternative descriptions of a particular body of data, the description containing fewer ... symbols will be regarded as simpler and will, therefore, be preferred over the other.

In the paper, he demonstrated that a wide variety of phenomena could be accounted for by adopting such a principle of *simplicity*.

Clearly, an evaluation metric can only contrast alternative analyses cast within the same theory (Chomsky 1965:37–47). One cannot, for example, compare in any meaningful way rules or representations formulated within an autosegmental framework and those formulated within the kind of segmental approach found in *SPE*. It is nevertheless striking that a slight translation of the sort of approach advocated by Halle (1962) makes it relevant for autosegmental representations, as illustrated by considering the examples already discussed in this chapter.

Consider in this regard the types of *symbols* manipulated by a hierarchical autosegmental theory. Essentially three types of symbols can be distinguished: (i) terminal elements (F), (ii) class nodes (C), (iii) associations of features and class nodes $(|)$.

(95)

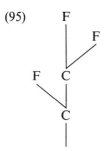

(Recall that some class nodes, for example, the articulator nodes Coronal and Dorsal, may function as terminal or as nonterminal nodes depending on the entire set of specifications in the relevant structure (see Sagey 1986).)

In such a hierarchical approach, one cannot simply count up the number of "symbols" in a representation to arrive at an adequate characterization of the representation's complexity. As noted by Clements (1985a), the presence of a linked terminal feature automatically implies the presence of all class node structure between the terminal node and the Root node. Such structure is an automatic consequence of the theory, serving to inherently restrict the class of possible structure-manipulating rules; it does not increase the complexity of a given representation.

Consequently, although associated terminal nodes imply the presence of the appropriate class nodes, the occurrence of a particular class node does not imply the presence of any particular terminal node (in any universal sense). Therefore, the number of stipulated specifications can be determined through counting the number of terminal nodes and of associations to terminal nodes in a given representation.

(96) *Representational Simplicity*

   The value of a representation is the inverse of the number of

   a. terminal F-elements

   b. associations to terminal F-elements

For example, the set of specifications for [a] given in (97a) includes two terminal nodes and two associations, while the set for [a] given in (97b) includes one terminal node and one association; (97c) has only one terminal node and no associations.[69]

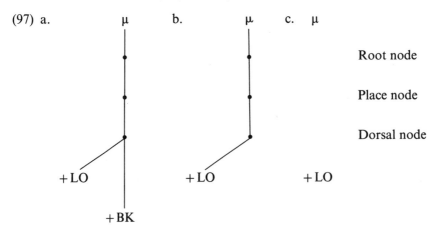

(97) a.   μ   b.   μ   c.   μ

                                                    Root node

                                                    Place node

                                                    Dorsal node

        +LO   +LO   +LO

        +BK

Given the principle in (96), representation (97b) is evaluated as simpler than (97a), and (97c) as simpler than both (97a) and (97b).

In this light, let us consider the phenomena in Yoruba, Haya, and Ainu that were discussed in the previous section. In all of these cases, we are dealing with a configuration where two compatible features are in a redundant relation with each other: some feature β is predictably present on the surface because of the presence of a second feature α.[70] In Yoruba, a vowel specified only as [+low] (α) receives the specification [−ATR] (β) at a stage preceding harmony. In Haya, the value [−high] (β) that is redundant for low vowels ([+low] = α) must *not* be present at the point where height harmony takes place. In Ainu, there is a lexical contrast with respect to backness for low vowels ([+low] = α), even though the contrast does not manifest itself on the low vowels at the surface (all surface low vowels are back ([+back] = β)).

According to the principle of Representational Simplicity, the simplest representation in all three of these cases would be a vowel solely specified as [+low]. We follow Halle (1962) in proposing that the reason the three cases differ in their behavior rests on the interplay between Representational Simplicity and the need to maintain intelligibility.

To understand intelligibility, consider a language like Finnish or English that contrasts the front and back low vowels [æ] and [a]. Since these vowels are phonetically and phonologically distinct in these languages, it is uncontroversial to distinguish them phonologically, for example, as follows:

(98) a. [æ]: [+low, −back]

   b. [a]: [+low]

Although the representation [+low, −back] for [æ] is more complex than the representation [+low], it must be maintained if the distinction between the two low vowels is to be maintained. Hence, Representational Simplicity is counteracted by a principle of Recoverability.

(99) *Recoverability*

   Phonological representations and phonetic content are related.

The most complete relation would be equivalence between phonological representations and phonetic content. However, the phonetic content is quite complex and includes much information that is either irrelevant or redundant. Thus, though satisfying Recoverability, complete equivalence ignores Representational Simplicity. The tension between Recoverability and Representational Simplicity is such that phonological representations are as impoverished as possible, yet are still rich enough that they relate unambiguously to phonetic content.

Recoverability could of course be expressed in a more directional sense, for instance, by saying that the phonetic content must be recoverable from the phonological representation. We maintain the more neutral expression of the relation given in

(99) since it is equally true that the phonological representation must be recoverable from the phonetic content.

What then of the case seen in Ainu? At first glance, one might think that Representational Simplicity would require all low vowels to be uniformly represented as [+low] since with regard to Recoverability, all low vowels surface *phonetically* as [a]. As pointed out by Halle (1962) with respect to a comparable case in Russian, however, such an analysis would not be valid because it does not capture the *phonological* properties of the relevant morphemes. Although the lexical contrast in low vowels on a stem does not manifest itself on the stem vowel itself, it does manifest itself on an adjacent suffix, as seen in pairs like *ram-u* 'to think' and *kar-i* 'to rotate'. Recoverability, therefore, forces an analysis precisely along the lines proposed in section 2.3.3.

The cases of Haya and Yoruba are very different. In each of these languages, there is neither a *phonetic* nor a *phonological* contrast in the behavior of low vowels. As a consequence, Recoverability will not prevent Representational Simplicity from imposing the single underlying representation [+low] for all low vowels.

Representational Simplicity immediately derives the desired result for Haya. Low vowels do not bear the redundant feature value [−high]; hence, they do not trigger lowering of a following high vowel. While a stem like *teg* will therefore induce lowering of the suffix in a form like *teg-el-a* 'set up a trap', a stem like *gab* does not induce comparable lowering: *gab-il-a* 'offer'. A theory incorporating Representational Simplicity predicts that a system like that of Haya should be unmarked and stable; a theory without such a principle either makes no predictions in this regard, or predicts that a rule like that of Haya should be marked and unstable because it is not "surface true" (there are nonhigh vowels that do not trigger spread of [−high], namely, the low vowels). Note in this regard that numerous Bantu languages (see note 63 for examples) exhibit precisely the type of rule found in Haya. The advantage of simplifying the formal statement of phonological rules is that the simpler rule encodes more directly properties that are crucially present on account of the alternation, rather than properties whose presence is necessitated by the theory itself. (See the discussion of Latvian Raising and Yawelmani Vowel Harmony in Archangeli 1984 for further examples of such rule simplification.)

In Yoruba, the phonological behavior of low vowels is different from the case of Haya because a redundant value is inserted phonologically. Prior to the application of [ATR] harmony, all low vowels become specified [−ATR]. Of importance is the following point: recall the evidence from section 2.3.1 showing that low vowels are underlyingly *unspecified* for [ATR] and acquire the value [−ATR] after the association of floating morpheme-level specifications of [ATR]. Such evidence demonstrates that Representational Simplicity holds of underlying representations even in cases where surface evidence appears to require more complex representations.

We conclude this section by considering four issues that arise out of this discussion of Representational Simplicity, issues that relate directly to the hypothesis of nonsegmental phonology advanced in the discussions of Tiv and Inupiaq, as well as to questions relating to theories of underspecification. First is the concept of *distinctness*.

2.4.1 Distinctness

According to definitions of distinctness such as those of Chomsky and Halle (1968), Kiparsky (1982), and Pulleyblank (1986a) (note also Yip 1989b), two segments are formally distinct only if they have contradictory specifications. According to such definitions, a segment specified [+F] is formally distinct from a segment specified [−F], but a segment specified [αF] is not formally distinct from a segment unspecified for [F]. Such definitions raise a variety of questions when incompletely specified representations are adopted. By this definition, the phonological representations of $/i_1/$ and $/i_2/$ in Barrow Inupiaq and of $/a_1/$ and $/a_2/$ in Ainu would not be formally distinct, raising the question of how these vowels can have phenomenally distinct behaviors.

Further, the oddity of such a definition is not restricted to the phonological component, as work in phonetics has shown. Keating (1985, 1988), Pierrehumbert and Beckman (1988), and Cohn (1989) argue that the input to the phonetic level is not necessarily a fully specified representation. This would mean that at no stage of the phonology would an [α]/∅ opposition ever involve formally *distinct* representations.

For *distinctness* to have some meaning within a theory allowing underspecified representations, it would therefore seem necessary to modify our understanding of the notion.

The problem just raised is directly attributable to viewing phonology in segmental terms. Consider the two ways in which representations can conventionally be considered to be distinct. First, as already discussed, representations can be distinct because they contain contradictory specifications: *bean* versus *beam*, *pat* versus *pot*, and so on. Second, representations can be distinct because they contain differing numbers of segments: *spa* is distinct from *paw*, *twitch* is distinct from *witch*, *hemp* is distinct from *hem*, and so on. Two representations can involve exactly the same sets of feature specifications and be distinct solely because of the length of the component segments, as is common in languages with distinctive consonant or vowel length. Crucial for this second class of cases, therefore, is the number of elements, not that two elements have contradictory specifications.

Consider in this regard the effect of shifting one's focus from the segment to the F-element. If differing numbers of *segments* should cause two representations to be distinct (that is, differing numbers of sets of F-elements linked in paths), then so too should differing numbers of *F-elements* cause two representations to be distinct.

Given F-elements as primitives, the representations [+low] and [+low, +back] are just as distinct as the sequences *hem* and *hemp*.[71]

2.4.2 Neutralization

Given representations that encode at least certain contrasts as the presence versus absence of some feature, whether binary or unary, it becomes possible to neutralize a contrast by a feature-filling process. This can be accomplished by association of F-elements as in Tiv, Yoruba, and Haya, and it can be accomplished by the insertion of an F-element as in Barrow Inupiaq and Ainu.

Feature insertion rules are not always neutralizing, of course. The rule inserting [−ATR] onto low vowels in Yoruba, for example, is not neutralizing since there is no [ATR] contrast on low vowels at any stage; in contrast, the rule spreading [−high] to suffixes in Haya neutralizes the high/mid contrast in those suffix vowels. A rule inserting some F-element F in some context C is neutralizing or nonneutralizing depending on whether F appears distinctively in context C.

It is entirely uncontroversial, therefore, that there should be a class of neutralizing, feature-filling rules. In fact, phonologists have often assumed that feature-filling rules, often of the neutralizing type, are the unmarked rule option (see Kiparsky 1985).

In such a framework, it is important to consider the status of absolute neutralization rules, that is, rules that eliminate the contrast between two distinct featural representations without contextual conditions. With respect to rule formalism, if neutralizing redundancy rules *with conditions* are allowed, then it is hard to see how one could eliminate formally the class of neutralizing redundancy rules *without conditions*.

But while formally permissible, rules of absolute neutralizauon pose problems in terms of Recoverability. Consider again the case of Ainu. We showed in section 2.3.3 that Ainu has a contrast in low vowels with respect to backness, just as it does in the mid and high vowels.

(100) *Ainu low vowels*

     a. +LO

     b. +LO
        +BK

While this contrast plays a role in the phonology of Ainu, it is eliminated by the surface. The attested *absolute* neutralization can be accomplished by the redundant insertion of [+back] on all low vowels.

Elimination of the contrast in (100) creates a lack of correspondence between phonological and phonetic representations, a problem for Recoverability (99). Essentially, the only way for Recoverability not to be violated is for some aspect of the phonetic representation *other than the low vowel itself* to correlate with the phonological difference between the two vowels. In Ainu, the relevant difference is clear in the transitivizing suffix that reflects the distinct representations in (100). In a case such as Barrow Inupiaq, discussed in section 2.2.2, the neutralized distinction between $[i_1]$ and $[i_2]$ is established by the two vowels' behavior with respect to the three rules Coronal Palatalization, Dorsal Assimilation, and Labial Assimilation. In general, therefore, absolute neutralization is predicted to be possible only in cases where there is robust evidence allowing the reconstruction of a contrast.

This is not to say, however, that there are no constraints on absolute neutralization other than Recoverability. Consider the neutralization rules required for Ainu and Barrow Inupiaq.

(101) a. Ainu $[+\text{low}] \rightarrow [+\text{back}]$

  b. Barrow Inupiaq $\mu \rightarrow [-\text{back}]$

The Ainu rule is an expression of the interdependency between lowness and backness; the Inupiaq rule is an expression of an apparent statistical asymmetry whereby front vowels are more commonly unspecified phonologically than back vowels. Such rules are clearly attested in nonneutralizing situations and are therefore predicted to occur in a neutralizing fashion given a sufficiently robust context.

One can imagine rules that do not express such interdependencies or asymmetries, for example, those in (102).

(102) a. Impossible $[+\text{low}] \rightarrow [-\text{back}]$

  b. Marked $\mu \rightarrow [+\text{back}]$

In chapter 3, we argue that rules such as the two in (102) would be impossible or highly marked depending on the case. With respect to absolute neutralization, the crucial point is that only a particular subset of the possible class of rules are substantively allowed, the class characterized in chapter 3 as "grounded." That is, both Recoverability and Grounding constrain the class of possible absolute neutralization rules.

As a final point, we note that an additional class of imaginable absolute neutralization rules are ruled out for formal reasons. Consider a language with a phonological contrast between advanced and retracted mid and high vowels.

(103)   i   u

    ɪ   ʊ

    e   o

    ɛ   ɔ

Such a class of vowels, attested as part of the inventory of a language like Okpę discussed in section 3.3.1.1, can be specified as in (104).[72]

(104)	i	ɪ	e	ɛ	u	ʊ	o	ɔ
	+HI	+HI			+HI	+HI		
	+ATR		+ATR		+ATR		+ATR	
					+BK	+BK	+BK	+BK

Hoffmann (1973) claims that in Okpę there is absolute neutralization between the pairs [ɪ/e] and [ʊ/o]. In section 3.3.1.1, we argue that this claim is not empirically substantiated. But consider the type of rule that would be required to derive such a neutralization. With underspecified representations, the vowels /ɪ, ʊ/, specified only as [+high] (abstracting away from [+back]), would have to both lose this specification and acquire the specification [+ATR], the F-element necessary for /e, o/. With fully specified representations, the change would be [+high, −ATR] → [−high, +ATR].

Whatever the degree of specification, the putative neutralization cannot be derived by a single primitive operation. Depending on the type of representation assumed, the rule would have to insert one feature and delete another, or else change two feature values. Both rule types are impossible in the theory of rules presented in chapter 4; hence, both putative types of absolute neutralization are ruled out formally.[73]

To conclude, we propose that neutralization of both contextual and absolute kinds can take place subject to a set of formal and substantive constraints. Formally, the rule may involve no more than a single operation, such as feature-filling insertion. Substantively, the rule must belong to a permissible class as defined by Grounding Theory. Finally, the contrast that is neutralized must be recoverable.

2.4.3   Are All Languages Like Tiv and Barrow Inupiaq?

We have argued at some length that the primitive building blocks out of which phonological representations are formed are F-elements, not segments. Segments are simply the by-product of linking together some set of F-elements. We have suggested, moreover, that the maximization of combination produces a pattern of 2^n contrasts, a possibility exemplified by Tiv in section 2.2.1; where combinations are minimized, an $n + 1$ pattern may result, as exemplified by Barrow Inupiaq in section 2.2.2. The two patterns, 2^n and $n + 1$, represent fairly extreme types of combination. As should be clear from the discussion of Yoruba, Haya, and Ainu, other languages exhibit intermediate positions in the typology of possible combinations. One question is important to address explicitly in this regard. In each language considered thus far, one combinatorial possibility was the absence of all specification. Does this lead to the conclusion that *all* languages have a role for an element that is absolutely unspecified? Does every language, for example, have a completely unspecified segment?

As a first point to note in this regard, consider again the example of [−ATR] in Yoruba. We have argued that low vowels must be unspecified underlyingly for [ATR], but that they receive a redundant specification very early in the phonology. In general, this means that feature specifications may be unspecified at the beginning of the phonology, allowing a completely unspecified consonant or vowel in underlying representation that is assigned some feature so early as to be almost indistinguishable from a situation where the feature was underlyingly present. Moreover, in the absence of some ad hoc constraint requiring that rules of redundancy be restricted to late stages of the grammar, it would presumably be impossible to prevent the early assignment of redundant feature values in appropriate cases. But this example begs the more important question. Can it be the case that even at the underlying stage, there is no element corresponding to a completely unspecified phoneme?

Consider in this regard the example of coronal consonants. Work such as that of Paradis and Prunet (1991) argues that coronal consonants may be underspecified for place features. Essentially, behavior that treats coronal consonants in an asymmetrical fashion is used to motivate the underspecified status of that class: the behavior is explicable only by *not* assigning a Coronal specification underlyingly. If we conclude that asymmetrical behavior of the appropriate type is accounted for by underspecification, we might ask whether coronals will invariably behave in an asymmetrical fashion.

The answer to this question is apparently negative. Considering data from Arabic, for example, McCarthy (1988) argues that the OCP prevents clusters of consonants with like place specifications from occurring within roots. If Coronal were underlyingly unspecified in Arabic, then coronal consonants should be exempt from such a constraint since the OCP would not prohibit a sequence of consonants without specifications. The fact that coronals behave in a manner comparable to other places of articulation, coupled with the fact that no place of articulation is singled out in an asymmetrical fashion, suggests that there is no "default" place in Arabic.

The obvious question is why not. Interestingly, the answer seems to be that Recoverability prevents it.

Consider the hackneyed example of an Arabic consonantal root: /ktb/ 'write'. In associating such a root to a template, whatever the precise details of the prosodic template itself, the second consonant must be at least partially specified in order for the association to take place correctly. The [t] of the root associates in a manner entirely comparable to any other consonant. If the [t] of /ktb/ were completely unspecified, this root would be incorrectly predicted to behave in a manner comparable to a biliteral root like /sm/ 'poison'. Note, moreover, that there is nothing special about second position as far as coronals are concerned. Roots may have an initial coronal as in /tbʕ/ 'succeed', just as they may have a final coronal as in /mqt/ 'detest'.

There seem to be essentially two ways of ensuring that coronals appear in the correct position: (i) empty Root nodes (see Sagey 1986) or empty Place nodes may be included in the representation as placeholders, (ii) Coronal may be underlyingly included in Arabic. The first possibility is undesirable for conceptual reasons, and it fails empirically. There seems virtually no independent evidence for allowing class nodes like the Root node and the Place node to exist without dominating some amount of feature content.[74] In the absence of independent motivation, the inclusion of such an unspecified class node here is completely ad hoc. At an empirical level, the simple inclusion of a class node makes the incorrect prediction that OCP effects sensitive to place should not involve coronals. Since the contrary is actually attested, this argues against the empty node analyses.

The conclusion is therefore straightforward. Representational Simplicity cannot force the postulation of representations where coronals are specified by default rules, because if the appropriate representations were indeed postulated, surface forms would be radically different from those in fact attested. That is, Recoverability blocks any simplification of representations including Coronal in such a templatically based pattern.

We conclude, therefore, that although Representational Simplicity forces the removal of a class of specifications from underlying representations in certain cases, Recoverability forces the inclusion of the same class in others.

2.4.4   Radical Underspecification, the Redundancy Rule Ordering Constraint, and Ternary Power

To close this discussion, we highlight a couple of the ways in which the arguments presented here are incompatible with earlier models of underspecification.

Consider first the case of *Radical Underspecification* (Archangeli 1984, 1988, Archangeli and Pulleyblank 1989, Kiparsky 1982, Itô and Mester 1986, Pulleyblank 1986a, 1988a, etc.). This model in its essence seeks to eliminate all phonological redundancy from underlying representations: contrasts are typically analyzed as αF versus ∅ oppositions.

Such a model is incompatible with analyses such as that of Barrow Inupiaq and Ainu presented here. Similarly, it is unclear how such an approach would deal with the characterization of Arabic root constraints. The central difference between the Radical and Combinatorial models is that Radical Underspecification *requires* the elimination of phonological redundancy; Combinatorial Specification *prefers* such elimination (Representational Simplicity) but counteracts the tendency toward such elimination by the principle of Recoverability.

Within much of the work in the Radical Underspecification model, the *Redundancy Rule Ordering Constraint* (RROC) has played an important role. Although the precise formulation of the RROC has varied, its central claim is that redundancy rules supply any feature value referred to in a phonological rule R by the point in the derivation at which rule R applies. For example, in Yoruba, the redundancy rule supplying [−ATR] to low vowels must apply prior to the rule of harmony, a rule that refers to the value [−ATR] in its structural description. Archangeli and Pulleyblank (1989) attribute such ordering to the automatic effect of the RROC. We note here, however, that it simply appears to be false that such ordering of redundancy rules invariably takes place. Although redundancy rules do apply *prior to* the application of relevant phonological rules in cases like Yoruba, redundancy rules can apply only *after* the application of relevant rules in cases like those discussed here for Haya and Ainu. If [−high] were redundantly assigned to low vowels in Haya prior to Post-Root Harmony (82), then harmony would incorrectly be triggered by low vowels; if [+back] were redundantly assigned to low vowels in Ainu prior to Dissimilation (91), then Dissimilation with the transitivizing suffix would incorrectly give an invariable . . . *a* . . . *i* pattern, ruling out . . . *a* . . . *u* entirely. We conclude that the RROC does not express a valid generalization about the operation of rules of redundancy.

It is worthwhile dwelling for a moment on the conceptual reason motivating the introduction of the RROC. As discussed in work such as that of Lightner (1963), Stanley (1967), Ringen (1975), Kiparsky (1982), and Pulleyblank (1986a), it is possible to derive ternary power in a theory that allows the specification of both values of a binary feature in addition to an absence of specification. In general, it was assumed that ternary power was undesirable, and constraints were therefore imposed to rule it out. The RROC was one such mechanism. Prior to the insertion of redundant values, Radical Underspecification envisioned representations with a binary contrast between αF and ∅; after the application of redundancy rules, governed by the RROC, representations would contrast +F and −F. Thus, if the RROC is abandoned, then what is the conclusion with respect to ternary power?

We suggest that ternary power with a binary feature is indeed available, although such power is not commonly utilized. For an explicit argument in favor of ternary power, see the discussion of Kalenjin in section 3.5.3. For the present, we address only the issue of why such power, if available, is not used more frequently. We suggest that the answer lies in the tendency to maximize combinatorial possibilities of F-elements, a tendency brought about largely by Representational Simplicity.

Consider a surface array of four vowels such as the following: [i, ɪ, e, ɛ]. These four vowels could in principle be represented with any of the following sets of F-elements:

(105) a. {[+high], [−high], [+ATR], [−ATR]}
       b. {[+high], [+ATR], [−ATR]}
       c. {[−high], [+ATR], [−ATR]}
       d. {[+high], [−high], [+ATR]}
       e. {[+high], [−high], [−ATR]}
       f. {[+high], [+ATR]}

  g. {[+high], [−ATR]}
  h. {[−high], [+ATR]}
  i. {[−high], [−ATR]}

Of these nine logical possibilities, ternarity is an issue in precisely the five combinations (a–e) that would be ruled out by Representational Simplicity. In the four possibilities sanctioned by Representational Simplicity, ternarity is a nonissue.[75] We suggest, therefore, that ternarity only arises as a possibility in cases where there is sufficient positive evidence to force one away from the set of preferred representations. Representational Simplicity does not rule out ternarity, but it makes it formally costly.

2.5   Simplicity in Associations: Morpheme Structure Conditions in Ngbaka

Representational Simplicity (96) was defined above as governing both feature content and associations. The focus of the evidence that has been discussed so far, however, has been exclusively feature content. In this section, we redress this imbalance by focusing on the issue of associations.

The central theme concerns the representation of exceptional linkings. We argue that general patterns of morpheme structure in Ngbaka, a Niger-Congo language spoken in the Central African Republic, support the notion that underlying representations are maximally simple. Exceptions to the general pattern of morpheme structure are shown to result from a particular type of increase in underlying complexity, an increase involving the preassociation of otherwise unremarkable features.

The pattern of vowel cooccurrence restrictions in Ngbaka has been quite widely discussed, for example, by Thomas (1963), Wescott (1965), Chomsky and Halle (1968), Clements (1982), Churma (1984), Itô (1984), Mester (1986), and Steriade (1987a). Surface representations in Ngbaka contrast the seven oral vowels given in (106).

(106) *Ngbaka surface vowels*

  i e ɛ a ɔ o u

Pairs of vowels like [i]: [e], and [u]: [o] are distinct from each other in terms of their feature for vowel height. This distinction could be represented (i) by invoking the F-element [+high] by itself ([i, u] = [+high]; [e, o] unspecified for [high]), (ii) by invoking the F-element [−high] by itself ([e, o] = [−high]; [i, u] unspecified for [high]), or (iii) by invoking both F-elements [+high] and [−high] ([i, u] = [+high]; [e, o] = [−high]). Considerations of Representational Simplicity would favor either of the first two options (the choice between them determined by markedness or language data), but the possibility of using both F-elements should be ruled out, or at least highly marked.

In work such as that of Mester (1986) and Steriade (1987a), Ngbaka has been taken to argue for the underlying presence of both values of contrastive features like [high]. That is, both [+high] and [−high] would be present in underlying representation. If such arguments are persuasive, then Ngbaka constitutes something of a problem for the notion of Representational Simplicity. Unlike a case such as that of Arabic, there is no templatic reason for including both values of features like [high]. In the absence of independent motivation for both values being present, therefore, one would not expect symmetrical behavior of the two values phonologically. In fact, however, we argue in this section that both values of F-elements are *not* required in Ngbaka. Moreover, an analysis in terms of combinatorial properties accounts for certain distributional properties that are not readily explained in alternative analyses using both values of contrastive features.

2.5.1 The Robust Patterns

The core pattern to account for in Ngbaka is the following. When vowels cooccur in a disyllabic word, only the restricted set of vowel sequences shown in (107) is possible.[76]

(107) *Ngbaka vowel cooccurrence*

V2	i	e	ε	a	ɔ	o	u
V1							
i	XXX	X	X	XXX	X	X	—
e	X	XXX	—	X	—	X	—
ε	X	—	XXX	X	—	—	X
a	X	X	X	XXX	X	X	X
ɔ	X	—	X	X	XXX	—	—
o	X	X	—	X	—	XXX	—
u	X	X	X	XXX	—	—	XXX

The overwhelming generalization that can be extracted from this table is that vowel sequences in Ngbaka tend to be identical. In the three classes of sequences distinguished by Thomas (1963), the percentage of cases involving identical vowels is as follows:

(108) *Identical vowel sequences*

CVCV (same tone)	79%
CVCV (different tones)	69%
CVV (usually different tones)	41%

(figures represent the percentage of each class having identical vowels)

In much the same manner as for Tiv, we derive the pattern of Ngbaka vowels by invoking the F-elements [+high], [+low], and [+round]; added to this set, the F-element [+ATR] derives the surface contrast between the pairs ε/e and $\supset/o$. Logically, these four F-elements produce the following 16 combinations. (Recall that circled F-elements are F-elements that are typically free in underlying representation.)

(109) *Ngbaka vowel representation*

    a.   F-elements

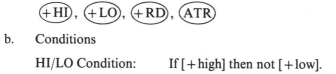

    b.   Conditions

            HI/LO Condition: If [+high] then not [+low].
            LO/HI Condition: If [+low] then not [+high].
            RD/LO Condition: If [+round] then not [+low].
            LO/RD Condition: If [+low] then not [+round].
            ATR/LO Condition: If [+ATR] then not [+low].
            LO/ATR Condition: If [+low] then not [+ATR].

c. i.

	u_1	u_2	i_1	i_2	o	$\supset$	e	ε
	+HI	+HI	+HI	+HI				
	+RD	+RD			+RD	+RD		
	+ATR		+ATR		+ATR		+ATR	

ii.

	*	*	*	*	*	*	*	a
	+HI	+HI	+HI	+HI				
	+RD	+RD			+RD	+RD		
	+ATR		+ATR		+ATR		+ATR	
	+LO	+LO	+LO	+LO	+LO	+LO	+LO	+LO

With respect to low vowels (109c-ii), every combination of [+low] with another F-element is ruled out since low vowels may be neither [+high], [+round], nor [+ATR]; with respect to high vowels, the potential contrast between [+high] vowels specified or not specified for [+ATR] is not exploited since all high vowels are [+ATR] on the surface. Given these combinations, the structure of Ngbaka morphemes can be derived as follows.[77]

First, it is possible for a morpheme to be completely unspecified for vocalic F-elements. In such cases, all vowels surface as [ε] (CVCV-D: 9%; CVCV-L: 14%; CVV: 3%).

(110) *No specifications:* ε...ε

    kέɓέ   'vite'

    mεkὲ   'appuyer, poser'

If a morpheme contains only the specification [+ATR], then all vowels surface as [e] (CVCV-D: 5%; CVCV-L: 6.5%; CVV: 4%).

(111) (+ATR): *e...e*

    yèlè   'étranger'

    kpetè   'gâté, abîmé'

To derive this pattern, [+ATR] links up and spreads throughout the morpheme.[78]

If a [+high] specification is present, it also links, then spreads throughout a morpheme, deriving a sequence of front high vowels (CVCV-D: 7%; CVCV-L: 6%; CVV: 8%).

(112) (+high): *i...i*

    síti   'mauvais'

    kpinì   'presser, essorer'

The [+high] morphemes show that [+high] also links and spreads, just like [+ATR].

The addition of [+ATR] to a [+high] morpheme would result in no surface change. There would therefore be no reason to postulate such a combination, and considerations of Representational Simplicity (96) militate in favor of the sole specification [+high].

In a similar fashion, morphemes bearing solely the specifications [+low] or [+round] account for the *a...a* (CVCV-D: 15%; CVCV-L: 19%; CVV: 15%) and ɔ...ɔ (CVCV-D: 15%; CVCV-L: 11%; CVV: 7%) patterns, respectively; as with [+ATR] and [+high], the F-elements [+low] and [+round] link and spread.

(113) a. (+low): *a...a*

        kamá   'frère ou soeur'

        kanà   'mère'

   b. (+round): ɔ...ɔ

        kɔtɔ́   'sortir'

        nɔkɔ́   'neveu, oncle utérin'

As with Tiv, the postulation of F-elements that are free in underlying representation predicts the possibility of underlying combinations of free F-elements. In considering the properties of such combinations, one can distinguish between sets that include compatible F-elements and sets that include incompatible F-elements. In cases involving compatibility, F-elements simply link up and spread in essentially the same fashion seen above.

(114) a. (+ATR) *and* (+round): *o . . . o* (CVCV-D: 11%; CVCV-L: 15%; CVV: 3%)

   wolo 'femelle, femme'
   lòngò 'piège à éléphant'

  b. (+round) *and* (+high): *u . . . u* (CVCV-D: 7%; CVCV-L: 7%; CVV: 1%)

   kulu 'âme'
   ngulù 'cochon'

In a manner parallel to that discussed above for the F-element [+high] by itself, the addition of [+ATR] to the set {[+round], [+high]} would produce exactly the same result as without [+ATR]. Representational Simplicity therefore selects the representation {[+round], [+high]}.

Turning to the F-element sets involving incompatibilities, we consider first the combinations involving [+high] and [+low], with and without [+round]. These combinations present essentially the same formal problem encountered above with respect to Tiv. It would be impossible for two incompatible F-elements to link simultaneously; such association would be blocked by the conditions in (109c) because the resulting representation would be ill formed, regardless of whether association is left to right (115a), right to left (115b), or to all possible bearers at the same time (115c).

(115) a. +HI   b. +HI   c. +HI

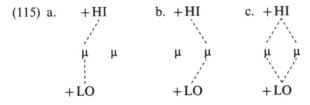

   +LO   +LO   +LO

Important in this regard is the fact that all of the robust combinations in (107) have been accounted for by the combination of free F-elements with the exception of two, *i . . . a* and *u . . . a*. This gap is resolved if we assume that the *i . . . a* and *u . . . a* patterns are precisely those that result from the combination of the incompatible features [+low] and [+high] (with and without [+round]), and if we assume that Ngbaka, like Tiv, assigns priority to the linking of [+high] (see section 2.2.1.7). That is, [+high] links from left to right in a one-to-one fashion, followed by the association of [+low]. Without [+round], this produces an *i . . . a* pattern (CVCV-D: 5.5%; CVCV-L: 1.5%; CVV: 19%), as in (116).

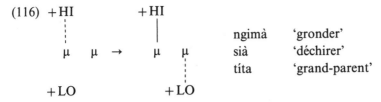

(116)

ngimà	'gronder'
sià	'déchirer'
títa	'grand-parent'

If [+round] is present in addition to [+high] and [+low], it links to the leftmost vowel, as in (117). Ordering the linking of [+round] with respect to the linking of [+high] is not crucial (CVCV-D: 4%; CVCV-L: 2%; CVV: 8%). Spreading of [+round] is impossible because the combination [+round, +low] is ruled out (109c).

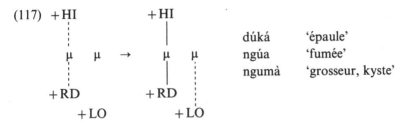

(117)

dúká	'épaule'
ngúa	'fumée'
ngumà	'grosseur, kyste'

As in Tiv, there appears to be no crucial evidence demonstrating the precise mechanism used to establish the priority of High Linking. The association process affecting [+high] could be ordered prior to that affecting [+low]; alternatively, one could imagine a priority clause such as "In the case of a conflict in linking between [+high] and [+low], associate [+high]." Of primary importance is the fact that the combinations {[+high], [+low]} and {[+high], [+low], [+round]} derive the two remaining robust patterns *i...a* and *u...a*.

Positing completely free underlying F-elements, there are five logically possible combinations, given in (118), that have not yet been discussed.

(118) a. {[+high], [+low], [+ATR]}

       b. {[+high], [+low], [+round], [+ATR]}

       c. {[+low], [+ATR]}

       d. {[+low], [+round]}

       e. {[+low], [+round], [+ATR]}

The first two sets, {[+high], [+low], [+ATR]} and {[+high], [+low], [+round], [+ATR]}, would produce results identical on the surface to the patterns attested with {[+high], [+low]} and {[+high], [+low], [+round]}, respectively, since [+ATR] is completely redundant given a [+high] specification. As a consequence, Representational Simplicity would select the representations without [+ATR].

The three remaining sets involve incompatibilities between [+low] and either or both [+ATR] and [+round]. No surface patterns appear to robustly use such sets of F-elements, and we tentatively assume that there are simply no established priorities to make possible the linking of these incompatible F-elements. Since the assignment of any of these pairs of features to a single path would result in ill-formed configurations comparable to those already seen in (115), association in such cases is ruled out.

To summarize, we posit the set of F-elements [+high], [+low], [+round], [+ATR] for Ngbaka. Morphemes include various combinations of these F-elements, and surface representations are derived by simple rules of association and spreading. Incompatible sets of F-elements cannot be realized on the surface except in cases involving [+high] and [+low], where left-edge priority is assigned to the linking of [+high]. Note that no more than one specification of a given F-element is possible for a single morpheme. For example, a morpheme may involve a single [+high] specification but may not involve multiple specifications (*[+high][+high]), a property expected under both the OCP and Representational Simplicity.

2.5.2   The Marked Cases: Prelinking
The above analysis accounts for all patterns involving 4% or more of the total, and accounts for just under 80% of the CVCV–different tones data set as a whole. The remaining cases distribute themselves across a wide variety of patterns, seven patterns involving between 1% and 3% of the total number, and eighteen additional patterns involving less than 1% each.[79]

Our proposal is that these less frequent patterns result from precisely the same combinations of F-elements as the robust cases; the difference lies in the lexical prelinking of certain F-elements. Since prelinking involves a more complex representation according to Representational Simplicity, such patterns therefore involve a more marked representation.

Consider again, for example, cases involving a [+high] specification. As seen in (112), a free [+high] F-element links and spreads to give a surface $i \ldots i$ pattern. If prelinked, the [+high] specification could be as in either of the representations of (119).[80]

(119) *Prelinked [+high]*

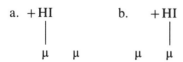

Since the structural description of High Spread would be underlyingly satisfied, not derived, in both of (119a,b), the Strict Cycle Condition (see below) blocks the application of lexical spreading in each such case. As a result, the only processes relevant in (119) would be the assignment of redundant values. Hence, (119a) would surface as $i \ldots \varepsilon$ (CVCV-D: 0.27%; CVCV-L: 0.5%; CVV: 2%), and (119b) would surface as $\varepsilon \ldots i$ (CVCV-D: 1.4%; CVCV-L: 0%; CVV: 0%): for example, *ziè* 'vomir' and *lèsi* 'silure', respectively.

Since for this and subsequent examples, it is crucial to make particular assumptions about the Strict Cycle Condition, we digress for a moment to discuss this issue before returning to the prelinked cases of Ngbaka.

2.5.3 The Strict Cycle Condition

There is a class of rules that has been observed to have the following properties:[81]

(120) a. Application takes place when the structural description of the rule is derived by morpheme concatenation.

  b. Application takes place when the structural description of the rule is derived by the prior application of a different phonological rule.

  c. Application is blocked when neither of the first two conditions is met.

Although it is fairly clear that there are rules exhibiting the properties outlined in (120), it is much less clear (i) exactly how to characterize the class of rules exhibiting these effects, and (ii) how to derive these effects theoretically. Works on these issues include Kiparsky 1973, 1982, 1985, 1991, Kean 1975, Mascaró 1976, Halle 1979, Clements 1982, Cole 1990, and numerous others. Three factors are prominent in these works: (i) whether the rule is an obligatory neutralization rule, (ii) whether the rule applies cyclically, (iii) whether the rule is feature-filling or structure-changing.

Both the characterization of the rule class exhibiting Strict Cycle effects and the manner in which such effects should be derived involve numerous issues concerning the interaction between morphology and phonology. Since such issues are to a great extent orthogonal to the formal concerns of the work here, we will not enter into a detailed discussion of Strict Cycle effects. As the Strict Cycle plays an important role in deriving some of the cases we discuss, however, we lay out here exactly which properties are crucial for our concerns, and we comment on the three properties mentioned in the last paragraph.

2.5.3.1 Association and Spreading In numerous cases, the association of a free autosegment to a free anchor must be able to take place even in a nonderived environment; spreading of a linked autosegment, on the other hand, exhibits standard Strict Cycle effects. That is, a linked autosegment spreads if the target is part of a separate morpheme, or if the linking was accomplished by an association process applying earlier on the relevant cycle. Works such as Levergood 1984, Pulleyblank 1986a, and Archangeli and Pulleyblank 1989 present versions of the Strict Cycle that

have precisely these effects. The crucial point with respect to association and spreading, therefore, is that association processes are not part of the class subject to Strict Cycle effects, while spreading rules are.

With regard to *cyclicity*, note that some of the association rules not showing Strict Cycle effects have been argued to be cyclic (see Pulleyblank 1986a); typically, the spreading rules exhibiting Strict Cycle effects are consistent with cyclic operation, although there is often no clear evidence either for or against cyclic application. In the case of Ngbaka, for example, we can assume that the rules of spreading under discussion are cyclic, although there is no strong evidence arguing for this position.

With regard to *neutralization*, it is not always clear whether to consider a process of association or spreading as neutralizing or not. In a case where a free, morpheme-level autosegment is associated, such association is the expression of a contrast; no neutralization is involved. On the other hand, in a context where there is a distinction between anchors linked to F and anchors not linked to F, then spreading of F neutralizes that distinction. Although specific configurations will differ, it would therefore appear that the paradigm case of association is nonneutralizing, while the paradigm case of spreading is neutralizing.

Finally, with regard to *feature filling* versus *structure changing*, the paradigm case of both association and spreading is feature filling, though it is possible for both association and spreading to apply in more marked cases to a target that is already specified for the feature involved.

2.5.3.2 Feature Insertion A large class of rules whose effect is to redundantly insert an F-element appears to be immune to Strict Cycle effects. That is, rules of feature insertion appear to apply even if the environment for their application is completely nonderived. For example, the rule inserting [−ATR] on low vowels in Yoruba applies within roots, in a completely nonderived fashion.

In the cases examined in this book, we have no strong evidence for the *cyclic* application of feature insertion rules, although in several cases, there is evidence that feature insertion takes place lexically and would be compatible with cyclic application (e.g., Yoruba, Pulaar, Indonesian). Although there is no a priori reason why feature insertion needs to be either *feature-filling* or *nonneutralizing*, it appears to be the case that all the rules examined in this book have both these properties. Considering again the Yoruba example, it was demonstrated above (i) that low vowels are unspecified for [ATR] underlyingly, and (ii) that there is no [ATR] contrast for low vowels. The first point means that the insertion of [−ATR] onto low vowels is feature-filling; the second point means that such insertion is nonneutralizing.

To summarize, we assume that the Strict Cycle Condition governs the application of spreading rules, but does not govern the application of rules associating free morpheme-level F-elements; nor does it govern the nonneutralizing insertion of redundant F-elements.

2.5.4 The Marked Cases: The Extent of Prelinking

Under the assumption that the Strict Cycle Condition blocks the nonderived spreading of a prelinked autosegment, the range of exceptional cases in Ngbaka is straightforwardly characterized. The robust cases in Ngbaka are analyzed as involving combinations of the free F-elements [+high], [+low], [+round], and [+ATR]; the marked cases involve exactly the same combinations of F-elements, but with varying degrees of underlyingly specified associations.

Consider, for example, cases involving single specifications of [+low] and [+round] that are entirely comparable to those seen in section 2.5.2 for [+high].

(121) *Prelinked [+low] and [+round]*

a. +LO   CaCɛ   (CVCV-D: 0.8%; CVCV-L: 1%; CVV: 0%)
     |
     μ   μ

b.   +LO   CɛCa   (CVCV-D: 0.5%; CVCV-L: 0%; CVV: 0%)
           |
     μ   μ

c. +RD   CɔCɛ   (CVCV-D: 0.5%; CVCV-L: 1%; CVV: 0%)
     |
     μ   μ

d.   +RD   CɛCɔ   (CVCV-D: 0%; CVCV-L: 0%; CVV: 0%)
           |
     μ   μ

An example of the *CaCɛ* pattern is *wágé* 'espèce d'igname'; an example of the *CɔCɛ* pattern is *kɔndɛ̀* 'coeur'; we were unable to find an underived example of the *CɛCa* pattern in Thomas 1963 although it is listed in table B as being an occurring (though rare) pattern. Thomas found no examples of the pattern *ɛ...ɔ*; that is, there are no examples of the configuration in (121d), where a single [+round] specification is posited, and where the [+round] specification is prelinked to the second mora. We discuss this gap below.

Unlike the F-elements [+high], [+low], and [+round], there appear to be absolutely no cases involving the prelinking of [+ATR]. That is, [+ATR] is unexceptionally free in underlying representation and therefore links and spreads in a fully harmonic fashion. This can be seen in (107) by the complete absence of mid vowel sequences disagreeing for [ATR] values: *e...ɛ, *e...ɔ, *ɛ...e, *ɛ...o, *ɔ...e, *ɔ...o, *o...ɛ, *o...ɔ.

Additional cases involving prelinking can be derived in conjunction with multiple F-elements. For example, corresponding to the cases in (119) and (121), it is possible to find morphemes with the additional specification [+ATR]. As noted above, in such cases [+ATR] associates and spreads in a regular fashion (noting that [+ATR] may not link to a vowel that is [+low]).

(122) *Prelinked [+high], [+low], or [+round] with free [+ATR]*

    a.  +HI   CiCe   (CVCV-D: 0.5%; CVCV-L: 0%; CVV: 2%)

            |

        μ   μ

         +ATR

    b.    +HI   CeCi   (CVCV-D: 0.27%; CVCV-L: 0%; CVV: 0%)

             |

       μ   μ

      +ATR

    c.  +LO   CaCe   (CVCV-D: 2%; CVCV-L: 0.5%; CVV: 0%)

           |

       μ   μ

      +ATR

    d.    +LO   CeCa   (CVCV-D: 2%; CVCV-L: 0.5%; CVV: 0%)

            |

       μ   μ

      +ATR

    e. 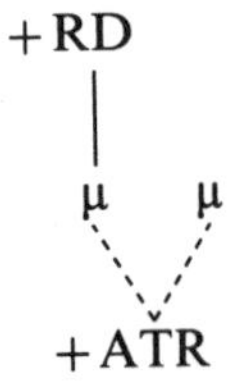 +RD   CoCe   (CVCV-D: 0.8%; CVCV-L: 0.5%; CVV: 0.9%)

           |

       μ   μ

      +ATR

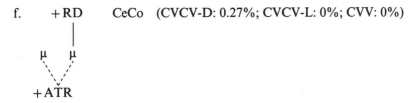

f.   +RD   CeCo   (CVCV-D: 0.27%; CVCV-L: 0%; CVV: 0%)

Examples of these patterns are as follows: *sibè* 'chanson', *zèdi* 'jeudi', *kákpe* 'esclave', *ndeyà* 'scorpion', *ngòmbè* 'fusil', *sekò* 'chimpanzee'. It is not always easy to find a monomorphemic example for each of the patterns. In addition to *sekò* for the *CeCo* pattern, for example, Thomas (1963:62) lists *setò* 'genie de forêt' as the only other form with this vowel sequence, but notes that the two forms could well be compounds. Given the rarity and formally marked status of the patterns under consideration, it should not be surprising, however, to find that certain patterns are unattested.

More complex patterns result when each of the F-elements in a set can be individually prelinked. Consider, for example, the combinations possible with [+high] and [+round].

If only one of the two F-elements is prelinked, the patterns in (123) are possible.

(123) *[+high] and [+round] with partial prelinking*

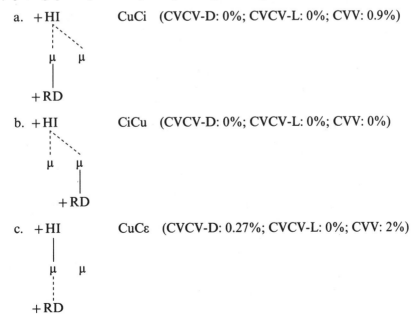

a. +HI   CuCi   (CVCV-D: 0%; CVCV-L: 0%; CVV: 0.9%)

b. +HI   CiCu   (CVCV-D: 0%; CVCV-L: 0%; CVV: 0%)

c. +HI   CuCɛ   (CVCV-D: 0.27%; CVCV-L: 0%; CVV: 2%)

d.   +HI   CɔCi   (CVCV-D: 0.5%; CVCV-L: 1%; CVV: 0.9%)
          |
      μ   μ
      ⋮
    +RD

As can be seen from the percentages, these patterns are very rare, and in the case of *CiCu*, completely nonexistent. Thomas (1963:62) provides a single example of the *CuCi* pattern, *sui* 'cendre', noting that this case is borrowed from the French *suie*. An example of *CuCɛ* is *budɛ̀* 'petit oiseau de la taille du mange-mil', and an example of *CɔCi* is *ʔɔti* 'laissé'.

Note that the pattern here that is completely unattested (*CiCu*) is comparable to the other unattested pattern seen above (ɛ...ɔ) in that both would involve the pre-linking of [+round] to the second vowel. Four related patterns are also completely unattested: a consideration of (107) shows that an initial high round vowel is never followed by a round mid vowel (*u...*ɔ*, *u...*o*); similarly, an initial mid round vowel is never followed by a round high vowel (*ɔ...*u*, *o...*u*). Therefore, the cases in (123) appear to represent the general pattern, in that there is no spreading of [+round] when trigger and target vowels differ in height.

These gaps are of some interest. The marked cases suggest that [+round] spreads only between vowels that agree in their [high] specifications. This condition, although true, is completely redundant for the robust cases. Consideration of robust sets of examples such as (113b) and (114a,b) shows that no conditions are required on the source or target of round harmony. In the robust cases, a putative height restriction is vacuously satisfied because of the spreading of the height features themselves; imposing such a restriction is unnecessary, however, since there are no robust patterns without height harmony with which to test the applicability of Round Spread. Since the nonrobust evidence requires height agreement, and since the robust data do not motivate the required restriction, one obvious interpretation of these facts is that the height restriction on round harmony constitutes an unmarked option cross-linguistically (see Steriade 1981).

If both the features [+high] and [+round] are prelinked, the patterns shown in (124) are possible.

(124) *Prelinked [+high] and [+round]*

a. +HI   CuCɛ (see (123c))
     |
       μ   μ
       |
     +RD

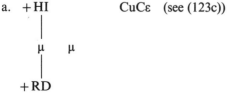

b. +HI   CiCɔ   (CVCV-D: 0.8%; CVCV-L: 0%; CVV: 4%)
    |
        μ   μ
                |
            +RD

c.   +HI   CɔCi   (see (123d))
            |
        μ   μ
        |
    +RD

d.   +HI   CɛCu   (CVCV-D: 0.5%; CVCV-L: 0%; CVV: 0%)
            |
        μ   μ
                |
            +RD

Two of the patterns so derived would be identical to patterns already derived via the prelinking of a single F-element; the two others are new. An example of the *CiCɔ* pattern is *biɔ* 'argile'; an example of the the *CɛCu* pattern is *pɛpu* 'vent'.[82]

All of the patterns in (124) could be supplemented by the inclusion of a free [+ATR] specification, as in (125). (Recall that there is no evidence for the prelinking of [+ATR].)

(125) *Prelinked [+high] and [+round] with free [+ATR]*

    a. +HI   CuCe   (CVCV-D: 1.1%; CVCV-L: 0%; CVV: 0%)
        |
            μ   μ
              \   /
               +ATR
        +RD

    b. +HI   CiCo   (CVCV-D: 0.27%; CVCV-L: 1.5%; CVV: 8%)
       |
           μ   μ
             \   /
              +ATR
              +RD

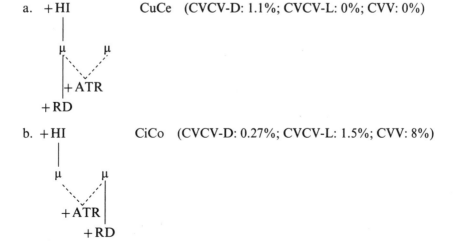

c.

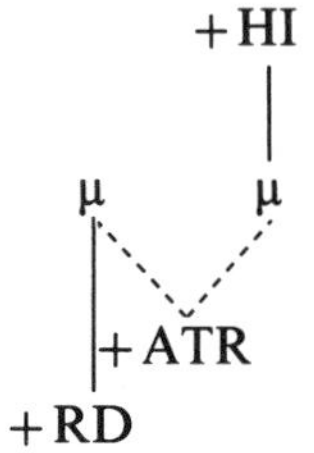

CoCi (CVCV-D: 0.8%; CVCV-L: 2.5%; CVV: 1.8%)

d.

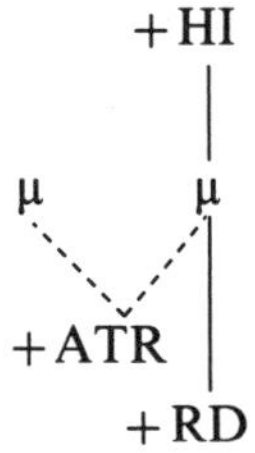

CeCu (CVCV-D: 0%; CVCV-L: 0%; CVV: 0%)

Examples of the first three patterns of (125) are *kukpè* 'écorce, peau', *pìlìzo*ⁿ 'pigeon domestique', *ngòmbi* 'harpe-luth'; the absence of forms with the pattern **CeCu* is discussed below.

Combinations involving prelinked F-elements other than [+high] and [+round] are much more restricted. Consider, for example, [+high] and [+low]. Because these F-elements are incompatible, they cannot be prelinked to the same mora. Prelinking [+high] therefore creates exactly two patterns, whether [+low] is free or prelinked.

(126) *Prelinked [+high] and free or prelinked [+low]*

a.

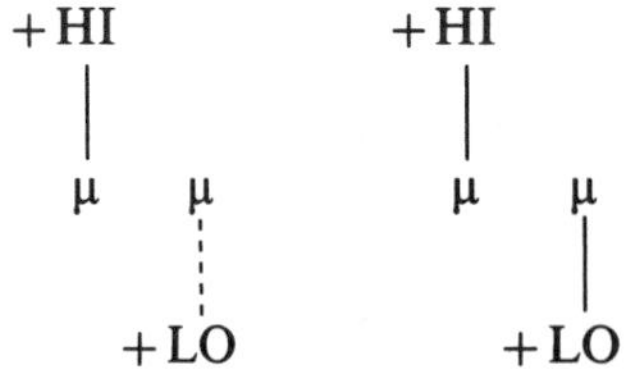

i . . . a

b.

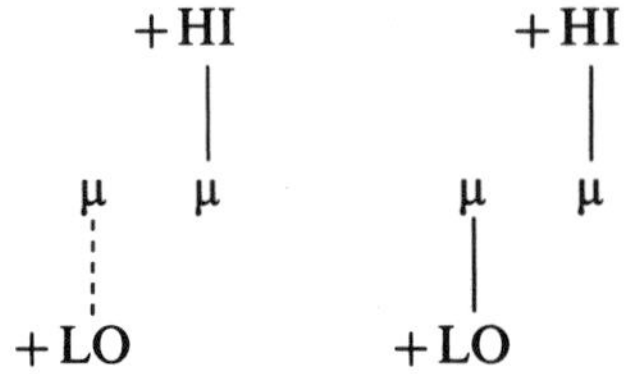

a . . . i (CVCV-D: 2%; CVCV-L: 0.5%; CVV: 3.5%)

The pattern in (126a) is identical to the result of regularly linking the free F-elements [+high] and [+low] (see (116)). Hence, prelinking [+high] derives only one new pattern, namely, *a . . . i*, as in *bàli* 'course'. Noteworthy in this regard is the fact that the *i . . . a* pattern (which we have argued derives from free F-elements) is much more frequent than the *a...i* pattern (which requires prelinking): *i...a* (CVCV-D: 5.5%; CVCV-L: 1.5%; CVV: 19%) versus *a...i* (CVCV-D: 2%; CVCV-L: 0.5%; CVV: 3.5%).

Prelinking of [+low], as opposed to or in addition to the prelinking of [+high], would derive no new patterns: prelinking to the initial mora results in *a...i*, while prelinking to the second mora results in *i...a*. Similarly, the inclusion of [+ATR] in addition to [+high] and [+low] would create no new patterns: [+ATR] (which is never prelinked) would link to whichever mora was assigned [+high], creating a result identical to that independently derivable by considerations of simplicity.

With or without prelinking and with or without [+ATR], the addition of [+round] to the patterns in (126) would produce exactly one new pattern, *a...u*, as in *nzámbú* 'pulpe de noix de palme' (CVCV-D: 0.5%; CVCV-L 1%; CVV: 2%).

Finally, it was suggested above that the absence of any priority clause prevents robust combinations of free [+low] and [+round] F-elements. Given prelinking, however, the following patterns are possible (with and without [+ATR]). In these patterns, we show only the prelinking of [+low]: the condition preventing [+round] and [+low] in a single path precludes [+round] from associating to the mora already associated to [+low].

(127) *Prelinked [+low] and free [+round], with and without free [+ATR]*

a. +LO   CaCɔ   (CVCV-D: 0.27%; CVCV-L: 1%; CVV: 0%)
    |
    μ   μ
               ⋮
          +RD

b.   +LO   CɔCa   (CVCV-D: 0%; CVCV-L: 0%; CVV: 0.9%)
            |
    μ   μ
    ⋮
 +RD

c. +LO   CaCo   (CVCV-D: 3%; CVCV-L: 0.5%; CVV: 4%)
    |
    μ   μ
          +ATR ⋮
          +RD

d.   +LO   CoCa   (CVCV-D: 2%; CVCV-L: 5%; CVV: 0%)

μ   μ

+ATR

+RD

Examples of three of these four patterns are *gazɔ* 'grelots de chevilles', *yàbo* 'genette', *kólá* 'dette'.[83]

To summarize, we have argued that combinations of free F-elements ([+high], [+low], [+round], [+ATR]) account for the 9 patterns that hold of the bulk of the attested Ngbaka data. These 9 patterns constitute 78.5% of the patterns involving a *CVCV* sequence with different tones (apparently the most robustly instantiated class), 82% of the patterns with a *CVCV* sequence on the same tone, and 68% of the patterns involving a *CVV* sequence. The remaining 20% to 30% of the data are distributed among an additional 25 patterns that result from the prelinking of F-elements. F-elements differ in their susceptibility to prelinking. Both [+high] and [+low] exhibit essentially all patterns made possible by prelinking. The F-element [+ATR], on the other hand, is never prelinked. The feature [+round] exhibits intermediate behavior: numerous patterns involving prelinking do exist, but three expected patterns (*i...u, e...u, ɛ...u*) are completely unattested, apparently because of a high degree of markedness involved in prelinking [+round] to μ_2 position.

The account of Ngbaka presented here posits a unified set of featural representations for both robust and marked cases, with relative rarity of the marked cases corresponding formally to the inclusion of prelinked underlying representations. Free underlying representations are preferred to prelinked representations because of Representational Simplicity (96), and where there is prelinking, the Strict Cycle Condition blocks the application of otherwise regular spreading rules.

Thus, we have accounted for the morpheme structure constraints of Ngbaka by positing four F-elements in conjunction with simple rules of association and spreading. For the majority of lexical items, these four F-elements are free; for a subset, certain F-elements may be prelinked. The majority correspond to the general pattern (the "XXX" in (107)); the prelinked subset accounts for deviation from this general pattern.

2.5.5 Morpheme Structure Conditions: OCP Accounts

Before concluding this discussion of Ngbaka, we compare our proposal with alternative accounts employing morpheme structure conditions, in particular, the accounts of Itô (1984), Mester (1986), and Steriade (1987a). We suggest that there is an inherent contradiction in OCP-based accounts of the morpheme structure conditions of

Ngbaka: although the robust cases depend crucially on invoking the OCP, a number of the more marked cases involve OCP violations. In the account presented here, on the other hand, the OCP is strictly respected, although its importance is limited to deriving the restriction on F-elements to at most one token of each per morpheme (see the conclusion to section 2.5.1).

Recent morpheme structure accounts crucially depend on an OCP-type prohibition against sequences of identical [high] specifications: *[αhigh][αhigh] (note, in particular, Mester 1986). Given this prohibition, a form like [síti] 'mauvais' must involve a structure like (128a), not (128b).

(128) a. +HI   b. * +HI +HI

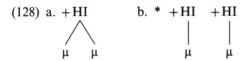

By postulating that structures like (128a) are completed with features that are dependent to [high], one derives the condition that "If a sequence of vowels agrees in height, then the vowels are identical." For example, a pattern like $u \ldots i$ is ruled out because [+round] is dependent on [high].[84]

(129)   RD
         |
        HI

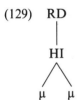

Since there cannot be two identical values for [high], there cannot be two values for [round].

Such an account is problematical on various counts. At the level of generalization, since Wescott 1965, it is usually assumed that (i) if high vowels cooccur in a word in Ngbaka, they must be identical; (ii) if nonhigh, nonlow vowels cooccur, they too must be identical; (iii) high and nonhigh vowels, on the other hand, may freely cooccur. These generalizations are argued to result automatically from the OCP-based account. Since sequences of *[+high][+high] and *[−high][−high] are ruled out, any vowels specified by distinct feature values F and G must of necessity involve distinct values for [high], as in (130).

(130)

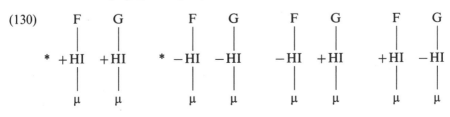

Empirically, however, these descriptive generalizations seem quite questionable. Certain patterns that are predicted to occur are virtually nonexistent, and certain patterns that should not occur appear about as frequently as some that are expected. Consider, for example, the combination of high and nonhigh vowels such as *i...e* and *e...i*. Both patterns are predicted to occur, but both are almost completely unattested: *i...e* (CVCV-D: 0.5%; CVCV-L: 0%; CVV: 2%); *e...i* (CVCV-D: 0.27%; CVCV-L: 0%; CVV: 0%). A consideration of Thomas's tables shows that the rarity of cases combining different values of [high] is completely independent of tonal and prosodic factors.

In addition, Thomas's tables show that there are cases of supposedly impossible combinations that are at least as frequent as the possible ones (though still not robustly attested). For example, consider the frequency of the pattern *o...e*: CVCV-D: 0.8%; CVCV-L: 0.5%; CVV: 0.9%. Although poorly exemplified, this "prohibited" pattern has more examples than the supposedly "predicted" patterns *i...e* and *e...i*. The generalizations on which the OCP-based dependent feature accounts have been based are faulty. It follows that a different account is necessary once a more adequate statement of the feature distribution is found.

The OCP-based account is also problematical on theoretical grounds. Since Mester's proposal, a large body of evidence has been gathered in favor of a theory of feature relations that would *not* allow the dependency shown in (129) (see Clements 1985a, Sagey 1986, McCarthy 1988, Yip 1988b, 1989b, Odden 1989, Wiswall 1991b, etc.). Within an approach such as that of Sagey (1986), barring a sequence of identical [high] specifications would not prevent a sequence of nonidentical [round] specifications since [high] and [round] would appear on independent tiers, as in (131).

(131) a.

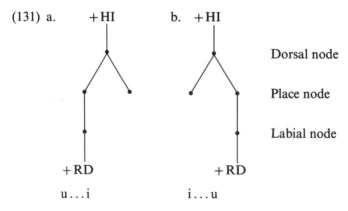

To supplement the OCP-based prohibition on sequences of identical specifications of [high], it would be necessary to stipulate that values of Dorsal/[high] could not branch, as in (132).

(132) *   αHI

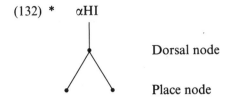

Dorsal node

Place node

Under this view, the elegant account of morpheme conditions proposed by Mester would only be possible within recent theories of the organization of phonological features if conditions supplemental to the OCP were assumed. Furthermore, the constraint in (132) is overly restrictive since it disallows configurations like that in (131).

This brings us to the third challenge for the OCP-based dependency account, the treatment of exceptions. From the table in (107), as well as the discussion above, it can be seen that a variety of patterns exist that should not exist according to an account such as Mester's: *u...i, o...e, ɔ...ɛ*, and so on. Since such exceptions are attested, even if nonrobustly, one must assume that the basic morpheme structure condition governing Ngbaka constitutes a *tendency* rather than an absolute. But this is a highly problematical assumption in an OCP-based account: if the basic morpheme structure condition of Ngbaka, *[αhigh][αhigh], is to have its source in the OCP, then one would not normally expect it to have lexical exceptions (McCarthy 1986a). McCarthy argues that it is not possible to consider the OCP as a tendency (rather than as an absolute constraint) and still derive the robust cross-linguistic properties that are attributed to it. Moreover, even allowing exceptions to the OCP still fails to explain why certain violations are possible and not others. With respect to the patterns considered regular under the OCP account, there are certain significant asymmetries that receive no explanation, for example, the fact that there are four or five times as many examples with an *i...a* pattern as with an *a...i* pattern. Another example already mentioned is that some of the patterns considered acceptable under the OCP account appear to be either less frequent or only marginally more frequent than some of the unacceptable patterns. We find, for example, the following percentages for *o...e* (an "unacceptable" pattern) and *a...ɔ* (an "acceptable" pattern): *o...e* (CVCV-D: 0.8%; CVCV-L: 0.5%; CVV: 0.9%); *a...ɔ* (CVCV-D: 0.27%; CVCV-L: 1%; CVV: 0%). There appear to be two conclusions. First, strictly interpreted, the OCP-based account should allow no exceptions at all of certain types—and yet exceptions exist. Second, the OCP-based account provides no explanation for a range of asymmetries that are attested in the Ngbaka data.

In the approach argued for here, the "exceptions" do not violate any conditions, and all underlying representations, both robust and exceptional, respect the OCP. "Exceptionality" is simply the result of unpredictable associations, which are consequently present in underlying representations.

2.5.6 Conclusion

The analysis of Ngbaka proposed here has numerous implications. As in the case of Tiv, the interaction of processes of association and spreading can account for surface patterns of morpheme structure, and, as in Tiv, conditions of cooccurrence (109c) govern linked paths rather than free sets of F-elements. In addition, contrary to the conclusions drawn by Itô (1984), Mester (1986), and Steriade (1987a), there seems to be no need to specify both values of a feature like [high]. On the contrary, the asymmetrical account presented here has both empirical and theoretical advantages over accounts that have posited the presence of both values of [high]. Given Representational Simplicity, the structurally simpler representations in the Ngbaka lexicon (those with only free specifications) are correctly predicted to be more frequent than the more complex representations (those including linked specifications). And from a theoretical perspective, the account does not require lexically governed exceptions to the OCP: no morphemes require two tokens of any F-element.

We close this discussion by noting that Tiv and Ngbaka do not appear to be unique in deriving properties of morpheme structure through the interaction of association and spreading. Our preliminary work on Susu (Houis 1963), a Mande language of Guinea, suggests that a very similar situation holds in that language.[85] We present in table form in (133) the patterns of vowel cooccurrence found in disyllabic forms.

(133) *Susu vowel cooccurrence*

V1 \ V2	i	e	ε	a	ɔ	o	u
i	XXX	X	X	XXX	X	X	X
e	X	XXX	—	X	—	—	X
ε	X	—	XXX	X	X	—	X
a	XXX	X	X	XXX	—	X	XXX
ɔ	*	—	X	X	XXX	—	*
o	*	X	—	X	—	XXX	*
u	X	X	X	XXX	—	??	XXX

Data base: Houis 1963, 641 forms

XXX	≥5.5%
*	2%–3.2%
X	<2%
??	the *u . . . o* pattern occurs, but frequency figures are not provided
—	no examples

The 11 robust patterns ("XXX") account for 72%–78% of the data base: with the exception of the patterns involving [+high] and [+low] (*i* ... *a, a* ... *i, u* ... *a, a* ... *u*), these patterns can be explained by positing free F-elements that link via rules of association and spreading. With respect to the forms combining specifications of [+high] and [+low], the major contrast between Ngbaka and Susu is that for Susu, there is no clear preference for the association of [+high] over the association of [+low]; both low-high (*a* ... *i, a* ... *u*) and high-low (*i* ... *a, u* ... *a*) forms occur with close to equal frequency. As with Ngbaka, (i) [ATR] is never prelinked, (ii) prelinking of [+round] to the second mora is rare, and (iii) Round Spread appears to be height-dependent. Also as with Ngbaka, the nonrobust patterns, large in terms of the number of patterns though small in terms of the amount of actual data, can be accounted for via prelinking.

We have argued so far that the notion of a phonological segment is entirely unnecessary, and that phonological representations are composed of specifications of feature-sized F-elements, an issue we return to in section 2.7. We have demonstrated that such F-elements may form the contrastive core of morphemes (Tiv, Ngbaka) and that patterns of feature cooccurrence are freer among unlinked features than among linked ones. In cases involving incompatible specifications, the number of contrasts derivable with underlyingly free F-elements (Tiv, Ngbaka) is much higher than can be derived with underlyingly linked F-elements (Barrow Inupiaq). Moreover, we have shown that considerations of simplicity will in general prevent predictable F-elements from being included underlyingly (Haya, Ngbaka) even when they function actively in the phonology (Yoruba). We have shown, however, that contrastive features may be contrastive even for classes not manifesting the contrast on the surface (Ainu).

One important conclusion from the work presented to this point is that one cannot predict whether a feature will be phonologically active by examining surface contrasts. A feature that is redundant on the surface may be inert (Haya), active (Yoruba), or even distinctive (Ainu). In the following section, we examine this issue further. We show that completely noncontrastive F-elements may play active roles in the phonologies of languages like Pulaar and Javanese.

2.6 Complete Predictability of F-Elements

In this section, we consider whether there is a necessary relation between the predictability of a feature and its status in phonological rules. Essentially, we ask whether completely predictable features are also completely inactive phonologically. We note first in this regard that it is entirely uncontroversial that features required to distinguish morphemes underlyingly may play an active role in the phonological rules of a language. Tiv, Haya, and Ngbaka all illustrate this point. It is also the case that features that are contrastive in general, yet predictable in some context, may play an active role even with respect to the predictable context. [ATR] values on low vowels in Yoruba and [back] values on low vowels in Ainu illustrate this in different ways. In this section, we pursue the latter point, looking at cases where features are *entirely* predictable. Given Representational Simplicity, such predictability would suggest that the features in question are not present in underlying representation at all. As we will show with respect to the distribution of [ATR] in Pulaar and Eastern Javanese, however, such completely redundant features may nevertheless play active roles in the phonology.

2.6.1   Pulaar

The underlying vowels of Pulaar (Paradis 1986), a Niger-Congo language of the West Atlantic branch spoken in Mauritania, exhibit the type of canonical five-vowel system that can be derived by the interaction of three F-elements, [+high], [+low], and [+back].

(134) *Pulaar vowel representation*

   a. F-elements

   +HI, +LO, +BK

   b. Conditions

   HI/LO Condition: If [+high] then not [+low].
   LO/HI Condition: If [+low] then not [+high].

   c.

	*	*	u	i	a_1	a_2	o	e
	+HI	+HI	+HI	+HI				
	+LO	+LO			+LO	+LO		
	+BK		+BK		+BK		+BK	

Combinations of [+high] and [+low] are ruled out by the conditions in (134b), and /a_2/ is selected over /a_1/ because of Representational Simplicity.

The feature [ATR] in Pulaar plays no contrastive function in this system, its values being completely predictable. The predictability is of a rather interesting nature, however. Paradigmatically, the tongue root values of nonmid vowels can be predicted from the [+high] or [+low] F-element: a [+high] vowel is advanced, a [+low] vowel is retracted. The tongue root values of mid vowels, on the other hand, are syntagmatically determined: a mid vowel immediately followed by an advanced vowel is also advanced; elsewhere, mid vowels are retracted. That is, although completely predictable, [ATR] values play an active role in the phonology of Pulaar. This harmonic behavior is illustrated in (135): the left-hand column shows roots with the underlying mid vowels paired with high-voweled suffixes, while the right-hand column shows the same roots paired with mid-voweled suffixes.[86]

(135) *Root + class marker*

[+ATR]	[−ATR]	
sof-ru	cɔf-ɔn	'poussin SG/DIM.PL'
ser-du	cɛr-kɔn	'crosse d'un fusil SG/DIM.PL'
ᵐbeel-u	ᵐbɛɛl-ɔn	'ombre SG/DIM.PL'
peec-i	pɛɛc-ɔn	'fente PL/DIM.PL'
beel-i	ᵐbɛɛl-ɔn	'flaque PL/DIM.PL'
dog-oo-ru	ⁿdɔg-ɔ-w-ɔn	'coureur SG/DIM.PL'

Since the distribution of [ATR] is entirely predictable based on other F-elements, we propose the following analysis of the Pulaar vowel system, assuming without comment that the underlying active F-elements are [+high], [+low], and [+back], as seen in (134a).

To derive the correct surface forms with respect to [ATR], two rules are necessary. The first, (136), inserts [+ATR] on high vowels.

(136) *Pulaar [+ATR] Insertion*

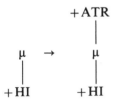

The second, (137), spreads [+ATR] leftward.

(137) *Pulaar [+ATR] Spread*

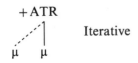

Examples such as those in (138) establish clearly the right-to-left nature of this process. In (138a), both columns have a final suffix with a mid vowel. The two columns differ in that the left-hand column also has a high-voweled suffix intervening between the stem and the final suffix. It is only the stem vowel that alternates: the lack of alternation in the final suffix is explained if harmony applies from right to left.

(138) *Root + verbal suffixes*

	[+ATR]		[−ATR]	
a.	6et-ir-dɛ	'peser avec'	6ɛt-dɛ	'peser'
	hel-ir-dɛ	'casser avec'	hɛl-dɛ	'casser'
	ɗokk-iɗ-dɛ	'éborgner'	ɗɔkk-ɔ	'borgne' (noun)
	feyy-u-dɛ	'abattre'	fɛyy-a	'abattre' (imperfective)
b.	duk-ɔ	'dispute-SG'		
	duk-ɔ-y-ɔn	'dispute-DIM.PL'		
	duk-oo-ji	'dispute-PL'		

The triplet in (138b) shows the vowel [ɔ] surfacing to the right of a high vowel except in the third form, where a high-voweled suffix is added and the vowel surfaces as [o].

[ATR] harmony does not affect [+low] vowels; rather, low vowels block the propagation of [+ATR], as shown in (139). The stems in (139) all have mid vowels, and all surface as [−ATR] despite the [+ATR] vowel of the final suffix. The difference between the forms here and those in (135) and (138) is that the mid vowels and triggering [+ATR] vowels in (139) are separated by a low vowel.[87]

(139) *Root + verbal suffixes*

a.	bɔɔt-aa-ri	'dîner'	*bootaari
	pɔɔf-aa-li	'respirations'	*poofaali
	nɔdd-aa-li	'appel'	*noddaali
	ⁿgɔr-aa-gu	'courage'	*ⁿgoraagu
b.	ɔɔñanⁿgel	'torsion-DIM'	*ooñanⁿgel
	gɔɔ6anⁿgel	'gorgée-DIM'	*goo6anⁿgel
	kɛlanⁿgel	'cassure-DIM'	*kelanⁿgel

The behavior of the low vowel can be accounted for through the interactions of two separate constraints: a prohibition against the cooccurrence of [+ATR] and [+low] (140a) (see chapter 3), and the Locality Condition (140b) (see chapter 1).

(140) a. *   +ATR   b. *   +ATR

The general analysis of Pulaar, then, is (i) [ATR] is not present in underlying representations; (ii) [+ATR] is inserted by rule only onto high vowels; (iii) [+ATR] spreads leftward, but does not affect low vowels.[88]

In summary, this discussion of Pulaar establishes four things. First, surface phonological contrasts do not necessarily reflect underlying morphophonological contrasts in a language. There is an [ATR] contrast in mid vowels at the surface in Pulaar, but this contrast is entirely derivative and need not be reflected in underlying representations.

Second, F-elements whose distribution is entirely predictable may participate in phonological rules.

Third, cooccurrence conditions not only are relevant for underlyingly active F-elements but may also hold over the distribution of F-elements whose presence is completely predictable: in Pulaar, although the distribution of [+ATR] is determined in part by the F-elements of the particular vowel and in part by location (i.e., to the left of a [+ATR] vowel), [+ATR] is still prohibited from combining with [+low].

Finally, conditions on feature cooccurrence may be restricted to specific rules or may be general. In Pulaar, for example, we have shown evidence for two conditions, the first restricting the appearance of [+ATR] to high vowels, the second restricting the appearance of [+ATR] to nonlow vowels. The first of these conditions governs only the rule inserting [+ATR]. If it were to hold of [+ATR] Spread, then the harmony rule would incorrectly affect only high vowels. By contrast, the condition restricting the occurrence of [+ATR] to nonlow vowels governs both [+ATR] Insertion and [+ATR] Spread. See chapter 3 for a detailed discussion of the theory of such conditions.

2.6.2 Javanese [ATR] Harmony

Eastern Javanese (Schlindwein 1988) provides a second case in which the distribution of [ATR] is entirely predictable: [−ATR] is assigned in closed syllables and spreads leftward to vowels of like height.[89] Interestingly, in Eastern Javanese there is strong evidence that the active [ATR] specifications must be inserted by rule, and cannot be present underlyingly. Thus, Eastern Javanese is comparable to Pulaar: the F-element active in the phonology cannot be present in underlying representation (at least, not without otherwise unmotivated ad hoc stipulations).

Underlyingly, Eastern Javanese exhibits the same five-way contrast just seen in Pulaar, and we assume the same underlying distribution of F-elements (see (134)). Also as in Pulaar, the feature [ATR] becomes active during the phonology. In Eastern Javanese, however, the active value is [−ATR]. Consider the ten vowels distinguishable on the surface in Eastern Javanese.

(141) i ɪ e ɛ ə a ɔ o ʊ u

We follow Schlindwein (1988) (i) in analyzing [ə] as epenthetic, and (ii) in accounting for the values of [ATR] in terms of two rules, Insertion and Harmony. We focus here on the latter phenomena, those involving [ATR].

The general pattern of [ATR] in Javanese is that vowels in closed syllables are [−ATR], and that in sequences of vowels of like height, if the rightmost is in a closed syllable (and so is [−ATR]), the whole sequence is [−ATR]. This is illustrated in (142) for high vowels. The left-hand column contains words with no closed syllables, and all high vowels are [+ATR] (e.g., *titi* 'careful', *tɪtɪ). The right-hand column contains words with a closed final syllable: here, all vowels surface as [−ATR] (e.g., *mʊrɪt* 'student', *murit).

(142) *[ATR] distribution: High vowels*

titi	'careful'	nʊl	'zero'
buri	'back'	mʊrɪt	'student'
turu	'sleep'	plɪpɪr	'edge'
bali	'return'	adʊs	'bathe'

The examples in (143) show exactly the same pattern with mid vowels.[90]

(143) *[ATR] distribution: Mid vowels*

ombe	'drink'	bɔbɔt	'weight'
bodo	'stupid'	lɛrɛn	'stop'
kere	'beggar'	gɔlɛʔ	'get'
rame	'noisy'	aŋɛl	'difficult'

In addition, a few roots include both high and mid vowels: where the second is in a closed syllable, harmony does not take place.

(144) *[ATR] distribution: High and mid vowels*

    ijɛn   'alone'   entʊʔ   'obtain'

We demonstrate below that [ATR] values such as those observed in (142)–(144) must be assigned by two rules along the lines of (145) and (146).[91]

(145) *Eastern Javanese [−ATR] Insertion*

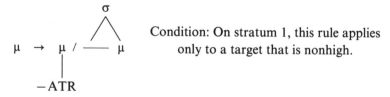

Condition: On stratum 1, this rule applies only to a target that is nonhigh.

(146) *Eastern Javanese [−ATR] Spread*

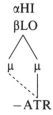

We argue that Eastern Javanese presents a case comparable in significant respects to Yoruba: the simpler representation is required by the phonology even though at a later stage the phonology makes use of a more complex representation. In contrast with Yoruba, however, in Eastern Javanese the relevant F-element is not present for *any* class of vowels/morphemes in underlying representation.

The demonstration that [−ATR] is inserted by rule rather than being present "in the right place" in underlying representation has three parts. First, [−ATR] Insertion applies in derived closed syllables as well as in syllables that are closed due to the underlying representation of the morpheme. Second, the distribution of [−ATR] on mid and high vowels differs depending on the morphological structure. Third, some underlying high vowels lower to mid: these derived mid vowels are assigned [−ATR] by the mid vowel pattern, not by the high vowel pattern.

2.6.2.1 [ATR] in Derived Closed and Open Syllables
Schlindwein reports that the suffixes *-ʔ* 'CAUSATIVE' and *-n* 'LOCATIVE' create closed syllables thàt subsequently undergo [−ATR] Insertion. She gives one example, repeated here in (147). (The causative is accompanied by nasalization of the initial stem consonant; hence, [k] alternates with [ŋ].)

(147) *[ATR] in derived closed syllables*

       kere 'beggar'   ŋɛrɛʔne   'beggar-CAUSATIVE-SUBJUNCTIVE'

Whether or not [ATR] is present in underlying representation, (147) shows that [−ATR] must be inserted by rule. Otherwise, the alternations caused by suffixation are not explained. (147) also shows that [−ATR] Insertion on mid vowels must follow the suffixation of *-ʔ* 'CAUSATIVE'.

Derived open syllables, on the other hand, do not surface with [−ATR], even though the underlying representation includes a sequence that does surface as a [−ATR] closed syllable if no suffix is added. In (148a), if no suffix is added, the form surfaces with a final closed syllable: the vowel is specified [−ATR]. However, if the demonstrative suffix *-e* is added, the syllable is opened and surfaces as [+ATR]. ((148b) is included to show how a stem with a final open syllable patterns: in such a case, an allomorph *-ne* of the demonstrative is added. The choice of allomorph depends on whether the stem ends in a vowel or a consonant.)

(148) *[ATR] in derived open syllables*

       a. tʊmɪs   'side dish'   tumise   'this side dish'
       b. buri   'back'   burine   'this back'

Again, whether or not [ATR] is present in underlying representation, to account for the alternations in (148) (*tʊmɪs* vs. *tumise*) it is necessary that [−ATR] be inserted by rule. Further, [−ATR] Insertion on high vowels must follow affixation of *-(n)e* 'DEMONSTRATIVE'.[92]

2.6.2.2   [ATR] on High and Mid Vowels   The distribution of [−ATR] in open sylla- bles differs depending on whether the vowel is mid or high. As Schlindwein (1988) demonstrates, differences in the patterns of the two sets of vowels are explained if mid vowels are subject to [−ATR] assignment earlier in the derivation than are high vowels. Compare the forms in (148) containing high vowels with the forms in (149) containing mid vowels: the suffixes are identical. In (149b), the [−ATR] pattern is found even though there are no closed syllables on the surface.

(149)   *[ATR] in derived open syllables*

a.	kere	'beggar'	kerene	'this beggar'
b.	bɔbɔt	'weight'	bɔbɔte	'this weight'

The contrast between high and mid vowels illustrated in (148) and (149) is explained if mid vowels are subject to [−ATR] assignment after the suffixation of the causative *-ʔ* and the locative *-n* but before any other suffixation; assignment of [−ATR] to high vowels, in contrast, follows all suffixation. The derivations of *bɔbɔte* and *tumise* in (150) illustrate this analysis.

(150)

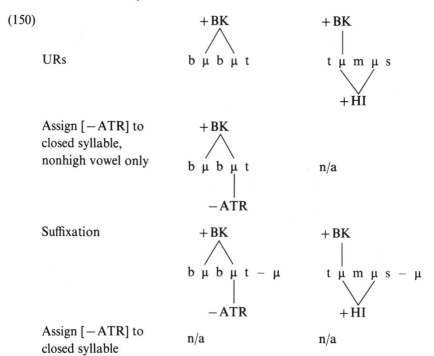

URs		
Assign [−ATR] to closed syllable, nonhigh vowel only		n/a
Suffixation		
Assign [−ATR] to closed syllable	n/a	n/a

[−ATR] Spread

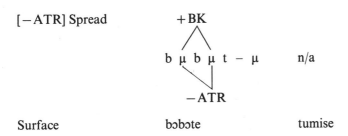

	+BK	n/a
	b μ b μ t − μ	
	−ATR	

Surface   bɔbɔte   tumise

Schlindwein adduces further support for the different applications of [−ATR] Insertion. For instance, syllables opened by [ə] Insertion have different [ATR] patterns depending on vowel height.

(151) *Syllables opened by schwa*

    a. /dins/   dinəs   'employed'
          /budk/   budək   'deaf'
          /ubrk/   ubrək   'commotion'
    b. /empr/   ɛmpər   'resemblance'
          /bosn/   bɔsən   'tired'
          /ork/   ɔrək   'shake'

2.6.2.3 [ATR] on Derived Mid Vowels In addition to derived open and closed syllables demonstrating that [−ATR] must be inserted by rule (regardless of whether it is present in underlying representation or not), evidence for the insertion of [−ATR] is found in the behavior of derived mid vowels.

High vowels become mid in forms suffixed by the causative -ʔ and the locative -*n*. These mid vowels are in closed syllables because of the suffix that triggers the lowering, and [−ATR] is assigned. (Note that the derived [−ATR] mid vowel does not necessarily surface in a closed syllable. Also, recall that the reason for an absence of [−ATR] Spread in cases such as (152) is that harmony requires agreement in height.)

(152) *[ATR] distribution: Derived mid vowels*

    buri   'back'   mburɛʔne   'back-CAUSATIVE-SUBJUNCTIVE'
                     mburɛni   'back-SIMPLE LOCATIVE'

Values for [ATR] depend on the environment a vowel is in, but not on whether the environment is derived or underlying. Thus, rules are needed to insert [−ATR]; once [−ATR] is assigned, it spreads leftward, conditioned by a "like height" restriction. To include specifications for [ATR] in underlying representation would be to make arbitrary choices about which value should be present in any given environment.

2.6.3 Conclusion

The formal model of Combinatorial Specification does not restrict which F-elements may be manipulated by phonological rules. In this section, we considered two cases in which the phonology manipulates an F-element that is not present at all in underlying representation.

These examples follow in progression from the cases considered in the previous section: in Haya and Ngbaka, only underlying F-elements are manipulated by rule; in Yoruba and Ainu, both underlying F-elements and predictable instances of those same F-elements are manipulated by rule; in Pulaar and Eastern Javanese, derived, completely predictable instances of F-elements are manipulated by rule.

A second point worth noting about these five languages is that the underlying representations of linked F-elements all correspond to a five-vowel system, *I, E, A, O, U*: in Haya, the surface reflects this; in Yoruba, a free underlying [−ATR] creates an [ATR] contrast in the mid vowels when it associates; in Pulaar and Eastern Javanese, the insertion of [ATR] creates distinctions that are not present underlyingly, in the mid vowels in Pulaar and in all nonlow vowels in Eastern Javanese. Thus, despite surface diversity, Combinatorial Specification formally states that in these languages, the linked vowel system is the standard *I, E, A, O, U* system. (Section 3.6.1.3 takes up the issue of why this five-vowel system is "standard.")

One result of the analyses presented here is that the number of legitimate F-element combinations appears to increase during the derivation. In the following section, we consider two cases of the opposite sort, where F-elements have more combinations in underlying representation than are permitted at the surface.

2.7 Incompatibility of F-Elements

F-elements that cooccur on a path, that is, F-elements that are linked to each other, must be compatible with each other. Most of the F-element combinations seen so far are of this "compatible" type. On the other hand, when two F-elements are incompatible, they may only cooccur in a formal representation where they are not linked to each other. Interesting cases of this "incompatible" type arise when one of the F-elements concerned is floating. We demonstrate in this section that certain types of mismatches between the F-element combinations that occur in underlying representation and the sounds that are manifested in surface realizations are expected under Combinatorial Specification. The cases considered involve a free F-element that does not have an eligible anchor available within its morpheme; this may be because there is simply no F-bearing unit (as in Chukchi), or because available F-bearing units have incompatible underlying F-elements (as in Yoruba, Maasai, and Nupe).

In formal terms, the model developed thus far allows for a full range of combinations of F-elements in the construction of representations. Given a pair of F-elements, α and β, the four types of underlying combinations shown in (153) are logically possible.

(153) a. α   b. α   c. $\boxed{\alpha}$ d. $\boxed{\alpha}$

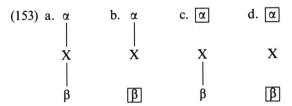

If α and β are compatible F-elements (e.g., [+back] and [+high] in a vowel system contrasting [i] and [u]), then all four representations are possible. If, however, α and β are incompatible (e.g., [+high] and [+low] in Tiv and Ngbaka, or [+low] and [−back] in a language with [a] but not *[æ]), then the configuration in which α and β are on a path is ruled out (153a).

We have already given examples of all the relations in (153) when α and β are *compatible* F-elements. The relation between [−high] and [+back] in Yoruba is an example of (153a); the relation in Yoruba between [−high] and [−ATR] is an example of (153b,c); the underlying free F-elements [+high] and [+round] in Tiv illustrate (153d).

With respect to incompatible F-elements, we have already noted that (153a) is impossible. Examples of (153b,c) have been seen in some of the exceptionally linked cases of Ngbaka (e.g., (121)–(127)). Finally, the configuration (153d) is illustrated with the free specifications [+high] and [+low] in both Tiv and Ngbaka.

In the following, we discuss a variation of the (153b/c) type, cases where an F-element is free but there is simply no potential anchor available for it to link to.

2.7.1 Chukchi Vowel Harmony

Chukchi, a Chukotko-Kamchatkan language spoken on the Chukotka peninsula in Eastern Siberia, has a classic dominant/recessive [ATR] vowel harmony pattern: morphemes (stems and affixes) are either "dominant" or "recessive"; if a surface form contains any dominant morpheme, then all surface vowels in that form are of the dominant set; otherwise (i.e., where there is no dominant morpheme anywhere in the form), all vowels are of the recessive set. In Chukchi, dominance is defined by the presence of a [−ATR] vowel (one of the set transcribed as [e, a/ɛ, o]—see (155)); forms where all vowels are recessive surface with [+ATR] vowels (the vowels transcribed as [i, e/ä, u]—again, see (155)). We take our data and general understanding of the phenomenon from work by Bogoras (1922), Anderson (1980), Comrie (1981a), and Kenstowicz (1979); we follow Kenstowicz (1979) and Calabrese (1988) in treating [−ATR] as the dominant F-element (but depart from these authors' analyses in a number of significant respects, particularly in our treatment of the dominant and recessive vowels transcribed as [e]).[93]

The underlying vowels of Chukchi can be represented with the linked F-elements [+low] and [+round] as shown in (154a). These two F-elements do not cooccur phonologically in Chukchi; their incompatibility is expressed by the conditions in (154b). Hence, three configurations involving linked F-elements are possible, as given in (154c). To account for the observation that *morphemes* are either dominant or recessive, we represent [−ATR] as a free F-element in the underlying representation of dominant morphemes: it links and spreads by rule. Because it is underlyingly free, [−ATR] is not included in the chart in (154c).

(154) *Chukchi vowel representation*

   a. F-elements

   $+$LO, $+$RD, $\boxed{-\text{ATR}}$

   b. Conditions

   RD/LO Condition: If [+round] then not [+low].
   LO/RD Condition: If [+low] then not [+round].

   c.
*	A	U	I
+LO	+LO		
+RD		+RD	

The association of a morpheme-level [−ATR] to the three vowels of (154c) produces the retracted vowels given in (155a); if no dominant [−ATR] value is assigned to such vowels, they surface with the nonretracted forms of (155b).

(155) *Chukchi surface vowels*

	A	U	I	Epenthetic
a. Dominant vowels	a/E	o	e_d	[−ATR]
b. Recessive vowels	e_r/ä	u	i	([+ATR])
c. Neutral vowels			ɪ (or ə)	

The symbol "e" is used for both dominant *I* and recessive *A*. We simply note this point here, distinguishing between the two cases diacritically ("e$_d$" and "e$_r$," respectively); in section 3.3.1.2, we discuss the phonological representation of these vowels in some detail.

The transcriptions here follow Bogoras (1922). The vowel transcribed here as ε is an "obscure" vowel, which alternates word-finally with a full [a] in word-medial position. The recessive [ä] occurs adjacent to [q] and to [ʔ]; it is described as a "long obscure vowel, in rest position of all the muscles of the oral cavity" (Bogoras 1922:643). It corresponds to a dominant [a]; see for example the first pair in (158c,d).

The vowel transcribed here as *ɪ*, following Bogoras (1922), corresponds to *ə* in Comrie's (1981a) transcription. Comrie (1981a:244) states that "schwa is neutral with respect to vowel harmony" and that its distribution is largely, although not completely, predictable. Bogoras (1922:657–58) provides a number of the environments in which his *ɪ* is predictable based on syllable structure requirements. As a final point concerning transcriptions, Bogoras distinguishes *k*, a palatal, from *q*, a velar.

Given this preamble concerning orthographic conventions, we can now turn to the harmonic patterns of Chukchi. We begin by laying out an analysis of the basic pattern of harmony, and then discuss the evidence for a fundamentally nonsegmental analysis.

We analyze "recessive" morphemes as unspecified for [ATR]. As such, a completely unspecified "recessive" verb root may appear without a suffix or with an equally unspecified "recessive" suffix (156a). In such cases, all vowels surface as [+ATR], a value that can be assigned very late in the phonology, even as late as the phonetics (see the "default values" box in section 2.2.1.3). We analyze "dominant" morphemes as containing a floating [−ATR] specification. For example, if a dominant suffix is added to the recessive roots of (156a), all vowels in the derived forms, both root and suffix vowels, are [−ATR]. This can be seen in (156b).

(156) *Recessive verbs with recessive and dominant affixes*

	[+ATR]			[−ATR]	
a.	e₍ᵣ₎le₍ᵣ₎ré₍ᵣ₎kɪn	'he feels dull'	b.	aláráma	'while feeling dull'
	íuʔrkɪn	'it thaws'		e_doʔma	'while thawing'
	pírirkɪn	'he takes'		pe_dré_dyo	'taken'

A root like *AlArA* 'feel dull' surfaces as [+ATR] with the recessive suffix *-kɪn* in (156a), *e₍ᵣ₎le₍ᵣ₎ré₍ᵣ₎kɪn*, but as [−ATR] with the suffix *-ma* in (156b), *aláráma*.

In similar fashion, the recessive noun roots plus affixes (if any) in (157a) are unspecified for [ATR] and surface as [+ATR]. The same roots in (157b) surface as [−ATR] because of the affixation of a dominant [−ATR] suffix.

(157) *Recessive nouns with recessive and dominant affixes*

	[+ATR]			[−ATR]	
a.	lile₍ᵣ₎	'eye'	b.	le_dlálhɪn	'eye-ABS'
				le_dlálhĭchɪn	'the aforesaid eye'
	ré₍ᵣ₎mkɪn	'people-ABS'		rámkĭchɪn	'people-EMPH'
	milute₍ᵣ₎	'hare'		me_dlotálhɪn	'hare-ABS'
	riquqe₍ᵣ₎	'fox'		re_dqoqálhɪn	'fox-ABS'
	te₍ᵣ₎mune₍ᵣ₎	'bivalve shell'		tamonálhɪn	'bivalve shell-ABS'
	ke₍ᵣ₎le₍ᵣ₎	'evil spirit'		kaláchɪn	'a particular evil spirit'

The concatenation of two morphemes with [−ATR] F-elements results in surface forms that are [−ATR], that is, indistinguishable from cases with a single [−ATR] specification. Consider the examples in (158). First, unspecified nouns (158a) are compounded with a [−ATR] adjective (158b); next, [−ATR] nouns (158c) are compounded with the same adjectives (158d).

(158) *Recessive and dominant roots with dominant affixes*

a.	ré_rmkɪn	'people'	b.	ramkíyŋɪn	'big people'
	ŋé_rwän	'woman'		ŋawánčɪŋɪn	'large woman'
c.	válE	'knife'	d.	valaíŋɪn	'large knife'
	aˀttɪn	'dog'		aˀttíyŋɪn	'large dog'

In the examples given so far, recessive stems vary depending on the [ATR] value of an affix. There are also numerous examples where recessive affixes vary as a function of the stem type; examples are provided in (159).

(159) *Dominant and recessive roots with recessive affixes*

	[+ATR]		[−ATR]	
a.	me_rnigítul	'piece of calico'	qáatol	'piece of reindeer (meat)'
b.	utte_rmil	'size of a tree'	qaáme_dl	'size of a reindeer'
			rorame_dl	'size of a reindeer fly'
c.	e_rkké_rnu	'as a son'	rɪrkáno	'as a walrus'
	lilé_rnu	'as an eye'	qoraɪnré_dtilo	'as a herdsman'
	ŋé_rwänu	'as a wife'	wíyolo	'as an assistant'
d.	qe_rlíne_rn	'pen'	te_dwe_dnan	'paddle, oar'
e.	une_rlčíčhɪn	'thong of thong-seal hide'	me_dmɪčé_dčhɪn	'thong of seal hide'
f.	ye_rtɪsˀqíurkɪn	'he comes once'	tɪmɪsˀqé_durkɪn	'he kills once'

The alternations illustrated in (156)–(159) demonstrate the basic pattern of Chukchi vowel harmony.

(160) *Chukchi [−ATR] Link/Spread*

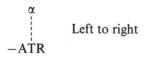

Left to right

Chukchi [−ATR] Link/Spread associates the free [−ATR] to the leftmost available vowel, then spreads the [−ATR] F-element rightward. As with Tiv High Link/

Spread (see (27)), there are no formal restrictions on the argument of this rule; this means that a free [−ATR] autosegment may link by this rule and a linked [−ATR] autosegment may also spread by the same rule. Moreover, if this rule is postponed until after all affixation and compounding, then harmony will affect the entire form: free tokens of [−ATR] will associate at the left edge and spread rightward.

Two important issues remain. The first issue, which we will postpone discussing until section 3.3.1.2, concerns the role of [e] as both the [+ATR] version of a low vowel and the [−ATR] version of a high vowel. The second issue of interest for Combinatorial Specification is the observation, made by Bogoras (1922), Kenstowicz (1979), and Comrie (1981a) and treated autosegmentally by Kenstowicz (1979), that morphemes are either dominant or recessive, even when they have no alternating vowels of their own: "[t]here are a number of words with neutral, probably auxiliary vowels ..., which produce the ablaut, as *tɪm* TO KILL; and quite a number of suffixes of the same phonetic character ... have the same effect ..." (Bogoras 1922:647). Comrie's observation is especially pertinent: "... a given morpheme is necessarily either dominant or recessive, even if [it] contains only the vowel schwa, indeed even if it contains no vowel at all ..." (Comrie 1981a:245). Bogoras's list of such morphemes includes *tɪm* 'to kill', which alternates with *nm*, and *tɪmg* 'to choke', which alternates with *mg*; it also includes a number of suffixes without vowels: *-lh-* 'SUBSTANTIVAL SUFFIX', *-čh* 'SUBSTANTIVAL SUFFIX', *-sʸq* 'over, top of', *-nv* or *-n* 'place of'. Comrie illustrates the dominant effect of *-nv/-n* 'place of' with the example *tɪle-* 'to go', *tɪla-n* 'road, way' (*tɪle-n).

Kenstowicz (1979) explores the distribution of [ə], showing that in many instances it is epenthetic. The result of this demonstration is that a number of verb roots are underlyingly vowelless, and receive vowels by epenthesis only. As Kenstowicz notes, such roots can be dominant (161a) or recessive (161b).

(161) *Vowelless roots*

a.	təm-ək	ga-nmə-le$_d$n	'kill'
	təw-ək	ga-twə-le$_d$n	'tell'
	jəp-ək	ga-jpə-le$_d$n	'put on clothes'
b.	ŋət-ək	ge$_r$-ntə-lin	'cut off, divide'
	gər-ək	ge$_r$-grə-lin	'lasso'
	rəg-ək	ge$_r$-rgə-lin	'dig, scratch'

As Kenstowicz (1979) points out, this additional information demonstrates that vowel harmony is induced by certain morphemes and not by others: it is irrelevant whether the inducing morpheme has a vowel, harmonic or otherwise. We analyze this by representing the dominant morphemes with a floating [−ATR] F-element. The existence of such morphemes in Chukchi is not a surprising result if F-elements are primitives and may be linked or free in underlying representation, precisely the formal properties of Combinatorial Specification.[94]

The behavior of dominant morphemes is explained by the underlying presence of a free [−ATR] F-element. The vocalic content of a morpheme containing such a free F-element is unimportant, as is the presence of such a vowel. Harmony results when the free [−ATR] F-element associates and spreads, whether initial association is to a tautomorphemic or heteromorphemic vowel.

(162)   tm   'kill'

If the segment is taken as basic, however, alternatives must be found to the simple type of representation given in (162). Either such a morpheme is diacritically marked to exceptionally induce harmony, or some abstract vowel must be postulated for such morphemes, a vowel that would trigger harmony but subsequently delete.

The contrast between theories is clear. Combinatorial Specification predicts the existence of data such as those found in Chukchi; a segmental model predicts that the Chukchi type of case should not exist. That Chukchi does exist is therefore a problem that necessitates the addition of abstract segments and feature-changing absolute neutralization or ad hoc diacritics to the segment-based model. And as the next three languages demonstrate, Chukchi is not an isolated example of this phenomenon.

2.7.2   Exceptions to Yoruba [ATR] Harmony

Tongue root harmony in Yoruba (section 2.3.1) associates and spreads [−ATR]; unlike in Chukchi, however, only nonhigh vowels may undergo [ATR] harmony. High vowels are consistently [+ATR] on the surface. One might expect, therefore, that a high vowel stem would consistently condition advanced prefixes. While this is the general pattern, in a survey of forms with the ò/ọ̀ agentive/instrumental prefix (see Archangeli and Pulleyblank 1989: appendix), two forms with only high vowels were nevertheless noted to condition a [−ATR] prefix.

(163)   *Anomalous harmony with productive prefixes*

  a. mu   'drink'
     ọ̀mu   'drinker'
     ọ̀mùtí   'drunkard'   (ọtí 'spirits')

  b. titun/tuntun 'newness'
     ọ̀tun   'newness'

These forms are parallel to those in Chukchi that are vowelless but induce harmony: if *mu* 'drink' and *-tun* 'new' are represented with a free [−ATR] F-element in underlying representation, the patterns are exactly as expected.

A fairly large number of examples of this type occur with high-voweled verb stems involving a class of unproductive nominalizing prefixes.

(164) *Anomalous harmony with unproductive prefixes: High-voweled roots*

    a. bí   'give birth to'
       ẹ̀bí   'birth'

    b. kú   'die'
       ẹ̀kú   'costume worn by the Egúngún'

    c. rí   'exhibit a certain appearance'
       ẹ̀rí   'evidence'

    d. wù   'please person'
       ẹwù   'a pleasurable feeling'

That the [ATR] values of the prefixes in such cases are determined by the verb root, and are not intrinsic properties of the prefixes, is clear from a consideration of the same prefixes when they occur with mid-voweled stems. Phonetically, both [+ATR] prefixes like [e] (165a,b) and [−ATR] prefixes like [ẹ] (165c,d) occur. The phonetically [+ATR] prefix occurs only with [+ATR] roots; the phonetically [−ATR] prefix occurs only with [−ATR] roots.

(165) *Anomalous harmony with unproductive prefixes: Mid-voweled roots*

    a. gbé   'perish'
       ègbé 'annihilation'

    b. rò   'think'
       èrò   'thought'

    c. ló̩   'transplant'
       ẹ̀ló̩   'transplanting'

    d. so̩   'be interlocked'
       ẹ̀so̩   'place where two glued edges meet'

If the prefixes are unspecified for [ATR], then their distribution is completely straightforward. If, on the other hand, it were assumed that the prefixes in (164) and (165) were underlyingly [−ATR], then there would be no explanation for the following gap. If a [−ATR] prefix were attached to a root unspecified for [ATR] (e.g., ẹ + *CE*), then either of two patterns could result. First, since the general rule of harmony applies only from right to left, one would predict an absence of harmony as in forms like *ate* 'hat': *[ẹCe]. No such forms occur. To remedy this incorrect prediction, one might posit an ad hoc rule for such forms that would spread [−ATR] from left to right. This would result in cases where a [+ATR] root surfaces as [−ATR] when concatenated with the appropriate class of prefixes: [Ce]/*[ẹCẹ]. Again, no such forms occur. We conclude, therefore, that such nominalizing prefixes cannot be specified for [ATR] underlyingly, with the result that the surface occurrence of [−ATR] derives from a property of the appropriate roots.[95]

The Yoruba data are interesting because they cannot be resolved by the "abstract segments and feature-changing absolute neutralization" alternative considered briefly for Chukchi. A nondiacritic, segmental account of Yoruba harmony exceptions would include [−ATR] in the underlying representations of vowels that surface as [i] and [u]. Thus, [−ATR] would not have a restricted distribution, predicting that all vowels should undergo harmony. This makes exactly the wrong predictions in the two-domain cases: recall that only [+ATR] mid vowels may be to the left of a high vowel flanked by two nonhigh vowels, èlùbọ́ 'yam flour', *ẹlubọ. In such cases, [−ATR] is incorrectly predicted to spread from the final vowel leftward, since under the feature-changing absolute neutralization hypothesis [−ATR] would be able to occur on all vowels: once feature-changing absolute neutralization took place, *ẹlubọ would be predicted to occur (derived from intermediate ẹlu̧bọ) while the attested pattern, exemplified by èlùbọ́, would be predicted not to exist. The alternative under feature-changing absolute neutralization would be to complicate the rule so that it targets only nonhigh vowels: that is, the rule would stipulate a pattern that is true independently of the rule of harmony. Hence, artifacts of the segmental hypothesis would be the positing of more complex rules and the invoking of feature-changing absolute neutralization.

2.7.3 Maasai [ATR] Harmony

Maasai (Tucker and Mpaayei 1955, Levergood 1984), a Nilo-Saharan language spoken in southern Kenya and northern Tanzania, presents a similar case, except that the free F-element is [+ATR], which cannot associate to [+low] vowels (*If [+low] then not [+ATR]*).[96] There are, however, a few stems with only [+low] vowels that nonetheless induce [+ATR] harmony.

The general pattern is illustrated in (166a,b) and (167a,b). Like Chukchi, Maasai exhibits a pattern of dominant harmony, though as mentioned, the active value is [+ATR]. The examples in (166a) and (167a) are ones in which all morphemes are recessive; that is, there are no [+ATR] morphemes and both stems and affixes are realized with [−ATR] vowels. The example in (166b) adds a dominant [+ATR] suffix -*ie*- 'APPLICATIVE' while (167b) involves a dominant stem *dot* 'pull'; all vowels except the initial low vowel of (166b) are therefore [+ATR].

(166) *Stem alternation due to suffix*

      a. a – ɪ – [pɛrr]
         INFINITIVE – CLASS II – split

      b. aa – i – [perr] – ie – ki
         1SG – CLASS II – split – APPLICATIVE – PASSIVE

(167) *Prefix alternation due to stem*

    a. ɛ – [jɪŋ] – U
        3 – enter – MOTION TOWARD

    b. e – [dot] – u
        3 – pull – MOTION TOWARD

Like the high vowels of Yoruba, Maasai [a] blocks right-to-left harmony, as shown in (168). (168a,b) show that the second person prefix alternates between [ɪ] and [i] depending (in this case) on the presence or absence of the applicative suffix. In (168c), the applicative suffix follows a low stem, and the prefix does not harmonize, demonstrating that the low vowel blocks harmony.

(168) *Opaque low vowel in root*

    a. ɪ – [tɔn]
        2 – sit

    b. i – [ton] – ie
        2 – sit – APPLICATIVE

    c. ɪ – [as] – ie   (*i – [as] – ie)
        2 – do – APPLICATIVE

To summarize, some morphemes, like -*ie*- 'APPLICATIVE', never alternate: they are always [+ATR]. Others alternate between forms with and without [+ATR] depending on the other morphemes that they are concatenated with. The low vowel [a] does not undergo harmony; rather, it blocks the propagation of [+ATR].

In light of this general pattern, the data in (169) are surprising. The prefix surfaces as [+ATR] in (169), despite a stem containing only the [+low] vowel *a*. This behavior of the "class II" prefix in (169) cannot be attributed to some special property of that prefix. In examples like those in (168), the same prefix is seen to alternate between [i] and [ɪ] in a perfectly regular fashion. The behavior of the prefix in (169) is therefore not due to some property such as a lexical specification of [+ATR].

(169) *Anomalous behavior of two* a-*roots*

    a. a – i – [ñaŋ] – U
        INFINITIVE – CLASS II – buy from – MOTION TOWARD

    b. a – i – [ñal] – ɪta
        1SG – CLASS II – annoy – CONTINUOUS

Both examples of idiosyncratic [i-] precede the palatal nasal [ñ], suggesting that this consonant might induce [+ATR] on the preceding vowel. There are two arguments against this conclusion. First, Tucker and Mpaayei (1955:52) state that *a*-roots may have either [i-] or [ɪ-] as the prefix, although the [−ATR] version [ɪ-] is more common:

they provide only the two examples given in (169), although the implication is that there are other such roots. Second, the palatal ñ does not induce [+ATR] on vowels to its left. In morpheme-internal contexts, [−ATR] vowels precede ñ, shown by (170a). Similarly with prefixes, [−ATR] vowels may precede ñ, as in (170b).

(170) a. akíñ   *akíñ   'to peel'
        εmíñɔr   *εmíñɔr 'part of animal's intestines'
    b. ε-ñáwá   ɪ-ñáwáííé 'udder-SG/PL'
       ε-ñaaláti ɪ-ñaalát   'quid of tobacco-SG/PL'
       ε-ñamu   ɪ-ñámin   'plunder, loot-SG/PL'

Apparently, then, there is no general rule assigning [+ATR] to vowels preceding ñ. The data in (169) must be accounted for by some other means.

In order that [+ATR] surface on the prefix in these forms, we posit that the underlying representation of the stems in (169) contains a free [+ATR]; this F-element cannot link to the stem vowel but does link to the prefix (provided of course that the prefix is not also [+low]). The exceptional cases in Maasai, then, are seen to be entirely analogous to the Chukchi and Yoruba examples: the pattern found in Maasai is precisely what is expected under the F-element-based Combinatorial Specification.

Furthermore, an "abstract-segment-and-absolute-neutralization" account fails in Maasai. Under such an account, the stems -ñaŋ- and -ñal- would have underlying [+ATR, +low] vowels, which would then trigger harmony and later undergo neutralization to become [+low, −ATR] vowels. There is compelling evidence in Maasai against an absolute neutralization account: the prohibition against assigning [+ATR] to a [+low] vowel is restricted to the rule associating free tokens of [+ATR] and the rule spreading [+ATR] leftward. Under rightward harmony, [a] alternates with [o]. Consider the alternation between [a] and [o] in the dative suffix, -akɪ/-oki, in the following examples: a-ɪ-[sʊj]-akɪ '1SG-CLASS II-wash-DATIVE' versus a-[bol]-oki '1SG-open-DATIVE'. (This phenomenon is discussed in some detail in section 4.3.2.) These cases demonstrate that in those contexts where the combination [+low, +ATR] must be allowed, the surface result is [o], not [a] nor [ə]. It follows that the stems in (169) cannot be simply [+low, +ATR] or else the surface forms would be *aiñoŋu and *aiñolita, rather than the correct aiñaŋʊ and aiñalɪta. Thus, to posit a [+ATR, +low] vowel to account for the patterns in (169) would lead to a paradox in the explanation of the distribution of -akɪ/-oki and other such suffixes: some instances of [+low, +ATR] would have to be resolved as [a] and others as [o].

2.7.4 Nupe Labialization and Palatalization

A somewhat different case is found in Nupe, a Kwa language spoken in central Nigeria (Hyman 1970, 1973, Harms 1973, Purcell 1989). In Nupe, consonants are optionally labialized when followed by either of the round vowels, [u] or [o], as shown in (171a), and consonants are optionally palatalized when followed by either of the front vowels, [i] or [e], as shown in (171b). In addition, labialized consonants never precede [i] or [e]; similarly, palatalized consonants never precede [u] or [o].

(171) a. *Labialization*

[egũ]	[egʷũ]	'mud'
[egó]	[egʷó]	'grass'
[po]	[pʷo]	'to roast'
[bú]	[bʷú]	'to invoke'

     b. *Palatalization*

[egi]	[egʸi]	'child'
[ege]	[egʸe]	'beer'
[bé]	[bʸé]	'to come'
[bí]	[bʸí]	'to crush'

Palatalized, labialized, and plain consonants may, however, precede the [+low] vowel [a]. Three-way near-minimal pairs are given in (172).

(172) *Low vowel stems*

a. [ega]	'stranger'		b. [tá]	'to tell'
[egʷa]	'hand' (*[ega])		[tʷá]	'to trim' (*[tá])
[egʸà]	'blood' (*[egà])		[tʸá]	'to be mild' (*[tá])

The distribution of consonants preceding the low and nonlow vowels contrasts in two ways. First, labialization and palatalization with nonlow vowels is optional, while with low vowels there is no optionality. Second, with low vowels, three different types of consonants may appear, while with nonlow vowels, only two types are possible per vowel quality. This is summarized in (173) (*vbl* = 'variable'; *lex* = 'lexically determined').

(173)

Preceding consonant	i	e	a	o	u
Palatalized	vbl	vbl	lex	*	*
Plain	vbl	vbl	lex	vbl	vbl
Labialized	*	*	lex	vbl	vbl

That is, with a nonlow vowel, consonantal behavior is variable, alternating between plain and whichever of palatalized or labialized is appropriate; with a low vowel, consonantal behavior is fixed, each low stem exhibiting exactly one consonant type.

There are two ways of accounting for this distribution: (i) via spreading of F-elements from vowel to consonant, or (ii) via spreading of F-elements from consonant to vowel. Before contrasting the two approaches, let us consider what the two have in common. Both analyses posit a three-way underlying height contrast in vowels, derivable by the two F-elements [+high] and [+low].

(174) *Partial Nupe vowel representation*

    a. F-elements

       +HI, +LO

    b. Conditions

       HI/LO Condition: If [+high] then not [+low].
       LO/HI Condition: If [+low] then not [+high].

  c.

*	I/U	A	E/O
+HI	+HI		
+LO		+LO	

Under an account that posits spreading from the vowels to the consonants, [−back] and [+round] would also be necessary on vowels prior to the rules of Palatalization and Labialization. The vowels [i] and [e] would be specified [−back] while the vowels [u] and [o] would be specified [+round].[97] Under this account, optional palatalization results from spreading the [−back] value of [e] and [i] and optional labialization results from spreading the [+round] value of [o] and [u].[98]

Such an account, however, does not extend obviously to the [+low] vowels, unless abstract low vowels (ɛ and ɔ) are posited in underlying representation (essentially the account offered in Hyman 1970, 1973). This is because [+low] does not combine with either [+round] or [−back] in Nupe, at least in surface realizations. The question appears to be whether underlying representations can include F-elements in combinations that do not appear together in surface realizations—the "abstractness" issue.

Within a theory of Combinatorial Specification, the issue of abstractness takes on a rather different appearance. An account is available, following the lines of Chukchi, Yoruba, and Maasai, where morphemes may contain *free* instances of F-elements that are incompatible with some underlyingly linked F-element(s) in the same morpheme. In Nupe, [+round] and [−back] may be present as free autosegments even in a morpheme with a (linked) [+low]; they then associate to the rightmost available consonant as in (175), since the vowel is unavailable.

(175) a. +LO   b. +LO   c. +LO

             \   \   \

      t   a   t   a   t   a

                              +RD   +BK

    [tá]   [tʷá]   [tʸá]

    'to tell'   'to trim'   'to be mild'

Under such an account, no neutralization is required; the observed pattern is predicted to be possible by the interaction of height features with the set of F-elements
required for the processes of Labialization and Palatalization. One might ask, moreover, whether it would even be possible to rule out such a possibility. Unless free
specifications were disallowed in underlying representations, or unless relations between autosegments could be established without requiring association, it would be
difficult to rule out the possibility of cases where a free specification may be incompatible with a linked one. That is, it would be impossible to rule out the kind of case
that Nupe constitutes.[99]

In addition, the optionality/obligatoriness of the appropriate contexts involved in
the Nupe pattern can be straightforwardly specified: association of free F-elements is
obligatory, spreading of already linked F-elements is optional. Compare, for example, the derivation of *t^{y}á* 'to be mild' (176a) with the derivations of *bi/b^{y}i* 'to crush'
(176b).

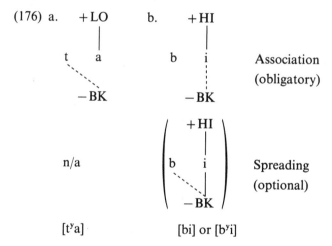

An alternative to the account just presented would be to assign the F-elements
[−back] and [+round] to consonants underlyingly, as in (177).

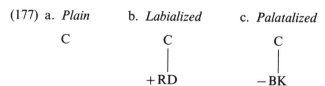

Under this account, vowels would be specified underlyingly only for height features,
as in (174). A vowel's specifications for [back] and [round] would be derived by
spreading the feature of the preceding consonant. Given such an analysis, the appearance of plain, palatalized, and labialized consonants before a low vowel would

straightforwardly reflect the various underlying possibilities open to consonants. Because of the incompatibility of the [−back] and [+round] consonant features with the [+low] specification of the vowel, such cases would not be able to exhibit spreading.

With nonlow vowels, however, the situation is markedly less straightforward since all mid and high vowels must receive on the surface either the value [−back] or the value [+round]: a vowel like the [+back, −round] vowel [ɨ] is not found in Nupe. This could be achieved by redundantly assigning the value [−back] to an unspecified consonant, resulting in a proper [−back] vowel (see note 98 for discussion of a similar rule that is necessary in the account proposed here). But if [−back] is redundantly assigned to any consonant not otherwise specified for [back] or [round], then it should also be assigned when such a consonant precedes a low vowel; such a move would incorrectly remove the possibility of having a plain consonant before a low vowel (as in *tá* 'to tell').

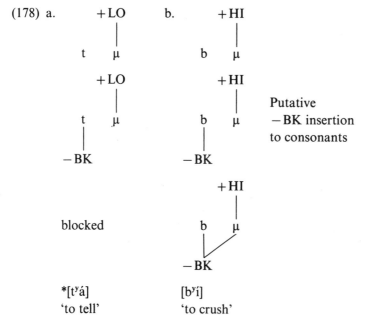

It would be necessary to assign a redundant [−back] feature to a consonant under the following conditions: (i) only if the consonant is not [+round], (ii) only if the following vowel is not [+low]. In addition, after spreading of the [−back] or [+round] value from the consonant to the nonlow stem vowel, it would be necessary to posit an optional rule delinking the feature from the consonant, since palatalization and labialization of consonants before nonlow vowels is optional.

A number of questions arise with any account of Nupe that will require information beyond what is available in the sources cited. The important points for our purposes here are that (i) under both accounts, the distribution of consonants to the left of [a] is a result of the incompatibility of [+low] with both [−back] and [+round] and (ii) such asymmetries are entirely expected within Combinatorial Specification. Combinatorial Specification allows the free combination of the F-elements of a language: certain F-elements are incompatible yet may still cooccur in a single representation provided that they are not linked to each other. This is exactly what is seen in Nupe, under either account.

2.7.5   Conclusion

To conclude, in this section we have sketched four cases in which certain morphemes contain free F-elements underlyingly that have no available anchor within the morpheme, either because of unavailability (Chukchi) or because of incompatibilities (Yoruba, Maasai, and Nupe). Two additional cases had already been presented: in both Tiv and Ngbaka, underlying free [+high] and [+low] are resolved by [+high] linking to the leftmost vowel followed by linking of [+low]. As discussed in the introduction of this section, the model of Combinatorial Specification predicts that representations should exist that include incompatible specifications, provided that such incompatibilities never occur on a path with each other. The examples considered in this section demonstrate that this prediction is correct: in the cases examined, it was sometimes necessary to posit free incompatible specifications—in no case was it necessary that the incompatible F-elements cooccur in a single path.

These cases constitute a strong argument for nonsegmental phonology, a model of phonology in which the F-elements and associations are the primitives out of which representations are constructed. The segment is inadequate for the expression of the regularities in these languages; once the regularities are expressed, the notion of segment is irrelevant.

2.8   General Summary and Conclusions

We have argued in favor of Combinatorial Specification by providing a number of examples showing the importance of the F-element as a phonological primitive and showing that the segment is a purely derivative construct. We have shown that whether F-elements are underlyingly linked or free, the establishment of lexical distinctions takes place at the level of the F-element. In certain cases, we have demonstrated that there can be mismatches between underlying and surface representations. One class of such cases, exemplified by Ainu and Barrow Inupiaq, involves contrasts that are neutralized by the insertion of redundant features. The second involves lexical representations with incompatible F-elements: some morphemes include free

F-elements that cannot link to a tautomorphemic anchor. This can be either because the morpheme contains no potential anchor (Chukchi) or because association is blocked by the presence of an implicational condition (Yoruba). Further examples of each type are found in Maasai, Nupe, Tiv, and Ngbaka. Mismatches such as these are predicted to exist if the F-element is taken as the basic combinatorial unit; they are predicted *not* to exist if the segment (rather than the F-element) is primitive.

The patterns attested in languages such as these are entirely compatible with Combinatorial Specification: no principles need to be added to the simple postulation of sets of F-elements that combine subject to implicational conditions.

The results here contrast sharply with any segment-based model. A segment-based theory predicts that languages should not behave in the manner exemplified in this chapter. All instances of the vowel [i] should behave in a single manner; all instances of the vowel [a] should behave alike. Morphemes should be composed of sets of segmental units. Cases that diverge from such expected segmental patterns require modifications or embellishments of the segment-as-primitive hypothesis. As discussed above, certain cases might be accounted for by assuming absolute neutralization; others might be accounted for by the establishment of diacritically distinguished classes of forms, each triggering different rules. It is also possible to assume an essentially "segment-based" theory, but to allow "floating features" as a type of special add-on feature.

Our central point in this regard is not that segment-like properties are never observed; rather, it is that such properties are predicted to occur and to be of a particular type by a theory based on subsegmental units. Allowing features to be both linked and free, the theory assigns a range of properties to sets of linked, segment-like sets of features. In particular, incompatibility is a property that cannot hold of such sets. With a segment-based theory, on the other hand, distinctions in terms of subsegmental elements are anomalous.

It should be noted, however, that cases involving subsegmental contrasts that are neutralized on the surface (as in Ainu and Barrow Inupiaq), and cases involving floating features that are incompatible with other tautomorphemic specifications (as in Maasai, Nupe, etc.), both appear to be relatively rare when compared with the more ordinary cases of "segment-like" contrasts.[100] Even within a single language, cases like those discussed for Yoruba and Maasai suggest that the number of exceptions to be accounted for by positing incompatible F-elements in underlying representations is fairly limited. If our assessment of the frequency of these phenomena is correct, the question arises why such phenomena should be less robust than other effects derived from Combinatorial Specification, and why an F-element account is preferred over an account that overtly indicates that these are unusual patterns by employing formal devices such as diacritics or feature-changing absolute neutralization.

We believe that the relative rarity of such cases is due to the fact that the required underlying representations put much greater demands on learning. Recoverability imposes the condition that phonological representations must relate to phonetic substance. If the relation between phonetic substance and phonological representation is a direct one, then we assume that it is easily learned. In a case where there is no direct phonetic motivation for distinguishing between two tokens, a distinction will be learned only if there is phonological evidence from alternations. For instance, in Yoruba, if a child has not encountered the derived form *òmu* 'drinker', but does know *mu* 'drink', then we expect that the child might spontaneously create *òmu 'drinker', but would not spontaneously create the correct form. Thus, there is a degree of instability inherent in such underlying representations, which, we believe, would often lead to the loss of the free F-element in precisely these forms. We postulate that since such contrasts make greater demands on learning strategies, they are correspondingly rarer. Historical factors will add to the rarity of these cases. If cases where there is a phonological contrast but no phonetic one involve historical mergers, then the class of cases potentially exhibiting the relevant effects will only be the class of cases that have undergone merger. Hence, general considerations of learnability and diachronic change will interact with the purely formal theory of feature specifications to produce the observed asymmetries.

In this chapter, we have argued for Combinatorial Specification, an impoverished formal model in which representations are composed of combinations of F-elements. Before concluding this discussion, we wish to stress a certain general point about the mapping between phonetic symbols and sets of specifications. We then consider the significance of Combinatorial Specification for a variety of feature specification issues.[101]

2.8.1 Transcriptions versus Descriptions

It is important to recognize that a linguist's choice of phonetic symbols is not pre-analytic. When a phonetic string is mapped onto a symbolic representation, decisions are made that depend on a wide array of sometimes conflicting criteria.

We argue that F-elements, not phonetic symbols, are ultimately of theoretical significance. The decision, for example, to specify a vowel as [+high] and [+back] plays an important role in the phonology of a language; that the symbol "u" or "ɷ" or "ɨ" might be selected to graphically symbolize such a feature set is only of theoretical significance to the extent that it reflects our analysis of the vowel in question.

Consider, for example, the relation between the value of the first formant (F_1) and vowel height. In a general sense, it is clear that lowness of F_1 correlates with highness of a vowel. In terms of specifics, however, the picture is not always clear. For example, a vowel symbolized as [ɪ] in Dinka (Jacobson 1980) has an average F_1 value of 300 Hz; the vowel symbolized the same way in English is given by Peterson and

Barney (1952) as having an F_1 value of 390 Hz (for a male speaker). Phonetically, is it clear that we are dealing with the "same" vowel? Add to this picture the F_1 values for the vowels in Dinka and English that are symbolized as [i], namely, 215 Hz (Dinka) and 270 Hz (English). Comparing the two pairs of vowels for Dinka and the two pairs of vowels for English, we see that in each case "i" has a higher F_1 value than does "ɪ." But in absolute terms, the formants of Dinka [ɪ] are actually closer to those of English [i] than to those of English [ɪ]. The problem compounds itself as one considers the class of "mid" vowels. For example, Jacobson cites the "mid" vowel [e] in Dinka as having an F_1 value of 400 Hz; but recall that Peterson and Barney cite the "high" vowel [ɪ] of English as having a comparable F_1.[102] In other words, both "high" and "mid" vowels may have comparable F_1 values. In fact, the problem may be even more severe. For a language like Akan, Lindau (1978) found that the "mid" vowel [e] actually has a lower F_1 value than does the "high" vowel [ɪ].[103]

One must ask, of course, what exactly such figures mean. Could one conclude, for example, that the Dinka data, or the English data, or the Akan data, have been mistranscribed?[104] To answer this, one must consider the actual goals of a transcription.

The choice of symbols generally serves two purposes. First, the choice of a particular vowel symbol constitutes a claim about the general location of the relevant sound in the vowel space. For example, assigning the symbol [i] to a vowel might plausibly constitute a claim that no other (front) vowel is higher in the language, that no other vowel has a lower F_1 value. If this were the sole purpose for a transcription, then one could conclude that a case like Akan has been mistranscribed because of the relative F_1 values of [e] and [ɪ]. But at least as important as this first point is the fact that a symbol reflects an analysis of the patterns of opposition and alternation observed in the language. A vowel in the same approximate location in the vowel space may be symbolized differently depending on properties of the language in question. Hence, the appropriate vowel is often transcribed (symbolized) as "e" in Akan because it patterns phonologically like a mid vowel, and the acoustically related vowel "ɪ" is transcribed as a high vowel because of its phonological behavior.[105] In sum, a particular transcription constitutes a claim about a combined phonetic/phonological *analysis* of a sound.

Significantly, the above focus on the first formant is quite arbitrary. Apart from depending crucially on F_1 and F_2, vowel identification can depend on factors such as the third formant and fundamental frequency (see, for example, Fant 1968). Reference has already been made to variables such as whether the speaker is male or female, presumably a factor whose primary source is in the varying lengths of the vocal tract. The more such factors are added to the list of variables involved in vowel identification, the greater the role of interpretation, of abstracting away from extraneous variables, in assigning appropriate symbolic representations.[106]

The main conclusion of the above discussion is that the assignment of symbolic representations to particular vowels constitutes part of a phonological *analysis*. One cannot, therefore, analyze a phonological system by first seeking to establish symbolic representations and only then embarking on an analysis of such representations. The fallacy of such an approach lies in the assumption that symbolic transcriptions are preanalytic. Hence, when faced with vowels transcribed as [e] or [ɪ], for example, we are dealing with a case where someone has analyzed two vowels as mid and high, respectively. Whether such vowels are "actually" mid or high is an analytic question whose answer lies in a combined examination of the segments' phonetic and phonological properties.

In closing this discussion, we should stress that the determination of F-elements for some sound is not (completely) arbitrary. A vowel with an F_1 value of 500 Hz, for example, could not plausibly be considered [+high]. While a detailed consideration of the limits on phonetic variation is beyond the scope of this work, as is a detailed consideration of the types of areas where cross-linguistic variation may be expected, some preliminary discussion of these questions with respect to the tongue root is given in section 3.3.

In the phonological analyses presented here, phonetic symbols are used as a mnemonic shorthand. Various realizations are often possible in principle for a given set of F-elements, and some role for language-specific rules of phonetic interpretation is assumed (see Liberman and Pierrehumbert 1984). The crucial and theoretically significant aspect of a phonological analysis consists solely of the analysis in terms of F-elements.

2.8.2   Feature Specification Issues

Combinatorial Specification is a formal model of F-element interaction. The central focus of Combinatorial Specification is to determine which F-elements are necessarily present in a representation, to establish their formal linking status, and to consider their mutual compatibility/incompatibility. To conclude this chapter, we briefly examine Combinatorial Specification with respect to a variety of phenomena that an adequate theory of phonology must account for. Our conclusion is twofold: (i) Combinatorial Specification expresses the basic insights provided by Radical Underspecification; and (ii) a number of cases that were problematical for Radical and Contrastive Underspecification theories receive a straightforward account under Combinatorial Specification.[107]

2.8.2.1   Asymmetry/Malleability   By *asymmetry*, we refer to cases in which [αF] plays an active role in some phonological rule(s) while the opposite value [−αF], is not critical in any phonological rules. The phenomenon and the account under Combinatorial Specification are exemplified by many of the languages discussed here, perhaps most notably by Tiv and Ngbaka: [αF] is present in representations while [−αF] is not, and [αF] can be manipulated by rules. *Malleability* refers to cases in which a variety of assimilation rules converge on the same target: the target's surface representation depends on which set of rules applies. Our discussion of Barrow Inupiaq provides an example of malleability and of the Combinatorial Specification account of the phenomenon: prior to rule application, the target's representation includes none of the spreading F-elements. The F-elements that are assigned via rule determine the various surface representations of the target.

The basic issue with regard to asymmetry and malleability is that phonological systems exist in which one feature value, [αF], plays a crucial and active role while the opposite value, [−αF], remains inert and malleable. The analysis under Combinatorial Specification is that such crucial, active F-elements are present in representations (and so can be manipulated by rules) while the inert, malleable F-elements are absent (and so cannot be manipulated, nor can they block the assimilation of active F-elements). Essentially the same account is offered under Radical Underspecification. Radical Underspecification and Combinatorial Specification differ from Contrastive Underspecification, however, in that formal asymmetries of the type just outlined are predicted to occur even with features establishing lexical contrasts, while Contrastive Underspecification rules this out.

2.8.2.2 Role of Active yet Predictable F-Elements Phonological systems have multiple active F-elements. In some cases, the language includes some active F-element [αF] that is predictably accompanied by some other active F-element [βG]. For example, in Yoruba, both [+low] and [−ATR] are active F-elements, yet [+low] predictably is accompanied by [−ATR].

Such predictable F-elements are seen to function in languages in a variety of ways, exemplified by Haya, Yoruba, and Ainu and presented schematically in (179). The predictable F-elements may be absent underlyingly and remain inert throughout the derivation ([−high] on [+low] in Haya). The predictable F-elements may be absent underlyingly but be active at a later stage in the derivation ([−ATR] on [+low] in Yoruba). The predictable F-elements may be underlyingly active in some paths but inert in other paths ([+back] on [+low] in Ainu).

(179) *[βG] is predictable on the basis of [αF]*

	Haya	Yoruba	Ainu
UR	[αF]	[αF]	[αF] vs. [αF, βG]
Later stage	[αF]	[αF, βG]	[αF] vs. [αF, βG]

The Combinatorial Specification analyses for these cases have been presented in this chapter. There are three further points of interest.

First, there is another possible representation under Combinatorial Specification, namely, that [αF, βG] is the *only* underlying representation for a path involving [αF] (i.e., [αF] alone does not exist). We have found no clear cases of this type. The question arises, therefore, whether a condition should be introduced into the theory of Combinatorial Specification in order to eliminate the possibility of such languages. The proposal offered here is that no additional conditions are necessary: Representational Simplicity (96) determines that [αF] is sufficient.[108]

Second, Radical Underspecification incorrectly predicts that languages of the Ainu type simply do not exist. In a version of Radical Underspecification incorporating the Redundancy Rule Ordering Constraint (RROC), all input representations in an Ainu-type case would be expected to be [αF, βG] for a rule referring to [βG]. In a version of Radical Underspecification *not* incorporating the RROC, all input representations in such a case would be expected to be [αF]. With or without the RROC, Radical Underspecification fails to derive patterns of the Ainu type. Since Combinatorial Specification neither forces redundancy-free underlying representations nor includes the RROC, Ainu-type languages receive a straightforward account.

Finally, languages like Ainu also resist analysis under Contrastive Underspecification. For example, the two /a/s in Ainu do not contrast with each other in any feature specifications and so should receive identical representations (see Steriade 1987a). If only one underlying representation is available for surface [a], then the only solution available to express the two types of low vowels is to indicate their distinct behaviors via the use of a diacritic. In short, under Contrastive or Radical Underspecification, an underlying distinction characterized in terms of predictable or redundant information is impossible.

2.8.2.3 Lexical "Exceptions"

The above discussion introduces the issue of how to represent "lexical exceptions"—that is, how to represent morphemes that do not follow the general patterns of a language. One of the advantages of Radical Underspecification is the ability to express certain types of lexical exceptions through phonological representations rather than through the use of diacritics. Consider, for example, an F-element that typically spreads but fails to do so in an arbitrary class of lexical items even though present. Yoruba exemplifies this case: some loanwords are disharmonic. The phenomenon can be handled under both Radical Underspecification and Combinatorial Specification through representations with an underlyingly *linked* token of the harmonic element, [−ATR], in conjunction with the Strict Cycle Condition (see Levergood 1984, Archangeli and Pulleyblank 1989, and sections 2.5.3 and 3.2.4.2).[109] Another possibility involves lexical items whose paths are incompatible with a harmonic F-element, yet which appear to consistently induce harmony, illustrated in our discussions of Nupe, Yoruba, Chukchi, and Maasai. As shown above, these patterns succumb to an analysis in Combinatorial Specification; a comparable analysis is possible under both Radical and Contrastive Underspecification.

There are also lexical exceptions involving F-elements that are typically inert in the language, exceptions that resist explanation under Radical Underspecification. Consider, for example, languages like Kalenjin (Antell et al. 1973, Halle and Vergnaud 1981; see also section 3.5.3) and Turkana (Dimmendaal 1983), which have a general [αF] harmony but where particular affixes idiosyncratically resist the harmony rule. Under Combinatorial Specification, a possible analysis is that the idiosyncratic morphemes include [$-\alpha$F], thereby preventing harmony from applying. Representations with [αF], [$-\alpha$F], and "[0F]" for a single class of F-element combinations are consistent with Combinatorial Specification. Such representations are not consistent with Radical Underspecification, which allows only a [βF]/"[0F]" contrast within a single class of combinations. Nor are they consistent with Contrastive Underspecification, which allows only a [βF]/[$-\beta$F] contrast within a single class.

2.8.2.4 "Redundancy-free" Representations   A further implication of Combinatorial Specification is that representations are not necessarily "redundancy-free"; this contrasts with Radical Underspecification, which strives to remove all redundancy (see Mohanan 1991 for discussion of this issue). We have given an example of this in our discussion of Ainu (section 2.8.2.2). Although the feature specification [$+$back] is completely redundant/predictable on low vowels on the surface, it cannot be systematically excluded underlyingly.

2.8.2.5 Epenthesis Identity   Hualde (1991) discusses a case from Arbizu Basque with properties similar to those of Ainu, posing a real problem for Radical Underspecification: surface [e] is derived both from a completely unspecified mora and from a mora with some F-element(s) (established on the basis of phonological alternations). Under Combinatorial Specification, representations of the two /e/s in Arbizu Basque would be formally comparable to the representations of the two /i/s in Barrow Inupiaq or of the two /a/s, in Ainu.

Interestingly, although some cases of completely unspecified moras in Arbizu Basque are underlying, others are the result of prosodic epenthesis. An insight provided by Radical Underspecification is *epenthesis identity*: where epenthesis is purely prosodic, the surface form of the inserted vowel should be identical to that of any underlying featureless vowel. Somewhat surprisingly, Combinatorial Specification preserves this insight in Arbizu Basque, a language that Radical Underspecification incorrectly predicts should not exist.

2.8.2.6 Markedness   A final issue that arises in studies of feature specification is how to represent markedness. By *markedness* we refer roughly to the cross-linguistic statistical skewings of F-element behavior. For example, certain F-elements typically enjoy an active role cross-linguistically (e.g., [+low]); certain features tend to be active, although the active F-element may vary (e.g., [high]); certain F-elements are used contrastively much less frequently (e.g., [ATR]). The formal model of Combinatorial Specification makes no direct claims about the relation between markedness and whether a particular F-element is active or not.

Three general approaches to feature/F-element markedness exist: (i) markedness is encoded in feature theory itself, (ii) markedness is encoded in the theory of feature specification, and (iii) markedness theory is independent of theories of both features and feature specification. Combinatorial Specification is a theory of feature specification that does not encode markedness. On this score, Combinatorial Specification is comparable to the Radical and Contrastive Underspecification approaches, as we show below.

If the statistical asymmetries were encoded in the theory of F-elements, features would be monovalent (see Anderson and Ewen 1987, Ewen and van der Hulst 1987, van der Hulst 1988, 1989, Avery and Rice 1989). The basic idea behind this approach can be interpreted as claiming that the statistical asymmetries are so strong that they should be formalized as absolute properties. In effect, this aspect of the theory ceases to involve markedness per se, replacing notions of relative markedness by absolute prohibitions.

An interesting question to consider is the effect of such a move on the three theories of feature specification. First, there is no effect on Combinatorial Specification: the formal model simply allows the combination of F-elements, but does not make any stipulations on the F-elements themselves. This contrasts with Radical Underspecification, which disallows both [αF] and [−αF] underlyingly. If all features are monovalent, this restriction is irrelevant. Some distinctions would remain, however, between Radical Underspecification and Combinatorial Specification since underlying redundancies between monovalent features would be ruled out by Radical Underspecification, but tolerated in appropriate circumstances in Combinatorial Specification.

With regard to Contrastive Underspecification, the theory's defining property is that underlying representations are determined by finding pairs of segments that contrast by their specifications for some feature (e.g., i and e standardly contrast for [high]): any features that do not serve to contrast two segments are not included underlyingly (continuing the example, i would be specified [+high] and e would be specified [−high]; e would not be specified [−low] unless the system also included a low front vowel æ). If all features are monovalent, this means of determining which features are absent is irrelevant: no such contrastive pairs could exist. Thus, the formal models of both Radical and Contrastive Underspecification depend on feature theory including binary features. Combinatorial Specification, by contrast, does not depend on whether feature theory ultimately provides binary or unary features.

Encoding markedness in a theory of feature specification could involve specifying only the marked values of the (binary) features, a position taken in some views of Radical Underspecification (e.g., Kiparsky 1982, 1985, Grignon 1984, Pulleyblank 1986a): under this approach, unmarked values would be unspecified underlyingly. Other views of Radical Underspecification (e.g., Archangeli 1984, 1988, Abaglo and Archangeli 1989, Archangeli and Pulleyblank 1989) maintain that markedness is not equivalent to initial specification. Under the latter view, *marked* and *specified* are not synonymous, nor are they synonymous under Contrastive Underspecification. Similarly, Combinatorial Specification puts no intrinsic restrictions on which F-elements may be active and which are inert.

One of Mohanan's (1991) criticisms of theories that omit feature specifications is that such theories do not encode markedness. We agree with the essence of this observation, which leads to the third possibility: that markedness is encoded in a theory that is independent of theories of both features and feature specification. This is the approach explored in this book. In chapter 3, we present the Grounding Conditions, a theory of F-element interaction that is in large part a theory of markedness. We explore issues involving the marked and unmarked status of active versus inert features, along with a variety of other issues that involve markedness and F-element specifications—for example, structure preservation, and what may be opaque or transparent to a given rule. A further result demonstrated in chapter 3 is that Combinatorial Specification and the Grounding Conditions together are capable of expressing the central insights of Contrastive Underspecification without engendering the problems that model faces.

Chapter 3
Grounding Conditions

Le phonème est la somme des impressions acoustiques et des mouvements articulatoires, de l'unité entendue et de l'unité parlée, l'une conditionnant l'autre: ainsi c'est déjà une unité complexe, qui a un pied dans chaque chaîne.
Ferdinand de Saussure, *Cours de linguistique générale*

In chapter 2, we established that representations are composed of F-elements and that F-elements may combine with each other in paths. Were such combinatorial possibilities completely unconstrained, then the number of possible combinations would be extremely large. For example, if one were to assume 20 F-elements (a fairly conservative estimate), then there would be 2^{20} possible F-element combinations, that is, 1,048,576.

While it is true that languages exhibit a fairly rich array of combinatorial possibilities, it is also true that the range noted above appears far too high when actually attested combinations are considered. The F-element combinations that natural languages exploit are a small subset of the logically possible combinations of their active F-elements. We are led to the conclusion that phonological theory requires some kind of conditions limiting the combinations of F-elements.

Introducing conditions in an unconstrained manner, however, would create at least as many problems as it would solve. Even if conditions are formally restricted, for example, to implicational statements like *If p then q* and *If p then not q*, the number of such conditions would be extremely high. To return to the example just cited, in a system with 20 F-elements, there are 760 implicational statements (positive or negative) involving the combination of exactly 2 F-elements.[1] We are led to ask, "What are the conditions on the conditions?"

In this chapter, we explore the hypothesis that conditions used in natural language directly reflect physical correlates of the F-elements involved. Thus, such conditions are physically *grounded*. As an example, consider certain physical properties associated with the F-element [+nasal]. On the one hand, velic opening allows air to pass freely through the nasal cavity, resulting in a configuration where there is no appreciable buildup of pressure. This produces a situation amenable to periodic vocal cord vibration (Ladefoged 1989). Nasal segments are typically characterized by such modal voicing in languages of the world (Ladefoged and Maddieson 1986). Apart from the fact that velic lowering produces a configuration conducive to voicing, this is presumably due to difficulties involved in the perception of voiceless nasals (Ohala 1975, Ladefoged and Maddieson 1986). The result is a phonetically based implicational relation between nasality and voicing: *If [+nasal] then [+voiced]*. Since this implicational condition reflects a physical correlation between [+nasal] and [+voiced], it is permitted under the Grounding Hypothesis. A proscribed condition would be one like *If [+nasal] then [−voiced]*: this condition is ruled out since it does not directly reflect physical correlates of [+nasal] and [−voiced]. (See Stevens, Keyser, and Kawasaki 1986 on relations between the physical correlates of features, and D. Pulleyblank 1989, Cohn 1990, and Gerfen, to appear, for discussion of the phonological role of conditions involving [+nasal].)

Such physically grounded conditions form the substantive core of Grounding Theory, a hypothesis with numerous testable predictions. We demonstrate that Grounding Theory has a wide range of desirable consequences, explaining phonological and phonetic properties of specific languages (rule formalization and rule application, phenomena such as opacity and transparency, neutralization; see Kiparsky 1973), properties of cross-linguistic variation, diachronic change, and so on. In addition to these results, Grounding Theory derives the robust Structure Preservation effect (Kiparsky 1985) and the robust properties of Contrastive Underspecification, at the same time both permitting certain attested phenomena that are proscribed by both these theories and accounting for a variety of phenomena that neither addresses.

In the following sections, we lay out the formal and substantive theory of Grounding Conditions. We then exemplify the proposal by exploring a range of facts involving the interaction of the feature [ATR] with tongue height features. The final section of this chapter addresses a variety of implications of the model, including discussion of Structure Preservation and Contrastive Underspecification.

3.1 The Grounding Hypothesis

In this section, we lay out the formal model of implicational statements responsible for determining the well-formedness of paths. We then address the substantive instantiation of such formal conditions, providing a specific example of the model by examining the interaction of tongue height and tongue root features. We argue that the types of patterns predicted to occur by Grounding Theory are those actually attested; the types of patterns predicted to be impossible, on the other hand, do not appear to exist.

3.1.1 Formal Properties of Path Conditions

In this book, we focus on F-elements and the relations between them. Thus, the type of conditions that we focus on are those that define relations between F-elements. Evidence from languages in chapter 2 shows that conditions on such relations hold only of F-elements *in paths*. For instance, the distribution of vowels in Tiv verbs motivates single morphemes with both [+ high] and [+ low] floating, yet the association of these F-elements is restricted such that they do not link up in a single path. As a result, the conditions we are concerned with are those over F-elements in paths, that is, *path conditions*.[2]

(1) *Path condition*

   A path condition is an implicational statement that determines whether paths between F-elements are well formed or ill formed.

There are four aspects to note about this definition of path conditions: (i) they are implications (ii) that define well-formedness or ill-formedness of (iii) relations (encoded as a path) (iv) between F-elements. We now consider formal implications of each of these components of path conditions.[3]

First, path conditions are *implicational statements*. Of the class of logically possible implicational relations between F-elements, we claim that two such relations are required for the expression of linguistically significant relations, namely, the implications of (2). We argue that both positive and negative formulations of conditions, as appropriate, can be important for an understanding of phonological systems because of the substantive content of phonological representations.[4] Formally, such implications have the structure given in (2).

(2) *Implicational statements*

   a. Positive   If *p* then *q*.

   b. Negative   If *p* then not *q*.

A positive path condition (2a) makes the requirement that a path involving some F-element *p* is well formed only when the F-element *q* is also present on the path. For example, a language could require that all low vowels be back (*If [+ low] then [+ back]*), or that all vowels with an advanced tongue root be high (*If [+ ATR] then [+ high]*). The truth values for such an implication are shown in (3a).

(3)   Representation

Condition	p present q not present $(p, \neg q)$	p present q present (p, q)	p not present q present $(\neg p, q)$	p not present q not present $(\neg p, \neg q)$
a. If p then q	F	T	T	T
b. If p then not q	T	F	T	T

A negative path condition (2b) prohibits the cooccurrence of two F-elements on a path. That is, it states that in order for some F-element p to be present in a path, the F-element q must not be present; the presence of q on a path with p would render the representation ill formed. For example, a language might prohibit voicing from appearing on obstruents (*If [− sonorant] then not [+ voiced]*), or a language might rule out low vowels with an advanced tongue root (*If [+ low] then not [+ ATR]*). The truth values for a negative implication are shown in (3b).

In a fully specified representation all of whose features are binary, there is no difference between a positive condition and a corresponding negative one. For example, the conditions *If [+ low] then [− ATR]* and *If [+ low] then not [+ ATR]* both prohibit the representation [+low, +ATR] and allow the representations [+low, −ATR], [−low, +ATR], [−low, −ATR]. Within a theory adopting full specification, therefore, a single type of implicational condition would be required, either positive or negative equivalently.

In partially specified representations, however, and in representations allowing a class of monovalent features, the situation is different. Consider for example a language in which Dorsal, Labial, and Coronal define single articulated consonants, and in which no double articulations are permitted. Given monovalent articulator nodes, such implications can only be expressed negatively: *If Dorsal then not Labial*, and so on. In a theory where absence of specification cannot be referred to (see Pulleyblank 1986a, Clements and Ṣonaiya 1989, Akinlabi 1993), this relation cannot be expressed positively. In marked contrast, consider a situation where a Labial glide must obligatorily be Dorsal (labiodental [w] vs. labial [ʋ]); such a relation can only be expressed positively, *If Labial then Dorsal*.

Note that no logical distinction is made by formulating a condition positively, as in (3a), or negatively with negated consequent, as in (3b). Independent of the expression of an implication, the theory and/or the analysis determines whether features are monovalent or binary, and if binary, whether one or the other value is phonologically present; whatever is determined on this count establishes the expression of any relevant implicational relationship as involving a positive or a negative consequent. Note in this regard that for the chart in (3), in a case where p or q is a binary feature, then

¬*p* and ¬*q* indicate either (i) the opposite feature value to that designated by *p* or *q*, or (ii) the absence of a specification *p* or *q* in the representation; in a case where *p* or *q* is a monovalent feature, then ¬*p* and ¬*q* refer solely to the absence of a specification *p* or *q*. It should be stressed that representational properties determine the appropriate formal expression of an implicational relationship, not vice versa.

Second, we assume that path conditions simply determine whether a path relation between F-elements is *well formed* or *ill formed*, consistent with our position that representations at all levels are well formed (Well-formedness Principle (24), chapter 1). As such, path conditions are *inert*, their role in language being solely to state the well-formedness of phonological representations. Important for certain results below, the conditions proposed here do *not* have the effect of automatically inducing changes in F-element representations: they neither insert nor remove particular F-elements or paths. Such inertness results from the Well-formedness Principle: path conditions define well-formedness and ill-formedness, and the Well-formedness Principle insists on well-formed representations. Given the model thus far, the "inertness" position is the null hypothesis.[5] The proposal here is that ill-formed representations, defined by universal and language-specific conditions, are invariably disallowed.

Third, since path conditions define *relations* between F-elements, the well-formedness of a path in a language can only be determined by reference to F-elements that are active in that language. An inactive F-element is not present in any representation. Therefore, it does not occur in any paths with other features and it cannot be referred to in any path condition. That is, if some F-element *r* is not present in a particular language's representations, then there can be no active path conditions *If r then q, If r then not q, If p then r, If p then not r*. We assume, therefore, the following metaconstraint on conditions:

(4) *Activation Condition*

    A path condition Φ is active in some language L only if representations in L include values for both the antecedent and consequent of Φ.

Just as in the determination of whether a path condition should be expressed positively or negatively, the representations of a language determine the relevance of a condition—a condition referring to some F-element α could not in and of itself cause α to be considered active. Were this not the case, then spurious conditions could have completely unwanted results. To see this, imagine that a language actively uses the F-elements [−back] and [+round], and that the language exhibits no evidence of tongue root activity. To rule out the possibility of front rounded vowels, such a language could, without the Activation Condition, invoke a condition such as *If [−back, +round] then [+ATR]*. Since [ATR] is not active, and since no front round vowel could therefore have the value [+ATR], such vowels would be ruled out by the invoking of a completely irrelevant condition.

It is particularly important in this regard to distinguish between two sources for a representation p, $\neg r$ (p without r): some F-element p occurs in combination without some F-element r. On the one hand, such a representation might occur in a particular lexical item in a language where both p and r are active. If the condition *If p then r* were imposed in this language, then the representation p, $\neg r$ would be ill formed. On the other hand, the representation p, $\neg r$ could occur in a language because r was not an active F-element at all. In this case, since r occurs in no representations at all, no path condition could refer to r and the path condition *If p then r* could not be invoked. A condition like *If p then r* can only be used to rule out configurations where both p and r are present.

Finally, path conditions define relations between *F-elements*. This raises the possibility that the very nature of F-elements themselves may determine properties of path conditions. In the next section, we explore this possibility, that the formal flexibility of path conditions is curtailed by the physical nature of the F-elements involved.

3.1.2 Substantive Properties of Path Conditions

As just outlined, the set of formal implicational statements is extremely rich, far too rich when actually occurring conditions are considered. We argue that the set of path conditions attested in human languages is restricted to implications that are rooted in physical properties of the vocal tract or speech signal (see Stevens, Keyser, and Kawasaki 1986): the flexibility of the formal theory is substantively constrained by physical properties. In this section, we concentrate on what it means to be "physically grounded"; in the remainder of the chapter, we explore ways in which grounded implications manifest themselves in various languages.

To focus the discussion of grounding, we examine the interaction of the tongue root position ([±ATR]) and tongue body height ([±high] and [±low]). These F-elements form an appropriate starting point for this study because their physical interaction is relatively well understood compared to that of many other feature pairs (see references throughout this section). The tongue body and the tongue root are physically connected. This connection takes on particular importance because of the incompressibility of the tongue. Constriction of the tongue in one area requires its expansion in another and, conversely, expansion of the tongue in one area requires its constriction in another (see Ladefoged et al. 1972). As a result, a gesture in one dimension typically correlates with a compensatory gesture in another dimension.[6]

Consider first the relation of the tongue root with upward movement of the tongue body, formally represented as [+high]. In the achievement of an upward displacement of the tongue body, there tends to be a constriction advancing the tongue root (see Perkell 1971, Ladefoged et al. 1972, Jacobson 1980). That is, raising of the tongue body tends to correlate with tongue root advancement. This is depicted in (5).[7]

(5) *[+high] implies [+ATR], not [−ATR]*

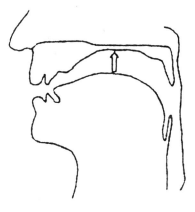
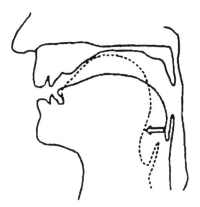

The opposite effect results from lowering the tongue body (formally [+low]): downward displacement of the tongue body tends to correlate with tongue root retraction, as sketched in (6).

(6) *[+low] implies [−ATR], not [+ATR]*

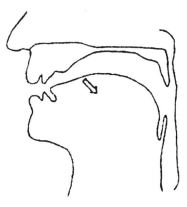
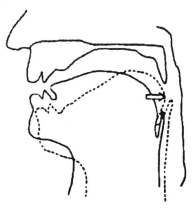

These correlations are supported by work such as MacKay's (1976) study of the degree of tongue root advancement in English vowels. Supporting work suggesting that the "tense/lax" distinction in English involves the tongue root (see Halle and Stevens 1969, Perkell 1971), MacKay came to the conclusion that the degree of tongue root advancement varies with tongue height, with greater advancement in high vowels than in mid, and greater advancement in mid vowels than in low.[8]

The interrelation is succinctly described by Jacobson (1980).

(7) Physiologically, one of the means to raise the body of the tongue is to pull the root of the tongue forward, since, as an incompressible body of constant mass, if the tongue is constricted in one area it will expand in another. Thus it is not an unusual expectation for higher vowels to have a tongue root which is more advanced [than] that for lower vowels ... (p. 185)

MacKay (1976) also found that greater advancement occurs with front vowels than with back: the model offered here predicts that this, too, should be reflected in phonological patterning. While we believe that this is correct (see the discussions of Kinande and Akan in this chapter and of Lango in chapter 5, for example), we focus here on [ATR] in connection specifically with the tongue height features.[9]

Labeling Grounded Path Conditions

Grounded conditions are referred to as either *X/Y Condition* or simply as *X/Y*. X refers to the antecedent and Y to the consequent. For example, *HI/ATR Condition* or *HI/ATR* refers to the condition in (8a), *If [+high] then [+ATR]/If [+high] then not [−ATR]*.

The two formal path conditions are given in (8a,b), corresponding to (5) and (6), respectively.

(8) *Grounded path conditions:* α/ATR

a.	HI/ATR Condition:	If [+high] then [+ATR].	If [+high] then not [−ATR].
b.	LO/ATR Condition:	If [+low] then [−ATR].	If [+low] then not [+ATR].

The formal statements of these conditions encode two types of relations. Synergistic, or *sympathetic*, gestures are encoded in the positive implication, while *antagonistic* gestures are encoded in the negative implication (see Perkell 1971, Ladefoged et al. 1972). We note a close relation between Stevens, Keyser, and Kawasaki's (1986) notion of "enhancement" and the notion of "sympathetic" relation. In cases like those of (8), one could say that tongue root advancement *enhances* tongue body raising, and that tongue root retraction *enhances* tongue body lowering (see Halle and Stevens 1969). Since positive and negative expressions of implications constitute different aspects of the same physical dependence, we consider them versions of a single condition.

It is important to note that the interdependency between tongue root and tongue body movements constitutes a tendency, not an absolute correlation. For example, while high vowels tend cross-linguistically to involve an advanced tongue root, it is nevertheless possible for a given language to contrast different tongue root values for high vowels. It is this aspect of the interdependency that makes the topic of particular interest phonologically, and we return to it in detail shortly.

The second substantive type of implication involves changes in tongue height implied by a movement of the tongue root: movement of the tongue root tends to be accompanied by a sympathetic movement of the tongue body, as described for example by Hall and Hall (1980).

(9) [A]s the tongue root is moved forward, the tongue body is compressed and
    therefore raised. Conversely, as the tongue root is retracted, the tongue body
    is pulled down and therefore lowered. Either, or both, gestures, therefore,
    may result in some difference in the position of the tongue body during the
    articulation of the two vowel sets [those with and those without tongue root
    advancement] ... (p. 207)

The figures in (10) schematically illustrate the effects on tongue body height when the tongue root position is altered.

(10) *Implications of tongue root position*

    a. [+ATR] implies [+high], not [−high].
    b. [+ATR] implies [−low], not [+low].

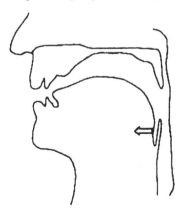
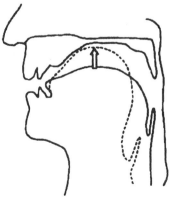

   c. [−ATR] implies [−high], not [+high].
   d. [−ATR] implies [+low], not [−low].

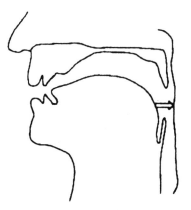 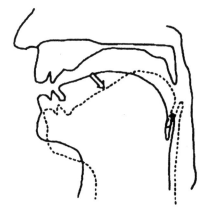

These dependencies are expressed formally in the following four path conditions, two relating advancement of the tongue root to tongue body height (as in (10a,b)) and two relating retraction of the tongue root to tongue body height (as in (10c,d)).[10]

(11) *Grounded path conditions: ATR/[vowel height] and RTR/[vowel height]*

    a. ATR/HI Condition: If [+ATR] then   If [+ATR] then not
                          [+high].   [−high].

    b. ATR/LO Condition: If [+ATR] then   If [+ATR] then not
                          [−low].   [+low].

    c. RTR/HI Condition: If [−ATR] then   If [−ATR] then not
                          [−high].   [+high].

    d. RTR/LO Condition: If [−ATR] then   If [−ATR] then not
                          [+low].   [−low].

The conditions in (8) and (11) together constitute the set of grounded path conditions involving [ATR], [high], and [low]: we claim that only these conditions reflect the physiologically preferred configurations of tongue body height and tongue root.

Before turning to the phonological support for precisely these conditions, we place them in the context of a formal theory of conditions.

3.1.3 Grounding Theory

The central issue at this point is to define the relationship between the substantive conditions noted above and the formal apparatus of path conditions discussed in the preceding section. The essence of our proposal is that in the unmarked case, languages are grounded in their phonetic substance. This is formally stated as the Grounding Conditions.

(12) *The Grounding Conditions*

    I. Path conditions invoked by languages must be phonetically motivated.

    II. The stronger the phonetic motivation for a path condition Φ,

        a. the greater the likelihood of invoking Φ,

        b. the greater the likelihood of assigning a wide scope to Φ within a grammar,

      and vice versa.

We call path conditions that are in accord with Grounding Condition I *grounded path conditions*.

It is important to distinguish two rather different types of claims involving the notion of grounding. First, Grounding Condition I makes an absolute claim regarding the class of possible path conditions. It states that a path condition may be invoked in natural language only if it reflects a physical dependence between two F-elements. The phonetic relation may be sympathetic or antagonistic, it may be physiologically or acoustically motivated—but it must exist. A path condition not expressing such a phonetically motivated relation may not be invoked in any natural language.

With respect to the tongue body height and tongue root features, the substantive conditions given in (8) and (11) are proposed to be the exhaustive list of grounded path conditions that may be invoked by languages. Given the formal device of positive and negative versions of implicational conditions, this set constitutes 37.5% of the logically possible conditions. Assuming the three features [±high], [±low], and [±ATR], 16 conditions involving an implication between two F-elements are possible; of these 16 conditions, 10 are ruled out as not belonging to the grounded set given in (8) and (11). That is, 62.5% of the logically possible implications are excluded from the substantively allowed class. The logically possible conditions that are excluded are given in (13).

(13) *Proscribed conditions*

If [+high] then [−ATR].	If [+high] then not [+ATR].
If [+low] then [+ATR].	If [+low] then not [−ATR].
If [−high] then [+ATR].	If [−high] then not [−ATR].
If [−high] then [−ATR].	If [−high] then not [+ATR].
If [−low] then [+ATR].	If [−low] then not [−ATR].
If [−low] then [−ATR].	If [−low] then not [+ATR].

If [+ATR] then [−high].   If [+ATR] then not [+high].
If [+ATR] then [+low].   If [+ATR] then not [−low].
If [−ATR] then [+high].   If [−ATR] then not [−high].
If [−ATR] then [−low].   If [−ATR] then not [+low].

The Grounding Hypothesis states that if a path condition does not express a grounded relationship, it can *never* be invoked in natural language.[11] The predictions here are absolute: the hypothesis would be refuted by a language that invoked a path condition that did not express a physiological or acoustic relation between two F-elements. With respect to [ATR], [high], and [low], evidence for one of the conditions in (13) would refute the hypothesis advanced in Grounding Condition I.

In contrast to the absolute predictions made by Grounding Condition I, Grounding Condition II makes predictions about cross-linguistic and intralinguistic tendencies.

Consider the implicational statements given in (14).

(14) a. If [+low] then [−ATR]; if [+low] then not [+ATR].

   b. If [+high] then [+ATR]; if [+high] then not [−ATR].

   c. If [−back] then [+ATR]; if [−back] then not [−ATR].

   d. If L-tone then [+ATR]; if L-tone then not [−ATR].

All four statements are phonetically motivated. The first two have already been discussed. The third is motivated in a manner similar to the condition involving [+high]: raising or fronting of the tongue body will tend to be accompanied by tongue root advancement, not tongue root retraction (as briefly noted above). The fourth condition is also phonetically motivated: lowering the larynx is one way of causing the type of lowered pitch appropriate for a L-tone; since larynx lowering is also a way of increasing the volume of the pharyngeal cavity, one expects a correlation between tonal values and values for [ATR] (see Painter 1976, Lindau 1979, Denning 1989).

Although the four conditions in (14) are all phonetically motivated, each appears to have a different status with respect to strength.[12] Our basic hypothesis in this regard is that there will be a correlation between the robustness of a phonetic relation and the tendency for that relation to express itself phonologically, both (i) in terms of the number of languages that invoke the relation, and (ii) in terms of the scope of the relation within the language that invokes it. The strength hypothesis is only half developed in this book, however. We note cases where phonological evidence suggests that certain conditions are more robust than others, but we leave largely unaddressed the question of whether phonological robustness correlates straightforwardly with phonetic strength.

Of the four conditions in (14), phonological patterns suggest that (14a) is the strongest. Languages with an [ATR] contrast in low vowels appear to be fairly rare;

languages with an [ATR] contrast in low vowels but not in high vowels ((14a) invoked, (14b) not invoked) appear to be extremely rare.[13] Our conclusion, admittedly fairly impressionistic, is that most languages have low vowels that are not [+ATR]; hence, the condition in (14a) is a very strong one. With regard to (14b), there seems to be a very clear tendency for high vowels to be [+ATR], but there exists a large class of languages where high vowels exhibit an [ATR] contrast.[14] We conclude that the condition in (14b) is strong, but not as strong as that in (14a). Moving on to the third and fourth conditions in (14), we note a marked reduction in strength. While numerous languages can be shown to exhibit the first two conditions in (14), manifestations of the latter two appear to be much less frequent. Moreover, while the first two conditions may commonly govern representations as a whole, the latter two often seem restricted to particular rule-governed contexts. For example, in Lango (Woock and Noonan 1979, as well as chapter 5), a rule of regressive [ATR] harmony incorporates a restriction involving the class of high front vowels. The correlation between frontness and tongue root advancement does not govern the inventory as a whole in Lango ([i, ɪ, u, ʊ] all occur), but it does affect the operation of a particular rule. Similarly, the type of tonal relation expressed in (14d) affects a very specific aspect of the interpretation of low vowels in Kinande (section 3.4.1.2) but does not restrict [ATR] values in general to vowels of a particular tonal type.

We propose, therefore, that every grounded path condition be assigned a particular strength. The strength value encodes the degree to which it is likely that a language incorporates a particular condition. We claim that the frequency of occurrence of a condition cross-linguistically will correlate with the extent to which the condition will apply widely throughout a grammar, and we speculate that such phonological manifestations of strength will correlate with the robustness of the phonetic motivation for a condition. Although it is perhaps unlikely that a language will be governed by a weak condition, a weak, but grounded, condition may be invoked in a marked case, often with respect to a particular rule. Since quantitative analysis of phonetic and cross-linguistic patterns is clearly beyond the possibilities of the current study, we will restrict indications of strength to impressionistic values: a condition may be *very strong* (14a), *strong* (14b), *medium* (14c), or *weak* (14d).[15]

We illustrate these strength differences by considering a pattern of sound changes observed by Elugbe (1982) to have taken place in the Ẹdoid language family of Nigeria.

3.1.3.1 Differing Strengths: Language Change in Ẹdoid
With regard to diachronic effects on language, a theory of grounded conditions of varying strengths makes the clear prediction that strongly antagonistic feature combinations should be the most prone to phonological change while strongly sympathetic feature combinations should be the most stable. For example, high front advanced vowels and low back

retracted vowels should be very stable, while low advanced vowels and high retracted vowels should exhibit both synchronic and diachronic variability. Where the evidence for an antagonistic representation is weak, change is expected to occur.

In a discussion of the vowels of Proto-Ẹdoid, Elugbe (1982) posits that Proto-Ẹdoid had a 10-vowel system; in our terms, Proto-Ẹdoid had no constraints on the combination of ATR with tongue body features. However, of the 20 present-day Ẹdoid languages considered by Elugbe, all but 1 have reduced the vowel inventory by one, two, or three vowels. The vowels that shift are [+high, −ATR] vowels and [+low, +ATR] vowels. The patterns of shift are shown in (15). Vowels without reduction "routes" in (15) did not shift.

(15) *Vowel reduction routes in Ẹdoid* (Elugbe 1982: 109)

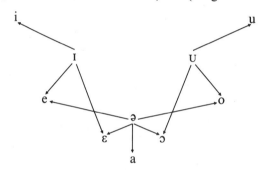

Significantly, the shifts shown in (15) are restricted in two ways: (i) which combinations shift and (ii) where they go. Inspection reveals that the F-element combinations that are subject to shift are those that contain the most antagonistic F-element combinations, [+high, −ATR] (defined as antagonistic by HI/ATR and RTR/HI) and [+low, +ATR] (defined as antagonistic by LO/ATR and ATR/LO). Moreover, the strength of the condition defining the antagonism determines the frequency of the change. In the table in (16), the numbers of daughter languages imposing the three conditions LO/ATR, HI/ATR, and BK/ATR are indicated.[16]

(16) *Ẹdoid: 20-language sample* (Elugbe 1982)

LO/ATR	(*ə)	19 languages: 95%
HI/ATR	(*ɪ, *ʊ)	12 languages: 60%
HI/ATR & BK/ATR	(*ɪ)	2 languages: 10%
No conditions	(i/ɪ, e/ɛ, ə/a, o/ɔ, u/ʊ)	1 language: 5%

Assuming that Elugbe's analysis of Proto-Ẹdoid as a 10-vowel system is correct, it is interesting to note that the status quo is maintained in only a single language, Dẹgẹma. This is not surprising if the Grounding Hypothesis is correct: in the unmarked case, strong conditions are imposed. With regard to the strength of conditions,

LO/ATR is imposed in the 19 languages other than Dẹgẹma—clearly establishing it as a very strong condition (see Ladefoged 1968). HI/ATR is strong, holding in 12 out of 20 languages, but by no means as frequent as LO/ATR. Finally, BK/ATR is much weaker, holding only of 2 languages.

Four inventories are therefore attested in the daughter languages.[17] First, the full 10-vowel system is possible where no conditions are imposed.

(17) i/ɪ   u/ʊ   Dẹgẹma
      e/ɛ   o/ɔ
            ə/a

Where LO/ATR is the only condition imposed, a 9-vowel system results.

(18) i/ɪ   u/ʊ   Ẹgẹnẹ, Ẹrụwa, Isoko, Uvbiẹ, Ẹmhalhẹ
      e/ɛ   o/ɔ
            a

With HI/ATR supplementing LO/ATR, a 7-vowel pattern is derived.

(19) i   u   Okpẹ, Urhobo, Ẹdo, Aoma, Avbianwu,
      e/ɛ   o/ɔ   Auchi, Unẹmẹ, Ghotuọ, Ọlọma, Uhami,
            a   Ehuẹun, Ukue

Finally, if BK/ATR is imposed in addition to both LO/ATR and HI/ATR, 8 vowels result.

(20) i   u/ʊ   Epie, Ibilo
      e/ɛ   o/ɔ
            a

Interestingly, the relatively weak condition BK/ATR holds only in conjunction with HI/ATR, not as a general condition. That is, not all front vowels are advanced, nor are all back vowels retracted; only front high vowels surface systematically with the value defined by BK/ATR.

The patterns of F-element combinations (whether phonological or phonetic) that result from the shifts observed in Ẹdoid are understandable in terms of the notion of antagonistic F-elements (note discussion in section 3.3.1). Without a theory such as the Grounding Conditions model, which brings out the intimate physical connection between F-elements, it would be surprising that only 3 of the 10 Proto-Ẹdoid vowels are subject to shift; it would also be surprising that the directions of shift are restricted depending on the segment undergoing the change.

We conclude, then, that the diachronic patterns of vowel reduction in Ẹdoid languages confirm predictions made by the Grounding Conditions model: that the

Grounding Conditions identify the antagonistic F-element combinations that are the most likely to undergo change and that the phonetic interpretation of these combinations of antagonistic F-elements determines the direction the change is likely to take.

In general, we have argued in this introduction to Grounding Condition II that stronger conditions are (i) likely to be invoked (IIa) and (ii) likely to have the widest scope possible, governing representations in general, and therefore any rules operating on such representations (IIb). By contrast, weaker conditions are (i) not particularly likely to be invoked and (ii) likely to hold only of representations created by a particular rule or rules, or of particular stages in the derivation.

Grounding Theory therefore combines the absolute prohibition of some patterns with the claim for other patterns that a cross-linguistic survey will show a tendency for languages to curtail the types of paths invoked. Grounding Condition I makes the absolute claim that paths considered well formed by any language must be phonetically grounded. Grounding Condition II makes a statement about *markedness*: the path conditions allowed by Grounding Condition I will tend to be invoked or not invoked as a function of their strength factor. Crucially, an isolated example of a language not invoking a strong path condition in some domain, or an isolated example of a language invoking a weak, but grounded, condition, does not constitute a counterexample to the hypothesis. What would falsify Grounding Condition II would be the existence of a data base showing that languages do not maximize the use of strongly grounded path conditions.

The examples presented in this book constitute a data base that is consistent with the Grounding Conditions: the languages explored here typically make use of path conditions, both in the composition of representations in general and in the application of particular rules, and the path conditions invoked are of a grounded character.[18]

Two final points should be noted. First, the substantive conditions given in (8) and (11) are not intended to be *all* the conditions relevant for the feature [ATR]; they are proposed as those conditions that govern the interaction of [ATR] with the height features [high] and [low]. [ATR] interacts with additional properties as well, as noted in (14) and as seen in various syllable-related examples in this and the previous chapter (recall the syllable-related case discussed with regard to Eastern Javanese in chapter 2). In this chapter, we restrict our attention to features governing vowel height.

Finally, we wish to place the Grounding Hypothesis within the type of "formal versus natural" debate found in works such as Stampe 1979, Donegan and Stampe 1979, Anderson 1981. Following Anderson, we assume that phonological phenomena result from an interplay of formal and substantive phenomena, with factors of various kinds responsible for the full array of attested phonological patterns. The grounding claim is not that *all* processes are necessarily "natural" in their behavior, though we agree with Anderson that they typically will be, but rather that implicational conditions (if and when imposed) will be of a "natural" type.

3.1.4 Conclusion

We have presented a formal and substantive model of Grounding Conditions. The two central proposals that manifest themselves in numerous ways from now on are (i) that permissible cooccurrence conditions are drawn from a phonetically motivated set (Grounding Condition I), and (ii) that the absence of a strong condition is more costly to a grammar than the presence of such a condition (Grounding Condition II). We conjecture that initial hypotheses posited by a language learner reflect physically motivated conditions quite closely, but that more marked configurations, derived formally by removing strong conditions from the grammar or by adding weak ones, are developed in the face of positive evidence.

In the next section, we explore the role of [ATR] in a variety of languages, demonstrating that in all cases examined, the distribution of [ATR] values is either constrained by a grounded path condition or is unconstrained. In no case is the distribution of [ATR] crucially constrained by an ungrounded path condition. This same point holds for all examples involving [ATR] that are presented in this book.

3.2   The Distribution of [ATR]

This section exemplifies the Grounding Theory with respect to [ATR], [high], and [low]. It is divided into three parts. Section 3.2.1 addresses the predictions made by the Grounding Conditions about languages in which all specifications for [ATR] are completely predictable. Section 3.2.2 explores the role of grounded conditions in phonological rules. Section 3.2.3 presents cases in which [+ATR] is the active F-element; section 3.2.4 presents cases in which [−ATR] is active. Significantly, in all cases, the path conditions governing the distribution of [ATR] are grounded, as predicted by Grounding Condition I.

3.2.1   Predictable Values of [ATR]

Before examining how [ATR] combines with vowel height features in the representation of morphemes, it is important to ask how to characterize the distribution of [ATR] in languages where it plays no role at all. This is an important issue because in the majority of the world's languages, it would appear that [ATR] plays no contrastive role (Maddieson 1984). By far the most common vowel system is some variant of the triangular five-vowel system *I, E, A, O, U*; in such a system, there is no need for [ATR].[19] Assuming an account for this failure of [ATR] to function actively in most vowel systems, the next issue is to examine which value of [ATR] will function actively in the establishment of lexical contrasts in those languages where such contrasts are made (see Kiparsky 1981). Although the phonological rule base on which decisions are to be made concerning the latter issue is still quite small, there is a body of opinion that the active value should be [+ATR], a position receiving some synchronic support in the patterns observed for Lango in chapter 5. By and large, we leave this aspect of the issue of markedness for further research. For present purposes, we assume (21), taking (21a) with greater confidence than (21b).[20]

(21) *[ATR] Markedness Statement*

    a. [ATR] tends *not* to be used actively.

    b. If used actively, the active value of [ATR] tends to be [+ATR]; the passive value of [ATR] tends to be [−ATR].

In contrast to this pattern, features like [high], [low], and [back] tend to be used actively; thus, these features have a positive first clause in their Markedness Statements (see Ladefoged and Maddieson 1990). The active values combine in the manner described in chapter 2 to produce a five-vowel pattern *I, E, A, O, U*; see section 3.6.1.3. Such a system may be specified further, however, with features playing no contrastive role in a standard five-vowel system, features like [round] and [ATR].

Focusing on [ATR] there are numerous ways by which values could be assigned to vowels. Given (21a), in the least marked language (at least with respect to [ATR]), [ATR] is assigned by rule, not present underlyingly. Further, by (21b), [+ATR] is the specification that is assigned. By the Grounding Conditions, the least marked language is one in which [+ATR] is assigned subject to the substantive conditions in (8) and (11), specifically the ATR/HI, HI/ATR, ATR/LO, and LO/ATR Conditions.

As illustration, consider the combination of [+ATR] with high, mid, and low vowels, respectively. With a high vowel, the assignment of [+ATR] satisfies all four conditions; with a mid vowel, ATR/HI does not hold, although all other conditions are respected; with a low vowel, the assignment of [+ATR] would require abandonment of three out of four conditions (ATR/HI, ATR/LO, LO/ATR). The prediction is that the maximally grounded five-vowel system would therefore have [+ATR] high vowels and [−ATR] mid and low vowels. (Recall that the Activation Condition (4) prevents the conditions in (22a) from holding until [+ATR] is activated (via insertion).)

(22) *Grounded unmarked pattern*

    a. [ ] → [+ATR], subject to ATR/HI, HI/ATR, ATR/LO, LO/ATR

    b. I   U   i   u
       E   O → ε   ɔ
          A   a

This pattern is the one found in languages like Greek, Zulu, and Ainu. In Maddieson's survey, it appears to be the most common instantiation of the five-vowel [I, E, A, O, U] pattern.

One point needs to be noted about the applicability of the HI/ATR Condition: the effect of the Activation Condition is that HI/ATR is not relevant until [+ATR] is inserted. But suppose that there were no Activation Condition: in this case, the representation prior to Unmarked [ATR] Insertion would be ill formed, thereby exerting pressure for the early application of [+ATR] Insertion. This runs counter to the evidence that redundant values are inserted late, if at all (see the "default values" box in section 2.2.1.3; also see Keating 1985, 1988, Pierrehumbert and Beckman 1988, Cohn 1989). Further, in the case of such completely redundant features, there appears to be a tendency for completely passive behavior of [ATR], behavior that is consistent with late assignment. We take this as further support for the Activation Condition and the Well-formedness Principle.

To summarize, the array in (22) is formally unmarked because (i) [ATR] plays no active role in the phonology (21a), (ii) when assigned, the active [ATR] F-element is [+ATR] (21b), and (iii) the assignment of [ATR] values is governed by the relevant substantive conditions ((8) and (11)). The thesis developed here distinguishes between various types of situations that depart from the absolutely unmarked pattern described in (22): more marked situations can be derived by modifications of any of these three properties.

Consider, for example, a somewhat more marked situation of the following type. As in the system already described, [ATR] plays no active role in the phonology. However, unlike the system described in (22), [−ATR] is assigned: this is more marked than (22) because it selects the marked value for (21b). According to a theory incorporating the Grounding Conditions, the inventory in (23) would be predicted.

(23) *Grounded marked pattern*

    a. [   ] → [−ATR], subject to RTR/LO, LO/ATR, RTR/HI, HI/ATR

    b. I   U   i   u

       E   O → e   o

           A   a

Maximal imposition of the Grounding Conditions in this type of pattern ensures that [−ATR] is assigned only to low vowels, the crucial condition being RTR/LO: *If [−ATR] then [+low]*. Although vowel patterns of this type are found in languages like Swahili, Luvale, and Garo, it appears from Maddieson's survey to be less common than the unmarked [i, ɛ, a, ɔ, u].

Independently of specific vowel systems, the general prediction from the combination of the [ATR] Markedness Statement and the Grounding Conditions is that there should be a strong preference for high [+ATR] vowels and low [−ATR] vowels. Furthermore, in the mid range the preference should be for [−ATR] vowels, although this preference should not be as strong as with the peripheral vowels. Maddieson's survey supports these results, as the table in (24) illustrates.[21]

(24) *Vowel frequency* (Maddieson 1984)

Number of languages with short vowels of the type indicated

[i]	271	[u]	254
[ɪ]	54	[ʊ]	48
[e]	83	[o]	88
[ɛ]	116	[ɔ]	100
"e"	113	"o"	113

[a]   274

Total sample = 317 languages

To summarize, the most common five-vowel systems are derived as follows. Combinations of tongue height features in conjunction with either [round] or [back] produce five vowels unspecified for tongue root position. Tongue root specifications are filled in by the assignment of either [+ATR], the unmarked pattern, or [−ATR], the marked pattern: both types of assignment are governed by the full set of applicable substantive conditions expressed in (8) and (11).

3.2.1.1 Conditions and Representations

Two general points should be stressed concerning the dependency of conditions on representations (rather than allowing representations to depend in some way on a language's choice of conditions).

First, because of the Activation Condition, Grounding Condition II maximizes only those conditions that govern features that are *active* in the language in question—it does not refer to conditions involving features that are not used distinctively and are not manipulated by phonological processes. Without this assumption, Grounding Condition II would predict the imposition of conditions even if the relevant features were not present. This would predict, for example, that in a language where [ATR] is inactive (the most common type of language), [+high] vowels, of necessity devoid of any [ATR] specification since [ATR] is inactive, would be ill formed because they would not respect the HI/ATR Condition: *If [+high] then [+ATR]*. To illustrate further, in Wolof and Yoruba (see sections 3.2.4.1 and 3.2.4.2) the RTR/HI and RTR/LO Conditions are relevant, but the ATR/HI and ATR/LO Conditions are not. This is expected since [−ATR] ("RTR"), not [+ATR], is active in these two languages. In contrast, ATR/HI and ATR/LO can play significant roles in languages where [+ATR] is active, for example, Pulaar (section 3.2.1.3) and Kinande (sections 3.2.3.1 and 3.4.1.2).

Second, the active F-elements in a language determine the precise versions of relevant conditions. The dependencies between features such as [±ATR], [±high], and [±low] do not vary as a function of the particular value that is specified for a binary feature. Grounded conditions govern the cooccurrence of particular types of elements, whether the formal specifications involved are of one value or the other. For example, the incompatibility of a high vowel and tongue root retraction is the same whether the high vowel is specified as [+high] or by the absence of a [high] specification, and whether the tongue root retraction is specified by [−ATR] or by the absence of tongue root specification. For example, in Yoruba (section 3.2.4.2), where [−high] is active, the positive version of RTR/HI, *If [−ATR] then [−high]*, is active since the positive version refers to [−high] (while the negative version refers to [+high]). In Wolof (section 3.2.4.1), we propose that [+high] is active: this means that the negative version of RTR/HI, the version referring to [+high], is relevant for Wolof (*If [−ATR] then not [+high]*). (See also section 3.6.1.3.)

Again, both of these points follow once we assume that path conditions in a language can only constrain F-elements that are present, as stated in the Activation Condition.

3.2.1.2 Absolute and Statistical Predictions   Before discussing cases where the role of [ATR] is not entirely passive, we distinguish between two types of predictions made by the Grounding Conditions as formulated in (12).

Consider a five-vowel system that is marked in two ways. First, [−ATR] rather than [+ATR] is assigned (see (21b)). Second, contra Grounding Condition II, the strong conditions of HI/ATR and RTR/HI do not hold on the output of this rule; [−ATR] is inserted subject to no path conditions at all and therefore affects all vowels.

(25) *Uniform [−ATR]*

   a. [   ] → [−ATR]

   b. I   U   I   U
       E   O → ɛ   ɔ
           A   a

Such a vowel system is by no means the unmarked five-vowel system. In Maddieson's (1984) survey, this pattern occurred in only two cases (Quechua and Southeastern Pomo; four others have [−ATR] high vowels with "generic" mid vowels "e" and "o," Luiseño, Hebrew, Tzeltal, and Mundari). Moreover, to replace the unconditioned assignment of [−ATR] by the unconditioned assignment of [+ATR] would produce even more undesirable results. Maddieson lists no systems of the type in (26).[22]

(26) *Uniform [+ATR]*

    a. [   ] → [+ATR]

    b. I   U   i   u

         E   O   →   e   o

              A   ạ

Consider the patterns described in (25) and (26). Such patterns are characterized as unlikely by the Grounding Conditions because they can only be derived by failing to implement strong conditions. In particular, the grounded conditions HI/ATR and RTR/HI fail to be invoked in (25), and LO/ATR and ATR/LO fail to be invoked in (26). Since all of these conditions are grounded (Grounding Condition I) and all of these conditions are strong (Grounding Condition II), they are expected to hold. It is important to note that Grounding Condition II does not absolutely rule out such systems, but assigns them a cost greater than that assigned to the systems in (22) and (23). Moreover, the pattern in (26) is analyzed as more marked than the pattern in (25) because the conditions that do not hold in (26), LO/ATR and ATR/LO, are stronger than the conditions that do not hold in (25), HI/ATR and RTR/HI.

In a theory without a principle akin to the Grounding Conditions, the patterns in (25) and (26) would be the least marked [ATR] patterns since they involve no extrinsic conditions on the cooccurrence of [ATR] with other features. The fact that such patterns are largely unattested demonstrates the inadequacy of such a theory. Evidence for the correctness of the general approach to conditions taken here is presented in various cases below, where increasingly more marked systems arise from the incremental suppression of grounded conditions.

Before we turn to such marked cases, consider vowel systems like those in (27), which are excluded by a theory including the Grounding Conditions, but logically possible in a theory without them.

(27) *Impossible patterns*

    a. [   ] → [−ATR], subject to *If [−ATR] then [+high]/not [−high]*

        I   U   ɪ   ᴜ

        E   O   →   e   o

            A   ạ

    b. [   ] → [−ATR], subject to *If [−ATR] then [−low]/not [+low]*

        I   U   ɪ   ᴜ

        E   O   →   ε   ɔ

            A   ạ

Like the grounded systems described in (22) and (23), these systems involve the assignment of some value of [ATR] in conjunction with a condition on [ATR] assignment. But unlike the systems described so far, these patterns are *absolutely* ruled out by Grounding Condition I:[23] the condition imposed to derive (27) does not belong to the set of conditions in (11). Substantively motivated conditions may be removed from a language's grammar, but any condition that is imposed must belong to the substantively motivated set.

3.2.1.3 Grounding and Pulaar [ATR] Harmony

Before concluding our discussion of cases where the distribution of [ATR] is entirely predictable, we reconsider the pattern of [ATR] in Pulaar (see Paradis 1986 and section 2.6.1). The underlying F-element inventory is unmarked with respect to [ATR] since [ATR] is not present (see [ATR] Markedness (21a)).[24] Unlike the cases discussed so far, however, [+ATR] is active in the language: it spreads leftward. Since [ATR] is not present underlyingly, it must be inserted. Our point in this section is that both the rule inserting [+ATR] and the rule spreading [+ATR] are grounded rules: [+ATR] Insertion is grounded by the ATR/HI Condition and [+ATR] Spread is grounded by the ATR/LO Condition. We review only the relevant properties of [ATR] harmony from chapter 2.

The first relevant fact is that in the absence of harmony, Pulaar exhibits a vowel system like the unmarked pattern of (22): [ATR] values are predictable; [+ATR] is redundantly assigned. Unlike in the cases shown so far, however, ATR/HI *cannot* be a condition on Pulaar in general. This is because of the additional fact that the predictable [+ATR] F-element of high vowels spreads leftward to any *mid* vowel. Recall forms of the type in (28), where the class suffixes of the first column (singular or plural suffixes) have a high vowel, while the class suffixes of the second column (diminutive plural) have a mid vowel.

(28) *Root + class marker*

[+ATR]	[−ATR]	
sof-ru	cɔf-ɔn	'poussin SG/DIM.PL'
ser-du	cɛr-kɔn	'crosse d'un fusil SG/DIM.PL'
ᵐbeel-u	ᵐbɛɛl-ɔn	'ombre SG/DIM.PL'
peec-i	pɛɛc-ɔn	'fente PL/DIM.PL'
beel-i	ᵐbɛɛl-ɔn	'flaque PL/DIM.PL'
dog-oo-ru	ⁿdɔg-ɔ-w-ɔn	'coureur SG/DIM.PL'

Such forms demonstrate that the [+ATR] F-element predictably assigned to high vowels spreads from right to left, affecting mid vowels. If the ATR/HI Condition (*If [+ATR] then [+high]/not [−high]*) were imposed generally, then [+ATR] mid vowels could not be derived at all. Note, however, that the ATR/HI Condition is not abandoned completely. Instead of constituting a general condition on representations, it holds solely of the output of [+ATR] Insertion (reproduced as (29)): a [+ATR] value *inserted by [+ATR] Insertion* must be on a path to [+high].[25]

(29) *Pulaar [+ATR] Insertion—Condition on targets: ATR/HI*

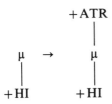

We have demonstrated that [+ATR] Insertion is grounded in Pulaar: although not all relevant path conditions hold of Pulaar representations, the one that does not, ATR/HI, holds of [+ATR] Insertion itself. The question next arises whether the harmonic rule, Pulaar [+ATR] Spread, is a grounded rule or not. Two conditions are crucially relevant: ATR/HI and ATR/LO. Unlike in the case of insertion, ATR/HI cannot be considered to hold of [+ATR] Spread because ATR/HI would restrict the targets to only the [+high] vowels, incorrectly ruling out mid vowels as targets. ATR/LO, a condition that so far has been assumed to hold of representations in Pulaar, permits [+ATR] to spread to mid vowels, but rules out low vowels as targets.

Consider relevant data such as the following. The low vowel [a] surfaces as [−ATR] regardless of context: even when followed by a high vowel, [a] is [−ATR]. This is exactly what is expected if ATR/LO holds of representations in Pulaar, including the output of [+ATR] Spread. (The symbol ạ indicates a [+ATR] low vowel.)

(30) *Low vowels are nonundergoers*

bɔɔt-aa-ri	'dîner'	*bootạạri
pɔɔf-aa-li	'respirations'	*poofạạli
nɔdd-aa-li	'appel'	*noddạạli
ⁿgɔr-aa-gu	'courage'	*ⁿgorạạgu

Importantly, the claim of the Grounding Conditions is that the Pulaar rule, governed by ATR/LO, is preferred to a similar rule spreading [+ATR], differing only by the absence of any condition, direct or indirect, on the height of the target.[26] Compare traditional graphic formulations of the Pulaar rule, with and without a condition restricting the rule from applying to a low target.

(31) a. *Governed by ATR/LO*   b. *Not governed by ATR/LO*

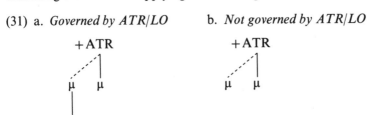

If the markedness of a rule increases with the complexity of a rule formulation, then traditional formulations of harmony would select the rule without the ATR/LO Condition (31b) as less marked than the rule including the ATR/LO Condition (31a). However, in terms of the formal model presented here, the rule of [+ATR] Spread that does not target low vowels is the less marked rule, because of the Grounding Conditions.

A second point of interest is that [a] not only fails to undergo harmony, but also blocks the transmission of the harmonic [+ATR] value: the mid vowels preceding a low vowel in (30) surface phonetically with a default retracted tongue root specification, not with the [+ATR] value that could potentially be supplied by the final high vowel.

(32) *Low vowels are opaque*

bɔɔt-aa-ri	'dîner'	*bootaari
pɔɔf-aa-li	'respirations'	*poofaali
nɔdd-aa-li	'appel'	*noddaali
ŋgɔr-aa-gu	'courage'	*ŋgoraagu

If the spreading rule were to apply across the low vowel, a configuration like that in (33) would be created. But as demonstrated in chapter 1, such a representation is ruled out since it violates Locality. (Syllable structure and associations of consonants to prosodic structure are omitted in this diagram.)

(33) *Locality Condition violation*

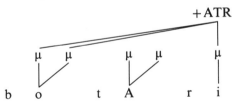

Sections 3.5 and 4.7 focus in more detail on issues raised by opacity and transparency effects. For the present, the crucial point is that the ATR/LO Condition substantively characterizes the class of opaque elements, opacity being formally derived by the Locality Condition.

A third point of interest is that Pulaar has three suffixes that induce [+ATR] Spread but have only mid vowels (Paradis 1986:145–50). We illustrate this pattern with the suffixes for class 9 (*-gol*) and class 8 (the diminutive singular, *-gel*); regular forms involving the class 21 suffix (diminutive plural, *-kɔn*) are included for purposes of comparison.

(34) *Mid-voweled suffixes inducing harmony*

Class 9	Class 8 dim. sg.	Class 21 dim. pl.	
lef-ol	lef-el	lɛf-ɔn	'ruban'
keer-ol	keer-el	kɛɛr-ɔn	'borne'
ceelt-ol	ceelt-el	cɛɛlt-ɔn	'coupure'
cef-ol	cef-el	cɛf-ɔn	'incantation'

We suggest what appears to be the minimal hypothesis, that the vowels of these suffixes are underlyingly assigned [+ATR] and therefore induce the general leftward spreading of [+ATR].[27]

Our analysis then requires both [+high] and (exceptional) [+ATR] vowels in underlying representation, but it has no [+high, +ATR] vowels in underlying representation. This might be interpreted as suggesting that underlying representations in Pulaar are governed by an *ungrounded* condition (*If [+high] then not [+ATR]* or *If [+ATR] then not [+high]*). This is not a necessary conclusion, however: there is absolutely no need for the absence of [+high, +ATR] vowels to be the result of a condition blocking their existence. This gap can be straightforwardly attributed to Representational Simplicity. All high vowels are [+ATR] on the surface; there is no phonological contrast between [+high] and [+high, +ATR] vowels. Representational Simplicity therefore selects [+high] over the more complex [+high, +ATR] for underlying forms. We conclude therefore that there is no need for an ungrounded condition such as *If [+high] then not [+ATR]* in this language: underlying representations are controlled only by LO/ATR and ATR/LO, conditions that rule out [+low, +ATR] vowels.

To summarize, although predictable in its distribution except for three special morphemes, [ATR] nevertheless plays an active role in the phonology of Pulaar. Three classes of vowels must be distinguished, the vowels belonging to each class being determined by grounded conditions on [ATR]. One class contains vowels that are redundantly assigned the active value [+ATR]: this class is defined by the ATR/HI Condition. The second class contains the vowels that are prohibited from receiving the active value [+ATR]: this class is defined by the ATR/LO Condition. The remaining class contains the vowels that may be harmonically assigned the active value [+ATR], namely, the mid vowels that are constrained neither by ATR/HI nor by ATR/LO. Thus, the Pulaar system is one step away from being completely grounded: ATR/HI is a condition on [+ATR] Insertion, but crucially it is not a condition on representations in general. In Pulaar, there is robust phonological evidence (in the form of harmonically derived [+ATR] mid vowels) that forces the language learner to posit a less grounded grammar: ATR/HI holds of a rule, but not

Pulaar Grounding

1. [ATR] is not active underlyingly (unmarked according to [ATR] Markedness (21a)).
2. [+ATR] is active (unmarked according to [ATR] Markedness (21b)).
3. ATR/HI holds of Pulaar [+ATR] Insertion, though not of representations (semimarked with respect to Grounding Condition II; consistent with Grounding Condition I).
4. ATR/LO holds of representations, therefore governing Pulaar [+ATR] Spread (unmarked with respect to Grounding Conditions I and II (12)).

Markedness Labels

After the discussion of each language in this chapter, we summarize the status of the analysis with respect to the Grounding Conditions. Terms found in these summaries are used as follows:

Unmarked: Respects any relevant markedness statement, or strong grounded condition holds of *representations*.

Semimarked: Grounded condition (weak or strong) invoked specifically for some *process*, but not for representations in general.

Marked: Some relevant markedness statement does not hold, or a strong grounded condition is not invoked.

One could also imagine the inclusion of an *impossible* class of cases, patterns of rules or representations that invoke ungrounded conditions. None appear to occur in our data, hence the Grounding Hypothesis.

of all representations—were it a condition on all representations in Pulaar, there would be no evidence of Pulaar [+ATR] Spread.[28]

An analysis of Pulaar invoking Grounding Theory makes numerous predictions, some involving markedness and some involving impossible patterns.

For example, it is predicted that there could be a language differing from Pulaar only in terms of the predictability of [ATR] assignment, not in terms of the classes of segments involved, that is, in terms of [ATR] Markedness (21a). For such a pattern, [+ATR] would be assigned idiosyncratically to certain high vowels in lexical representations, with spreading only from this lexically specified class. In the next section, we demonstrate that Kinande is essentially this type of language.

A second class of languages predicted to occur is one with fewer path conditions. Regardless of the values for the [ATR] Markedness Statement, such a language is more marked (see Grounding Condition II). Akan is one such language; discussion of Akan follows discussion of Kinande.

A third class of cases predicted to occur is a set of languages involving [−ATR] as the active value, that is, cases that are marked with regard to [ATR] Markedness (21b). Various types are predicted to occur. For example, there could be a language essentially comparable to Pulaar but involving the opposite value of [ATR]. If [−ATR] Insertion were fully grounded in such a case, [−ATR] would be assigned only to *low* vowels in accord with the RTR/LO Condition (11). With a partially grounded rule of spreading comparable to that of Pulaar, mid vowels would contextually undergo harmony and high vowels would block harmony because of the ATR/HI Condition (11). Although such cases are predicted to occur, we do not know of any, although Yoruba and Eastern Javanese (both discussed in chapter 2) come close in significant respects.

The second class of predictions involves rules that should not occur: Grounding Condition I predicts the impossibility of rules of insertion or spreading that are subject to ungrounded path conditions. To lay out the types of predictions made, in the following section we sketch the ways that conditions interact with rules in general; we then exemplify the range of systems predicted not to exist, and consider in more detail systems predicted to exist.

3.2.2 Grounding Conditions and Phonological Rules

The above discussion of Pulaar claims that the *rule* of [+ATR] Insertion has a grounded condition on its Target: the rule inserts [+ATR] only if the Target is [+high]. In this section, we make explicit certain aspects of the formal proposal concerning such rule conditions, and we also lay out a sample of the types of predictions made by the substantive proposals concerning [ATR].

The first question we address is what exactly it means for a rule to be governed by a particular condition. We focus on rules of *insertion*, *association*, and *spreading*.[29] When a particular implicational condition governs some rule, we take the antecedent of the condition to correspond to the Argument of the rule—namely, the F-element that is inserted, associated, or spread (see sections 4.1 and 4.2.5 for more on Arguments).

The necessity of this conclusion can easily be seen from a case like the following. In (35a), [+ATR] spreads under the condition that the Target be [+high].[30]

(35) a. +ATR

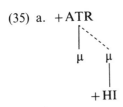

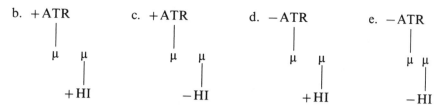

Under standard assumptions, the rule formulated in (35a) should apply to the configuration given in (35b), but should fail to apply to the configurations in (35c–e). Consider in this regard the truth tables for two possible expressions of the condition on the relation between [+ATR] and [+high], under the interpretation that if the conditional is not satisfied, the rule cannot apply.

(36) *Antecedent = Argument: If [+ ATR] then [+high]*

	Antecedent	Consequent	Conditional
Representation (35b)	T	T	T
Representation (35c)	T	F	F
Representation (35d)	F	T	T
Representation (35e)	F	F	T

If the *antecedent* of the implicational condition is interpreted as the element that spreads, then the condition is satisfied in representation (35b) but not in (35c). Spreading is therefore applicable in the correct form. (Note that since the antecedent of the condition is not satisfied in (35d,e), the condition is logically satisfied; but since the rule specifically spreads "[+ATR]," it still does not apply in such configurations.)

Compare this result with what obtains if the *consequent* of the implicational condition is interpreted as the element that spreads.

(37) *Consequent = Argument: If [+high] then [+ATR]*

	Antecedent	Consequent	Conditional
Representation (35b)	T	T	T
Representation (35c)	F	T	T
Representation (35d)	T	F	F
Representation (35e)	F	F	T

In this case, the condition is satisfied both in representation (35b) and in representation (35c). Spreading is therefore incorrectly predicted to occur in both forms. In fact, the visible effect of imposing the condition *If [+high] then [+ATR]* on a rule of [+ATR] Spread is actually the same as that of imposing no condition at all.

We conclude, therefore, that the imposition of a grounded condition on the application of a rule is to be interpreted by satisfying the *antecedent* of the condition with the element undergoing the rule, the Argument, and by satisfying the *consequent* of the condition with an element on a path with the antecedent (whether the path condition is a condition on the source or on the Target).

As a final point, note that the path satisfying the relevant condition must be present in the *output* of a rule imposing a condition on the Target of the rule of association, spreading, or insertion. For example, in (35b), the ATR/HI Condition is satisfied by the output of the spreading rule, not by the input. With a condition imposed on the Argument itself, however, the appropriate configuration must be found in the *input*. For example, if ATR/HI is imposed on the Argument as in (38a) (meaning that [+ATR] spreads only from a [+high] vowel; see, for example, the discussion of Lango, chapter 5), then spreading is only applicable in a configuration where the input meets the condition, (38b), but not (38c–e).

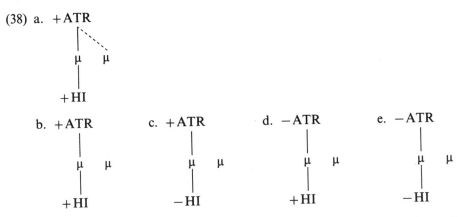

(38) a. +ATR

b. +ATR   c. +ATR   d. −ATR   e. −ATR

Having clarified what it means for a condition to be relevant when a rule applies, we now address predictions made by this model about rules and their effects, exploring implications in three domains: (i) the formulation of rules, (ii) "redundancy rules," and (iii) effects of rule application.

3.2.2.1 Restrictions on Phonological Rules

This chapter and the previous one present a large number of phonological rules that target F-elements in one way or another. A number of these rules have restrictions on their Argument or Target. If Grounding Condition I is correct, the set of restrictions in rules involving conditions on paths should be selected from the set of grounded path conditions.

Rules need conditions on paths in a variety of instances, for example, if a rule creates a path (by insertion, association, or spreading) between some F-element Φ and a *subset* of the language's Φ-bearing units. An instance of this is seen in Pulaar [+ATR] Insertion (29): [+ATR] is inserted only on [+high] vowels, even though mid vowels are also legitimate bearers of [+ATR] (as seen by the effect of

Pulaar [+ATR] Spread). A second case is Menomini, discussed in section 4.7.3. In Menomini, [+ATR] spreads only to nonlow vowels, even though low vowels can also bear [+ATR] in this language. Numerous other examples are seen throughout the text.

It is easy to determine which path-creating rules are proscribed by the Grounding Conditions: they are simply the ones where the element that undergoes rule application or the element that is targeted for rule application is restricted in some ungrounded fashion. Ungrounded path conditions involving [ATR], [high], and [low] have been given in (13), repeated in (39) for convenience.

(39) *Proscribed conditions*

If [+high] then [−ATR].	If [+high] then not [+ATR].
If [+low] then [+ATR].	If [+low] then not [−ATR].
If [−high] then [+ATR].	If [−high] then not [−ATR].
If [−high] then [−ATR].	If [−high] then not [+ATR].
If [−low] then [+ATR].	If [−low] then not [−ATR].
If [−low] then [−ATR].	If [−low] then not [+ATR].
If [+ATR] then [−high].	If [+ATR] then not [+high].
If [+ATR] then [+low].	If [+ATR] then not [−low].
If [−ATR] then [+high].	If [−ATR] then not [−high].
If [−ATR] then [−low].	If [−ATR] then not [+low].

Any rule including one of the constraints in (39) as a condition on its application is proscribed by Grounding Theory. A relatively unconstrained rule may create a weakly grounded or ungrounded configuration by not invoking a condition at all, but no rule can create as its sole output a path involving the antecedent (as Argument) and the consequent of an ungrounded condition.

For example, it should be impossible to find a language comparable to Pulaar but where [−ATR] is assigned to high vowels and spreads from high vowels; the required rule of [−ATR] Insertion would not be grounded, since the necessary rule condition would be *If [−ATR] then [+high]*, a member of the set of ungrounded path conditions given in (39). Similarly, it should be impossible to find a language with a set of rules comparable to those of Pulaar, but where the class of vowels to which [+ATR] is assigned is the *mid* vowel class; as with the case just mentioned, the [ATR] Insertion rule would not be grounded.

In (40), we show schematically these and some other rules of insertion and spreading that the Grounding Conditions predict do not exist in any language; the problem in each case is that the condition on the rule is not a grounded path condition. The list in (40) is by no means exhaustive; as can easily be established by referring back to (39), numerous other rules are predicted to be impossible.

(40) *Proscribed rules*

Insert/Link/Spread [−ATR] onto   (imposing *If [−ATR] then*
[+high]   *[+high]*)
Insert/Link/Spread [+ATR] onto   (imposing *If [+ATR] then*
[−high, −low]   *[−high], [−low]*)
Insert/Link/Spread [+ATR] onto   (imposing *If [+ATR] then*
[+low]   *[+low]*)
Insert/Link/Spread [+ATR] onto   (imposing *If [+ATR] then*
[−high]   *[−high]*)
Insert/Link/Spread [−ATR] onto   (imposing *If [−ATR] then*
[−low]   *[−low]*)
etc.

It is important to stress that Grounding Theory rules out particular implicational conditions, not particular feature combinations. For example, many languages allow both advanced and retracted versions of high vowels (Eastern Javanese, for example). Although retracted high vowels are more marked than advanced high vowels, the combination of retraction and tongue body height is not ruled out by Grounding Theory. Impossible, however, is an implicational condition that *requires* the marked configuration whereby high vowels are retracted (39), as is an implicational condition *disallowing* the unmarked configuration whereby high vowels are advanced (39). No rule could *specifically* target high vowels as the recipients of [−ATR], to the exclusion of mid and low vowels.

The Grounding Theory makes strong claims about possible and proscribed rules: the necessity of any proscribed rule would falsify the strongest version of the Grounding Condition model.

3.2.2.2 Rules of Redundancy

The Grounding Hypothesis has two results for so-called redundancy rules, rules that supply absent F-elements.

First, given the claim that languages maximize the use of grounded conditions, it would be expected that redundancy rules should often "duplicate" conditions. That is, a redundancy rule might mirror the effect of a condition. Consider the example of a language in which the ATR/LO Condition holds, *If [+ATR] then not [+low]*, and hence where all low vowels are redundantly assigned [−ATR]. The ATR/LO Condition would prevent [+ATR] from associating to vowels that are [+low]. Further, a redundancy rule assigning [−ATR] would apply specifically to low vowels. That is, a rule inserting [−ATR] would be restricted in its application to the class of low vowels by the imposition of RTR/LO on the insertion rule, *If [−ATR] then [+low]*. Note that the class of vowels receiving [−ATR] by redundancy rule is exactly the class of vowels that cannot bear [+ATR]. This, then, is the duplication problem.

The Grounding Hypothesis formally removes the need for such duplication in the unmarked case. Consider the rule that inserts [−ATR]. Contrary to the assumption above, this rule need not stipulate that all Targets are [+low]. The reasoning is as follows. By Grounding Condition II, strong conditions are maximized in the unmarked case. The conditions that are relevant are those that refer to active F-elements. Activating [−ATR] (by inserting it) renders RTR/LO relevant. RTR/LO restricts insertion of [−ATR] to [+low] Targets. By Grounding Condition II, the language would be more complex if the condition did not hold. Formally, therefore, Grounding Theory does not require the duplication of conditions and redundancy rules since such rules can be governed by conditions affecting representations in general. Conditions only need to hold specifically of rules if they do not hold generally in the language.

In addition, the class of possible redundancy rules is greatly curtailed by Grounding Theory. As illustrated in the example above, in the unmarked case, context-free redundancy rules are grounded by conditions holding generally in the language. Additionally, context-dependent rules inserting redundant F-elements can only be governed by grounded conditions, just like other types of phonological rules (see section 3.2.2.1). For example, in Wolof and Yoruba, [−ATR] Insertion is grounded by the RTR/LO Condition: [−ATR] is inserted only on [+low] vowels. In Pulaar, the rule inserting [+ATR] is grounded by the ATR/HI Condition: [+ATR] is inserted only on [+high] vowels. These rules are in accordance with a general claim of the Grounding Conditions: any path conditions referred to in a rule must be grounded.

(41a) shows the grounded and ungrounded context-dependent rules inserting [−ATR]; (41b) gives the grounded and ungrounded rules inserting [+ATR]. (The rules in (41) are formulated with respect to tongue height features only, since this is our present focus.) Under the Grounding Conditions, all and only the rules in the left-hand column are permitted as context-dependent insertion rules. Any other rules inserting values for [ATR] must be context-free. Instances of rules from the right-hand column would constitute counterexamples to the theory advanced here.[31]

(41) *Grounded rules*   *Ungrounded rules*

   a. Insert [−ATR] on [+low].   Insert [−ATR] on [−low].
       Insert [−ATR] on [−high].   Insert [−ATR] on [+high].
                               Insert [−ATR] on [−high, −low].

   b. Insert [+ATR] on [+high].   Insert [+ATR] on [−high].
       Insert [+ATR] on [−low].   Insert [+ATR] on [+low].
                               Insert [+ATR] on [−high, −low].

That "redundancy" rules are grounded is a consequence of the more general claim of the Grounding Condition model, namely, that if there are path conditions on any rule, such conditions are grounded.

3.2.3 Lexical Specifications of [+ATR]

The next two sections focus on languages that are marked with respect to the *active* status of [ATR]: they represent the marked option for the [ATR] Markedness State- ment (21a), in that [ATR] is active rather than inert. Given an active status for [ATR], the unmarked situation is for [+ATR] to be the active value, according to the [ATR] Markedness Statement (21b): the languages discussed in this section, Kinande and Akan, provide examples of this type. In addition, we suggest that when phonological systems exhibit the active use of [ATR] features, they tend to display evidence of enhancing *sympathetic* relations between F-elements, and of minimizing *antagonistic* relations between F-elements, as defined by the Grounding Hypothesis.

3.2.3.1 Kinande Kinande, a Bantu language spoken in Zaire, has a system of [ATR] harmony (Valinande 1984, Mutaka 1991,[32] Schlindwein 1987, Steriade 1987a, Hyman 1989) that is restricted in a variety of relevant ways.[33] To begin, although it is possible to distinguish morphemes on the basis of [ATR], this contrast is found only with vowels of a particular height class. Specifically, [+ATR] may occur in a morpheme only when the morpheme contains a high vowel (see ATR/HI (11)). To illustrate, with infinitive forms like those in (42a), stem and preceding affixes surface with [+ATR] values;[34] with forms like those in (42b), both stem and prefixes surface with [−ATR] values.[35]

(42) *Stems with high vowels*

    a. [+ATR]   e-rɪ-lịb-a   [ɛrɪlíːbà]   'to cover'

                e-rɪ-hụk-a   [ɛríhúːkà]   'to cook'

    b. [−ATR]   e-ri-lim-a   [ɛrɪlíːmà]   'to cultivate'

                e-ri-hum-a   [ɛrɪhúːmà]   'to beat'

Stems with nonhigh vowels, on the other hand, uniformly appear with [−ATR] values, and uniformly condition [−ATR] values.

(43) *Stems with nonhigh vowels*

    e-ri-hek-a   [ɛrɪhέːkà]   'to carry'

    e-ri-kar-a   [ɛrɪkǎːrà]   'to force'

    e-ri-boh-a   [ɛríbɔ̌ːhà]   'to tie'

The above examples illustrate cases that are uniformly [−ATR], as well as cases where high vowel stems trigger the harmonic spreading of [+ATR] onto vowels to the left of the stem. In the cases in (42a), the vowels that undergo harmony are also high. However, *mid* vowels can also undergo the effects of [ATR] harmony, seen in the following data involving a [+ATR] agentive suffix. Note in (44a–b, f–g) that the underlying difference in high vowels seen in (42) is neutralized with the agentive suffix.[36]

(44) *Stems with the [+ ATR] agentive suffix*

    a. o-mʉ-lịb-ị   [ɔ̀mùlíꜜ:bì]   'coverer'

    b. o-mʉ-lịm-ị   [ɔ̀mùlíꜜ:mì]   'farmer, cultivator'

    c. o-mʉ-hẹk-ị   [ɔ̀mùhéꜜ:kì]   'porter, carrier'

    d. o-mʉ-kar-ị   [ɔ̀mùkǎ:rì]   'forcer'

    e. o-mʉ-bọh-ị   [ɔ̀múbőꜜ:hì]   'tier'

    f. o-mʉ-hʉm-ị   [ɔ̀mùhűꜜ:mì]   'beater'

    g. o-mʉ-hʉk-ị   [ɔ̀múhűꜜ:kì]   'cook'

Focusing for the moment on the pattern with nonlow vowels, Kinande can be assumed to have a vowel system that deviates only slightly from a completely unmarked (inert) system (22) where [ATR] plays no contrastive role. As in such a completely unmarked system, [+ATR] is the active F-element; unlike such a system, Kinande contrasts morphemes containing an active [+ATR] specification with morphemes containing no underlying specification for [ATR]. Where present, the specified [+ATR] value spreads leftward.

While this much of an analysis is fairly obvious, there remains an interesting problem. If there were no grounded path conditions governing the assignment of [+ATR], then morphemes with any sequence of vowels would be potential [+ATR] morphemes. The fact that [+ATR] is generally restricted to morphemes including a high vowel (exceptions are discussed below) remains to be formally accounted for.

This fact, we suggest, receives an explanation from the Grounding Hypothesis. In a completely grounded system, the cooccurrence of [+ATR] with vowels of different heights is completely predictable: in a completely grounded system, [+ATR] is permitted only on high vowels. In a completely ungrounded system, [+ATR] could cooccur with vowels of any height, without restriction. In a system where [ATR] plays a contrastive function, conditions must not be fully in force or no contrast would be possible. We suggest in our discussion of Kinande and other languages that the tendency is for languages to *relax* conditions, not abandon them, and to impose conditions on specific rules when they cannot hold generally.

For Kinande, we follow Schlindwein (1987) in assuming that lexical specifications of [ATR] are floating underlyingly, and that a free [+ATR] specification is associated uniquely to a [+high] Target.[37] In terms of grounding, the initial association of [+ATR] is subject to the ATR/HI Condition given in (11). Since the ATR/HI Condition on the association process would be violated if [+ATR] were to associate to any nonhigh vowel, a morpheme-level specification of [+ATR] can only surface if there is a high vowel to link to.

(45) *General Association (Kinande)—Condition on Target: ATR/HI*

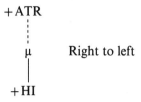

+ATR

μ   Right to left

+HI

With respect to the examples above, the roots in (42a) are therefore analyzed as containing a [+ATR] specification that associates via (45) to the high vowel of the root, as shown in (46a), while those in (42b) and (43) have no such specification, as shown in (46b,c), respectively.

(46) *URs of three roots*

    a. E−rI−lib−A   b. E−rI−lIm−A   c. E−rI−hEk−A

          +ATR

   [èrílǐ:bà]   [èrìlǐ:mà]   [èrìhɛ̌:ka]
   'cover'   'cultivate'   'carry'

Supplementing the rule of association is a harmony rule (47) that spreads [+ATR] from right to left: this rule is responsible for the harmonic aspect of the surface form in (46a).

(47) *General Harmony*

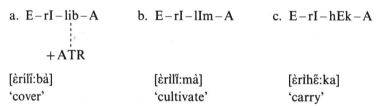

    +ATR

   μ   μ

Harmonic Patterns   Unlike the rule of General Association, harmony is not restricted to high vowels. That is, association is more strictly grounded than subsequent spreading. Classified in terms of Targets, various cases of harmony can be distinguished.

First, harmony can affect high vowels to the left of a [+ATR] source; examples were shown in (42a) and (44). (The [+ATR] specifications in (48) are represented on separate planes because they are provided by distinct morphemes; see McCarthy 1981, 1986a.)

(48) *High vowels undergo harmony*

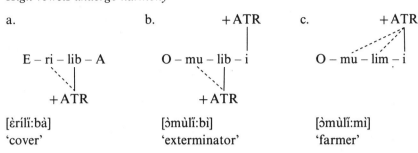

a.

E – ri – lib – A
+ATR

[èrílǐ:bà]
'cover'

b.   +ATR

O – mu – lib – i
+ATR

[ɔ̀mùlǐ:bì]
'exterminator'

c.   +ATR

O – mu – lim – i

[ɔ̀mùlǐ:mì]
'farmer'

Second, harmony can affect a mid vowel to the left of a [+ATR] source. This is possible because the ATR/HI Condition (11) governs the application of General Association but not spreading.

(49) *Mid vowels undergo harmony*

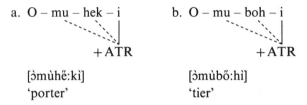

a. O – mu – hek – i
+ATR

[ɔ̀mùhě:kì]
'porter'

b. O – mu – boh – i
+ATR

[ɔ̀mùbǒ:hì]
'tier'

The third class of cases involves a low vowel to the left of a [+ATR] vowel. We assume, following Hyman (1989), that low vowels in this context undergo harmony, but we put off discussion of low vowels until later in this section.

Incompatible Roots   A fourth class of cases exists, a class that constitutes exceptions to the general pattern that [+ATR] occurs only in morphemes with [+high] vowels (see Mutaka 1990, 1991). In certain forms, [+ATR] prefixes are conditioned by certain root morphemes that are atypical in two respects: (i) the root does not include any high vowels, (ii) the nonhigh root vowels of the harmony-inducing morphemes are all [−ATR]. That is, prefixes are [+ATR] in spite of the apparent absence of a [+ATR] trigger within the root, illustrated by the contrast between (50a), the regular case, and (50b), the special case.

(50) *[−ATR] roots triggering [+ATR] prefixes*

a. e-ri-se   [èrí:sê]   'rat's dung'
   e-ri-ses-a   [èrìsɛ́:sâ]   'to arrange (a bed)'
   e-ri-sak-a   [èrísǎ:kà]   'to incise'
   e-ri-tsuku   [èrìtsÚ:kÙ]   'coldness'
   e-ri-bumba   [èríbÙ:mbà]   'clay'

  b. e-rɩ-hembe   [ɛríhɛ̀:mbɛ̀]   'horn'
     e-rɩ-bere   [ɛríbɛ̃:rɛ̀]   'breast'
     e-rɩ-tako   [ɛrítǎ:kɔ]   'buttock'
     e-rɩ-samba   [ɛrìsà:mbà]   'eagle'
     e-rɩ-lolo   [ɛrìlɔ̃:lɔ̀]   'sin'
     e-rɩ-tema   [ɛrítɛ̃:mà]   'cheek'
     e-rɩ-kala   [ɛríkǎ:là]   'ember'
     e-rɩ-sesa   [ɛrísɛ́:sà]   'kind of grass'
     e-rɩ-saka   [ɛrìsǎ:kà]   'kind of rat'

  c. a-ma-hembe   [àmáhɛ̀:mbɛ̀]   'horns'
     a-ma-bere   [àmábɛ̃:rɛ̀]   'breasts'

  d. e-sɩ-seke   [ɛsísɛ̀:kɛ̀]   'reeds'
     o-lu-seke   [ɔlúsɛ̀:kɛ̀]   'reed'
     e-sɩ-sako   [ɛsísǎ:kɔ]   'tattoos'
     o-lu-sako   [ɔlúsǎ:kɔ]   'tattoo'

The examples in (50a) demonstrate that the prefixal sequence [ɛrɪ] does not bear a lexical [+ATR] specification. The examples in (50b) illustrate certain class 5 roots that introduce a [+ATR] value that links to the class prefix, not a root vowel. Comparing examples such as those in (50c) with the corresponding examples in (50b) shows that the root vowels remain [−ATR] if there is no available high vowel to link to; even if a mid root vowel is present (a vowel that does undergo harmonic spreading), such a vowel is not affected in such cases. Finally, the examples in (50d) illustrate an additional condition on such prefixal association (51), namely, that the Target must be [−back] (Mutaka 1991).[38]

(51) *Special Association (Kinande)—Conditions on Target: ATR/HI, ATR/BK*

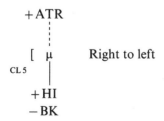

Combinatorial Specification in conjunction with grounded restrictions on the cooccurrence of F-elements predicts the possibility of patterns like that in (50). By postulating underlying representations with a free [+ATR] F-element, it is predicted that certain morphemes could exist where a morpheme-level specification [+ATR] is present, but where there is no root high vowel to associate to.[39] The morpheme-level specification would only be able to surface if an eligible anchor were supplied via affixation. In Kinande, this occurs when a high front vowel appears in an appropriate prefix, exactly as in (50b).[40]

This analysis is illustrated with the example of 'horn'. Such a root is underlyingly assigned a representation that includes a free, morpheme-level [+ATR] specification.

(52) *UR of a mid-voweled root with a free [+ATR]*

   hEmbE

   +ATR

Since the rule associating [+ATR] targets only high vowels, the [ATR] specification of such a morpheme cannot link to either root vowel. Where a morpheme containing a high vowel is supplied via affixation, linking becomes possible (53a); where no high vowel is present, there can be no linking, hence no realization, of the [ATR] specification (53b).

(53) *Derivations*

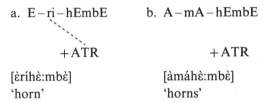

   a. E − ri − hEmbE   b. A − mA − hEmbE

            +ATR   +ATR

   [ɛ́ríhɛ̀:mbɛ̀]   [àmáhɛ̀:mbɛ̀]
   'horn'   'horns'

Two points about such cases should be noted. First, there is no *universal* application of a set of association conventions (Goldsmith 1976, Pulleyblank 1986a, etc.). When the language-specific association rules of Kinande fail, no association of any kind is possible. Hence, the [+ATR] specification of the root *hEmbE* cannot link to a mid vowel even though such a combination of features is possible in Kinande. Note, moreover, that the failure of "conventional" association cannot be attributed to some principle such as disjunctive ordering. In the Kinande case, the more general conventional association would have to be considered disjunctive with respect to the more specific rule of Special Association. In a case like that in (53b), however, the specific rule does *not* apply. As a result, normal considerations of disjunctivity would permit the application of any conventional mode of association, incorrectly predicting linking in such a case.[41] (For a thorough discussion of the issue of association by rule versus association by convention, see chapter 4.) As a second point, the lexical [+ATR] specification fails to surface in derived forms involving these special roots. In diminutive and augmentative forms, for example, even a high-voweled prefix surfaces as [−ATR]. Compare the forms in (54) with those in (50) employing the same roots.

(54) *Forms derived from some mid-voweled roots with a free [+ATR]*

e-hi-hembe	[èhíhὲːmbὲ]	'small horns'
e-hi-bere	[èhíbɛ̆ːrὲ]	'small breasts'
e-hi-tako	[èhítǎːkɔ̀]	'small buttocks'
e-hi-samba	[èhìsàːmbà]	'small eagles'
e-hi-lolo	[èhìlɔ̆ːlɔ̀]	'small sins'
e-hi-tema	[èhítɛ̆ːmà]	'small cheeks'

Following Mutaka (1991), we assume that erasure of the floating [+ATR] specification takes place at a derivational stage that is prior to affixation of the diminutive and augmentative prefixes, but after affixation of the regular class prefixes. Although this issue warrants much closer examination within a general consideration of the morphology/phonology interaction (see Mutaka 1990, 1991 for some discussion), Mutaka (1990) suggests that the relevant distinction is a stratal one: free [+ATR] specifications link to stratum 1 prefixes, but undergo stray erasure prior to stratum 2 affixation. For present purposes, the crucial point is that incompatibility is defined by the grounded condition ATR/HI on General Association.

Left-to-Right Spreading The general pattern of spreading illustrated above takes place from right to left. There is a more restricted pattern, however, that takes place from left to right. Consider, for example, the harmonic behavior of the benefactive suffix *ɪr/ir*.

(55) *Left-to-right spreading*

a. e-ri-lim-a   [èrìlíːmà]   e-ri-lim-ir-a   [èrìlìmíːrà]   'work/work for'

b. e-rɩ-lɩm-a   [èrílíːmà]   e-rɩ-lɩm-ɩr-a   [èrílìmíːrà]   'exterminate/ exterminate for'

c. e-rɩ-lɩban-a   [èrìlìbǎːnà]   e-rɩ-lɩban-ir-a   [èrìlìbàníːrà]   'disappear/ disappear for someone'

Forms such as *e-ri-lim-ir-a* [èrìlìmíːrà] 'work for' (55a) show that the suffix *ɪr/ir* is underlyingly unspecified for [ATR], appearing as [−ATR] with a root not containing a [+ATR] specification. With a [+ATR] root like *-lim-* 'exterminate', however, the suffix surfaces with a [+ATR] value: *e-rɩ-lɩm-ɩr-a* [èrílìmíːrà] 'exterminate for' (55b).

Such cases require the positing of a left-to-right rule that spreads [+ATR].[42] Unlike the more general right-to-left rule, this process applies only to a high-voweled Target. The rule does not spread, for example, the [+ATR] value of a root such as *-lịb-* 'disappear' when the immediately following vowel is low: *e-rị-lịban-ir-a* [èrìlìbànǐːrà] 'disappear for someone' (55c).[43] Similarly, left-to-right spreading does not take place if the potential Target is mid. Some relevant examples were seen in (54); additional examples are given here.

(56) *Left-to-right spreading inapplicable*

    a. e-rị-ịno   [έrǐːnɔ̀]   'tooth'

    b. a-ka-ịko   [ákǐːkɔ̀]   'fireplace'

    c. mọ-tụ-a-tsakụr-ịre   [mótwàtsàkwíːrὲ] 'we voted'

We conclude, therefore, that the rule of right-to-left harmony in (47) must be supplemented by the left-to-right rule in (57).

(57) *Suffixal Harmony—Condition on Target: ATR/HI*

Of interest in the present context is that the substantive condition required for left-to-right spreading is a grounded one: ATR/HI. That is, if [+ATR] is to spread by this rule, then the Target must be [+high].

Phrasal Harmony The final harmonic process to be discussed in Kinande operates at the phrasal level. Like the general rule (47), Phrasal Harmony (58) spreads from right to left; like the suffixal rule (57), however, Phrasal Harmony is quite narrowly grounded in that it targets only high vowels.

(58) *Phrasal Harmony*

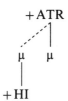

Consider the effect of Phrasal Harmony on nouns that appear with [−ATR] vowels in isolation. When the rightmost vowel of such a noun is high, it is targeted by Phrasal Harmony.

(59) *Phrasal Harmony*

a. e-mį-tį mį-kųhį   [èmítí míkù:hì]   'short trees'
   e-mi-ti   [èmí:tì]   'trees'
   mį-kųhį   [míkù:hì]   'short'

b. e-bį-tsųngų bį-kųhį [èbìtsùngú bíkù:hì]   'short potatoes'
   e-bi-tsungu   [èbìtsù:ngù]   'potatoes'
   bį-kųhį   [bíkù:hì]   'short'

c. o-mų-tahį mų-kųhį   [ɔ̀mútàhí múkù:hì]   'short branch'[44]
   o-mu-tahi   [ɔ̀mʊ́tã́:hì]   'branch'
   mų-kųhį   [múkù:hì]   'short'

d. e-kį-gǫtsį kį-rįto   [èkígótsì kìrí̃:tɔ̀]   'heavy big rat'
   e-ki-gotsi   [èkígɔ́:tsì]   'big rat'
   kį-rįto   [kìrí̃:tɔ̀]   'heavy'

e. o-mų-kękųlų mų-kųhį [ɔ̀múkèkùlú múkù:hì]   'short old woman'
   o-mu-kekulu   [ɔ̀-mʊ́-kɛ̀kʊ̀:lʊ̀]   'old woman'
   mų-kųhį   [múkù:hì]   'short'

As observed by Schlindwein (1987), once harmony has spanned the word boundary, it proceeds iteratively to both high and nonhigh vowels. Between words, harmony requires that the targeted vowel be high; once into the new word, harmony applies by the regular right-to-left rule that targets both high and nonhigh vowels. That is, Phrasal Harmony (58) feeds a postlexical application of General Harmony (47).

When the noun preceding a [+ATR] adjective ends with a nonhigh vowel, there is no harmonic effect. The examples in (60) illustrate this absence of harmony with both mid and low final vowels.

(60) *Phrasal Harmony inapplicable*

a. e-mi-hamba mį-kųhį   [èmìhámbá míkù:hì]   'short knives'
   e-mi-hamba   [èmìhá:mbà]   'knives'

b. e-mi-twero mį-kųhį   [èmítwèrɔ́ míkù:hì]   'short nails'
   e-mi-twero   [èmítwɛ̃́:rɔ̀]   'nails'

c. e-bi-seke bį-kųhį   [èbísèkɛ́ bíkù:hì]   'short sugar canes'
   e-bi-seke   [èbísɛ̀:kɛ̀]   'sugar canes'

Finally, Phrasal Harmony applies strictly from right to left. In cases where a [+ATR] noun precedes an adjective unspecified for [ATR], no harmonic change occurs, and the adjective surfaces with [−ATR] values.

(61) *Phrasal Harmony inapplicable*

a. e-kị-kalị ki-ri	[ɛ̀kíkàlì kí:rì]	'tall woman'
e-kị-kalị	[ɛ̀kíkà:lì]	'woman'
ki-ri	[kí:rì]	'tall'
b. e-nyụnyụ nyi-ri	[ɛ̀nyùnyù nyí:rì]	'long bird'
e-nyụnyụ	[ɛ̀nyű:nyù]	'bird'
nyi-ri	[nyí:rì]	'long'
c. o-mụ-kalị mu-li-mu-li	[ɔ̀múkàlì múlìmú:lì]	'tall woman'
o-mụ-kalị	[ɔ̀múkà:lì]	'woman'
mu-li-mu-li	[múlìmú:lì]	'tall'
d. e-kị-sịkị ki-buya	[ɛ̀kísíkì kìbű:yà]	'pretty log'
e-kị-sịkị	[ɛ̀kísí:kì]	'log'
ki-buya	[kìbű:yà]	'pretty'

In conclusion, spreading at the phrasal level combines properties of different word-level rules of Kinande. Like the general word-level rule, Phrasal Harmony takes right to left as its defined directionality. And like the suffixal word-level rule, Phrasal Harmony imposes the grounded condition that targets must be high.

To summarize, we observe that in Kinande, unlike in a language like Pulaar, [ATR] plays an underlyingly active role; it serves a lexically distinctive function. To account for the surface distribution of [ATR], five rules must be distinguished in Kinande: General Association (45), Special Association (51), General Harmony (47), Suffixal Harmony (57), Phrasal Harmony (58). Although a superficially complex pattern results, it has been shown that for all processes except General Harmony, the Kinande system is grounded in that it imposes the ATR/HI and ATR/BK Conditions. The superficial complexity of the system is argued to result from the coordination of several formally simple rules, where each rule imposes a particular set of grounded conditions.

Kinande Grounding

1. [ATR] is active in underlying representation (marked according to [ATR] Markedness (21a)).
2. [+ATR] is active (unmarked according to [ATR] Markedness (21b)).
3. ATR/HI holds of General Association, Suffixal Harmony, and Phrasal Harmony (consistent with Grounding Conditions I and IIa; semimarked with respect to Condition IIb (12)).
4. ATR/HI and ATR/BK hold of Special Association (consistent with Grounding Conditions I and IIa; semimarked with respect to Grounding Condition IIb (12)).

Before closing this discussion of Kinande, we consider the status of low vowels
with respect to harmony. The low vowel pattern is of particular interest since it
illustrates a transparency effect, an effect that we attribute to the phonetic interpretation of antagonistic F-element cooccurrences. (See section 4.7 for more on transparency effects.)

Harmonic Behavior of Low Vowels   The facts concerning the harmonic behavior of
low vowels are not altogether clear. Following Hyman (1989), we have assumed
above that low vowels can be targeted by General Harmony (47). The reasons for this
assumption concern primarily the phonetic realization of the penultimate low vowels
in forms such as the following:

(62) *Advanced low vowels*

      a. ò-mʉ́-kàlị̀   [ɔ̀múkə̀:lì]   'woman'

      b. ò-mʉ́-kàlị̀-kàlị̀   [ɔ̀múkàlìkə̀:lì]   'a real woman'

      c. è-kị̀-tsàlị̀   [ɛ̀kìtsə̀:lì]   'pea'

      d. ò-mʉ̀-kàngị̀   [ɔ̀mùkə̀:ngì]   'barrier'

Because of the [+ATR] vowel to their right, these low vowels surface with a [+ATR]
variant. Several points are important in this regard.

First, Hyman observes that the raised variants of low vowels are found when
the vowels undergo prepausal lengthening. Such metrical lengthening, the details of
which need not concern us here, is a general process of Kinande, affecting vowels of
all heights. Second, N. M. Mutaka (personal communication) has noted that all the
examples with raised penultimate low vowels are on a L-tone. The forms in (62) can
be contrasted with forms such as the following where low vowels appear on a H-tone:

(63) a. ò-mʉ̀-kátị̀   [ɔ̀mùká:tì]   'bread'

      b. ò-mʉ́kámị̀   [ɔ̀múká:mì]   'brewer'

In addition, recall that short low vowels in [+ATR] contexts have generally been
considered to be unaffected by harmony.

(64) *Unadvanced short low vowels: Advanced and retracted environments*

	[+ATR]	tʉ-ka-kị-lịm-a	[tùkákílì:mâ]	'we exterminate it'
vs.	[−ATR]	tu-ka-ki-lim-a	[tùkákìlì:mâ]	'we cultivate it'
	[+ATR]	tʉ-ka-kị-hʉk-a	[tùkákíhù:kâ]	'we cook it'
vs.	[−ATR]	tu-ka-mu-hum-a	[tùkámùhù:mâ]	'we beat him'
	[+ATR]	o-mʉ-tahị mʉ-kʉhị	[ɔ̀mútàhí múkù:hì]	'short branch'
vs.	[−ATR]	o-mu-tahi	[ɔ̀mʊ́tă:hì]	'branch'

The low vowels in (64) have been considered by authors such as Schlindwein (1987) and Mutaka (1991) to be transparent. That is, harmony passes right through them, without affecting them. We follow Hyman, however, in assuming that such transparency is only apparent, taking the forms in (62) as evidence that low vowels undergo harmony in a [+ATR] environment. It is incumbent on such an analysis, of course, to provide an account for the various forms that do not appear to undergo change, forms such as those in (63) and (64). Before making a suggestion for such cases, we note that it would clearly be desirable to conduct an instrumental investigation of the low vowels of Kinande in various contexts, to determine whether there is actually a general harmonic effect on low vowels.

Anticipating a more detailed discussion in section 3.3.1, we suggest that antagonistic feature combinations may result in the neutralization or near-neutralization of a contrast. In the case in question, the [+ATR] instruction of an advanced low vowel may be neutralized phonetically by the [+low] instruction of such a vowel. In Kinande, it would appear that such neutralization takes place except when a low tone enhances the [+ATR] effect, perhaps by causing an additional expansion of the pharynx by larynx lowering (see Denning 1989, Meechan 1992).[45,46]

Viewed along these lines, the Grounding Hypothesis serves to identify two types of transparency. Consider the schematic diagram in (65), where Y is the transparent segment.

(65) *Transparency—antagonistic or sympathetic*

First, as suggested for Kinande, if α is antagonistic to a feature in Y, then its effect may not be apparent on the surface. We label this *antagonistic transparency*. Second, it may be that Y is redundantly specified as α, that α is sympathetic with respect to some relevant feature of Y. For example, the discussion of Ngbaka in section 2.5 indicated that [+ATR] can harmonically spread through a high vowel, even though high vowels are ultimately redundantly specified as [+ATR] (ATR/HI Condition). We refer to this as *sympathetic transparency*.[47] In each of these types of transparency, there is no phonological skipping of a transparent class. The illusion of transparency is the result of canonical spreading in conjunction with grounded conditions, either antagonistic or sympathetic, that affect the phonetic output. These effects as well as others involving the relation between grounded conditions and rules are discussed in some detail in section 3.5.

It is worth stressing in this regard that we do not propose to turn conditions on and off at different stages of a derivation of the type seen in Kinande. That is, we do not propose that at some stage [+ATR] is allowed to appear on low vowels, while at some subsequent stage (for the relevant cases) [+ATR] is removed from such vowels. Our proposal employs a static appeal to the phonetics: since lowering of the tongue body and advancement of the tongue root are two articulations that are both articulatorily and acoustically antagonistic, we suggest that phonetic implementation of the two features simultaneously results in certain languages in one feature counteracting or neutralizing the other.

To conclude this discussion of Kinande, we again note the phonological similarity between Pulaar and Kinande. In Pulaar, [ATR] values are completely predictable, with [+ATR] redundantly assigned to high vowels; in Kinande, [ATR] is a lexical property of certain roots, but as in Pulaar, its association to vowels depends on the vowel being [+high], and in the class 5/10 cases, being [−back] as well. In Pulaar, [ATR] Spread targets the class of vowels that can be assigned [+ATR] according to the grounded path conditions of (11), that is, the class of nonlow vowels. In Kinande, while the role of ATR/LO is not entirely clear, we observe the grounded path condition of ATR/HI imposed on targets when spreading is from left to right at the lexical level, and when spreading is from right to left at the phrasal level.

The Grounding Condition approach makes a variety of predictions about languages exhibiting a Kinande-type pattern. For example, such languages would be impossible if [−ATR], rather than [+ATR], were the value that associates specifically to high vowels, or if [−ATR] specifications were lexically associated to high vowels. For such possibilities to be realized, a condition restricting [−ATR] to high vowels would be needed, but such a condition would not be grounded.

A second set of impossible languages would involve systems comparable to Kinande but where [+ATR] was lexically assigned to low vowels, was to associate specifically to low vowels, or was to be assigned or associate specifically to mid vowels. Any of these systems would require either a condition restricting [+ATR] to low vowels or a condition restricting [+ATR] to mid vowels, but neither of these conditions would be grounded. In fact, we know of no such languages.

A type of possible language would be one that is comparable to Kinande in having a lexically present free [+ATR] but one that is less grounded than Kinande in terms of how [+ATR] links. Akan, considered in the next section, is of this type.

3.2.3.2 Akan Up to this point, we have considered languages where the [ATR] feature is entirely predictable, and cases where the feature is limited in its initial distribution to an extremely restricted class of segments. There are of course well-studied systems where the feature has a much wider, less restricted distribution. One must ask how, or whether, substantive conditions on [ATR] play a role in such systems. We consider this broader issue through an examination of Akan. We argue that ATR/LO plays an extensive role in the language's phonology, while ATR/HI plays a subsidiary role in a variety of contexts.

Akan (Stewart 1967, 1983, Schachter and Fromkin 1968, Clements 1981, 1984, Dolphyne 1988) has an [ATR] harmony system with 10 surface vowels (see Stewart 1967, Painter 1973): [i, ɪ, e, ɛ, ə, a, ɔ, o, ʊ, u].[48] It is clear from work since Clements 1981, however, that at the lexical level, only 9 vowels are distinguished, the result of imposing LO/ATR (see Kiparsky 1985): [i, ɪ, e, ɛ, a, ɔ, o, ʊ, u]. For a 10-vowel [ATR] system, none of the substantive constraints discussed for languages like Pulaar and Kinande would hold. Even for the lexical 9-vowel inventory of Akan, not all of the substantive conditions given in (8) and (11) are adhered to: (i) not all high vowels are [+ATR] (i.e., the HI/ATR Condition plays no general role); (ii) not all [+ATR] vowels are high (demonstrating that the ATR/HI Condition is also not generally respected); (iii) not all [−ATR] vowels are low (i.e., the RTR/LO Condition does not play a general role). Considered in these terms, the Akan vowel system is more marked than the systems of Pulaar and Kinande because it is less grounded, according to Grounding Condition II. By imposing fewer conditions on the combinatorial properties of the relevant F-elements, a greater number of combinations are derived, corresponding to a greater number of surface realizations. With a lexical 9-vowel system like that of Akan, robust positive evidence of marked feature combinations forces the language learner to adopt representations with fewer substantive constraints than the cross-linguistically unmarked system (see Stampe 1979).

In the following discussion, we have two central aims. First, we illustrate the treatment within a grounded framework of a fairly ungrounded harmony system. Second, we present evidence that even though the Akan system as a whole does not obey conditions like ATR/HI and ATR/BK, individual processes show evidence for the applicability of such constraints. (See the discussion of Lango in chapter 5 for a somewhat different case that illustrates the same two points.)

In Akan harmony, we observe first that in the vast majority of cases, individual [ATR] values for vowels are predictable from a single specification of [ATR] at the level of the morpheme (Stewart 1967, Clements 1981). There is no reason for assigning [ATR] values to particular vowels. Examples like those in (66) illustrate roots that induce [+ATR] values; examples like those in (67) illustrate roots that induce [−ATR] values. Note that the same prefix or suffix appears as [+ATR] in one case and as [−ATR] in another depending on the root value for the [ATR] feature.[49]

(66) *[+ATR] roots*

e-bu-o	'nest'
o-kusi-e	'rat'
e-sĩnĩ	'piece'
o-fiti-i	'he/she pierced (it)'
o-be-tu-i	'he/she came and dug (it)'
o-susu-i	'he/she measured (it)'
e-tene	'it (news) spreads'

(67) *[−ATR] roots*

ɛ-bʊ-ɔ	'stone'
ɔ-kɔdɪ-ɛ	'eagle'
ɛ-pʊ̃nʊ̃	'door'
ɔ-cɪrɛ-ɪ	'he/she showed (it)'
ɔ-bɛ-tʊ-ɪ	'he/she came and threw (it)'
ɔ-fʊrʊ-ɪ	'he/she went up'

Assuming the unmarked pattern whereby [+ATR] is the active [ATR] F-element, as explicitly argued by Stewart (1967), we derive these forms by assigning a morpheme-level [+ATR] specification to the roots in (66) and by assigning no [ATR] specification to the roots in (67). The [+ATR] forms are derived by associating the morpheme-level specification and spreading it to both prefixes and suffixes; the remaining forms, with no [+ATR] specifications, are realized as [−ATR] at the surface.

Described in these terms, Akan constitutes a quintessential example of an autosegmental system. What is interesting, however, is the manner in which various facts deviate from the standard autosegmental ideal. In the following discussion, we first consider evidence that low vowels resist cooccurring with a [+ATR] value, manifestations of ATR/LO (11b), and then we consider evidence that the value [+high] exhibits preferential status with respect to [+ATR], manifestations of ATR/HI (11a).

Low Vowels Unlike the [ATR] values of mid and high vowels, the [ATR] values of low vowels in Akan are completely predictable from the context.

In a root containing only low vowels, low vowels are invariably [−ATR], and condition [−ATR] variants of adjacent affixes.

(68)	kasa	'to speak'
	ɔ-kasa-ɪ	'he/she spoke'
	ɔ-rɪ-kasa	'he/she is speaking'
	bɛ-da	'come sleep'
	ɔ-fata	'he/she deserves'
	ɔ-ba-a	'he/she came'
	ɔ-bɛ-ba	'he/she will come'
	mɛ-ba	'I will come'

Both within roots and for affixal morphemes, low vowels surface as [+ATR] only in contextually restricted environments. The distribution is as follows.

First, low vowels are [−ATR] when adjacent to a [−ATR] vowel.

(69) a. bañcɪ   'cassava'
         a-kʊkɔ   'fowl'
         a-pʊncɪrɛnɪ-ɪ   'frog'
         jʷarɪ   'to bathe'
         yarɪ   'to be ill'
         wa-tʊ   'he/she has thrown (it)'
         ma-çʷɛ   'I have looked at (it)'

    b.   a-mɪna   'hole'
         a-bɛrɛwa   'old woman'
         pɪra   'to sweep'
         wʊwa   'bee'

The examples in (69) illustrate cases where [a] precedes a nonlow retracted vowel
(69a) and where [a] follows a nonlow retracted vowel (69b).

In addition, [a] is [−ATR] when occurring to the right of a (nonlow) advanced
vowel.

(70) sika   'money'
     kosua   'egg'
     m-moja   'blood'
     e-cʷã   'scar'
     bisa   'to ask'
     o-kura   'he/she is holding'

When preceding a [+ATR] vowel, however, the low vowel is raised and fronted,
giving the low [+ATR] vowel [a̡] (Clements 1981). In verbs, this raising takes place
only in front of high advanced vowels; in nouns, raising takes place before any
advanced vowel.[50]

(71) a. *Verbs*

         pa̡tiri   'to slip'
         ŋʷa̡nsĩ   'to sneeze'
         ka̡ri   'to weigh'
         wa̡-tu   'he has dug it'

    b.   *Nouns*

         a̡-furuma   'navel'
         na̡ñcʷi-e   'cow'
         ya̡funu   'belly'
         kaŋka̡bi   'millipede'
         ba̡-yi-ɛ   'witchcraft'

kʷajo   [proper name]

a̧-ko   'parrot'

a̧-go   'velvet'

pɪra̧ko   'pig'

One might interpret the cases in (71) as evidence for the application of canonical harmony to low vowel targets. As demonstrated by Clements (1981), however, such cannot be the case. There are essentially three differences between the harmony observed with mid and high vowels, and the limited harmony observed in (71) for low vowels.

First, a low vowel is a Target only for a trigger to its right. Unlike with nonlow vowel Targets, harmony does not take place from left to right (compare (70) with (66)). Second, the effect of an advanced vowel on a low vowel appears to have a categorial condition (noun/verb) that is not present with nonlow vowels. Finally, examples like kaŋka̧bi 'millipede' and pɪra̧ko 'pig' show that the effect of an advanced trigger on a low vowel is local; the vowel preceding the low vowel adjacent to the trigger is unaffected whether low or nonlow.[51]

These differences serve to demonstrate that the process of "Raising" as it affects low vowels cannot be collapsed with the general harmony process. As a corollary, the general harmony process must be prevented from applying to low vowels. Within the context of the present work, this means that harmony is constrained by the ATR/LO Condition. Moreover, it can be demonstrated that the ATR/LO Condition, in conjunction with Locality, is *directly* responsible for blocking harmony and creating opacity, rather than *indirectly* causing opacity via the association of an opaque [−ATR] specification. The argument is structured as follows: (i) certain facts concerning the distribution of [ATR] in underlying forms demonstrate that low vowels are initially unspecified for [ATR], (ii) certain facts concerning the phonetic realization of low vowels demonstrate that low vowels are unspecified for [ATR] postlexically. Since low vowels are unspecified for [ATR], their opacity cannot be the result of preassociation.

The distributional facts arguing for not initially specifying low vowels as [−ATR] are as follows. Within a stem, [a] precedes [−ATR] vowels, as in yarɪ 'to be ill' (69a), and follows [−ATR] vowels, as in pɪra 'to sweep' (69b). Within an advanced stem, a low vowel may precede a [+ATR] vowel (where it will undergo the special rule discussed above), as in ka̧ri 'to weigh' (71), and a low vowel may also follow a [+ATR] vowel, as in sika 'money' (70).

Within the analysis where low vowels are unspecified for [ATR] underlyingly, this distribution is trivially accounted for. General Association and Harmony are blocked by ATR/LO from assigning a morpheme-level [+ATR] specification to a low vowel, as shown in (72).

(72) a. y A r I   b. p I r A   c. k A r i   d. s i k A
                                                  ⋮   ⋮
                                               +ATR   +ATR

The opacity effect derived by ATR/LO in Akan can be straightforwardly contrasted with the transparency effect derived by the same condition in Kinande. In Kinande, ATR/LO is not imposed phonologically, but makes its effect felt at the phonetic level through the counteraction of the opposing values, [+ATR] and [+low]; in Akan, ATR/LO makes its effect felt phonologically, ruling out the cooccurrence of [+ATR] and [+low] in all phonological representations.

In an alternative approach where low vowels are underlyingly linked to a [−ATR] specification as in (73), the analysis becomes more stipulative.

(73) a. y a r I   b. p I r a   c. k a r i   d. s i k a
         | | | ⋮   ⋮ |
        −ATR   −ATR   −ATR+ATR   +ATR−ATR

Cases like (73c) require that a morpheme-level [+ATR] specification be allowed to follow the [−ATR] specification of a low vowel; cases like (73d) require that a morpheme-level [+ATR] specification be allowed to precede the [−ATR] specification of a low vowel. But if the morpheme-level specifications precede and follow segment-level specifications, such an analysis incorrectly predicts the possibility of two unattested classes: it should be possible for roots with low vowels to have a *preceding* or *following* [+ATR] value that associates outside of the root, as in (74).

(74) a.   C   a...   b. ...C   a
               | |
            +ATR −ATR   −ATR +ATR

In a case like (74a), prefixes would be advanced while suffixes would be retracted; in a case like (74b), suffixes would be advanced while prefixes would be retracted. Neither type of case appears to exist. We conclude from these distributional facts that low vowels are underlyingly unspecified for [ATR].

It might be possible to prelink low vowels with a [−ATR] specification, but to have the morpheme-level specification on a different tier (Cole 1987, McCarthy 1989a): under this view, the two would be unordered with respect to each other.[52] Two points are important in this regard. First, the motivation for positing "morpheme-level" tongue root features is the observation that *all* tongue root values for a morpheme can be determined by a single underlying tongue root value. If both [+ATR] and [−ATR] specifications are included for a morpheme (even if on different tiers), this point is no longer as clearly maintained in the analysis. That is, it is less straightforward to call a [+ATR] specification a "morpheme-level" specification when it is not the only tongue root specification on the morpheme.[53] Nevertheless, let us assume that [+ATR] values are unordered with respect to [−ATR] values on low vowels by virtue of appearing on a different tier. While this would resolve the distributional problem shown in (73) and (74), it leads to our second point: except for the presence of [−ATR] on low vowels, in most respects, the analysis required would be entirely comparable to the analysis *without* [−ATR] at all, differing only in that it would lose results available in an analysis where low vowels are unspecified for [ATR].

First, recall that the central motivation for assigning [−ATR] to low vowels in the first place was to derive their opacity from the No Crossing Constraint. Obviously, if [−ATR] is not on the same tier as [+ATR], opacity of low vowels cannot be due to crossing. The solution to this problem is to appeal to Locality (which in any event has been demonstrated to derive the No Crossing Constraint; see section 1.5.2.2). If Locality is the relevant condition, however, then the presence of [−ATR] on low vowels is completely superfluous—it plays no role in the phonology of harmony.

Second, if [−ATR] is present in the phonology, whether on the same tier as [+ATR] or on a different tier, then certain additional problems arise. To illustrate such problems, consider the possibility of resolving the multitier problem by specifying low vowels with [−ATR] and by assuming moreover that [−ATR] is the sole active value for [ATR] in Akan. Such an approach is untenable for various reasons. As noted by Berry (1957) and Stewart (1967), there are certain asymmetries in the distribution of [ATR] that argue in favor of [+ATR] being the specified value. One example is that over word boundaries, [−ATR] is replaced by [+ATR] and not vice versa, a pattern to be discussed below. In addition, a [−ATR] analysis runs into contradictions when confronted with some of the data shown above. The examples in (69), (70), and (71) show that within roots, low vowels may both precede and follow vowels of both [−ATR] and [+ATR] values. Such data demonstrate either (i) that not all low vowels would be specified for [−ATR] early on, or (ii) that spreading of [−ATR] would not take place from a low trigger. But either conclusion would be incompatible with the data in (68), which show that prefixes are consistently [−ATR] when preceding a low vowel. That is, a [−ATR] account would require simultaneously that low vowels be consistently [−ATR] and that low vowels be [−ATR] as a function of lexical idiosyncrasy, a contradiction. The general conclusion seems to be that if [−ATR] is specified at all, then (i) it must be specified in conjunction with [+ATR], and (ii) it must be constrained in some way so as to be phonologically inert. Such inertness is purely stipulative if [−ATR] is present phonologically, but derives from the feature representation if [+ATR] is the sole active F-element.

Having established that low vowels are underlyingly unspecified for [ATR], we address the question of whether they receive a [−ATR] specification during the course of the phonological derivation.

The examples in (71) showed that low vowels are raised and fronted in certain environments when preceding a [+ATR] vowel. With [a], this effect can be seen word-internally since low vowels do not otherwise undergo harmony; across word boundaries, the effect is seen with all vowels. (As Clements (1981) points out, in the word-internal cases, nonlow vowels to the left of [+high, +ATR] vowels always undergo General Harmony, so the application of this second rule would not be apparent.) Some representative examples are given in (75), where, as in (71), raising is indicated by a subscripted dot (Clements 1981).

(75) *Raising of nonlow vowels*

Stem	Definite	Indefinite	
a. bayırɛ	bayırɛ nʊ	bayırɛ̣ bi	'yam'
b. ɔwɔ	ɔwɔ nʊ	ɔwɔ̣ ni	'snake'
c. bañcɪ	bañcɪ nʊ	bañcɪ̣ bi	'cassava'
d. ɔsʊnʊ	ɔsʊnʊ nʊ	ɔsʊnʊ̣ bi	'elephant'
e. ŋŋʷa	ŋŋʷa nʊ	ŋŋʷạ bi	'snail'

Raising is clearly a late, probably phonetic, rule. As noted by Berry (1957), Clements (1981), Kiparsky (1985), and Dolphyne (1988), the rule is gradient in nature. Raising a mid vowel such as [ɛ] produces a surface vowel that is described as intermediate between [ɛ] and [e], *not* as identical to [e].

In addition, Clements (1981:155) states that the degree of raising and fronting in this environment varies noticeably depending on the syntactic juncture involved, and that this variation is also speaker-dependent. Clements further observes that the effect may extend beyond the immediately preceding vowel: "... Vowel Raising ... influences the articulation of preceding syllables as well, causing them to acquire increasingly raised variants in a gradual 'crescendo' as the conditioning syllable is approached ..." (Clements 1981:157). In a discussion of this *cline* effect (Kiparsky 1985), Berry (1957:130) notes that the effect may take place not only over several syllables, but also "... through a sequence of distinct words ...". Based on these descriptions, we follow Kiparsky (1985) in concluding that the effect is derived by interpolation of [+ATR] rather than by a categorical spreading rule (see Pierrehumbert and Beckman 1988, Keating 1988, Cohn 1989 on interpolation).

Consider two possible representations (76a,b) for the phonological input to the phonetics in a phrase like *Ama ayıra sika nʊ* 'Ama has lost the money' (Berry 1957).

(76) a. ama ayıra sika nʊ   b. a m a   a y ı r a   s i k a   n ʊ

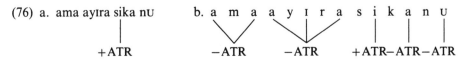

The gradient crescendo may begin as early as *ama*, extending through to the [+ATR] specification of *sika*. If the underspecified representation in (76a) is adopted, it is straightforward to adopt Pierrehumbert and Beckman's (1988) proposal for deriving the attested cline as the phonetic interpolation of a local feature transition, perhaps with the positing of a boundary [−ATR]. That the interpolation occurs across a sequence of vowels might suggest that the effect is, in fact, nonlocal. However, as Pierrehumbert and Beckman (1988:161) emphasize in their discussion of the interpolation of tone in Japanese, "When the two tones are well separated, ... they are nonlocal only when viewed from the phoneme tier. When viewed from the tone tier, they are indeed local, referring only to adjacent elements on the tier or in the prosodic tree."[54] It is the absence of specifications for [−ATR] throughout the representations that allows interpolation to be a local effect. (See also chapter 1 on Locality.)

If, on the other hand, we assume along the lines of (76b) that each low vowel is specified as [−ATR], then there is no obvious motivation for a phonetic cline; a stable string of retracted vowels would be expected. Note in this regard that no rules discussed by Clements (1981, 1984) or by Schachter and Fromkin (1968) that apply subsequent to harmony require that the gradient [+ATR] vowels ever be on a phonological path with [+ATR].

Akan Postlexical [+ATR] Harmony

We do not formalize the rule of Akan postlexical [+ATR] harmony because we do not have a clear understanding of how rules creating gradient effects are to be represented. In this regard, we disagree with the conclusion drawn by Kiparsky (1985) that the lexical and postlexical rules are one and the same rule, the difference being that the postlexical application of the rule violates lexical marking conditions. In Akan, the two effects cannot be the result of a single rule: postlexically, the rule is restricted to [+high] triggers while lexically, there is no such restriction. Moreover, the rules apply differently to classes of nouns and of verbs. Thus, while the two rules are quite similar, they are not identical and so cannot clearly be a single rule with both lexical and postlexical application.

For whatever reason, such nearly identical pairs of rules do not appear to be that uncommon. See Hyman 1990b for a pair of nearly identical tone rules, and section 3.2.3.1 on Kinande for a set of rules governing [ATR] harmony; several of our analyses in chapter 4 involve pairs of nearly identical rules, such as the Maasai rules spreading [ATR] and the Eastern Javanese rules inserting [−ATR]. (See chapter 5 for a possible explanation of such sets of similar rules.)

Before leaving the question of the Akan cline, we note two important implications of the analysis presented here. First, consider the status of the ATR/LO Condition, which prohibits the cooccurrence of [+ATR] with [+low]. If these two features cooccur on a path at some level of Akan, then ATR/LO must not hold of the relevant level. On the face of it, the mere existence of the vowel [a] would seem to warrant such a relaxing of the grounded ATR/LO Condition. But note that under an interpolation analysis, there is no necessary phonological cooccurrence of [+ATR] with [+low]. The fact that there is a phonetic transition does not mean that there is cooccurrence of the type represented by a phonological path.

Kiparsky (1985:125) suggests that "postlexical rules which spread features in violation of lexical marking conditions ... are intrinsically gradient." It should be noted, however, that gradient effects are *not* restricted to feature combinations that are defined by path conditions as marked—note the tonal facts of Japanese (Pierrehumbert and Beckman 1988), for example. Thus, the effects mentioned in the quotation from Kiparsky 1985 are a subset of the gradient effects allowed in general. Under the Grounding Condition model, if gradient effects are the result of rules of phonetic interpolation, then gradience does not result from the cooccurrence of F-elements on paths and hence should not be subject to the set of path conditions that hold in a particular language. Recall in this regard that "Vowel Raising" affects *all* vowels, assigning a gradient [+ATR] realization to nonlow vowels as well as to low vowels. Low vowels are not singled out to be affected by [+ATR], an effect that would be ungrounded.

The second implication concerns opacity. Forms like those in (77) illustrate the fact, already noted, that low vowels interrupt general harmonic spreading.

(77) a. pırąko   'pig'

    b. fuñanı   'to search'

    c. o-bisa-ı   'he/she asked (it)'

    d. ɔ-kạri-i   'he/she weighed (it)'

Since low vowels are specified for [−ATR] neither underlyingly nor at the late level where clines are derived, this means that the opacity in (77) cannot be the result of the convention prohibiting crossed association lines (Goldsmith 1976, Clements 1981). Following the proposal in section 1.5.2, and as already seen for a comparable case in Pulaar (section 3.2.1.3), we propose that opacity results from (i) the inability of a [+ATR] specification to link to a [+low] vowel, in conjunction with (ii) the ill-formedness of any configuration where harmonic spreading would skip a low vowel (Locality/Precedence). That is, opacity is directly the result of the antagonistic relation identified by the ATR/LO Condition. (See section 4.7 for discussion of the formal configurations that give rise to neutrality.)

Highness and Frontness We have just shown that the formal "canonicity" of harmony in Akan is disturbed by the imposition of ATR/LO: general linking and spreading of [+ATR] cannot affect low vowels. In addition to this evidence for grounded conditions operating in Akan, there is abundant evidence for the relevance of the ATR/HI Condition: *If [+ATR] then [+high]/not [−high]*. It must first be stressed that ATR/HI, unlike ATR/LO, cannot be considered a condition on representations in general. Numerous examples, including cases of lexical contrast, show that both [+ATR] and [−ATR] mid and high vowels exist in Akan. Nevertheless, in specific contexts we find either that [+ATR] is restricted to high vowels, or that [+high, +ATR] is a preferred trigger for harmony.

Recall the discussion of clines and the relevant data given in (71) and (75). Although the discussion so far has concentrated on the effects of interpolation on low vowels, it is equally relevant that in verbs, the sole class of triggers for raising is *high* vowels. That is, not all vowels are triggers; only the class with the sympathetic combination of [+high, +ATR] is strong enough to induce a raising effect. Note that it is not crucial for this point that raising be specifically phonetic, as suggested above, or phonological. The central claim of the Grounding Hypothesis is that phonologies exhibit formal reflections of phonetic properties. This effect of high vowels on [−ATR] vowels to their right can also be observed in compounds; see Dolphyne 1988.

It has also been observed (Stewart 1967; note also Berry 1957) that with monomorphemic verb stems, [+ATR] is possible only in a stem containing at least one high vowel.[55] For example, in a monosyllabic verb root in Asante, we observe a full range of retracted vowels, but only two advanced vowels.

(78) *Monosyllabic verb roots*

Retracted	sɪw	'sharpen'
	sɛw	'spread out'
	saw	'dance'
	sɔw	'catch'
	sʊw	'bear fruit'
Advanced	siw	'plug a hole'
	suw	'be worn out/decay'

Whether or not further investigation warrants a synchronic treatment along the lines of that proposed above for a similar restriction in Kinande (section 3.2.3.1), such a restricted distribution illustrates a clear tendency for the feature value [+ATR] to be closely tied to the feature value [+high].

As a final observation concerning the feature [+high], consider an additional rule whereby only [+ATR] vowels precede palatal consonants that are followed by [a]. In (79a), the regular harmonic effect is seen on nonlow vowels; in (79b), the interpolative effect of [+ATR] is seen on the low vowel.[56] The forms in (79c) show that the phenomenon cannot be explained by positing a floating [+ATR] in the palatal-[a]

forms: a floating [+ATR] could dock to the final nonlow vowel in these examples, but there is no evidence for such docking.

(79) a. o-cʷa-ɪ   'he cut it'
     wu-be-jʷarɪ   'you will bathe'
     o-jʷanɪ-ɪ   'he fled'
     o-sʸanɪ-ɪ   'he descended' [cf. dialectal o-sanɪ-ɪ]
     o-ñanɪ-ɪ   'he woke up'
     e-cʷa   'scar'
     ejʷa (asɪ)   'market'
     ojʷañ   'sheep'

   b. a̱-cʷa   'he has cut it'

   c. jʷarɪ   'to bathe'
      jʷanɪ   'to flee'
      jaɪ   'to abandon'
      cʷarɪ (mu)   'to cross'
      çʷanɪ   'to peel; hatch'
      sʸanɪ   'to descend'
      ñanɪ   'to awaken'

Under the assumption that the palatalized consonants in such examples are [+high] and/or [−back], the appropriate redundancy rule requires either (i) the ATR/HI Condition (that [+ATR] is inserted only on a *high* consonant), or (ii) the ATR/BK Condition (that [+ATR] is inserted only on a *front* consonant),[57] or (iii) both ATR/ HI and ATR/BK.

A final instance of the influence of ATR/HI in Akan is found with the affixation of vowel-initial suffixes. A stem-final high [+ATR] vowel triggers the general rightward harmony rule, illustrated in (80a). However, a stem-final nonhigh [+ATR] vowel loses its [+ATR] specification under suffixation (80b,c). (See chapter 5 for a somewhat similar process in Lango.)

(80) *Loss of [+ATR] on nonhigh vowels* (Dolphyne 1988:23)

   a. di   o-di-i   'he ate it'
      hu   o-hu-i   'he saw it'
                o-numi-i   'he sucked it'

   b. wie   o-wiɛ-ɛɪ   o-wiɛ-ɛyɛ   'he finished it'
      surɔ   o-surɔ-ɔɪ   o-surɔ-ɔyɛ   'he was afraid'
      hwire   e-hwirɛ-ɛɪ   e-hwirɛ-ɛyɛ   'it got pierced'

   c. wie   a-wiɛ-yɛ   'the end'
      sie   a-siɛ-yɛ   'cemetery'

d. hwɛ   ɔ-hwɛ-ɪ   'he looked at it'
   tɔ   ɔ-tɔ-ɪ   'he bought it'
            ɔ-tʊ-ɪ   'he baked it'

The paradigm is completed with (80d), which shows that nonhigh vowels that are not [+ATR] exhibit no special behavior in this environment.

Of importance here is that the rule deleting [+ATR] targets an *ungrounded* configuration, one combining [+ATR] with [−high], and makes it more grounded: the output is in accord with ATR/HI while the input is not.

We conclude, therefore, that even though high retracted vowels do occur in Akan, there is nevertheless evidence for the presence of grounded conditions involving high vowels in the operation of various morpheme-level constraints and intra- and inter-word processes. To summarize, the distribution of [+ATR] in Akan is grounded, but only minimally so: the ATR/LO and LO/ATR Conditions are the only ones that hold of the language as a whole; ATR/HI (and perhaps also ATR/BK) hold under specific circumstances.

Akan Grounding

1. [ATR] is active in underlying representation (marked according to [ATR] Markedness (21a)).
2. [+ATR] is active (unmarked according to [ATR] Markedness (21b)).
3. ATR/LO, LO/ATR hold of all rules (unmarked with respect to Grounding Conditions I and II (12)).
4. ATR/HI holds in various specific situations: verb roots, triggers of regressive phrase-level and compound harmony, conditioning of harmony induced by palatal and palatalized consonants (consistent with Grounding Conditions I and IIa; semimarked with respect to Grounding Condition IIb (12)).

The case of Akan illustrates our hypothesis that grounded conditions represent *tendencies*, not *absolutes*. Languages vary in which conditions are relevant and in the number of conditions that are relevant. The greatest falsifiability of the Grounding Hypothesis lies not in *how many* conditions hold but in *which* conditions hold: we claim that path conditions are restricted to only those that are phonetically grounded. Whether a language imposes conditions extensively (like Pulaar) or in a more limited fashion (like Akan), the conditions imposed are members of the set of grounded conditions.

The existence of grounded path conditions does not depend on assuming a particular active value for a feature. Just as [+ATR] is in a sympathetic relation to tongue body raising and in an antagonistic relation to tongue body lowering, so [−ATR] is in exactly the opposite relation with respect to comparable gestures. By making the use of [−ATR] as an active F-element a marked situation rather than a proscribed one, we predict the existence of languages where [−ATR] is active, but in a grounded fashion. Note that for [−ATR] to be active, both clauses of the [ATR] Markedness Statement in (21a) and (21b) are given marked values. But the Grounding Conditions themselves should still hold. We demonstrate that this is the case in Wolof and in Yoruba: in both languages, RTR/HI and RTR/LO serve an important function in constraining the assignment or spreading of [−ATR].

3.2.4 Lexical Specification of [−ATR]

In the preceding sections, we have proposed a substantive set of constraints governing the feature [ATR], constraints that are grounded in physiological properties. We have demonstrated that these constraints derive cross-linguistic patterns of behavior of [ATR] in inventories, and that they contribute to an explanation of the behavior of [ATR] in cases where it functions actively.

In the examples considered so far, the active F-element is [+ATR], which we have hypothesized to be the unmarked situation where [ATR] is active (see (21)). However, as with the Grounding Conditions, we view the Markedness Statement to be a tendency, not an absolute. At this point, we turn to an examination of languages in which [−ATR] is the active F-element. Recall that where [−ATR] is active, the relevant versions of grounded path conditions are those referring to [−ATR], not to [+ATR].

In addition to demonstrating why we propose that the [ATR] Markedness Statement (21b) is a tendency, not an absolute, the languages considered here also reveal that the Grounding Conditions govern a variety of effects of rule application. We present Wolof [−ATR] harmony and review relevant aspects of Yoruba [−ATR] harmony (see section 2.3.1): in both languages, [−ATR] is the active F-element. We demonstrate that the grounded conditions RTR/HI and RTR/LO are relevant in both languages, although the conditions have quite different effects because of their interaction with rules involving slightly different formal properties.

Before beginning the discussion of languages with a lexically active [−ATR], we would like to reemphasize that the [ATR] Markedness Statement in (21b) is provisional (i.e., the proposal that [+ATR] is preferred as the active value over [−ATR]): [−ATR] might be the preferred [ATR] value. Since markedness proposals reflect cross-linguistic tendencies, as the data base of rules involving [ATR] grows and becomes more reliable, we will be in a better position to evaluate the substantive side of the markedness hypothesis.

3.2.4.1 Wolof Wolof (Ka 1988) belongs to the West Atlantic subgroup of the Niger-Congo language family; it is spoken in Senegal and the Gambia. Wolof har-

mony is interesting because it has two vowels that are consistently specified for a particular [ATR] value on the surface, although the values for [ATR] are different for the two vowels concerned: (i) [+high] vowels are always [+ATR] and (ii) long [+low] vowels are always [−ATR]. Harmonically, long low vowels behave as though their [−ATR] value were definitively present, triggering harmony regardless of their position in a string. In contrast, high vowels behave in a somewhat inconsistent fashion: *initial* high vowels appear to trigger harmony; all other high vowels are transparent. We argue that the range of properties attested in Wolof is consistent with positing [−ATR], not [+ATR], as the active F-element in Wolof.

The distribution of [ATR] F-elements with respect to [+high] and [+low] is important not only in determining which F-element is active but also in understanding the role of the Grounding Conditions in Wolof. We argue that RTR/LO, RTR/HI, and HI/ATR are all relevant in Wolof, and that no ungrounded conditions are required.

Harmony and Nonhigh Vowels   Wolof distinguishes eight vowels on the surface, as shown in (81). The vowels can be long or short, except for [ə], which can only be short.[58]

(81) *Wolof surface vowels*

    [−ATR]   ɛ a ɔ
    [+ATR]   i e ə o u

  a. Active F-elements

    +HI, +LO, +BK, ⟨−ATR⟩

  b. Conditions

    HI/LO Condition: If [+high] then not [+low].
    LO/HI Condition: If [+low] then not [+high].

c.	*	*	U	I	A_1	A_2	O	E
	+HI	+HI	+HI	+HI				
	+LO	+LO			+LO	+LO		
	+BK		+BK		+BK		+BK	

[−ATR] is not included in the combinations in (81c) because it is a free F-element in underlying representation, shown by the box in (81a). To indicate that [−ATR] is active but not in a path in underlying representation, capital letters are used to designate the "archiphonemes" resulting from the various combinations of F-elements. The two starred combinations are ruled out by the conditions in (81b). Of the two possibilities, A_1 and A_2, Representational Simplicity selects the latter: we know of no evidence requiring A_1 in Wolof.

Within a word, nonhigh vowels generally agree for [ATR], as shown in (82). (Wolof data lists here and elsewhere include both the standard Wolof orthography and a phonetic transcription in square brackets.) (82a) includes polymorphemic forms with [+ATR] variants of the mid vowels; (82b) shows forms with the same morphological structure where the mid vowels are [−ATR]. As (82c,d) indicate, nonhigh forms typically exhibit the same value for [ATR] on all vowels. (We discuss exceptions to this generalization shortly.)

(82) *Harmony: Nonhigh vowels*

    a. [−high, +ATR] ... [−high, +ATR]

jënd-ël	[jəndəl]	'buy for'
lééb-ël	[leebəl]	'tell stories for'
fóót-ël	[footəl]	'do laundry for'
gën-é	[gəne]	'be better in'
réér-é	[reere]	'be lost in'
dóór-é	[doore]	'hit with'
bëgg-óón	[bəggoon]	'wanted'
réér-óón	[reeroon]	'was lost'
ñów-óón	[ñowoon]	'came'

    b. [−high, −ATR] ... [−high, −ATR]

wax-al	[waxal]	'speak for'
bey-al	[bɛyal]	'cultivate for'
woor-al	[wɔɔral]	'fast for'
xam-e	[xamɛ]	'know in'
dem-e	[dɛmɛ]	'go with'
xool-e	[xɔɔlɛ]	'look with'
takk-oon	[takkɔɔn]	'tied'
reer-oon	[rɛɛrɔɔn]	'had dinner'
jox-oon	[jɔxɔɔn]	'gave'

    c. [−high, +ATR] ... [−high, −ATR]

    none

    d. [−high, −ATR] ... [−high, +ATR]

    none

Stems with exclusively mid vowels and/or short low vowels demonstrate that rightward harmony exists in Wolof. At this point, either [−ATR] or [+ATR] could be the active F-element. The ensuing discussion argues that the active harmonic feature is [−ATR], motivated through the inspection of forms with low or high vowels. If [−ATR] is active, Grounding Theory predicts possible asymmetries with low and high vowels: low vowels (possibly in some context) are expected to always be [−ATR] while high vowels (again, possibly in some context) are expected to never be [−ATR]. Both of these predictions are borne out; we examine low vowels first.

Low Vowels   In general, low vowels alternate, as do mid vowels. This is illustrated by the suffix alternations -al/-əl in the first data sets in (82a,b). There are two exceptions to this generalization, one phonological and the other lexical. From inspecting the behavior of these exceptions, we find evidence supporting [−ATR] as the active F-element in Wolof.

The surface forms of the suffixes in (83) confirm that low vowels alternate in the harmonic environment. In (83a), low vowels follow a [+ATR] stem, surfacing as [ə]. In (83b), low vowels follow [−ATR] stems and surface as [a].[59]

(83)   *Alternating low vowels*

a.   [+ATR] ... ə

sófóór-ëm	[sofoorəm]	'his/her driver'
tëcc-ët	[təccət]	'to smash'
génn-ëndóó	[gennəndoo]	'to go out together'
dóór-ënté	[doorənte]	'to hit each other'
wétt-ëli	[wettəli]	'to give company to'
tër-ëdi	[tərədi]	'to be agitated'

b.   [−ATR] ... a

tool-am	[tɔɔlam]	'his/her field'
màtt-at	[maattat]	'to bite continuously'
dend-andoo	[dɛndandɔɔ]	'to be neighbors'
xool-ante	[xɔɔlantɛ]	'to look at each other'
fecc-ali	[fɛccali]	'to fill completely'
xam-adi	[xamadi]	'to be impolite'

Long low vowels differ from short low vowels in two ways. First, they do not alternate: long low vowels are always [−ATR]. Second, regardless of their position in a string, long low vowels induce [−ATR] on subsequent vowels—as predicted if [−ATR] is the active value. (84)–(86) illustrate the behavior of the long low vowels. The forms in (84) show that where a long low vowel occurs as the first vowel in a sequence, subsequent vowels are [−ATR]. The first two members of each set show that the suffixes alternate depending on the stem vowel. The third member of each set shows that after long low vowels, only [−ATR] variants surface.

(84) *Initial long low vowels*

    a. réér-é   [reere]   'to be lost in'
        xool-e   [xɔɔlɛ]   'to look with'
        xaar-e   [xaarɛ]   'to wait in'

    b. dóór-lé   [doorle]   'to help hit'
        dee-le   [dɛɛlɛ]   'to lose a relative'
        jaay-le   [jaaylɛ]   'to help sell'

    c. sófóór bëlé   [sofoor bəle]   'that driver'
        golo bale   gɔlɔ balɛ]   'that monkey'
        mbaam male [mbaam malɛ] 'that donkey'

    d. góór góógulé [goor googule]   'that man just mentioned'
        cere boobule   [cɛrɛ bɔɔbulɛ] 'that couscous just mentioned'
        gaal googule   [gaal gɔɔgulɛ] 'that boat just mentioned'

The behavior of medial long low vowels is shown in (85): nonhigh vowels to the right are [−ATR], regardless of values for [ATR] to the left.

(85) *Medial long low vowels*

    a. yóbbuwaale   [yobbuwaalɛ]   'to carry away also'
        génnaale   [gennaalɛ]   'to go out also'
        woowaale   [wɔɔwaalɛ]   'to call also'
        jamaale   [jamaalɛ]   'to pierce also'

    b. dóóraate   [dooraatɛ]   'to hit usually'
        yabaate   [yabaatɛ]   'to lack respect for'

    c. jéémëntuwaaleeti   [jeemǝntuwaalɛɛti]   'to try also without conviction
                                             once more'

      < jéém-   -antu-   -aale-   -ati
         'to try' 'DEPRECIATIVE' 'ASSOCIATIVE' 'REITERATIVE'

The forms in (86) are borrowed words. The same harmonic pattern is found in borrowings: vowels following /aa/ are [−ATR].[60]

(86) *Borrowed words*

    a. ʔaajo   [ʔaajɔ]   'need' (from Arabic)
        saafara   [saafara]   'holy water' (from Arabic)
        taalibe   [taalibɛ]   'disciple' (from Arabic)

    b. séytaane   [seytaanɛ]   'devil' (from Arabic)
        kumaase   [kumaasɛ]   'to start' (from French)
        tamaate   [tamaatɛ]   'tomato' (from French)

To summarize, two generalizations hold of long low vowels in Wolof. First, long low vowels are [−ATR]. Second, nonhigh vowels to the right of a long low vowel are [−ATR].

These generalizations are simple manifestations of grounded conditions. The first observation can be expressed by a rule inserting [−ATR] on long vowels, a rule conditioned by RTR/LO: *If [−ATR] then [+low]*. This condition selects only the [+low] vowels as Targets of the rule. All long low vowels without [−ATR] in their underlying representation (i.e., unexceptional vowels) receive the F-element via this rule.

The second observation is expressed by ensuring that low vowels are assigned [−ATR] *before* the application of regular harmony. In this way, all long low vowels are [−ATR] when harmony applies and so they trigger harmony, regardless of their position in the string.

The evidence from low vowels thus suggests that [−ATR] is the active F-element and that the harmony rule extends the domain of a [−ATR] specification rightward.

Further support for the analysis of [−ATR] as active comes from the behavior of the agentive suffix *-kat*. The short low vowel in *-kat* never alternates, as seen in (87).

(87) *Nonalternating /a/*

    a. [+ATR] ... kat

fóót-kat	[footkat]	*[fɔɔtkat]	*[footkət]	'laundry person'
yëglé-kat	[yəglekat]	*[yaglɛkat]	*[yəglekət]	'announcer'
tëgg-kat	[təggkat]	*[taggkat]	*[təggkət]	'drummer'

    b. [−ATR] ... kat

togg-kat	[tɔggkat]	'cook'
jàngale-kat	[jaangalɛkat]	'teacher'
faj-kat	[fajkat]	'curer'

This morpheme also induces [−ATR] on subsequent vowels, as illustrated in (88). (Compare the behavior of *-am* in these cases with its behavior in (83).)

(88) *Nonalternating /a/ induces harmony*

    a. [+ATR] ... kat ... [−ATR]

ligééy-kat-am	[ligeeykatam]	'his/her worker'
luxus-kat-am	[luxuskatam]	'his/her magician'

    b. [−ATR] ... kat ... [−ATR]

jàngale-kat-am	[jaangalɛkatam]	'his/her teacher'
xonjom-kat-am	[xɔnjɔmkatam]	'his/her witch'

The behavior of *-kat* 'AGENT' follows from the underlying representation of the morpheme if two assumptions are made, (i) *-kat* is underlyingly assigned [−ATR] and (ii) the harmonic transmission of [−ATR] takes place in a regular fashion, from left to right, in such forms. This is consistent with [−ATR] as the active F-element.

High Vowels   Further support for positing [−ATR] as the active harmonic value comes from the behavior of high vowels: although high vowels are never [−ATR] (or are always [+ATR]), they appear to trigger harmony *only* when in initial position. Thus, high vowels do not exhibit the pattern expected when a combination is always accompanied by the harmonic F-element. Rather, medial high vowels behave as though [+ATR] were *absent* since they do not interfere with harmony (89), while initial high vowels behave as though [+ATR] were *present* since they appear to induce harmony (92). These contradictory facts argue against an underlying [+ATR] F-element.

(89) shows that noninitial high vowels are transparent to Wolof [−ATR] harmony. That is, if nonhigh vowels flank a high vowel, the nonhigh vowels still agree for [ATR], regardless of the presence of the high vowel. In (89a), the nonhigh vowels surface as [+ATR], while in (89b), they surface as [−ATR]. The absence of cases of the types in (89c) and (89d) indicates that high vowels neither block nor initiate harmony.[61]

(89) *Transparency: Medial high vowels*

  a. [+ATR] ... [+high] ... [+ATR]

gëstuléén	[gəstuleen]	'do research!'
tóxiléén	[toxileen]	'go & smoke!'
tërijiléén	[tərijileen]	'go sleep!'
séénuwóón	[seenuwoon]	'tried to spot'
tëriwóón	[təriwoon]	'went & slept'
yóbbujinë	[yobbujinə]	'he went to bring'

  b. [−ATR] ... [+high] ... [−ATR]

tekkileen	[tɛkkilɛɛn]	'untie!'
moytuleen	[mɔytulɛɛn]	'avoid!'
soppiwuleen	[sɔppiwulɛɛn]	'you have not changed'
xolliwoon	[xɔlliwɔɔn]	'peeled'
teeruwoon	[tɛɛruwɔɔn]	'welcomed'
yebbijina	[yɛbbijina]	'he went to unload'

  c. [−ATR] ... [+high] ... [−high, +ATR]

  d. [+ATR] ... [+high] ... [−high, −ATR]

Antagonistic Transparency   The data in (89) suggest that high vowels are transparent, although in a rather different way than cases seen so far. Recall that we have looked at two types of transparency. In section 3.2.3.1, we argued that there is an antagonistic transparency effect in Kinande when a [+ATR] harmonic value hits a vowel with the antagonistic F-element value [+low]; in Ngbaka (section 2.5), a sympathetic transparency effect results from spreading [+ATR] onto a high vowel that would otherwise receive [+ATR] redundantly because of the sympathetic feature specification [+high]. In the case of Wolof, although the harmonic F-element [−ATR] would indeed be antagonistic to the F-element [+high], there is absolutely no evidence that high vowels receive the F-element [−ATR]. Unlike in Kinande, there is no salient context in which retracted high vowels are perceived. It thus seems unlikely that harmony actually assigns [−ATR] to high vowels.[62] We propose, therefore, that the high vowels are, as suggested by the term *transparency*, skipped over by the harmonic process.

We digress briefly from our discussion of grounding to consider how such skipping can be formally accomplished. First, imagine that a process of spreading skips a high vowel, along the lines shown in (90).

(90) *Ill-formed gapped representation*

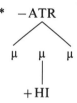

Such an analysis, while it represents perhaps the canonical autosegmental approach to "transparency" (see Archangeli and Pulleyblank 1987, Steriade 1987b, Ka 1988, etc.), violates the Locality Condition. Since this analysis is impossible given Locality, either another analysis must be available, or Locality itself must be abandoned or modified.

Such drastic measures are not necessary because a rule-based account of this case is available without any elaboration of independently required aspects of the theory. We propose that "contextual neutrality" of the Wolof type results not from a rule of spreading per se, but from a context-sensitive rule of F-element insertion: context-sensitive rules and rules that insert F-elements are each independently motivated. Thus, [−ATR] is inserted (on a nonhigh vowel) when the targeted vowel follows a [−ATR] specification. This rule is applicable in (91a,b), but is inapplicable in (91c,d) because of the absence of a contextual [−ATR]. (These examples are schematic in that [ATR] is represented as linking directly to moras, and the only prosodic structure included is moras.)

(91) *Representations after Association*

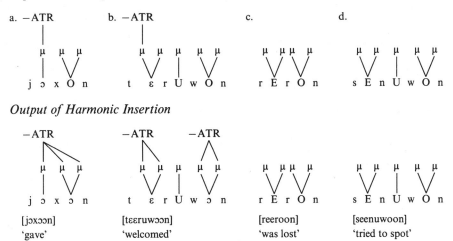

Output of Harmonic Insertion

[jɔxɔɔn]   [tɛɛruwɔɔn]   [reeroon]   [seenuwoon]
'gave'   'welcomed'   'was lost'   'tried to spot'

Two points are relevant with respect to these forms, the first involving formal properties of transparency effects, the second involving substantive issues.

Formal issues are discussed at some length in section 4.7. Several questions, all treated in chapter 4, are of importance. The technical question must be addressed of why the insertion of an F-element relates the representations /jɔxOOn/ and [jɔxɔɔn] in a manner resembling the effect of a spreading rule. As already discussed with respect to Yoruba (section 2.3.1.3), insertion results in merger when there is an identical F-element in a local environment, as determined by the OCP.[63] Since both feature insertion and spreading can result in multiply linked representations, the precise formal relation between insertion and spreading must be examined. In particular, it must be made clear why a rule inserting an F-element can result in a transparency effect, while a spreading rule cannot. A second formal issue involves the stipulation of an identity condition in the Wolof rule of Harmonic Insertion: the rule inserts [−ATR] only when following a [−ATR] specification. Identity conditions, already a crucial component of the OCP, are also addressed in chapter 4 (see section 4.7.2.2).

For present purposes, the crucial aspect of the Wolof case is not the formal characterization of harmony, but the substantive identification of the class of transparent segments, identification that is defined by the relevant grounded conditions. Specifically for Wolof, the grounded ATR/HI Condition prevents insertion from assigning a [−ATR] value to a high vowel in a case like (91b). More generally, the segments bypassed by an insertion rule are those that are ineligible to receive the harmonic F-element because of some grounded condition.

Finally, such transparency can result only from a rule of F-element insertion since a spreading rule would invariably have its effect curtailed because of the Locality Condition (see (90)).

Initial High Vowels We have shown that noninitial high vowels are transparent to [ATR] harmony and have proposed that [−ATR] is the harmonic value. There is one set of data, however, that might at first appear to argue against such a proposal. As (92) exemplifies, initial high vowels are followed systematically by [+ATR] vowels.[64]

(92) *Initial high vowels*

gis-é	[gise]	'to see in'	*[gisɛ], *[gɪsɛ]
suul-é	[suule]	'to bury with'	*[suulɛ], *[sʊʊlɛ]
jiit-lé	[jiitle]	'to help lead'	*[jiitlɛ], *[jɪɪtlɛ]
sumb-lé	[sumble]	'to help start'	*[suumblɛ], *[sʊʊmblɛ]
nir-óó	[niroo]	'to look alike'	*[nirɔɔ], *[nɪrɔɔ]
xul-óó	[xuloo]	'to quarrel'	*[xulɔɔ], *[xʊlɔɔ]
tiit-óón	[tiitoon]	'was scared'	*[tiitɔɔn], *[tɪɪtɔɔn]
suul-óón	[suuloon]	'was buried'	*[suulɔɔn], *[sʊʊlɔɔn]
ligéé-ël	[ligeeəl]	'to work for'	*[ligɛɛal], *[lɪgɛɛal]
suul-ël	[suuləl]	'to bury for'	*[suulal], *[sʊʊlal]
jiw-ëndóó	[jiwəndoo]	'to plant together'	*[jiwandɔɔ], *[jɪwandɔɔ]
wut-ëndóó	[wutəndoo]	'to look for together'	*[wutandɔɔ], *[wʊtandɔɔ]

Before considering the implications of a [+ATR] analysis of such data, we propose an account in terms of [−ATR]. The issue is how to explain why initial high vowels are never followed by [−ATR] vowels (unless of course the vowel is both long and low, or follows such a vowel) in spite of the fact that such forms would be predicted by Combinatorial Specification: underlying representations of stems with initial high vowels could include a free [−ATR] specification, which would then associate to a noninitial mid or low vowel. Although such a pattern is logically possible, there are no surface forms that would correspond to such an underlying representation. In chapter 4, we discuss a number of comparable cases. Our proposal is that the absence of such surface effects results from a rule whose application is *noniterative*, in Wolof, a noniterative rule of [−ATR] association: [−ATR] can associate only to the leftmost vowel, and where that vowel is [+high], association is impossible because of RTR/HI.

Up to this point, we have demonstrated that Grounding plays a role in the distribution of [ATR] in Wolof; we have also argued that [−ATR] is active, not [+ATR], supporting our view that the choice between [+ATR] and [−ATR] is determined by markedness considerations, not absolutes. In the next section, we complete the argument for an active [−ATR] by considering the implications of positing an active [+ATR].

Active [+ATR]? The second part of our argument for an active retracted tongue root F-element is to consider some of the problems that would arise if [+ATR] were to be analyzed as the active F-element. We examine the [+ATR] alternative in some detail for two reasons. First, a central point of this section is that [−ATR] is the active F-element, a position that goes against an apparently robust cross-linguistic pattern (21). Thus, it is necessary to seriously entertain the possibility that [+ATR] is the active F-element, in order to be assured that it is not.[65] Second, in a language like Ngbaka (section 2.5), we proposed a "no-skipping" analysis where apparent transparency results from spreading a sympathetic F-element. The potential applicability of such a hypothesis for Wolof should therefore be seriously considered. We show in this regard that if [+ATR] is the harmonic value, then the formal model must be greatly enriched. If [−ATR] is the harmonic F-element, no changes are required in the formal model.

The [+ATR] analysis must account for three basic properties: (i) the behavior of *-kat* 'AGENT', (ii) the opacity of long low vowels, and (iii) the behavior of high vowels, "harmonic" initially and transparent medially. Even assuming that the active harmonic element were [+ATR], both (i) and (ii) could be accounted for by [−ATR] specifications. In the case of *-kat*, a [−ATR] value would be present in underlying representation; in the case of long low vowels, a [−ATR] specification could be inserted by a grounded redundancy rule. Rightward spread of [+ATR] would then be blocked by the prohibition against crossed association lines (as derived by Locality) and [−ATR] would be filled in on unspecified vowels by default. Apart from noting that such a proposal requires the specification of [−ATR] in addition to the postulated harmonic [+ATR], we do not address further this aspect of the [+ATR] possibility.

The behavior of high vowels would require a more complex treatment. The distribution of [+ATR] in forms with high vowels presents a paradox if [+ATR] is the active F-element: (89) argues that harmony precedes the redundant insertion of [+ATR] on high vowels, while (92) argues for the opposite order. Dealing with this paradox, which does not arise if [−ATR] is the active F-element, is the biggest problem for the [+ATR] account.

One solution to the paradox would be to restrict the locus of the redundant insertion of [+ATR] to the leftmost vowel of a form, that is, to the cases in (92) involving initial high vowels. Such a positionally determined redundancy rule (a rule with both an F-element condition and a "position-in-the-word" condition) poses a variety of problems. Such a rule is completely "opaque": at the surface, initial high vowels are no more [+ATR] than noninitial high vowels; noninitial high vowels are no less [+ATR] than initial ones. Consequently, the assignment of [+ATR] to initial high vowels captures no generalization concerning the redundant values of [ATR] on the class of high vowels. On the contrary, the motivation for such an insertion rule appears to be a direct artifact of the theory assumed. To account for the equivalence in [ATR] values on high vowels at the surface, such an approach would presumably require a second rule that inserts [+ATR] onto high vowels generally, *after* the application of harmony. That is, two rules inserting [+ATR] onto high vowels would be required, one applying prior to harmony (initial high vowels only), the second applying after harmony.

An alternative would be to insert [+ATR] on all high vowels prior to spreading, then add conditions to the spreading rule to restrict which medial high vowels may act as triggers. In the set of cases where the vowels preceding the high vowel are [+ATR] (e.g., *góór góógulé* [goor googule] 'that man just mentioned' (84d)), a free [+ATR] value would be posited for the appropriate morpheme, and harmony would also apply from the medial high vowel; in contrast, for forms where the vowels preceding the high vowel are [−ATR] (e.g., *gaal googule* [gaal gɔɔgulɛ] 'that boat just mentioned' (84d)), no free [+ATR] would be posited and no spreading would take place from the medial high vowel. The problem is how to characterize the class of medial high vowels that trigger harmony if all high vowels are assigned [+ATR] prior to harmony, particularly when the very same vowel may trigger harmony in one case and not in another (e.g., the medial high vowel of [gɔɔgulɛ/googule]).

This point is illustrated in (93). In (93a), the underlying representation is shown, with a free [+ATR] on the stem *góór* 'man' but not on the stem *gaal* 'boat'. The second stage, (93b), shows the association of the free [+ATR] and the redundant insertion of [+ATR] on high vowels.

(93) *Assuming active [+ATR] in Wolof*

    a. Underlying   +ATR
       representation

                    g O O r   g O O g U l E   g A A l   g O O g U l E

    b. Associate &   +ATR   +ATR   +ATR
       insert [+ATR] | | |

                    g o O r   g O O g u l E   g A A l   g O O g u l E

To derive [goor googule] correctly, spreading from the medial [+ATR] would have to take place; to derive [gaal gɔɔgulɛ], spreading would have to be blocked.

The required rule could not restrict spreading to the class of [+ATR] specifications that are initial; such a restriction would incorrectly derive *[goor googulɛ]. Nor could the rule be restricted so as to apply only from a noninitial [+ATR]: apart from not accounting for harmony in the first two syllables of [goor googule], such a rule would incorrectly predict partial harmony in 'the boat just mentioned', incorrectly deriving *[gaal gɔɔgule]. The most plausible account might be one along the following lines. First, a general rule would spread a word-initial [+ATR] specification. Second, a more specific rule would spread a [+ATR] specification that *follows* a [+ATR] specification. In the representation of [goor googule] in (93), this would mean that both [+ATR] values would spread; in [gaal gɔɔgulɛ], the single [+ATR] specification would not spread since it is not initial and it does not follow a [+ATR] value.

In forms containing two noninitial high vowels, however, the account just sketched would incorrectly predict that the second such vowel would induce spreading.

(94) *Two medial high vowels*

xaritam boobule	[xaritam bɔɔbulɛ]	'that friend of his/hers just
	*[xaritam bɔɔbule]	mentioned'
cf. (89b) tekkileen	[tɛkkilɛɛn]	'untie!'
këriñëm bóóbulé	[kəriñəm boobule]	'that coal of his/hers just
		mentioned'
cf. (89a) gëstuléén	[gəstuleen]	'do research!'

Thus, the behavior of medial high vowels would be problematical if [+ATR] were the active F-element.

Moreover, finding some solution to the medial high vowel problem would not resolve all difficulties. Another problem would be how to characterize the requirement that the [+ATR] inducing harmony is typically associated to the first vowel in the form.

We have already shown that characterizing the trigger as the leftmost [+ATR] specification fails—being "initial" cannot mean "initial on the [ATR] tier." Another possibility would be to characterize the spreading element as the [+ATR] associated to the leftmost vowel of the form. Under this hypothesis, the rule would incorrectly predict *non*iterative spread of [+ATR] from the initial vowel. Howard (1972) argues that a rule may apply iteratively only if the Target of the rule satisfies Argument conditions (and a further legitimate Target exists, of course). Iterativity of a spreading rule is shown schematically in (95). The representation in (95a) is subject to a rule spreading F rightward from vowel to vowel. The first iteration spreads F to μ_2, shown in (95b); μ_2 satisfies Argument conditions, so the rule can reapply (iterate), creating the representation in (95c).

(95) *Iterative F Spread*

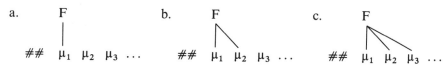

Contrast the iteration in (95) with the effect when the rule is conditioned to spread F only from the first vowel in the word, that is, from $\#\# C_0$ ____. Under a strict interpretation of the positional restriction, only one iteration is possible, from μ_1 to μ_2. Spreading from μ_2 to μ_3 is impossible because μ_2 does not satisfy the "initial-vowel" condition.

(96) *F Spread from leftmost V*

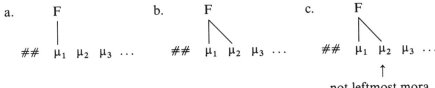

The situation in (96) is exactly that which would be predicted if spreading of [+ATR] were triggered only by the leftmost vowel in a form. But this is not the attested pattern. Thus, we conclude that the Argument of the rule cannot be conditioned by its position in the string.

The upshot of this demonstration is that the patterns observed in Wolof are, quite simply, not the expected patterns if [+ATR] were the active, harmonic F-element. By contrast, as already shown, the patterns observed are among the expected, possible patterns if [−ATR] is the active, harmonic F-element. We conclude, then, that [−ATR] is the active F-element in Wolof, in spite of a markedness tendency to the contrary.

Summary: Markedness   First, we have already presented languages where [ATR] appears not to be active at all (e.g., Tiv, Barrow Inupiaq, Haya, Ainu); we have also discussed languages where [+ATR] is the active F-element (Pulaar, Kinande, Akan). Wolof now is added to the set of languages in which [−ATR] is active (see also the discussion of Yoruba and Chukchi): this array of languages supports our hypothesis that the marking conditions (like (21)) represent tendencies in languages, not cross-linguistic laws. We will even see in languages like Kalenjin (section 3.5.3) and Lango (chapter 5) that both [+ATR] and [−ATR] may cooccur actively in a single language, and that a full 10-vowel pattern is possible by combining [±ATR] with a 5-vowel system (with considerable evidence bearing on issues of markedness and grounding).

Summary: Grounding   We have proposed that grounded path conditions may take as their domain either (i) representations in general, both underlying and derived, or (ii) specific rules. Wolof presents an example with a condition of each type.

First, throughout all stages of the language, [+high] and [−ATR] do not combine. This holds of underlying representations and of the association of [−ATR]. Additionally, it holds of Wolof [ATR] harmony, as shown by the transparency of high vowels. This is exactly the expected pattern if the HI/ATR and RTR/HI Conditions hold: neither allows [−ATR] and [+high] in combination on a path.

By deriving transparency by the postulation of path conditions, Grounding Theory predicts that only a limited class of conditions—namely, the grounded class—is allowed to characterize the set of transparent elements. Whether generally or as a property of a specific rule, transparency is cross-linguistically limited to a small subset of the logically imaginable cases. Under this view, for example, a rule comparable to that of Wolof, except with the roles of mid and high vowels reversed (i.e., high vowels alternating and mid vowels transparent), would be impossible: such a language would be proscribed since no grounded path condition could specifically restrict the association of [−ATR] to high vowels.

Low vowels also exhibit the effects of grounded processes. In a single class of cases—namely, when [+low]—a vowel that is long in Wolof is necessarily [−ATR]. This restriction is an instance of the RTR/LO Condition holding of a process that inserts [−ATR] on long vowels: the condition restricts the targets of [−ATR] Insertion to combinations with [+low]. Because of the particular F-elements present in Wolof, RTR/LO defines compatibilities between F-elements, not incompatibilities. The effect of constraining [−ATR] Insertion by this condition is to select a subset of the eligible [−ATR] bearers to undergo [−ATR] Insertion. Thus, although all non-high vowels may be [−ATR] in Wolof, only [+low] vowels are targeted by the process of [−ATR] Insertion that affects long vowels.

Beyond these grounded conditions, one holding generally and one holding of a particular rule, [−ATR] combines freely in Wolof.

Wolof Grounding

1. [ATR] is active (marked according to [ATR] Markedness (21a)).
2. [−ATR] is active (marked according to [ATR] Markedness (21b)).
3. RTR/LO holds specifically of [−ATR] Insertion (consistent with Grounding Conditions I and IIa; semimarked with respect to Grounding Condition IIb (12)).
4. RTR/HI and HI/ATR hold of all representations (unmarked with respect to Grounding Conditions I and II (12)).

Vowel harmony in Yoruba provides further examples of two of the same conditions: RTR/HI holds of representations in general and RTR/LO holds of a specific rule. We turn now to this case.

3.2.4.2 Yoruba Vowel Harmony and Grounding Conditions   Reviewing from section 2.3.1: the general vowel harmony pattern in Yoruba is that [−ATR] harmony targets mid vowels, is triggered by some mid and all low vowels, and is blocked by high vowels.[66] The general pattern of leftward spreading is accounted for by the four properties listed in (97).

(97) *Formal properties of Yoruba vowel harmony*

      a. [−ATR] is active.

      b. [−ATR] is free in underlying representation.

      c. [−ATR] associates from right to left.

      d. [−ATR] spreads from right to left.

Central to this analysis is the postulation of [−ATR] as the active F-element, (97a).

In our discussion of Yoruba in chapter 2, we presented several arguments for [−ATR] as the active F-element. In this section, we explore the role of the Grounding Conditions in the distribution of [ATR] in Yoruba, RTR/LO and RTR/HI being particularly relevant. As with Wolof, in Yoruba these conditions take on very different roles from each other. We argue that RTR/HI holds of Yoruba in general, and consequently affects the nature of representations as well as the manner in which rules apply. In contrast, RTR/LO does not hold of representations at all stages, but does hold specifically of the application of [−ATR] Insertion.

We consider the patterns resulting from RTR/LO first, reviewing particulars of the analysis only where they are relevant to the grounded path conditions.

The RTR/LO Condition: If [−ATR] then [+low]; if [−ATR] then not [−low]   In sequences mixing low and mid vowels, the distribution of [ATR] is asymmetrical, accounted for in part by the right-to-left spreading of [−ATR] (97d). To the left of a low vowel, mid vowels are always [−ATR] (*èpà* 'groundnut', *ọjà* 'market' vs. **èpà, *ojà*, etc.), while to the right of a low vowel, mid vowels may be [−ATR] but need not be (*àjẹ̀* 'paddle', *aṣọ* 'cloth' vs. *ate* 'hat', *àwo* 'plate').

Leftward spreading of [−ATR] accounts for the asymmetry with [a] only if *all* low vowels trigger [−ATR] Spread. As argued in section 2.3.1, [−ATR] cannot be present on all low vowels in underlying representation. Therefore, a rule inserting [−ATR] is required, a rule that is restricted in its application to low vowels. This restriction is precisely the RTR/LO Condition.

(98) RTR/LO holds of Yoruba [−ATR] Insertion.

The class of vowels subject to [−ATR] Insertion is exactly the class defined as preferring [−ATR] by the substantive path conditions governing [ATR]. Since it is the values [+low] and [−ATR] that are active in Yoruba, it is the positive version of

RTR/LO that is relevant (*If [− ATR] then [+ low]*), not the negative version (*If [− ATR] then not [− low]*).

***The RTR/HI Condition:* If [− ATR] then [− high]; if [− ATR] then not [− high]**   We now turn to the role of the RTR/HI Condition in Yoruba, arguing that it holds of representations in Yoruba, not of specific rules. We first show that three separate facts about the general distribution of [ATR] in forms with high vowels are accounted for if RTR/HI holds of specific rules or of specific points in the derivation. According to Grounding Condition II, a strong condition, such as RTR/HI, should hold, and should hold as widely as possible. This hypothesis is supported not only by the multiple repetitions of the same condition throughout the grammar of Yoruba but also by the distribution of [− ATR] in loan vocabulary. We first review the three general properties of [ATR] distribution in forms with high vowels.

First, in Standard Yoruba there are no high [− ATR] vowels on the surface. This is expressed by the following condition:[67]

(99) RTR/HI holds of Yoruba surface representations.

Second, the pattern of harmony involving mid vowels and an abutting high vowel is symmetrical where the pattern of mid and low vowels is asymmetrical: with a string of peripheral high vowels, mid vowels can have either value for [ATR] to the left or to the right. In (100a), high vowels precede both [− ATR] and [+ ATR] mid vowels; in (100b), high vowels follow both [− ATR] and [+ ATR] mid vowels. The forms in (100c) show that the [− ATR] mid vowels can precede a peripheral *sequence* of high vowels as well as a single high vowel.[68]

(100) *Symmetry with peripheral (sequences of) high vowels*

a.	ilẹ̀	'land'	ilé	'house'
	itọ́	'saliva'	ìgò	'bottle'
b.	ẹ̀bi	'guilt'	ebi	'hunger'
	ọ̀kín	'egret'	orí	'head'
c.	ẹ̀bùrú	'shortcut'		
	ẹ̀gúsí	'a food made from seeds of melon'		

That the values of [ATR] on mid vowels do not interact with a peripheral sequence of high vowels is explained if the RTR/HI Condition holds of the rule that associates a free [− ATR].

(101) RTR/HI holds of Yoruba [− ATR] Association.

When attempting to associate a free [− ATR] specification, the right-to-left scanning for an anchor skips any high vowel, such high vowels being ineligible because of RTR/HI.

The third relevant observation concerns the distribution of [ATR] in forms with (strings of) *medial* high vowels where such forms have two domains of nonhigh vowels, one on each side of the high vowel string. The two-domain pattern is illustrated in (102). The final nonhigh vowel is unconstrained: it can be any mid vowel ([+ATR] or [−ATR]) (102a,b) or the low vowel (102c). By contrast, the initial nonhigh vowel is restricted: it cannot be a [−ATR] mid vowel. The medial high vowel is *opaque*: it blocks the leftward spreading of [−ATR] from mid and low vowels (102b,c).

(102) *Opacity of medial high vowels*

  a. $V_f = [+ATR]$ MID   àbúrò   'younger sibling'
                                òyìbó   'any European'
                                èsúró   'Redflanked Duiker'
                                *ẹsuro, etc.

  b. $V_f = [−ATR]$ MID   àkùrò   'a type of farmland'
                                èlùbọ́   'yam flour'
                                odídẹ   'Grey Parrot'
                                *ọdidẹ, etc.

  c. $V_f = [−ATR]$ LO   abíyá   'armpit'
                                yorùbá   'Yoruba'
                                òjìyá   'Daniellia Ogea'
                                *yọruba, etc.

The properties of the two-domain pattern are predicted if Yoruba [−ATR] Spread (97d) is constrained by the RTR/HI Condition: so constrained, when [−ATR] spreads, it cannot associate to vowels unless they are specified [−high]. Consequently, high vowels are ineligible targets for harmony. In addition, the Locality Condition rules out the possibility of skipping such a vowel by the harmonic spreading process.

(103) RTR/HI holds of Yoruba [−ATR] Spread.

RTR/HI is relevant in three different contexts, (99), (101), and (103). This repetition raises the question of whether RTR/HI holds of all representations or only of specific rules. The treatment of loanwords in Yoruba provides an interesting argument that conditions are imposed on languages rather than on rules, all else being equal. This is in accord with Grounding Condition II, that in the unmarked case, the role of path conditions is maximized. Within a language, the maximal role of a path condition is that it hold of all representations. Thus, in a language like Yoruba, the first hypothesis is that RTR/HI holds of the language.[69]

Instances of high [−ATR] vowels would provide evidence forcing RTR/HI to be at best a rule condition rather than a language condition: however, there are no such vowels in Standard Yoruba. Nevertheless, the general pattern in Yoruba would in principle be consistent with positing RTR/HI as a condition on [−ATR] Association and on [−ATR] Spread, rather than proposing that it hold of the language as a whole. If this were the correct analysis, then Grounding Condition II should be changed, to derive that in the unmarked case, path conditions hold of specific *rules* in languages. However, the behavior of words borrowed into Yoruba offers evidence that conditions hold of derived and underived representations in general, rather than simply holding of specific rules.

English provides a source for many Yoruba loans. Whether English has an [ATR] distinction or a tense/lax distinction is a subject of debate (see for example note 8, Halle and Stevens 1969, Perkell 1971, Ladefoged et al. 1972, MacKay 1976, Lindau 1978, 1979, Ladefoged and Maddieson 1990). Whatever the resolution of this debate, the English *tense* mid vowels correspond to *advanced* mid vowels in Yoruba (104a), and English *lax* mid vowels correspond to *retracted* mid vowels in Yoruba (104b) (Salami 1972, Akinlabi 1993).

(104)   *English*   *Yoruba*

   a. slate [e]   síléètì
       brake [e]   bíréèkì
                            bíréèkù

       stove [o]   sítóòfù
       globe [o]   gílóòbù
                            gúlóòbù

   b. bread [ɛ]   búrẹ̀dì
       propeller [ɛ]   pòròpẹ́là
       drawer [ɔ]   dúrọ́ọ̀

The behavior of the tense and lax high vowels is relevant for the issue of whether conditions hold of languages or of rules. If the RTR/HI Condition holds of the language, then borrowed words should obey the condition; if it holds only of the rules, then borrowed words could correspond more directly to the source. As the pairs in (105a,b) show, English high vowels correspond only to [+ATR] high vowels in Yoruba, regardless of their tense/lax value in English, contrasting sharply with the pattern for borrowed mid vowels seen in (104a,b).

(105)   *English*   *Yoruba*

   a. grease [i]   gírísì
       free [i]   fíríì
       school [u]   súkúrù
                            súkúù

       glucose [u]   gúlúkóòsì

b. fridge [ɪ]   fíríijì   *fɪrɪɪjɪ, etc.
    slippers [ɪ]   sílípáàsì   *sɪlɪpaasɪ, etc.
    clipper [ɪ]   kílípà   *kɪlɪpa, etc.
                          kílíbà
    brick [ɪ]   bíríkì   *bɪrɪkɪ, etc.
    book [ʊ]   búùkù   *búʊ̀kʊ̀, etc.
    cook (noun) [ʊ]   kúùkù   *kúʊ̀kʊ̀, etc.
                          kúkù

The basic observation is that [−ATR] does not surface on high vowels, even in the loan vocabulary. This is an expected distribution if RTR/HI is a condition on the language; it is a complete accident if RTR/HI is simply a condition on specific rules.

Knowledge of loanwords is not necessary in order to learn the basic properties of a language. Rather, the behavior of loanwords is expected to follow from robust properties of the grammar of the host language. Consequently, the evidence from English loanwords in Yoruba is particularly telling: with the RTR/HI Condition holding generally, their behavior is straightforward; without a general condition, their behavior is anomalous.

We conclude, then, that the maximal utilization of a path condition is to invoke it for all representations in a language; but in the event that positive evidence requires that a path condition not be maximized, it will still tend to hold of specific rules (e.g., RTR/LO in Yoruba).[70] That is, we take facts such as those in Yoruba to argue for the scope clause of the Grounding Conditions.

Yoruba Grounding

1. [ATR] is active (marked according to [ATR] Markedness (21a)).
2. [−ATR] is active (marked according to [ATR] Markedness (21b)).
3. RTR/LO holds specifically of [−ATR] Insertion (consistent with Grounding Conditions I and IIa; semimarked with respect to Grounding Condition IIb (12)).
4. RTR/HI holds of all representations (unmarked with respect to Grounding Conditions I and II (12)).

To summarize briefly, two conditions are important for an account of [ATR] in Yoruba: RTR/LO determines the class of vowels targeted by [−ATR] Insertion, the [+low] vowels. RTR/HI holds of the language in general, thereby restricting the application of [−ATR] Association and [−ATR] Spread as well as the way in which loanwords are assimilated. These properties are very similar to those seen in Wolof: in both languages, grounded conditions are responsible either for general F-element combination or for F-element combination that results from specific rules. Significantly, in both languages, all path restrictions on the distribution of [−ATR] are grounded, in accordance with Grounding Condition I.

3.2.5 Conclusion

This section has provided evidence in support of the [ATR] Markedness Statement (21) and the Grounding Conditions (12). We review this support here; in the next section, we address some of the predictions made by the proposed model.

3.2.5.1 [ATR] Markedness   The [ATR] Markedness Statement (21) allows a variety of language types, all of which have been shown to exist. The statement itself is repeated here.

(106) *[ATR] Markedness Statement*

    a. [ATR] tends not to be used actively.

    b. If used actively, the active value of [ATR] tends to be [+ATR]; the passive value of [ATR] tends to be [−ATR].

These statements predict languages of basically three types: (i) completely unmarked languages in which neither value for [ATR] is active (consistent with (106a)), (ii) the most marked languages in which [−ATR] is active (marked with respect to both (106a) and (106b)), and (iii) "in-between" languages in which [+ATR] is active (marked with respect to (106a) but unmarked with respect to (106b)).

    We have demonstrated that languages of all three types exist: [ATR] is inactive (Tiv, Barrow Inupiaq, Ainu), [−ATR] is active (Wolof, Yoruba, Eastern Javanese), and [+ATR] is active (Pulaar, Kinande, Akan). Of importance, too, is the contrast between Pulaar and Eastern Javanese: even where [ATR] is essentially redundant, the active value may be either [+ATR] (Pulaar) or [−ATR] (Eastern Javanese). The lists in (107) assign languages discussed so far to classes established by whether [+ATR] or [−ATR] is active.

(107) *[+ATR] languages*   *[−ATR] languages*

    Pulaar   Wolof

    Kinande   Yoruba

    Akan   Eastern Javanese

    Maasai   Chukchi

    Okpẹ

    The general point is that even when [ATR] is active, there is no single fixed active [ATR] F-element. Rather, this is a dimension along which we find language-particular variation, a point already made under Radical Underspecification (see, for example, Abaglo and Archangeli 1989 for arguments supporting this claim with respect to [high]). We assume that the F-elements for various features have different strengths of preference in the two clauses of their Markedness Statements (see Mohanan 1988). For example, it appears to be the case that if [±nasal] is active, [+nasal] consistently behaves as the active F-element, not [−nasal]. This presents a striking contrast to [ATR], where languages with active [ATR] may divide almost evenly between those with active [+ATR] and those with active [−ATR]. (See also note 20 and section 3.6.1.3.) As an interim proposal, we suggest that such strengths can be expressed as a value between $\emptyset$ and 1, where $\emptyset$ would indicate impossibility and 1 would indicate invariable selection. Any value greater than .5 would therefore indicate that a feature is likely to occur, and a value less than .5 would indicate the opposite tendency. For example, we assume that features like [high], [low], and [back] would have values greater than .5, expressing the likelihood that they occur in a system; [ATR], on the other hand, would have a value less than .5.

As the data base of phonological analyses grows, we will be in a better position to evaluate quantitatively the relative markedness of the language types noted above. At this point, we observe that distinctions in the strengths of tendencies appear to exist, but we do not attempt to actually introduce values without a more adequate data base. We speculate, moreover, that strengths will reflect interactions of phonetic properties—the Grounding Hypothesis.

We assume that statements comparable to (106) are constructed for all features (Kiparsky 1981). The format for a binary feature is given in (108a,b) and for a monovalent feature in (108a) alone, where *F* is the feature involved.

(108) *Format for markedness statements*

    a. F tends to be used [*X-amount*] actively.

    b. If F is used actively, its active value tends [*Y-amount*] to be [αF]; the passive value of F tends [1 − *Y-amount*] to be [−αF].

3.2.5.2 Grounding Conditions   The languages examined here have suggested the postulation of the Grounding Conditions (12), repeated here.

(109) *The Grounding Conditions*

    I. Path conditions invoked by languages must be phonetically motivated.

    II. The stronger the phonetic motivation for a path condition Φ,

        a. the greater the likelihood of invoking Φ,

        b. the greater the likelihood of assigning a wide scope to Φ within a grammar,

    and vice versa.

Languages considered here require some subset of the conditions governing the interaction between [ATR], [high], and [low], as indicated in (110).[71]

(110) *Relevant conditions: HI/ATR; LO/ATR; ATR/HI; ATR/LO; RTR/HI;*
      RTR/LO

Language	Condition on representations	Condition on specific rules only
Pulaar	HI/ATR LO/ATR ATR/LO	ATR/HI ([+ATR] Insertion)
Kinande	LO/ATR ATR/LO	ATR/HI (General Association, Special Association, Suffixal Harmony, Phrasal Harmony)
Akan	ATR/LO LO/ATR	ATR/HI (roots, phrase-level harmony, compound harmony, palatalization cases)
Yoruba	RTR/HI	RTR/LO ([−ATR] Insertion)
Wolof	RTR/HI HI/ATR	RTR/LO ([−ATR] Insertion)

Reviewing these conditions leads to two important points. First, every necessary condition is a grounded condition: no ungrounded conditions are necessary. This is the claim made by Grounding Condition I.

Second, every language requires some conditions, the expectation given Grounding Condition IIa. Further, the Yoruba treatment of loanwords argues that conditions over a language as a whole are preferred to conditions over a series of rules. Both of these points support Grounding Condition IIb, that conditions are maximized.

This concludes the basic exemplification of Grounding Theory. In the following sections, we turn to empirical predictions of the theory. We begin by considering aspects of the phonetics of tongue root phenomena, arguing that a class of cases that have been highly problematical for phonological analyses receive a virtually trivial account when analyzed in terms of antagonistic phonetic properties. We then consider the relation between Grounding Theory and Combinatorial Specification, arguing, among other things, that the central properties of Contrastive Underspecification (Clements 1987, Steriade 1987a) and Structure Preservation (Kiparsky 1985) are derived through the interaction of conditions with F-element combinations. Finally, we anticipate the more detailed discussion of rule properties in chapter 4 by showing some of the ways in which Grounding Theory constrains the operation of phonological rules.

3.3   The Acoustic Realization of [ATR]

The central thesis of this chapter is that formally significant reflections of phonetic properties are observed in phonological systems. In this section, we review certain acoustic properties of tongue root manipulations and suggest that certain types of phenomena generally considered to require phonological explanations are more properly accounted for within the phonetics.

Both tongue body raising and tongue root advancement cause lowering of F_1 acoustically; similarly, both tongue body lowering and tongue root retraction cause raising of F_1.[72] This is not surprising since "the muscle actions corresponding to 'advanced tongue root' are a subset of those corresponding to 'high'" (Perkell 1971:136). In quite direct terms, therefore, the acoustic effects of the pairs *tongue body raising/tongue root advancement* and *tongue body lowering/tongue root retraction* enhance each other, while the effects of the pairs *tongue body raising/tongue root retraction* and *tongue body lowering/tongue root advancement* counteract each other (see Stevens, Keyser, and Kawasaki 1986). Perkell suggests that the effects of "overlapping commands to the same structures have additive effects" (1971:136), while antagonistic combinations result in "some kind of cancellation" (Perkell 1971:138). Phonetically, therefore, the grounded implications motivated above for the features [ATR], [high], and [low] receive support.

Two points are important in this regard, the first regarding the possibility of absolute phonetic identification of vowels, the second regarding overlap in acoustic realizations.

In section 2.8.1, we demonstrated that a particular phonetic transcription is not pretheoretic—that such a level involves a considerable degree of analysis. Moreover, we showed that vowels considered phonologically the same might have rather different formant values (cf. English (Peterson and Barney 1952) and Dinka (Jacobson 1980)) and that within a single language, there might be overlap in the formant values for vowels of different height (e.g., Akan (Lindau 1979) and Shilluk (Jacobson 1980)).[73] Such properties are straightforwardly understood when the sympathetic or antagonistic nature of pairs of F-elements are considered.

To see this, consider a schematic representation for a canonical high vowel "I" and a canonical mid vowel "E."

(111)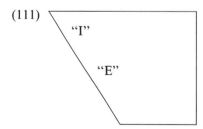

By enhancing the high vowel specification with the value [+ATR], a vowel approaching cardinal [i] can be achieved (HI/ATR: *If [+high] then [+ATR]*) (see Halle and Stevens 1969). If, however, such a high vowel is combined with the value [−ATR], then the result is antagonistic (HI/ATR: *If [+high] then not [−ATR]*); the effect is to raise somewhat the first formant that would otherwise have been lowered by the high specification. Similarly, "E" may also have its first formant raised or lowered depending on the [ATR] specification. We see, therefore, that tongue height features and tongue root features can work together to additively increase or decrease F_1, or they can subtract from each other, counteracting to some degree the effect of the other feature.

Any theory of language that includes features like [high], [low], and [ATR] must somehow encode the actual extent to which the tongue moves as a result of a particular feature specification, or the extent to which formants are affected. Following *SPE*, we assume that such quantitative assignments take place in the phonetics. The issue of interest here concerns the precise values assigned phonetically to such movements.

Assuming as in (111) that the symbols "I" and "E" represent the effect specifically of the [±high] component of a vowel, the additional effect of [±ATR] can be sketched as shown in (112).

(112)

If the effect of tongue root movement on F_1 is relatively small, the result is an absence of overlap between the four surface vowels that are defined by the free combination of [±high] and [±ATR]: $i \gg \text{I} \gg e \gg \varepsilon$. Such a "canonical" interaction between vowel height and [ATR] can be observed in languages like DhoLuo (Jacobson 1980) and Ebira (Ladefoged and Maddieson 1990). If, however, the effect of tongue root movement is larger, then phonetic overlap may result: $i \gg e \gg \text{I} \gg \varepsilon$. That is, a retracted high vowel may occur that is phonetically "lower" than an advanced mid vowel. Such a pattern has been documented for languages like Akan (Lindau 1979) and Ịjọ (Ladefoged and Maddieson 1990).

3.3.1   Addition of Components: Apparent Neutralization

We discuss in terms of the above issues two languages, Okpẹ and Chukchi, that putatively exhibit phonological neutralization involving [ATR]. We argue, however, that no phonological neutralization takes place—that the phonetic results are directly derivable from unmodified phonological representations.[74] In the discussion of these languages, we make two basic points.

First, we note that the putative neutralizations involve antagonistic F-element combinations, combinations that are only possible in languages where not all grounded conditions are invoked, that is, in languages that are marked with respect to Grounding Condition II. For example, [+high, −ATR], a combination that figures in the apparent neutralization in both Okpẹ and Chukchi, is defined as antagonistic by the RTR/HI Condition and by the HI/ATR Condition, yet neither condition is generally enforced in the phonology of either language.

Second, we argue that the type of antagonism observed in such cases explains the possibility of apparent neutralization along the acoustic lines sketched above. We suggest that, depending on the precise phonetic instantiation of the relevant F-elements, the pronunciation of one representation can be auditorily similar, perhaps in some cases even truly identical, to the phonetic instantiation of a different phonological representation. The potential phonetic similarity of various formally distinct feature combinations marks off certain F-element combinations as inherently unstable: given two possible representations, one with and one without antagonistic, ungrounded feature combinations, one is led to expect the antagonistic case to be subject to both synchronic and diachronic modification in the direction of a more grounded representation.[75]

3.3.1.1 Okpẹ Harmony and Neutralization   Hoffmann (1973) and Omamor (1988) examine tongue root harmony in Okpẹ, an Ẹdoid language (Niger-Congo) spoken in Nigeria. Interestingly, although the system behaves phonologically as though [ATR] combines freely with all vocalic F-elements (in at least some environments), the surface realizations led Hoffmann to describe Okpẹ as having seven vowels phonetically, [i, e, ẹ, a, ọ, o, u]. Here, we first present the evidence that [ATR] phonologically combines freely with all F-elements in the language, and we then consider the issue of the surface realizations of ι, υ, a (where, as elsewhere, a represents a [+ATR, +low] vowel).

The F-element combinations that we assume for Okpẹ are shown in (113). [+ATR] is free in underlying representation, a property of particular morphemes, not particular vowels; hence, the relevant combinations with and without [+ATR] are omitted in (113). Of A_1 and A_2, A_2 is preferred because of Representational Simplicity.

(113) *Okpẹ vowel representation*

    a. F-elements

        +HI, +LO, +BK, (+ATR)

b. Conditions

HI/LO Condition:	If [+high] then not [+low].
LO/HI Condition:	If [+low] then not [+high].

c.

*	*	U	I	A₁	A₂	E	O
+HI	+HI	+HI	+HI				
+LO	+LO			+LO	+LO		
+BK		+BK		+BK			+BK

We use the symbols in (114) to designate combinations in (113c) with and without the feature [+ATR].

(114) *Symbols used for Okpẹ vowels*

With [+ATR]	i	e	ạ	o	u	
Without [+ATR]	ị	ẹ	a	ọ	ụ	

The harmonic pattern in Okpẹ verbs is exemplified with prefixes and suffixes in (115)–(117). These lists show both the phonological pattern and the surface realizations described by Hoffmann. The general pattern is that the affixes take on the [ATR] value of the root. Note in this regard that low vowel affixes can be targeted by the [+ATR] value of harmony, but there are no [+ATR] low vowels in roots. We derive this pattern by imposing the condition ATR/LO (*If [+ATR] then not [+low]*) on the association of a free, morpheme-level specification, but by imposing no such condition on the harmony rule itself.[76]

As (115) shows, high vowels induce tongue root harmony on prefixes and suffixes. In addition, prevocalic high vowels become glides, as can be seen in the infinitive and the continuous.[77]

(115) *High vowels*

	Imperative		Infinitive		Continuous, 1pl inclusive		
/i/	tí	[tí]	ètyó	[ètyó]	ạ'tyạ́	[é'tyɛ́]	'pull'
/u/	rú	[rú]	èrwó	[èrwó]	ạ'rwạ́	[é'rwɛ́]	'do, make'
/ị/	rị́	[ré]	ẹ̀ryọ́	[èryɔ́]	a'ryá	[á'ryá]	'eat'
/ụ/	sụ́	[só]	ẹ̀swọ́	[èswɔ́]	á'swá	[á'swá]	'sing'

There are a variety of points to explain about the data in (115). First, in the infinitive, the prefix alternates between [e] and [ɛ], accounted for by straightforward root-controlled [ATR] Harmony. Given this analysis of mid vowels, the data for the continuous can be analyzed as similarly harmonic, but with a low vowel both in prefix and in suffix positions.[78] The proposed low [+ATR] vowel is realized as [e] unless it is word-final (following a glide), where it is realized as [ɛ]. As for the high vowels that are described as phonetically [e] and [o] in the imperative, Hoffmann notes that the prefixes of forms such as the infinitive and the continuous show that the tongue root value of these roots is [−ATR], while the fact that they undergo glide formation in the same tenses attests to the status of these root vowels as [+high] (compare the forms in (116)). To be accounted for, therefore, is the apparent surface realization of these [+high, −ATR] vowels as mid [+ATR] vowels.

(116) demonstrates the harmonic pattern when roots have mid vowels; (117) illustrates the behavior of a low-voweled stem. In these data sets, the effect of harmony is seen only in the prefixes, since the suffix vowels in the infinitive and the continuous delete when following nonhigh vowels. Note that the absence of glide formation in the forms in (116) establishes that the feature value [−high] is appropriate for the root vowels transcribed as [e] and [o] in these cases.

(116) *Mid vowels*

	Imperative		Infinitive		Continuous, 1pl inclusive		
/e/	sé	[sé]	èsé	[èsé]			'fall'
/o/	só	[só]	èsó	[èsó]	a̗'só	[é'só]	'steal'
/ẹ/	dẹ́	[dɛ́]	ẹ̀dẹ́	[ɛ̀dɛ́]			'buy'
/ọ/	lọ́	[lɔ́]	ẹ̀lọ́	[ɛ̀lɔ́]			'grind'

(117) *Low vowels*

	Imperative		Infinitive		Continuous, 1pl inclusive		
/a/	dá	[dá]	ẹ̀dá	[ɛ̀dá]	á'dá	[á'dá]	'drink'

These forms require a vowel deletion rule in addition to the harmony and glide formation rules needed for (115).[79] Given some account of glide formation and vowel deletion, the net conclusion that Hoffmann (1973) reaches regarding the harmonic behavior of high, mid, and low vowels is that their phonology involves straightforward root-controlled [ATR] Harmony while the phonetic realizations of low [+ATR] vowels and high [−ATR] vowels require certain adjustments.

One possibility is to treat Okpẹ as an instance of absolute neutralization of a formal phonological type (see Hoffmann 1973, Pulleyblank 1986c, Calabrese 1988). Such a treatment would involve essentially the analysis of harmony sketched above, followed by feature-changing rules. For [+high, −ATR], both F-elements would change into their opposite values, [−high, +ATR], while for [+low, +ATR], either one F-element would change ([+low] to [−low], giving [e]) or both F-elements would change ([+low, +ATR] to [−low, −ATR], giving [ɛ]).[80] In short, this type of analysis would treat the pattern of neutralization in Okpẹ as involving a mismatch between underlying and surface phonological representations, with the purported mismatch resolved by a large-scale change in phonological representations.

Such an analysis seems undesirable for conceptual reasons, and in Okpẹ, for empirical reasons as well. Conceptually, allowing rules whose effect is to simultaneously change more than one value allows a type of power that is not clearly motivated by attested alternations in natural languages. For example, the rules in (118b,c) would both be predicted to be possible if the rule type (118a) were permitted.

(118) a. $[\alpha F, \beta G] \rightarrow [-\alpha F, -\beta G]$

   b. $[-\text{nasal}, +\text{voiced}] \rightarrow [+\text{nasal}, -\text{voiced}]$

   c. $[-\text{sonorant}, +\text{constricted glottis}] \rightarrow [+\text{sonorant}, -\text{constricted glottis}]$

Rule (118b) would context-freely convert voiced oral segments into voiceless nasal segments, while (118c) would convert glottalized obstruents into nonglottalized sonorants. It is not difficult to imagine any number of such improbable rules.

   In addition, if the phonology were allowed to delink or delete both of the offending F-elements in an antagonistic combination, this would predict a completely unattested type of pattern of interaction with redundancy rules. As an example, consider the antagonistic combination $[+\text{low}, +\text{ATR}]$ and assume that both $[+\text{low}]$ and $[+\text{ATR}]$ are delinked: this could result in a vowel with no F-elements at all (depending on which other F-elements are present). But a vowel with no F-elements at all is the malleable vowel consistent with all F-element combinations in the language. (See, for example, the behavior of /i/ in Yoruba (Pulleyblank 1988c) and the behavior of /e/ in Gengbe (Abaglo and Archangeli 1989).) As a result, the erstwhile $[+\text{low},$ $+\text{ATR}]$ vowel could be realized as whatever vowel in the system, if any, is phonologically unspecified. When actually attested patterns are considered, however, it is significant that despite a considerable degree of variability, the advanced low vowel never develops into a $[+\text{high}]$ vowel, for example, in spite of evidence in various languages for such a vowel being underspecifiable. As a relevant data set, note that in all the developments of the $[+\text{low}, +\text{ATR}]$ vowel of Proto-Ẹdoid (section 3.1.3.1), diachronically related vowels are phonetically close to the original. This type of distribution would be accidental under a phonological account of the Okpẹ-type apparent neutralization. Since the strictly phonological account predicts randomness rather than the systematicity actually observed, we conclude that an unconstrained phonological approach is on the wrong track.

   We conclude, therefore, that an adequate phonological theory should not allow the formalization of rules that neutralize contrasts by large-scale alterations of feature values.

   Within the proposal made here, rules of the type in (118) are impossible under the theory of rule parameters outlined in chapter 4: a single rule may affect no more than a single feature or node. For example, a rule could spread or delete a feature like $[+\text{nasal}]$, or a node like the Place node, but a single rule could not simultaneously

affect pairs of features as in (118). Moreover, within a standard approach to phonological rules, it would not be possible to express a change such as that putatively
observed in Okpẹ as involving two rules: (i) [+high] → [−high], (ii) [−ATR] →
[+ATR]. As formulated, both of these rules would affect more than the intended
class; and even if they were appropriately restricted, there would still be unintended
results. For example, if the rule affecting [+high] was modified to affect only high
retracted vowels, it would then be necessary for the rule affecting [ATR] to apply to
(derived) mid vowels; in this case, however, the rule would overapply to instances of
[−high, +ATR] vowels that were not derived by the prior application of the neutralization rule affecting vowel height.

In any event, such a phonologically based analysis is unable to explain certain
phonological, and apparently also phonetic, facts about Okpẹ, facts that are explained if the phonological representation is left intact. First, the phonological resolution to Okpẹ vowels predicts that there could be some subsequent phonological
rule that classes the erstwhile [+high, −ATR] vowels with [−high] vowels or with
[+ATR] vowels (and similarly for the erstwhile [+low, +ATR] vowels). We know
of no such rules. Second, despite the apparent auditory identity between the surface
realizations of high [−ATR] vowels and mid [+ATR] vowels, there is some evidence suggesting that the two are actually phonetically distinct. Omamor (1973) gives
values for F_1 and F_2 of the relevant Okpẹ vowels based on a preliminary study of one
speaker, shown in (119). F_1 of the high [−ATR] vowels is consistently higher than F_1
of the mid [+ATR] vowels. In addition, F_2 is usually lower for the high [−ATR]
vowels than it is for the mid [+ATR] vowels, although here there is some overlap.

(119) *F_1 and F_2 of Okpẹ vowels*

	F_1	F_2			F_1	F_2
i	300	2550		u	400	750
	325	2300			400	850
	350	2375				
ị	500	2250		ụ	500	1200
	600	2000			600	1225
e	400	2275		o	400	1050
	425	2275			450	1200
	450	2300			450	1325
	475	2200				
ẹ	no examples given			ọ	675	1150
					725	1225

This preliminary acoustic evidence suggests that even though perceptual studies describe the vowels as identical or near-identical, there are subtle phonetic distinctions

that correlate with the distinct phonological representations. Thus, there is neither phonetic nor phonological evidence for neutralization of high [−ATR] vowels with mid [+ATR] vowels in Okpẹ.

As shown here, Okpẹ phonology allows [+high, −ATR] and [+low, +ATR], even though these constitute combinations of features in an antagonistic relation, combinations that show that certain grounded path conditions do not hold in Okpẹ. Rather than invoke phonological neutralization processes that are in any event of questionable motivation, we propose that the phonological representations remain unchanged, and that the phonetic interpretations of such representations involve a trade-off between the lowering of F_1 produced by the [+high] specification and the raising of F_1 produced by the [−ATR] specification (see (112)). Note that in Okpẹ, the quantitative instantiation of tongue root movement is relatively large in comparison with the instantiation of tongue body movement. As seen for Akan in section 2.8.1, in the case of [+high, −ATR], tongue root retraction is considerable enough to produce a high vowel with a higher F_1 than the corresponding mid vowel; in the case of [+low, +ATR], tongue root advancement is considerable enough to produce the quality of a "mid" vowel, with advancing to a greater extent in nonfinal vowels [e] than in final vowels [ɛ]. With respect to the Ẹdoid family of which Okpẹ is a member, there appears to be evidence that the overlapping pattern is quite general. Laniran (1985) states that a perceptual study of Èmálhè, an Ẹdoid language closely related to Okpẹ, suggests a similar pattern. She also refers to an acoustic study by Donwa (1983) on Isoko, another Ẹdoid language, where such acoustic overlap is also claimed to exist.

Note that if one were to seriously pursue the implicit assumption that all phonologically high vowels must be phonetically higher than all phonologically mid vowels, then serious complications involving reversal would be required for languages like Akan, Shilluk, and Ịjọ. In these cases, it has never been suggested that the contrast between vowels like mid "e" and high "ɪ" is neutralized. But if a "high" vowel cannot be phonetically lower than a "mid" vowel, then one would be forced to say that after the application of phonological harmony, phonological [+high, −ATR] becomes [−high, +ATR] (as under the standard, purely phonological, analysis of Okpẹ), but also that [−high, +ATR] becomes [+high, −ATR]. Both for conceptual reasons involving the power of mechanisms required for such reversal, and for empirical reasons involving a complete absence of evidence for the derived feature specifications, such analyses would seem highly undesirable.

Under the view of Okpẹ-type "neutralization" proposed here, there is no discrepancy between the phonology and the phonetics per se; there is simply language-specific variation in the precise quantitative realization of tongue root and tongue body features. No shift in phonological representations is necessary or desirable. Grounding Theory predicts that such discrepancies will correspond directly to antagonistic F-element combinations, combinations that can occur only when a particular grounded path condition is suspended in the phonology of a given language.

3.3.1.2 Chukchi Dominant [e] (e_d) and Recessive [e] (e_r) Chukchi presents a case similar to Okpẹ in that the retracted front high vowel apparently neutralizes with the advanced low vowel (see Jakobson 1952, Anderson 1980). We suggest that the neutralization effect is again a result of the phonetic interpretation of antagonistic F-elements rather than the result of a phonological rule changing F-elements.[81]

Recall from section 2.7.1 that Chukchi has a dominant/recessive harmony system. Dominant vowels are transcribed as [e_d, a, o] and recessive vowels as [i, e_r, u]. These alternations are briefly illustrated in (120); see chapter 2 for full discussion and exemplification. (120a) illustrates the [i] ~ [e_d] alternation, (120b) the [e_r] ~ [a] alternation, and (120c) the [u] ~ [o] alternation. Relevant vowels are underlined.[82]

(120) *[+ATR]*   *[−ATR]*

a.	pírirkın	'he takes'	pe_dré_dyo	'taken'
	íu'rkın	'it thaws'	e_do'ma	'while thawing'
	lile_r	'eye'	le_dlálhın	'eye-ABS'
b.	ge_rmné_rlin	'he whetted'	valamnálın	'the knife whetter'
	ve_r'gčúrmın	'grass border'	va'gran	'grass house'
	te_rn-lé_rut	'good head, clever'	tan-rán	'good house'
c.	qunné_re_rkık	'single daughter'	qon-gıtkáta	'one legged'
	nuté_rsʸqäqíŋkı	'underground'	notasʸqayé_dŋgüpü	'from underground'

The F-element representations posited in the earlier discussion of Chukchi are repeated in (121). (121d) shows the possible representations once [−ATR] links and spreads by Chukchi [−ATR] Link/Spread, the rule responsible for harmony.

(121) *Chukchi vowel representation*

a. F-elements

+LO, +RD, (−ATR)

b. Conditions

RD/LO Condition: If [+round] then not [+low].
LO/RD Condition: If [+low] then not [+round].

c.

	*	A	U	I
+LO	+LO			
+RD			+RD	

d. e$_r$ u   i   a   o   e$_d$

+LO			+LO		
	+RD			+RD	
			−ATR	−ATR	−ATR

The pattern observed to hold in Chukchi is in essence entirely comparable to that of Okpẹ. Assuming that [+high] and [+ATR] are phonological or phonetic default values for Chukchi vowels, the surface combinations requiring phonetic interpretation are as follows. First, a [+low] vowel may be either [−ATR], the dominant case, or [+ATR], the recessive case. As in Okpẹ, the sympathetic relation between [+low] and [−ATR] found in the retracted low vowel results in [a]; also as in Okpẹ, the antagonistic relation found between [+low] and [+ATR] results in the much more advanced vowel transcribed as [e]. With regard to high vowels, the presence of the recessive feature [+ATR] results straightforwardly in [i] and [u]. In combination with the dominant, and antagonistic, feature [−ATR], Chukchi vowels react phonetically in the manner already described for Okpẹ: considerable tongue root retraction results in the perceived vowels' being transcribed as [e] and [o].[83]

Treated in this way, it is an accident of the phonetics that there is (putative) neutralization of the contrast in Chukchi between the [+high, −ATR] vowel e$_d$ and the [+low, +ATR] vowel e$_r$. Since no features reflect such neutralization, it is claimed that no phonological effects should result.[84]

While we make no pretense here of resolving the issue of precisely how great a range is possible for rules of phonetic interpretation, we do note in closing that many logically possible cases are clearly ruled out. For example, it would not be possible to have a language identical to Chukchi, but in which the advanced, recessive vowels surface as [e, ə, o], that is, with the sympathetic [+high, +ATR] combinations realized as [e, o] but the antagonistic [+low, +ATR] combinations realized straightforwardly as [ə]. Also impossible would be a language in which the retracted, dominant vowels surface as [ɪ, e, ʊ], that is, with the antagonistic combination [+high, −ATR] being realized straightforwardly but the sympathetic combination [+low, −ATR] advancing and raising to [e].

3.3.2 Summary

Two basic points have been made in the discussion of these languages. First, we note that the putative neutralizations involve antagonistic F-element combinations, combinations that are only possible in languages where not all grounded conditions are invoked. For example, [+high, −ATR], a combination that figures in the apparent neutralization in both Okpẹ and Chukchi (and in the diachronic change in Ẹdoid), is defined as antagonistic by the RTR/HI Condition and by the HI/ATR Condition. Second, we argue that the antagonism observed in such cases explains the possibility of apparent neutralization. With a pair of features like [high] and [ATR], feature values conditioning movements in opposite directions can counteract each other, creating an inherently unstable combination. The effects in Okpẹ and Chukchi (and Ẹdoid) are not at all surprising given the substantive nature of the path conditions: the F-elements defined as antagonistic by path conditions are exactly those that involve antagonistic articulatory gestures or acoustic effects. In such antagonistic cases, the phonetic realization necessarily involves a certain give-and-take between the two features; the precise instantiation of this give-and-take varies from language to language.

3.4   Grounded Conditions and Combinatorial Specification

In chapter 2, we argued that featural representations result from the combination of F-elements, and that the combinations occurring in a particular language are constrained by the imposition of implicational conditions. Within the context of the present chapter, we refine this proposal by restricting the class of implicational conditions to the class of *grounded* conditions.

To illustrate with a case already discussed, the free combination of [ATR] with a 5-vowel system would give 10 surface vowels, as in Kinande and in an Ẹdoid language like Dẹgẹma (section 3.1.3.1). Imposition of ATR/LO would reduce the derived inventory to 9 vowels (as in Akan, Isoko, etc.); imposition of both ATR/LO and ATR/HI would reduce the derived inventory to 7 vowels (as in Pulaar, Auchi, etc.); and so on. The central claim is that surface inventories result from the combination of selected F-elements as constrained by the imposition of grounded conditions.

In this section, we discuss two implications of this proposal. First, we consider more generally the role of grounded conditions in a grammar. At various points throughout this chapter and chapter 2, we have argued that conditions govern not only inventories but also active phonological alternations. We suggest here that the effects of Structure Preservation are derived in this way. Second, we suggest that the central insights of Contrastive Underspecification are similarly derived by the interaction of grounded conditions with Combinatorial Specification. For both Structure Preservation and Contrastive Underspecification, we demonstrate that the central effects are derived, although the theories as a whole are not equivalent to the proposal made here: divergences constitute a further source of evidence in favor of the modular approach based on the interaction of Combinatorial Specification and Grounding Theory.

3.4.1   Deriving the Structure Preservation Effect
One of the central theses in this work is modularity. We argue that it is the interaction of various semi-independent subtheories that accounts for the types of complex pho-

nological behavior observed in natural language. In this section, we consider such modularity in terms of the interaction of Combinatorial Specification and grounded conditions with morphosyntactic levels, arguing that the central properties of Structure Preservation (Kiparsky 1985) are thereby derived.

(122) By STRUCTURE PRESERVATION I mean that marking conditions ... must be applicable not only to underived lexical representations but also to derived lexical representations, including the output of word-level rules. (Kiparsky 1985:92)

The Structure Preservation hypothesis contains essentially three components. First, a class of "marking conditions" is proposed. Second, it is claimed that this class of conditions governs both underlying representations and derived lexical representations. Third, it is claimed that the conditions do not (necessarily) hold of postlexical representations.

Consider these three points as they relate to the Grounding Hypothesis. With respect to the class of marking conditions itself, one can simply view Grounding Theory as a substantive proposal regarding the composition of the class of marking conditions. Kiparsky explicitly views the marking conditions as relating to issues of markedness; the Grounding Hypothesis suggests that markedness is rooted in phonetic properties. Since this entire chapter on grounding can be considered a fleshing out of a proposal for marking conditions, we do not dwell further on this issue here.

The claim that conditions hold of both underlying and derived lexical representations follows directly from the proposal that the use of strongly grounded path conditions in a grammar is maximized in the unmarked case (Grounding Condition II). If conditions hold preferentially of all morphosyntactic domains rather than some subset of domains, then they will normally hold of the entire lexicon.[85]

Finally, the observation that postlexical rules need not obey Structure Preservation can be obtained by simply turning off the relevant path conditions at the postlexical stage.

In comparing the Structure Preservation proposal with that of Grounding Theory, several issues are important. Foremost are issues involving the interplay between formal and substantive stipulations. Grounding Theory imposes substantive stipulations on the composition of the class of marking conditions to a much greater extent than does Structure Preservation. On the other hand, Structure Preservation makes extremely restrictive claims about the domain assignments for conditions, unlike Grounding Theory, which essentially says no more than that conditions hold to the maximal extent possible. Finally, in cases where a condition does not hold of representations as a whole, Structure Preservation says nothing; Grounding Theory, on the contrary, says that even if a particular path condition does not hold of representations in general, it can still hold of specific rules. On the first and third issues, then,

Grounding Theory is the more restrictive approach; on the second, the more restrictive approach is Structure Preservation.

3.4.1.1 Domains and Structure Preservation Effects

In this section, we focus on areas where Structure Preservation and Grounding Theory make predictions that diverge in fact, or in appearance only. We argue that the Grounding Hypothesis comes closer to deriving the range of effects that we observe in tongue root harmony systems, suggesting overall that Structure Preservation is both too restrictive and not restrictive enough.

Introducing a Condition on Stratum 1   One of the robust observations accounted for by Structure Preservation is that the kinds of conditions that govern underlying representations also govern early derivation, stratum 1 for example. On the face of it, Grounding Theory might seem to lose this generalization: what would prevent a language from having a particular set of conditions hold of underlying forms, but not of stratum 1 and subsequent strata? Or conversely, what would prevent a language from imposing a condition on stratum 1 that did not hold of underlying representations?

Consider first the putative case where a condition holds underlyingly but not of stratum 1. Note first in this regard that rules and conditions are assigned to particular phonological domains. We assume that the first such domain is stratum 1. Hence, the earliest domain to which a condition can be assigned is stratum 1. The effect of assigning a condition to stratum 1 is that all underlying representations and all stratum 1 derivations must conform to the condition. Given that path conditions define the well-formedness of F-element combinations, both "segmental inventories" and stratum 1 alternations are therefore defined by the same class of stratum 1 conditions.

But suppose that in some language, underlying representations did not respect a path condition α that was nonetheless imposed at stratum 1. To establish the existence of this situation would require evidence of an underlying representation that violated path condition α. However, since the role of Grounding Conditions is to *block* representations that are not in accord with a path condition, an underived representation that violated α would be blocked from entering stratum 1 by the existence of path condition α on that stratum.

The net effect is that if a path condition holds of stratum 1, it will also give the appearance of governing underived representations.

Introducing a Condition on Stratum n   The demonstration in the preceding section extends to any stratum n and the output of stratum $n - 1$. If a path condition holds at stratum n, then any violations of that path condition at the output of stratum $n - 1$ will be blocked from entering stratum n by the path condition, thereby removing the evidence motivating the existence of such a structure at stratum $n - 1$. This situation is shown schematically in (123a,b). Three schematic feature representations are given at stratum $n - 1$: [F], [G], and [F, G]. In (123a), at stratum n the condition *If [F] then [G]* is introduced. As a result, [F] is blocked from entering stratum n. Similarly, as shown in (123b), if the path condition is negative, [F, G] is blocked from entering stratum n.

(123) *Trying to introduce a condition on stratum* n

   a. Introduce the positive version of a condition

Representations	[F]	[G]	[F, G]
Stratum $n - 1$	OK	OK	OK
Stratum n: *If [F] then [G]*	blocked	OK	OK

   b. Introduce the negative version of a condition

Representations	[F]	[G]	[F, G]
Stratum $n - 1$	OK	OK	OK
Stratum n: *If [F] then not [G]*	OK	OK	blocked

Since [F] (or [F, G]) is blocked from entering stratum n, there is no evidence present in the later stratum for such a representation having existed on stratum $n - 1$. But the absence of such representations at stratum $n - 1$ is consistent with the relevant path condition also holding of stratum $n - 1$. By Grounding Condition II (strong path conditions are maximized), the formal grammar would therefore include the condition at both strata.

Blocking versus "Repair" Since stratum n is an arbitrarily selected stratum, the net result of the above demonstration is that all conditions that hold for any n (including the word level) will hold for all earlier strata. This is one of the main effects of Structure Preservation (122): conditions hold of underived and derived lexical representations, including the word-level representations. We conclude that if grounded conditions are accepted as *blockers*, there is no need for the additional notion of "Structure Preservation": the structure-preserving effect is simply one of the results of Grounding Theory.

   Note that a possible analysis of (putative) absolute neutralization (such as Okpẹ and Chukchi, section 3.3.1) might be that a particular representation, say, [+high, −ATR], is created at some stratum $n - 1$, but that a grounded condition is introduced at stratum n to rule out such a combination and to trigger a "repair" strategy (*SPE*, Piggott and Singh 1985, Singh 1987, Calabrese 1987, 1988, Rice 1987, Paradis 1988, Yip 1988b, Mohanan 1991, Myers 1991, etc.). The proposal here relates closely to repair strategy proposals in a number of ways. First, the proposal that rule conditions must be grounded defines the class of configurations that could be considered to require "repair." Second, the theory of rule parameters in chapter 4 defines the ways in which "repairs" could be realized. Note in this regard that we claim that "repair" processes exhibit the same range of formal properties as other processes, such as spreading, insertion, and so on, that are not motivated by an ill-formed input.

Importantly, however, in a theory that allows conditions to trigger changes, not just to block representations, the Structure Preservation effect is no longer derived. Nothing intrinsic to the notion of "repair" would rule out the possibility of allowing ill-formed representations to enter some stratum, to be subsequently repaired on that stratum. Hence, it would not follow that conditions on stratum n must hold of stratum $n - 1$. We reject such a weakening of the theory of constraints. On conceptual grounds, requiring that all representations be well formed at all stages is more restrictive. On substantive grounds, Grounding Theory not only defines certain classes of representations as being likely to trigger changes of a "repair" type (those with antagonistic relations), but also defines other classes of representations as being likely to result for reasons of enhancement (those with sympathetic relations). Grounding Theory is therefore broader in its coverage than repair strategies, and this within a more restrictive theory. We note in closing that cases apparently requiring repair-motivated adjustments such as Okpẹ and Chukchi are better analyzed without phonological neutralization at all (see section 3.3.1).

In general, the theory advocated here allows path conditions to formally *block* representations, but not to formally trigger *changes* in representations. Although the substantive markedness of a particular configuration may constitute pressure to change it in some way, we do not assume that such representations are formally ill formed if a language allows them at some stage of a derivation.

Summary Structure Preservation is essentially restricted to making statements about the domains of conditions; by contrast, Grounding Theory makes additional claims about the nature of phonological rules and their effects (section 3.2.2), as well as claims about the phonetic realization of various types of feature combinations (section 3.3.1). The two theories are therefore not notational variants of each other; rather, there are important empirical differences between them. In the next section, we consider more of these differences. We show that the Grounding Conditions allow for various types of languages that would be ruled out by Structure Preservation, illustrating with three languages already discussed: Yoruba, Akan, and Kinande.

3.4.1.2 Beyond Structure Preservation In the previous section, we demonstrated that the robust structure-preserving effect is derived from the Grounding Conditions. This results if path conditions are neither introduced nor removed during the course of a derivation. However, there are cases in which path conditions apparently are either added or lost. We consider examples of each type in this section. We demonstrate that the Grounding Conditions account for data proscribed by Structure Preservation. These cases combine with other implications of Grounding Theory (such as the implications for phonological rules discussed in section 3.2.2) to show that Grounding Theory has a broader scope than does Structure Preservation.

The first case we consider involves adding a condition during the lexical derivation, logically possible under the Grounding Conditions but impossible under Structure Preservation.

Introducing a Condition: Yoruba Low Vowels   As shown in (123), were a condition *If [F] then [G]* to be introduced at some domain *n*, then any instances of [F] alone would be impermissible in the input to domain *n*. Consequently, no evidence for any representation including [F] but not including [G] would remain in domain *n*.

Crucial in the above demonstration is the restriction *in the input to domain n*. It would be possible for a scenario to exist where the domain *n − 1* contains a general rule assigning [G] to all instances of [F]. As a result of such a rule, no instances of [F] without [G] would remain in the input to domain *n*. (124) schematizes this case.

(124)   *A general rule assigning [G] to [F]*

	[F]	[G]	[F, G]
Input to stratum *n − 1*	[F]	[G]	[F, G]
Rule: [F] → [G]	[F, G]	n/a	n/a
Output of stratum *n − 1*	[F, G]	[G]	[F, G]
Stratum *n*: *If [F] then [G]*	OK	OK	OK

We have already presented languages with essentially this property. In section 3.2.4.2, we showed that in Yoruba all [+low] vowels are redundantly assigned [−ATR]. Once the rule of Yoruba [−ATR] Insertion applies, the LO/ATR Condition can hold of all subsequent strata. Pulaar, in section 3.2.1.3, presents a comparable case, in which [+ATR] is assigned to [+high] vowels and subsequently HI/ATR holds of all representations.

Two points are of interest. First, the Grounding Conditions (109) state that in the unmarked case, path conditions hold. As a result, the preferred Yoruba grammar is that which adds the relevant condition once redundant [ATR] F-elements are inserted. Second, we know of no evidence in Yoruba of a later process creating a violation of the introduced path condition, a result consistent with the condition holding generally in later stages of the derivation.[86]

To summarize, languages may add path conditions. Evidence that a condition *If [F] then [G]* has been added arises if the language has a general rule inserting [G] on all instances of [F]. Yoruba provides an example of exactly this sort. The pattern is entirely compatible with the Grounding Condition model but would be at least a technical counterexample to Structure Preservation (122), since Structure Preservation states that a single set of conditions holds of both underived and derived representations. In languages like Yoruba, this appears not to be the case: conditions hold of derived representations that do not hold of underlying representations.

Removing Conditions: Phonetic Interpolation in Akan   Structure Preservation rules out the loss of conditions until the word level is attained: at that point, conditions no longer hold. By contrast, the formal model of Grounding Conditions exerts pressure *preventing* the loss of conditions at any stage in the derivation. By Grounding Condition II, path conditions hold in the unmarked case: loss of a condition constitutes going from a less marked state to a more marked state.[87] Thus, the two models make different predictions. The Grounding Condition model states that it is marked for any strong condition to be lost (though unmarked for a weak condition to be lost), while Structure Preservation states that all conditions are lost at a particular point in the derivation, immediately after word-level rules.

Despite the prediction that strong conditions will not be lost, it is important to consider the nature of condition loss, to determine the extent to which such cases do exist. One can only determine that a path condition has been removed if some rule creates a violation of that condition. Without such a rule, the representations do not change, so there is no evidence that a path condition has been removed.

Akan might appear to provide a case in which a negative condition is lost (Kiparsky 1985). As shown in section 3.2.3.2, although low vowels are opaque to harmony lexically, they appear to undergo harmony postlexically. Kiparsky proposes that this is due to the loss of a marking condition at the postlexical level of representation.

As suggested above, however, there is no real evidence that [+ATR] is ever on a phonological path to [+low] in Akan. The across-the-board gradient nature of harmony above the word level argues for deriving the relevant forms by an application of phonetic interpolation affecting all vowels in the appropriate environments: crucially, low vowels are not singled out for special treatment. In short, ATR/LO holds of *all* phonological levels of Akan.

We speculate that cline-forming rules in general may not need to obey path conditions, because of their low-level syntagmatic motivation. Note that by definition, if clines do not involve the creation of *paths*, then no *path conditions* may be violated as the specific result of cline formation. We conclude that, contrary to first appearances, the Akan data do not constitute a case where a condition that holds lexically does not hold postlexically.[88]

Never Imposing Conditions: Weak Interpretation in Kinande   Kinande presents another case that might appear to involve the removal of a condition. Here we review only the behavior of low vowels in harmonic domains, and as with Akan, the data allow an alternative analysis that does not require positing a condition lexically and then removing it postlexically.

In Kinande, as shown in section 3.2.3.1, low vowels appear to be transparent to
[+ATR] harmony at the lexical stage. However, at the surface, long low L-toned
vowels are [+ATR] in [+ATR] words. This observation raises the possibility that the
LO/ATR and ATR/LO Conditions, which might be considered to hold of the lexicon, are abandoned postlexically.

We have argued above, however, that there is no real evidence even for the lexical
prohibition of [+ATR] with [+low]. Morpheme-level specifications of [+ATR] link
specifically to high vowels (ATR/HI) and then spread leftward in a less constrained
fashion, targeting both high and nonhigh vowels (no conditions). We suggested that
the transparency of low vowels is apparent only, but that their advanced nature is
phonetically salient only in particular contexts.

We identified two types of transparency in section 3.2.3.1: (i) antagonistic
(Kinande), (ii) sympathetic (Ngbaka). Both classes of targets are identified by
grounded conditions, but neither is formally transparent in the sense of being an
ineligible target for a spreading rule. For such cases, there will be no evidence for
the removal of a condition involved in defining "transparency" if there is no *formal*
transparency to define.

3.4.1.3 Conclusion In robust terms, the transderivational effects of the Grounding
Conditions are comparable to the effects attributed to Structure Preservation
(Kiparsky 1985). There are, however, both formal and substantive differences.

Formally, Structure Preservation claims that conditions are not added lexically.
We demonstrated that the Grounding Conditions allow the limited introduction of
path conditions, that it is possible in principle to find evidence for the introduction of
conditions, and that the phenomenon is attested (Yoruba).

In addition, Structure Preservation turns conditions off after the word level; under
Grounding Theory, the least marked grammar maintains all strong conditions (see
Hyman 1990b, Kaisse 1990, Rice 1990), although turning a condition off is certainly
possible. The postlexical behavior of low vowels in Akan appears at first to suggest
that the ATR/LO Condition no longer holds postlexically. We propose instead that
the surface distribution of [+ATR] in such a language is a composite of a lexical
[+ATR] harmony rule that respects the LO/ATR Condition and a late (postlexical
or phonetic) rule interpolating [+ATR]. If interpolation rules do not create phonological paths, there is no reason why they should be subject to path conditions.
Consequently, LO/ATR can hold postlexically as well as lexically in Akan. The
prediction resulting from this conclusion is that clines can only be blocked by specifications that are present (see Keating 1988, Cohn 1989). This contrasts with phonological assimilation rules, in which opacity can result from absent specifications, as in
Yoruba.

Finally, it has been suggested that there exists a class of cases where conditions appear to have been turned off only because they were never in fact on. In a case like Kinande, for example, the solid lexical evidence is for the imposition of ATR/HI (which subsumes ATR/LO) on the initial process of association. There is no strong evidence that ATR/LO ever governs lexical derivations, hence no reason to assume that the cooccurrence of [+ATR] and [+low] involves the loss of a condition.

In terms of substance, the Grounding Conditions constitute on the one hand an instantiation of the types of marking conditions assumed by Structure Preservation, and on the other hand an elaboration and extension of such conditions. We have argued that, unlike Structure Preservation, the effects of grounded conditions can be felt in the phonetics; we have argued in addition that grounded conditions can impose restrictions on the class of eligible triggers or targets for rules even in cases where the conditions in question do not govern representations as a whole.

3.4.2 Contrastive Underspecification

Contrastive Underspecification (Clements 1987, Steriade 1987a, Christdas 1988, Mester and Itô 1989, etc.) takes as highly significant the observation that there are cases where feature values play a phonological role only within the class of elements for which the features concerned are distinctive.[89] Schematically, if some feature [F] is used to contrast segments A and B, but receives a value redundantly for segment C, then specifications would be as follows (where *0F* stands for "unspecified for F"):

(125)   A   B   C
      [F] αF $-\alpha$F   0F

As illustration, consider the case of Khalkha Mongolian (Steriade 1987a). In Khalkha, seven surface vowels are attested: [a, e, o, ö, i, u, ü]. Rialland and Djamouri (1984) argue convincingly that the well-known process often referred to as "back" harmony (see Poppe 1954, Chinchor 1978–79, Steriade 1979, Anderson 1980, etc.) involves the spread of [−ATR]. Of interest is the fact that there is a gap in the surface inventory as far as [ATR] is concerned. Whereas with round vowels both [+ATR] and [−ATR] variants are possible, for nonrounded vowels an [ATR] contrast is possible for nonhigh vowels, but for the high unrounded vowel [i], there is no [−ATR] counterpart.

(126) *Khalkha Mongolian vowel inventory*

	[+ATR]	[−ATR]
i	ü	u
	ö	o
	e	a

The attested gap in the high vowels, that /i/ is unpaired with a [−ATR] counterpart, is extremely important. Whereas all other vowels participate in harmony, the front vowel [i] does not; in addition, [i] is transparent to the harmonic process.

Steriade's proposal is that the transparency of the front high vowel is a direct result of the gap in the Khalkha inventory. In the cases where vowels contrast on the basis of their [ATR] values, both values are included in the relevant phonological representations, hence [+ATR] for [ü, ö, e] and [−ATR] for [u, o, a]; where there is no contrast involving [ATR], for [i], no [ATR] value is included. Harmony affects the vowels specified for [ATR]; the vowel unspecified for [ATR] is neutral to harmony.

There are two aspects to the Contrastive Underspecification proposal, both as they affect this particular case in Khalkha, and as they affect phonological systems generally. First, both values of the harmonic value are present for the harmonic class. Second, the neutral class (i.e., the class that does not undergo harmony) does not exhibit an underlying contrast in the harmonic feature. Considering the second point leads to an understanding of the first point. Steriade (1987a:360) suggests that the neutrality is due to Structure Preservation in the sense of Kiparsky (1985) and Itô and Mester (1986): "a segment which cannot bear an underlying specification for F ... cannot be subject to a lexical rule that assigns it a value for F."[90] As discussed in section 3.4.1, for Kiparsky (1985), Structure Preservation is the result of a set of marking conditions, conditions that we have argued to be selected from the class of grounded conditions.

The crucial point is the following. Given a class of conditions, arguably grounded, that define a class of nonundergoers, the distinction between neutral segments, like Mongolian [i], and harmonic segments, like all other vowels of Mongolian, is adequately achieved. If the harmonic class is specified for only one value of the harmonic feature, the neutral class is defined by the relevant set of marking conditions; if the harmonic class is specified for both values of the harmonic feature, the neutral class is *still* defined by the relevant set of marking conditions. That is, marking conditions define the neutral class whether the harmonic class is fully or partially specified: the issue of degree of specification is therefore a separate one, not tied necessarily to the account of neutrality.

We conclude that the crucial aspect of Contrastive Underspecification is not specifying harmonic segments for both values of the harmonic feature, but rather is *imposing a set of marking conditions*. The proposal made here, the imposition of grounded conditions, therefore derives the effects of Contrastive Underspecification when taken in conjunction with Combinatorial Specification, and constitutes a claim about the types of contrastive inventories that can be derived. The approach is thus fundamentally modular.

Empirical and conceptual issues arise. On the one hand, one must seek a formal analysis for cases like Khalkha Mongolian. On the other hand, one must determine whether the claims of Contrastive Underspecification are entirely comparable to those of Grounding Theory in combination with Combinatorial Specification.

Consider first the actual implementation of the sketched analysis of Khalkha. As argued by Rialland and Djamouri (1984), the value of [ATR] that is crucially present is [−ATR]. The problem for a grounded account of the harmonic pattern is therefore to determine why this feature does not associate to the vowel [i]. On the one hand, RTR/HI and HI/ATR are relevant: both conditions rule out the combination of [−ATR] with [+high]. These conditions are necessary but not sufficient for Khalkha, however, since by themselves they would incorrectly rule out the second member of the pair [ü/u] as well (see (126)). One must assume, therefore, that in conjunction with RTR/HI and HI/ATR is a condition that distinguishes between [i] and [ü/u]. While this might be a condition involving an incompatibility between tongue root retraction and spread lips, a more plausible suggestion would be to prohibit the combination of tongue root retraction with tongue body fronting, for which we have seen some evidence in the discussion of E̩doid (see sections 3.1.3.1 and 3.1.2; further evidence is found in Lango, see chapter 5). Rialland and Djamouri note in this regard that the usual transcriptions of Khalkha are misleading in that *ü* appears to represent a front vowel. They provide phonetic evidence that the vowel is actually back, suggesting that a more adequate transcription of *ü* (a [+ATR] back vowel) would be [u], while a more adequate transcription of *u* (a [−ATR] back vowel) would be [ʊ]. We conclude, therefore, that the cooccurrence restrictions observed in Khalkha appear to straightforwardly reflect grounded restrictions between tongue root movement and tongue body fronting and raising. The transparency itself can be formally derived along the lines of our analysis of Wolof in section 3.2.4.1. (See also section 4.7 for a discussion of the formal properties of neutrality.)

With regard to comparability of Contrastive Underspecification and Grounding Theory/Combinatorial Specification, the central point here is that Combinatorial Specification in conjunction with Grounding Theory derives the robust effects attributed to Contrastive Underspecification: grounded conditions govern both the combination of F-elements in underived representations ("inventories") and the combination of F-elements in derived representations ("Structure Preservation"). At the same time, it is clear that they are not equivalent. Various attested relations between F-elements are inconsistent with the claims of Contrastive Underspecification that both values of a feature used distinctively are present in the relevant class. Since these cases have already been discussed (section 2.8.2), we will not dwell on them further.

A final point in this discussion of Khalkha Mongolian is that grounded conditions identify the neutral vowel. We explore the relation between grounding and the question of which vowels may be neutral in the next section.

3.5   Grounded Conditions and Rules

We argued in chapter 2 that phonological representations are composed of sets of F-elements, and we have proposed in this chapter that combinations of the members of these sets are defined as well formed or ill formed by implicational conditions whose basis is in the phonetics. In chapter 4, we discuss the way in which phonological rules relate different representations. Anticipating that discussion, here we examine one way in which grounded conditions determine the correct operation of such relations. Our basic claim, which derives directly from Grounding Condition I, can be stated as follows:[91]

(127)   *Grounded rule conditions*

Where a path condition is imposed on the source or target of a rule, the condition must be grounded.

Throughout this chapter, we have presented numerous cases where grounded implications restrict the application of some phonological rule, for example, with rules of redundancy (e.g., Pulaar [+ATR] Insertion (section 3.2.1.3); this is also the topic of section 3.2.2) and rules of harmony (e.g., Pulaar [+ATR] Spread (section 3.2.1.3)), as well as more idiosyncratic rules (e.g., palatal-induced harmony in Akan (section 3.2.3.2)). We have also shown that one and the same condition may have very different effects in different languages. For example, in Pulaar, ATR/HI holds of [+ATR] Insertion while in Kinande the same condition holds of [+ATR] Association. This single condition performs quite distinct functions in the two languages, with distinct results: in Pulaar, all [+high] vowels are [+ATR], while in Kinande, some [+high] vowels are not specified for [ATR].

In this section, we direct our attention to a further ramification for phonological rules, namely, predictions about neutral elements (those that appear to neither trigger nor undergo a harmony process). We refer to a neutral segment as *opaque* when it does not allow harmony to continue progressing beyond it; we refer to a neutral segment as *transparent* when it allows propagation of the harmonic F-element to continue, despite exhibiting no alternation with respect to the harmonic feature. There are two issues involved in the problem of characterizing neutrality: (i) determining the formal means by which opacity or transparency is to be expressed and (ii) determining the possible neutral classes with respect to a specific rule. In this section, we focus on the second issue, arguing that in general, neutral classes can be defined in terms of grounded conditions. We defer discussion of the formal characterization of such rules to section 4.7.

The central claim is that the classes of segments that exhibit transparency and opacity effects are classes for which the spreading feature is not distinctive (see

Kiparsky 1981, Clements 1981, 1987, Clements and Sezer 1982, van der Hulst and Smith 1986, Steriade 1987a, etc.). Where the harmonic feature is not distinctive, the surface value can be either the opposite of the harmonic value (involving an incompatibility with the spreading value) or the same as the harmonic value (involving redundant assignment of the spreading value). The essence of this proposal can be seen by reconsidering the contrast between cases such as the transparency exhibited by high vowels in Wolof and the opacity exhibited by high vowels in Yoruba, both due to RTR/HI, and the contrast between the transparency attested by low vowels in Kinande and the opacity attested by low vowels in Pulaar, both resulting from ATR/LO.

The question of which vowels may be neutral to a given rule receives a very specific answer under the Grounding Condition model: systematic instances of opaque and transparent segments must be defined by grounded conditions. *Antagonistic* neutrality with respect to α is therefore limited to classes of targets that are defined by a grounded path condition as incompatible with α; *sympathetic* neutrality with respect to α is established for classes where α is redundant. This proposal leads to a wide range of predictions about possible and impossible types of neutrality in harmony systems in general, and in [ATR] systems in particular.

3.5.1 Systematically Impossible Neutrality
The Grounding Conditions rule out the systems listed in (128).

(128) *Proscribed opaque and transparent vowels*

      a. [+low] opaque in [−ATR] harmony

      b. [+high] opaque in [+ATR] harmony

      c. Only mid opaque in any [ATR] harmony

      d. Only mid transparent in any [ATR] harmony

Low vowels cannot be opaque to [−ATR] harmony (128a): either the low vowels would have to be singled out for redundant specification as [+ATR], or a condition would be required to prevent the cooccurrence of the two F-elements [+low] and [−ATR]. The former possibility would have to invoke the ungrounded condition (*If [+ATR] then [+low]*; see (129a)); the latter possibility would rule out the cooccurrence of two F-elements that are compatible under any set of grounded conditions (129b) (*If [−ATR] then not [+low]*).

(129) *[+low] opaque in [− ATR] harmony: proscribed*

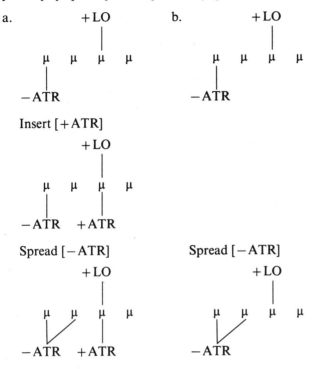

In precisely the same fashion, high vowels cannot be opaque to [+ATR] spread (128b) because (i) high vowels cannot be redundantly [−ATR], and (ii) [+high] and [+ATR] are always compatible.

In (128c,d), the proscribed pattern singles out the *mid* vowels for opacity or transparency, while high and low vowels alternate. Such systems are proscribed because the only grounded conditions that prevent [αATR] from appearing on mid vowels also prevent it from appearing on high vowels (RTR/LO) or on low vowels (ATR/HI). Similarly proscribed would be transparency derived by positing a path condition on a redundancy rule aimed at assigning either [+ATR] or [−ATR] to mid vowels in an across-the-board fashion: such a path condition could only be ungrounded and is therefore impossible.

3.5.2 Systematically Possible Neutrality

Note that in both (128a,b), transparency is possible: the requirement would be that [−ATR] harmony precede a rule inserting [−ATR] redundantly on low vowels, or that [+ATR] harmony precede a rule inserting [+ATR] on high vowels (both constituting grounded rules of redundancy). The latter is our analysis of the distribution of

[ATR] in Ngbaka in chapter 2 (see van der Hulst and Smith 1986, Ewen and van der Hulst 1987).

Further, as noted above, opacity is possible where grounded conditions identify the opaque element as being in an antagonistic relation to the harmonic F-element. There are two ways that this might be expressed formally. First, as in our account of Yoruba vowel harmony in chapter 2, a grounded condition identifies a class of vowels as ineligible targets. In Yoruba, the RTR/HI Condition identifies high vowels as ineligible bearers of [−ATR] and they are therefore opaque: harmony cannot associate [−ATR] to these vowels (130) and cannot "skip" them because of the Locality Condition.

(130) *Conditions and Locality*

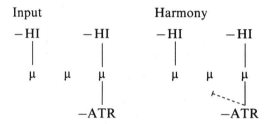

An alternative exists: rather than appealing to the RTR/HI Condition to limit the targets, we could suggest that the ATR/HI Condition identifies targets for redundant [+ATR] insertion: [+ATR] would be inserted on all high vowels, and Locality would again block spreading beyond the high vowel. This is, of course, the traditional "No Crossing Constraint" violation account for harmony.

(131) *Redundant [+ATR] and Locality*

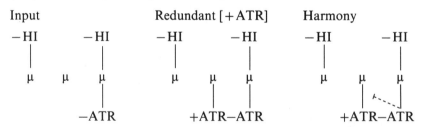

Crucially, the class of opaque elements in a language like Yoruba is identified by grounded conditions regardless of the formal representation of opacity. Opacity results either directly from the interaction of grounded conditions with Locality, or indirectly, via the interaction of Locality with the output of grounded redundancy rules.

There remains a residue of cases involving neutrality, however, which cannot be explained simply in terms of the grounded conditions holding between the harmonic F-element and the neutral segment(s). We turn to this residue in the next section.

3.5.3 Idiosyncratic Neutrality

It is not the case that all instances of neutrality are systematic. Consider, for example, the opaque vowels in Kalenjin (Antell et al. 1973, Halle and Vergnaud 1981). Kalenjin, a Nilotic language, has a 5-vowel system crosscut by [ATR], giving 10 surface vowels; it also has a [+ATR] Harmony rule triggered by any root or suffix that is invariably [+ATR], as in (132b,c). Contrast these with the form in (132a), which shows recessive affixes with a recessive root: all vowels surface as [−ATR].[92]

(132) *Kalenjin [+ATR] Harmony*

   a. Unspecified root and affixes: all [−ATR]
      kI − A − pAr − In   [kɪabarɪn]   'I killed you-SG'

   b. [+ATR] root: all [+ATR]
      kI − A − ke:r − In   [kiage:rin]   'I saw you-SG'

   c. [+ATR] suffix: all [+ATR]
      kI − A − kEr − E   [kiagere]   'I was shutting it'

      cf. [kɪagɛr]   'I shut it'

In addition to dominant ([+ATR]) and recessive (unspecified) roots and affixes, there are three opaque affixes, affixes that invariably surface as [−ATR] (133a,b) and prevent propagation of the harmonic [+ATR] (133c,d) *ma-* 'NEGATIVE', *ka-* 'PERFECTIVIZER', and *-kɛ* 'REFLEXIVE'. (The opaque affixes are underlined in the left-hand column of (133).

(133) *Opacity in Kalenjin [+ATR] Harmony*

   a. kI − A − (i)un − <u>kɛ:</u>   [kiaungɛ:]   'I washed myself'
                                    *[kiaunge:]

   b. <u>ma</u> − tI − (i)un − <u>kɛ:</u>   [matiungɛ:]   'don't wash
                                    *[matiunge:]   yourself'

   c. kA − <u>ma</u> − A − ke:r − Ak   [kamaage:rak]   'I didn't see you-PL'
                                    *[kamaage:rak]

   d. kA − <u>ma</u> − <u>ka</u> − kO − ke:r − A   [kamagagoge:ra]   'and he hadn't seen
                                    *[kamagagoge:ra]   me'

In Kalenjin, the opacity of these three morphemes cannot be attributed to membership in a grounded class because [+ATR] combines freely in this language, both underlyingly and as a result of harmony. Here, then, opacity is an idiosyncratic property of certain morphemes, one that can be expressed by specifying these vowels as [−ATR] in underlying representation, as in (134).

(134) k A − m a − A − k e: r − A k   →   k A − m a − a̱ − k e: r − a̱ k

$$
\text{−ATR} \quad \text{+ATR} \qquad\qquad\qquad \text{−ATR} \quad \text{+ATR}
$$

Spreading of [+ATR] cannot affect the [−ATR] vowel, and Locality prevents the spread of [+ATR] from crossing past the lexically specified [−ATR] vowel. Note that such a case constitutes the ternary use of the feature [±ATR]. At the point where harmonic spreading takes place, vowels may be (i) unspecified for [ATR], (ii) specified as [+ATR], (iii) specified as [−ATR].

The Kalenjin example demonstrates that certain idiosyncratically opaque elements cannot be defined by grounded conditions, thereby raising the issue of whether Grounding Theory is completely irrelevant to cases of idiosyncratic opacity. This is not the case. First, we have seen with a case like Akan (section 3.2.3.2) that appeals to crossing violations are insufficient to derive opacity, and that direct reference to grounded conditions is necessary. In addition, Grounding Theory predicts that, in fact, lexical (idiosyncratic) specifications for a harmonic F-element may be opaque because of conditions on the rule itself. For example, one might imagine a language similar to Kalenjin in having free combination of [+ATR], but similar to Pulaar in allowing only [+high] vowels to serve as sources for the harmonic feature. In this case, any lexical [+ATR] specification linked to a nonhigh vowel will be opaque, just as the [−ATR] specification is opaque in Kalenjin. In chapter 4, we argue that Menomini presents this type of case, restricting both sources and targets of [+ATR] harmony by the ATR/LO Condition, despite allowing [+ATR, +low] vowels in the language in general. In such cases, neutrality is due to idiosyncratic, lexical specifications but is systematically characterized by imposing a grounded condition in the rule itself. Finally, although the amount of data is insufficient to warrant strong conclusions, we note that all three exceptional morphemes requiring the preassociation of [−ATR] in Kalenjin are [−high]—that is, prelinking is consistent with the requirements of RTR/HI: *If [−ATR] then [−high]/not [+high]*.

3.5.4 Summary

To conclude, for any rule, the class of Targets may be either featurally undefined or defined by some set of path conditions. Conditions may be imposed on specific rules or may hold more generally in the language. Since Grounding Condition I states that any path conditions invoked by a language must be grounded, this theory predicts severe restrictions on the cooccurrence conditions that a language may invoke: it is these conditions that define systematic neutrality (where they hold of a language in general) and that may characterize idiosyncratic neutrality (where the conditions hold only of a source and/or target in a specific rule, but do not hold of the language in general). The neutrality effects are simply an expected subset of the phenomena resulting when Grounding Theory interacts with rules. As noted in the introduction to this section, the focus here has been on the range of *substantive* effects derived by the Grounding Conditions; in section 4.7, we examine the range of *formal* effects involved in cases of transparency and opacity.

3.6 Conclusion

The central claim of this chapter is that the conditions governing the combination of features are of a substantively constrained nature. Conditions may or may not be imposed in a particular language; but where imposed, a condition can only be of the substantively grounded set. The unmarked case is for strong conditions to be imposed maximally (Grounding Condition II); ungrounded conditions are absolutely ruled out (Grounding Condition I).

   Formally, constraints on the cooccurrence of F-elements on paths involve implicational statements of the form in (135).

(135) *Path condition format*

    a. Positive   If [F] then [αG].

    b. Negative   If [F] then not [$-\alpha$G].

The sole direct effect of such conditions is to block representations that do not conform.

   The version of a condition that is relevant, positive or negative, depends on which F-elements are active: if [αG] were active, then the positive version of (135) would hold; if [$-\alpha$G] were active, then the negative condition would hold; if both values were active, then both positive and negative conditions would hold. In this way, the Grounding Hypothesis is essentially symmetrical. Moreover, for each feature, a markedness statement determines the extent to which the feature is likely to be active and when a feature is active and binary, which value is likely to be active (e.g., (21), (106), (108)).

   In concluding this chapter, we discuss the relation of the Grounding Hypothesis to a theory of markedness, and we raise certain issues regarding modality and modularity.

3.6.1 Implications of Markedness
The model presented here makes markedness claims of two types: (i) concerning conditions, (ii) concerning features. Grounding Condition II states that languages

prefer strong conditions to have the widest distribution possible. In addition, each feature has its own two-part markedness statement of the form in (108).

In the following sections, we briefly present certain implications of the markedness component of the grounding model, looking at learnability, language change, and typology. Essentially, this section sketches outlines of prospective research since at this point we have not explored any of these areas with the care that each deserves.

3.6.1.1 Learnability   One role for markedness theory could be to establish a point of departure for language learning: *Take the unmarked case as the initial state.* In terms of the Grounding Conditions, there could be at least two possible interpretations of this hypothesis. First, one could assume that all grounded conditions hold initially, and that positive evidence is required to move to a more marked representation. Alternatively, one could assume that all conditions of a certain strength hold initially; positive evidence could cause the language learner to relax a strong condition or to impose a weak condition.

In terms of feature markedness, certain features such as [high] and [low] have a strong tendency to be active, while others, [ATR] for example, have a weaker tendency to be active (see (106)). Thus, a feature like [ATR] would be absent initially (its unmarked state), whereas features like [high] and [low] would be present (their unmarked state). Following Kiparsky (1981), we have assumed that there is a markedness statement for each feature that determines whether [+F] or [−F] is the unmarked F-element (108b).

There are a variety of ways in which a system may become more marked. With respect to features, there are two options: (i) some features may be present where their absence is unmarked, or absent where their presence is unmarked; and (ii) the marked value of a feature may be present rather than the unmarked value.[93] In addition, some strong grounded condition(s) may not hold. We briefly consider the nature of these types of marked properties in light of the learnability of such a system. Our main point is that to learn violations of markedness requires robust evidence (see Chomsky 1982).

[F] tends not to be used actively. To learn that a weakly occurring feature like [ATR] is active requires positive evidence. Such evidence takes the form of alternations (recall ATR Insertion in Pulaar and in Eastern Javanese) or simply finding impressive morphemic distinctions due to [F].

If [F] is used actively, its active value tends to be [αF]; the passive value of [F] tends to be [−αF]. To learn that a weaker value of a feature, [−αF], is active again requires evidence. Finding morphemic distinctions due to [F] is insufficient since either [αF] or [−αF] could be responsible for the distinction. What is necessary here is to find alternations whose distribution is impossible if only [αF] is active, but explained if [−αF] is active. Importantly, the patterns motivating [−αF] must be vigorous enough to be learnable. We argued in section 3.2.4 that the patterning of [−ATR] in both Yoruba and Wolof presented sufficient evidence to motivate [−ATR] over the unmarked [+ATR].

In the unmarked case, languages maximize the use of strong path conditions (Grounding Condition II). To learn that some condition is inactive requires a phonological violation of the condition. As argued in sections 3.3.1 and 3.4.1.2, determining whether a surface form constitutes a phonological violation of a condition is not necessarily straightforward. Since the surface form alone is inadequate in determining the phonological patterning of F-elements, to learn that some condition does not hold requires robust phonological evidence.

If the need for impressive evidence for certain features' presence is correct, then markedness and learnability considerations put constraints on rule systems as well as on representations: a language with marked representations (either due to the F-elements that are present or due to strong conditions that are inactive) is expected to have solid evidence supporting the marked state. This predicts a clear asymmetry: strong evidence should be involved in establishing the use of marked feature values, while peripheral evidence is consistent with use of the opposite, unmarked, value.

3.6.1.2 Language Change   If we are correct in the assumption that language learners assume the unmarked state and move to more marked grammars only in the face of evidence, then if evidence becomes less evident, languages should change to a less marked state. There are three ways in which a language can become less marked, corresponding to the three types of markedness discussed in the previous section: (i) activation of a particular feature can change to the unmarked state (active or inactive, depending on the feature, (108a)); (ii) an inactive feature value can become the active one, (108b); (iii) an inactive strong condition can become active (Grounding Condition II).

Also of interest is exploring the ways in which evidence might become less impressive. The Grounding Conditions suggest a particular way in which evidence might weaken.

The Grounding Conditions identify particular F-element combinations as antagonistic; it is these combinations that are subject to the greatest degree of variation in their phonetic implementation (see section 3.3.1 and Meechan 1992). Because of the antagonistic F-elements, such combinations are inherently unstable and subject to phonological reanalysis. For example, features like [+high] and [−ATR] phonetically counteract each other to a certain extent; as a result, such a combination may be phonetically very close to a mid vowel, with consequent reanalysis possible in that direction. The general result is varying degrees of confusion for the language learner in the case of antagonistic combinations unless there is strong evidence supporting the phonological representation. Change is expected to occur where the evidence is

weak and confusion arises because of the mismatch between phonological and phonetic representations.

In addition, the Grounding Conditions model identifies sympathetic F-element
combinations, that is, those that are inherently stable and so should show minimal
diachronic variation. Thus, not only does the model suggest which sounds are likely
to show variation over time, it also predicts which sounds are more likely to remain
constant.

A preliminary discussion supporting these claims, based on Elugbe's (1982) analysis of the vowels of Proto-Ẹdoid, was presented in section 3.1.3.1. See also Akinlabi,
Archangeli, and Pulleyblank, in preparation.

3.6.1.3 Typology The model presented in this chapter makes typological claims,
about F-element distribution, about rule systems, and about rules.

F-Element Combinations Under simple assumptions, the model laid out thus far
conspires to establish the five-vowel system *I E A O U* as the least marked vowel
system. This result is consistent with the survey in Maddieson 1984.

Two sets of assumptions are necessary. First, we assume that the three features
[high], [low], and [back] are normally active. That is, the markedness statements for
all three features (see (108)) assign them high activation levels. Second, we assume
that there are four grounded conditions governing the cooccurrence of these three
features.

(136) *Conditions governing [±HI], [±LO], [±BK]*

HI/LO Condition:	If [+high] then [−low]/not [+low].
LO/HI Condition:	If [+low] then [−high]/not [+high].
LO/BK Condition:	If [+low] then [+back]/not [−back].
FR/LO Condition:	If [−back] then [−low]/not [+low].

Given the four grounded conditions in (136), any combination of feature values of
[high], [low], and [back] gives the five-vowel system *I E A O U*. For example, consider
the set of combinations that results from combination of the F-elements [+high],
[+low], and [−back].

(137) a. Active F-elements

+HI, +LO, −BK

	1	2	3	4	5	6	7	8
b.	+HI	+HI	+HI	+HI				
	+LO	+LO			+LO	+LO		
	−BK		−BK		−BK		−BK	
c.	*	*	I	U	*	A	E	O

The three active F-elements create eight combinations. Combinations 1 and 2 are ruled out by the HI/LO and LO/HI Conditions; combination 5 is ruled out by the LO/BK Condition. The result is therefore five combinations, 3, 4, 6, 7, and 8, corresponding to *I U A E O* respectively, (137c).

Of interest with respect to the issue of vowel typology is the fact that *any* combination of values for the features [high], [low], and [back] derives the same five-vowel system—provided that the four grounded conditions in (136) are invoked. The resulting systems would not be expected to behave phonologically in an identical fashion, but they would all have the same set of surface vowels. Given the robustness of the five-vowel pattern cross-linguistically, we take this as an important result. Significantly, too, the status of particular values of [high], [low], and [back] as marked or unmarked is immaterial to the typological generalization. We therefore do not commit ourselves here to a particular set of claims in this regard. The attested stability is directly attributable to the fact that positive and negative versions of conditions make equivalent claims about the well-formedness of representations. For example, a front low vowel is ruled out in (137) by virtue of the fact that LO/BK prohibits the cooccurrence of a [+low] specification with a [−back] specification—a negative condition; if the same five vowels had been specified with [+back] rather than [−back], then a front low vowel would be ruled out by the positive condition *If [+low] then [+back]*.

More marked vowel systems can be derived in a variety of ways, for example, by changing the cooccurrence restrictions on the active F-elements (compare Tiv and Barrow Inupiaq from chapter 2), by removing F-elements from the system (to create a three- or four-vowel system), or by adding F-elements to the system, F-elements whose activation level is weak enough that they are not found in the most unmarked system (e.g., [round] and [ATR]). Numerous examples of this type have been examined with respect to the feature [ATR] in this chapter. Alternatively, along the lines suggested in section 3.6.1.1, a more marked system can be derived by removing conditions. For example, removal of the LO/BK Condition would derive a sixth vowel, the front counterpart of the back low vowel. On the issue of removing conditions, it is perhaps worth noting that there is no reason a priori to assume that even the HI/LO and LO/HI Conditions cannot be relaxed in appropriately marked systems. By allowing the marked combination of [+high] and [+low], the range of coalescence and diphthongization effects observed in work of a "particle" type (Schane 1984, de Haas 1988, Anderson and Ewen 1987, van der Hulst 1988, 1989, Kaye, Lowenstamm, and Vergnaud 1985, Hayes 1990, etc.) can be derived.

Systems   The proposed model makes three kinds of typological claims with respect to phonological systems.

First, the model predicts that conditions need only be stipulated for specific rules where the condition is suspended more generally in the language. For example, in

Pulaar, ATR/HI does not hold generally: [e/o] contrast with [ɛ/ɔ]. However, ATR/HI does hold of the rule inserting [+ATR]. Since Grounding Condition II results in the maximization of strong conditions, the model predicts that if a condition C does not hold generally in some language, it is nonetheless likely to hold of any rules whose Argument is the antecedent to C; the stronger condition C is, the more likely this is to be true. (This point is explored further in chapter 5.)

Second, in languages where the conditions do not hold generally, rules requiring conditions are predicted to be more stable and less subject to diachronic change than rules that do not require conditions. This prediction follows from Grounding Condition II.

Finally, the evidence required to establish rules referring to F-elements with weak activation levels is predicted to be generally more salient than that for rules referring to unmarked F-elements. This is because to be learnable, marked F-elements require strong evidence (see section 3.6.1.1).

Rules In section 3.2.2, we discussed a variety of claims about possible and proscribed phonological rules. Among these was a typology of opacity and transparency with respect to rules propagating [ATR]. The limiting effect of grounded conditions in determining possible and impossible redundancy rules was discussed in section 3.2.2.2.

3.6.1.4 Summary In this section, we have looked briefly at a number of predictions made by the markedness aspects of the Grounding Condition model, touching on learnability, language change, and typology. Each of these areas warrants a research program, which we have yet to conduct in any detail. The general conclusion to draw from this discussion is the same point made throughout this whole section: implications of Grounding Theory extend well beyond restrictions on F-element cooccurrence.

3.6.2 Modality, Modularity, and Universal Grammar
Phonological behavior is fundamentally modular according to the theory being developed here. A subtheory of feature organization (Combinatorial Specification) interacts with a subtheory of implications (Grounding Theory), which in turn interacts with modules concerned with phonological rules, phonological domains, and so on. The subtheory of implications is itself intrinsically modular in a manner that has far-reaching ramifications. There are three crucial components of Grounding Theory: (i) formal implicational statements, (ii) substantive patterns of phonetic interaction, (iii) constrained instantiations of substantive implications (Grounding Conditions I and II).

Formally, both the implicational schemata and the expression of the Grounding Conditions share an important property with Combinatorial Specification: they are modality-independent. That is, no direct reference is made to the spoken modality used for all the languages that we have considered. The implications of this separation are considerable. Broadly speaking, two types of theories can be envisaged.

First, one could imagine that the phonological component consists of little more than a set of *skeletal formal statements* to the effect that the phonology manipulates formal objects, that such formal objects are hierarchically organized, that there are implicational relations between such formal objects, and that the implications may vary in strength, have particular formal effects, and so on. Such a formal phonological component would interact directly with the phonetics to derive the types of effects that have been discussed here.

(138) *Learned Theory*

> a. F-elements: $\{X, Y, \ldots\}$
> b. Implications: If p then q; if p then not q.

Alternatively, one could imagine that the phonological component contains *both formal and substantive content*. That is, in addition to defining the types of formal objects and implications as given in (138), the phonological component itself would actually include substantive instantiations of implications such as HI/ATR, ATR/ LO, and so on.

(139) *Hard-wired Theory*

> a. F-elements: $\{\pm\text{high}, \pm\text{ATR}, \ldots\}$
> b. Implications: If $[+\text{high}]$ then $[+\text{ATR}]$; if $[+\text{high}]$ then not $[-\text{ATR}]$; ...

The role of grounding would be very different in the two theories. For the Learned Theory, the Grounding Conditions would directly govern the relation between the formal phonology and the primary phonetic data. For the Hard-wired Theory, the Grounding Conditions would constitute (part of) the purely phonological definition of what constitutes a permissible implicational relation.

At issue, therefore, is the degree of modularity exhibited in the construction of a theory of the phonology/phonetics interface. Moreover, it should be possible to test the predictions of each hypothesis in this regard. For example, while the Learned Theory predicts a range of substantive cross-linguistic variation that might not be expected with the Hard-wired Theory, the Hard-wired Theory predicts a somewhat looser relation to phonetic realization than does the Learned Theory.

In addition, the potential separation of phonology from phonetics raises extremely interesting questions about languages employing different modalities. Recent research on sign languages, in particular American Sign Language, shows evidence of organizational principles in visual signs that are comparable in significant ways to those of oral language phonologies (see, for example, Padden and Perlmutter 1987, Wilbur 1987, Corina and Sagey 1988, Brentari 1990, Ann 1990, 1991). The door is therefore opened to an investigation of the role of modal implementation in determining the correct structure of phonological theory.

The Grounding Condition model offers the possibility of an account of phonological phenomena that is modality-independent. Grounding Conditions I and II require no reference to articulatory/acoustic/gestural/visual features, nor does the formal definition of path conditions as implicational statements. Specific instantiations of path conditions can be derived from the F-elements allowed by the modality in question; which path conditions satisfy Grounding Condition I is determined by inspection of the physical apparatus of production (vocal tract; hands) and perception (ears; eyes). Thus, Grounding Theory suggests a research program for phonological systems regardless of the modality.

Chapter 4
Parametric Rules

If the representations are right, the rules will follow ...
John McCarthy, "Feature Geometry and Dependency"

4.1 Introduction

The phonological system of a language is comprised of two parts, representations and relations between representations. Up to this point, our focus has been on representations, with the combinations allowed by the formal model of Combinatorial Specification being restricted by the constraints possible under the Grounding Conditions. A theme inherent in this work is that the different subtheories do not duplicate each other's properties. Hence, as we turn our attention to the algorithms relating structures, our intent is to isolate the variables by which such algorithms differ and to define those variables in a way that does not duplicate the structures themselves.

At issue is the range of language-particular variation possible in the systematic relations between phonological representations. At one extreme is the position that all such relations are governed by universal automatic mechanisms, or *conventions*. The effect of a convention is constant given a particular input: there is a fixed effect, and the point or points in the derivation at which the convention holds are also fixed. There is nothing language-particular about a convention. Implicit in the research paradigm that focuses on representations is the idea that most, if not all, algorithms are conventions, or near-conventions (see McCarthy 1988).

In contrast to conventions are *rules*. The effect of a rule is at least partially language-dependent both in its function and in its application. This chapter constitutes an argument that rules vary independently of representations: taking care of the representations is not enough. The argument is made by demonstrating that formally comparable abstract representations relate to quite distinct surface representations. Given this result, the challenge is to determine the type and range of variation available in the characterization of such rules.

We make this argument primarily through a study of the phenomena that have been explained as the association and spreading of F-elements. These two types of relations form an interesting pair with respect to the issues noted above because there are arguments in the literature that both are effected by convention (Goldsmith 1976), that all association and some spreading is effected by convention (Williams 1976, Halle and Vergnaud 1982), and that association is effected by convention but spreading is effected by rule (Pulleyblank 1986a). (See chapter 1 for elaboration of this point.) In section 4.6, we demonstrate that the range of variation that character-izes association processes is just as large as that found in spreading rules. The evi-dence presented leads to the conclusion that there is no motivation for a general "association convention." Rather, association, like spreading and so on, is accom-plished by rule.

Many other conventions that have been proposed in the literature are statements that define well-formed representations, for instance, the Obligatory Contour Princi-ple, which prohibits adjacent tier-internal identical elements. We examine a number of OCP effects in this chapter and demonstrate that these different effects result from the application of different rules, each in a manner consistent with the OCP as defined in chapter 1.

Other types of well-formedness are determined by Locality, for instance, the prohi-bition against crossed association lines (see section 1.5.2). Standard analyses of neu-tral segments attribute opacity to the No Crossing Constraint and transparency to the lack of a No Crossing Constraint violation. We reject the No Crossing Constraint as the sole source of neutrality in section 4.7, showing that formal properties of neutrality effects, both transparency and opacity, result from the interaction between different representations and a variety of rule types. This complements the discussion of the role of the Grounding Conditions in determining substantive properties of neutrality effects. (See section 3.5.)

The demonstration in this chapter that alternation-particular variation occurs with association, with OCP effects, and with neutrality, regardless of the representations, argues strongly that rules are a central, not a peripheral, aspect of the phonological component: getting the "right" representation is important, but insufficient. We pro-pose a narrowly restricted class of rules, derived by assigning values to four binary parameters, Function, Type, Direction, and Iteration, laid out in section 4.2. Values for these parameters identify the rule-governed relation between two representations with respect to a particular F-element: we use the term *Argument* to identify the F-element affected by a rule. F-elements typically are in a path with some anchor; rule-governed relations may hinge on differences in the structure of such paths, fre-quently with respect to a subset of potential anchors for the Argument F-element. The term *Target* refers to the class of anchors identified as relevant for specific rules:

we take the default Target to be any anchor licensed by the language for the Argument F-element. In section 4.2.5, we explore the various types of requirements that may be imposed on Arguments and Targets.

Before introducing the parameters and elaborating on Arguments and Targets, we address the theoretical issues behind the proposal for parametric rules as opposed to some other view of rules.

4.1.1   Why Change Our Concept of the Nature of Rules?

Formal rules characterize how underlying and surface representations are related. We aim here to isolate the components of such relations and to determine the type of variation found within each such component: the components constitute the parameters, and the variation gives the possible settings for each parameter. (See Clements 1981, Clements and Sezer 1982, Archangeli and Pulleyblank 1987, Paradis 1986, Steriade 1987a, Piggott 1988, Yip 1988b for other discussion of parametric rules.)

The parametric approach contrasts significantly with the more standardly employed "rule pictures." The idea with pictures is to graphically depict the input representation and the output representation. There have been few attempts at a constrained theory of graphically represented rules. (See both Archangeli 1984 and Pulleyblank 1986a for attempts to limit the types of graphic notations available for use in rules.) Yet if there are no limits on possible rules, there is no theory: anything is an acceptable rule. One of the reasons why few attempts have been made to rigorously constrain the graphic notation may be the focus on representations. Implicit in this focus might be an assumption that phonologists know too little about representations to make exploring rules a worthwhile endeavor. Our view contrasts with this: since phonologies are systems of representations and rules, in order to determine whether the representational model is appropriate, it is important to consider how the rule algorithms are expressed.

A result of the graphic means of expressing rules is that the rule itself necessarily encodes information that is not manipulated by the rule—and indeed is never manipulated by any rule.[1] The pictures do not distinguish (explicitly or implicitly) between elements that are crucially included in the rule's representation and those that are only incidentally present, because of the structure involved and the method of depicting rules. Graphic approaches also treat rules in a holistic fashion rather than componentially: the entire picture together determines the nature of the rule.

The parametric approach differs on both counts. The parameters isolate specific components of processes that can vary, and determine the degrees of variability found with each component established. We demonstrate here that a wide range of surface phenomena can be derived from a very small number of interacting parameters, with the set of theoretically possible rules much closer to the set of actually attested rules than with graphic approaches. This contrasts dramatically with any approach positing a large number of parameters or unlimited variation for any given parameter (which are different ways of construing the graphic model). We argue that to allow additional parameters or parametric values predicts significantly more phenomena than are attested cross-linguistically, providing multiple analyses of certain patterns. To the extent that a smaller set of parameters and/or values can account for the observed phenomena, there is no need to extend this set beyond the four that are motivated here.

4.2   The Four Parameters

In this section, we introduce and illustrate the four parameters, Function, Type, Direction, and Iteration.

4.2.1   Function: Insert or Delete

Rules relate representations. Given the assumption that Precedence relations in an input representation are retained in an output representation (see chapter 1), only two changes are possible: the addition of some material or the deletion of some material. This chapter explores the model through a study of insertion rules.

(1) *Parameter*: Function
     Values: INSERT or DELETE

The effect of INSERT is that the output contains some material not present in the corresponding input. The effect of DELETE is the converse: the input contains some material not present in the output. The nature of the material that is added or lost is defined by the Type parameter.

4.2.2   Type: Path or F-Element

Since rules relate two different representations and since representations consist of F-elements and paths, it follows that rules manipulate F-elements and/or paths. Rules vary on this score: we refer to this as the *Type* parameter.

(2) *Parameter*: Type
     Values: PATH or F-ELEMENT

An INSERT/PATH rule has the effect of introducing paths between tokens of the Argument, an F-element, and the relevant Targets, a subset of the anchors. An INSERT/F-ELEMENT rule has the effect of introducing tokens of the Argument in paths with any specified Targets. The two DELETE rules remove information. A DELETE/PATH rule has the effect of removing a path, that is, delinking. The result may or may not be a free F-element, depending on the representation involved. A DELETE/F-ELEMENT rule removes an F-element.[2]

To see the difference between rules inserting paths and F-elements, consider Yoruba [−ATR] Insertion and [−ATR] Spread. Graphic representations of these rules are presented in (3a,b), repeated from (67) and (68) in chapter 2.

(3) a. *Yoruba [−ATR] Insertion: INSERT/F-ELEMENT*

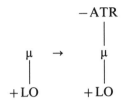

b. *Yoruba [−ATR] Spread: INSERT/PATH*

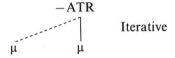

The effect of Yoruba [−ATR] Spread on representations like those in (4) is straightforward. In *ọkọ̀* 'vehicle' (4a), addition of a path between [−ATR] and the relevant Target, μ_1, produces a well-formed output and the rule applies.

(4) *Yoruba [−ATR] Spread*

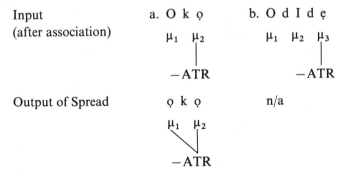

In contrast, with *odidẹ* 'Grey Parrot' (4b) insertion of a path between [−ATR] and μ_2 is ill formed as a result of the RTR/HI Condition that holds of Yoruba; insertion of a path between [−ATR] and μ_1 is ill formed because of Locality: in this form, the rule cannot apply without violating either grounded conditions or Precedence.

The effects of Yoruba [−ATR] Insertion, an INSERT/F-ELEMENT rule, are shown in (5).

(5) *Yoruba [−ATR] Insertion*

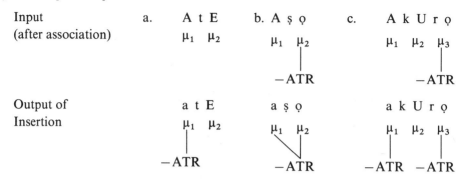

In *ate* 'hat' (5a), insertion of [−ATR] on a [+low] vowel is straightforward: a new token of [−ATR] is introduced in a path with the Target. The cases shown in (5b,c) require more comment. Consider *aṣọ* 'cloth' (5b) first. Here, the input already contains a token of the Argument. To introduce a *new* token of the Argument in a path with the Target would create an OCP violation: the identical elements on the [ATR] tier would be associated to adjacent anchors (see section 1.5.1). As a consequence, the value of [−ATR] that is inserted by the rule is automatically merged with the pre-existing specification in conformity with the OCP. In this way, the rule introduces a token of the Argument in a path with the relevant Target and all representations are well formed.[3] The third case, *àkùrò* 'type of farmland' (5c), has a token of the Argument in the input representation, which associates to the rightmost vowel. As already shown with *odídẹ* 'Grey Parrot' (4b), [−ATR] Spread does not apply "across" a high vowel. However, in (5c), the initial vowel, μ_1, is an eligible target for [−ATR] Insertion. Were the effect of [−ATR] Insertion to be simply the insertion of an association line, as it is in (5b), the result would be an ill-formed structure, one that infringes upon Locality by creating a Precedence violation. Thus, in this case, application of [−ATR] Insertion adds a token of the Argument in a path with the relevant Target. Neither the OCP nor Locality is violated.

Of interest and importance here is that an INSERT/F-ELEMENT rule may introduce a relation between an F-element and a Target, either by insertion of the F-element (and path) as in (5a,c) or by the insertion of an F-element that automatically merges with a value already present, effectively causing the insertion of a path as in (5b). In contrast, an INSERT/PATH rule does no more than insert a path: if the input contains no tokens of the Argument, the INSERT/PATH rule cannot apply.

In this chapter, we explore the parametric model with a primary focus on the variation occurring in the class of INSERT rules, particularly the class of INSERT/PATH rules. We show that variation in the surface effects of rules of this class results from the combination of settings for two other parameters, Direction and Iteration, as well as conditions on Argument and/or Target. We turn now to the final two parameters.

4.2.3 Direction: Left to Right or Right to Left

Historically, the parameters of directionality and of iterativity are closely connected, proposed together as an alternative to the simultaneous mode of rule application advocated in *SPE* (see Johnson 1972, Howard 1972, Anderson 1974, Kenstowicz and Kisseberth 1977). We adopt both notions here, addressing the issue of directionality first.

We begin by noting that directionality is well established in prosodic theory, both in theories of stress (see Hayes 1981, Prince 1983, Halle and Vergnaud 1987a) and in theories of syllabification (see Itô 1986, 1989). Although it was considered at one point that directionality might be a property only of metrical rules (Halle and Vergnaud 1981), there is ample evidence from autosegmental processes in favor of such a parameter.

Yoruba [−ATR] Spread (section 4.2.2) and Wolof [−ATR] Spread (section 3.2.4.1) both involve directional asymmetries, with vowels predictably appearing as [−ATR] either to the left (Yoruba) or to the right (Wolof) of low vowels that are [−ATR]. Importantly, the asymmetry in Yoruba is the mirror image of the comparable asymmetry in Wolof. In Yoruba, a low vowel may be *followed* by any mid vowel, regardless of its value for [ATR], but only [−ATR] mid vowels may immediately *precede* low vowels.[4]

(6) *Yoruba asymmetries*

    a. Vowels following low vowels: [+ATR] and [−ATR]

        ate   [ate]   'hat'
        aṣọ   [ašɔ]   'cloth'

    b. Vowels preceding low vowels: [−ATR] (*[+ATR])

        ẹpà   [ɛkpà]   'groundnut'
        ọjà   [ɔjà]   'market'

Conversely, in Wolof, long low vowels may be *preceded* by vowels with either [ATR] specification but all *following* nonhigh vowels are [−ATR].

(7) *Wolof asymmetries*

    a. Preceding [+ATR] vowel, following [−ATR] vowel

        yóbbuwaale   [yobbuwaalɛ]   'to carry away also'
        génnaale   [gennaalɛ]   'to go out also'

b. Preceding $[-\mathrm{ATR}]$ vowel, following $[-\mathrm{ATR}]$ vowel

| woowaale | [wɔɔwaalɛ] | 'to call also' |
| jamaale | [jamaalɛ] | 'to pierce also' |

Such asymmetries indicate that $[-\mathrm{ATR}]$ Spread differs in the two languages: in Yoruba, its effect is to the left of the Argument, and in Wolof, to the right. Such pairs of rules suggest a parameter of *Direction*; we give this parameter two values, *LEFT TO RIGHT* (Wolof) and *RIGHT TO LEFT* (Yoruba).

(8) *Parameter*: Direction
    Values: LEFT TO RIGHT or RIGHT TO LEFT

We define Direction as identifying whether the effect of the rule is found to the RIGHT/LEFT of relevant edges. Edges are defined both by the phonological ends of a form (the boundaries of the appropriate phonological constituent) and by linked tokens of the Argument. It is important to distinguish between linked and free F-elements.

In the case of an Argument that is free, edges are defined (i) by morphosyntactic boundaries (or the phonological constituents derived therefrom (see Selkirk 1984, Nespor and Vogel 1982, 1986, Hayes 1989, Inkelas 1989, etc.), and (ii) by linked F-elements on the same tier as the Argument. For example, edges for A in (9) are the left-hand boundary and the pair formed by B/W; edges for C are B/W on the left and D/Z on the right.

(9)
$$
\begin{bmatrix}
A & B & C & D \\
 & | & & | \\
U & V & W & X & Y & Z
\end{bmatrix}
$$

In the case of an Argument that is linked, the edges are determined by the Argument's own linkings. In (9), for example, in a case where B is the Argument, B/W would constitute a right edge for a rule whose direction is right to left, and a left edge for a rule whose direction is left to right.[5]

4.2.4 Iteration: Iterative or Noniterative

Spreading rules contrast as to whether they affect multiple targets or only a single target: we take this to be the difference between *iterative* and *noniterative* application (see Johnson 1972, Howard 1972, Anderson 1974, Jensen and Stong-Jensen 1976, Kenstowicz and Kisseberth 1977, Kiparsky 1985, Hewitt and Prince 1989, etc.). By way of introduction, we present a relevant minimal pair, the contrast in tone spreading between Kinande and Tonga, Bantu languages spoken in Eastern Zaire and Zambia, respectively.

We examine Kinande first, relying on Mutaka 1990.

4.2.4.1 Noniterative H-Tone Spreading in Kinande In Kinande, a H-tone spreads from right to left, spreading only to one target. Additional moras are unaffected.

Consider the following examples involving simple infinitive forms. Prefixes such as the preprefix and infinitive marker *e-ri-* and the prefix *na-* 'just' are underlyingly toneless, as can be seen from the fact that they surface as L when in combination with a toneless verb root.[6]

(10) *Toneless prefixes*

    a. e-ri-hum-a . . .   'to hit'

    b. e-ri-na-hum-a . . .   'to just hit'

In contrast, the same morphemes surface with a H-tone when immediately preceding a H-toned verb root.

(11) *H-tone on prefixes*

    a. e-rí-tum-a . . .   'to send'
       e-ri-ná-tum-a . . .   'to just send'
    b. e-rí-korogot-a . . .   'to scrape'
       e-ri-ná-korogot-a . . . 'to just scrape'
    c. e-rí-bangalal-a . . .   'to be overactive'
       e-ri-ná-bangalal-a . . . 'to just be overactive'

Mutaka (1990) argues extensively in favor of a two-part analysis whereby the root H-tone first spreads noniteratively from right to left, and then delinks from the rightmost vowel. This analysis is illustrated in (12).[7]

(12) *Derivations showing H-spreading and H-delinking*

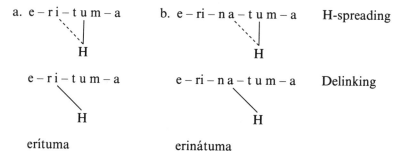

For present purposes, the crucial aspect of this derivation is the fact that spreading affects only a vowel that is adjacent to the H-toned vowel of the verb root: the forms are not **erítuma* and **erinátuma*. The failure of such vowels to undergo tonal spreading cannot be attributed to some intrinsic property of the vowel since the same vowel will undergo or fail to undergo spreading depending on its proximity to the H-tone trigger.

4.2.4.2 Iterative H-Tone Spreading in Tonga We now turn to Tonga (Meeussen 1963, Carter 1971, 1972, Goldsmith 1982, 1984a, Pulleyblank 1986a).

To account for the distribution of H-tone in Tonga, Pulleyblank (1986a) argues for rules of spreading and delinking that are both very similar to those just seen for Kinande. A lexical H-tone spreads leftward *to an unbounded set of targets*, subsequently delinking from the rightmost vowel.

(13) *H-spreading and H-delinking in Tonga*

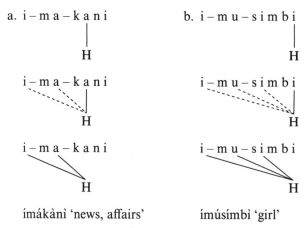

        ímákànì 'news, affairs'   ímúsímbì 'girl'

Crucial to an account of the distribution of H-tone in Tonga is the observation that H-tone spreading affects all vowels to the left of the Argument. This is comparable to the spreading of [−ATR] in both Yoruba and Wolof, where unbounded spans of vowels may similarly undergo rule application.

4.2.4.3 Iteration In all but one respect, the effects of the Kinande and Tonga spreading rules are virtually identical. The sole difference is in whether spreading affects a single vowel or the entire string of available vowels. Without some means of formally expressing precisely this difference in rules, the disparate effects of H-spread in these two languages would be anomalous. We use the parameter of *Iteration* to indicate this difference.

(14) *Parameter*: Iteration
      Values: ITERATIVE or NONITERATIVE

A NONITERATIVE rule identifies an Argument and locates exactly one potential Target for that Argument. If the Argument so identified meets all the conditions for rule application, then the rule applies once and stops; if not all conditions are met, then the rule does not apply at all. In the case of an ITERATIVE rule, the rule successively identifies Arguments until an edge is reached, whether or not application is possible on each iteration. In section 4.4, we present a variety of examples further illustrating Iteration effects.

We have now introduced the four primary parameters, Function, Type, Direction, and Iteration. Before commencing further exploration, we comment briefly about conditions on Argument and Target and on how to formalize rules.

4.2.5   Argument and Target Requirements

Since a rule defines a well-formed relation between a particular F-element (the Argument) and a class of anchors (the Target), any conditions holding generally of those F-element–anchor pairs in a language will necessarily hold of the Argument-Target pairing identified in a rule. However, a rule may impose further requirements on the Argument and/or the Target.

We focus on two types of such requirements, those on content and those on structure. With respect to feature content, grounded conditions may limit the Argument or the Target to a grounded subset of the class of anchors for the Argument in question. Menomini (section 4.7.3) provides an example: although low vowels exhibit an [ATR] contrast, both the Argument and the Target of [+ATR] Spread are restricted by ATR/LO; low vowels are neither sources nor targets *for this rule*. Numerous examples of this basic type are seen throughout this book. We refer to such requirements as *A(rgument)-Conditions* and *T(arget)-Conditions* and place them in the "Other requirements" space in formal rule statements (see (18)).

In terms of structure, the range of autosegmental possibilities for representations, as already discussed, is that there may or may not be a path between an F-element and an anchor (see section 4.6.3). If there is no such path, both F-element and anchor are *free*; if there is such a path, the two are *linked*. While it would be quite conceivable that languages impose one of these structural possibilities on either the Argument or the Target, we propose here that only the former, *free*, is available as a formal requirement. That is, rules may require that an Argument or a Target be free, or rules may impose no structural requirement, thereby allowing both free and linked F-elements to satisfy the latter type's structural description. We suggest, moreover, that Arguments and Targets differ with respect to the unmarked or marked status of these options. For Targets, we suggest that the unmarked situation is for a rule to apply only to a Target that is free with respect to the Argument F-element (see Kiparsky 1985). For example, a rule of association or spreading will more commonly be feature-filling than feature-changing. For Arguments, on the other hand, we suggest that the least marked rule takes as an Argument an appropriate F-element, whether free or linked. Of direct relevance to early proposals concerning the properties of association (see Goldsmith 1976, Clements and Ford 1979), this predicts that a language with linking and spreading (e.g., Tiv High Link/Spread in chapter 2) is to be preferred to a language that allows linking alone (e.g., Wolof [−ATR] Association in chapter 3). We abbreviate these requirements as *A(rgument)-Structure* and *T(arget)-Structure.*[8]

It is also possible for rules to impose certain restricted types of contextual requirements. We do not discuss such contextual requirements systematically in this work (although for some discussion, see section 4.7.2.2).

The requirements introduced briefly in this section are of a rather different status than the four parameters Function, Type, Direction, and Iteration. Whereas values for each of Function, Type, Direction, and Iteration partition rule effects into two mutually exclusive classes, the imposition of requirements on either Argument or Target does not. The free option for structure selects a subset of the F-elements or anchors selected when no conditions are imposed on structure; similarly, a grounded condition such as ATR/HI selects a subset of the F-elements or anchors identified when no such condition is imposed generally in the language.

4.2.6   Rule Formalization

A potentially important issue remains to be addressed: how to represent specific rules.

To emphasize the parametric limitations on interrule variation, we choose a chart representation for the formal representation of rules. Specific instantiations of rules are illustrated below with the Tonga and Kinande H-tone spread rules discussed above. These rules are given a graphic representation in (15),[9] and parametric formulations in (16) and (17).

(15) a. *Tonga H-Tone Spread*

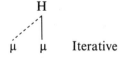

μ   μ   Iterative

b. *Kinande H-Tone Spread*

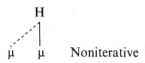

μ   μ   Noniterative

Under the parameter-value pairing approach, these two rules would be formulated as in (16) and (17). The Function and Type values together show that these rules IN-SERT PATHs; in each case, the path is added between a H-TONE (the Argument) and FREE tone-bearers to its left (RIGHT TO LEFT). The two rules differ in whether the Target may be any number of anchors to the left (ITERATIVE in Tonga) or whether only a single Target is considered (NONITERATIVE in Kinande).

For purposes of expository reference only, the first line in each figure gives the name of the rule. On the second line, the nondefault substance of each rule is listed (see below for more on defaults). These statements constitute the actual learned content of a rule, since by hypothesis, all other settings are supplied by the theory of parametric rules itself. To illustrate, in the case of Tonga (the rule parametrically formulated in (16)), the nondefault settings are H-TONE, RIGHT TO LEFT. These two factors are sufficient to parametrically define the rule given graphically in (15). In addition to these nondefault properties, we give the complete parametric formulation of each rule to make all rule properties explicit. As can be seen in (16) and throughout this chapter, rule charts first identify the Argument affected by the rule, then give values for the four binary parameters, and finally give structural and other requirements, if any, on the Argument or the Target of the rule.[10]

(16) *Tonga H-Tone Spread*

   Nondefault rule settings: **H-TONE; RIGHT TO LEFT**

Argument:	H-TONE	Default	Nondefault
Parameters	Function	INSERT	
	Type	PATH	
	Direction		RIGHT TO LEFT
	Iteration	ITERATIVE	
Structure requirements	A-Structure	NONE	
	T-Structure	FREE	
Other requirements	A-Conditions		
	T-Conditions		

(17) *Kinande H-Tone Spread*

Nondefault rule settings: **H-TONE; RIGHT TO LEFT; NONITERATIVE**

Argument:	H-TONE	Default	Nondefault
Parameters	Function	INSERT	
	Type	PATH	
	Direction		RIGHT TO LEFT
	Iteration		NONITERATIVE
Structure requirements	A-Structure	NONE	
	T-Structure	FREE	
Other requirements	A-Conditions		
	T-Conditions		

One property characterized in the chart remains to be addressed, the two columns headed by *default* and *nondefault*. We assume that each parameter has a preferred (or default) value. For example, we assume that INSERT and PATH are the default values for the Function and Type parameters, respectively. We take PATH as the default over F-ELEMENT because path manipulation does not affect the content of a representation. Rather, it simply changes structural relations: path manipulations alter relations between elements that are present, while F-element manipulations alter the set of elements that are present. We take INSERT to be the default over DE-LETE: adding relations and elements is consistent with Prosodic Licensing (Itô 1986) and with Recoverability, while removing something during a derivation increases the challenge of figuring out the form of the input representation, and so reduces Recoverability. Defaults for A-Structure (NONE) and for T-Structure (FREE) are discussed in section 4.2.5.

The above exhausts the binary parameters of rules. By contrast, grounded conditions (which may be imposed on rules as A-Conditions and T-Conditions) do not present a binary choice: the domain over which a grounded condition holds and the relative strength of the grounded condition(s) contribute to an evaluation of the degree of markedness of a particular condition. Thus, we do not include "default/nondefault" categories for these requirements.

The approach sketched here, in which each parameter has a default value, makes predictions about rule typologies, language change, and language acquisition, and contributes to the systematic evaluation of different grammars. We do not explore these predictions in this book. An alternative approach, which would not make such predictions, would be to simply list the parameters paired with the relevant value for the rule. Since incorporating default and nondefault options makes interesting predictions, we prefer it as a model.

The rule charts identify the Argument, each parameter, and each type of requirement; additionally, the default and nondefault values are distinguished. The general chart format is depicted in (18); values for each binary parameter are provided in the appropriate columns.[11]

(18) *Rule format*

Argument:	(some F-element)	Default	Nondefault
Parameters	Function	INSERT	DELETE
	Type	PATH	F-ELEMENT
	Direction	LEFT TO RIGHT	RIGHT TO LEFT
	Iteration	ITERATIVE	NONITERATIVE
Structure requirements	A-Structure	NONE	FREE
	T-Structure	FREE	NONE
Other requirements	A-Conditions	(grounded conditions/context)	
	T-Conditions	(grounded conditions/context)	

As a final point, since we treat rules as componential, it is appropriate to represent them as such, hence the parametric approach and chart representation. Importantly, however, the means of characterizing rules, whether graphically, parametrically, or by some other means, is important to the extent that it clarifies the nature of the rules themselves. The chart representation has this effect. The parametric chart representation for the most part translates rather readily into a graphic notation; of importance is the fact that the converse is not true. There are numerous imaginable graphic rules that cannot receive a parametric formulation, showing that the parametric model is more restrictive than the graphic model in that it allows fewer well-formed rules.

There are also a few cases of parametric rules that cannot readily be represented in graphic form. Consider, for example, the effect of Yoruba [−ATR] Insertion, discussed in section 4.2.2. The effect of this rule varies in a way that is not easy to represent graphically since the differences depend on whether or not the input string already contains a token of the Argument. This mismatch supports our decision to represent rules simply by listing their parametric values. To represent the Yoruba rule graphically requires either a complex formalization, or the abandonment of any rigorous interpretation of what it means to satisfy the structural description and change of a rule.

4.2.7 Summary

Our intent in this chapter is to explore a range of effects that should, we argue, be attributed to rules. The above discussion has introduced the robust effects of the values for each of the four basic parameters that we propose. Of interest now is to explore a number of the perhaps surprising effects of the interactions of various settings for these parameters, in particular, the different surface effects that result from varying the settings for Direction and Iteration as well as the effects of different requirements on Argument and/or Target. In doing so, we demonstrate how a very wide variety of surface patterns can be derived from this small set of binary parameters, Function, Type, Direction, and Iteration.

4.3 Direction

The first parameters that we explore in depth are those restricting the window in which the rule applies, Direction and Iteration; of these, we focus first on Direction.

The need for directionality in formal linguistic theory is well established: various modules of the grammar require both left-to-right and right-to-left directions for the explanation of particular phenomena. Syntactic theory, for example, makes use of directionality in assigning case and thematic roles (see Travis 1984). With respect to phonology, standard theories of stress and syllabification argue that prosodic constituents are constructed directionally, a domain being scanned either from left to right or from right to left (see, for example, Hayes 1981, Itô 1986, Halle and Vergnaud 1987a). With regard to F-element alternations, Howard (1972) offers detailed motivation for directionality from a strictly linear point of view; many of his arguments translate readily into nonlinear representations.

The contrast between Wolof and Yoruba [−ATR] Spread discussed in section 4.2.3 argues that both LEFT TO RIGHT and RIGHT TO LEFT are necessary values for the Direction parameter. This same contrast is seen in Wolof and Yoruba [−ATR] Association: in Wolof, association takes place from the left edge, while in Yoruba, it takes place from the right edge.

Although the general need for left-to-right and right-to-left directionality is reasonably uncontroversial, the fact that we do not posit a *bidirectional* parameter setting deserves some comment. In early autosegmental work, bidirectionality was taken as a defining trait of autosegmentalism. For example, Halle and Vergnaud (1981) proposed metrical analyses of directional harmony systems, but autosegmental analyses specifically of bidirectional patterns. In such work, autosegmental bidirectionality followed automatically from the autosegmental well-formedness condition proposed by Goldsmith (1976). When evidence was presented, however, that autosegments should not spread automatically (Pulleyblank 1985, 1986a), bidirectional spreading ceased to be an automatic consequence of the appropriate set of autosegmental representations. The issue then became the following: in addition to left-to-right and right-to-left cases of spreading, and the like, is it necessary to postulate bidirectional rule application?

Logically, of course, the answer appears to be negative. Basic bidirectionality can be derived by the conjunction of left-to-right and right-to-left application. At issue, therefore, is whether there is any empirical evidence for assuming that apparent bidirectionality is the result of a single rule, instead of the result of a conjunction of unidirectional rules. We argue against true bidirectionality and in favor of unidirectional rules.

First, we demonstrate that there are cases where a single unidirectional rule can create a "bidirectional" effect on the surface. Second, we show that there are cases of apparent bidirectionality where two rules must be posited because of differences in the way the left-to-right and right-to-left rules operate. If rules must be posited that apply in different directions *but also differ in minimal additional ways*, then it is clearly predicted that rules applying in different directions could also cooccur *without differing in any ways other than directionality*. That is, cases of *derived* bidirectionality are predicted to occur.

We conclude that since the multiplication of parameter settings is not desirable, and since two unidirectional values derive the effects of bidirectionality, the Direction parameter is strictly binary: LEFT TO RIGHT and RIGHT TO LEFT.

4.3.1 Bidirectionality through a Unidirectional Rule in Margi

Some cases of apparent bidirectional spreading can be derived by a single unidirectional rule. Hoshi (1989), for example, argues that the bidirectional effect in Nez Perce (Aoki 1962, 1966) can be derived from a unidirectional rule provided that association of the harmonic feature ([ATR]) takes place after all affixes have been added. The delayed association ensures that the harmonic feature is at a periphery; thus, harmony itself applies in a single direction, rather than bidirectionally.[12]

(19) a. *Representation after all affixation*

$$
\left[\ldots\mu\ldots \left[\left[\left[\ldots\mu\ldots\mu\ldots \right] \begin{array}{c} \ldots\mu\ldots \\ -\mathrm{ATR} \end{array} \right] \ldots\mu\ldots \right] \right]
$$

b. *Representation after left-to-right association*

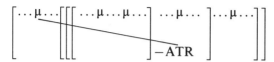

c. *Representation after rightward spread*

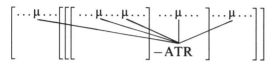

In a language like Nez Perce, the motivation for either a formally bidirectional or a formally unidirectional spreading rule would appear to be more conceptual than empirical. In other cases, however, there is empirical motivation for the unidirectional analysis.

Consider the spreading of tone in Margi, a Chadic language of Nigeria (Hoffmann 1963, Williams 1976, Pulleyblank 1986a, Tranel 1990). Stems in Margi can be demonstrated to belong to one of four classes: (i) L, (ii) H, (iii) LH, or (iv) toneless.[13] From surface tonal patterns, bidirectionality of tone spreading appears to be required because of the interaction of the four tone classes with suffixal tone possibilities. As illustration, consider the interaction of H-tone and toneless stems in combination with both toneless and H-tone suffixes.

When a H-tone stem is followed by a toneless suffix, the suffix surfaces as H (20a); when following a L-tone stem, the suffix surfaces as L (20b).

(20) a. *H-tone stem and toneless suffix*

tsá + ri   →   tsárí   'to knock at'
tá + nya   →   tányá   'to use all in cooking'

      b. *L-tone stem and toneless suffix*

nə̀ + ri   →   nə̀rì   'to tell a person'
fàfə̀ + na   →   fàfə̀nà   'to wipe off'

When a toneless stem precedes a H-tone suffix, the stem surfaces as H (21a); before a L-tone suffix, a toneless stem surfaces as L (21b).[14]

(21) a. *Toneless stem and H-tone suffix*

məl + ía   →   mə́lía   'to make (ready)'
ŋal + bá   →   ŋálbá   'to bite a hole'

b. *Toneless stem and L-tone suffix*

hər + ɗà   →   hə̀rɗà   'bring me'

skə + ɗà   →   skə̀ɗà   'wait for me'

While such facts might seem to suggest the necessity for a rule of bidirectional tone spreading, an alternative is possible, a unidirectional analysis along the lines of the schematic derivation in (19). Margi differs from the schematic picture (19) in one important respect—tone association is cyclic. As we demonstrate below, the cyclic property provides an argument in favor of the formally unidirectional analysis of superficial bidirectionality, an argument that derives from an account of the following generalization concerning derivational affixes. Derivational affixes in Margi fall into two tonal classes, high and nonhigh. High affixes are systematically H-toned on the surface, and condition the appearance of a H-tone on adjacent toneless vowels. Nonhigh affixes, on the other hand, exhibit asymmetrical behavior, depending on whether they are prefixed or suffixed. In the suffixed cases, as already seen in (20), the tone of the nonhigh suffix is determined by the stem. In prefixes, however, nonhigh affixes are systematically L. We propose that this asymmetry is to be accounted for in terms of unidirectional tone spreading, a proposal that is incompatible with a bidirectional account of Margi.

First, (22) shows derivations of *tányá* (20a) and *ŋálbá* (21a), illustrating how a bidirectional appearance can be derived by unidirectional spreading.

(22) *Margi cyclic tone rule derivations*

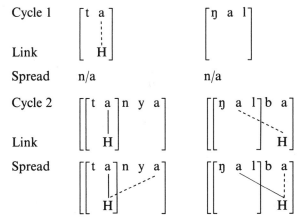

Pulleyblank (1986a:89–91) argues that such a unidirectional account straightforwardly explains certain distributional facts about the tone of Margi affixes. The pattern of interest is the following. As stated already, two tonal classes of derivational suffixes are attested, those that are toneless and those that introduce a H-tone. Unlike what we find with the four tonal possibilities for stems, this two-way distinction essentially exhausts the range of tonal possibilities for derivational suffixes.[15] Similarly, with prefixes, two different tonal classes must be identified.[16] While there is a class of H-tone prefixes that corresponds to the H-tone suffixes of examples like those of (21), there is no class of prefixes that exhibits the type of alternating pattern exhibited by Margi toneless suffixes (see (20)). Instead, the second tonal possibility for prefixes is membership in a class that consistently surfaces with a L-tone.

(23) a. *H-tone prefix*

           ská + wì   'lest (I) run-EXCLUSIVE II'
           ská + sá   'lest (I) go astray-EXCLUSIVE II'

    b. *L-tone prefix*

           gà + wì   'ran-NARRATIVE'
           gà + sá   'erred-NARRATIVE'

As argued in Pulleyblank 1986a, it is possible to provide a uniform analysis of both prefixes and suffixes as involving a H-tone versus toneless contrast if association in Margi takes place in a cyclic, directional (left-to-right) fashion. To posit bidirectional spreading would predict incorrect forms such as *gá+sá for 'erred-NARRATIVE', as shown by comparing the two derivations in (24).

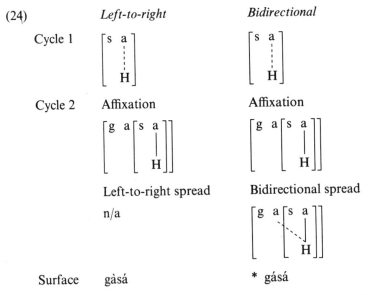

(24)   *Left-to-right*   *Bidirectional*

Where linking and spreading take place from left to right, association to the stem is effected on a cycle prior to the addition of a prefix. Since spreading takes place only from left to right, the prefix is unaffected and surfaces without a H-tone. By contrast, if spreading were to be bidirectional, then tone from the stem would be expected to spread to the prefix, deriving an incorrect form, *gásá, with a H-tone prefix. Note that it is not the case that prefixes and stems belong to different domains of some kind. For example, the negative tense marker [kálá] 'without' causes regular left-to-right spreading of its H-tone onto a following toneless stem. Consider the behavior of a toned stem, whether L-toned, H-toned, or LH-toned ((25a–c), respectively). In all cases, the stem tones are unaffected by the prefix whose tone is consistently H.

(25) a. L stem   ndàlà   kálá ndàlà   'ooze'

     b. H stem   tsá   kálá tsá   'kill'

     c. LH stem   shìlí   kálá shìlí   'come'

     d. Toneless stem   ɓàl   kálá ɓál   'break'

When this prefix is attached to a toneless stem, however, both prefix and stem surface on a H-tone (25d). Compare the simple infinitive form for 'break' [ɓàl], which surfaces with a default L-tone, with the form derived by prefixation: [kálá ɓál].

To summarize, two properties of tone in Margi must be accounted for. First, the tonal interdependence of stems with suffixes superficially suggests bidirectionality: tonal values of a stem affect a toneless suffix, tonal values of a suffix affect a toneless stem. Within a theory positing strictly unidirectional rules of spreading, such surface "bidirectionality" in Margi is the result of having free underlying tonal features, in conjunction with rules of association and spreading that take place in the same direction, left to right in this case. The second property to be accounted for is the asymmetry in the tonal realizations of nonhigh prefixes. By assuming cyclic tonal association and a left-to-right direction for tone spreading, toneless prefixes are predicted to surface systematically on a L-tone. Suffixes and prefixes are analyzed in a unified fashion underlyingly, lexically represented as either H-tone or toneless depending on the morpheme, with toneless prefixes receiving their surface tone invariably by default, while toneless suffixes receive a default tone only if there is no stem tone to their left.

In contrast, an analysis involving formal bidirectionality cannot explain the suffix/prefix asymmetry. To distinguish between the behavior of prefixes and suffixes, all nonhigh *prefixes* must be stipulated to be underlyingly L-tone, while all nonhigh *suffixes* must be stipulated to be underlyingly toneless. Such an approach offers no explanation of the ad hoc underlying difference that must be posited for the two affix types.[17]

We express the two tonal effects, association and spreading, in a single rule. There are no A-Structure requirements ("NONE"), indicating that either of the formal states of association—free or linked—satisfies this rule. Thus, the rule causes both association (of free tones) and spreading (of linked tones).

(26) *Margi Tone Association and Spread*

Nondefault rule settings: TONAL NODE

Argument: TONAL NODE		Default	Nondefault
Parameters	Function	INSERT	
	Type	PATH	
	Direction	LEFT TO RIGHT	
	Iteration	ITERATIVE	
Structure requirements	A-Structure	NONE	
	T-Structure	FREE	
Other requirements	A-Conditions		
	T-Conditions		

Nez Perce can be analyzed in precisely the same fashion, except that association must be noncyclic in Nez Perce in order to derive the correct surface forms. Okpę and Chukchi, in addition to Nez Perce, exhibit this same type of phenomenon (see sections 2.7.1, 3.3.1.1, 3.3.1.2). Since an analysis of these languages is available in terms of the combination of unidirectional association and spreading, they provide no motivation for an additional *bidirectional* value for Direction.

4.3.2 Bidirectionality from Multiple Spreading Rules in Maasai

In contrast with the type of case just seen, certain languages truly appear to require both left-to-right and right-to-left spreading. Importantly, as we show in this section, evidence in favor of spreading in both directions does not necessarily mean that a *bidirectional* parameter setting must be posited. An alternative is to posit two unidirectional rules instead of one bidirectional one. In this section, we explore a relevant case and argue that apparent bidirectional spreading in Maasai necessarily results from the combination of at least two unidirectional rules.

In Maasai, apparent bidirectional harmony results from a pair of rules applying in opposite directions. The motivation for two separate rules derives from the asymmetrical behavior of low vowel targets with respect to the harmonic F-element [+ATR], behavior that depends on whether the low vowel is to the right or to the left of the Argument in question.[18]

Maasai (Tucker and Mpaayei 1955, Levergood 1984, Cole and Trigo 1988) is often considered to have a nine-vowel system lexically: [i, ɪ, e, ɛ, a, ɔ, o, ʊ, u]. As in Akan, the low vowel [a] seems to have no [+ATR] counterpart. In contrast to such an analysis, we argue that there is a [+ATR] counterpart to the low vowel that occurs only in restricted circumstances. This tenth vowel, which is transcribed as [o], results from a rule of left-to-right [+ATR] spreading, but does not result from a rule of right-to-left [+ATR] spreading.

The basic vowel harmony pattern is analyzed by Levergood (1984) as a [+ATR] dominant bidirectional system. As the examples in (27) show, the [ATR] values of both prefixes and suffixes may depend on the [ATR] value of the stem. The first member of each pair shows a [+ATR] root with a particular set of affixes; those same affixes are seen with a [−ATR] root in the second member of each pair.[19,20]

(27) *Root-controlled harmony*

a.	/kI – ñorr – U/	kiñorru
	1PL-love-EXTRA FUTURE	'we shall love'
	/kI – IdIm – U/	kɪdɪmʊ
	1PL-be able-EXTRA FUTURE	'we shall be able'
b.	/mI – kI – itoki/	mikintoki
	NEG-1PL-do again	'we shall not do again'
	/mI – kI – rAñ/	mɪkɪrañ
	NEG-1PL-sing	'let us not sing'
c.	/ɛ – ŋor – IšO/	ɛŋorišo
	3SG-hunt-INTRANS	's/he spears things'
	/ɛ – IsUj – IšO/	ɛɪsʊjɪšɔ
	3SG-wash-INTRANS	's/he does washing'

In addition to root-controlled harmony, some suffixes are invariably [+ATR]. Such suffixes, when in an appropriate environment, trigger harmony themselves. The first member of each pair in (28) shows a suffix triggering harmony on the preceding root; the second member shows the same root without a [+ATR] suffix, in which case all vowels exhibit the default pattern and surface with a [−ATR] vowel.

(28) *Suffix-induced harmony*

a.	/A – rOk – u/	aroku
	1SG-black-INCEPTIVE	'I become black'
	/A – tV – rOk – A/	atɔrɔka
	1SG-PAST-black-INCEPTIVE	'I became black'
b.	/A – tV – dOl – ie/	atodolie
	1SG-PAST-see-APPLIED	'I saw it with s.t.'
	/A – dOl/	adɔl
	1SG-see	'that I could see'

   c. /IsUj – IšO – re/   isujišore
       wash-INTRANS-APPLIED   'wash with s.t.!'

      /IsUj – IšO/   ɪsujɪšɔ
       wash-INTRANS   'wash!/do the washing!'

The forms in (27) and (28) illustrate the robust harmony pattern in Maasai: [+ATR], from a suffix or from a root, spreads to the entire form. (There are no inherently [+ATR] prefixes.)

Given this much data, Maasai [ATR] harmony could receive an analysis comparable to that sketched in the preceding section for cases like Nez Perce and Margi: late association of the harmonic F-element followed by a unidirectional harmony rule. However, there is one crucial difference between Maasai and the other types of bidirectional cases considered: the variable behavior of the low vowel /a/ in Maasai.

If /a/ occurs in a *prefix*, it blocks harmony from a [+ATR] root. As shown in the second member of each pair in (29), if a prefix containing /a/ intervenes between a [+ATR] root and a nonlow prefix, the /a/ blocks spreading of [+ATR] to the preceding nonlow prefix. The first member of each pair demonstrates that the nonlow prefix vowel can surface as [+ATR] when no low vowel intervenes.

(29) *Opaque /a/ in prefixes*

     a. /kI – dot – Un – ie/   kidotuñe
        1PL-pull-MT-APPLIED   'we shall pull it out with s.t.'

       /kI – tA – dot – Un – ie/ kɪtadotuñe
        1PL-PAST-pull-MT-APPLIED 'we pulled it out with s.t.'

     b. /IE – m – E – niŋ/   lemeniŋ
        MS-NEG-3SG-hear   'who does not hear him/her'

       /IE – m – AA – niŋ/   lɛmaaniŋ
        MS-NEG-1SG-hear   'who does not hear me'

In an entirely parallel fashion, if /a/ occurs in a *root*, it blocks harmony from an invariant [+ATR] suffix to a nonlow affix preceding the root. The second member of each pair in (30) shows that such a prefix does harmonize if the root is nonlow.

(30) *Opaque /a/ in roots*

     a. /I – As – IšO – re/   ɪasišore
        2SG-do-INTRANS-APPLIED   'you work'

       /I – duŋ – IšO – re/   iduŋišore
        2SG-cut-INTRANS-APPLIED 'you cut with s.t.'

b. /kI – ŋAr – ie/   kɪŋarie
  1PL-share-APPLIED   'we share with s.o.'

/kI – duŋ – ie/   kiduɲie
  1PL-cut-APPLIED   'we cut with s.t.'

The nature of this blocking suggests that if Maasai [ATR] harmony were to be a postcyclic, unidirectional rule, then association and spreading would have to take place from right to left, not from left to right.

If harmony in Maasai were the result of a single bidirectional rule, then the behavior of the low vowel /a/ ought to be consistent in stems, prefixes, and suffixes: any occurrence of /a/ should block the propagation of harmony. Contrary to this expectation, if an /a/ occurs in a suffix following a [+ATR] stem, it *undergoes harmony* and raises, surfacing as [o]. The first member of each pair in (31) shows the suffix undergoing harmony and surfacing with an [o]; the second member shows the [a] form of the suffix when following a [−ATR] root. The relevant [a/o] pairs are underlined.[21]

(31) *Harmonic /a/ in suffixes*

    a. /AA – ipot – I – tA – I/   aaipotit<u>o</u>i
       1SG-call-?-CONT-PASS   'I am being called'

      /AA – rIk – I – tA – I/   aarɪkɪt<u>aɪ</u>
       1SG-nauseate-?-CONT-PASS   'I am being nauseated'

    b. /A – tV – pet – A/   atapet<u>o</u>
       1SG-PAST-smear-PAST   ' I smeared it'

      /A – tV – pEt – A/   atɛpɛt<u>a</u>
       1SG-PAST-keep close to-PAST   'I kept close to it'

    c. /A – tV – dot – U – A/   atadotu<u>o</u>
       1SG-PAST-pull-MT-PAST   'I pulled out (s.t.)'

      /A – IŋOr – U – A/   aiŋɔrʊ<u>a</u>
       1SG-look at-MT-PAST   'I came looking for (s.t.)'

Comparison of the forms in (29) and (30) with those in (31) reveals the asymmetrical behavior of /a/: prefix /a/ and root /a/ block the *leftward* spreading of [+ATR] but suffix /a/ undergoes the *rightward* spreading of [+ATR].

Two general approaches to the Maasai pattern can be distinguished. The first is a purely rule-based approach: two rules of [+ATR] harmony are posited, a right-to-left rule constrained by ATR/LO (hence, low vowels are opaque), and an unconstrained left-to-right spreading of [+ATR] (hence, /a/ is harmonic). This is the position that we argue for.

The alternative is a representational account, in essence, the account of Levergood (1984). Harmony is analyzed as the result of a single bidirectional rule, the behavior of low vowels being explained by distinct representations: low vowels in roots and prefixes would be represented differently from low vowels in suffixes. Under the representational account, low vowels in suffixes would be characterized in some way so as to undergo harmony, while those in stems and prefixes would be characterized so as not to undergo it (for instance, via a [−ATR] specification, Levergood's (1984) analysis).[22]

The harmony-inducing suffixes of Maasai provide an interesting way of distinguishing between the rule-based and representational analyses. Recall from (28) that certain suffixes are invariably [+ATR] and induce harmony. Under the rule-based account, leftward spreading from such a [+ATR] suffix is predicted to be blocked by a preceding low-voweled suffix, just as it is by a low-voweled root or prefix. As (32) demonstrates, this is the correct prediction. The first member of each pair shows a suffix with /a/ followed by a [+ATR] suffix: [+ATR] harmony is blocked by /a/ and so does not affect the root. The second member of each pair shows that the very same suffix /a/ does undergo [+ATR] harmony when following a [+ATR] root. The relevant [a/o] pairs are underlined.

(32) *Variable behavior of suffix /a/*

      a. /E – tV – nUk – Ar – ie/   ɛtʊnʊka̱rie
         3SG-PAST-bury-MA-APPLIED   's/he buried it with (s.t.)'

         /E – ibuk – Ar – ie/   eibuko̱rie
         3SG-pour-MA-APPLIED   's/he poured it away with s.t.'

      b. /A – IpUt – AkIn – ie/   aɪpʊta̱kiñe
         1SG-fill-DATIVE-APPLIED   'I fill it for s.o. with s.t.'

         /A – duŋ – AkIn – ie/   aduŋo̱kiñe
         3SG-cut-DATIVE-APPLIED   'I cut for s.o. with s.t.'

      c. /E – IpUt – A – rI – ie/   ɛɪpʊta̱riyie
         3SG-fill-MA-N-APPLIED   'it will get filled up'

         /E – isud – A – rI – ie/   eisudo̱riyie
         3SG-hide-MA-N-APPLIED   's/he will hide him/herself'

The form in (33) is particularly interesting because it shows both effects simultaneously. The [+ATR] of the root *-bol-* cannot spread to the prefix *I-* because of the intervening opaque *-tA-* yet it does spread rightward to both suffixes, changing the low *-A-* to *-o-*.

(33) *Variable behavior of /a/*

    /I – tA – bol – A – kI/   ɪta̱bolo̱ki
    1SG-(PAST)-open-PRES/SUBJ-DAT 'I opened it for s.o.'

These data provide strong support for the conclusion that Maasai [ATR] harmony actually results from two rules, a leftward spreading rule that targets nonlow vowels and a rightward spreading rule that targets all vowels, including low vowels.

Compare this with the representational analysis discussed above. To posit a bidirectional rule relies crucially on distinct representations for the two types of low vowels, those that are opaque and those that are harmonic. The prediction under the bidirectional analysis is that a particular vowel will always be of one class or the other, harmonic or opaque, but not both. As (32) demonstrates, this prediction is false. Rather, two rules are necessary. Once the two rules are present in the language, positing different types of representations not only is redundant, but would then predict four classes of cases, not two (left to right/right to left with or without opacity).

Perhaps the most important point illustrated by these data is that representations alone are insufficient to account for opacity effects: exactly the same vowel is opaque in one instance and an undergoer in another *within a single language*. We return to this point in section 4.7.

The rule of leftward spreading is formalized in (34). This rule spreads [+ATR] from right to left. It fails to assign [+ATR] to low vowels because of the ATR/LO Condition, reflected in the rule under the Target specifications.

(34) *Maasai Leftward [+ATR] Spread*

Nondefault rule settings: +ATR; T-Condition: ATR/LO; RIGHT TO LEFT

Argument:	+ATR	Default	Nondefault
Parameters	Function	INSERT	
	Type	PATH	
	Direction		RIGHT TO LEFT
	Iteration	ITERATIVE	
Structure requirements	A-Structure	NONE	
	T-Structure	FREE	
Other requirements	A-Conditions		
	T-Conditions	ATR/LO	

The effect of the ATR/LO Condition on the harmony rule is that only targets that are [−low] may receive [+ATR] specifications. That is, low vowels block Leftward [+ATR] Spread. (35a) shows the effect of Leftward [+ATR] Spread in (32b), *aɪpʊtakiñe* 'I fill it for s.o. with s.t.': the /a/ of the dative suffix *-AkIn-* blocks spreading of [+ATR] onto the root *-IpUt-* (35a). The rule cannot apply *across* a [+low] vowel because the result would violate the Locality Condition, specifically the Precedence Principle: the [+low] vowel intervenes between the Argument and the Target (35b).

(35) *Opaque /a/*

    a. A – I p U t – A k i n – i e   →   aɪpʊtakiñe

                           +ATR

    b. *A – i p u t – A k i n – i e   →   *aiputakiñe

                           +ATR

Now consider the rule of rightward spreading: it has no Target specifications, and so affects all vowels. No structural conditions are imposed on the Argument; hence, both linked and free tokens of [+ATR] are legitimate Arguments.

(36) *Maasai Rightward [+ATR] Spread*

    Nondefault rule settings: +ATR

Argument:	+ATR	Default	Nondefault
Parameters	Function	INSERT	
	Type	PATH	
	Direction	LEFT TO RIGHT	
	Iteration	ITERATIVE	
Structure requirements	A-Structure	NONE	
	T-Structure	FREE	
Other requirements	A-Conditions		
	T-Conditions		

(37) shows rightward spreading in (31a), *aaipotitoi* 'I am being called'. Rightward [+ATR] Spread targets the /a/ of *-tA-* 'CONTINUOUS', which ultimately surfaces as [o]. Leftward [+ATR] Spread cannot affect the prefix because leftward spreading requires a nonlow Target.

(37) *Harmonic /a/*

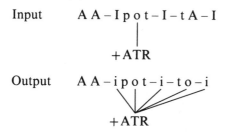

Input   A A – I p o t – I – t A – I
                          |
                      +ATR

Output   A A – i p o t – i – t o – i
                      +ATR

Application of this rule to a low vowel creates a [+ATR, +low] pairing, an antagonistic combination that ultimately results in [o].[23]

Maasai shows that it is necessary to allow languages to have two distinct rules spreading the same argument in opposite directions. Moreover, this conclusion is completely independent of the general issue of whether or not "bidirectional" is permitted as a value for Direction. Since a language like Maasai must posit two rules going in opposite directions, then even a theory incorporating a "bidirectional" parameter must make allowance for such a possibility.

4.3.3 Summary

In this discussion, we have examined two types of putative bidirectional spreading rules and shown that the evidence for bidirectionality is not compelling. In one type of case, spreading processes are better analyzed as involving a single direction (Margi); in a second type of case, the surface effect of "bidirectionality" results from the conjunction of two rules applying in different directions (Maasai).

The requirement that there be directional rules, left-to-right in some instances and right-to-left in others, establishes a typology of rule sets.[24]

(38) *Typology of direction types*

    a. Left to right only

    b. Right to left only

    c. Both left to right and right to left

Individual phonologies may include more than one rule applying in a particular unidirectional fashion. For example, there are two distinct rules of spreading that apply from right to left in Kinande (see section 3.2.3.1), and three distinct rules of spreading in Lango that apply from left to right (see chapter 5). As we have shown, it is also possible to have conjunctions of rules applying in different directions. The example discussed here is Maasai; another interesting language illustrating this property is Lango (chapter 5). This general phenomenon, sets of rules affecting a single Argument and varying by one or more parameter settings, is empirically motivated further in section 4.6; chapter 5 explores the hypothesis that attested rule sets comprise an interesting systematic subset of the imaginable rule sets and suggests a means of evaluating such rule sets.

The basic point concerning bidirectionality to be derived from the typology in (38) is the following. Since rules may or may not impose structural, grounded, and contextual conditions, and since rules may apply in different directions, it follows that a system is possible where two rules with either no conditions or the same conditions, but with differing directions of application, could coexist in a language's phonology (see Gerfen 1991 on Izi). That is, the model clearly predicts the possibility of a language where two rules applying in opposite directions—but otherwise identical—combine to produce the appearance of bidirectional application. Given that such a pattern is predicted to exist by a theory positing the two parameter settings LEFT TO RIGHT and RIGHT TO LEFT, there is absolutely no motivation for introducing a third parameter value such as "bidirectional."

4.4 Iteration

As shown in the discussion of H-Tone Spread in Tonga and Kinande, a minimal pair based on the Iteration parameter, *noniterative* rules are distinguished from *iterative* rules in that noniterative rules look for a single target, rather than applying successively to multiple targets. In this section, we explore effects of this parameter on association processes, INSERT/PATH rules that require a FREE Argument. We demonstrate first that there is an empirical distinction between iterative and noniterative association; this distinction also explains contrasting restrictions on the distribution of harmonic elements. Subsequent sections continue the exploration of iterativity effects, including polarity and exotic association patterns such as "edge-in" and "default docking."

For a given Argument, an ITERATIVE rule successively accesses a sequence of Targets while a NONITERATIVE rule has access to a single Target. In rules where the Argument is necessarily FREE, the effects of these settings are markedly different. Consider the representation (39) in a language where (i) X and Y are members of the same prosodic class of anchors, and (ii) the feature F can link to X but cannot link to Y because of grounded conditions in the language. Since F is free, association between F and any of X_{1-3} is, in principle, well formed.

(39) *Schematic input representation*

$$Y_1 \quad X_1 \quad Y_2 \quad X_2 \quad X_3$$

$$F$$

The potential *targetability* of X_{1-3} can be seen from the fact that were F to be underlyingly linked, as in (40), then such linking could take place to any of X_{1-3}.

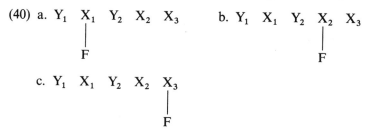

(40) a. Y_1 X_1 Y_2 X_2 X_3 b. Y_1 X_1 Y_2 X_2 X_3

      F   F

  c. Y_1 X_1 Y_2 X_2 X_3

                      F

Consider first the possibility of linking the free value F in (39) in a NONITERATIVE fashion. With a LEFT TO RIGHT rule, the only accessible anchor is Y_1. Association fails because Y is not an eligible F-bearer given applicable grounded conditions. The rest of the targets are inaccessible: F remains free (41a).

Since this is the first case discussed, we review in slightly more detail: an Argument, F in this case, is identified. The Function INSERT and the Type PATH establish that the rule associates F to an eligible anchor. The Direction LEFT TO RIGHT means that targets are examined beginning from a left edge. Since there are no relevant linked features, and since F in particular is not linked, the edge determining directionality is therefore the morphosyntactic boundary preceding Y_1. Finally, since the rule is NONITERATIVE, exactly one potential target is considered, the anchor adjacent to the left edge. As stated above, rule-governed association then fails because the potential anchor does not satisfy substantive conditions on the rule.

Compare this with a comparable rule applying from RIGHT TO LEFT and in a similarly NONITERATIVE fashion. Since in this case, Direction establishes the final boundary as the relevant edge, the first potential anchor encountered by the rule is X_3. Since X_3 is an eligible F-bearer, the rule succeeds, and F is associated (41b).

(41) *Noniterative association*

  a. Y_1 X_1 Y_2 X_2 X_3 Left to right

       F

  b. Y_1 X_1 Y_2 X_2 X_3 Right to left

     F

Now consider the ITERATIVE association of F, first from LEFT TO RIGHT (42a). In this case, the leftmost target is Y_1: the rule fails because Y is not an F-bearer. However, the rule, being ITERATIVE, is not restricted to anchors adjacent to the edge. Continuing from left to right, the next Target is X_1. Since X_1 is an F-bearer, the rule succeeds, giving the representation in (42a). At this point, there are no further FREE tokens of the Argument in the representation, so the rule can no longer apply. That is, once iterative association succeeds, further application is bled by its own success.

This differs from the *SPE*-style view of rule application in which potential targets are identified, and application to all identified targets takes place simultaneously. The two types of algorithms have different empirical results: identifying successive targets means that a rule whose A-Structure is FREE may simply link the Argument; identifying all potential targets and then simultaneously affecting them all has the effect of association *and* spreading. As seen in the discussion of Chaha (section 4.4.1), association rules are not necessarily accompanied by spreading of the Argument. We take this as an argument in favor of the iterative mode of application and against the simultaneous mode (see Howard 1972, Anderson 1974, Jensen and Stong-Jensen 1976, Kenstowicz and Kisseberth 1977, Kiparsky 1985).

The representation in (42b) results if the rule scans from RIGHT TO LEFT: the rightmost target is an F-bearer and so the rule succeeds immediately.

(42) *Iterative association*

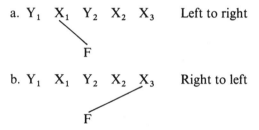

    a. Y_1 X_1 Y_2 X_2 X_3 Left to right

                              F

    b. Y_1 X_1 Y_2 X_2 X_3 Right to left

                  F

The above demonstration illustrates the schematic association patterns expected of ITERATIVE and NONITERATIVE INSERT/PATH rules applying to FREE Arguments. It remains to be shown that rules do, indeed, have these effects. In this section, we examine the behavior of labialization and palatalization morphemes in Chaha and the differing rules associating [−ATR] in Yoruba and Wolof, showing that in each pair, one language has precisely the distribution expected if the association rule is ITERATIVE (42) while the other has the pattern expected of NONITERATIVE association (41).

4.4.1 Chaha Labialization and Palatalization

The palatalization and labialization morphologies of Chaha (a Gurage language of Ethiopian Semitic) are discussed by Johnson (1975), McCarthy (1983), and Hendriks (1989). Labialization surfaces on *the rightmost labializable consonant*, which on independent grounds are the labials and velars. If there are no labializable consonants, labialization does not surface. Palatalization surfaces on *the rightmost consonant if palatalizable*, where palatalizable consonants are independently established to be the coronal and velar obstruents. Palatalization does not surface if the rightmost consonant is not palatalizable.[25] We analyze the association of the two morphological features as formally identical except for the Iteration parameter: labialization associates iteratively and palatalization noniteratively. This distinction, we argue, accounts for the difference between "the rightmost labializable consonant" and "the rightmost consonant if palatalizable."

4.4.1.1 Chaha Labialization   The third person masculine singular object in Chaha is indicated by labialization, illustrated in (43)–(45). In (43), the rightmost consonant of the stem is labializable and so becomes rounded when labialization is introduced as part of the object suffix.[26]

(43) *Rightmost consonant of stem is labializable*

	No object	With object	
a.	dänägä	dänäg^{w}än	'hit'
b.	nädäfä	nädäf^{w}än	'sting'
c.	näkäbä	näkäb^{w}än	'find'

In (44), the final consonant of the stem is a coronal and so is not labializable. However, the penultimate consonant of the stem is labializable, and so is rounded.

(44) *Medial consonant of stem is labializable, final is not*

	No object	With object	
a.	näkäsä	näk^{w}äsän	'bite'
b.	käfätä	käf^{w}ätän	'open'
c.	bäkärä	bäk^{w}ärän	'lack'

Note that the docking of labialization in (43c), *näkäb^{w}än*, and in (44c), *bäk^{w}ärän*, demonstrates that it is the *rightmost* labializable consonant that receives the morphemic feature since in both examples, there is a labializable consonant farther to the left. Comparison of *käf^{w}ätän* with *bäk^{w}ärän* demonstrates that there is no preference for labials over velars as the Target, despite the fact that labial consonants must include a Labial node (i.e., the immediately dominating node for the labializing feature [+round]). (This fact is significant for an evaluation of the "default docking" proposal (Mester and Itô 1989), a proposal that is discussed in section 4.6.1.)[27]

The forms in (45a) provide examples where only the leftmost stem consonant is labializable, and it receives the labializing feature. An example with only coronals is

found in (45b): since there is no labializable consonant, the morphologically introduced rounding does not surface.

(45) a. *Only leftmost consonant of stem is labializable*

No object   With object

qätärä   qʷätärän   'kill'
mäsärä   mʷäsärän   'seem'
mäkʸärä   mʷäkʸärän   'burn'

   b. *No labializable consonants*

No object   With object

sädädä   sädädän   'chase'

In the distribution of labialization (46), association operates from RIGHT TO
LEFT: this accounts for why the *rightmost* labializable consonant of the stem receives
the [+round] feature. In addition, the rule must be ITERATIVE: if it fails to find a
labializable consonant at the right edge, it continues leftward until a labializable
consonant is found. This accounts for the data in (44)–(45).

(46) *Chaha Labialization*

Nondefault rule settings: +ROUND; RIGHT TO LEFT; A-Structure:
                            FREE

Argument:	+ROUND	Default	Nondefault
Parameters	Function	INSERT	
	Type	PATH	
	Direction		RIGHT TO LEFT
	Iteration	ITERATIVE	
Structure requirements	A-Structure		FREE
	T-Structure	FREE	
Other requirements	A-Conditions		
	T-Conditions		

Independent of the rule itself, the anchors of [+round] are labials and velars, that
is, the labializable consonants. The Target itself must be free of [+round], as shown

by (47) (see Hendriks 1989): the morphological labialization skips over the root's labialized /mʷ/ and docks on the unlabialized velar to the left.

(47) *Target is free of [+round]*

Personal (3sg masc)	Impersonal	
tägmʷämʷäṭim	tägʷmʷämʷaṭʸim	'rinse'

4.4.1.2 Chaha Palatalization The palatalization pattern in Chaha is illustrated with the masculine and feminine second person singular imperative in (48)–(49). The forms in (48a,b) show that a final consonant is palatalized in the appropriate morphological class if it is a palatalizable consonant, a coronal in (48a) and a velar in (48b).

(48) *Imperative—rightmost consonant of stem is palatalizable*

	Masculine	Feminine	
a.	gʸäkʸət	gʸäkʸətʸ	'accompany'
	nəməd	nəmədʸ	'love'
	nəkəs	nəkəsʸ	'bite'
b.	wəṭäq	wəṭäqʸ	'fall'
	fəräx	fəräxʸ	'be patient'

The forms in (49) show that if the rightmost consonant is not palatalizable, no palatalization surfaces, even when there is a coronal or velar farther to the left. (Recall that only coronal and velar *obstruents* are palatalizable.)

(49) *Imperative—rightmost consonant of stem is not palatalizable*

Stem-final consonant = coronal sonorant

Personal	Impersonal	
bänär	bʷänär	'demolish'
qäṭär	qʷäṭär	'kill'
sʸägär	sʸägwär	'change'

It is crucial that palatalization limit its focus to the rightmost consonant: if this peripheral consonant is not palatalizable, the rule does not apply. In precisely this point, Chaha Palatalization (50) differs formally from Chaha Labialization (46), whose domain extends to the left edge of the form. This is exactly the difference provided by the two settings for the Iteration parameter. While Chaha Labialization is ITERATIVE, Chaha Palatalization must be NONITERATIVE.[28]

(50) *Chaha Palatalization*

    Nondefault rule settings: −BACK; RIGHT TO LEFT; NONITERATIVE;
                                 A-Structure: FREE

Argument:	−BACK	Default	Nondefault
Parameters	Function	INSERT	
	Type	PATH	
	Direction		RIGHT TO LEFT
	Iteration		NONITERATIVE
Structure requirements	A-Structure		FREE
	T-Structure	FREE	
Other requirements	A-Conditions		
	T-Conditions		

4.4.2 Association of Free [−ATR] in Yoruba and Wolof

As shown above, rules associating FREE F-elements may be either ITERATIVE or NONITERATIVE. In this section, we explore the effect of such rules in harmony systems. As shown with Chaha, the difference between an ITERATIVE and a NON-ITERATIVE rule associating a FREE Argument is seen when the peripheral target is an ungrounded anchor. With an ITERATIVE rule, even if the peripheral anchor is rejected, nonperipheral anchors are considered (in a progressive directional manner) until a grounded anchor is found or the end of the domain is reached. Such a harmonic pattern can be observed with the association of [−ATR] in Yoruba.

4.4.2.1 Iterative Association in Yoruba

As argued in section 2.3.1, Yoruba vowel harmony involves a floating [−ATR] that associates and then spreads. Both association and spreading take place from right to left, subject to the grounded condition RTR/HI: [−ATR] associates only to nonhigh vowels. The crucial forms for a demonstration of iterativity are those in which a mid vowel is followed by one or more high vowels: [−ATR] mid vowels are possible in this environment. Compare (51a), where a morpheme-level [−ATR] specification (if any), links to the rightmost vowel, with (51b,c) where a morpheme-level [−ATR] skips over one or two peripheral high vowels (data taken from (100) in chapter 3). Such data show that floating [−ATR] specifications link up in an iterative fashion.

(51) *Symmetry with peripheral (sequences of) high vowels*

    a. ilẹ̀   'land'   ilé   'house'

       itọ́   'saliva'   ìgò   'bottle'

    b. ẹ̀bi   'guilt'   ebi   'hunger'

       ọ̀kín   'egret'   orí   'head'

    c. ẹ̀bùrú   'shortcut'

       ẹgúsí   'a food made from seeds of melon'

A final high vowel is rejected as a Target because of RTR/HI. As the forms in (51b,c) demonstrate, the rule still may apply, accessing nonhigh vowels to the left of one or more high vowels occurring at the right edge. This shows that the rule associating the free [−ATR], formalized in (52), must be ITERATIVE in Yoruba.[29,30]

(52) *Yoruba [−ATR] Association*

    Nondefault rule settings: −ATR; RIGHT TO LEFT; A-Structure: FREE

Argument:	−ATR	Default	Nondefault
Parameters	Function	INSERT	
	Type	PATH	
	Direction		RIGHT TO LEFT
	Iteration	ITERATIVE	
Structure requirements	A-Structure		FREE
	T-Structure	FREE	
Other requirements	A-Conditions		
	T-Conditions		

4.4.2.2 Noniterative Association in Wolof Contrasting with the ITERATIVE association pattern exemplified by Yoruba, the theory also predicts the possibility of a harmony system in which the harmonic F-element is associated *noniteratively*. The distinguishing property of such a case is that the free harmonic F-element is completely unable to associate in forms where the peripheral target is an ungrounded anchor. Such cases typically surface with no manifestation of the harmonic F-element. Wolof exemplifies such a case, as does Khalkha Mongolian (see section 3.4.2).

    Recall from section 3.2.4.1 that Wolof [−ATR] harmony involves a floating F-element that associates and spreads from left to right, subject to RTR/HI. Crucially for the point at hand, roots with initial high vowels *never* induce [−ATR] harmony; relevant forms are repeated from (92) in chapter 3.

(53) *Initial high vowels*

gis-é	[gise]	'to see in'	*[gisɛ], *[gɪsɛ], etc.
suul-é	[suule]	'to bury with'	*[suulɛ], *[sʊʊlɛ], etc.
nir-óó	[niroo]	'to look alike'	*[nirɔɔ], *[nɪrɔɔ], etc.
xul-óó	[xuloo]	'to quarrel'	*[xulɔɔ], *[xʊlɔɔ], etc.
jiw-ëndóó	[jiwəndoo]	'to plant together'	*[jiwandɔɔ], *[jɪwandɔɔ], etc.
wut-ëndóó	[wutəndoo]	'to look for together'	*[wutandɔɔ], *[wʊtandɔɔ], etc.

The analysis we propose for Wolof is that association of the free [−ATR] is NON-ITERATIVE, as formalized in (54).

(54) *Wolof [−ATR] Association*

Nondefault rule settings: −ATR; NONITERATIVE; A-Structure: FREE

Argument:	−ATR	Default	Nondefault
Parameters	Function	INSERT	
	Type	PATH	
	Direction	LEFT TO RIGHT	
	Iteration		NONITERATIVE
Structure requirements	A-Structure		FREE
	T-Structure	FREE	
Other requirements	A-Conditions		
	T-Conditions		

There are two possible underlying representations for morphemes in Wolof, one with and one without a free [−ATR]. In the latter case, the rule of harmony is irrelevant because there is no [−ATR]. It is the other logical possibility, in which [−ATR] is present in the underlying representation, that is of interest.[31] Where the morpheme containing a free [−ATR] has an initial nonhigh vowel, left-to-right association assigns the [−ATR] value to the initial vowel, and harmonic spreading derives the completed surface [ATR] pattern. But the situation is rather different given a form with an initial high vowel.

(55) g I s – E

  – ATR

The association rule in (54) cannot associate a free [– ATR] in a form like /gIs-E/: the high vowel is not a grounded [– ATR] anchor because of RTR/HI. (Recall that since no high vowels are ever [– ATR], RTR/HI holds generally in Wolof. Thus, it need not be specified in the rule itself.) Since the rule is NONITERATIVE, the noninitial mid vowel is never even considered as a Target. As a result, the floating F-element cannot associate.

In a situation where an autosegment cannot associate, only exceptional circumstances would lead a speaker to posit such a specification at all. For example, were such a language prefixing, the free F-element could associate to the leftmost prefix vowel if one were available; the exceptional verb stems in Maasai (section 2.7.3) are plausibly best analyzed along these lines. Patterns such as those seen in class 5 of Kinande (section 3.2.3.1) as well as the exceptional morphemes in Yoruba and Chukchi (section 2.7) also bear directly on this point, showing that morphemes may indeed have specifications that can only surface if there is concatenation with an appropriate morpheme. We note in concluding this aspect of the discussion that Representational Simplicity interacts with this NONITERATIVE pattern to derive the result that no floating [– ATR] would be posited in a form like *gise*: the less complex underlying representation, which is preferred given Representational Simplicity, is the one without the floating [– ATR].

The contrast between association in languages like Wolof and Yoruba and in the two Chaha rules is predicted to occur given the model presented here. Association rules are necessary; association rules can be either ITERATIVE or NONITERATIVE. As demonstrated here, such association rules may combine with spreading rules, producing strikingly different effects, depending on the setting of the Iteration parameter.

4.5   Rule Functions versus Rule Effects

So far in this chapter, we have focused on laying out an approach to rules that revolves around the four binary parameters, Function, Type, Direction, and Iteration. It might seem that such a list is significantly too restrictive. Numerous rule types have been proposed in the autosegmental literature that do not have obvious interpretations given only the parameters formulated here. We address this issue here, considering whether rule effects like polarity, metathesis, dissimilation, fusion, consonant harmony, and so on, are derived from the interaction of the parameters just listed, or whether they need to be included as primitive functions. In this section, we focus on polarity and dissimilation, although additional rule effects are discussed later in other sections.

4.5.1   Polarity Effects: Yoruba Object Clitics

As background to our analysis of polarity, consider first a rule such as Yoruba [−ATR] Insertion, discussed in section 4.2.2. This rule is a case of ITERATIVE F-element insertion: the rule applies to targets throughout the relevant domain. Recall in particular that because of the OCP there is automatic merger of F-elements inserted by such a rule. The assignment of [−ATR] to low vowels in a form like *ata* 'pepper' results in a single, multiply linked [−ATR] value, not in two separate values, a result that would be at odds with the OCP.

Such a pattern contrasts with that derived by the NONITERATIVE application of F-element insertion. In establishing precisely what is expected of a NONITERATIVE insertion rule, it is important to recall the effect of noniterativity. If a rule spreads some Argument, the first requirement is to locate an Argument. Having located an Argument, the establishment of edges as determined by Direction makes reference to the Argument, and Iteration determines whether Targets are examined in a bounded or unbounded fashion. A crucial difference with a rule that inserts an F-element is that the Argument is not *located*, it is *inserted*. Since edges of the domain of rule application cannot be determined with reference to an Argument not yet inserted, the result is that edges for INSERT/F-ELEMENT are simply the morphosyntactic edges of the morphological form being considered for rule application. The distinction between ITERATIVE and NONITERATIVE application is therefore clear: ITERATIVE rules apply to all eligible anchors within the domain; NONITERATIVE rules apply strictly to the first or last anchor of the domain, if eligible, exactly as just shown with the NONITERATIVE INSERT/PATH rule of Chaha.

Consider schematic inputs such as those in (56).

(56)   *Inputs to INSERT/F-ELEMENT*

   a.

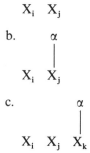

   $$X_i \quad X_j$$

   b. α
       $|$
       $X_i \quad X_j$

   c. α
            $|$
       $X_i \quad X_j \quad X_k$

Assume that $X_{i,j,k}$ are all eligible bearers of α. If a rule of INSERT/F-ELEMENT were to assign α in an ITERATIVE fashion, then *all* anchors in (56) would receive α. Moreover, because of the OCP, all cases would involve a single, multiply linked token of α in their output, as in (57).

(57) *Outputs of INSERT/F-ELEMENT/LEFT TO RIGHT/ITERATIVE*

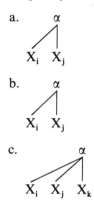

But consider the result if the rule of INSERT/F-ELEMENT applies in a NON-ITERATIVE fashion. This means that the only anchors that could be affected by the rule of insertion would be the rightmost and the leftmost instances of X. Application of insertion to the forms in (56) would derive the forms in (58), where LEFT TO RIGHT directionality is assumed.

(58) *Outputs of INSERT/F-ELEMENT/LEFT TO RIGHT/NONITERATIVE*

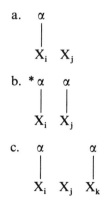

Two points are crucial. First, the automatic merger seen in cases of ITERATIVE insertion is unavailable here because a NONITERATIVE rule restricts its window to exactly one potential anchor. Any anchor that is nonperipheral is unavailable for rule manipulation by a NONITERATIVE process. Second, the application of insertion to (56b) to derive (58b) is ill formed because it violates the OCP: the identical F-elements α are associated to adjacent prosodic anchors. Given the Well-formedness Principle, this means that rule application would be blocked in such a case. In contrast, application to (56c) results in the well-formed configuration (58c): the anchors of the identical F-elements are not adjacent.

The clear prediction of this approach to NONITERATIVE rules of F-element insertion is that such rules will apply only in the event that an anchor adjacent to the edge of the domain is *not* associated to a token of the Argument: the effect is polarity, and the behavior of H-tone in Yoruba object clitics provides just such an example.[32]

As shown in section 1.5.1.2, the distribution of tone on object clitics in Yoruba is variable yet entirely predictable. The monosyllabic clitics show polarity. As seen in (59a,b), repeated from chapter 1, the clitic vowel is H-toned when attached to a L- or M-toned verb. By contrast, the clitic is M-toned when attached to a H-toned verb (59c).

(59) *Polarity with object clitics in Yoruba*

a. rà	á	'buy it'		lù	mí	'beat me'
b. jẹ	ẹ́	'eat it'		pa	mí	'kill me'
c. rí	i, *rí í	'see it'		rí	mi, *rí mí	'see me'

In chapter 1, we argued for an analysis of the distribution of H-tone on the object clitics involving a rule inserting a H-tone on the clitic vowel. Here, we propose a formal statement of the required rule. The forms in (59a,b) uncontroversially involve insertion of a H-tone from right to left. The rule is formalized in (60).

(60) *Yoruba H-Tone Insertion*

Nondefault rule settings: **H-TONE; F-ELEMENT; RIGHT TO LEFT; NONITERATIVE; T-Condition: OBJECT CLITIC**

Argument:	H-TONE	Default	Nondefault
Parameters	Function	INSERT	
	Type		F-ELEMENT
	Direction		RIGHT TO LEFT
	Iteration		NONITERATIVE
Structure requirements	A-Structure	NONE	
	T-Structure	FREE	
Other requirements	A-Conditions		
	T-Conditions	OBJECT CLITIC	

The crucial setting with respect to deriving the polarity effect (i.e., deriving the contrast between (59a,b) and (59c)) is the NONITERATIVE value. The effect of applying (60) is the addition of a H-tone on the final vowel of the object clitic. Because the parameter setting is NONITERATIVE, no Targets other than the word-final vowel are accessed. With a H-toned verb, insertion of a H-tone on the clitic is therefore blocked because such insertion would create an ill-formed representation—one containing an OCP violation. This is shown in (61).

(61)

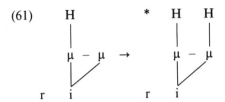

Since the H-tone cannot be inserted, the object clitic remains toneless, ultimately surfacing with a M-tone.

As the Yoruba polarity effect shows, the general point is that the NONITERA-TIVE insertion of an Argument α is blocked whenever the site of insertion is adjacent to a token of α. Moreover, the clear prediction is that polarity effects are to be found strictly at the edges of domains (see Pulleyblank 1986a).

4.5.2 Dissimilation Effects: Japanese Rendaku

We have just argued that "polarity" effects are derivative, not primitive. A further question might be whether all polarity effects must therefore be analyzed in terms of the NONITERATIVE parameter value. We suggest in this section that this is not the case. We discuss here the Rendaku pattern (usually called "dissimilation" in Japanese), in conjunction with Lyman's Law, whereby obstruents surface as voiced when preceding only sonorants and voiceless obstruents, but as voiceless when preceding any voiced obstruent—a polarity effect involving voicing (Itô and Mester 1986, Ishihara 1989, 1991).

In the case of Rendaku, we propose that the polarity/dissimilation effect is the result of an INSERT/F-ELEMENT rule whose A-Structure is FREE. Such a rule has no effect at all on either of the input configurations of (56) owing to the OCP, as shown in (62a,b).

(62) *Outputs of INSERT/F-ELEMENT/A-Structure FREE*

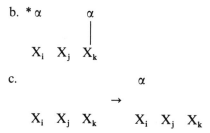

b. * α   α
                |
   X$_i$ X$_j$ X$_k$

c.   α

              →
   X$_i$ X$_j$ X$_k$ X$_i$ X$_j$ X$_k$

The general Rendaku phenomenon is that [+voiced] is inserted at the left edge of the second member of certain compounds in Japanese. The inserted voicing specification associates at the left edge of the compound's second member. (The data given here are taken from Ishihara 1991.)

(63) *Rendaku*

    a. hooki   hosi   →   hookibosi
       'broom'   'star'   'comet'

       sentaku   hasami   →   sentakubasami
       'laundry'   'scissors'   'clothespin'

    b. inu   tosi   →   inudosi
       'dog'   'year'   'year of the dog'

       kome   tawara   →   komedawara
       'rice'   'straw bag'   'straw rice-bag'

    c. kuro   satoo   →   kurozatoo
       'black'   'sugar'   'brown sugar'

       baka   samurai   →   bakazamurai
       'fool'   'samurai'   'fool samurai'

    d. naga   kutu   →   nagagutu
       'long'   'shoes'   'boots'

       hara   kuro   →   haraguro
       'stomach'   'black'   'wicked'

Of interest for our discussion here is the Lyman's Law effect: a voiced obstruent in the second member of the compound prevents Rendaku from taking place.

(64) *Lyman's Law*

    a. kami   hubuki   →   kamihubuki, *kamibubuki
       'paper'   'snowstorm'   'confetti'

    b. naga   tabi   →   nagatabi, *nagadabi
       'long'   'trip'   'long trip'

c. baka	sawagi	→	bakasawagi, *bakazawagi
'fool'	'uproar'		'spree'
d. onna	kotoba	→	onnakotoba, *onnagotoba
'woman'	'language'		'feminine wording'

If the rule of Rendaku is formulated so as to insert a FREE [+ voiced] specification, the Lyman's Law effect follows automatically from the OCP.[33]

To illustrate this, we give the two partial derivations in (65), the first showing a case where the second member of the compound does not contain a voiced obstruent, the second showing a case where the second member of the compound contains a voiced obstruent.[34]

(65) a. [[H A R A] [K U R O]]   compounding

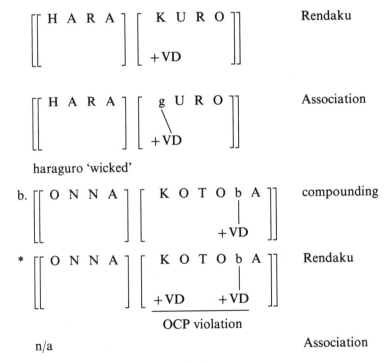

haraguro 'wicked'

onnakotoba 'feminine wording'

Given the Well-formedness Principle, which prohibits ill-formed representations at all stages of a derivation, if there is a voiced obstruent in the second member of the compound, the OCP prevents application of Rendaku—otherwise, an ill-formed representation results, an OCP violation on the voicing tier as shown in the second step of (65b). Rule application is therefore blocked, and a voiceless obstruent results. It is crucial for this analysis that the inserted voicing specification be FREE. If it were linked, then the intervening vowels (and consonants) would prevent adjacency of the identical [voiced] tokens and the form would be well formed, comparable to the acceptable insertion of an independent token of $[-\text{ATR}]$ on the low vowel /a/ in a case like Yoruba àkùrò 'type of farmland' (see section 4.2.2 as well as general discussion of adjacency and twin peaks configurations in section 1.5.1). Because of this contrast, we conclude that FREE is necessary as the Argument designation of Rendaku (66), crucially responsible for the derived polarity effect.

(66) *Rendaku*

Nondefault rule settings: + VOICED; F-ELEMENT; A-Structure: FREE;
T-Condition: MORPHOLOGICAL

Argument:	+VOICED	Default	Nondefault
Parameters	Function	INSERT	
	Type		F-ELEMENT
	Direction	LEFT TO RIGHT	
	Iteration	ITERATIVE	
Structure requirements	A-Structure		FREE
	T-Structure	FREE	
Other requirements	A-Conditions		
	T-Conditions	MORPHOLOGICAL	

Certain points should be mentioned with regard to this rule. First, we do not address the morphological issue of how precisely to characterize the second member of a compound as the domain of Rendaku, nor do we attempt to characterize the precise set of compounds that undergo the rule. See Itô and Mester 1986, Nishikawa 1987, Ishihara 1989, 1991, for discussion of this issue. Second, we note that the value for Iteration is completely irrelevant for this rule. At most one token of [+ voiced] can be inserted since any further tokens would create an OCP violation.

To conclude, we have shown that the polarity effect attested in Rendaku can be directly traced to positing the A-Structure condition FREE. Given this condition, the effect is derived by the interaction of Rendaku with lexical specifications of voicing.

4.5.3 Summary

The above discussion explores implications of Iteration and A-Structure settings for the analysis of "polarity" and "dissimilation"—but there are significant general implications that go far beyond such specific phenomena.

First, a conclusion implicit in the above analysis is that there is no formal rule type corresponding to notions of "polarity" or "dissimilation." Such phenomena are simply expected by-products of particular arrays of parameter settings in conjunction with particular arrays of input representations (see Chomsky 1981, Jaeggli 1986, Baker, Johnson, and Roberts 1989 for this type of modularity argument in syntax with regard to the phenomenon of "passive"). It is not always clear whether a particular set of alternations even constitutes polarity, for example, or whether it constitutes dissimilation. Ainu "dissimilation" (section 2.3.3) would have formal rule settings comparable to those of Yoruba "polarity" (in spite of the difference in labels) while it would have different settings than Japanese "dissimilation" (in spite of similar labels). According to the hypothesis here, although such terminology may serve a descriptive purpose, it has no linguistic importance. As seen by comparing Yoruba object clitics with Japanese Rendaku, there is no claim that every surface phenomenon that could be assigned the label "polarity" will necessarily have precisely the parameter settings in (60). The crucial aspect of the Japanese case is that the inserted Argument be FREE, while for a case like Yoruba object clitics, the crucial aspect is the NONITERATIVE setting, both *marked* parameter values.

This brings us to the second major point deriving from the above discussion. There are many phonological phenomena to be observed in natural languages. The existence of some superficial phenomenon, however, is not justification for postulating a formal rule parameter. Just as we have argued that there are no formal rule functions "polarize" and "dissimilate," so we take seriously the hypothesis that rule functions are limited to exactly two, INSERT/DELETE. The claim, therefore, is that the rule effects posited in the autosegmental literature are derivatives of these two functions. (We return to this point in section 4.7, in discussing the variety of configurations responsible for surface neutrality effects.)

Several classes of rules can be established, at least for the purposes of exposition. Rules of "insertion," "deletion," "association," "delinking/dissociation," and "spreading" are straightforwardly derived by the interaction of the Function parameter, INSERT/DELETE, with the Type parameter PATH/F-ELEMENT. Rules of "dissimilation" and "polarity" derive from the interaction of F-ELEMENT rules with the NONITERATIVE parameter setting (Yoruba, Ainu), or with an A-Structure condition FREE (Japanese). Work such as that of Saito (1981), McCarthy (1986a), Besnier (1987), and Archangeli and Pulleyblank (1987) on "metathesis" in a language like Rotuman (Churchward 1940) suggests that the apparent reordering of elements results not from a rule function "metathesize" but from a simple conjunction of delinking and reassociation. Similarly, "fusion/merger" (e.g., Clements 1985a, Piggott 1989, Avery and Rice 1989) can be analyzed as the result of feature spreading of a type made routine since the postulation of hierarchical feature structure (Clements 1985a, Sagey 1986). Processes of "fission" (e.g., McCarthy 1984a) and "copy" (Steriade 1986a) can be similarly decomposed into components (for some discussion of fission and copy, see section 4.7).

The central conclusion of this discussion emphasizes the modular nature of the parametric approach to rules. Complex superficial rule effects derive from the interaction of a small set of simple formal parameters.

4.6 Association by Rule

Up to this point, we have focused on relations involving Direction and Iteration. In this section, we explore an array of interactive effects derived by varying the settings for these parameters and others. The central concern is a characterization of various patterns of association. In sections 4.3 and 4.4, we have proposed that at least some instances of association are effected by rule, not by convention. In this section, we explore this implication further by considering a variety of types of association, for example, "default docking" (Mester and Itô 1989) and "edge-in" association (Yip 1988a). We reach two conclusions. First, the parameters of Direction and Iteration are sufficient for producing the attested association effects; no additional parameters or parametric values are required. Second, association of free F-elements is effected by rule; an association convention is neither motivated nor necessary.

There are two parts to the argument against an association convention (or conventions). First, we demonstrate that the association of free F-elements is subject to the same range of parametric variation as is the spreading of linked F-elements. Different parametric value combinations achieve the effect of the various association conventions proposed in the literature. Given this result, to include a convention to achieve some particular association effect is unrevealing. Second, if there is an association convention, some means of subverting its effect is necessary in order to allow the range of association effects attested in natural language. In short, an association convention is not necessary; the parameters alone are sufficient to account for the attested phenomena and to predict the type of variation actually attested in association patterns.

The first pattern we turn to is the "default docking" of palatalization in Japanese mimetics.

4.6.1 "Default Docking" in Japanese Mimetics

The "default docking" phenomenon involves the directional association of an F-element to a restricted class of anchors. If a form contains no such anchors, association links the autosegment to the last grounded F-bearer encountered in the string (whether "last" means rightmost or leftmost depends on the value for Direction). We show here that the effect of default docking is a predicted result of rule interaction and can therefore be expressed without adding any new parameters.

Mester and Itô (1989) argue for the mechanism of "default docking," based on a detailed examination of Japanese mimetics. We rely heavily on their analysis here.[35]

Japanese mimetics may come in two versions, one without any palatalized consonants and one with palatalization. Examples are given in (67).[36]

(67) *Japanese mimetics*

a.	poko-poko	'up and down movement'
	p^{y}oko-p^{y}oko	'jumping around imprudently'
b.	kasa-kasa	'rustling sound, dryness'
	kas^{y}a-kas^{y}a	'noisy rustling sound of dry objects'
c.	pota-pota	'dripping in large quantities'
	pot^{y}a-pot^{y}a	'dripping in large quantities'
d.	zabu-zabu	'splashing'
	z^{y}abu-z^{y}abu	'splashing indiscriminately'
e.	noro-noro	'slow movement'
	n^{y}oro-n^{y}oro	'(snake's) slow, wriggly movement'

Mester and Itô (1989) demonstrate that the distribution of palatalization in mimetics is regular. The generalizations fall into two classes, illustrated in (68)–(69) and (71). In one class of cases, it is the initial consonant that is palatalized, as shown in (68). This pattern is straightforwardly accounted for by a rule that associates a floating [−back] specification from LEFT TO RIGHT.[37]

(68) *Generalization: Initiality*

h^{y}oko-h^{y}oko	'lightly, nimbly'	*hok^{y}o-hok^{y}o
g^{y}obo-g^{y}obo	'gurgling'	*gob^{y}o-gob^{y}o
p^{y}oko-p^{y}oko	'jumping up and down'	*pok^{y}o-pok^{y}o

The next set of data shows that the left-to-right rule must be NONITERATIVE. Mester and Itô (1989:283–84) point out that palatal consonants cannot precede the vowel /e/ (except in the swear word *t^{y}e?* and certain recent loans like *t^{y}ekku* 'check' and *s^{y}erii* 'sherry'). This appears to be a general constraint in Japanese, holding of mimetics as a subcase. Interestingly, in mimetics where the leftmost vowel is /e/, palatalization is not possible, even on the second consonant, as seen in (69).

(69) *Generalization: *C^ye*

keba-keba	'gaudy'	*k^yeba-k^yeba	*keb^ya-keb^ya
neba-neba	'sticky'	*n^yeba-n^yeba	*neb^ya-neb^ya
gebo-gebo	'gurgling'	*g^yebo-g^yebo	*geb^yo-geb^yo
teka-teka	'shining'	*t^yeka-t^yeka	*tek^ya-tek^ya

By positing a NONITERATIVE LEFT TO RIGHT rule, we account for the absence of palatalization on the second consonant in the forms in (69): the rule is unable to apply to the initial consonant because of the constraint against C^ye sequences and is unable to apply to the second consonant because to do so would require iteration. It is the nonexistence of the starred forms in (69) that leads Mester and Itô (1989) to propose Default Docking: were the palatalization feature simply subject to a left-to-right association convention where right-to-left docking to a coronal is not possible (see below), forms like *keb^ya-keb^ya would be predicted. This effect is achieved here via a NONITERATIVE rule, a rule type that is necessary independently of the mimetics facts.

The rule that accounts for the distribution illustrated in (68)–(69) is given in (70).[38]

(70) *Japanese Mimetics General Palatalization*

Nondefault rule settings: − BACK; NONITERATIVE; A-Structure: FREE

Argument:	−BACK	Default	Nondefault
Parameters	Function	INSERT	
	Type	PATH	
	Direction	LEFT TO RIGHT	
	Iteration		NONITERATIVE
Structure requirements	A-Structure		FREE
	T-Structure	FREE	
Other requirements	A-Conditions		
	T-Conditions		

In the second class of cases, noninitial coronals receive the palatalization prosody in preference to initial consonants, whether the initial consonant is coronal or not. Since mimetics consist of two identical bimoraic units, this pattern is observed only in forms with a medial consonant. The data in (71a) show that palatalization of a medial coronal is favored over palatalization of the initial consonant. The forms in (71b) show that when both consonants are coronals, it is the rightmost one that is palatalized. Finally, (71c) shows that word-initial coronals can be palatalized, so that the pattern in (71b) must be due to the right-to-left application of the association rule targeting coronals, not to some prohibition in mimetics against word-initial palatalized coronals.[39]

(71) *Generalization: Coronal dextrality and dominance*

    a. metʸa-metʸa   'destroyed'
       kasʸa-kasʸa   'rustling'
       hunʸa-hunʸa   'limp'

    b. dosʸa-dosʸa   'in large amounts'
       nosʸo-nosʸo   'slowly'
       netʸa-netʸa   'sticky'

    c. tʸoko-tʸoko   'childish small steps'
       zʸabu-zʸabu   'dabble in liquid'
       nʸoki-nʸoki   'sticking out one after another'

The pattern can be accounted for by an association rule linking [−back] from the right edge. The necessary rule is given in (72).[40]

(72) *Japanese Mimetics Coronal Palatalization*

    Nondefault rule settings: −BACK; RIGHT TO LEFT; A-Structure: FREE;
                                 T-Condition: FR/COR

Argument:	−BACK	Default	Nondefault
Parameters	Function	INSERT	
	Type	PATH	
	Direction		RIGHT TO LEFT
	Iteration	ITERATIVE	
Structure requirements	A-Structure		FREE
	T-Structure	FREE	
Other requirements	A-Conditions		
	T-Conditions	FR/COR	

The rule as stated affects only FREE [−back] specifications: as a result, once the specification is linked by the first iteration of the rule, further association is impossible: the Argument is no longer free. If the FREE condition on Arguments were not included, one might expect to find combinations of association and spreading of a sort that would derive unattested forms like those in (73).

(73) *Generalization: Monopalatality*

      a. *kʸasʸa-kʸasʸa   cf. (71a)

      b. *dʸosʸa-dʸosʸa   cf. (71b)

To summarize, the above analysis involves two rules, a right-to-left association that can only dock to Coronals, and a left-to-right noniterative association that docks to all palatalizable consonants. Neither rule is unusual. First, Coronal Palatalization is comparable formally to cases like Kinande [+ATR] Association, discussed in section 3.2.3.1: the free F-element associates to a grounded subset of the F-bearers. Moreover the particular subset of F-bearers to which the palatalization feature docks is precisely the same (the coronals) as seen in another palatalization rule, that of Barrow Inupiaq (section 2.2.2.2). Second, Japanese General Palatalization is both formally and substantively comparable to palatalization in Chaha in that it applies to all paths with which [−back] is compatible and in that it is noniterative. Thus, both rule types required for Japanese mimetics occur independently in other languages.

Is it necessary, therefore, to enrich the formal apparatus of autosegmental theory by adding the association mechanism of "default docking"? Quite clearly, the answer is negative. First, as just demonstrated, the default docking effect is not necessary as a primitive operation because it can be derived by independently necessary rule types. It results when (i) one rule imposes conditions on the Target while another rule imposes no such conditions and (ii) the two rules operate in opposite directions. In Japanese, it is the interaction of the more specific ITERATIVE RIGHT TO LEFT rule that targets only coronals with the more general NONITERATIVE LEFT TO RIGHT rule that derives the surface appearance of "default docking."

Second, it should be stressed that default docking could not be considered to be a general algorithm for associating free specifications. The *iterative* nature of the right-to-left aspect of Japanese "default docking" is not always a property of association: for example, Chaha palatal association (section 4.4.1) and Wolof [−ATR] association (section 4.4.2.2) are noniterative. The restriction of anchors to a subset of the potential anchors is not always a property of association: for example, neither Chaha labial association nor Chaha palatal association has this property (section 4.4.1). Finally, docking of autosegments that are left over after a restrictive pass of association (the "default" docking effect) is not found in patterns like the class 5 cases in Kinande (section 3.2.3.1) or in cases like Yawelmani glottal association (section 4.6.5).

4.6.2 Edge-in Association

An alternative to directional association or default docking has been proposed by Yip (1988a), who argues that floating F-elements associate from the edges in. In a melody with multiple F-elements, the first and the final specifications associate peripherally, then the second and the penultimate associate next to those, and so on. The basic structure of Yip's argument may be summarized as follows: if the edge-in effect is not due to a convention, then multiple rules are required; therefore, this effect must be due to convention.

There are three problems with this argument. First, even if an edge-in convention is postulated, multiple rules of types not accounted for by an edge-in algorithm are required in various languages, for example Japanese (mimetics; section 4.6.1), Kinande ([ATR]; (section 3.2.3.1), and Kukuya (tone association; section 4.6.4). Second, as will be demonstrated shortly, the two rules necessary to derive edge-in effects are independently motivated in systems where they do not cooccur. Finally, Yip's examples do not incontrovertibly motivate a type of association that is truly "edge-in"; rather, all Yip's examples are consistent with an analysis comparable to that proposed for Japanese mimetics or for Kukuya tone association: a noniterative rule applies in one direction and an iterative rule applies in the opposite direction. The crucial point is that association in the "noniterative" direction affects a *single* element. This contrasts with the predictions of the edge-in proposal, which states that association proceeds from the edges inward, where one would expect the possibility of *multiple* elements linking inward from both edges.

The reason for the difficulty in demonstrating the need for an edge-in algorithm in this regard is the relatively small number of autosegments that typically need to be associated. Yip's examples involve at most 3 or 4 F-elements/segments usually mapping to at most 3 or 4 positions, thereby giving 1-2*-3 or 1-2-3-4 patterns as the most complicated ones actually attested. Both of these patterns are consistent with the association of a single element, the final element, at the right edge, followed by the association of the remainder in a one-to-one fashion from the left edge in conjunction with left-to-right spreading if free anchors remain. Once a single element is associated at the right edge, nothing further suggests an edge-in pattern.

As a consequence, exactly the mechanism necessary to account for the mimetics pattern—namely, two rules, one of which is noniterative—derives the basic "edge-in" effect. We suggest, therefore, that Yip's evidence does not motivate a particular *convention* of association, but constitutes strong evidence for an approach to association such as that argued for here, where associative processes are expected to exhibit the range of behavior attested by other types of phonological rules. Yip's (1988a) data base includes the initial association of consonants and vowels in certain Semitic languages and Cupeño, and the association of tones in Wuxi Chinese. We look at one of these cases here, Tigrinya, to exemplify the proposed analysis of "edge-in" effects.

Consider the following representative data from Tigrinya:

(74) *Edge-in association in Tigrinya*

Perfect	säbärä	mäskära
Frequentative	säbabärä	mäsäkakära
	'silver'	'plait'

To derive these patterns, the last consonant of a triliteral or quadriliteral root is mapped to the final syllable. Preceding consonants are then mapped from left to right, with all empty consonantal positions filled through association to some element of the melody, even if the mappings are one-to-many.

Under the model presented here, such a pattern is accounted for by the interaction of two rules, a rule of RIGHT TO LEFT NONITERATIVE association affecting FREE Arguments and a rule of LEFT TO RIGHT ITERATIVE association affecting all Arguments, regardless of linking status. The interaction of these rules is illustrated in (75). (We use a syllabic template, roughly following McCarthy and Prince 1986, 1990.)

(75) *Schematic derivation of Tigrinya edge-in effects*

Right-to-left noniterative association

Left-to-right iterative association

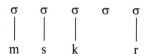

Left-to-right spreading

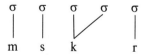

Add vowel melody: mäsäkakära

As noted earlier, a crucial point with regard to such a conjunctive use of association rules is that *both* are independently required in cases where they occur individually. The RIGHT TO LEFT/NONITERATIVE/A-Structure: FREE case involved precisely the settings required for Chaha Palatalization (section 4.4.1). The LEFT TO RIGHT/ITERATIVE settings with no conditions on the Argument are exactly the settings required for Margi Tone Association and Spread (section 4.3.1). Thus, the "edge-in" effect is derivative.

Our analysis of Tigrinya requires that an ITERATIVE rule apply to inputs with multiple F-elements, contrasting with the majority of our examples, which have a single F-element; Kukuya (section 4.6.4) has the same property, although with slightly different structural conditions on the Argument. Before turning to Kukuya, we take a moment to explore the formal effects of Iteration more thoroughly.

4.6.3 Excursus on Iterative Rule Application

In considering iterative and noniterative rules in section 4.4, we briefly addressed the issue of the rule application algorithm characterized by "ITERATIVE," arguing that iteration must be interpreted as identifying Targets successively rather than simultaneously. Association with multiple F-elements, as in the Tigrinya example, motivates the same type of algorithm from a rather different perspective.[41] At issue is the effect of an iterative association rule on an input with multiple F-elements as potential Arguments, and multiple anchors as potential Targets (76a). The desired result, exemplified above in Tigrinya, is that the F-elements X, Y, Z associate in a one-to-one fashion to the anchors (76b).

(76) a. Input   X   Y   Z ...   b. Output   X   Y   Z ...
                                                    | | |

         μ_1 μ_2 μ_3 ... μ_1 μ_2 μ_3 ...

Simultaneous application would first require identifying which F-elements would associate to which anchors—for example, that Z would associate to μ_3. To accomplish this without being able to refer to the association of X and Y would require some kind of counting mechanism to identify Z as the third Argument and μ_3 as the third Target. Yet counting admits unwarranted possibilities into phonological theory (see McCarthy and Prince 1986, Halle and Vergnaud 1987a). By contrast, successive application simply associates pairwise: once the first Argument-Target pair is identified and associated, the next iteration identifies the next pair, and so on. No counting is required. This iterativity effect is implicit in the various association conventions proposed in the literature (see chapter 1 for a brief review); our effort here is to make the successive effect explicit.

How is the appropriate Argument-Target pair identified? The Direction parameter locates the edge at which a rule takes effect; the Locality Condition allows a phonological relation to be established only under conditions of adjacency. Thus, the Arguments and Targets specified in a rule can only be elements that are adjacent to the edge(s) defined by Direction.

Where the input contains only free tokens of the Argument (as in the original input in Tigrinya), morphosyntactic boundaries establish the relevant edges and the appropriate' Argument and Target are those adjacent to the correct boundary. Additionally, where an input contains linked tokens of the Argument, each such token establishes an edge. Consequently, each successful iteration of an association rule creates a new edge; this new edge defines the location of the next Argument-Target pair. The first two iterations relevant for (76a) are given in (77).[42]

(77) a. Input   X   Y   Z ...

                               μ_1 μ_2 μ_3 ...
      b. First iteration   X   Y   Z ...
                               |
                               μ_1 μ_2 μ_3 ...
      c. Second iteration   X   Y   Z ...
                               | |
                               μ_1 μ_2 μ_3 ...

Where the A-Structure condition of a rule is FREE, association proceeds unambiguously as shown in (77): once an F-element is *linked*, it no longer meets the A-Structure requirements of the rule.

Note that separating out each iteration in the application of an iterative rule is for expository purposes only! Such stages are intended to explicitly illustrate the manner in which we assume iterative processes operate. They do *not* represent accessible stages of a derivation—linguistically significant levels include only the input and output representations.

Where there are no structural requirements on the Argument (A-Structure: NONE), the situation is somewhat more interesting than the above cases because the rule can affect both linked and free F-elements. (Margi (section 4.3.1) and Kukuya (section 4.6.4) are two relevant examples.) There are two types of cases to consider: those with only linked F-elements at the relevant stage of derivation, and those with both linked and free F-elements ((78a,b), respectively). For expository purposes only, we systematically assume LEFT TO RIGHT rules in the following discussion. In our first example, the input representation contains only *free* targets; the "second iteration" of the rule is the crucial one for our discussion here.

(78) *A-Structure: No conditions*

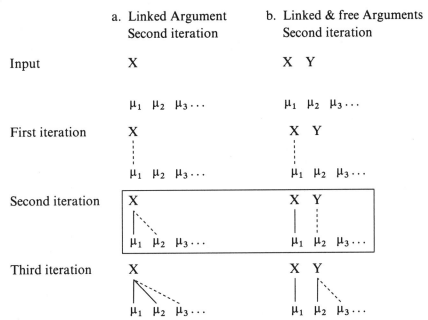

	a. Linked Argument Second iteration	b. Linked & free Arguments Second iteration
Input	X	X Y

In derivations such as these, the first iteration is completely straightforward: the leftmost free Argument links to the leftmost Target. On the second iteration, the situation becomes more informative.

Consider first the case where the input to this iteration contains only a linked F-element, (78a): path insertion results in spread (cf. the several harmony examples presented here). The linked X identifies the edge; since the A-Structure: NONE setting allows both free and linked Arguments, X is a legitimate Argument for the rule in addition to defining an edge. Adjacency is satisfied (nothing intervenes between X and itself), and the rule applies as shown.

Consider now a case where the input to the iteration under consideration contains both linked and free F-elements, (78b). The linked X identifies the relevant edge for both the *linked X* (as with (78a)) and the *free Y* (as with (77)). Why is this ambiguity resolved by linking Y, not X, to μ_2? We propose that resolution is a result of the interaction of standard successive rule iterations with Prosodic Licensing (Itô 1986: F-elements are not realized unless they are associated to prosodic structure) and Recoverability, rather than being defined into the rule theory itself. If the ambiguity is resolved in favor of the free F-element, more F-elements become prosodically licensed; hence, recoverability is improved. By contrast, if the ambiguity is resolved in favor of the linked F-element, the free F-element may never become prosodically licensed, depending on subsequent rule application or lack thereof, and so the F-element left free may never be realized. As a consequence, linked F-elements are affected only once there are no free ones left in an appropriate position.

We now turn to cases in which the domain contains linked targets. The cases of particular interest in this regard are those involving rules with the settings A-Structure: NONE and T-Structure: NONE, that is, cases where both free and linked F-elements constitute eligible Arguments, and both free and linked anchors constitute eligible Targets.

Consider the input configurations in (79a–c). Assuming a left-to-right rule, X/μ_1 defines the edge for association of the free Y in (79a) while the morpheme boundary defines the edge for association of the free Y in (79b) and the free X in (79c). The first case (79a) is comparable to the one just considered: rule application to the free Argument on the first iteration supersedes application to the linked Argument for precisely the reasons given above, Prosodic Licensing and Recoverability.

(79) *A-Structure: No conditions; T-Structure: No conditions*

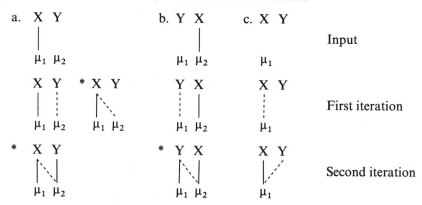

Of interest are the second and third cases, (79b,c). On the first iteration, it is clear both in terms of left-to-right directionality and in terms of its being floating that Y should associate in (79b) and that X should associate in (79c). The case is somewhat ambiguous, however, with regard to potential versus actual application of a second iteration. Should association stop once at the end of the first iteration, or should it continue? Since this case appears to be resolved differently in (79b) and (79c), we address it here.

There are four formal configurations in which rules can apply: (80a) from a FREE Argument to a FREE Target, (80b) from a FREE Argument to a LINKED Target, (80c) from a LINKED Argument to a FREE Target, and (80d) from a LINKED Argument to a LINKED Target.

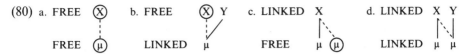

(80) a. FREE Ⓧ   b. FREE   Ⓧ Y   c. LINKED X   d. LINKED X Y

FREE ⓜ   LINKED μ   FREE   μ ⓜ   LINKED μ μ

Consider the applicability of rules with different structural restrictions to configurations of these four kinds. First, rules may impose the restriction FREE on both the Argument and the Target (A-Structure: FREE and T-Structure: FREE). Such rules would apply only in configuration (80a), where both the F-element and the anchor are initially unassociated. Second, rules could relax the FREE restriction on either the Argument or the Target. If it were relaxed on the Argument (A-Structure: NONE and T-Structure: FREE), the resulting rule would apply in configurations (80a,c), that is, any configuration involving an unassociated anchor. If it were relaxed on the Target instead (A-Structure: FREE and T-Structure: NONE), then the rule so defined would apply in cases (80a,b), configurations involving an unassociated F-element regardless of the structural properties of the anchor. Note in this regard that the association of Y in (79c) fits the pattern just described: Y, a free F-element, links to μ_1 even though the mora is already linked. In contrast, (79a,b) do not meet the patterns so far since neither involves either a free F-element or a free anchor.

We are left with the crucial configuration. What class of structural configurations is designated by a rule setting where the FREE restriction is imposed neither on the Argument nor on the Target, that is, the settings A-Structure: NONE and T-Structure: NONE? We propose that such a rule selects the union of results obtained in the two individual patterns where NONE is imposed as a structural condition on either Argument or Target, namely, the configurations in (80a–c), but not that in (80d).

(81) | *A-Structure* | *T-Structure* | *Configurations meeting structural requirements* | |
|---|---|---|---|
| FREE | FREE | FREE-to-FREE | (80a) |
| NONE | FREE | FREE-to-FREE | (80a) |
| | | LINKED-to-FREE | (80c) |
| FREE | NONE | FREE-to-FREE | (80a) |
| | | FREE-to-LINKED | (80b) |
| NONE | NONE | FREE-to-FREE | (80a) |
| | | FREE-to-LINKED | (80b) |
| | | LINKED-to-FREE | (80c) |

The effect of this proposal is that the iterative application of a rule with unrestricted structural requirements (A-Structure: NONE and T-Structure: NONE) will cause any free feature to associate and any free anchor to undergo association or spreading —precisely the sort of pattern about to be argued for in Kukuya.

In concluding this discussion, we note that contour segments are significantly more marked than noncontoured segments, and rules in general can be argued to create contours only when something forces such linking. For instance, a contour will result from a rule with no restrictions on either the A-Structure or the T-Structure, namely, when there is a free Argument but no free anchor, depicted in (82).

(82) *A-Structure: NONE; T-Structure: NONE*

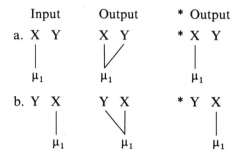

In (82), a contour is derived from the association of an otherwise floating feature because Prosodic Licensing and Recoverability override the undesirability of producing a contour. However, neither principle would require spreading in examples like (79a,b) on the second iteration, since spreading would not improve Recoverability,[43] and both potential Arguments are already prosodically licensed at the end of the first iteration. In contrast, if a rule imposes a Target condition that makes it impossible for the rule to apply without creating a contour (perhaps automatically triggering delinking), then the T-Structure: NONE setting can result in rule application even to a linked anchor. For example, in Yoruba (Pulleyblank 1986a), the tonal node of a L-tone spreads onto a mora bearing a H-tone to create a rising contour.

Association patterns of the types seen in (78) and (79) are illustrated in the Kukuya example in the next section: in forms with insufficient anchors, contours result; in forms with insufficient autosegments, both association and spreading results. These are the association effects of a rule whose A-Structure and T-Structure are without restriction (i.e., NONE).

4.6.4 Tone Association in Kukuya

In the last sections, we argued that the parametric approach to rules derives the "default docking" and "edge-in" effects through the conjunction of two rules, one iterative and one noniterative. This might be interpreted as meaning that the adoption of a theory of parametric rules results in a proliferation of rules. In fact, however, there are numerous cases where the parametric proposal actually results in a reduction of rules. In Margi (section 4.3.1), for example, a single rule derives both the association and spreading of tones. In this section, we consider a somewhat similar case in Kukuya, a Bantu language spoken in the People's Republic of the Congo (Paulian 1974), where *three* processes—association, spreading, and contour formation—can be expressed as a single rule parametrically.

Hyman (1987) demonstrates that Kukuya exhibits a pattern of tonal melodies that is startlingly similar to perhaps the classical case of tonal melodies, that of Mende, a Mande tone language (Leben 1973, 1978, Goldsmith 1976). Like roots in Mende, Kukuya roots select from the five tonal melodies, L, H, LH, HL, LHL,[44] as exemplified in (83).[45]

(83) *Five tonal melodies in Kukuya*

Tone	Monomoraic CV	Bimoraic CVCV
L	bà	bàlà
	'grasshopper killer'	'to build'
H	bá	bágá
	'oil palms'	'show knives'
LH	sǎ	sàmí
	'weaving knot'	'conversation'
HL	kâ	kárà
	'to pick'	'paralytic'
LHL	bvǐ̃	pàlî
	'he falls'	'he goes out'

Following the now-standard argument presented by Goldsmith (1976), we take the restricted number of tonal melodies as evidence that tones are unassociated in underlying representation and that roots are assigned one of the five tonal melodies. Association of the tonal melodies proceeds, for the most part, from left to right (motivated by the location of the falling contour in forms like *pàlî* 'he goes out'). Initially, tones link in a one-to-one fashion, and where there are too many tones, contours are created, (82a). The effect is seen in the monomoraic column for words with more than one tone in their melody; it is also seen in the bimoraic column for the LHL melody. Where there are too few tones, rightward spreading takes place, as seen in the bimoraic columns for L- and H-toned words (see (78a,b)).

The general pattern just described is expressed by a single rule, as shown in (84). Crucial for the pattern of spreading and contour formation, no structural conditions are imposed on either the Argument or the Target. That is, the F-elements satisfying the Argument of a rule may be either linked or free, as may the anchors that constitute Targets. It is noteworthy that these particular rule settings derive the effect of Goldsmith's (1976) well-formedness condition: all tones end up associated to some tone-bearing unit and all tone-bearing units end up associated to some tone.

(84) *Kukuya Tone Association*

Nondefault rule settings: TONAL NODE; T-Structure: NONE

Argument: TONAL NODE		Default	Nondefault
Parameters	Function	INSERT	
	Type	PATH	
	Direction	LEFT TO RIGHT	
	Iteration	ITERATIVE	
Structure requirements	A-Structure	NONE	
	T-Structure		NONE
Other requirements	A-Conditions		
	T-Conditions		

In a significant sense, the proposed analysis of Kukuya constitutes coming around full circle with respect to conjunctions of association, spreading, and contour formation. In the first explicitly autosegmental work, Goldsmith (1976) proposed that autosegments linked, spread, and created contours as the result of a single well-formedness condition. Subsequent work arguing against automatic contour formation (Clements and Ford 1979) and against automatic spreading (Pulleyblank 1986a) had the following implication: since less is accomplished by convention, more rules must be posited. Hence, any theory that assumes only that one-to-one association is accomplished by convention must posit rules, where appropriate, for spreading, and additional rules, where appropriate, for contour formation. The ironic result of proposing that association takes place entirely by parametric rule, never by convention, is that we return to a theory where association, spreading and contour formation can be expressed as a single process.

Before we leave this discussion of Kukuya, it is important to note one complication of the general association pattern that occurs with trimoraic roots.

(85) *Tonal melodies in Kukuya, continued*

	Trimoraic
Tone	CVCVCV
L	bàlàgà
	'to change route'
H	bálágá
	'fence'
LH	mʷàrəgí
	'younger brother'
HL	káràgà
	'to be entangled'
LHL	kàlə́gì
	'he turns around'

The general rule of Kukuya Tone Association accounts for all but one cell in the paradigm in (85). As seen in the form *mʷàrəgí* 'younger brother', LH roots surface with a LLH pattern rather than the LHH pattern predicted by (84).

To derive the attested LLH pattern, an additional rule must be postulated, one that associates the final H of a polytonal melody prior to the application of Kukuya Tone Association.

(86) *Kukuya Final H Association*

> Nondefault rule settings: H-TONE; RIGHT TO LEFT; NONITERATIVE;
> T-Condition: L ____ # #

Argument:	H-TONE	Default	Nondefault
Parameters	Function	INSERT	
	Type	PATH	
	Direction		RIGHT TO LEFT
	Iteration		NONITERATIVE
Structure requirements	A-Structure	NONE	
	T-Structure	FREE	
Other requirements	A-Conditions	L ___ ##	
	T-Conditions		

The effect of Kukuya Final H Association is to link a H-tone to the final root vowel.[46] By ordering this rule prior to Kukuya Tone Association, the full array of attested surface patterns is derived: a monomoraic input is comparable to (82b) and the bi- and trimoraic inputs are comparable to (79d,e).

It should be noted that any approach to Kukuya employing some kind of association convention will run into problems with the forms motivating Kukuya Final H Association. Assuming a convention that links, spreads, and creates contours would require either an analogous rule (an "initial tone association rule"; see Goldsmith 1976, Haraguchi 1977, Clements and Ford 1979, Clements and Goldsmith 1984, etc.) applying prior to the convention, or some kind of patch-up rule applying after conventional association is complete (see Hyman 1987). Even an edge-in algorithm, which might at first glance seem motivated by the LLH pattern, would require patch-up for either LLH or HLL depending on assumptions concerning medial spreading. (Note that it is not simply that H-tones do not spread; consider the simple H pattern.) Kukuya, in this regard, simply cannot be considered to exhibit a *conventional* pattern of association.[47]

Our general conclusion is that Kukuya exhibits a pattern of association that, although very different from the pattern seen in other cases so far, is straightforwardly derived by the parametric model. The general pattern of association collapses three subpatterns, linking, spreading, and contour formation, into a single rule by virtue of the absence of structural conditions on both the Argument and the Target of the rule.

4.6.5 T-Conditions: Yawelmani Glottal Association

We have shown that rules of association may vary in terms of Direction, in terms of Iteration, in terms of the structural conditions on Arguments and Targets, and in the possibility of imposing contextual conditions on Arguments. In this section, we discuss a final point, that conditions can be imposed on the Targets of association processes.

Consider the formal parameter settings crucial for a rule to constitute "association," namely, INSERT/PATH. As has been amply illustrated, these parameter settings derive effects of *association* and/or *spreading*, depending on (i) structural conditions on the Argument and (ii) the nature of the representations that provide input to the relevant rule.

Where the rule involved results in spreading, there are numerous examples where Targets are restricted to some subset of the overall class of appropriate anchors. For example, Tiv, Ngbaka, and Susu (sections 2.2.1 and 2.5) exhibit height-dependent spreading of [+round]; Menomini (section 4.7.3) exhibits a related height dependency on the spreading of [ATR]. Kinande (section 3.2.3.1) has rules like Suffixal

Harmony and Phrasal Harmony, both of which restrict their Targets to high vowels. Lango, a complex case of harmonic spreading discussed in some detail in chapter 5, makes extensive use of Target conditions on the spreading of [ATR].

If association were the result of a convention, then it would be expected to differ from spreading by applying systematically to all eligible anchors for whatever feature is undergoing association. In fact, however, association processes exhibit similar restrictions on their classes of Targets. Restrictions may be prosodic in nature; see, for example, Kenstowicz 1987 on Kizigua, where tones associate to metrically stressed syllables. Alternatively, restrictions may involve the types of F-element cooccurrence restrictions that we have examined here. In Kinande (section 3.2.3.1), despite the fact that the language allows [+ATR] on all vowels, General Association links a floating [+ATR] to [+high] vowels only (ATR/HI), and Special Association imposes the additional restriction that the Target be [−back] (ATR/BK). In Maasai, [+ATR] associates only to nonlow vowels (section 2.7.3), although all vowels, including low vowels, are eligible anchors for [+ATR] (section 4.3.2). In Japanese mimetics (section 4.6.1), the right-to-left association of [−back] is restricted to coronals, although both labials and dorsals can be palatalized.

Given this similarity between conditions on spreading and conditions on association, we conclude that if spreading is effected by rule, then so is association. In addition, given the range of cross-linguistic variation exhibited by spreading (and association) rules, we conclude that if spreading is the result of a convention, then the notion of convention has been robbed of all interesting and testable content.

To round out the evidence in favor of allowing conditions on the Targets of association rules, we provide one further example of restricted association here, that of Glottal Association in Yawelmani Yokuts. This case is interesting because it is not subject to reanalysis in terms of "edge-in association," "default docking," or some other type of "association convention."

In Yawelmani Yokuts (Newman 1944, Archangeli 1983, 1991), a morphologically provided glottalization feature induces glottalization only on sonorants, despite the fact that Yawelmani has a full range of both glottalized sonorants and obstruents. We take the F-element to be [+constricted glottis] ([+CG]). To correctly associate [+CG] requires a Target condition restricting the set of eligible anchors to those that are [+sonorant].

The forms in (87)–(89) show the distribution of glottalization with one of the several suffixes that provide a floating glottal feature. As seen in these lists, the floating F-element does not always have a surface reflex.[48]

If the second consonant of the stem is a sonorant, a glottalized sonorant results (87).

(87) *Glottalization of sonorants*

       Default   Stem   σ–(ʔ)aa
       template   melody

   a. Biconsonantal roots

σ	caw-	caaw'aahin	'shout'
$σ_{μμ}$	c'um-	c'oom'aahin	'devour'
Φ	nin-	neen'aahin	'quieten'

   b. Triconsonantal roots

σ	ʔilk-	ʔel'kaahin	'sing'
$σ_{μμ}$	dull-	dol'laahin	'climb'
Φ	yawl-	yaw'laahin	'follow'

Otherwise, if the stem is biconsonantal, a full-fledged glottal stop surfaces after the stem-final obstruent (88).[49]

(88) *Glottal stop realization*

σ	max-	maxʔaahin	'procure'
$σ_{μμ}$	dos-	dosʔoohin	'report'
Φ	hot'-	hot'ʔoohin	'build a fire'

Otherwise (i.e., when the stem has three consonants but the second consonant is an obstruent), glottalization does not surface at all (89).

(89) *Absence of glottalization*

σ	hogn-	hognaahin	'float'
$σ_{μμ}$	ʔidl-	ʔedlaahin	'hunger'
Φ	ʔagy-	ʔagyaahin	'pull'

We address here the issue of how glottalization, [+CG], docks on a sonorant, as seen in (87).[50] There are two points to consider: (i) that [+sonorant] segments are the sole Targets in this rule and (ii) that Targets in this rule must be postvocalic. We argue that the former is a property of the docking rule itself and the latter is a general property of glottalized sonorants in Yawelmani. We address the latter issue first.

    Whether syllable-initial or syllable-final, glottalized sonorants in this language occur only postvocalically.[51]

(90) "[E]ach of the simple nasals, semivowels, and laterals is balanced with a glottalized consonant which is treated as a distinct phoneme with the following limitation: *it can never appear initially in a word or in a syllable that follows a closed syllable.*" (Newman 1944:15; emphasis added)

Given this distribution, it might at first appear that association "by convention" is the more appropriate account: independently of the association process at issue, the floating glottal F-element would not be able to link to an initial sonorant because initial sonorants simply cannot be glottalized. Hence, if the second consonant is a sonorant, that will be the first eligible anchor for the floating F-element since that consonant is always postvocalic. If the second consonant is not a sonorant, then when the third consonant (if any) is reached, the floating F-element may not link up even if it is sonorant because the third consonant is always postconsonantal (because of the templatic morphology; see Archangeli 1983, 1991).

However, we cannot simply invoke the standard one-to-one, left-to-right association convention because there are two constraints on the association of the glottal feature that are not constraints either on the distribution of glottalization or on the distribution of glottalized sonorants. Consider first the general distribution of glottalization in Yawelmani: *any* consonant except /h/ and fricatives may be glottalized. Moreover, glottalized obstruents, unlike glottalized sonorants, may occur freely in stems. As shown in (91), there are no restrictions on such glottalized obstruents comparable to the postvocalic condition found on glottalized sonorants.[52]

(91) *Yawelmani consonant inventory, with examples of glottalized consonants*

p, b, p'	lap'ʔaʔ	'one who has whipped'
t, d, t'	hiwt'iwlaxoʔ	'becomes very happy'
ṭ, ḍ, ṭ'	ʔoṭ'k'a	'steal!'
k, g, k'	bok'en	'will find'
c, z, c'	pic'pic'xoonit	'is being counted repeatedly'
l, l'	lool'istiisa	'inheritance-o'
m, m'	ʔaluum'wiy-	'to put into the mouth slowly'
n, n'	k'an'aaʔin	'goal touchers-o'
w, w'	t'aw'awseelaw	'goal-L'
y, y'	ʔay'ak'c'i	'one who is throwing a lance-o'

As seen above, glottal association affects only sonorants. Given the range of glottalized consonants in (91), the process associating [+CG] must therefore stipulate that the floating [+CG] may dock to only a subset of the language's [+CG]-bearers, the [+sonorant] class.[53]

The association of [+CG] must also be constrained to apply only within roots since the glottalization does not surface on an otherwise legitimate sonorant in a suffix when there is no eligible sonorant in the stem. This is shown in (92). The stem *waxl-* does not have a sonorant in the relevant position. The suffix *-in* contains a postvocalic sonorant but glottalization does not surface on that segment.

(92) *[+ CG] Association is root-bounded*

> waxlaasin   waxl-(ʔ)aas-in   'one who is always weeping-POSS'
> *waxlaasin'
>
> cf.
> t'ul'as   t'ul-(ʔ)aas   'one who is apt to burn things-SUBJ'

To summarize, Yawelmani Glottal Association (93) formally inserts a path, with a free [+ CG] as the Argument. The rule must state that the Target is [+ sonorant] and that the rule applies only within the root domain. Since we have not explored the "domain of application" issue in this work, we provisionally provide the descriptive statement "root-bounded" as a T-Condition in the rule statement.

(93) *Yawelmani Glottal Association*

> Nondefault rule settings: + CONSTRICTED GLOTTIS; A-Structure:
>   FREE; T-Structure: NONE; T-Conditions:
>   CG/SON, ROOT-BOUNDED

Argument:	+CG	Default	Nondefault
Parameters	Function	INSERT	
	Type	PATH	
	Direction	LEFT TO RIGHT	
	Iteration	ITERATIVE	
Structure requirements	A-Structure		FREE
	T-Structure		NONE
Other requirements	A-Conditions		
	T-Conditions	CG/SON; ROOT-BOUNDED	

In this section, we have shown that it is necessary to constrain association of the glottal feature in Yawelmani by both a domain condition, ROOT-BOUNDED, and by a path condition, that the Target be [+ sonorant]. If association is due to a rule, such constraints deserve no special comment: both domains and targets suffer restrictions in rules. By contrast, if association were the result of a convention, then the existence of these two constraints would be entirely unexplained.

4.6.6   Conclusion

In linear models of phonology such as *SPE*, very few effects could be directly attributed to representations; systematic correspondences between representations had to be assigned to rules. Part of the excitement surrounding early work in nonlinear models derived from the hope that articulated approaches to representations could automatically derive such systematicity, without recourse to language-specific rules. We have argued here that such hopes are at least to a certain extent ill founded. It would appear, perhaps not surprisingly, that systematicity between representations involves an intricate interaction between correct representations, on the one hand, and a restrictive set of formal rule parameters, on the other.

The topic of this section has been a case study of one of the foremost candidates for "automaticity": the "convention" responsible for the association of free specifications. We conclude that there is nothing at all "conventional" about the way in which autosegments associate.[54] Association takes place from left to right, from right to left; it takes place iteratively and noniteratively; it takes place by itself or in conjunction with spreading and/or contour formation; it applies to all anchors for the relevant feature, or to subsets of the relevant anchors. In short, association of free F-elements exhibits precisely the same sort of variation that defines other phonological processes such as spreading.

Moreover, just as sets of rules may interact to produce complex surface patterns, so may sets of association rules interact to produce complex association patterns: bidirectionality, default docking, edge-in association, and so on. No single type of interaction can be defined as uniquely valid. Multiple association rules may apply in a single direction (Kinande); multiple association rules may apply in opposite directions (default docking/edge-in); iterative association rules may precede noniterative rules (default docking); iterative rules may follow noniterative rules (edge-in).

One might counter, however, that by assuming association to be "just another rule," one loses an account of the special nature of association, of the fact that it is one of the commonest attested phonological processes. This counterargument is flimsy: there are two somewhat interrelated reasons for expecting association to be extremely common. First, unless a free F-element associates, it is not Prosodically Licensed (Itô 1986). Except in very special circumstances, such as the configurations leading to downstepped tonal realizations, F-elements that are not prosodically licensed simply do not surface phonetically. Recoverability, therefore, militates against even including such a feature in lexical representations. The result is the following: for a language to circumvent the restrictions imposed by Recoverability, positing FREE F-elements necessitates the positing of rules that will accomplish association.

The second reason that association rules are so common concerns the nature of the formal defaults assigned by the theory of parametric rules proposed here. Consider a schematic rule (94) all of whose parameter values are the default values.

(94) *The "Default" Rule*

   Nondefault rule settings: α

Argument:	α	Default	Nondefault
Parameters	Function	INSERT	
	Type	PATH	
	Direction	LEFT TO RIGHT	
	Iteration	ITERATIVE	
Structure requirements	A-Structure	NONE	
	T-Structure	FREE	
Other requirements	A-Conditions		
	T-Conditions		

This rule, the result of the full complement of default settings, defines a process whereby an F-element α would associate from left to right and spread automatically —precisely the "convention" assumed in works such as Williams 1976 and Clements and Ford 1979. Consider in this light a slight change in the above settings, namely, replacing the default T-Structure: FREE setting with the nondefault T-Structure: NONE, a change whose result would be to allow the creation of contours. With this single change, the resulting rule would derive the effect of Goldsmith's (1976) "convention," whereby autosegments automatically linked, spread, and created contours. Finally, consider making the single change in (94) of replacing the default A-Structure: NONE setting with the nondefault A-Structure: FREE. This single change would automatically derive the one-to-one "convention" proposed by Pulleyblank (1986a). In other words, the nondefault parameter settings in (95) derive three of the basic proposals that have been made concerning unidirectional association "conventions."

(95) *Some parametric association types*

| | Effect of rule | | |
	One-to-one	Spread	Contours
Nondefault rule settings: α	yes	yes	no
Nondefault rule settings: α; T-Structure: NONE	yes	yes	yes
Nondefault rule settings: α; A-Structure: FREE	yes	no	no

From a formal perspective, the special property about these three rules is not "conventional" status, but simply that they represent three of the most formally desirable rule configurations.

Association rules can of course vary in ways other than those in (95). We have illustrated variation in terms of Direction, Iteration, conditions on the Arguments, and conditions on Targets. In (96), we display rules of association alongside rules of spreading, illustrating the types of variation found in this regard.

(96) *Variation in "association" and "spread" rules*

Parameter		ASSOCIATION RULES A-Structure: FREE	SPREAD RULES A-Structure: NONE
Direction:	Left to right	Tiv Low Link	Ngbaka Round Spread
	Right to left	Yoruba [−ATR] Association	Yoruba [−ATR] Spread
Iteration:	Iterative	Chaha Labialization	Pulaar [+ATR] Spread
	Noniterative	Chaha Palatalization	Lango Progressive [+ATR]/μ Spread
A-Conditions:		Kukuya Final H Association	Tiv Round Spread
T-Conditions:		Yawelmani Glottal Association	Menomini [+ATR] Spread

The association of free F-elements is subject to the same range of variation as rules of spreading: association of free F-elements is effected by rule, not by convention.

As we conclude this discussion of association, it is useful to reconsider the broader implications of the "association by rule" conclusion. Note in this regard that we have not posited some special rule type "Associate!" On the contrary, as with cases such as the polarity/dissimilation effects discussed in section 4.5, we propose that superficial phenomena of association result from the action in concert of various independent rule components. The wide range of variation shared by rather different processes like "association" and "dissimilation" derives from the range of possible combinations of independently motivated parameter settings. In addition, we note with association, as with cases of polarity and dissimilation, that similarity of phenomena at a superficial level does not necessarily result from identical formal analyses. Both of these themes, componentiality and phenomenological indeterminacy, are reflected in our discussion of neutrality effects, the focus of the next section.

4.7 Neutrality: Transparency and Opacity

The componentiality and phenomenological indeterminacy just discussed with respect to association can be observed in a range of phenomena. While it is not within the scope of this study to address these issues everywhere that they are relevant, we conclude this chapter by examining one additional set of phenomena that has figured centrally in the autosegmental literature, namely, neutrality effects.

Neutrality effects encompass both *opacity*, the blocking of successive rule application by some elements, and *transparency*, the ability of some elements to be ignored during rule application. By way of illustration, consider the contrast between the Yoruba and Wolof harmony effects. In both cases, [−ATR] is the Argument and both harmony rules affect only nonhigh vowels. For present purposes, the most significant difference between the two rules resides in the way each responds to high vowels. In Yoruba, high vowels prevent further application of the harmony rule: *èlùbọ́*, **ẹ̀lùbọ́* 'yam flour'. Yoruba high vowels are *opaque*. In Wolof, the harmony rule may apply across a high vowel: *tekkileen* [tɛkkilɛɛn] 'untie!' (cf. *gëstuléén* [gǝstuleen] 'do research!'). Wolof high vowels are transparent.

The classical autosegmental approach to this distinction is extremely elegant: *opacity* is attributed to the structural property of being linked; *transparency* is attributed to the structural property of being free. For example, the Yoruba form would be represented by assigning the opaque high vowel a [+ATR] specification, as in (97a); the [+ATR] specification would block harmonic spreading. The Wolof form would be represented by excluding such a specification, as in (97b); the harmonic [−ATR] would therefore spread over the transparent high vowel.

(97) *Classical neutrality effects*

    a. *Yoruba opacity*   b. *Wolof transparency*

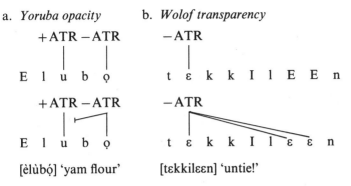

       [èlùbọ́] 'yam flour'   [tɛkkilɛɛn] 'untie!'

While this representational approach to neutrality effects at first appears quite successful, consideration of a wide number of cases has shown it to be problematical. Some of the central problems are as follows.

The representations required to "derive" neutrality effects are not independently motivated. This is true in two distinct senses. On the one hand, the gapped configuration postulated for a case like Wolof in (97b) is completely unmotivated cross-linguistically. Apart from cases specifically involving harmony-with-transparency, the cases under consideration, such structures have not been motivated. This issue was discussed in chapter 1, where it was concluded that gapped configurations should be universally ruled out because they violate Locality. To allow gapped structures for transparency effects requires the weakening or abandoning of general locality constraints (see Schein and Steriade 1986, Cole 1987, Steriade 1987b), a move that has serious and undesirable consequences in general.

In contrast, formally linked structures of the type in (97a) are amply motivated in a wide number of languages. Nevertheless, the problem in a case like (97a) is that within Yoruba there is no motivation independent of opacity for assigning [+ATR] to high vowels; on the contrary, there is considerable independent evidence in Yoruba that high vowels are *not* assigned such a specification at the lexical stage of the derivation where harmony takes place (Pulleyblank 1988c). Similar arguments were given for Akan (section 3.2.3.2); it was shown that opaque low vowels are unspecified for [ATR] at both early and late stages, rendering highly suspect an analysis of opacity at an intermediate stage as due to an [ATR] specification. Maasai (section 4.3.2) provides a related example where the same vowel, the low vowel /a/, acts both as opaque and as an undergoer. As noted in the discussion of Maasai, neutrality effects cannot be straightforwardly derived from representational properties if the neutrality effects vary for the same representation.

Maasai is relevant in demonstrating an additional point. Opaque elements need not belong to the same morpheme as the Argument. For example, in Maasai, root /a/

is opaque to the spreading of [+ATR] from a suffix. Given the morphemic tier hypothesis (McCarthy 1981, 1986a, Cole 1987), one would expect a root [ATR] specification to be on a different tier from a suffix specification. The representational analysis of opacity could only account for the Maasai pattern by assuming an ad hoc mechanism to conflate tiers.[55]

The crucial point here is the role of *independent* motivation. At best, only *indirect* attribution to structural factors can be made when there is no independent evidence for the structural configurations that are posited. The *direct* source of neutrality is the rule or condition that often stipulatively derives the required configuration, for example, the rule that inserts or redundantly requires a [+ATR] specification on high vowels in Yoruba but not in Wolof.

The types of neutrality effects under discussion have figured prominently in this work, particularly in section 3.5, where we argued that Grounding Theory identifies the class of elements that may be neutral. At issue now is the question of how such neutrality effects are formally expressed: the challenge is to show that the variety of attested neutrality effects can be obtained without introducing additional rule parameters expressly for that purpose. This is an important point: the parametric approach fails if it cannot account for a particular class of phenomena without introducing a parameter specifically designed for the phenomenon in question.[56]

We demonstrate here that the aggregate effects of Grounding Theory, the Locality Condition, and Parametric Rule Theory predict the range of attested types of neutrality. No new or special properties need to be introduced: neutrality follows from independently motivated subtheories. We turn first to *canonical neutrality*, effects predicted by the Locality Condition.

4.7.1 Neutrality as a Locality Effect

In the canonical neutrality phenomena, rules of harmonic spreading interact with designated classes of neutral segments, neutrality manifesting itself as either opacity or transparency. We argue here that such effects are predicted by the way in which the Well-formedness Principle and the Locality Condition restrict rule application. By Well-formedness, only well-formed outputs are possible; by Locality, gapped configurations (98) are ill formed.

As established in chapter 1, a representation is ill formed if it involves a gapped configuration. Ill-formedness is attributed to the Precedence clause of the Locality Condition, *Precedence relations cannot be contradictory.* In (98), α is linked to non-adjacent anchors: the configuration is ill formed as a result of contradictory precedence relations.

(98) *Gapped configuration—ill formed*

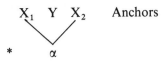

In the set of ordered paths involving α and its anchor tier, namely, $\{X_1/\alpha < Y < X_2/\alpha\}$, we find the contradictory statement that α both precedes and follows Y. The clear prediction is that feature spreading cannot skip over intervening anchors: opacity results, not transparency.

(99)

$$\alpha \qquad \qquad \alpha$$
$$| \qquad\qquad\qquad \rightarrow \qquad \diagdown$$
$$X \quad X_1 \ Y \ X_2 \qquad\qquad X \quad X_1 \ Y \ X_2$$

4.7.1.1 Canonical Opacity   The classical autosegmental approach to opacity is to derive it by invoking the No Crossing Constraint of Goldsmith (1976). For example, Clements (1981) proposes that in Akan, the opaque low vowel /a/ is associated to [−ATR]. As a result, the prohibition against crossed association lines prevents [+ATR] from spreading across /a/; further, the [−ATR] specification of /a/ spreads to preceding vowels. We call this form of opacity *representational opacity*, since the opacity is due to specific properties of the representation (100).

(100)

$$\alpha \qquad\quad \beta \qquad\qquad\quad \alpha \qquad\quad \beta$$
$$| \qquad\quad | \qquad\qquad \rightarrow \quad \diagdown \qquad\quad |$$
$$A_i \ \ A_i \ \ A_j \ \ A_i \qquad\quad A_i \ \ A_i \ \ A_j \ \ A_i$$

This general approach is familiar from similar accounts of Maasai (Levergood 1984), Wolof (Ka 1988), Kikuyu (Clements and Ford 1979, 1981) (by no means an exhaustive list of such analyses), as well as being crucial in the analysis of translaryngeal harmony offered in Steriade 1987b, Wiswall 1991a,b.

In the analyses presented here, we have shown evidence that *crossing* is not exclusively responsible for opacity, arguing that opacity effects cannot in all cases be directly attributed to properties of the representation. However, as noted above, under Precedence, if a harmonic feature cannot link to some otherwise legitimate anchor, then harmonic spreading must stop since anchors cannot be skipped. For what reason might an anchor be antagonistic to the harmonic F-element? In the bulk of the cases of opacity examined here, a grounded implicational condition defines the relation between the spreading feature and some targeted anchor as incompatible. Hence, the combination of the Precedence clause of the Locality Condition with grounded antagonistic combinations defines the core class of opacity: *antagonistic opacity*.

Several arguments have already been presented in favor of this appeal to antagonistic opacity. For example, in Maasai (section 4.3.2), one and the same segment may be opaque for one rule but an undergoer for another—there is no representational property that uniquely defines the behavior of the opaque class. In Akan (section 3.2.3.2), distributional properties defined *prior* to harmony, as well as phonetic interpolation effects that take place *after* harmony, both indicate that the opaque low vowel should be represented as devoid of [ATR] specifications. Opacity effects involving low vowels during the harmonic process itself can therefore not be attributed to the presence of a [−ATR] specification on the low vowel. A third case would be Yoruba, where high vowels are opaque to [−ATR] Spread because of their incompatibility with that feature. The opacity cannot be attributed to crossed association lines since there is considerable evidence that high vowels in Yoruba are unspecified for vocalic features, including [ATR] (Pulleyblank 1988c).

One might imagine, therefore, that *antagonistic opacity* is proposed to completely supplant analyses of *representational opacity* based on crossed association lines. This would actually be a rather paradoxical position, however. Recall that we derive the prohibition against crossed association lines from the Precedence clause of the Locality Condition. Since both opacity as defined by antagonistic grounding effects and opacity as defined by crossed association lines are derived by Precedence, there is no reason intrinsic to opacity for selecting one of the two systematically over the other. The expectation would therefore be the following: where general considerations of Combinatorial Specification lead one to posit the presence of the harmonic feature on an opaque element, Locality (via crossed association lines) will account for the opacity; where general considerations of Combinatorial Specification lead one to exclude a specification from an opaque element, Locality (via the gapped configuration) will account for the opacity. We have shown several examples of opacity where the opaque elements are *not* specified for the harmonic feature. In the discussion of Kalenjin (section 3.5.3), we presented the opposite kind of case, one where the opaque element must be specified for the harmonic feature. The conclusion is that opacity of both types is a predicted effect of the interplay among Locality, Wellformedness, antagonistic configurations (Grounding Theory), and representations (Combinatorial Specification).

4.7.1.2 Canonical Transparency By disallowing gapped configurations, Locality rules out the spreading of some F-element α across a non-α-bearer. For example, spreading from consonant to consonant is ruled out in a CVC sequence. Likewise, it might appear that spreading from vowel to vowel would be ruled out in a VCV sequence. However, under the proposal in chapter 1, that Locality is tempered by the Anchor Hypothesis (*Anchor-paths establish cross-tier ordering*), vowel-to-vowel spreading in a *VCV* sequence is in fact well formed: the consonant is ignored. We call this *prosodic transparency*.

To elaborate, since features of vowels take moras as their anchors, the class of anchor-paths relevant for establishing the order of vowel features is therefore defined on the mora tier.

(101) *Prosodic transparency*

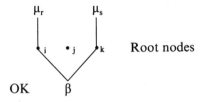

In (101), the ordered set of anchor-paths for β is $\{\mu_r/\beta < \mu_s/\beta\}$. There is no contradiction in precedence relations in such a configuration: μ_r precedes μ_s on the mora tier; since both are linked to β, and since an element cannot precede or follow itself, no contradictory cross-tier orderings are established. The representation is well formed. Cases of this type abound; for example, virtually every example of harmony discussed in this book involves prosodic transparency.

4.7.1.3   Root Nodes and Moras as Anchors for α   In (101), only moras are β-bearers. Thus, the presence of Root$_j$ is not relevant in determining the well-formedness of (101): Root nodes are not anchors for β. In such a case, by the Anchor Hypothesis, the Root nodes play no role in determining cross-tier ordering. What, then, are the expected neutrality effects where some F-element γ allows *both* Root nodes and moras as its anchors? Does allowing the configuration in (102) alter the Precedence relations just considered?

(102)

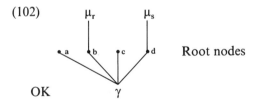

In a "CVCV" sequence like (102), the F-element γ is associated to all anchors, *Root$_{a,c}$* and $\mu_{r,s}$. The representation is well formed: γ is associated to all four Root nodes, so at the Root tier there are no precedence contradictions. Recall that precedence relations hold only between elements whose paths do not intersect. Here, the paths to the four anchors all intersect at γ.

Cases become interesting when only some of the anchors are in a path with γ. Consider first the "CVCV" sequence in (103): the paths of both consonants and the second vowel intersect at γ, but that of the first vowel does not. Consequently, precedence relations for γ may be determined. (Effectively, a syllable from (102) has been incorporated at the right edge of (98).)

(103)

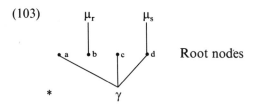

Like (98), (103) is ill formed, and for precisely the same reasons. The set of anchor-paths for γ is {Root$_a$/γ, Root$_c$/γ, μ$_s$/γ}. With respect to the mora tier, the ordering is {μ$_r$ < μ$_s$/γ}: there are no contradictions, so the representation is well formed at this level. At the Root level, however, a contradiction arises: in the set {Root$_a$/γ < Root$_b$ < Root$_c$/γ < Root$_d$}, γ both precedes and follows *Root$_b$*. Precedence relations at the Root level are contradictory, so the representation is ill formed.

Next, a syllable from (102) is incorporated at the left edge of (101), giving (104): again the representation is well formed. Again, precedence relations can be determined with respect to γ because the second consonant does not include γ in its path.

(104)

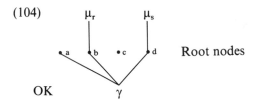

The anchor-paths are {Root$_a$/γ, μ$_r$/γ, μ$_s$/γ}. Precedence at the moraic level is identical to that in (101): there are no contradictions in {μ$_r$/γ < μ$_s$/γ}. At the Root level, too, there are no contradictions: {Root$_a$/γ < Root$_b$ < Root$_c$ < Root$_d$}. Note that although γ is in a *path* with both *Root$_b$* and *Root$_d$*, these Root nodes are not anchors for γ. As a result, the Root node ordering is {Root$_a$/γ < Root$_b$ < Root$_c$ < Root$_d$}, which is perfectly consistent. The representation is well formed.

Consider in addition a representation like (105).

(105)

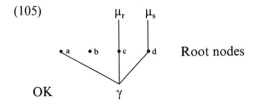

In this case, the anchor-paths are $\{Root_a/\gamma, \mu_r/\gamma, \mu_s/\gamma\}$. At the moraic level, this case is comparable to well-formed configurations already shown. There are no contradictions with regard to Precedence: $\{\mu_r/\gamma < \mu_s/\gamma\}$. At the Root level, the configuration is equally well formed: $\{Root_a/\gamma < Root_b < Root_c < Root_d\}$. In a manner essentially comparable to (104), $Root_c$ and $Root_d$ in (105) are on paths to γ, but they do not count in the calculation of Precedence since the anchors in those paths are the moras, not the Root nodes.

To summarize, the combined effect of the Anchor Hypothesis and Precedence is to rule out gapped configurations like (98); at the same time, they cooperate to permit a specific class of gapped configurations, as in (101). The same result obtains where the set of anchors includes both Root nodes and moras: configurations like (103) are ruled out, while configurations like (104) and (105) are allowed.

The consequence is clear. The theory predicts a class of representations like those in (104) and (105). The issue is, Do they occur?

With respect to (105), we have already shown a relevant configuration in section 2.2.2.2. In Barrow Inupiaq, the [−back] feature of appropriate front vowels palatalizes a coronal consonant *even over an intervening noncoronal consonant*. The result is a gapped configuration corresponding to the schema in (105). We suggest that formal configurations of the type shown in (104) are similarly attested. We give here an example arising from a harmonic process in Nyangumarta that involves both consonants and vowels.

4.7.1.4 Nyangumarta Palatal Harmony   Like many Australian languages, Nyangumarta (O'Grady 1964, Hoard and O'Grady 1976, Archangeli 1986, Sharp 1986) has only three vowels, /I, A, U/. Certain suffix vowels alternate among these three, depending on the quality of the final stem vowel. This general pattern is illustrated in (106).

(106) *Nyangumarta vowel harmony*

     a. yirri-rni-rni   'see-REALIS-1SG.NOM'
         kalku-rnu-rnu   'hold-REALIS-1SG.NOM'
         wirla-rna-rna   'hit-REALIS-1SG.NOM'

     b. wirri-limi-rni   'put-FUTURE-1SG.NOM'
         kalku-lumu-rnu   'hold-FUTURE-1SG.NOM'
         yurpa-lama-rna   'rub-FUTURE-1SG.NOM'

The data in (106) motivate rules of [+high] spread and [+round] spread affecting /A/.[57]

Nyangumarta [+high] harmony is also triggered by palatal consonants ([j, ly, ny, y]), both the general spreading to the right and a noniterative spreading to the left.

The role of consonants in harmony is illustrated by the contrast between forms with and without the suffix *-yV-* '3PL.NOM', shown in (107). In (107a), [+high] harmony takes place, spreading rightward to *-ntV* '2SG.ACC' and leftward to *-rnV-* 'REALIS'; by contrast, in (107b), harmony is based on the final root vowel, as in (106).

(107) *Harmony induced by palatal consonants*

    a. yirri-rni-yi-nti   'see-REALIS-3PL.NOM-2SG.ACC'
       kalku-rni-yi-nti   'hold-REALIS-3PL.NOM-2SG.ACC'
       wirla-rni-yi-nti   'hit-REALIS-3PL.NOM-2SG.ACC'

    b. yirri-rni-nti   'see-REALIS-2SG.ACC'
       kalku-rnu-ntu   'hold-REALIS-2SG.ACC'
       wirla-rna-nta   'hit-REALIS-2SG.ACC'

Regressive spreading from the palatal nasal /ny/ is illustrated in (108): the suffix *-nyi* '1PL.INCLU.NOM' causes the preceding vowel to surface as [i], not [a].

(108) *Regressive harmony induced by palatal consonants*

    a. wirla-nami-nyi   'hit-IRREALIS-1PL.INCLU.NOM'
       wirla-nama-rna   'hit-IRREALIS-1SG.NOM'

    b. wirla-nama-lpi-nyi   'hit-IRREALIS-REMOTE-1PL.INCLU.NOM'
       wirla-nama-lpa-rna 'hit-IRREALIS-REMOTE-1SG.NOM'

Since [+high] accepts both Root nodes and moras as its anchor, the [+high] harmony rule might be construed as applying to both consonants and vowels. In this case, a configuration like the schematic (102) would result from harmony, predicting that all consonants would show effects of [+high]. Conversely, the rule might be more restrictive, targeting only moras and deriving representations comparable to the schematic (104). If so, no consonants would show the effect of the harmony process. In fact, the latter appears to be the case: consonants are unaffected by the Nyangumarta harmony rule.

This brief sketch suggests that consonants in Nyangumarta are prosodically transparent, in accord with the predictions of the Anchor Hypothesis and Locality. That is, the prosodic condition on rule Targets means that all nonmoraic elements (consonants) are skipped. Combining these results with the earlier discussion of representational and antagonistic opacity, we conclude that a strict formal principle, the Locality Condition, governs configurations of canonical harmony, directly or indirectly deriving formal neutrality effects.[58]

4.7.2 Apparent Counterexamples

The canonical neutrality effects discussed in the preceding section identify a large class of cases involving either opacity or transparency. There are, however, a number of apparent counterexamples, cases that might appear to involve opaque or transparent elements but cannot be analyzed strictly in terms of Locality effects. Consider, for example, the case of apparent transparency in (109): α appears to have spread from X to X, skipping Y.

(109) *Ill-formed transparency configuration*

Given the Locality Condition, this configuration is not a possible formal result for a spreading rule. One must look for alternative formal mechanisms, therefore, to derive such apparent transparency. A satisfying result of the model presented here is that no new formal apparatus is required: interactions between the independently motivated modules predict precisely this class of effects. The neutrality effect may result from interactions with Grounding Theory; it may also result from properties specific to the harmony rule itself. We consider each type in turn.

4.7.2.1 Grounding Effects   The problematical property of (109) is that the harmonic F-element α is not associated to Y, despite Y being an anchor for α: were α associated to Y, the representation would be well formed (110). The configuration reflects the canonical rule spreading α (nondefault rule settings: α).

(110) *Canonical spreading*

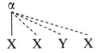

If the configuration in (110) is to be considered well formed, it is clear that both X and Y constitute well-formed anchors for α. At issue, then, is whether the phonological configuration in (110) could result in the appearance of transparency at the surface level. The possibility arises through the interaction of such configurations with Grounding Theory: we have already discussed two types of such interaction (section 3.5). On the one hand, *sympathetic neutrality* may result from a pattern where, independent of spreading environments, all instances of Y surface with α. For example, high vowels in Ngbaka (chapter 2) can be targeted by the [+ATR] harmonic value, as in *sibè* 'chanson', *zèdi* 'jeudi' (111a). But even in sequences where there is no source of [+ATR], high vowels still surface as advanced because of the redundant grounded relation between vowel height and tongue root advancement (HI/ATR), as in *budè* 'petit oiseau de la taille du mange-mil', **bʊdè*, and *ʔti* 'laissé', **ʔtɪ* (111b).

(111) a.   s   I   b   E   →   s   i   b   E   →   s   i   b   e

          +ATR   +ATR   +ATR

b. b   U   d   E   →   [budɛ]   (*[bʊdɛ])

An alternative to such *sympathetic neutrality* is *antagonistic neutrality* of the type demonstrated to hold of low vowels in Kinande (section 3.2.3.1). We argued that for such a case, the appearance of transparency is simply a lack of phonetic salience (see section 3.3.1). In cases like [ɔmùká:tì] 'bread' and [ɔmúká:mì] 'brewer', the [+ATR] specification of the final high vowel spreads leftward, clearly and robustly deriving the advanced [u] of the prefix [mʊ/mu] (112). We have argued that despite appearances, the low penultimate vowel is phonologically [+ATR] in such a context, but that the [+ATR] value is not salient because of its incompatibility with a [+low] specification.[59]

(112)   +ATR

          O m u k a̧ t i

Only when the [+low, +ATR] vowel is both lengthened and L-toned is the effect of [+ATR] perceived.

Formally, therefore, cases such as these constitute canonical examples of harmonic spreading; substantively, Grounding Theory accounts for the superficial appearance of transparency.

4.7.2.2   Rule-based Effects: Contextual Neutrality   The second possible way of deriving neutrality effects is through properties specific to the relevant rule itself, a *contextual neutrality* effect. Either transparency or opacity may result, depending on the requirements imposed by the rule.

Contextual Transparency   In the preceding discussion of apparent counterexamples, we identified (113a) as a well-formed formal configuration that can in certain cases derive the effect that has been attributed to the ill-formed (113b). An alternative well-formed representation with a potentially comparable surface effect is given in (113c): there are simply two tokens of the F-element α, one associated on each side of the ineligible anchor Y.

(113) a. α   b.   α   c. α   α

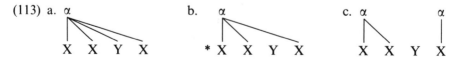

We demonstrate below that this configuration is a predicted result of a rule insert-ing α on X; by adding a contextual condition, the appearance of harmony-with-transparency is derived.

We begin with the observation that INSERT/F-ELEMENT rules may trivially exhibit transparency effects. Where such rules are ITERATIVE, anchors not meeting the contextual requirements of the rule neither undergo the rule nor block it: this class of anchors is, in effect, transparent. Consider, for example, the by now familiar example of Yoruba [−ATR] Insertion, which targets low vowels. In a form like *agírá* 'snuff' or *àkura* 'type of fish', the medial high vowel has no effect on the insertion of [−ATR]. A twin peaks configuration results (114).[60]

(114) A g I r A →   a g I r a

              | | |

           −ATR   −ATR

A further effect of an INSERT/F-ELEMENT rule is that it may result in the same kind of configuration that results from an INSERT/PATH rule, a multiply linked F-element (see section 2.3.1). In a Yoruba form like *àjẹ̀* 'paddle', the insertion of [−ATR] on the low vowel (which is adjacent to a vowel already associated to [−ATR]) cannot create an illicit OCP violation. Instead, iterative rule application results in the multiply linked F-element (115). (On the effect with a NONITERA-TIVE rule, see section 1.5.1.2.)

(115) A   j   E   Underlying representation

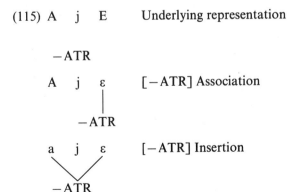

     −ATR

  A   j   ε   [−ATR] Association

              |

     −ATR

  a   j   ε   [−ATR] Insertion

     \   /

  −ATR

The twin peaks configuration of (114) corresponds to transparency; the plateau of (115) corresponds to spreading. These two effects, predicted by the settings INSERT/F-ELEMENT, create the configuration in (113c). What remains is to explain why some such INSERT/F-ELEMENT rules apply only to inputs already containing a token of the Argument F-element, thereby deriving a harmonic effect. But this is readily accomplished by a contextual condition on the Argument: in this case, the contextual condition restricts insertion to sites to the right or left of an existing token of the relevant F-element.[61]

An example of such contextual transparency was seen in the analysis of Wolof given in section 3.2.4.1. We argued there that the harmonic effect in a language like Wolof is derived by a rule that inserts *F-elements*, rather than *paths* (in conventional terms akin to *insertion*, rather than *spreading*, of the harmonic element). In Wolof, the rule inserts [−ATR], contextually restricted to apply only to the right of a token of [−ATR]. This is shown by the derivations of *deme* [dɛmɛ] 'go with' and *tekkileen* [tɛkkilɛɛn] 'untie!' in (116).

(116) a. Underlying representation (with suffixes)

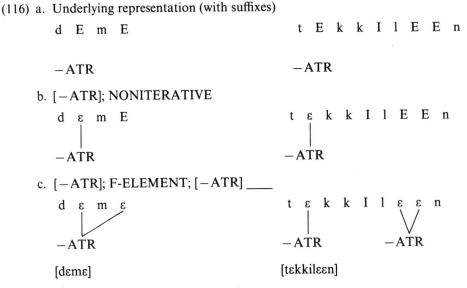

b. [−ATR]; NONITERATIVE

c. [−ATR]; F-ELEMENT; [−ATR] ____

[dɛmɛ]   [tɛkkilɛɛn]

Importantly, in step (116c), where [−ATR] is inserted by a context-sensitive rule, two effects are possible: (i) insertion of [−ATR] on a prosodic anchor adjacent to an existing [−ATR], which results in merger of the two tokens of [−ATR], as in [dɛmɛ], comparable to (115); (ii) insertion of [−ATR] on a prosodic anchor that is not adjacent to the prosodic anchor of an existing [−ATR], which involves no merger—the output has an additional token of [−ATR], as in [tɛkkilɛɛn], comparable to (114).

The patterns of various harmony systems that are amenable to this type of analysis include Khalkha Mongolian (see references in section 3.4.2), Finnish (see Goldsmith 1985 and references therein), Hungarian (see Ringen 1988 and references therein) as well as the types of consonant harmony systems discussed in works such as Shaw 1991a.

It should be noted in the current context that the Wolof-type pattern of feature insertion does not remove the need for postulating true rules of spreading. Rules of the type INSERT/PATH and contextually conditioned rules of the type INSERT/F-ELEMENT are not equivalent. As illustrated schematically in (117), the two types of rules may produce different effects, depending on the input configuration. In (117a), the anchor of Argument α, X_i, is adjacent to an eligible target, X_j, and the effect of spreading is derived whether the rule inserts a path or an F-element. The difference arises when the eligible target X_j is *not* adjacent to the Argument's anchor, as in (117b).

(117)

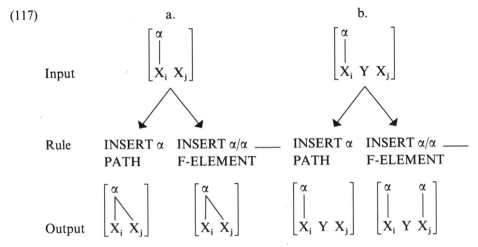

X = eligible bearer of α
Y = ineligible bearer of α

The INSERT/PATH rule derives opacity effects, while employing an appropriately conditioned INSERT/F-ELEMENT rule results in transparency. Moreover, since Path rules are less marked than F-element rules, they should be more common. That is, since INSERT/PATH rules result in opacity where INSERT/F-ELEMENT rules result in transparency, the prediction is that opacity effects should be more robustly attested cross-linguistically than transparency effects.

In closing, we note two predictions of the account of such contextual transparency. First, contextual transparency is restricted to iterative rules: were the rule noniterative, then there would be no application where the harmonic source was immediately followed by an ineligible Target. That is, if X represents a harmonic source, Y an ineligible Target, and Z an eligible Target, then a noniterative rule would always be blocked from applying in a configuration ... $XYZ_1Z_2Z_3$. ... If the rule were iterative, as in Wolof, then the entire string of Targets (Z_1, Z_2, etc.) would undergo the rule. Predicted to be impossible would be a process skipping an ineligible Target, and affecting a single element, that is, a rule that would affect only Z_1 in the above configuration.

Second, central to our proposal that some cases of harmonic transparency are due to imposing a rule context on an INSERT/F-ELEMENT rule (rather than to special properties of an INSERT/PATH rule) is the prediction that there is independent motivation for both INSERT/F-ELEMENT rules and contexts on rules. This book has already included a variety of examples of INSERT/F-ELEMENT rules; before continuing our discussion of contextual neutrality, we digress briefly to focus on motivation for contexts on rules, particularly "identity" as a context.

Excursus on Identity Conditions   Imposing a context on a rule is not a controversial proposal. Elsewhere in this book, we have posited contextual conditions on rules without comment. Examples include phonological and morphological contexts for INSERT rules, both of F-elements (e.g., Akan [+ATR] Insertion, section 3.2.3.2) and of Paths (e.g., Kukuya Final H Association, section 4.6.4), as well as DELETE/F-ELEMENT rules (e.g., Kukuya H Deletion, section 1.5.1.1). Perhaps more deserving of comment is the positing of a contextual *identity* condition. We briefly address "identity" and its role in grammar in this excursus.

An identity condition may be thought of as a dyadic predicate, where the relation holding between the two arguments is the relation of "sameness."

(118) *Identity Predicate*

   IDENTICAL-TO (X, Y)

This relation is important in a wide variety of phonological contexts. The paradigm case involves the OCP: "Within a tier, *identical* elements are prohibited."[62] In order for a sequence X, Y to be prohibited by the OCP, it must be a sequence that satisfies the Identity Predicate (118).

Apart from cases involving the OCP, identity conditions are widely attested. For example, in Tiv (sections 2.2.1.5 and 2.2.1.6), [+round] spreads only to vowels that agree in height, that is, in configurations where there is identity with respect to the feature [high]. Similar identity conditions on the operation of spreading rules are observed in Eastern Javanese (section 2.6.2) and Yawelmani (see below, this section). Identity conditions are also crucial in the account of Menomini that we present later in this chapter. Two points are worth noting about such cases. First, they are not reducible to the OCP. Consider the configurations in (119), appropriate for a pattern such as that in Tiv, where all representations respect the OCP.

(119)   +RD   +RD   +RD   +RD
           | | | |
    a. μ_i μ_j b. μ_i μ_j c. μ_i μ_j d. μ_i μ_j
           \ / | \
           +HI   +HI   +HI

As illustrated in (120), in the type of rule under consideration, rule application in such forms must be restricted to cases (119a) and (119d).

(120)

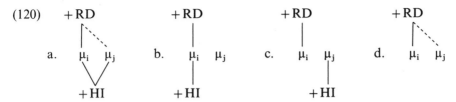

By imposing the Identity Predicate on the Argument and Target of the rule of Round Spread with respect to the feature [high], the desired result is obtained. This result is completely orthogonal to the OCP, however, since all four cases would be well formed, both in terms of their input and in terms of their output.

Note that one might attempt to make the OCP relevant by invoking a "linked feature" condition on the harmonic process (Cole 1987, Cole and Trigo 1987, 1988). For this to be possible, both values of [±high] would have to be present when the rule applies (122), with the rule formulated as in (121).

(121) *Round Spread—Linked feature version*

$$+RD$$
$$\mu_i \quad \mu_j$$
$$\alpha HI$$

(122)

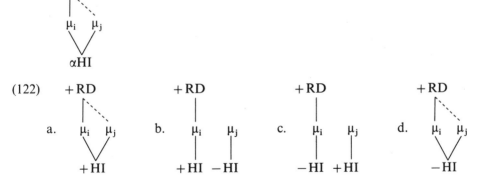

Before turning to the problems with this type of account, we should note that "linked" structures themselves are simply one type of configuration involving identity. A linked configuration involving some feature α encodes the observation that two adjacent anchors are identical with respect to α.

Two types of problems arise with the "linked feature" analyses.[63] First, there is often no independent motivation for having both feature values present. In Tiv, for example, there is evidence for the presence of [+high], but there is no evidence for the presence of [−high]. Postulation of [−high] values as in (122), therefore, would be an ad hoc artifact of the linked feature condition itself. Were the linked feature condition to be invoked within the representations that are independently motivated, then Round Spread in a language like Tiv would erroneously be restricted to sequences of high vowels (case (119a)).

A second problem concerns the applicability of this type of rule in sequences that span morpheme boundaries. It is often, perhaps typically, the case that rules of the type under consideration apply in morphologically derived contexts. The Yawelmani rule seen below, typical in this respect, applies within roots as well as between roots and suffixes. As a result, the contextual identity cannot, at least initially, be attributed to branching structures since the individual morphemes may each individually introduce relevant feature values, values for [high] in the examples in (119). In a case where multiple tokens of a feature are introduced by the morphology, configurations such as (123) would result. (We ignore here whether the relevant features would appear on the same or distinct tiers; see McCarthy 1981, etc.)

(123) +RD

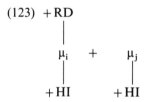

In order to conflate configurations such as the one in (123) with those in (122), it would be necessary to *fuse* the two specifications of [+high], the specifications that were introduced by different morphemes. But in this case, fusion itself would have to make reference to the Identity Predicate, since only identical sequences of [high] would be fused.

In the model presented here, there is no rule function "fuse," although fusion might result as part of end-of-stratum tier conflation (McCarthy 1986a). The "linked feature" account would predict that dependent harmonies are (i) morpheme-internal (as in Tiv and Ngbaka, see chapter 2) or (ii) both polymorphemic and late (as in Yawelmani, see below): in polymorphemic cases, harmony would necessarily follow tier conflation and fusion. However, there are other cases where the early application of feature-dependent harmony excludes such a possibility. For example, Haya Post-Root Harmony (section 2.3.2; Byarushengo 1975) takes place only between the root and certain suffixal extensions (i.e., prior to tier conflation) at the stem level. Further, Post-Root Harmony is dependent on values for [round].

The general Post-Root Harmony phenomenon in Haya is discussed in section 2.3.2: [−high] spreads from the root to the extension vowel. Here we focus on a restriction on the rule: if the target vowel is [+round], the source vowel must also be [+round] in order for [−high] spreading to take place. This is illustrated in (124): neither high vowels nor low vowels trigger Post-Root Harmony, (124a,b). Mid vowels trigger Post-Root Harmony to the nonround causative suffix -*Is*, (124c,d); only *round* mid vowels trigger Post-Root Harmony to the *round* reversive suffix -*U:lUl*, (124d).

(124) *Haya Post-Root Harmony* (Byarushengo 1975)

			Root	Causative	Reversive	
a.	HIGH	[i]	-sib-	sib-is-a	sib-u:lul-a	'pleat'
		[u]	-kub-	kub-is-a	kub-u:lul-a	'fold'
b.	LOW	[a]	-gab-	gab-is-a	gab-u:lul-a	'offer'
c.	MID	[e]	-teg-	teg-es-a	teg-u:lul-a	'set up a trap'
d.	MID ROUND	[o]	-kom-	kom-es-a	kom-o:lol-a	'tie up'

This pattern can be expressed by a rule spreading [−high], subject to an identity condition on the target: if the target is [+round], the trigger is also [+round]. To express this pattern in terms of a "linked feature" constraint would require the ad hoc fusion of the root's [+round] specification with that of the suffix. Fusion would not be principled because the harmony process takes place at the stem level, prior to end-of-stratum tier conflation (and universal fusion).

To conclude this discussion of harmony processes, admitting *identity* as a condition on rules as well as on conventions (like the OCP) allows explanation of attested patterns, while the "linked feature" account incorrectly predicts the nonexistence of a class of attested cases. The "linked feature" approach can be preserved only by resorting to ad hoc representations and ad hoc fusion of features.

In addition to spreading rules, processes of delinking can make reference to identity. In Tonga and Kinande (sections 4.2.4.2 and 4.2.4.1), for example, a rule delinks a H-tone *when the H-toned mora immediately follows another H-toned mora*. The rule applies only when there is identity with respect to tone. Another related rule is the vowel deletion rule of Tiv (section 2.2.1), which deletes a word-final mora. The rule has two conditions. The first is segmental and is therefore not relevant here. The second is that the mora targeted for deletion must share a value for [high] with the immediately preceding mora. That is, deletion is conditioned by an identity condition governing [high].

Particularly relevant to the discussion of identity conditions for INSERT/F-ELEMENT rules is the status of identity conditions for DELETE/F-ELEMENT rules. Consider the widespread process referred to as Meeussen's Rule in Eastern Bantu (see Goldsmith 1984b). This rule deletes a H-tone when it immediately follows another H-tone. Crucially, in order for the rule to apply, identity must be established between the tone that is to undergo deletion and a contextual tone to its left. Consider the following examples from Shona (Myers 1987):

(125) *Shona: Meeussen's Rule*

	Noncopular	Copular	
a.	ìshé	ndí-shè	'chief'
b.	bángà	í-bàngà	'knife'
c.	mù-rúmé	mú-rùmè	'man'
d.	chì-kórò	chí-kòrò	'school'

Deletion of a H-tone in cases such as this takes place only when there is a second H-tone to the left, as in (126).

(126)

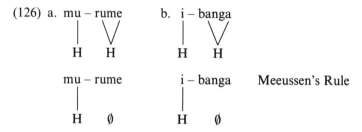

The basic claim of the parametric approach to rules is that a phonological rule expresses a systematic relation between two levels of representation in terms of a highly restricted class of parameters. In the deletion example in (126), a particular F-element, the second H-tone, is present at an early stage α of derivation, but is absent at the later stage β. The difference between this rule and a rule of insertion is simply a matter of whether α corresponds to the input stage (as in the deletion case) or to the output stage (as in an insertion case), and correspondingly, whether β constitutes output or input. Phrased differently, the basic claim of insertion and deletion rules is that representations may differ with respect to the presence or absence of some F-element. It would seem to be expected, therefore, that if the presence or absence of an F-element can be conditioned by the presence of an identical contextual F-element, then such a condition should be found both when the F-element is found in the input (deletion) and when it is found in the output (insertion). We conclude, therefore, that the existence of rules such as Meeussen's Rule, a deletion rule with a contextual identity condition, leads us to expect the existence of rules of the type seen in Wolof, an insertion rule with a contextual identity condition.

This introduces a further prediction of the model, that contexts on F-element rules are restricted to tier-internal conditions: the contextual F-element and the Argument are members of the same tier.[64] This is a result of the proposal that Locality constrains rule application. Unless mentioned as a special condition in the rule, prosodic anchors are not directly involved in F-element rules. But without access to prosodic anchors, Locality is respected only *within a tier*: it is impossible to characterize adjacency between α and β where the two are on different tiers without accessing their prosodic anchors. Thus, "long-distance" contextual transparency effects are possible only where the Argument and context are members of the same tier.

Perhaps surprisingly, opacity effects may also derive from contextual identity conditions, exemplified in Yawelmani.

Contextual Opacity in Yawelmani   Opacity can also result from restrictions imposed in an INSERT/PATH rule, giving *contextual opacity*. In such a case, a subset of the eligible anchors is selected as rule targets: the unselected set is opaque, because of the Locality Condition. Examples such as Tiv Round Harmony and Ngbaka Round Harmony (see chapter 2), Kinande Phrasal and Suffixal Harmony (section 3.2.3.1), and Maasai Leftward [+ATR] Spread (section 4.3.2) all exemplify the phenomenon; a further case is found in Yawelmani Round Harmony (Newman 1944, Kuroda 1967, Archangeli 1984, 1985, Steriade 1986a, Hong, in preparation).

In Yawelmani, [+round] spreads rightward onto vowels of like height (127a), but not onto vowels of different height (127b).

(127) *Yawelmani Round Harmony*

	Surface	Underlying		
a.	yawalhin	<yawaal-hin	'followed'	
	lihimhin	<lihm-hin	'ran'	
	hoginhin	<hogn-hin	'floated'	
	ʔugunhun	<ʔugn-hin	'drank'	
	ṭawhatinxoohin	<ṭaw-hatn-xoo-hin	'was trying to win from someone'	
	liʔhatinhin	<liʔ-hatn-hin	'wanted to sink'	
	doshotinhin	<dos-hatn-hin	'was trying to tell'	
	hudhatinxoʔ	<hud-hatn-xoo-ʔ	'want to know about'	
b.	hudhatinxoʔ	<hud-hadn-xoo-ʔ	'wants to know about'	*hudhatṵnxoʔ
	buk'k'aliw	<buk'k'-aal-w	'hill-LOC'	*buk'k'alṵw
	suhwa:hin	<suhw-aa-hin	'made by supernatural powers'	*suhwa:hṵn
	dosʔin'ay	<dos-(ʔ)in'ay	'while reporting'	*dosʔin'ọy
	go:ninxask'a	<goon-in-xas-k'a	'fall right down!'	*go:ninxọsk'a
	gobʔin'ay	<gob-(ʔ)in'ay	'while entering'	*gobin'ọy

The standard analysis of Yawelmani Round Harmony is that [+round] spreads rightward between vowels of like height. The "like height" restriction is a property of the rule itself; imposing such a condition derives *contextual opacity*.[65]

Attributing opacity to incompatibility fails in this case because [+round] combines freely with high and nonhigh vowels in the language, both in general and as a result of this rule.

Attributing opacity to the representation also fails. Since both high and nonhigh vowels may be opaque, all vowels would be specified as either [+round] or [−round]. Under such full specification, it would be necessary for the rule to be able to "override" specifications that are already present, or else no harmony effect would be seen at all. However, if the spreading of [+round] were allowed to override [−round] specifications, the specifications of [−round] could not be the source of opacity. In order to derive opacity, a "like-height" condition needs to be placed on the rule. However, as seen with our analysis above, the like-height condition itself is sufficient to derive opacity: any [−round] specifications would be superfluous.

4.7.2.3 Summary The phenomena considered in this section each evince a surface neutrality effect, yet none succumbs to a canonical neutrality analysis. Strikingly, however, each receives a straightforward analysis in terms of the model developed in this work: sympathetic and antagonistic transparency follow from the Grounding Theory; contextual neutrality, both transparency and opacity, are predicted effects of imposing restrictions on rules.

Prominent in this demonstration are two of the recurring themes of this work: phenomenological indeterminacy and modularity of the phonological component. The modularity claim is that complex arrays of surface phenomena are to be derived by the interaction of simple, independently motivated components; the phenomenological indeterminacy claim is that deceptively similar sets of data may be accounted for in rather different ways in different languages. These themes are at the heart of our discussion of the harmonic system of Menomini, the conclusion to this discussion of neutrality.

4.7.3 Menomini: A Case Study
Menomini vowel raising (Bloomfield 1962) constitutes a severe test for any theory of neutrality effects: three of the six vowel qualities in the system can be transparent, and a fourth is opaque; in addition, vowel quantity plays a role in transparency though not in opacity. In the following discussion, we demonstrate that the modular approach of this book straightforwardly accounts for the Menomini patterns; we demonstrate that neutrality effects crucially combine requirements on (i) the substantive set of F-elements, (ii) rule settings, (iii) Locality Condition considerations, and (iv) grounded implications. We argue that accounts based solely on structural representations can succeed in describing the Menomini facts only at the cost of making completely ad hoc assumptions.

4.7.3.1 Menomini Vowel Representations In the standard description of Menomini harmony (Bloomfield 1962), long mid vowels are described as raising to high vowels when followed by a high vowel; short mid vowels and the low vowel (long or short) are transparent to this rule. Crucial for an account of such harmony is an identification of the F-element responsible for such vocalic "raising." Our hypothesis is that raising is the result of tongue root advancement. That is, for phonetic reasons to be detailed below, [+ATR] is postulated to be the active harmonic value. Not only does this hypothesis account straightforwardly for the actual process of raising, it allows a grounded characterization of the class of Menomini vowels that triggers and undergoes the rule, namely, the class of vowels defined by ATR/LO (the nonlow vowel class).

Our proposal is that Menomini makes use of the three F-elements, [+low], [+ATR], [+round], subject to a path condition prohibiting [+low] and [+round] on a single path. These F-elements in conjunction with the relevant grounded condition give the combinations in (128c).[66]

(128) *Menomini vowel representation*

    a. F-elements

        +LO, +RD, +ATR

    b. Conditions

        LO/RD Condition: If [+low] then not [+round].
        RD/LO Condition: If [+round] then not [+low].

    c.

*	*	ạ	a	u	U	i	I
+LO	+LO	+LO	+LO				
+RD	+RD			+RD	+RD		
+ATR		+ATR		+ATR		+ATR	

Menomini is a paradigm example of a language that raises problems for the establishment of simple correspondences between sound and symbol (see section 2.8.1). We consider certain ramifications of this issue before proceeding to an account of harmony itself, since the feature specifications in (128) depart from those used in earlier accounts (Cole and Trigo 1987, 1988, Cole 1987, Steriade 1987a) in certain respects.

There is considerable variation in the way that certain vowels are realized. For example, Bloomfield (1962:7) reports that the vowel we transcribe as [a] ranges when short from a vowel "more open than the vowel of English *pet* ... all the way to that of the vowel in English *pit*"; when long, it is consistently lower, ranging from French *tête* through English *bad* and French *brave* to English *father* (Bloomfield 1962:4). The analytic problem is that this vowel ranges from what might be analyzed as a high retracted vowel all the way to what might be considered a low retracted vowel.

Similarly, the vowels we transcribe as [ɪ] and [ʊ] vary in their realization, particularly depending on whether they are short or long. When short, they are described as comparable to the vowels of English *pit* and *put*, respectively (Bloomfield 1962:8–9); furthermore, for some speakers, short [ɪ] appears to merge phonetically with [i] although it maintains distinct harmonic effects. Long [ɪ:] and [ʊ:], on the other hand, have realizations that are more like a "mid" vowel.[67]

Our analysis of such variability appeals to the notion of phonetically antagonistic F-element combinations (see section 3.3.1). Viewed in terms of the features [high] and [low], there would be no obvious explanation for the range of variation just described. But viewed in terms of the interaction of tongue body height with [ATR], it is the vowels that exhibit a tension with respect to their [ATR] value that are prone to vary (see Meechan 1992).

Abstracting away from values for [ATR], Menomini exhibits a three-vowel system: *I, A, U*. Assuming that the basic F-element inventory from which such a system could be derived contains [high], [low], [back], and [round], we observe the following. Combinations of either [back] or [round] with [high] would derive four-vowel systems, not three-vowel systems. By contrast, assuming that in typical systems low vowels are redundantly [+back] and [−round], the combination of [low] with either [back] or [round] would derive the desired three-vowel system. We postulate, therefore, that the evidence in Menomini for a basic three-vowel system constitutes evidence for selecting the feature [low]. As regards the choice between [back] and [round], we select [round] here for essentially arbitrary reasons. As for the values of these features that are active, we assume that Markedness Statements for these features establish [+low] and [+round] as active in the unmarked case (see Kean 1975, Archangeli 1984 for relevant discussion), as in (128a).

This brings us to the essential point, the issue of how [ATR] values interact with the basic *I, U, A* system. As argued in chapter 3, noncontrastive features are expected to enhance contrastive ones (see Stevens, Keyser, and Kawasaki 1986), either phonetically or phonologically; hence, the *I, U, A* system should result on the surface in a high front unrounded vowel, a high back rounded vowel, and a low back unrounded vowel. Consider in this light the expected interactions with [ATR]. Whether the result of phonetic interpretation or of phonological feature insertion, the assignment of tongue root advancement to the high vowels *I* and *U* results in a sympathetic combination, while the combination of tongue root advancement with the low vowel *A* produces an antagonistic combination; in a similar fashion, the combination of tongue root retraction with *A* is sympathetic, while the combination of retraction with *I* and *U* is antagonistic.

The important conclusion is that the vowels exhibiting considerable variability are precisely those identified by their tongue root values as involving antagonistic combinations, an expected result of Grounding Theory. Moreover, as will be demonstrated in the following sections, the characterization of Menomini vowels in terms of tongue root specifications provides a straightforward account of the range of attested harmonic patterns.[68]

4.7.3.2 Transparency: Menomini Raising Given the vowel system as represented in (128), Menomini harmony is readily characterized as involving a regressive [ATR] harmony pattern, triggered by and targeting only the nonlow vowels, as schematically illustrated in (129).

(129) *Schematic quality effects*

    a. High vowels trigger and undergo

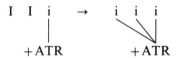

    b. Low vowels are "transparent"

    c. [+ATR] low vowels are "opaque"

This pattern is illustrated with the data given below. The forms in (130) show the raising effect when the triggering vowel is in an adjacent syllable.[69]

(130) *Menomini raising—adjacent syllables*

se:pe:w	[sɪ:pɪ:w]	'river'
si:piah	[si:piah]	'river-LOC'
oto:tɛ:mew	[ʊtʊ:tạ:mɪw]	'he has X as a totem'
otu:hpuakanew	[ʊtu:hpuakanɪw]	'he has X as a pipe'

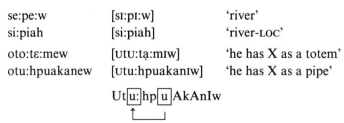

The data in (130) provide preliminary evidence that the harmony rule applies from right to left, and indicate that the rule targets only long vowels (131). As evidence for the latter point, note the initial short [ʊ] in [ʊtu:hpuakanɪw], *[utu:hpuakanew].

(131) *Schematic quantity effects*

   a. Long vowels are Targets

   b. Short vowels are not Targets

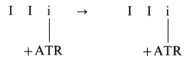

   c. Short vowels are "transparent"

The length restriction is further confirmed by the forms in (132); short vowels are neither affected by harmony nor do they impede it.[70]

(132) *Menomini raising—transparent short vowels*

to:ckenɛw	[tʊ:ckɪnạw]	'he nudges him'
tu:ckenihɛw	[tʊ:ckɪnihạw]	'he nudges him in body/belly'
to:hkopɛ:hsen	[tʊ:hkʊpạ:hsɪn]	'he lies with buttocks spread'
tu:hkopiahnɛw	[tʊ:hkʊpiahnạw]	'he walks with buttocks spread'
pe:hcekona:h	[pɪ:hcɪkʊna:h]	'sacred bundle'
pi:hcekona:htian	[pi:hcɪkʊna:htian]	'sacred bundle'
we:to:hkatowak	[wɪ:tʊ:hkatʊwak]	'they work together'
wayi:tu:hkatitwaʔ	[wayi:tu:hkatitwaʔ]	'??they work together??'
se:kahe:ʔkow	[sɪ:kahɪ:ʔkʊw]	'he puts drops in his eyes'
nesi:kahi:qkim	[nɪsi:kahi:qkim]	'??I put drops in my eyes??'
we:nepow	[wɪ:nɪpʊw]	'he dirties his mouth'
newi:nepim	[nɪwi:nɪpim]	'I dirty his (my?) mouth'

nIw⌈i:⌉n⒤p⌈i⌉m

Low vowels are transparent, whether short or long. Examples of short vowels are included in (132) (in addition to one long vowel example). Additional long vowel examples are given in (133). The low vowel transparency is formally derived by adding a condition restricting Targets of the rule by the grounded condition, ATR/ LO: *If [+ ATR] then [− low]/not [+ low].*

(133) *Menomini raising—transparent long low vowels*

ce:pa:hkow	[cɪ:pa:hkʊw]	'he cooks'
neci:pa:hkim	[nɪci:pa:hkim]	'cook-NOM'
so:poma:hkow	[sʊ:pʊma:hkʊw]	'he makes sugar'
nesu:poma:hkim	[nɪsu:pʊma:hkim]	'sugar-maker'

nIs⟨u:⟩p(Ⓤ)m(Ⓐ:)hk⟨i⟩m

The data presented thus far motivate a rule that inserts the F-element [+ATR] from right to left subject to the presence of a contextual [+ATR] specification (the contextual restriction is discussed in more detail below). The Target of the rule has two conditions: (i) it must be long, (ii) it must be nonlow, that is, subject to ATR/LO.

(134) *Menomini [+ ATR] Spread*

Nondefault rule settings: + ATR; F-ELEMENT; RIGHT TO LEFT;
A-Conditions: ____ ⟨ + ATR & ATR/LO⟩;
T-Conditions: ATR/LO, μμ

Argument:	+ATR	Default	Nondefault
Parameters	Function	INSERT	
	Type		F-ELEMENT
	Direction		RIGHT TO LEFT
	Iteration	ITERATIVE	
Structure requirements	A-Structure	NONE	
	T-Structure	FREE	
Other requirements	A-Conditions	___<+ATR & ATR/LO>	
	T-Conditions	ATR/LO, μμ	

In terms of formal parameter settings, Menomini is entirely comparable to a case like Wolof (section 4.7.2.2). What makes Menomini rather special is the variety of transparent vowels in the language, directly attributable to the restrictions on the Target. The Target must be long, which renders short vowels transparent; the Target is subject to ATR/LO, which renders the low vowels transparent, whether short or long.

Unless one is willing to abandon the restrictive definition of Locality adopted in chapter 1, the only possible alternative to the rule-based approach proposed here is one that analyzes the transparency of Menomini along the lines of Kinande or Ngbaka (section 4.7.2.1). The assumption under such an account would be that spreading is actually of the canonical type, with even "transparent" vowels targeted by harmony. Under such an account, one would assume a realization algorithm for the transparent vowels whose effect would be to neutralize or remove the salience of the harmonic feature.

(135) *Sympathetic or antagonistic neutrality*

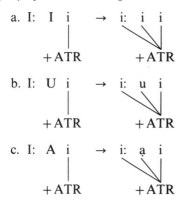

For a case like Menomini, such an account is completely untenable. The assignment of [+ATR] to the vowels *I*, *U*, *A* would produce the surface vowels [i, u, a̧], not the vowels [ɪ, ʊ, a] that are the appropriate realizations for such transparent vowels. Under the assumption that transparency was only apparent, the distinction between a short nonlow harmonic trigger ([i, u]) and a transparent vowel ([ɪ, ʊ]) would be completely lost.

One option might be considered in this regard, namely, to assume that the harmonic feature [+ATR] is *not* the feature that distinguishes the short, transparent vowels *ɪ*, *ʊ* from the harmonic triggers *i*, *u*. That is, the long vowels *i:*, *u:* would be distinguished from *ɪ:*, *ʊ:* by the feature [ATR], but the short vowels *i*, *u* would be distinguished from *ɪ*, *ʊ* by some other feature. For example, one might analyze the harmonic triggers *i*, *i:*, *u*, *u:* as high advanced vowels and the harmonic undergoers *ɪ:*, *ʊ:* as high retracted vowels, but the transparent vowels as mid vowels "e," "o." Under such an account, harmony would assign [+ATR] to *ɪ:*, *ʊ:*, correctly deriving [iː, uː]; harmony would also assign [+ATR] to the vowels "e" and "o" when they occur in a harmonic span, but the realization of these vowels would be comparable to "e" and "o" in nonharmonic spans. That is, neutralization would take place in these "mid" vowel sequences.

Such an approach is ruled out for both conceptual and empirical reasons. Conceptually, neither antagonistic neutrality nor sympathetic neutrality would be possible with mid vowels, because there are no grounded relations between [+ATR] and mid vowels that are either antagonistic or sympathetic. Empirically, such an approach fails because there are alternations in Menomini demonstrating that short ɪ, ʊ have feature specifications entirely comparable to their long counterparts.

Under a variety of prosodic conditions (which we do not discuss here), certain vowels lengthen while others shorten. The length alternations are independent of vowel quality. Of particular interest for our purposes, even the vowels ɪ and ʊ alternate for length. Crucial for the argument being made here, when a short and a long vowel alternate, the long version undergoes harmony if it is in the harmonic environment, regardless of whether the length is underlying or derived. The triplets in (136) show these three-way alternations.

(136) *Length and harmony triplets*

ɛːhkohnɛt	[ạːhkʊhnạt]	'as far as he walked'
ahkoːhnɛw	[ahkʊːhnạw]	'he walks so far'
ahkuːpiːkat	[ahkuːpiːkat]	'the water extends so far'
nekot	[nɪkʊt]	'one'
nekoːtɛːyaw	[nɪkʊːtạːyaw]	'one affair'
nekuːtikatɛːw	[nɪkuːtikatạw]	'one-legged being'
okemaːs	[ʊkɪmaːs]	'man's name: "Little Chief"'
okeːmaːhkatam	[ʊkɪːmaːhkatam]	'he is chief over it'
okiːmuːhkiw	[ʊkiːmuːhkiw]	'chieftainess'
omɛkeciw	[ʊmạːkɪciw]	'he has scars/scabs on his belly/body'
omɛkeːw	[ʊmạːkɪːw]	'he has a scab or a scar'
wɛːmekiːqkit	[wạːmɪkiːqkit]	'he has a scarred or scabby face'

Length and harmony alternations

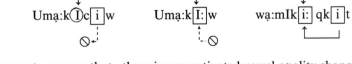

Unless one were to assume that otherwise unmotivated vowel quality changes accompany the changes in length (ɪ, ʊ vs. ɪː, ʊː), such examples clearly demonstrate that the harmonic alternant of the quality ɪ, ʊ is i, u.

In conclusion, the transparent vowels of Menomini must *not* be assigned the harmonic element during the course of spreading: transparency is not simply an apparent effect resulting from a configuration of canonical harmonic spreading. Since the Locality Condition rules out skipping such neutral elements, the only possibility within the parametric proposal elaborated here is to derive harmony by an iterative rule that inserts F-elements, subject to an appropriate contextual condition. Transparency, under this account, falls out from these rule settings.

4.7.3.3 Opacity: The Contextual Restriction One aspect of Menomini harmony has not yet been discussed: in all the harmony data seen so far, nonlow advanced vowels constitute the triggers of harmony; low advanced vowels do not trigger the rule.

(137) *Menomini raising—[ạ(:)] is not a trigger*

ku:hku:hsikamek	[ku:hku:hsikamɪk]	'pigsty'
ko:hko:hse:sɛh	[kʊ:hkʊ:hsɪ:sạh]	'little pig'
api:sa:kamiw	[api:sa:kamiw]	'it is a black liquid'
ape:saqnɛm	[apɪ:saqnạm]	'black dog'
ahpi:hciwɛw	[ahpi:hciwạw]	'he has so much muscular strength'
ahpe:htohnɛw	[ahpɪ:tʊhnạw]	'he walks so far/so fast'
masku:tiah	[masku:tiah]	'prairie-LOC'
masko:tɛ:w	[maskʊ:tạ:w]	'prairie'

As (137) shows, [ạ(:)] does not induce harmony. If harmony in this case resulted from a rule of spreading, this condition would be derived by imposing the grounded condition ATR/LO on the Argument of the rule: *If [+ATR] then not [+low].* But since the Argument is inserted, not spread, the same effect is achieved by imposing ATR/LO on the F-element constituting the contextual condition (represented in (134) by A-Condition: ____ ⟨+ATR & ATR/LO⟩.[71] That is, a [+ATR] specification triggers harmonic insertion, provided that it is *not* on a path to [+low]. As a result, [ạ] (long or short) is prevented from being an Argument of the rule.[72]

The fact that a [+ATR] specification on a low vowel does not suffice to initiate harmony in Menomini has an immediate implication concerning opacity. Not only is harmony not triggered by [ạ(:)], but [ạ(:)] also prevents further propagation of [+ATR], as shown in (138) and (139). In these lists, [ạ(:)] intervenes between a potential high vowel source and the target. No harmony takes place; the low [+ATR] vowel is opaque.

(138) *Menomini raising—opacity of short [ạ]*

so:wa:nɛhki:qsew	[sU:wa:nạhki:qsɪw]	'he has his hair blown back by the wind'
mo:nehpɛni:w	[mU:nɪhpạni:w]	'he digs potatoes'
we:qsakɛsewikamek	[wɪ:qsakạsɪwikamɪk]	'hospital'
pe:htɛhki:ʔtaw	[pɪ:htạhki:ʔtaw]	'he sticks his head in'

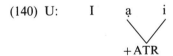

(139) *Menomini raising—opacity of long [ạ:]*

po:tawɛ:temi:w	[pU:tawạ:tɪmi:w]	'Potawatomi'
se:kenekɛwikamek	[sɪ:kɪnɪkạwikamɪk]	'saloon'
ke:skenɛ:hcihɛw	[kɪ:skɪnạ:hcihạw]	'he cuts off his fingers'

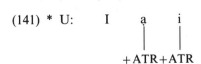

The account already developed for Menomini automatically accounts for this effect of opacity. The vowels of a form such as [mU:nɪhpạni:w] 'he digs potatoes' can be represented schematically as in (140).

(140)
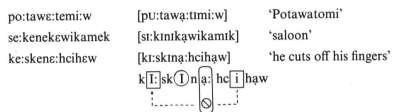

Application of harmony in such a case, if the rule were to apply, would cause the word-initial vowel to raise to [u:]. The case is of considerable interest because simple representational considerations of crossing could not account for the attested opacity since no association line would be crossed if the [+ATR] were to spread. The only way to derive opacity via crossed lines would be to posit a representation violating the OCP, as in (141).

(141) * U: I   ạ   i
               | |
             +ATR+ATR

In addition, since the vowel [I] has been clearly established to be transparent, opacity can in no way be attributed to that vowel. A crossed-line approach to opacity therefore fails.

Consider, however, the effect on (140) produced by the parametric rule in (134). The Argument of the rule is [+ATR]. This establishes the relevant edges. Given the two associations in (140), three domains for Argument/Target relations are established, illustrated in (142): (i) a domain from the right boundary to the first association, (142a), (ii) a domain from the first association to the second, (142b), and (iii) a domain from the second association to the left boundary, (142c).

(142) *Edges define domains*

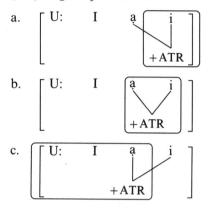

a.

b.

c.

In the first domain, there is no Free Target to which a rule could apply. In the second domain, the same is true. In the third domain, there is an eligible target (the initial [U:] is long, and rule application would obey the T-Condition ATR/LO), but the contextual [+ATR] necessary for rule application to be possible is on a path to [+low]. The A-Condition, ____ ⟨+ATR & ATR/LO⟩, is therefore violated and rule application is blocked.

The theory of parametric rules automatically derives the attested opacity in such a case.

It is worth pausing to explore the role of ATR/LO in Menomini, for it illustrates an important prediction of Grounding Theory. Three F-elements are posited for Menomini vowels: [+low], [+round], [+ATR]. Since [+ATR] freely crosscuts the system of vowels, grounded conditions governing the relation between [ATR] and the tongue body feature cannot hold of representations in general. Grounding Theory predicts, however, that if strong conditions do not hold of representations as a whole, the next most desirable grammar is one where relevant conditions hold of rules. For a rule whose Argument is [+ATR], the only relevant condition governing the relation between the tongue root and the tongue body is ATR/LO, and ATR/LO holds of both the Target and the contextual condition of Menomini harmony, the two places where it can hold.

4.7.3.4 Conclusion To summarize, in addition to its transparency effects, Menomini vowel harmony exhibits opacity effects. Crucially, opacity cannot be the result of language-internal F-element incompatibility: the opaque element *bears* the harmony Argument.[73] Moreover, Menomini clearly demonstrates a case of opacity that cannot be attributed to representational opacity; since no association lines would be crossed, spreading would create no violation of the No Crossing Constraint.[74] We conclude, therefore, that cases like Menomini must attribute opacity to rule effects.

The example is a rather striking illustration of the modular approach to phonological systems. The vowels are described by three statements, two concerning the features (Combinatorial Specification), and one concerning the prosodic structure of Menomini.

(143) *Menomini vowel system*

    a. The three basic vowels of Menomini form a triangular vowel space *I, A, U* (Combinatorial Specification).

    b. An active [+ATR] value crosscuts the system (Combinatorial Specification).

    c. Vowels may be either short or long.

The harmony rule also exploits the interaction of different phonological modules. The basic rule ("Insert [+ATR]") results in a rather complex array of transparent and opaque vowels owing to its three conditions.

(144) *Menomini "Insert [+ ATR]" rule conditions* (Parametric Rules)

    a. ____ [+ATR]

    b. Target is long.

    c. Both Target and Argument are subject to ATR/LO (Grounding).

The contextual condition in (144a) allows transparency. The prosodic and grounded conditions of (144b,c) define the transparent elements themselves. The application of this rule to representations including [+low, +ATR] vowels results in opacity.

To conclude, Combinatorial Specification, Grounding Theory, and Parametric Rule Theory each contribute by explaining some specific aspect(s) of this language. It is the combination of the effects of these contributions, along with the prosodic restrictions, that results in the exotic harmony pattern evidenced in Menomini.

4.7.4 Neutrality Effects: A Summary

In the preceding sections, we have addressed the question of whether opacity and transparency can be considered to result from a single rule type (spreading), operating on representations that differ with respect to whether the neutral element is present, and blocks spreading, or absent, and is ignored by spreading. We have argued against this position, concluding that transparency and opacity are both surface phenomena that may be derived from very different sources.

Representations can give rise to either transparency or opacity. As shown by the examination of Nyangumarta, transparency results if the harmonic F-element takes a prosodically defined class as its Target; elements outside the defined class can be transparent. Opacity results, on the other hand, when spreading would produce a violation of Locality, either by a direct Precedence effect (as in Yoruba) or by the effect of Precedence in ruling out crossed association lines (as in Kalenjin).

Grounding Theory can give rise to either opacity or the surface appearance of transparency. A case like opacity in Yoruba results because [−ATR] is phonologically incompatible with high vowels in the language: high vowels interrupt the progress of the rule. In other cases, a harmonic element spreads to an apparently neutral target, but a grounded effect masks the effect of harmony. In Kinande, for example, in addition to its combination with nonlow vowels, [+ATR] combines phonologically with [+low] vowels as a result of spreading. But because of the relative incompatibility of such a [+low, +ATR] combination, these vowels are realized with a salient [+ATR] component only when the advancement is enhanced by a vowel's being both long and L-toned. Elsewhere, the [+ATR] value of the low vowel appears not to be realized, an apparent transparency effect deriving directly from antagonistic neutrality. Sympathetic neutrality can also derive the appearance of transparency, as in Ngbaka, where high vowels end up redundantly assigned the value [+ATR], independently of whether or not they undergo harmony.

Finally, *rules* can give rise to either transparency or opacity. Transparency results when a rule inserts an F-element, with a contextual identity condition on the site of insertion, as in Menomini and Wolof. By contrast, opacity results with insertion when conditions are imposed on a contextual triggering element, as in Menomini; opacity also results when a spread rule restricts the Targets of a rule to a subset of the anchors for the harmonic F-element (as in Yawelmani Round Harmony).

The conclusion following from this demonstration is that neutrality is not a phenomenon that enjoys some formal status; it is a surface effect derived from a variety of sources, each source motivated independently of the neutrality effect that it contributes to.

4.8   Conclusion

Different levels of phonological representations encode different types of information: the underlying level, for example, necessarily encodes information crucial for lexical distinctions and access, information quite distinct from that required by the level that feeds into phonetic interpretation (see Mohanan 1986, Goldsmith 1989,

1990, Lakoff 1989). In order to satisfy the needs of the different levels, properties of the corresponding representations differ. Some means, then, is needed to systematically relate the representations appropriate for the different levels. Parametric Rule Theory articulates a specific hypothesis about the nature of such relations. The four rule parameters, Function, Type, Direction, and Iteration, combined with conditions on Argument and Target Structure, derive a typology of rule-governed relations, with variation in the possible relations identified by the range of possible values; further variation is derived from requirements imposed on Argument and Target.

Numerous other parameters are imaginable, as are other values for the parameters proposed here. In developing this particular set of parameters, we conjecture that the set of parameters used to characterize phonological relations mirrors properties of the representations themselves, while their values reflect the variation possible in each dimension (a type of formal "grounding"). Consider for example the Function parameter: the minimal difference possible between two related representations is that one contains information not present in the other, expressed by the values INSERT and DELETE. Within a standard autosegmental theory, the two types of information that combine to derive a phonological representation are F-ELEMENTs and PATHs, the two values for the Type parameter. The linear organization of representations derives the minimal values for Direction assumed here, while Iteration reflects the "one-versus-many" restriction that has been widely observed (particularly in the metrical literature) to hold of the counting predicate. Finally, in terms of the possibilities made available by autosegmental representations, the F-elements that form the substance of a representation may be free (not incorporated into a prosodic anchor) or linked (prosodically incorporated); A-Structure and T-Structure values focus on one of these two logical possibilities, FREE. In short, the proposed parameters manifest basic properties of representations; the values express minimal variation with respect to each such property. By restricting parameters to those "grounded" in formal properties of the representation, the theory predicts that no phenomena will be found requiring the addition of an ad hoc parameter that is motivated by construction-specific or phenomenon-specific properties, rather than by general properties of phonological representation.

Rules are defined by different parameter settings; parameter settings are established for *each* rule, not for the language as a whole. Internal to a language, a particular setting holding of one rule may not hold of any other rules in the language: Kinande tone rules require different Functions (one rule spreads, one delinks: section 4.2.4.1); Yoruba [−ATR] rules have different Types (one inserts an F-ELEMENT, the other a PATH: section 2.3.1); the two Maasai [+ATR] rules require opposite Directions (section 4.3.2); and the two Chaha rules, Palatalization and Labialization, differ in terms of Iteration, as do the two rules of Japanese mimetics (section 4.6.1). Limiting the domain of a parameter setting to a particular pattern of alternations contrasts with an approach where settings for a parameter are defined for the language as a whole.[75]

The four binary parameters predict 16 basic relations; our discussion has focused on the 8 involving the INSERT Function. These are motivated through consideration of a wide variety of surface effects, including straightforward association and spreading as well as polarity, dissimilation, exotic types of association, and neutrality effects: the model readily accounts for each. Note that the inclusion of even one additional binary parameter would double the number of basic relations; by limiting the set of parameters, a proliferation of unattested rule types is avoided. Conversely, elimination of any one of the four proposed parameters renders some class of phenomena anomalous, having no formal explanation. We conclude that given the range of phenomena considered in this chapter, there cannot be fewer parameters and more would be gratuitous.

In addition to its basic role in expressing relations between representations, the Parametric Rule Theory makes a variety of typological predictions.

A ranked typology of rules is predicted by the contrast between default and non-default values for the parameters: the more default settings a rule involves, the more common it should be cross-linguistically. Association/spreading is predicted to be the most common rule type of all: it involves exclusively default values. A-Conditions and T-Conditions contribute to this typology as well, with Grounding Theory also playing a role. The formally simplest and substantively most constrained grammar is one where grounded conditions hold of representations in general, and therefore hold of rules as a subcase. In languages where particular grounded conditions do not hold generally, rules with grounded conditions on Argument or Target should be common. Finally, rules with contextual conditions should be more rare than those without.

The default/nondefault values also predict a clear pattern with respect to learnability. A nondefault value is set only in the face of motivating evidence: the expectation is that the evidence would need to be robust in order to clearly establish the nondefault value. By contrast, phenomena that are not robustly attested in specific languages are predicted to be derivable from more general, less marked rules (as constrained by the Locality Condition and the Well-formedness Principle).

By way of illustration, consider the contrast between opacity in Yoruba, the expected case given a run-of-the-mill spreading rule and a class of non-Targets, and transparency in Wolof, accounted for by a contextual condition on the Argument with a nondefault Type setting. In Wolof, there is ample evidence for transparency: the harmonic span is typically polymoraic, affecting stems, suffixes, and even clitics— exactly the expectation given a marked set of rule parameter values. By contrast, the evidence for Yoruba opacity might be considered to be singularly lacking. The Yoruba harmony domain is limited to roots and stems: compounds, clitics, unassimilated loanwords do not undergo harmony (Fọlarin 1987, Akinlabi and Oyebade 1987, Archangeli and Pulleyblank 1989). Trimoraic roots and stems are relatively rare; rarer still are trimoraic roots/stems with two harmony domains separated by a high vowel. Yet the only disharmonic roots/stems are these two-domain forms. How then is the pattern of opacity acquired? Consider the types of properties concerning which there is ample evidence in Yoruba: (i) [−ATR] anchors only to nonhigh vowels (RTR/HI); (ii) harmony occurs in (bimoraic) roots/stems; (iii) harmony does not take place in longer forms. Since opacity is not robustly attested, why does it obtain?

We propose that such nonrobustly motivated patterns should fall out from general principles. Opacity in the Yoruba case is predicted by the interaction of the universal Locality Condition with two well-motivated properties specific to Yoruba, RTR/HI and the general [−ATR] Spread rule. Since representations are subject to Locality, the spreading of [−ATR] within a harmony domain is blocked by high vowels: opacity is the predicted interaction. The point here is analogous to observations made about phenomena like parasitic gaps in syntax (see Chomsky 1981, 1982, 1986): nonrobust phenomena result from the interaction of independently motivated properties of a system.

The focus of this chapter has been on properties of specific rules, arguing that an extremely limited class of rule parameters is sufficient to account for a wide range of natural language phenomena. As demonstrated in the case studies presented here, however, an understanding of phonological patterns often requires the postulation of several independent, though interacting, rules. In some cases, several rules govern the distribution of a single F-element in a specific language. The issues surrounding this kind of interaction of sets of rules are not the focus of this chapter, although the parametric approach serves to dramatize them. Nor are they an artifact of the model proposed here: consider, for instance, a case like Akan or Kinande, where a variety of apparently unrelated rules determine the distribution of [ATR] entirely independently of a parametric formulation. In the closing chapter, we turn to a discussion of the formal and substantive relations between such sets of rules, developing a proposal for evaluating interrule relations in terms of a hypothesis of optimization.

Chapter 5
Conclusion

Òkè méjì kì í bínú ẹni; bí a bá gun ọ̀kan, à sì máa rọ ọ̀kan. 'Two hills will not bedevil one; if one climbs one, one descends one.'
Oyekan Owomoyela, *A Kì í: Yorùbá Proscriptive and Prescriptive Proverbs*

5.1   Introduction

A basic premise of this study is that grammatical theory is profoundly modular (Chomsky 1981, 1986). We have argued that a complex range of phonological data is accounted for by the interaction of three largely independent submodules of the phonological component: Combinatorial Specification, Grounding Theory, and Parametric Rule Theory. We have attempted to motivate each of these phonological modules independently of the others, and to explore a range of effects that result from their interaction.

Following a rapidly growing body of literature started by works such as Clements 1985a and Sagey 1986, we assume that the raw material from which feature representations are constructed consists of a small number of binary features and an even smaller set of superordinate nodes that organize the features into larger natural classes. Feature representations result from the paradigmatic and syntagmatic combinations of such *F-elements*. Taking issue with earlier accounts of feature content such as Radical and Contrastive Underspecification, we argue for a theory of *Combinatorial Specification* in which the formal default is to allow for the free combination of F-elements. We demonstrate that languages may vary along several dimensions with respect to their combinatorial possibilities. First, inventories of active F-elements may differ. For example, vowels in Tiv derive from the combination of [+high], [+low], and [+round]; Ngbaka includes the same inventory but adds the F-element [+ATR]. Second, languages may differ with respect to whether sets of active F-elements may or may not cooccur in a path with each other. For example, Tiv allows the cooccurrence of [+low] and [+round]; Ngbaka disallows it. Finally, languages may differ with respect to whether F-elements are formally linked or free. For example, while features like [+high] and [+low] are underlyingly free in Tiv and Ngbaka, the same features are underlyingly linked in a language like Pulaar. A number of proposals in the literature have argued for limits on the degree of specification, proposing universal mechanisms for filling in unspecified values, and so on. We argue against such proposals, suggesting that the only formal constraints on F-element combination are Representational Simplicity and Recoverability.

Although completely free combination is attested in some cases, specific languages may impose substantive conditions on the class of allowable F-element cooccurrences. For example, Lango (see below) permits [+ATR] to combine with all 5 basic vowels {I, E, A, O, U}, deriving a 10-vowel system; other languages disallow certain combinations, for example, by restricting the presence of [+ATR] to nonlow vowels (e.g., Akan), or to high vowels (e.g., initial association in Kinande). We argue that the appropriate restrictions should be formalized as implicational *if-then* conditions whose substantive content is closely governed by phonetic properties, the *Grounding Hypothesis*. We propose that feature markedness is derived in large measure by the apparently trivial hypothesis that *the stronger a phonetic implication, the greater its role in phonological systems*. Implicational conditions constitute an integral part of a theory of markedness; they not only govern the composition of particular segmental inventories (such inventories derived by the combination of appropriate F-elements) but also determine the relative markedness of different inventories. The Grounding Conditions also play a central role in phonological rules, establishing the likelihood of both synchronic and diachronic changes.

While Grounding Theory substantively governs paradigmatic feature combinations and syntagmatic rule-governed alternations, we also suggest that alternations are narrowly constrained by a theory of formal rule parameters. The essence of the parametric proposal might be considered "micromodular": just as the interaction of different phonological modules produces a rich array of surface effects, so the interaction of a small set of rule parameters (Function, Type, Direction, Iteration) produces a rich array of rule-governed relations between representations. We argue that these four parameters exhaust the range of variation universally available, intrinsically restricting the range of possible grammars. Four binary parameters predict 16 formal rule types. Addition of any other binary parameter would immediately double the number of rule types. That is, increasing the number of parameters to five would imply 32 distinct rule types, and so on. While a set of 16 basic rules is plausibly motivated, a model with 32 or more basic rule types appears to predict a far wider range of distinct phenomena than is attested. Since adding parameters induces a rapid expansion of theoretically possible rule types, we suggest that the addition of further formal parameters should be undertaken only where there is robust empirical support, where the full range of additional rule types is attested: finding a *single* additional rule type is insufficient motivation for the introduction of a parameter whose effect would be the introduction of not 1 but *16* formal rule possibilities.

The set of four parameters proposed here, in conjunction with the representations provided by Combinatorial Specification and the substantive constraints imposed by Grounding Theory, is motivated through a consideration of robust processes of feature insertion and feature spreading. Yet these parameters are seen to also derive a range of more exotic phenomena involving complex association effects, OCP effects, neutrality effects, and so on. That broad empirical coverage requires no further formal properties supports the postulation of these particular parameters. Our working hypothesis is therefore that phenomena apparently requiring the postulation of additional parameters should be analyzed as involving rule types derived from the four basic ones. The introduction of further parameters appears to be empirically unmotivated and theoretically undesirable.

The preceding discussion assesses the extent to which the modular proposal of this book succeeds; we turn now to certain ways in which it fails. We distinguish three types of issues. First, there is a large class of phenomena that is essentially outside the scope of our proposals and about which few predictions are made. Second, there is a class of phenomena that falls within the scope of our proposals, but has not been investigated: numerous predictions are made about this class, but they have not been tested. Third, there is a class of phenomena that falls directly into the purview of our proposals, and that are not explained.

First, our attention has been limited to the phonological distribution of F-elements. We have largely ignored the role of the morphological and syntactic components and details of the phonetic component, as well as the role of prosodic structure in the phonological component. Moreover, we have ignored many questions that arise concerning the hierarchical organization of the F-elements we have examined. All of these areas are important, and all would interact in various ways with the subtheories of the phonological component with which we have dealt. However, our investigation does not explore these areas and so does not make direct predictions about the nature of the interaction with such aspects of grammatical theory.

Of the phenomena that fall squarely into the range of our proposals concerning F-element interaction, those considered here have been limited in several respects. We have considered vowels to the virtual exclusion of consonants, and even with regard to vowels, we have focused on a specific subset of the full range of vocalic features, paying particular attention to the tongue root. We have also limited the types of formal alternations under consideration to a subset of those expressible by the Function INSERT. Other alternations, such as deletion, reduction, coalescence, and so on, receive little or no attention (see section 4.5 for some related discussion). It is also the case that the language sample upon which our claims have been based is limited, both in terms of language families and in terms of typological and geographic distribution.

It is clear, therefore, that the various proposals made must be tested against a wider range of phenomena and for a wider class of languages. It is also clear that the model makes predictions that are readily testable with such an enlarged data base: attested syntagmatic and paradigmatic regularities among F-elements are expected to be expressible in terms of the restricted set of rule parameters proposed, and are expected to exhibit substantive restrictions of the types predicted by Grounding Theory.

One issue, however, lies squarely within the scope of the research presented here, and appears to pose serious problems for our formal proposals. The three basic components of the modular proposal of this book are F-elements, implicational conditions, and parametric rules. Combinatorial Specification governs the way in which F-elements combine; the Grounding Conditions govern the way in which implicational conditions are instantiated and combined. But whereas Parametric Rule Theory constitutes a theory of permissible *individual* rules, no account has been presented of the way in which rules *combine* within grammars. We have simply given lists of rules necessary for particular languages. "What constitutes a permissible rule inventory?" and "What constitutes permissible rule interactions?" are questions that have yet to be addressed.

In a variety of ways, the absence of an adequate theory of rule sets has serious repercussions. The fundamental concern is that the availability of a multiplicity of rules overgenerates by making possible a variety of unattested phonological systems, nullifying restrictions inherent in proposals such as the feature hierarchy and parametric rules.

For example, consider one effect involving the characterization of rules of autosegmental spreading. The Parametric Rule Theory sketched in chapter 4 allows only a single argument per rule. Within a hierarchical theory of feature structure, this means that single nodes are invariably the locus of feature assimilation processes. The explanatory advantage of such a theory could easily be lost if there were no limits on the nature of rule sets: cases of node spreading could be reinterpreted by a set of otherwise identical rules, each affecting a single feature. Under the hypothesis that there are no constraints on rule sets, *any* set of features could then serve as Arguments for such a set of rules, seriously undermining the restrictiveness of the parametric/feature-hierarchical theory.

A further prediction would be that a single language could contain any set of rules, even a set of several distinct rules affecting the distribution of a single F-element. Even with the restrictive class of rule types proposed here, the number of rule systems generated by the free combination of rules is infinite. Thus, despite a significant effort to limit the languages that are theoretically possible to a set that corresponds more closely to the set of attested languages, allowing multiple rules undermines this attempt.

An immediate response to this problem might be to limit the number of rules possible in a language, perhaps by limiting the number of rules allowed to determine the distribution of a single feature. One might propose, for example, that a language may have no more than one rule governing the distribution of any one F-element. But numerous counterexamples to such a proposal have been presented in the preceding chapters as well as elsewhere. In the analyses presented thus far, Akan and Kinande require at least four rules each affecting [ATR]; Lango, discussed later in this chapter, requires *six* rules affecting [ATR].

A related though somewhat different problem arises in a language like Yoruba (see Archangeli and Pulleyblank, to appear). Yoruba requires three rules to define the distribution of [ATR], [−ATR] Association, Spread, and Insertion: [−ATR] Association and [−ATR] Spread are *formally identical* (each involving the nondefault parameter settings −ATR, RIGHT TO LEFT), but [−ATR] Insertion crucially intervenes between the two (section 2.3.1). Under the view that grammars include lists of rules, the Yoruba example shows that such lists cannot even be restricted to distinct (nonidentical) rules. The necessity for multiple rules affecting a single Argument and for identical rules serves only to exacerbate the problem of rule inventories since it eliminates the most obvious way of controlling rule system overgeneration.

To embark on a comprehensive examination of issues concerning rule inventories would be to embark on an introductory chapter, not a concluding one. The issue seems sufficiently important, however, to warrant at least some preliminary discussion here. Following and extending ideas advanced by Prince (1990) and Prince and Smolensky (1991a,b), we suggest that the types of interrelations between rules and between rule interactions seen in languages like Kinande, Akan, and Yoruba are resolved in terms of "optimization": languages tend toward configurations that are optimal in terms of the formal and grounding factors discussed in this book.[1]

We develop the optimization hypothesis by examining the distribution of [ATR] in Lango, a language that requires six rules to characterize [ATR] distribution (whether the rules are formulated parametrically or in standard graphic autosegmental fashion). The general conclusions that we draw from this preliminary study of rule optimization are (i) that the modular approach to phonological systems taken here makes optimization of these systems straightforward, and (ii) that optimization of such systems may answer the once unaskable question, What constitutes a possible rule inventory?

5.2 [ATR] in Lango

Lango, a Nilotic language spoken in Uganda (Woock and Noonan 1979), places no constraints on the paradigmatic combination of [ATR] with other vocalic features. The language exhibits the full range of combinatorial possibilities predicted by the unconstrained interaction of an [ATR] feature with a basic 5-vowel system: from the set {I, E, A, O, U}, 10 surface vowels are derived: [i, ɪ, e, ɛ, ə, a, ɔ, o, ʊ, u].

Despite this freedom in F-element combination, rules determining the syntagmatic pattern of [ATR] invoke conditions on Argument and/or Target. Thus, although the language does not generally restrict F-element combinations, restrictions are nonetheless central to the distribution of [ATR], and every nonprosodic condition is a grounded condition as predicted by Grounding Theory.

There are at least six rules spreading [ATR] in Lango. Formally, these rules are readily expressible in parametric terms, each involving the noniterative (see Poser 1982) insertion of a path, with differences lying in direction of application. Other differences are expressed by grounded conditions or by a prosodic condition involving the distance possible between Argument and Target (whether the rule is able to cross two consonants (skipping a coda mora), or only one consonant (applying only to adjacent moras)).

In the ensuing discussion, we first lay out the six rules required and then consider their interaction within an optimization framework.

5.2.1 Two Progressive Harmony Rules

The forms in (1) demonstrate that the first person singular possessive suffix has two forms, advanced -ə́ and retracted -á. The choice of surface forms depends on the quality of the stem vowel: the suffix is [+ATR] ([ə]) if the stem vowel is [+ATR] ([i, e, ə, o, u]); otherwise, if the stem vowel is [−ATR] ([ɪ, ɛ, a, ɔ, ʊ), the suffix vowel surfaces as the [−ATR] [a].

(1) *Progressive harmony across nongeminate consonants*

[i]	cín	'hand'	cíŋə́	'my hand'
[e]	ŋèt	'side'	ŋètə́	'my side'
[ə]	(no example in Woock and Noonan)			
[o]	wót	'son'	wódə́	'my son'
[u]	ŋùt	'neck'	ŋùtə́	'my neck'
[ɪ]	yíb	'tail'	yíbá	'my tail'
[ɛ]	lɛ́b	'tongue'	lɛ́bá	'my tongue'
[a]	wàŋ	'eye'	wàŋá	'my eye'
[ɔ]	bwɔ́m	'wing'	bwɔ́má	'my wing'
[ʊ]	(no example in Woock and Noonan)			

This pattern is straightforwardly accounted for by assuming (i) that the suffix is underlyingly unspecified for [ATR] (or is underlyingly [−ATR]) in conjunction with (ii) a rule of rightward [+ATR] spreading. Where spreading does not take place, vowels surface with their [−ATR] form, this being either the manifestation of underlying representation or the result of default specification, an issue that is orthogonal to our central concerns here.

The data in (2) demonstrate that in certain cases, the triggers of rightward [+ATR] spreading are restricted to the high vowels /i/ and /u/, an instance of the grounded ATR/HI Condition imposed on the Argument of spreading. This restriction is imposed when two consonants separate the Argument from the Target, seen, for example, when comparing *wódǝ́* 'my son' from (1) with *dòkká* 'my cattle' from (2).

(2) *Progressive harmony across geminates: From high vowels only*

[i]	píg	'juice'	píggǝ́	'my juice'
[u]	òpúk	'cat'	òpúkkǝ́	'my cat'
[e]	gwèn	'chickens'	gwènná	'my chickens'
[ǝ]	ñǝ̀ŋ	'crocodile'	ñǝ̀ŋŋá	'my crocodile'
[o]	dòk	'cattle'	dòkká	'my cattle'
[ɪ]	àtín	'child'	àtínná	'my child'
[ɛ]	bèl	'wheat'	bèllá	'my wheat'
[a]	càl	'picture'	càllá	'my picture'
[ɔ]	kɔ̀m	'chair'	kɔ̀mmá	'my chair'
[ʊ]	lʊ̀t	'stick'	lʊ̀ttá	'my stick'

Where there is only one intervocalic consonant, [+ATR] spreads from a stem vowel of any height rightward (1); where there are two consonants, the source of harmony must be [+high] (2). That is, spreading in the latter case is subject to ATR/HI: [+ATR] is a legitimate Argument only where it is in a path with [+high].

We express the difference between spreading across one consonant and spreading across two in terms of prosodic structure. Where spreading progresses from syllable head to syllable head (2), an onset alone or both an onset and a coda may intervene. By contrast, where spreading progresses from mora to mora (1), coda consonants, being moraic, block it. The two rules are schematized in (3a,b) and formalized in (4) and (5), respectively.[2]

(3) *Progressive Harmony—schematic*

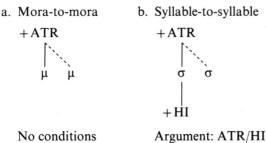

    a. Mora-to-mora   b. Syllable-to-syllable

    No conditions   Argument: ATR/HI

(4) *Lango Progressive [+ ATR]/µ Spread*

Nondefault rule settings: + ATR; NONITERATIVE; T-Condition: µ-µ

Argument:	+ATR	Default	Nondefault
Parameters	Function	INSERT	
	Type	PATH	
	Direction	LEFT TO RIGHT	
	Iteration		NONITERATIVE
Structure requirements	A-Structure	NONE	
	T-Structure	FREE	
Other requirements	A-Conditions		
	T-Conditions	µ–µ	

(5) *Lango Progressive ATR/HI Spread*

Nondefault rule settings: + ATR; NONITERATIVE; A-Condition: ATR/HI;
T-Condition: σ-σ

Argument:	+ATR	Default	Nondefault
Parameters	Function	INSERT	
	Type	PATH	
	Direction	LEFT TO RIGHT	
	Iteration		NONITERATIVE
Structure requirements	A-Structure	NONE	
	T-Structure	FREE	
Other requirements	A-Conditions	ATR/HI	
	T-Conditions	σ–σ	

These two rules are readily expressed in the parametric model; further, the parametric model singles out the two factors by which the rules differ: (i) whether or not ATR/HI is imposed on the Argument and (ii) whether spreading takes place between syllable heads or between moras.

It would of course be possible to collapse the graphic rules of (3a,b) or the parametric rules of (4) and (5) into a single statement were *SPE*-style angled brackets permitted in the theory; this is also true of the three regressive harmony rules discussed in the next section. Angled brackets are a device used to show common properties of two (or more) rules through what is *not* enclosed by the angled brackets; they also show differences between the rules by what *is* enclosed by the brackets. Finally, through an implicational statement relating two or more sets of angled brackets, they show the relation between these differences. The insight behind angled brackets is that in some cases a group of rules share an essential property, despite variation in the details. The challenge raised by this observation (and not met by the device of angled brackets) is to limit the range of these relations, both within and among rules: as sketched in section 5.3, optimization appears to answer this challenge.

5.2.2 Three Regressive Harmony Rules

There are three regressive harmony rules that also spread [+ATR], and all three require that the Argument be in a path with [+high]. That is, all three invoke the ATR/HI Condition. In addition, one rule invokes ATR/HI on the Target of harmony, and one rule requires that the Argument also be [−back]; that is, the rule invokes the grounded ATR/BK Condition (*If [+ATR] then [−back]/not [+back]*).[3] As with the progressive harmony rules, the parametric formulation emphasizes both the similarities and the differences between the rules, with differences centering on the particular set of grounded conditions imposed on the Argument and the Target.

The first of the regressive harmony rules is illustrated in (6): [+ATR] spreads leftward from the high vowel of a suffix like *-wu* '2nd person', affecting both high and nonhigh targets. This spreading crosses a single consonant.[4]

(6) *Regressive harmony: VC[+HI]*

[ɪ]	pɪ́	'for'	pìwú	'for you'
[ɛ]	lɛ̀	'axe'	lèwú	'your axe'
[ɔ]	jɔ̀	'people'	jòwú	'your people'

In contrast, the infinitive suffix *-(C)o*, also [+ATR], has a mid vowel rather than a high vowel: as the data in (7) show, this suffix does not trigger regressive harmony regardless of the number of consonants involved (cf. *ɪmmo* 'to visit', *wayo* 'to pull').

(7) *Absence of regressive harmony from a nonhigh Argument*

[i]	riŋŋo	'to run'
[e]	ketto	'to put'
[ə]	(no example in Woock and Noonan)	
[o]	pwoddo	'to beat'
[u]	rucco	'to entangle'
[ɪ]	lɪmmo	'to visit'
[ɛ]	nɛnno	'to see'
[a]	wayo	'to pull'

Comparing (6) with (7) argues that regressive harmony triggered by back vowels takes place only from high vowels.

As the next data set demonstrates, the Argument for regressive harmony is not restricted to high back vowels. In (8), the second person suffix -*(C)i* induces harmony toward the left. In this case, harmony is possible whether one consonant or two intervenes: *yíbí* 'your tail', *dèkkí* 'your stew'.

(8) *Regressive harmony: VC(C)i*

[i]	píg	'soup, juice'	píggí	'your juice'
[e]	ém	'thigh'	émí	'your thigh'
[ə]	ñɘ̀ŋ	'crocodile'	ñɘ̀ŋŋí	'your crocodile'
[o]	dòk	'cattle'	dòkkí	'your cattle'
[u]	búk	'book'	búkkí	'your book'
[ɪ]	yíb	'tail'	yíbí	'your tail'
[ɛ]	dɛ̀k	'stew'	dɛ̀kkí	'your stew'
[a]	màc	'fire'	mɘ̀ccí	'your fire'
[ɔ]	kɔ̀m	'chair'	kòmmí	'your chair'
[ʊ]	lùt	'stick'	lùttí	'your stick'

Interestingly, spreading from /u/ also applies across two consonants, but *only* if the target is also [+high], as illustrated in (9). Where the vowel that could undergo harmony is nonhigh, harmony does not take effect.

(9) *Regressive harmony: VCC[+HI]*

[ɪ]	nìŋ	'name'	nìŋwú	'your name'
[ʊ]	lùt	'stick'	lùtwú	'your stick'
[ɛ]	dɛ̀k	'stew'	dɛ̀kwú	'your stew'
[a]	kàl	'millet'	kàlwú	'your millet'
[ɔ]	kɔ̀m	'chair'	kɔ̀mwú	'your chair'

In summary, the process of regressive harmony in Lango occurs in three environments (10a–c). First, spreading takes place in any case where the [+ATR] Argument is in a path with [+high] and the Target is separated from the Argument by no more than a single consonant (data in (6)). If two consonants intervene between the Argument and the Target, then it continues to be the case that the source of [+ATR] must be high; in addition, either the Target must be [+high] (data in (9)), or else the Argument must be [−back] (data in (8)). The three rules are formalized in (11)–(13).

(10) *Regressive Harmony—schematic*

a. Mora-to-mora	b. HI-to-HI	c. HI-FRONT
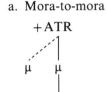	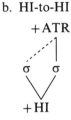	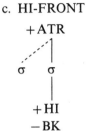
Argument: ATR/HI	Argument: ATR/HI	Argument: ATR/HI
	Target: ATR/HI	Argument: ATR/BK

(11) *Lango Regressive μ-μ Spread*

Nondefault rule settings: +ATR; RIGHT TO LEFT; NONITERATIVE;
                            A-Condition: ATR/HI; T-Condition: μ-μ

Argument:	+ATR	Default	Nondefault
Parameters	Function	INSERT	
	Type	PATH	
	Direction		RIGHT TO LEFT
	Iteration		NONITERATIVE
Structure requirements	A-Structure	NONE	
	T-Structure	FREE	
Other requirements	A-Conditions	ATR/HI	
	T-Conditions	μ-μ	

(12) *Lango Regressive High-High Spread*

Nondefault rule settings: +ATR; RIGHT TO LEFT; NONITERATIVE;
A-Condition: ATR/HI; T-Conditions: ATR/HI, σ-σ

Argument:	+ATR	Default	Nondefault
Parameters	Function	INSERT	
	Type	PATH	
	Direction		RIGHT TO LEFT
	Iteration		NONITERATIVE
Structure requirements	A-Structure	NONE	
	T-Structure	FREE	
Other requirements	A-Conditions	ATR/HI	
	T-Conditions	ATR/HI ; σ–σ	

(13) *Lango Regressive High Front Spread*

Nondefault rule settings: +ATR; RIGHT TO LEFT; NONITERATIVE;
A-Conditions: ATR/HI & ATR/BK;
T-Conditions: σ-σ

Argument:	+ATR	Default	Nondefault
Parameters	Function	INSERT	
	Type	PATH	
	Direction		RIGHT TO LEFT
	Iteration		NONITERATIVE
Structure requirements	A-Structure	NONE	
	T-Structure	FREE	
Other requirements	A-Conditions	ATR/HI & ATR/BK	
	T-Conditions	σ–σ	

Like the rules of progressive spreading, the regressive rules are strikingly similar. Moreover, like the progressive rules, the regressive rules distinguish whether the process applies between syllable heads or only between moras, and individual rules are distinguished by the particular grounded conditions that are imposed. Unlike the progressive rules, some of the regressive rules have grounded Target conditions imposed on them in addition to the type of Argument conditions previously encountered.[5]

5.2.3 Progressive [−ATR] Spread

At this point, we have exemplified five of the six rules defining the distribution of [ATR] in Lango. The remaining rule involves the progressive spread of [−ATR], rather than [+ATR]. The effect of this rule is illustrated in (14), data left over from the infinitive paradigm given in (7). The infinitive suffix -(C)o surfaces with a [−ATR] vowel provided that the vowel of the stem is back and [−ATR].

(14) *Progressive [−ATR] harmony*

[ɔ]	lwɔkkɔ	'to wash'
[ʊ]	lʊbbɔ	'to follow'

The data from (7) are repeated in (15) for comparison. In these forms, which do not have back [−ATR] vowels in their stems, there is no progressive [−ATR] harmony. The fact that /a/ does not trigger left-to-right spreading of [−ATR] in *wayo* indicates that /a/ is specified [+low], but not [+back], in accord with Representational Simplicity, and is comparable to the behavior of Haya low vowels with respect to [−high] spreading. (See sections 2.3.2 and 2.4.)

(15) *Absence of progressive [−ATR] harmony from a nonback Argument*

[i]	riŋŋo	'to run'
[e]	ketto	'to put'
[ə]	(no example in Woock and Noonan)	
[o]	pwoddo	'to beat'
[u]	rucco	'to entangle'
[ɪ]	lɪmmo	'to visit'
[ɛ]	nɛnno	'to see'
[a]	wayo	'to pull'

The rule of Progressive [−ATR] Spread is schematized in (16), with the parametric formalization in (17).[6]

(16) *Progressive [−ATR] Harmony—schematic*

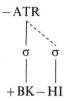

Argument: RTR/BK
Target: RTR/HI

(17) *Lango Progressive [−ATR] Spread*

Nondefault rule settings: −ATR; NONITERATIVE; A-Condition:
RTR/BK; T-Conditions: RTR/HI; σ-σ

Argument:	−ATR	Default	Nondefault
Parameters	Function	INSERT	
	Type	PATH	
	Direction	LEFT TO RIGHT	
	Iteration		NONITERATIVE
Structure requirements	A-Structure	NONE	
	T-Structure		NONE
Other requirements	A-Conditions	RTR/BK	
	T-Conditions	RTR/HI; σ–σ	

An interesting implication of the rule of [−ATR] Spread is the necessity of an active [−ATR] F-element. This may be the result of [−ATR] being present in underlying representations or of its being inserted at some point during the derivation. Either analysis is theoretically possible under the model presented here, and we know of no empirical arguments for choosing between the two options.

5.2.4 Summary

As shown here, Lango allows the feature [ATR] to combine freely with its otherwise standard five-vowel inventory, {I, E, A, O, U}. There are no general conditions restricting the distribution of this feature. In spite of such combinatorial freedom, however, all but one of the six rules defining the distribution of [ATR] make use of grounded conditions, restricting either the Argument or both the Target and the Argument. But it is not simply the role of grounded conditions that varies in these rules: rules also differ by their direction of application (left to right or right to left), their Arguments ([+ATR] or [−ATR]), and their relevant prosodic Targets (μ-μ or σ-σ). The chart in (18) shows the parameters by which the six rules vary.

(18) *Variation in the Lango rules*

Rule #	(4)	(5)	(11)	(12)	(13)	(17)
Argument	+ATR	+ATR	+ATR	+ATR	+ATR	−ATR
A-Conditions		ATR/HI	ATR/HI	ATR/HI	ATR/HI & BK	RTR/BK
T-Conditions				ATR/HI		RTR/HI
Direction	L-R	L-R	R-L	R-L	R-L	L-R
Prosodic Targets	μ-μ	σ-σ	μ-μ	σ-σ	σ-σ	σ-σ

If the theory is not constrained in some way, the requirements that Lango appears to make on a theory of rule interaction set the stage for an abuse of derivational power. Although the components are individually straightforward, their combined use seems unwarrantably rich. Free combination of F-elements, in this case [±ATR], is the unmarked option given Combinatorial Specification; each of the conditions placed on the various rules is a grounded condition as required by Grounding Theory; individually, the rules are standard rules of types derived by simple settings of Parametric Rule Theory.[7] But to allow six rules to govern the distribution of a single feature opens the door to potentially infinite sets of arbitrary rule combinations. Lango dramatizes the question of whether every imaginable set of rules constitutes a well-formed rule system. That is, given that theories must encompass the range of rules found in Lango, does it follow that theories must allow every logically possible rule system to exist? Are rule inventories constrained in some principled manner? We turn to these issues in the next section, beginning with the fundamental question, "What is the relation between rules and representations?"

5.3 Optimality

Since *SPE*, it is standard to think in terms of phonological *derivations*. A surface phonological representation is derived by successively applying a set of rules to an initial, underlying representation. Within such an approach, there are as many representations in a phonological derivation as there are applicable phonological rules. The notion of Optimality (see Smolensky 1986, Prince and Smolensky 1991a,b) presents a rather different picture. Certain levels of representation are defined largely or exclusively on morphosyntactic grounds (see Lakoff 1989, Goldsmith 1989, 1990).

This extremely limited set of representations is hypothesized to constitute the entire
set of phonological representations. Rules in this framework define well-formed relations between such representations. For example, a simple rule spreading α from left
to right would define (19b) as a well-formed surface form relating to the underlying
form (19a).

(19) a.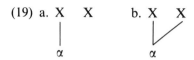

The default relation between two representations is *identity*; that is, the representations are identical to each other. Such identity makes each representation completely
recoverable from the other. In cases of nonidentity, the parametric approach to rules
given in chapter 4 defines a certain class of formal interrelations between levels as well
formed, namely, those expressible in terms of values for the four formal parameters
Function, Type, Direction, and Iteration, qualified in appropriate cases by grounded
conditions.

Optimality introduces a means of evaluating these relations: evaluation of the
parametric and grounding factors establishes some relations as "good" or "optimal"
and others as "bad" or "nonoptimal." The *optimization* hypothesis is that grammars
prefer relations between representations that are defined in formal and grounded
terms as optimal: synchronic and diachronic processes should gravitate toward optimal relations. Such evaluation, as we argue below, is composite, not holistic: a relation may be optimal with respect to one factor and nonoptimal with respect to
another. In order to optimize a particular set of relations, therefore, it is necessary
first to evaluate the factors that comprise those relations. We turn to this now.

In chapter 4, we suggested that every parameter has a default setting. Viewed
from the perspective of Optimality, a rule defined entirely by default parameter settings is formally optimal; similarly, a rule defined entirely by marked settings expresses the worst of the allowable relations between representations. Concretely, the
parametric rule proposal defines rules of iterative left-to-right association and spreading as optimal (INSERT/PATH/LEFT-TO-RIGHT/ITERATIVE) while a noniterative right-to-left process of deletion (DELETE/F-ELEMENT/RIGHT-TO-LEFT/
NONITERATIVE) would be nonoptimal. Other possible rules—for instance, right-
to-left association/spreading or noniterative association/spreading—fall somewhere
between these two extremes because their formal expression combines optimal and
nonoptimal factors.

The evaluation of the parametric values of a rule is supplemented by evaluation of
the relevant grounded conditions. Rule-governed relations resulting from or in representations with sympathetic feature combinations are optimal; these are created by

invoking a grounded condition on Argument or Target. Cases allowing representations with antagonistic feature combinations are nonoptimal; this will arise if no grounded conditions are invoked. The relative strengths of different grounded conditions are also relevant. For example, a sympathetic relation governed by a strong condition (e.g., [−ATR, +low] as governed by RTR/LO) is better than a sympathetic relation governed by a weak condition (e.g., [−ATR, +back] as governed by RTR/BK).

In the following discussion, we suggest that a fundamental trade-off between parametric and grounded optimization scales governs the pattern of rules observed.

(20) *Feature Optimality Hypothesis*

   Parametric factors and grounding factors offset each other.

In Lango, where parametric factors are optimal, harmony applies in a manner that is almost completely independent of the featural content of the representation. As parametric factors become less optimal, increasingly good substantive feature combinations are required to make rule application possible.

5.3.1 Lango Optimization

The six rules of Lango motivated in section 5.2 vary along three formal parameters, and variously invoke four different grounded conditions. In terms of formal parameters, *Arguments* range over [+ATR] and [−ATR], *Direction* ranges over left to right and right to left, and *Prosodic Target* ranges over application from mora to mora and from syllable to syllable. With respect to substantive implicational conditions, tongue root movement relates both to height (*ATR/HI*; *RTR/HI*) and to backness (*ATR/BK*; *RTR/BK*), restricting the *Argument* and/or *Target*. Except for the Prosodic Target, variation between mora-to-mora and syllable-to-syllable application, these components have already been ranked in previous chapters. We briefly review their rankings here and propose a ranking for Prosodic Target.

[ATR] Markedness (chapter 3, (21)) states that [+ATR] is the preferred active [ATR] value: thus, [+ATR] is stronger than [−ATR] (21a-1). In chapter 4, we proposed that the default value for Direction is toward the right; thus, left-to-right is better than right-to-left (21a-2). The final parametric factor is the specification of Prosodic Target. We suggest that rule application is stronger in smaller domains (see Mohanan 1988, to appear). Hence, application between moras is stronger than application between syllable heads: application between moras can cross at most an onset while application between syllable heads crosses both onsets and codas. In order to generate a scale combining the parametric factors, it is also necessary to establish the relative strengths of the different formal parameters with respect to each other. In this regard, we assume here that Argument is stronger than Direction, and Direction is stronger than Prosodic Target, as shown by the order "1-2-3" in (21a).

The grounding factors are ranked in three ways. First, following the Grounding Conditions, it is better for active conditions to hold than to not hold. Thus, with each condition that is relevant in Lango, it is better for that condition to hold, shown in (21b-1,2).[8] Second, ATR × HI is stronger than ATR × BK, again following findings in chapter 3: the phonological correlation between [ATR] and [high] is stronger than the phonological correlation between [ATR] and [back]. This ranking is shown in (21b) by the order "1-2."

(21) *Lango [ATR] distribution factors*

    a. Parametric factors

        1. Argument   +ATR ≫ −ATR
        2. Direction   L-R ≫ R-L
        3. Prosodic Target   μ-to-μ ≫ σ-to-σ

    b. Grounding factors

        1. Grounding 1   ATR × HI ≫ no such condition
        2. Grounding 2   ATR × BK ≫ no such condition
        3. Grounding 3   Conditions on Argument ≫ conditions on Target

Finally, again following the Grounding Hypothesis, it is better for active conditions to hold more generally in a language. A condition holding of the Argument may hold of both input and output representations, while a condition holding of the Target holds only of output representations, not of the input. Thus, grounded conditions on the Argument hold more generally than conditions on a Target: we conclude that conditions limiting the Argument are preferred over conditions limiting the Target, as shown in Grounding 3 (21b-3).

Inspecting the Lango rules in terms of the factors summarized in (21) reveals the trade-off between parametric and grounding strengths. To illustrate this, we show how these factors partition the six rules into sets, turning first to the parametric factors.

5.3.1.1 Parametric Factors in Lango Consider first the parametric factor *Argument*. The rules of Lango are differentiated in that one rule manipulates [−ATR] while the rest manipulate [+ATR]. Given [ATR] Markedness, the [+ATR] set is defined as stronger than the [−ATR] set. That is, rules manipulating [+ATR] are higher on the scale of optimality than a rule manipulating [−ATR], as shown in (22).

(22) *Partition by Argument*

OPTIMAL	NONOPTIMAL
+ATR	−ATR
all other rules	−ATR σ σ +BK −HI

These two sets are divided internally by the second factor, Direction. In the processes involving [+ATR], two rules apply from left to right and three from right to left; the Direction parameter ranks the two rules applying from left to right as more optimal. In the [−ATR] set, there is only left-to-right application: the relatively nonoptimal process spreading [−ATR] takes place only in the stronger direction, left to right. That is, in Lango, the parametric configuration giving right-to-left application with a [−ATR] Argument is simply too weak and never takes place. This partition is represented in (23).

(23) *Partition by Argument and Direction*

OPTIMAL			NONOPTIMAL
+ATR		−ATR	
L-R	R-L	L-R	R-L
+ATR μ μ	+ATR μ μ | +HI	−ATR σ σ | +BK −HI	no such rules
+ATR σ σ | +HI	+ATR σ σ | +HI		
	+ATR σ σ | +HI −BK		

The scale in (23), as well as that in (28) and the grounding scales discussed in section 5.3.1.2, constitutes a *lexicographic product* (Prince and Smolensky 1991a): weaker factors internally partition the divisions derived from stronger factors.[9] Prince and Smolensky explore the hypothesis that phonological phenomena can be accounted for by multiplying all relevant factors into a single lexicographic product and determining a cutoff point after which the combination of factors is simply too weak for an effect to be seen in the language, the point where the *identity* relation is better than a relation defined by rule application.

(24) *Lexicographic Optimization* (Prince and Smolensky 1991a)

    a. Create a lexicographic product from the relevant factors.

    b. Determine the cutoff relevant for the language.

Relevance is central. Lexicographic products only make plausible claims for individual cases when scales are composed specifically of the factors relevant for the language in question: if a factor is irrelevant in a language, it does not appear in a scale.[10]

The final parametric factor is Prosodic Target. Within the sets defined by Argument and Direction, Prosodic Target creates a further subclassification, with mora-to-mora rules preferred over syllable-to-syllable rules. With regard to this factor, both left-to-right and right-to-left rules affecting [+ATR] are subclassified so as to prefer left-to-right spreading. In the [−ATR] set, the rule applies from syllable to syllable (but see below).[11]

(25) *Partition by Argument, Direction, and Prosodic Target*

At first glance, the [−ATR] rule might seem to pose something of a problem for the hypothesis that the lexicographic product creates a scale with a single cutoff. Since mora-to-mora spreading is more highly valued than syllable-to-syllable spreading, the expected pattern for a single rule of [−ATR] spreading would be from mora to mora, not from syllable to syllable. However, application from syllable to syllable subsumes mora-to-mora spreading between syllables, and in Lango, all mora-to-mora spreading is across syllable boundaries. In the absence of some additional distinction, such as the grounded differences observed in the left-to-right [+ATR] rules, positing a left-to-right syllable-to-syllable rule is equivalent to positing two otherwise identical left-to-right rules, one applying from mora to mora and the other from syllable to syllable. That is, the formulation of this rule as applying specifically from syllable to syllable (as in (16)) is an artifact of traditional graphic manners of representing rules. Since mora-to-mora and syllable-to-syllable Prosodic Target specifications are both strong enough to induce the left-to-right spreading of [−ATR], they are both appropriately included in the optimization scale, as in (25).

The parametric factors divide the rules into five ranked sets. The optimal class contains the best values for each factor: [+ATR], left to right, and mora to mora. As the scale progresses toward the nonoptimal end, the combinations worsen: the second class involves left-to-right syllable-to-syllable spreading, then right-to-left mora-to-mora, and so on. Toward the nonoptimal end of the scale, we find the weakest parametric configuration that permits rule application in Lango: [−ATR] spreading left to right. Right-to-left spreading of [−ATR] is so weak that the *identity* relation (the absence of any rule application) is preferred in Lango.

Two important questions remain to be answered. First, it must be explained why particular grounded conditions are imposed on particular parametric configurations. Why, for example, is the condition that the Target be [+high] imposed on *right-to-left* mora-to-mora spreading but not on *left-to-right* mora-to-mora spreading? Second, it must be determined whether the type of ranking proposed above has any predictive power. Given some set of factors, can we predict whether a particular set of rules is possible or impossible? Central to an understanding of these issues is the way that the grounding factors combine with the parametric ones: the six rules observed in Lango all correlate *weakness* in the parametric scale with *strength* in the grounding scale and vice versa. To elucidate this trade-off, we turn to a discussion of the grounding scale.

5.3.1.2 Grounding Factors in Lango Two grounded relations are relevant in Lango, ATR × HI and ATR × BK. Under the Grounding Hypothesis, the imposition of more conditions is better than the imposition of fewer conditions, and ATR × HI is stronger than ATR × BK, giving rise to the scale in (26) (see Prince 1990 on optimal foot types).

(26) ATR × HI   ≫   ATR × HI   ≫   ATR × BK   ≫   no conditions
     ATR × BK
          1   2   3   4

Inspection of the rules in Lango establishes the cutoff on this scale between factor 2, ATR × HI, and factor 3, ATR × BK: ATR × BK alone is never sufficient to induce rule application. Since any factor weaker than ATR × HI is never strong enough to establish rule application in Lango, step 3 is irrelevant and therefore disregarded in subsequent lexicographic products.

Since no grounded conditions hold of left-to-right, mora-to-mora spreading, it might appear that we have excised an intermediate step from the scale in (26), leaving "$1 \gg 2 \gg 4$," rather than establish a cutoff point between factors $\{1,2\}$ and factors $\{3,4\}$. Such excision would run contrary to Lexicographic Optimization (24) since if the cutoff in (26) falls between steps 2 and 3, then step 4, too, should not be relevant. However, in a grounding scale, "no conditions hold" (step 4) has special status because a mapping between a parametric factor and "no conditions hold" is equivalent to the complete absence of a mapping between a parametric combination and the grounding scale. Such a parametric combination is strong enough in its own right to hold without any help from the grounding scale. The effect is that the "no conditions hold" factor appears to be boosted up in the scale whenever there is a reduction in the overall length of a grounding scale.

We turn now to the Lexicographic Optimization for grounding factors in Lango, starting with ATR × HI, the strongest relevant grounded condition.

One Lango rule does not invoke the ATR × HI condition; the other five do. The ATR × HI Condition manifests itself in a manner appropriate to the Argument of the rule concerned. Four of the rules governed by ATR × HI take [+ATR] as their argument; in such cases, ATR/HI establishes a preference for the sympathetic relation observed between tongue root advancement and tongue body raising. The fifth rule governed by ATR × HI takes as its Argument [−ATR]; RTR/HI establishes a preference for an absence of tongue body raising when in conjunction with tongue root retraction. In this latter case, the ATR × HI Condition blocks the occurrence of an antagonistic feature combination.

(27) *Partition by ATR × HI*

NONOPTIMAL	OPTIMAL
NO CONDITIONS HOLD	ATR × HI
+ATR $\mu \qquad \mu$	all other rules

Turning to the weaker of the grounded factors, ATR × BK, we note that this
condition is invoked in only two of the Lango rules, and only as a condition that is
supplemental to ATR × HI (see (26)): (i) of the two rules causing right-to-left spreading of [+ATR] from syllable to syllable, one requires that the Argument be [−back];
(ii) with the single rule affecting [−ATR], spreading takes place only when the Argument is [+back]. The partitioning when ATR × BK is included in the grounding
scale is given in (28).

(28) *Partition by ATR × HI and ATR × BK*

NONOPTIMAL		OPTIMAL
NO CONDITIONS HOLD	ATR × HI	ATR × HI ATR × BK

Given that imposing conditions is better than not imposing conditions, the rules at
the far right of the scale are optimal in terms of grounding. The rule at the far left of
the scale has the weakest grounding: no conditions hold at all.

The final relevant grounding factor determines whether conditions are imposed on
the Argument or on the Target, (21b-3). Given the suggestion made in the discussion

of (21), that the Argument factor is stronger, and since more conditions are better than fewer conditions, we derive the scale in (29).

(29) *Argument/Target scale*

Argument	$\gg$	Argument	$\gg$	Target	$\gg$	no conditions
Target						
1		2		3		4

Inspection of the Lango rules shows that a Target condition alone is never sufficient for rule application: the cutoff, then, is between steps 2 and 3.

The lexicographic product produced by incorporating the relevant portion of the Argument/Target scale of (29) (the part prior to "cutoff") with the scale of (28) produces the complete grounded partitioning given in (30).[12]

(30) *Partition by ATR × HI, ATR × BK, and Argument/Target*

The rules governed by the ATR × HI Condition alone are divided into two classes: (i) the class of cases where the condition holds only of the Argument (left-to-right spreading of [+ATR] from syllable to syllable, and right-to-left spreading from mora to mora), and (ii) the class where the condition is imposed on both Argument and

Target (right-to-left spreading from syllable to syllable). In a parallel fashion, the rules governed by the conjunction of the ATR × HI and ATR × BK Conditions are divided into two classes: (i) a class where the conditions hold only of the Argument (right-to-left syllable-to-syllable spreading), and (ii) a class where both Argument and Target exhibit conditions (left-to-right spreading of [−ATR]).[13]

5.3.1.3 Optimization of [ATR] in Lango   At this point, we have established two lexicographic products, one ranking the parametric factors relevant for the distribution of [ATR] in Lango (25), and one ranking the relevant grounding factors (30). It remains only to combine these two scales to create an overall characterization of the optimal distribution of [ATR] in Lango, whereby parametric weakness is offset by grounded strength, and parametric strength offsets grounded weakness, the Feature Optimality Hypothesis (20).

The notion of trade-off is illustrated in (31), where optimal configurations are indicated by numbers higher on the scale (*1*) and nonoptimal ones by numbers lower on the scale (*5*). The trade-off relation shows a mapping of the best of the parametric scale with the worst of the grounding scale and vice versa.

(31) *Trade-off*

OPTIMAL PARAMETERS			NONOPTIMAL PARAMETERS	
1	2	3	4	5
5	4	3	2	1
NONOPTIMAL GROUNDING			OPTIMAL GROUNDING	

The alignment of scales shown in (31) is illustrative: other mappings are imaginable. What is impossible in an offsetting relation is strength mapping to strength and weakness to weakness. For instance, the configuration in (32) is ill formed for precisely this reason: the strong parametric combination *2* is mapped to the strong grounding combination *2*, while the weak parametric *4* maps to the weak grounding *3*.

(32) *Trade-off*

A trade-off pattern of the type shown in (31) is instantiated by the two scales of Lango. Consider first the rule that is strongest on the parametric scale in (25). This rule, the left-to-right spreading of [+ATR] from mora to mora, requires no grounded conditions, unlike all other rules in Lango. Since strong grounded conditions hold in the unmarked case, this means that the formally strongest rule is nonoptimal in terms of grounding factors. In other words, grounding weakness is offset by parametric strength.

Balancing strength and weakness continues across the two scales as shown in (33): the second and third strongest parametric configurations pair with the second weakest grounding configuration (ATR × HI holding of the Argument), while the fourth parametric configuration pairs with two of the strongest grounding factors (ATR × HI holding of Argument and of Target, and both ATR × HI and ATR × BK holding of Argument).

(33) *Schematic illustration of trade-off*

OPTIMAL PARAMETERS				NONOPTIMAL PARAMETERS
+ATR				−ATR
L-R		R-L		L-R
μ–μ	σ–σ	μ–μ	σ–σ	μ–μ/σ–σ
	ARGUMENT	ARG & TARG	ARGUMENT	ARG & TARG
NONE HOLD	ATR × HI		ATR × HI ATR × BK	
NONOPTIMAL GROUNDING				OPTIMAL GROUNDING

Under trade-off, as the parametric configurations continue to weaken, the grounded ones strengthen, culminating in the weakest relevant parametric configuration, left-to-right [−ATR] spreading, being offset by the strongest relevant grounded configuration, ATR × HI and ATR × BK holding of both Argument and Target. (34) shows both the six rules and the trade-off between parametric and grounding factors.

(34) *Optimization of [ATR] in Lango*

OPTIMAL PARAMETERS					NONOPTIMAL PARAMETERS
+ATR					−ATR
L-R		R-L			L-R
μ–μ	σ–σ	μ–μ	σ–σ		μ–μ/σ–σ
+ATR ⌐ ⟍ μ μ	+ATR ⌐ ⟍ σ σ │ +HI	+ATR ⌐ μ μ │ +HI	+ATR ⌐ σ σ ⋁ +HI	+ATR ⌐ σ σ │ +HI −BK	−ATR ⌐ ⟍ σ σ │ │ +BK −HI
	ARGUMENT		ARG & TARG	ARGUMENT	ARG & TARG
NONE HOLD	ATR × HI			ATR × HI ATR × BK	
NONOPTIMAL GROUNDING					OPTIMAL GROUNDING

Lango is striking because of its six different rules determining the syntagmatic distribution of [ATR], a distribution that dramatizes the question of what constitutes a well-formed rule inventory. The Feature Optimality Hypothesis (20) sketched here ranks the relevant factors in the language: the factors relevant for Lango are, with the addition of one prosodic factor, precisely those motivated in the preceding chapters. Further, the ranking used here is explicit or implicit in the modular subtheories argued for in those chapters.

The mathematical operation of Lexicographic Optimization (24) ranks the parametric and grounding factors, ultimately creating two scales, which are then encoded in trade-off order (20): (i) each parametric combination pairs with certain grounding combinations, (ii) the grounding combinations improve as the parametric ones worsen, (iii) the parametric factors improve as the required grounding factors worsen.

5.3.1.4 Demonstration The charts in this section demonstrate how the statement of the optimal distribution of [ATR] in Lango (34) serves to select the optimal surface representation, given a particular underlying representation.[14]

The six steps of the Lango scale are placed across the top of each chart, followed by the step of the parametric scale (step 8, *[−ATR], right to left*) that is beyond step 7, *IDENTITY*, the Lango cutoff point.

Each left-hand column shows an underlying representation in conjunction with the four surface associations of [ATR] that could potentially correspond to it. The optimal surface representation for each underlying representation is revealed by inspecting the cells in the chart. Each cell marked with a dash "−" is one in which the parametric factors are not satisfied. The remaining cells, those where parametric factors are satisfied, subdivide into three classes. First, *G:OK* indicates that any imposed grounded conditions are also satisfied. Second, *G:** indicates that although the parametric factors are satisfied, the grounding factors are not. Third, in cases where only the right-to-left spreading of [−ATR] would express the relation between forms (factor 8), we leave moot the question of whether grounded conditions are satisfied since the parametric values themselves are never sufficient to establish a well-formed relation: *G:??*. The optimal surface representation for a given underlying representation is the one with the leftmost—or best—pairing that satisfies both the parametric and grounding factors: these are boxed for easy identification (" G:OK ").

In every set of cases, considerations of optimization correctly identify the surface form that corresponds to a given underlying form. For example, in a *VCV* case where the first vowel is the back nonhigh advanced vowel [o] and the second vowel is low (35), the optimal surface form is [o . . . ə], defined by the mapping in the first (leftmost) column; in a *VCCV* configuration where the first vowel is the high front advanced vowel [i] and the second vowel is low (36a), the surface form is [i . . . ə], defined by the optimal mapping that in this case falls in the second column, not the first. The forms in (35)–(40) progress across the table, with forms of gradually weaker formal configurations constituting the optimal pairings. In addition, in cases where it is relevant, forms are included that show configurations where the default, IDENTITY relation is the best option.

(35) *Factor 1 is optimal*

		1	2	3	4	5	6	7	8
		+ATR	+ATR	+ATR	+ATR	+ATR	−ATR	IDENT	−ATR
		L-R	L-R	R-L	R-L	R-L	L-R		R-L
		μ-μ	σ-σ	μ-μ	σ-σ	σ-σ	σ-σ		
			A: HI	A: HI	A: HI	A: HI	A: BK		
					T: HI	A: BK	T: HI		
UR: oCA									
	ɔ-a	−	−	−	−	−	−	−	G:??
	ɔ-ə	−	−	−	−	−	−	−	−
	o-a	−	−	−	−	−	−	G:OK	−
[wódə́]	o-ə	G:OK	G:*	−	−	−	−	−	−

(36) *Factor 2 is optimal*

		1	2	3	4	5	6	7	8
		+ATR	+ATR	+ATR	+ATR	+ATR	−ATR	IDENT	−ATR
		L-R	L-R	R-L	R-L	R-L	L-R		R-L
		μ-μ	σ-σ	μ-μ	σ-σ	σ-σ	σ-σ		
			A: HI	A: HI	A: HI	A: HI	A: BK		
					T: HI	A: BK	T: HI		
a. UR: iCCA									
	ɪ-a	−	−	−	−	−	−	−	G:??
	ɪ-ə	−	−	−	−	−	−	−	−
	i-a	−	−	−	−	−	−	G:OK	−
[píggə́]	i-ə	−	G:OK	−	−	−	−	−	−
b. UR: oCCA									
	ɔ-a	−	−	−	−	−	−	−	G:??
	ɔ-ə	−	−	−	−	−	−	−	−
[dòkká]	o-a	−	−	−	−	−	−	G:OK	−
	o-ə	−	G:*	−	−	−	−	−	−

(37) *Factor 3 is optimal*

		1 +ATR L-R μ-μ	2 +ATR L-R σ-σ A: HI	3 +ATR R-L μ-μ A: HI	4 +ATR R-L σ-σ A: HI T: HI	5 +ATR R-L σ-σ A: HI A: BK	6 −ATR L-R σ-σ A: BK T: HI	7 IDENT	8 −ATR R-L
a. UR: OCu									
	ɔ-U	−	−	−	−	−	G:*	−	−
	ɔ-u	−	−	−	−	−	−	G:OK	−
	o-U	−	−	−	−	−	−	−	−
[jɔ̀wú]	o-u	−	−	G:OK	G:*	G:*	−	−	−
b. UR: ACo									
	a-ɔ	−	−	−	−	−	G:*	−	−
[wayo]	a-o	−	−	−	−	−	−	G:OK	−
	ə-ɔ	−	−	−	−	−	−	−	−
	ə-o	−	−	G:*	G:*	G:*	−	−	−

(38) *Factor 4 is optimal*

		1 +ATR L-R μ-μ	2 +ATR L-R σ-σ A: HI	3 +ATR R-L μ-μ A: HI	4 +ATR R-L σ-σ A: HI T: HI	5 +ATR R-L σ-σ A: HI A: BK	6 −ATR L-R σ-σ A: BK T: HI	7 IDENT	8 −ATR R-L
a. UR: ICCu									
	ɪ-U	−	−	−	−	−	G:*	−	−
	ɪ-u	−	−	−	−	−	−	G:OK	−
	i-U	−	−	−	−	−	−	−	−
[niŋwú]	i-u	−	−	G:OK	G:*	−	−	−	−
b. UR: ECCu									
	ɛ-U	−	−	−	−	−	G:*	−	−
[dɛ̀kwú]	ɛ-u	−	−	−	−	−	−	G:OK	−
	e-U	−	−	−	−	−	−	−	−
	e-u	−	−	−	G:*	G:*	−	−	−

(39) *Factor 5 is optimal*

	1	2	3	4	5	6	7	8
	+ATR L-R μ-μ	+ATR L-R σ-σ A: HI	+ATR R-L μ-μ A: HI	+ATR R-L σ-σ A: HI T: HI	+ATR R-L σ-σ A: HI A: BK	−ATR L-R σ-σ A: BK T: HI	IDENT	−ATR R-L

a. UR: ECCi

	1	2	3	4	5	6	7	8
ε-ɪ	−	−	−	−	−	G:*	−	−
ε-i	−	−	−	−	−	−	G:OK	−
e-ɪ	−	−	−	−	−	−	−	−
[dèkkí] e-i	−	−	−	G:*	G:OK	−	−	−

b. See (37b) and (38b) for relevant IDENTITY cases

(40) *Factor 6 is optimal*

	1	2	3	4	5	6	7	8
	+ATR L-R μ-μ	+ATR L-R σ-σ A: HI	+ATR R-L μ-μ A: HI	+ATR R-L σ-σ A: HI T: HI	+ATR R-L σ-σ A: HI A: BK	−ATR L-R σ-σ A: BK T: HI	IDENT	−ATR R-L

a. UR: UCo

	1	2	3	4	5	6	7	8
[bwúmɔ́] ʊ-ɔ	−	−	−	−	−	G:OK	−	G:??
ʊ-o	−	−	−	−	−	−	G:OK	−
u-ɔ	−	−	−	−	−	−	−	−
u-o	−	−	G:*	G:*	G:*	−	−	−

b. UR: UCCo

	1	2	3	4	5	6	7	8
[lʊbbɔ] ʊ-ɔ	−	−	−	−	−	G:OK	−	−
ʊ-o	−	−	−	−	−	−	G:OK	−
u-ɔ	−	−	−	−	−	−	−	−
u-o	−	−	−	G:*	G:*	−	−	−

c. UR: ECCo

	1	2	3	4	5	6	7	8
ε-ɔ	−	−	−	−	−	G:*	−	G:??
[nɛnno] ε-o	−	−	−	−	−	−	G:OK	−
e-ɔ	−	−	−	−	−	−	−	−
e-o	−	−	−	G:*	G:*	−	−	−

5.3.2 Rule Inventories

Under optimization, the language-particular properties of a rule inventory reduce to three aspects: (i) correctly characterizing and ranking the relevant parametric and grounding factors, (ii) establishing the relevant cutoffs in the lexicographic scales created from these factors; and (iii) establishing the trade-off relations between the parametric and grounding scales.

The first to these, characterizing the relevant parametric and grounding factors, has been the focus of much of this book. The strongest hypothesis is that the class of factors is universally determined and universally ranked; the preceding chapters have examined this hypothesis at length and argued in favor of it. Rule systems that require the ill-formed ordering of these factors are proscribed. For example, one of the results from chapter 3 is that grounded conditions involving [ATR] and [high] are preferred to those involving [ATR] and [back]. Thus, a system like that depicted in (41) is impossible under universal optimization because the grounding factors are not ranked according to their strengths (compare with (34)): the order of ATR × HI with respect to ATR × BK has been switched.

(41) *An impossible optimization of [ATR]*

+ATR					−ATR
L-R		R-L			L-R
μ–μ	σ–σ	μ–μ	σ–σ		μ–μ/σ–σ
+ATR μ μ −BK	+ATR σ σ −BK	+ATR μ μ −BK	+ATR σ σ −BK	+ATR σ σ +HI −BK	−ATR σ σ −HI +BK
	ARGUMENT		ARG & TARG	ARGUMENT	ARG & TARG
NONE HOLD	ATR × BK			ATR × BK ATR × HI	

We turn now to a brief discussion of the two remaining issues, considering implications of lexicographic and trade-off orders for possible rule inventories.

First, Lexicographic Optimization (24) posits a *single* cutoff for each lexicographic scale: inherent in this hypothesis is the claim that relevant factors (primitive or composite) are contiguous in their scales. In this regard, it is noteworthy that in both the parametric and grounded scales of Lango, no factors are skipped in determining the attested relation between underlying and surface forms. The portions of both scales that are imposed to define well-formedness in Lango are continuous, as shown in (42).

(42) *Continuity in lexicographic order*

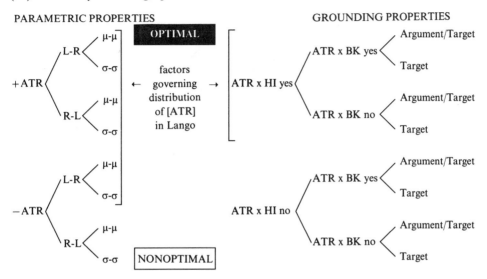

If only contiguous portions of optimization scales can be used in defining well-formed phonological relations, then an extremely restrictive condition is placed on the cross-linguistic nature of rule inventories. Lexicographic Optimization predicts, for example, that is would be impossible for a grammar to closely resemble that of Lango, but exclude specifically the rule spreading [+ATR] from left to right, from syllable to syllable. Allowing the other five rules but excluding that one would be possible only if the parametric scale were broken into noncontinguous sections.

Finally, the hypothesis that parametric and grounding strengths offset each other's weaknesses makes predictions about possible and impossible rule systems. Possible systems are those that maintain the trade-off relation between parametric and grounding factors; impossible systems are those that do not. Compare the well-formed mapping between the Lango parametric and grounding factors given in (33) with the ill-formed mapping in (43). Trade-off order is not observed in (43): the second-from-best parametric factor maps to a stronger grounded configuration than does the third-from-best parametric factor.

(43) *Schematic ill-formed mapping between factors*

OPTIMAL PARAMETERS				NONOPTIMAL PARAMETERS
+ATR				−ATR
L-R		R-L		L-R
μ–μ	σ–σ	μ–μ	σ–σ	μ–μ/σ–σ

	ARGUMENT	ARG & TARG	ARGUMENT	ARG & TARG
NONE HOLD	ATR × HI		ATR × HI ATR × BK	

NONOPTIMAL GROUNDING   OPTIMAL GROUNDING

Such a language would be identical to Lango except that left-to-right spreading of [+ATR] from syllable to syllable would require that both Argument and Target be conditioned by ATR/HI, not just the Argument. The hypotheses tentatively advanced in this chapter proscribe such a language.

The ill-formed rule systems sketched here are only a small sample of the variety of rule systems that are proscribed by optimization. Other proscribed systems can be imagined, by switching the order of various factors, by ignoring steps in the middle of a scale, and by manipulating the range over which factors hold: each such manipulation creates rule systems where "goodness" is expressed by nonoptimal configurations.

5.3.3 Summary

Optimality mirrors the combinatorial approach to characterizing the inventories of sounds in languages. Sounds are treated componentially, not holistically, allowing description of sound inventories in terms of their components (i.e., the active F-elements, the focus of chapter 2). Similarly with rules: in chapter 4, we isolated components of rules (the parameters with their default and marked values), and we suggest here that sets of default rule parameters combine to define optimal rule interactions. Finally, the grounded conditions of varying strengths motivated in chapter 3 provide a natural characterization of the factors that combine to define optimal grounding scales. Thus, Optimality restricts the ways in which the parametric and grounding components of rules may be combined to create rule inventories.

The exploration of Optimality given here is undoubtedly preliminary but serves to supplement work on areas such as stress and syllable structure (Prince 1990, Prince and Smolensky 1991a, Goldsmith 1990, Goldsmith and Larson, to appear, etc.). A wide range of questions are raised regarding the workings and implications of such a model. We have presented here a single, hopefully suggestive, example leading toward a particular set of answers. Clearly an adequate treatment of the issues raised by optimization can only be addressed through consideration of a large number of rule inventories, involving both [ATR] and other feature types. Our effort here is to suggest the plausibility of Optimality as a means of tackling a question that we have not been able to ask before, namely, how to evaluate sets of phonological rules governing autosegmental feature distribution.

5.4   Conclusion

This book has explored a range of phonological systems with the aim of delineating possible and impossible feature systems. The approach throughout has been strongly modular, with surface effects resulting from the interaction of both formal and substantive subtheories. Each modular subtheory presented pertains to a particular domain of inquiry; we have attempted to demonstrate not only that each such module is necessary independently, but also that their interactions produce interesting and desirable results.

The formal subtheories, Combinatorial Specification and Parametric Rules, define the range of possible feature representations and possible rules. The internal structure of these formal systems is componential: both representations and rules are composed of combinations of relevant primitives, F-elements, associations, and parametric rule values. A further similarity between these two formal modules arises where such systems are substantively constrained by grounded conditions: the necessary restrictions force better configurations. Phrased differently, phonetically motivated implicational constraints operating within each module serve to optimize the system in general.

Constraining the formal theory relies crucially on the relation between phonetic and phonological structures, the Grounding Hypothesis. With representations, Optimality takes the form of imposing grounded conditions, conditions that favor phonetically sympathetic combinations and disfavor phonetically antagonistic combinations. With rules, Optimality allows weak rule-governed relations between phonological representations to exist provided that they are improved by substantive strength, represented by imposing grounded conditions on the Argument (and Target) of a rule.

Our overall conclusion is that an extremely restricted set of formal elements interacts in a highly modular fashion with the implementational system to derive the
phonological systems—inventories of representations and rules—that we observe.
We have shown that phonological phenomena cannot be understood solely in terms
of formal patterns, in isolation from the physical properties of the system. At the
same time, the physical properties alone have been shown to be inadequate in defining the systematic behavior of sounds in particular languages. We have demonstrated
that it is through the interaction of the formal and substantive theories that an
explanation of feature patterns is found and, further, we have suggested that this
modular interaction is not random: rather, it systematically optimizes representations
and relations between representations.

Appendix: Exceptional Verb
Patterns in Tiv

In chapter 2, generalizations about Tiv verbs are made on the basis of a 937-verb corpus extracted from Abraham 1940. Thirty-four examples—under 4% of the total sample—are exceptional under our analysis. These are listed below, along with an indication of the type of exceptionality. In some cases, the classification is not exclusive: a form is listed only once although it can be viewed as an exception to more than one rule.

(1) a. *Trisyllabic Invisibility: 1 example*

    iCiCe   ímbise   'jam into, press in on' [1 example]

  b. *Persistent Invisibility: 1 example*

    CɔCe   kɔ́se   'abrade lightly with the fingernail and gently squeeze out pus' [1 example]

  c. *Failure of High Link/Spread: 6 examples*

Ci(C)eC∅	tíhel	'be flexible' [2 examples]
CuCaC∅	mùsan	'exchange' [1 example]
CeCaC∅	hèndan	'contradict a person' [3 examples]

  d. *Failure of High Lowering: 3 examples*

    (C)iCa   yína   'be less than' [3 examples]

  e. *Failure of High Link/Spread and High Lowering: 1 example*

    CiCaC∅   nyíman   'dispute' [1 example]

  f. *Failure of Place Spread: 8 examples*

(C)ie	cíe	'unexpectedly seen or heard' [2 examples]
Cihe	ríhe	'be long' [1 example]
Cuhe	wùhe	'pull out (grass, tree, etc.)' [1 example]
(C)ieC∅	yíer	'lean against' [2 examples]
CueCe	wúese	'happy' [1 example]
Cɔho	nyɔ́ho	'be or become sweet' [1 example]

g. *Apparent Place Spread but intervening nonlaryngeal consonant: 4 examples*

CaCa	kpàma	'annoy' [3 examples]
CɔCɔC∅	gbɔ̀rɔm	'be slack' [1 example]

h. *Delinking of [+high] from initial syllable: 4 examples*

(C)oCuC∅	sóghur	'shake thing to cause contents to fall out' [4 examples]

i. *Delinking of [+high] from initial syllable allowing linking of [+low]:*
   5 examples

Cɔ(C)uC∅	sɔ̀ngur	'gulp with grief' [4 examples]
CɔɔCu	sɔ̀ɔsu	'push thing through another to clean the latter' [1 example]

j. *Apparent delinking of [+round] from initial syllable: 1 example*

CaCoC∅	mgbághom	'approach' [1 example]

Two related classes of cases that might be considered exceptional are the following:

(2) (C)iaC∅	pìam	'place one thing on another' (< *pìame*)
	ndíal	'lick' (< *ndíale*)
	rìan	'lurk motionless in hiding' (< *rìane*)
CuaC∅	húan	'be or become silent' (< *húane*)

There are 9 examples of these patterns, though they include only 1 of the *CuaC* type. At issue is why High Link/Spread does not spread the initial [+high] specification to the second mora. Note that if spreading of [+high] does not take place, then the [+low] specification can link straightforwardly to the second mora, deriving the correct surface realizations.

To derive this result, one could assume that High Link/Spread applies only across syllables and not within syllables, noting that if this is so, then (26a,b) of chapter 2 must involve Place Spread, to account for the tautosyllabic effects, as well as High Spread, to account for the heterosyllabic effects.

The surface [ia] demonstrates that the F-elements [+high] and [+low] are present in underlying representation, the final consonant provides a clue that this form is trimoraic, and the [a] indicates that the underlying representation includes final Invisibility. We contrast the two views of High Link/Spread in the two derivations in (3): the surface effects of assuming that High Spread applies to heterosyllabic moras only are illustrated in (3a); the alternative of assuming that High Spread applies syllable-internally as well as across syllables is illustrated in (3b). As the two derivations demonstrate, the surface form is correctly derived only if High Spread is restricted to heterosyllabic application, as seen in the second step of the derivation in (3a).

(3)

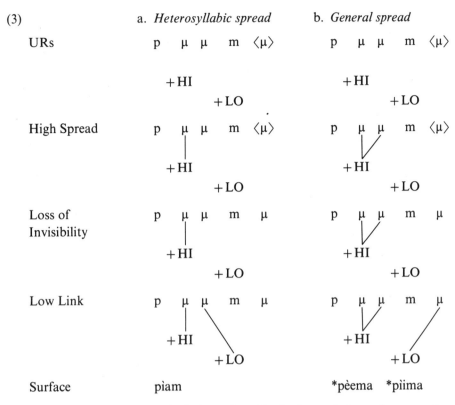

The derivation in (3a) correctly derives *pìam* (the final vowel absent because of vowel deletion) while the derivation in (3b) incorrectly derives either **pèema* or **pìima* depending on whether or not High Lowering is applicable to a long vowel. If the *(C)iaCØ* and *CuaCØ* patterns are to be viewed as regular, one must conclude, therefore, that High Link/Spread applies only heterosyllabically—that it *cannot* apply tautosyllabically. As a result, forms such as those in (26) in chapter 2 require Place Spread for the initial long vowel. For a language exhibiting a clear distinction between mora-to-mora and syllable-to-syllable spreading, see the discussion of Lango in chapter 5.

Notes

Chapter 1

1. Tongue root harmony is discussed in some detail in chapter 3. See that chapter for references to the large literature on this subject.

2. The examples in (2) are taken from Welmers 1973:34. Transcriptions have been modified to match those given in (1) from Ladefoged 1968. Note that the transcriptions in these examples from Igbo do not necessarily mesh with more standard transcriptions. In terms of the official orthography, the four advanced vowels are represented as *i, e, o, u* and the retracted vowels as *ị, a, ọ, ụ*; in terms of a more phonologically oriented system (see Welmers 1973), the advanced vowels would be transcribed as [i, e, o, u] and the retracted vowels as [ɪ/ɩ, a, ɔ, ʊ/ɷ]. How to transcribe such vowel systems is orthogonal to the point being made here, but for some discussion both in general terms and with respect to Igbo, see section 2.8.

3. The changes observed in this suffix with respect to vowel height and lip rounding are independent of the process of tongue root harmony.

4. Imaginable yet unattested patterns fall into two classes, *accidental gaps* (patterns that a theory predicts might occur but that have not yet been discovered) and *systematic gaps* (patterns that a theory predicts could never occur). Differentiation of these two types of gaps is important: identifying an "accidental gap" pattern in a natural language provides support for the theory, while identification of a "systematic gap" pattern constitutes a counterexample to it.

5. Although not the topic of research here, three broad types of interaction can be distinguished at least in principle: (i) there can be no interaction (e.g., SEMANTICS ↔ PHONOLOGY); (ii) there can be a one-way interaction (e.g., SYNTAX → PHONOLOGY); (iii) there can be a two-way interaction (e.g., MORPHOLOGY ↔ PHONOLOGY). See the illustration in (4).

6. The figure in (7a) is for expository purposes only and does not constitute a formal proposal for transparency. In chapter 4, we argue that cases of transparency where a vowel is apparently skipped do not formally involve a spreading configuration of the type seen in (7a).

7. A class of cases exists where harmony is possible between multiple consonants over vowels (see Shaw 1991a). Although we do not discuss such cases in this book, our treatment would be along the lines proposed for cases of transparency such as Wolof (sections 3.2.4.1, 4.7.2) and Menomini (section 4.7.3).

8. The list in (9) is not exhaustive. Other restrictions, such as geminate constraints, play a significant role in phonologies.

9. As should be clear from the discussion in this introduction, we are considering only a subset of the necessary phonological subtheories.

10. We assume that features are binary, for example [+high] and [−high], although the assumption of binarity is not crucial to the model presented in this book. Where we use [+ATR] and [−ATR], for example, it would be possible to redefine systems in terms of two monovalent features *ATR* and *RTR*. Adjustments to particular details would of course be required were such monovalency assumed for all features. For some additional discussion of binary versus monovalent features, see section 2.1.

11. On this issue, note, however, a proposal such as that of McCarthy (1988) that certain features like [±consonantal] and [±sonorant] should be analyzed as defining the Root tier rather than appearing on independent tiers themselves.

12. See also chapter 2. The notion "path" is used in various places in this book, for example, in defining Node Generation (21) and Precedence (55); in chapter 3, we argue that *paths* constitute the domain of grounded implicational conditions.

13. The types of cases that Avery and Rice (1989) take as motivation for their Node Activation Condition are accounted for in the framework proposed here by an interaction between Combinatorial Specification and Grounding Theory. Although we do not address the Node Activation Condition directly, some relevant discussion can be found in section 3.4.

14. Within a single language, certain features may change their ability to be moraic during the course of the phonology. Archangeli (1991), for example, demonstrates that consonants may be nonmoraic at an early stage in the derivation of Yawelmani, but moraic at a later stage. Thus, for some classes, prosodic anchors may change during the course of a derivation.

15. For alternative views on this issue, see work such as Paradis 1988, Calabrese 1988, Yip 1988b, and Myers 1991.

16. There is a large literature on the OCP including work such as Leben 1973, Goldsmith 1976, McCarthy 1986a, Mester 1986, Yip 1988b, and Myers 1987. For arguments against the OCP as a universal, see Odden 1986, 1988.

17. For an argument against the persistence of floating tones, however, see Clark 1985.

18. Myers also proposes a clause of Adjacency for linked features. We turn to this question below.

19. Following Yoruba orthographic conventions, /kp/ is represented by the letter *p* in the text; figures show the "phonological" form, /kp/, appropriate for such a labial-velar stop.

20. For similar cases in Shona, see Myers 1987.

21. We assume, following Yip (1980) and Pulleyblank (1986a), that the featural representation of a H-tone is [+upper], and that the featural representation of a L-tone is either [−upper] or [−raised]. We use *H* and *L* in figures, since the precise feature values for tones are orthogonal to the discussion.

22. Myers (1987) presents a similar case from Shona, where a single multiply linked H-tone becomes a L-tone, affecting all vowels to which it is linked. Comparable cases, involving other features, are found in discussions of the OCP (e.g., Rotuman; McCarthy 1986a) and in discussions of geminate inalterability (e.g., LuGanda; Clements 1985b).

23. We return to the Yoruba polarity example in section 4.5.1, in our discussion of iterativity effects in rules, at which point we formalize the rule.

24. As mentioned in note 19, the letter *p* in Yoruba orthography represents a labial-velar stop [kp].

25. The form in (40b) provides evidence that insertion must apply to the *rightmost* mora. Following Pulleyblank (1986a), M-tones are unspecified in Yoruba: were the tone inserted to the leftmost available mora, *pá mi* would surface instead of the attested *pa mi*.

26. It is possible, though not required, that a rule of feature insertion creates a plateau. For an example of such a plateau-creating rule, see the discussion of Yoruba tongue root harmony in section 2.3.1. For discussion of the formal distinction between the two types of insertion rule, see sections 4.2.2 and 4.5.1.

27. The orthographic sequence *Vn* in Yoruba indicates a nasal vowel. In this clitic, the initial mora, represented informally as *V*, receives its nontonal features from the final vowel of the verb root by a regular rule of progressive assimilation, not shown in the derivation in (45b). See Pulleyblank 1988c.

28. Where Myers's definition refers to the *p-bearing tier*, we modify it to refer to the *anchor tier*. Although the two definitions are identical in most configurations, there are cases where they differ. See the discussion of Nyangumarta in section 4.7 for one example.

29. Note, however, proposals such as those of Kaye and Lowenstamm (1982) and Kaye (1985) where certain features are considered to be unordered with respect to each other, receiving their phonetic ordering by the interaction of interpretive principles with syllable structure.

30. See McCarthy 1986a,b for two possible examples, one from templatic morphology in Hausa and one from diachronic change in Chaha.

31. Unlike the plateau configuration seen in (53), this representation is not saved by virtue of α actually being linked to μ_j, since it is not. Were such a linking present, the representation would be a well-formed plateau: it would no longer be meaningful to consider μ_j to precede or follow α.

Chapter 2

1. John McCarthy has pointed out to us the relevance of Lightner's (1965) work on vowel harmony in this regard. Lightner proposes morpheme-level harmony features that in certain cases correspond in a fairly straightforward fashion to the type of free features posited here and elsewhere in autosegmental work. The primary difference is that for Lightner these features were diacritic markings while in autosegmental theory they constitute true phonological features. See also Stewart 1967 in this regard.

2. Floating features are posited both as part of the representation of some morphemes and as the morpheme itself, for example, palatalization in Chaha and in Japanese. Examples of each type are found in this book.

3. For further discussion, see "The Death of the Phoneme" in Kaye 1989.

4. It is worth noting that even in a theory such as that of Kaye, Lowenstamm, and Vergnaud (1985), a theory that proposes segment-sized elements as the primitives of combination and phonological manipulation, segments are assumed to be composed of smaller components that play a crucial role in determining the result of combining different segmental units.

5. Note that we are not claiming that *all* cooccurrence restrictions are of this type. For example, restrictions on onset or coda clusters in English are not obviously explained in terms of restrictions on F-elements on paths with each other.

6. Thanks especially to Chip Gerfen for discussion that led to the inclusion of "prosodic categories" in the definition of *path*, as in Gerfen 1992.

7. The prohibition against [+high] and [+low] in a single path may not be universal. Analyses such as that of de Haas (1988) suggest that mid vowels derived by coalescing high and low vowels are precisely the [+high, +low] vowel. Note also works such as Schane 1984, Kaye, Lowenstamm, and Vergnaud 1985, Anderson and Ewen 1987, and van der Hulst 1989.

8. The presentation of formal properties of combination has benefited from discussion with Debbie Schlindwein Schmidt.

9. With regard to combinations as illustrated in (10), [+F] and [−F] count as *two* F-elements. The term *F-element* refers to *each* specification included in a representation. We do not absolutely rule out the use of both values of a binary feature in the establishment of lexical contrasts. However, under normal circumstances, such representations would be somewhat surprising. Consider the difference between (10b) and (10c), where the addition of a third F-element to the representation doubles the number of potentially contrasting segments. If the third F-element were to be the opposite value of either of the first two, then the number of new contrasts would be either zero or two, depending on whether absolute neutralization were also posited. If the [+low] of (10c) were, for example, [−high], then combinations 1 and 3 would be impossible since [+high] and [−high] are inherently incompatible specifications; under this account, combinations 6 and 8 would forcibly neutralize with either 5 and 7 (if [−high] were redundant) or with 2 and 4 (if [+high] were redundant). On the surface, therefore, the addition of [−high] would result in no new segments at all. Evidence for such a combination of F-elements would have to reside in a superficially opaque set of alternations where rules referred to a three-way distinction that disappears on the surface: such patterns do occur, although infrequently. For an example, see the discussion of Kalenjin in section 3.5.3. We tentatively assume that the rarity of such examples is due to learnability, not to some specifically grammatical constraint. Representations with both [+F] and [−F] are therefore theoretically possible, but predicted to demand special circumstances in order to arise. For additional discussion, see section 2.4.4.

10. The particular choice of features used in (10) is for purposes of illustration only. Claims concerning cross-linguistic frequency of feature use, such as "If there is one F-element, then it is [+high]; if there are two F-elements, then they are [+high] and [+round]," are *not* being made. For some discussion of which features are the first to establish contrasts, see Christdas 1988 and section 3.6.1.

11. Tiv is a Niger-Congo language spoken in Nigeria. The analysis presented here is based on the sample of 937 verbs found in Abraham 1940. Arnott (1958) and Pulleyblank (1988a) have also addressed the problem of the distribution of vowels in Tiv verbs. The analysis presented here extends that of Pulleyblank (1988a).

12. The small number of exceptional patterns are addressed in the Appendix; all robust patterns are discussed in this section.

13. Lombardi (1990) argues for an analysis of affricates in Classical Yucatec where certain morpheme structure conditions derive from properties of association. See also LaCharité, in preparation, for a discussion of the Yucatec pattern.

14. See sections 3.2.1, 3.2.5, and 3.6 for discussion on the concept of feature markedness, both within grammars and with respect to such learnability.

15. There is a class of exceptions to this statement, lexically marked by Invisibility. See section 2.2.1.7 for discussion. Note also that in certain classes of verbs discussed below, vowel identity in a *VV* or *VhV* sequence could be derived via Place Spread, but identity could also be derived by additional rules required for the Tiv vocalic system. We do not discuss such cases of ambiguity because the crucial point of the discussion here is the entirely predictable nature of surface specifications; where different aspects of the overall analysis converge on the same result, this point is unaffected.

16. With [e], Place Spread is apparent only. This is because /e/ has no features under the analysis offered here: consequently, it has no Place node. Thanks to Cari Spring for bringing this to our attention.

17. Several points are important with respect to the following examples. (i) Initial consonants have no bearing on the vocalic realization of a stem and are therefore parenthesized in the Tiv data sets both here and in subsequent sections. For example, the first form in (14), *ii* 'bury', could be replaced by one like *bii* 'touch' with no effect on the vowel sequences. (ii) Tiv verbs are maximally trimoraic, with *(C)VV* and *(C)VhV* sequences only possible as the first two moras of a verb; where a verb contains three moras, the third mora is invariably a short vowel preceded by one of the consonants [v, l, r, gh, m, n, s] (*gh* in Tiv represents a voiced velar fricative). (iii) The verb forms presented throughout this discussion of Tiv do not represent fully inflected surface forms. Surface forms of Tiv verbs involve the addition of tonal and segmental affixes to the bases under discussion. The acute/grave accents on the first vowel of a stem indicate whether the verb belongs to the H-tone or L-tone class. For discussion of the tonal phonology of Tiv verbs, see Arnott 1964, McCawley 1970, Leben 1973, Goldsmith 1976, Pulleyblank 1985, 1986a. (iv) Based on tonal patterns and consonant distribution and behavior under certain types of suffixation, Pulleyblank (1986a, 1988a) demonstrates that consonant-final verbs are derived from underlying vowel-final verbs by a rule of vowel deletion. Where consonant-final forms are included in displays, the vowel-final forms from which they are derived are included to the right (e.g., *gér* < *gére*). The highly productive rule of vowel deletion requires that the two vowels agree for the F-element [high] and that the intervening consonant be of the set [v, l, r, gh, m, n]. Note that the distribution of consonants in the final syllable of trisyllabic stems is highly restricted: the only consonant occurring in the third syllable that does not trigger vowel deletion is [s].

18. For a more detailed motivation of the unspecified analysis of [e], see Pulleyblank 1988a.

19. In both graphic representations of rules like (23) and simplified derivations like (25), we do not indicate hierarchical structure that would automatically result from Node Generation ((21) of chapter 1).

20. Cases involving a *VV* or *VhV* pattern in conjunction with a [+high] specification could result in the surface patterns [ii] and [ihi] as a result of either Place Spread or High Link/ Spread. We know of no evidence from Tiv that clearly establishes which rule is responsible for the *i ... i* pattern of such cases. The crucial point in this and certain other cases involving Tiv Place Spread is that the surface patterns are predictably derived from a set of free underlying specifications.

21. We adopt the term *Invisibility* from Poser 1984 and Inkelas 1989. It should be noted that our use of Invisibility in Tiv differs from the use in Inkelas 1989 in that it appears to be crucial to allow the lexical encoding of Invisibility on roots for Tiv.

22. See the Appendix for the small number of exceptions to the disyllabic generalization.

23. We know of no reason to order High Link/Spread and Round Link and so show both taking place in the second step of the derivation. Anticipating results of this section, we note in passing that Round Spread is applicable in this example because both vowels are [+high]. Round Spread must therefore follow High Link/Spread since the latter rule creates the agreement in vowel height required for the spread of [+round].

24. Sharon Inkelas (personal communication) has raised the possibility of accounting for the cases where there is no spreading by positing monomoraic underlying representations that are augmented to bimoraic status after the application of High Link/Spread. This hypothesis is problematical for a number of related reasons. Tonal F-elements as well as the F-elements under consideration here, [+high], [+low], and [+round], attach to syllable heads. This means that syllabification must precede the association of such F-elements. If epenthesis is an automatic by-product of syllabification (as argued in Itô 1986, 1989), epenthesis would precede association. In addition, there is a class of monomoraic verbs, albeit a small one, that must not undergo any process of epenthesis. Tonal properties distinguish such cases from bimoraic bases, and all bimoraic bases (with or without spreading) behave the same way with respect to the relevant processes. See Pulleyblank 1985, 1986a.

25. Consistent with the approach taken to redundant values outlined in the "default values" box in section 2.2.1.3, we include reference only to [+high] since there is no independent motivation for a reference to [−high]. That is, we schematize the rule with reference to an optional branching [+high] specification rather than with reference to a branching [αhigh]. We interpret the optional branching [+high] as meaning that the rule applies (i) if there is a multiply linked [+high] specification, (ii) if there is no [+high] specification at all. See also Hong, in preparation.

26. In the discussion of Ngbaka in section 2.5, we provide a second case where a configuration involving free [+high] and free [+low] assigns priority to the linking of [+high]. Relevant cases in Ngbaka involving [+low], [+ATR], and [+round] are also discussed, where no priority clause appears to exist.

27. An alternative to ordering the rules linking [+high] and [+low] would be to propose that the linking rules apply in opposite directions, [+low] from the right and [+high] from the left. This analysis fails since the $a \ldots e$ pattern in (24) (e.g., áser 'wrench off; break off') shows that [+low] must link from the left.

28. There are a small number of cases (nine examples) where the following patterns are observed: $(C)iaC\emptyset$, $CuaC\emptyset$. Either these cases must be viewed as exceptional, or the application of High Link/Spread and Low Link must be modified slightly. For a proposal along the latter lines, see the Appendix.

29. The analysis of $e \ldots a$ verbs presented here has benefited considerably from discussion with Sanford Schane.

30. We do not formulate the rule of High Lowering because of its involvement with two phenomena, palatalization and ablaut, that are not discussed here. Note that Pulleyblank (1988a) failed to observe the predictable relation between the patterns in (45) and (46). As a result, the $e \ldots a$ cases were treated as exceptions to the otherwise regular association of [+low], and the combination of [+high] and [+low] was considered to have a defective distribution. A possible analysis of the $e \ldots a$ pattern was to mark the initial vowel of the relevant verbs as Invisible with respect to [+low]. This resulted in final Invisibility with respect to [+high] in patterns such as $i \ldots e$ and initial Invisibility with respect to [+low] in patterns

such as $e \ldots a$. In the present analysis, these problems are resolved. In particular, the possibility of analyzing $e \ldots a$ patterns as involving Invisibility sensitive to particular F-elements ceases to have any motivation.

Positing a rule of High Lowering has important implications as well for the process of vocalic ablaut that is attested in various tenses (Arnott 1958, Pulleyblank 1988a); Pulleyblank suggested that the priority clause necessary to derive a surface [+high ... +low] pattern is abandoned in an ablaut context, resulting in the inability of [+high] and [+low] to associate and thereby producing an ablaut realization with mid vowels. Given the necessity for a rule of High Lowering that is independent of ablaut contexts, this type of blocked association involving incompatible F-elements is no longer motivated for Tiv. However, see section 2.5 for a possible case of this type in Ngbaka.

31. Barrow Inupiaq is an Inupiaq language spoken in and around Barrow, in northern Alaska; it is of the Eskimo branch of the Eskimo-Aleut language family. Data are taken from Kaplan 1981.

32. We agree with Kaplan that the epenthesis account is untenable, but for different reasons. The essence of the epenthesis account is that all instances of $/i_2/$ are inserted by an epenthesis rule that follows palatalization: the prediction is that all locations of $/i_2/$ are predictable. As shown in the text, coronal stops palatalize to the right of $/i_1/$, but do not palatalize to the right of $/i_2/$, regardless of intervening consonants. Thus, any surface [i] that does not trigger palatalization of a subsequent coronal stop is an instance of $/i_2/$, not $/i_1/$. In light of this, consider the pair *iglu* 'house' and *tinu* 'push'. The first vowel of each form does not trigger palatalization (*iglu and *tiñu) and so must be inserted under the epenthesis account. This suggests /glu/ and /tnu/ as the underlying representations for the forms. The pattern of consonants and vowels is identical in the two forms: a general rule of epenthesis would treat them identically, deriving either *gilu and *tinu* or *iglu* and *itnu. In short, the epenthesis account fails to explain the distribution of $/i_2/$ and so is untenable.

33. Although our analysis differs from his in crucial ways, it adopts as its central thesis a proposal by Bourgeois (1988): the difference between $/i_1/$ and $/i_2/$ is one of specification versus lack of specification rather than of which specifications are present.

34. Recent work has addressed the question of whether the back-front dimension is best represented as a Dorsal feature or as a Coronal feature. We follow Keating (1991) in treating [back] as a Dorsal property. We treat the relation between [−back] and Coronal as the result of a grounded relation between these two F-elements, rather than as evidence that the back-front property is best characterized as a daughter of the Coronal node (contra proposals in E. Pulleyblank 1989a, Genetti 1989, and Mester and Itô 1989).

35. The suffix -*tuq* in (49e) creates a coronal geminate when added to *tikiṭ* ([tikič]). Kaplan (1981) transcribes the result of palatalization as [tṭ] (i.e., [tč]): we take this to be palatalization of the (derived) geminate /tt/, with a single release, hence the appearance of [tč] rather than [čč].

36. The roots in (49) and elsewhere give evidence for why we assume that Barrow Inupiaq vowel F-elements are linked in underlying representation: their order is unpredictable.

(i)	VCi_1	VCu	VCa	VCi_2
$i_1 CV$	tiŋi 'take flight'	sisu 'slide'	iga 'book'	no cases found
uCV	qupi 'to cleave'	ulu 'woman's knife'	nuna 'land'	punniq 'loaf of bread'
aCV	savik 'knife'	saluk 'be thin'	pana 'spear'	panik 'daughter'
$i_2 CV$	no cases found	iglu 'house'	no cases found	ini 'place'

37. The dual of (50a,b) and the nominalizer of (50c,d) also involve gemination or degemination, as do a number of other processes in Barrow Inupiaq. Forms with and without both gemination and Dorsal Assimilation (if applicable) sometimes occur in free variation in the dual, as shown in (50): what does not occur is forms with only gemination or only Dorsal Assimilation where both are possible. The two must go together. We do not discuss further the alternations involving gemination/degemination observed in cases such as those of (50) and (51): for discussion, see Dresher and Johns 1990. Note also that there is no apparent gemination when there is no final consonant in the stem: *ulu/ulum* 'woman's knife' (**ullum*). This contrasts with the dual (50a,b), where gemination is an option (*nuna/nunnak* or *nunak* 'land'), and with the nominalizer (50c,d), where gemination is obligatory (*sana/sannaq* 'to carve').

38. Bourgeois (1988) uses Labial and Dorsal where we use [+round] and [+low], respectively. We know of no data distinguishing between the two analyses.

39. As noted by Kaplan (1981), certain morphological restrictions are applicable. For example, palatalization sometimes fails to apply with enclitics: *savik[λ]u* 'and the knife' versus *savik[t]auq* 'the knife too' (**savik[s]auq*); *savik[t]auq* 'the knife too' versus *aasiiv[s]auq* 'thus too' (Kaplan 1981:107). Also, Kaplan (1981:129) notes that "a final *k* other than the dual marker will not trigger vowel alternations" and presents the pair *tuullik* 'loon' versus *tuullak* 'loons-DUAL'. The exact morphological restrictions are orthogonal to our present concerns.

40. The precise details of the [t] ~ [s/č] alternation do not appear to be crucial to the topic of this section, hence are not discussed here.

41. It should be noted that the configuration in (55a) does not constitute a *gapped* configuration of the type ruled out by the Locality Condition discussed in chapter 1. For explicit discussion of this configuration, see section 4.7.1.3.

42. Cole (1987), Czaykowska-Higgins (1987), and Bessell (1990) propose a tongue root component; McCarthy (1989b) proposes a pharyngeal component.

43. This raises the possibility that the vocalic F-elements of Barrow Inupiaq are more properly analyzed as Dorsal, Coronal, and Labial, rather than [+low], [−back], and [+round] (see Bourgeois 1988, E. Pulleyblank 1989b). If the analysis were reformulated in terms of node specifications for vowels, nothing in the central thesis of Combinatorial Specification would be affected.

44. Technically, the relevant condition is one preventing the combination of articulator nodes, since [+low] is redundantly assigned in these examples. The need to posit this additional constraint is not problematical given the proposal developed in chapter 3 that representations are maximally, not minimally, constrained in the unmarked case.

45. We do not address the issue of whether the [+low] specification assumed here to characterize a low vowel is phonologically inserted on the low vowels derived via Dorsal Assimilation, or whether "lowness" is a phonetic property of such a vowel: we know of no phonological rules treating these vowels as [+low] and therefore do not assign a specification. See the "default values" box in section 2.2.1.3.

46. In a paper on Coeur d'Alene, Bessell (1990) notes several examples whose properties appear quite similar to those observed in Barrow Inupiaq, one case indeed being a description by MacLean (1986) of North Slope Inupiaq. Apart from Coeur d'Alene itself (Doak 1992, Bessell 1990), Menomini (Piggott 1971) and Kalispel (an Interior Salish language) are noted.

47. A theory that would force full or partial specification of the fourth vowel would therefore either abandon Representational Simplicity or supplement Recoverability by further constraints on specification.

48. However, see Ọla 1992 for an attempt at analyzing [ATR] harmony in Yoruba in terms of a [+ATR] value.

49. For other sources on Yoruba vowel harmony, see Awobuluyi 1967, Awobuluyi and Bamgboṣe 1967, Bamgboṣe 1967, 1986, Capo 1985, Courtenay 1968, Fọlarin 1987, Fresco 1970, George (Madugu) 1973, Mohanan 1991, Owolabi 1981, Oyelaran 1971, 1973, and Salami 1972.

50. Pulleyblank (1988c,d) demonstrates that the underlying vowel corresponding to surface [i] is malleable in ways consistent with its having no F-elements in underlying representation. Since the features of [i] are [+high], [−low], [−back], and [+ATR], the asymmetries involving [i] suggest that those F-elements are not present underlyingly, making available instead the values given in (61a). Note that Clements and Ṣonaiya (1989) and Akinlabi (1991, 1993) argue that it may be necessary to supply some degree of specification underlyingly even to /i/. Even if this turns out to be correct, their arguments concern dorsal features and nasality, not tongue root features. That is, their evidence is irrelevant for the concerns of this section since it does not suggest the presence of a [+ATR] specification in the phonology of Yoruba.

51. We choose to label conditions such as those in (61b) without using nonletter symbols like "+" and "−". Any condition referring specifically to the value [+ATR] therefore employs *ATR* in its label; any condition referring *specifically* to [−ATR] uses *RTR* in its label; any condition referring to both values of [ATR] uses *ATR* in its label (this situation arises whenever [±ATR] occurs as the consequent of a condition; see chapter 3). In Yoruba, therefore, we use the label *RTR/HI* because it is the value [−ATR] that is active in Yoruba. This use should not be interpreted as an argument for either a binary phonological feature [±RTR] or a monovalent feature RTR. As for the status of such implicational conditions, in chapter 3 we explore the set of substantive conditions governing the relation between tongue root features and tongue height features, arguing that only a very restricted set of conditions are allowed crosslinguistically.

52. We do not enter into a detailed argument here for general properties of the Yoruba harmony system; see Archangeli and Pulleyblank 1989.

53. In Standard Yoruba, *u*-initial words do not occur.

54. The account in (69a) is consistent with an analysis of Yoruba where all vowels are specified for some value for [ATR] (see Mohanan 1991). Arguments against (69a) therefore bear on Mohanan's (1991) arguments concerning Radical Underspecification. For a number of problems with the account of Yoruba sketched in Mohanan 1991, see note 57.

55. The OCP violation observed in (70b) would not arise if the morpheme-level specification were on a different tier from the phonologically determined specification of a low vowel. Such a representation could result from considerations of linear ordering along the lines discussed by McCarthy (1989a, Yip 1989a): since morpheme-level specifications are unordered with respect to any other specifications within a morpheme, they appear on a separate tier. Under such an account, the generalization that *all* low vowels trigger harmony would be accounted for by a morpheme structure condition requiring that every low vowel bear a [−ATR] specification; at a technical level, harmony would affect both types of [−ATR], morpheme-level and low-vowel. One problem arises with respect to this hypothesis. In a monomorphemic configuration of the type *mid...high...low* (see discussion below in the text), the initial mid vowel

is invariably [+ATR]. If, however, linked [−ATR] specifications on low vowels were posited in conjunction with a morpheme-level specification on a separate tier, then the normal expectation (McCarthy 1979, 1981) would be that the morpheme-level specification skips over the vowel prespecified as [−ATR]. This would derive an unattested pattern like *yǫruba. One type of case suggesting this mode of association is the Arabic binyan involving a prespecified t; a root such as √ktb associates to such a binyan by skipping over the t, even though it appears, crucially, on a different tier. A second example is the association pattern of morphemic specifications of labialization in Chaha. For discussion, see McCarthy 1983, Hendriks 1989, and section 4.4.1.

56. We follow Archangeli and Pulleyblank (1989:200) in our formulation of this problem.

57. Mohanan (1991) explores an alternative possibility for Yoruba vowel harmony, involving full specification and structure-changing spreading of both values of [ATR]. In order to account for the absence of harmony from high vowels in forms like ẹbi 'guilt', Mohanan proposes that final high vowels are extraprosodic and so cannot trigger harmony. Note that the Invisibility analysis makes the wrong prediction when sequences of high vowels occur at the end of a word. Since only a single unit may be Invisible, harmony is predicted to take place whenever a mid vowel is followed by two (or more) high vowels. Thus, attested forms like ẹ̀gúsí 'a food made from seeds of melon' are anomalous under the Invisibility account and therefore add to the arguments found in Tiv and Barrow Inupiaq against the full specification of features. For a detailed discussion of the relation between [−ATR] specifications and high vowels, see Archangeli and Pulleyblank 1989.

58. As discussed in chapters 3 and 4, we attribute the opacity of the high vowel in such a case to the conjunction of Locality and the presence of the implicational condition RTR/HI (61) that restricts the assignment of [−ATR] to vowels that are [−high]: (i) RTR/HI prohibits the spreading of [−ATR] to the medial high vowel, (ii) Locality prevents the spreading of [−ATR] to the initial mid vowel since it would have to skip the intervening high vowel.

59. The right-to-left directionality of association is clearly observed in cases such as èlùbọ́ 'yam flour' and odídẹ 'Grey Parrot'. Comparing such cases with examples like òyìbó 'any European' and èsúró 'Redflanked Duiker', we observe that the [−ATR] morpheme-level specification of the former cases links to the rightmost available mid vowel. Patterns like *ẹlubo are unattested in morphologically underived cases.

60. In (61), we propose that there is a condition on [−ATR] in Yoruba allowing it to be associated only to a [−high] vowel. Throughout this section, we allow [−ATR] to link to low vowels as well. Such association to low vowels raises the potential for a formal inconsistency: if low vowels are specified as "[+low]," not as "[+low], [−high]," then how can a condition requiring [−high] be satisfied by a low vowel? There are several ways to resolve this apparent inconsistency. On the one hand, low vowels could be assumed to have the representation [+low, −high]. This could be the result of an underlying specification or it could be the result of an insertion rule applying prior to the association of [−ATR]. Alternatively, one could replace the condition in (61) by a disjunctive condition allowing [−ATR] in combination with either [−high] or [+low]. A final possibility is to assume that the condition *If [−ATR] then [−high]* is satisfied if [−ATR] is combined with either [−high] or [+low] (even if [−high] is not actually specified for a [+low] vowel). The logic of this last possibility is that since the class of low vowels is a proper subset of the class of nonhigh vowels, any condition requiring membership in the larger class automatically includes the possibility of membership in the smaller class. There are empirical differences between these various possibilities for regulating

the association of [−ATR] to low vowels, but we do not have evidence forcing the selection of one particular approach. For some related discussion, see note 70 in chapter 3.

61. Substantively, this condition is altogether plausible, as witnessed by phenomena such as those observed in Pulaar (section 2.6.1) and Kinande (section 3.2.3.1).

62. The statements in (81) do not mention [−high] because [−ATR] can only link to [−high] in Yoruba: since this is a general property of the language, it need not be repeated in specific rules. See chapter 3 and Archangeli and Pulleyblank 1989 for further discussion.

63. Schlindwein (1989) makes exactly the same point with respect to a comparable process of post-root harmony in Yaka. Versions of the same harmony process are found in other Bantu languages as well, for example, Kinande (Valinande 1984), Kimatuumbi (Odden 1989, Clements 1989), and Cibemba (Hyman 1992). Note that this aspect of the general combinatorial proposal made here is essentially of the type that would be proposed under a model of Contrastive Underspecification (Clements 1987, Steriade 1987a). See section 3.4.2 for discussion.

64. See Byarushengo 1975 for more examples of this process. The rule affects the vowel /u/ in addition to /i/ but only if the root contains /o/. We do not discuss this condition in this section but note that it can be formally expressed as the following condition on the rule of harmony: if the target of harmony is [+round], the argument of harmony is characterized by [+round]. (This condition can also be expressed in terms of backness provided that the low vowel [a] is unspecified for this feature.) See also section 4.7.2.2, where such identity conditions are briefly examined.

65. See the discussion of feature markedness in section 3.2.5 on why we have selected [+low] and [+back] over the opposite values, or the feature [round]. Of note, however, is that the analysis would not change were [−low] rather than [+low] posited as the relevant value. Like the values for [back], values for [low] play no role in the process discussed here.

66. Schlindwein (1989, 1990) has independently arrived at a comparable analysis of the Ainu dissimilation facts, for reasons very similar to those that motivate the analysis here.

67. Recall that (89) is an informal statement of the rule: the "subject to the OCP" statement is convenient at this point in the discussion, but should not be construed as a "±OCP" option on rules. Rather, as laid out in chapter 1, we assume that the OCP holds of all representations. Its relevance as a blocker in this case follows from the noniterative property. See section 4.5.1 for discussion.

68. Preliminary exploration of Djingili vowel harmony (Conway et al. 1990) indicates that Djingili representations are comparable to those of Barrow Inupiaq, with four underlying vowels corresponding to three surface vowels. See also van der Hulst and Smith 1985.

69. We ignore the role of prosodic structure since our focus is on the interactions of F-elements.

70. With respect to low vowels in these three languages, the interesting property is the contrast between representations of the type in (97a) and (97b). For this reason, our discussion focuses only on this contrast, not on the contrasts with (97c). For a discussion of Representational Simplicity with respect to associations, see section 2.5.

71. This understanding of distinctness has implications for the Strict Cycle Condition (Mascaró 1976, Kiparsky 1982, 1985, etc.). Consider a rule such as the one inserting [−ATR] onto low vowels in Yoruba. If the class of rules exhibiting Strict Cycle effects is the class of "obligatory neutralization" rules, then the insertion of [−ATR] is unproblematical because it is not neutralizing. Even though the output of the rule is *distinct* from the input, this

would not invoke the Strict Cycle. Similarly, if the class of rules exhibiting Strict Cycle effects were to be the class of feature-filling rules (Kiparsky 1991), then no problem would be encountered since the rule inserting [−ATR] is feature-filling. If, however, Strict Cycle effects are attributed to some version of the Elsewhere Condition, making crucial reference to "distinctness," as in Kiparsky 1982, 1985, then there are a number of potential problems. For a case like the Yoruba insertion of [−ATR] onto low vowels, such a definition would erroneously predict that insertion would be blocked. For a brief discussion of the Strict Cycle Condition, see section 2.5.3.

72. The point being made here is valid whatever the details of the assumed specifications, as can be verified by appropriately substituting [−ATR] for [+ATR], [−high] for [+high], and so on.

73. Although we will dwell no further on this question, it should be noted that prohibiting such rules is very desirable. To allow the formal device of inserting and deleting features by a single rule, or to change multiple feature values, would derive a wide array of unattested rule types. For example, one could imagine a rule that would neutralize the distinction between oral obstruents and nasal sonorants, or that would neutralize the distinction between voiceless obstruents and voiced sonorants, and so on. This class of unattested cases cannot be derived by the application of feature-filling redundancy rules, nor can it be derived by rules that can effect no more than a single primitive rule operation.

74. Note, however, Avery and Rice 1988, 1989 on this issue.

75. Furthermore, markedness would rank for preference the four possibilities in (f–i). For discussion, see chapter 3.

76. This table is a slight modification of Thomas's (1963) table B. Thomas gives three tables of vowel cooccurrence patterns: one for *CVCV* forms with different tones, one for *CVCV* forms with like tones, and one for *CVV* forms, generally with different tones. We select the *CVCV* forms with different tones as the basis of our discussion because various indications in both the table and the text suggest that this is the most highly exemplified class; hence, the distribution of percentages of cases to particular patterns is more significant. It was impossible to create a table based on averages across all three types because raw numbers were not available to establish the relative weightings between Thomas's different tables.

In the table given here, we indicate the robust patterns by *XXX*; nonrobust patterns are indicated by a single *X*; completely unattested patterns are indicated by—.

Two points concerning the table should be noted. (i) Two patterns (. . . *u* . . . *i* and . . . *ɔ* . . . *a*) that are completely unattested in table B are assigned *X* in our table because they are exemplified by examples in the *CVV* table (0.9% for each) (these are the only two cases where a 0 exemplification in table B corresponds to examples elsewhere). (ii) Cases with 4% or more in table B are considered robust. The top end of the robust group (15%, 11%, 9%) was easy to establish, the bottom end much less so. We allowed ourselves to be guided by table A and table C in establishing a cutoff point. The patterns at the bottom end of what we consider robust have the following percentages, where parenthesized values indicate percentages in tables A and C, respectively: 5.5% (1.5%/19%), 5% (6.5%/4%), 4% (2%/8%). Patterns that we consider nonrobust have percentages dropping to below 1% in either or both of tables A and C: 3% (0.5%/4%), 2% (0.5%/3.5%), 2% (0.5%/0%), 2% (0.5%/0%), 2% (0.5%/0%). To a certain extent, providing an exact cutoff is not important since we provide analyses even of the infrequent cases; the crucial point is that such patterns should be in some way more marked than the patterns that are robustly attested. In the text below, we include Thomas's percentages for reference purposes; the first percentage in each case indicates the number of *CVCV*– different tones cases (*CVCV-D*—the table we use here), the second, the number of *CVCV*–like tones cases (*CVCV-L*); the third, the number of *CVV* cases (*CVV*).

77. The analysis presented here is similar in spirit to that proposed by Churma (1984) in that properties of vowel cooccurrence in Ngbaka are derived by the application of rules rather than by the positing of static morpheme structure conditions. Like Churma, we posit rules of [ATR], [back]/[round], and [high] harmony. The accounts differ markedly, however, in their treatment of forms involving low vowels, in their treatment of exceptions to the robust patterns, and in the range of cases assumed to exhibit height harmony.

78. We do not schematize the Ngbaka rules of association and spreading; they are comparable to rules already presented in this chapter for other languages, notably Tiv.

79. See note 76 for a discussion of why 4% was used as a cutoff for determining robustness.

80. Logically, one could also prelink [+high] to both moras. Since this would derive the same surface pattern as positing a free F-element, however, there would be no motivation for such prelinking: the simpler representation would be posited since Representational Simplicity refers to associations as well as to F-elements.

81. With respect to the Strict Cycle Condition, see also note 71.

82. We take this example from Mester 1986. Tone is not marked in Mester's work and we were unable to locate the example in Thomas 1963.

83. We did not find an example of the pattern *Cɔa* (127b) in Thomas 1963. However, we did find the example *sɔyà* 'espèce de banane à cuire'. According to the table of possibilities for a *CɔCa* pattern with different tones, there should be no such case. From an examination of other cases provided by Thomas, a possible explanation for this apparent discrepancy is that *sɔyà* is polymorphemic (see Thomas 1963:45).

84. Actually, Mester uses [back]; since the choice of [back] or [round] as contrastive in Ngbaka is orthogonal to the issue of morpheme structure, we use [round] here to facilitate comparison with the account of Ngbaka given in this section.

85. Lombardi (1990) proposes a similar analysis for affricates in Classical Yucatec, and Myers (1990) notes comparable properties with vowels in Mandarin rimes.

86. Pulaar affixation also includes mutation of the root-initial consonant: this is illustrated, for example, by the contrasts between *sof-* and *cɔf-* in (135). We do not address this phenomenon here. See Paradis 1986 for discussion. A further point of note is that there are three mid vowel suffixes that appear to exceptionally trigger [+ATR] harmony (Paradis 1986:145–50). We discuss these suffixes in section 3.2.1.3.

87. We thank Carole Paradis for supplying us with the forms in (139b), showing the lack of harmony across short /a/. The suffix *-gel* in (139b) is one of the exceptional harmony-inducing suffixes mentioned in note 86 and discussed in section 3.2.1.3.

88. Note that if the opposite order for [+ATR] Insertion and [+ATR] Spread were posited, there would be no evidence for [+ATR] Spread since no [+ATR] specifications are present in the representation until after [+ATR] Insertion has applied. James Myers (personal communication) notes that this relation between the two rules raises conceptual problems. He suggests that either the rules are intrinsically ordered or else they constitute "one rule" in some sense

because of their interdependency. A possible resolution to this problem is to relate the two rules in terms of "optimization", along the lines proposed for Lango harmony in chapter 5, and for Yoruba harmony in Archangeli and Pulleyblank, to appear.

89. As Schlindwein (1988) points out, the pattern in the data she collected differs from the better-known pattern found in the dialect of Javanese described by Dudas (1976), where [−ATR] spreads from mid vowel to mid vowel only if the two vowels agree for rounding.

90. A nasal-consonant sequence, as in *ombe* 'drink', is standardly taken to be the onset of the second syllable.

91. We have assumed that the F-elements for Javanese are the same as those in Pulaar (see (134)). This would mean that [+high], not [−high], is the active value for Javanese. The cooccurrence restriction limiting the assignment of [−ATR] on stratum 1 to nonhigh vowels would therefore be expressed as a negative condition: *If [−ATR] then not [+high]*. In chapter 3, this particular condition, referred to as *RTR/HI*, is discussed in some detail. For the purposes of Javanese, an equivalent analysis could be obtained by translating the "nonhigh vowel" condition into a positive condition involving [−high] in conjunction with an appropriately revised set of vocalic F-elements. Although Schlindwein (1988) does not include relevant data, her discussion of the facts indicates that low vowels do not induce [ATR] harmony on mid vowels. For this reason, we include the condition that the source and target of harmony agree with respect to both [high] and [low]. Forms like *mʊrɪt* and *gɔlɛʔ* show that there is no requirement that source and target agree for [back].

92. An alternative would be to delete [−ATR] from vowels in open syllables, or insert [+ATR] in that context. Such an approach is problematical since [−ATR] appears in open syllables in harmonic contexts (see (142) and (143)).

93. Kenstowicz (1976,1979) notes that Skorik (1961) describes the surface vowels of Chukchi as [i, e, ɛ, a, ɔ, o, u], where [i, e] and [o, u] alternate harmonically. Our discussion here relies on the data discussed by Bogoras (1922).

94. Hong (1991) shows that vowel harmony in Manchu is comparable to that in Chukchi, including the existence of neutral-voweled roots that induce [−ATR] on affixes, where normally neutral-voweled roots are found only with [+ATR] suffixes.

95. Akinbiyi Akinlabi (personal communication) has pointed out the existence of sets of forms such as the following: *mí* 'to breathe', *ẹ̀mí* 'life', *èémí* 'breath (noun)' (derived from *ẹ̀mimi*). In such a set, the relatively unproductive prefix in *ẹ̀mí* surfaces with a [−ATR] value while the more productive prefix in the reduplicated form surfaces with a [+ATR] value. We analyze such roots as involving a floating [−ATR] specification underlyingly. This [−ATR] F-element associates to the prefix *E-* of *ẹ̀mi* but is stray-erased prior to the morphology of *èémí*. See section 3.2.3.1 for an analysis of similar facts in the harmony system of Kinande. Consistent with this proposal for Yoruba, Akinlabi (1986) and Akinlabi and Oyebade (1987) have developed lexical accounts of Yoruba in which prefixation as in *ẹ̀mi* is assigned to an earlier stratum than the type of reduplication seen in *èémí*.

96. For additional discussion of the domain of the constraint against combining [+low] and [+ATR] in Maasai, see section 4.3.2.

97. Our analysis here follows closely that of Purcell (1989).

98. Free combination of [−back] and [+round] with the vowel specifications of (174) would produce two unattested combinations: (i) both [−back] and [+round], (ii) neither [−back] nor

[+round]. The first possibility can be ruled out by the postulation of conditions ruling out front rounded vowels.

(i) FR/RD Condition: If [−back] then not [+round].
     RD/BK Condition: If [+round] then not [−back].

The second possibility, absence of specifications for [−back] and [+round], would be expected to give a surface vowel that is back and unrounded. Following Purcell (1989), we account for the absence of such a vowel by assuming a redundancy rule assigning the F-element [−back]. This rule is prevented from applying to [+round] vowels because of the two conditions in (i), the FR/RD Condition and the RD/BK Condition; it is prevented from applying to [+low] vowels because of conditions preventing the occurrence of low rounded vowels.

(ii) LO/BK Condition: If [+low] then not [−back].
      FR/LO Condition: If [−back] then not [+low].

Since vowels not specified for either [−back] or [+round] would give the same surface result as a vowel underlyingly specified [−back], we assume that Representational Simplicity (96) causes [−back] to be inserted by a general rule, rather than being present in underlying representation on [i] and [e].

99. A possible objection to this analysis would be the following. The analysis involving free underlying values of [−back] and [+round] predicts the possibility of *both* values occurring on a single morpheme. If the morpheme were nonlow, then one value could link to the vowel, and the other could link to the consonant, producing either an obligatorily palatalized consonant before [u] or [o] or an obligatorily labialized vowel before [i] or [e]. To rule these possibilities out might appear to require prohibiting a combination of *free* [−back] with *free* [+round] within a single morpheme, constituting a counterexample to our claim that relations between unassociated F-elements cannot be expressed. We suggest, however, that the absence of morphemes combining free values of [−back] and [+round] is due not to some condition prohibiting such a combination, but to the absence of a priority clause that would associate one of the values preferentially (note related cases in Tiv (section 2.2.1.7) and Ngbaka (sections 2.5.1 and 2.5.2)). In the absence of some type of priority, neither value can link; hence, Representational Simplicity would result in the absence of [back]/[round] specifications in such a morpheme rather than the presence of both.

100. Unfortunately, the data bases on which such judgments can be based are inadequate at the present time; the judgments themselves are therefore largely impressionistic.

101. An additional issue that deserves exploration in light of the theories introduced in this work is that of language acquisition, raised briefly in the preceding subsection. We venture no further on this topic, not because it is not of interest but because our lack of knowledge of acquisition and learnability would render any such discussion speculative at best.

102. In fact, Ladefoged (1975) records a value of 400 Hz for English [ɪ], and for women, Peterson and Barney (1952) record an average F_1 value of 430 Hz for English [ɪ].

103. A clear illustration of the discrepancies between absolute formant values and analyses into vocalic "segments" can be found in the six sets of formant values given on page 108 of Ladefoged and Maddieson 1990.

104. It might be thought that the above problems arise specifically when consideration is given to acoustic features, but that segments can be satisfactorily and unambiguously described if

attention is paid to their articulation. However, work such as that of Jackson (1988) shows that this is not correct. Jackson demonstrates that the "same" vowel in different languages can be produced in very different ways articulatorily.

105. A similar situation is found in Igbo (Ladefoged 1968), discussed in section 1.1. Ladefoged's transcription is given in (i).

(i) i   e   ɛ   a   o   ɔ   u   ʊ

According to fairly conventional interpretations of transcriptions, one might mistakenly interpret "e" as representing a [+ATR] vowel, and "ɛ" as representing a [−ATR] vowel. In fact, however, Ladefoged demonstrates on the basis of cineradiographic tracings (see (1) of chapter 1) that "e" is a retracted vowel while "ɛ" is advanced. Because of the role that these vowels play in the harmonic pattern of Igbo, more phonologically oriented transcriptions might represent the retracted high vowel as [ɪ] or [i] and the advanced mid/low vowel as [e] (see Welmers 1973).

106. In addition, articulatory variables are clearly important; see for example, Perkell 1971, Ladefoged et al. 1972, Lindau and Ladefoged 1986 (a paper that discusses both articulatory and acoustic variability), and Jackson 1988.

107. In chapter 3, we return to a discussion of Contrastive Underspecification, suggesting that the central insights of that theory result from the interaction of Combinatorial Specification with Grounding Theory, a theory of substantively constrained implicational conditions.

108. Note in this regard the discussion of Arabic in section 2.4.3.

109. This type of case appears to present a challenge for Contrastive Underspecification concerning whether the feature is "contrastive" or not, and whether it is "prosodic" or not. Clements (1987) proposes that features functioning "contrastively" have both values specified and that features functioning "prosodically" have a single value specified. The problem is how to establish the "contrastive" or "prosodic" status of a feature that is not treated uniformly throughout the vocabulary or phonology of a language. For example, a harmonic feature may generally behave "prosodically" and therefore be analyzed as monovalent, while in certain morphemes it does establish a contrast and does not spread (note, for example, the behavior of [ATR] in native versus loan vocabulary in Yoruba). Where a feature does not exhibit uniform behavior across different morpheme classes with respect to its "contrastiveness" and "linked/free" status, it is unclear how (prosodic) Contrastive Underspecification would treat it.

Chapter 3

1. This number is $2*(n*(n-1))$, where in this case $n=20$: $n*(n-1)$ defines the number of positive (or negative) conditions; multiplying by 2 defines the total number of conditions, positive and negative. Note that *If a then b* is a distinct implication from *If b then a*.

2. We qualify the term *condition* with *path* to distinguish those statements that express restrictions on paradigmatic F-element combinations from other types of conditions. As a general observation, it is not the case that conditions are reserved exclusively for the particular type of F-element relation examined here. For example, the Obligatory Contour Principle is a condition governing sequences of specifications, while a theory of syllabification can make use of *if-then* statements that are similarly not path conditions (see Itô 1986).

3. This section has benefited from discussion with Jennifer Cole and K. P. Mohanan, neither of whom is likely to agree completely with the final text.

4. Such conditions have a long history in generative phonology: Stanley 1967 includes an early proposal for *if-then* conditions, the type of implicational statements we make use of here.

5. To allow conditions to play a dynamic role would require a stage in the derivation where ill-formed representations are created, followed by a stage where the ill-formed representations are "repaired." See Calabrese 1988 and Paradis 1988 for two models of constraints and repair; see Peng 1990 for arguments against a stage of the derivation including ill-formed representations. For some discussion of repair strategies, see section 3.4.1.1.

6. In addition to some relevant material in section 2.8.1, section 3.3 considers certain acoustic properties of [ATR] that relate to the articulatory discussion of this section. Note that Lindau (1979) argues that the feature [ATR] should probably be more properly considered a feature of pharyngeal expansion rather than solely tongue root movement. Just as retracting the tongue root decreases the volume of the pharyngeal cavity, so does raising of the larynx (see Jacobson 1980, Denning 1989, Meechan 1992). Similarly, the pharyngeal cavity can be caused to expand by advancing the tongue root or by lowering the larynx. Moreover, Denning and Meechan both raise the possibility that a feature of larynx lowering/raising may be necessary to supplement a more strictly tongue root feature. Although we accept the basic correctness of Lindau's observation, we continue to use the term *ATR* because of its wide acceptance in the phonological literature, and we focus here specifically on articulatory and acoustic effects of tongue root movement as they relate to tongue body height, with fairly restricted comments about tongue body fronting/backing and laryngeal effects.

7. The relation between tongue height and tongue root features plays an important role in works such as Steriade 1987a and Calabrese 1988. The present proposal differs from such previous ones in attempting to derive the class of attested conditions explicitly from phonetic properties.

8. Lindau (1979) and Ladefoged and Maddieson (1990) argue against the appropriateness of distinguishing between English vowels like [i, u] and [ɪ, ʊ] by a tongue root feature (cf. Halle and Stevens 1969, Painter 1973), Lindau notes that Perkell (1971) shows greater differences in tongue height than in the position of the tongue root for such pairs of vowels, and that Ladefoged et al. (1972) find variation among speakers of American English as to whether the tongue root is involved in such contrasts. She also notes that the larynx is not consistently lower for vowels like [i, u], as it would be in a language such as Akan. Ladefoged and Maddieson add that statistical analyses of tongue shapes in English (Jackson 1988) do not support the postulation of a separate variable for the root of the tongue, whereas similar analyses of Akan do. Two points seem important with respect to these arguments. First, even if it is correct that [ATR] is not the appropriate feature for English, this does not affect the implicational relations between the tongue root and the tongue body. Second, it is not clear that the evidence presented strongly argues for distinguishing between independent features of [ATR] and [tense]. On the one hand, work such as that reported in Jacobson 1980 shows that there can be considerable variation in the precise phonetic realization of [ATR] even in cases where the "ATR-ness" of the phenomenon seems uncontroversial. In particular, some cases appear to use the tongue root almost exclusively while others may use larynx height. Absence of larynx movement in English is therefore not conclusive. In addition, the enhancement of one feature by another (see Stevens, Keyser, and Kawasaki 1986, Stevens and Keyser 1989) leads to cases where the primary feature phonologically may not be the primary feature phonetically. A case in point is Hombert's (1976) study of the role of tonal contours in the perception of high tones in Yoruba: although there is clear phonological evidence that contours are derived from

sequences of level tones in Yoruba (see Pulleyblank 1986a, Akinlabi 1984), the strongest perceptual cue for high and low tones in certain contexts is not the level of pitch, but the presence or absence of a rising contour (for high) or a falling contour (for low). Therefore, one cannot conclude in isolation that because changes in tongue height appear phonetically primary, phonetically secondary tongue root movement is also phonologically secondary, and vice versa.

This brings us to one final point. At a phonological level, the feature [ATR] (for a language like Akan) and the feature [tense] (for a language like English) appear to be in complementary distribution. Languages use one or the other but not both (though note Lindau-Webb 1987 on Agwagwune). If languages with 4 or even 5 vowel heights are postulated (independent of the tongue root) (see Ladefoged and Maddieson 1990, Khabanyane 1991, Clements 1991a), then it should be possible to derive from 8 to 10 vowel "heights" by superimposing the feature of tongue root advancement/retraction. Even if one restricts oneself to 4 vowel heights and if one excludes low vowels from such a pattern since they so rarely exhibit tongue root variants, such an approach would still predict seven vowels, for example, each of /i/, /e/, and /ɛ/ having two [ATR] variants (without regard to the front/back distinction), in conjunction with a nonalternating /æ/. A survey such as that of Maddieson (1984), however, produces no plausible candidates for such a language. Following Halle and Stevens (1969), we conclude, therefore, that the complementary distribution between [ATR] and [tense] should be explained by analyzing the relevant cases as manifestations of a single feature.

9. For some discussion of the relation between tongue root movement and features other than vowel height, see Halle and Stevens 1969, Lindau 1979, Ladefoged and Maddieson 1990, Khabanyane 1991.

10. *RTR* ("retracted tongue root") is used in condition titles where [−ATR] is the antecedent. This convention is used for expository convenience only and is not intended to imply a need for two tongue root features. (For an argument in favor of two independent features, [RTR] and [ATR], however, see Goad 1991.)

11. Whether or not a condition is grounded depends on the precise definition of the F-elements concerned. For example, we assume that [−high] and [−low] indicate an absence of tongue body raising and tongue body lowering, respectively. Since the absence of tongue body movement does not imply either tongue root advancement or retraction, conditions like *If [−high] then [+ATR]* and *If [−high] then [−ATR]* are not grounded. If, however, one were to modify the definition of [high] such that [−high] involves active lowering of the tongue body, then the situation would change: *If [−high] then [+ATR]* would continue to be ruled out because it would not be grounded, while *If [−high] then [−ATR]* could now be considered a grounded relation. The resolution of such questions is an empirical issue.

12. Our understanding of the role of strength was strongly influenced by Mohanan (1988, to appear) and has benefited considerably from discussion with James Myers. For a model that approaches strength in terms of a hierarchical ranking, see Calabrese 1988.

13. Wolof is arguably one such case (see section 3.2.4.1), although for an analysis to the contrary, see Ndiaye 1991.

14. Kinande (section 3.2.3.1) and Akan (section 3.2.3.2) are two such languages discussed in this chapter. See also Eastern Javanese, discussed in chapter 2.

15. The proposal here is nondeterministic in the sense that individual cooccurrence conditions are not hierarchically ranked with respect to each other. In this way, the proposal differs from

that of Calabrese (1988). For Calabrese, violations of conditions at "higher" places in a hierarchical order is possible only if conditions at "lower" places in the hierarchy are also violated. For example, a very strong condition such as LO/ATR can be violated only if HI/ATR, a somewhat weaker condition, is also violated. We do not adopt Calabrese's proposal in this regard because of marked cases that are counterexamples to such a hierarchy. In Wolof (section 3.2.4.1), for example, the LO/ATR Condition does not hold: Wolof exhibits a contrast between [a] and [ə]; it respects HI/ATR, however, in that all high vowels are redundantly [+ATR]. For the hierarchical ranking approach, Wolof should be impossible; for the nondeterministic approach taken here, Wolof is highly marked (but it is not ruled out) because the one specific condition that does not hold is very strong.

16. For some discussion of BK/ATR, see note 6 and section 3.1.2. For a case illustrating its phonological application, see the discussion of Lango in chapter 5.

17. A perhaps inevitable danger of using a relatively large sample of languages is that one may take issue with details of the analysis of particular cases. In the analysis of Okpẹ presented below, for example, Okpẹ is argued to constitute a system with 10 phonological vowels.

18. We have not endeavored rigorously to determine whether the prediction is in fact correct that the unmarked case is where conditions hold of all stages of the derivation. Rather, we have focused on languages in which path conditions do not hold generally, in order to demonstrate that even in such cases, the grounded path conditions are still relevant for some aspect of the language.

19. Systems with five vowel qualities account for 30.9% of the systems in Maddieson's survey of 317 languages; in such systems, it is not obvious that [ATR] is necessarily active. Systems with fewer than five vowel qualities also do not obviously require [ATR]. Together, systems with up to five vowels account for 44.8% of the languages in the survey. Having six vowels does not necessarily support the inclusion of an active [ATR] either; systems of six vowels, the next largest group of vowel patterns (18.9%), often have a central, nonlow vowel as the sixth vowel. We interpret these figures from Maddieson 1984:127 as being indicative that [ATR] tends not to be used actively in the languages of the world. Ladefoged and Maddieson (1990) refer to [ATR] as one of the "minor" vowel features, as opposed to the "major" features that determine vowel height, frontness/backness, and rounding. At the same time, we acknowledge that there are weaknesses in interpreting a survey such as Maddieson's. For instance, Nez Perce has a five-vowel system on the surface ([i, æ, a, ɔ, ʊ/u]) and is therefore counted in the 30.9% of five-vowel systems recorded by Maddieson. Hall and Hall (1980), however, argue that Nez Perce exhibits a basic three-vowel system with a superimposed [ATR] distinction on two of the three vowels. It is often difficult from a segment inventory to determine precisely which F-elements are phonologically appropriate. Note the difficulties in this regard discussed in section 2.8.1.

20. We suspect that each clause of such markedness statements for individual features must be assigned a "strength" in much the same way as discussed above for conditions. The strength value for (21a) would determine the likelihood that [ATR] is used in a grammar, and the strength value for (21b) would determine the likelihood that [+ATR] is the active F-element in systems where [ATR] is used. In general, certain features are relatively likely to be used in natural languages, while others are relatively unlikely; certain features are very skewed in their use of specific feature values, while others exhibit common use of both values. Since the focus of our research has been on the interaction of F-elements in languages, not on the frequency of

their presence in languages, we do not speculate on the strengths assigned to the clauses of the [ATR] Markedness Statement beyond specifying for each a positive or negative tendency.

21. With respect to all vowel heights, the table in (24) takes note only of short vowels. Thus, a language that has both long and short [i] is represented only once in this chart, while a language that has only long [iː], and no short [i], is not included at all. With respect to mid vowels, Maddieson uses the symbols *"e," "o"* for two purposes: "Vowels described as being mid may in fact lie between higher and lower mid positions, or they may have simply been transcribed or labeled as mid vowels without any further specification in the source consulted for the language in question. In either case, such vowels are distinguished notationally from higher mid vowels by being enclosed in double quote marks ..." (Maddieson 1984:123). Such vowels comprise more than a third of the mid vowels of each category; thus, it is difficult to know exactly how to interpret these figures with respect to the [ATR] Markedness Statement. As for low vowels, [a] constitutes the largest group of short vowels. We argue in section 3.4.1.2 that a [+ ATR, + low] vowel does not have a single acoustic interpretation; consequently, we do not include a [+ ATR] counterpart to [a] in (24).

22. A low vowel with an advanced tongue root is indicated here by [a̰].

23. The only language with any such properties cited by Maddieson is Karok (Bright 1957): it apparently has both mid [+ ATR] vowels and high back [− ATR] vowels, but no high back [+ ATR] vowels, [i, iː, eː, a, aː, oː, ʊː, ʊ]. Bright (1957:11) describes the high back vowels, long and short, as "a back rounded vowel, lower-high but tense"; we found no evidence that [ATR] values are significant in the phonological processes of Karok. The phonetic realization of the high back rounded vowel in Karok may be due to a grounded connection between [ATR] and [back] (*If [− ATR] then [+ back]*), as briefly mentioned in the text. See also note 6.

24. There are three morphemes that exceptionally require a lexical specification for [ATR]; we discuss them later in this section.

25. For preliminary discussion of how to interpret rule formulations with respect to such conditions, see section 3.2.2.

26. In Pulaar, ATR/HI holds directly of the rule inserting [+ ATR], since ATR/HI does not hold generally of the language. By contrast, ATR/LO holds indirectly of the rule spreading [+ ATR] since it holds of all representations in Pulaar.

27. Paradis (1986) analyzes these forms as involving a floating high vowel that triggers harmony in a regular fashion but is not itself realized. This alternative is also completely consistent with the tenets of the Grounding Hypothesis.

28. Because the distribution of [+ ATR] in underlying representations is so rare, our statement of Pulaar Grounding in section 3 2.1.3 includes the claim that [ATR] is not active underlyingly.

29. In chapter 4, these are the processes defined by the function *insert*. Note that rules that insert floating F-elements (i.e., rules that insert F- elements without creating paths), cannot be subject to path conditions since no path is created. Other types of rules, *deletion* and *delinking*, typically remove paths. This raises the interesting possibility that rules removing paths can only invoke (antagonistic) grounded path conditions, creating preferred representations by removing incompatible combinations of feature specifications. We do not address this issue because of the almost complete absence of deletion rules in the cases we examine in this study.

30. Requiring that the Target of a rule be [+ high] is seen in Pulaar for an insertion rule (section 3.2.1.3), in Kinande for an association rule (section 3.2.3.1), and in Lango for a spreading rule (chapter 5).

31. On this point, the model presented here contrasts sharply with Radical Underspecification, a model of feature representation that also allows the insertion of absent values (see Mohanan 1991). Radical Underspecification places no formal restrictions either on the types of environments for rules inserting redundant values or on the relation between conditions and rules. Such restrictions serve to limit the effect of Representational Simplicity in establishing underlying representations: predictable information can be removed from a representation only insofar as it can be supplied by either (i) a context-free rule or (ii) a grounded rule.

32. Mutaka 1991 is a much-revised version of a paper originally written in 1986.

33. We owe a very special thanks to N. M. Mutaka for discussing material in this section, as well as for tone marking and providing supplemental data.

34. The initial "augment" vowel in the following examples is outside the regular domain of [ATR] harmony. In a non-[ATR] environment, it will surface as [−ATR]; in an [ATR] environment, it may optionally surface as either [+ATR] or [−ATR]. The augment's optional appearance as [+ATR] is consistent with its becoming a harmonic target only at the postlexical level since in general, postlexical harmony in Kinande is optional. Moreover, the distribution of the augment is syntactically determined (Mutaka n.d., Seki 1986). See Mutaka 1991 for some discussion of harmonic properties of the augment, as well as Mutaka 1990 for a general discussion of the interaction between morphology and phonology in Kinande.

35. In the following data from Kinande, [+ATR] values are represented orthographically by a cedilla under the appropriate vowel symbol, following a fairly standard practice in Bantu linguistics; all vowels without such a cedilla are [−ATR]. In the tonal transcriptions, [`] represents a low tone, ['] represents a high tone, [ˆ] represents a falling tone, and ["] represents a phrasal high tone. The distinction between ['] and ["] is in their distribution, ["] occurring only prepausally (see Hyman and Valinande 1985, Mutaka 1990).

36. The form in (44d) and similar examples raise questions concerning the status of the low vowel [a] with respect to harmony. We assume, following Hyman (1989), that low vowels undergo harmony, but that the phonetic effect of such harmony is salient only in a restricted set of circumstances to be discussed at the end of this section.

37. Conditions on processes of association are discussed in some detail in chapter 4.

38. Although we do not discuss the front/back dimension in any detail, we assume that tongue root advancement tends to correlate with tongue dorsum fronting, and vice versa. See section 3.1.2 and related discussion in section 3.2.3.2 on Akan, section 3.1.3.1 on Ẹdoid, and the discussion of Lango in chapter 5.

39. See section 2.7 for a variety of such cases.

40. The role of morphological diacritics in triggering this association is not clear. N. M. Mutaka (personal communication) notes that the appearance of [+ATR] prefixes with [−ATR] roots appears to occur only with classes 5 and 10. It should be noted in this regard that the class 5 singulars seen in (50) take class 6 plurals with the prefix ma-, a low vowel prefix that would not show the effects of harmony. Similarly, the class 10 plurals of (50) take singulars from class 11, a class that is immune to Special Association because it has a back vowel in the prefix. We note, therefore, that there is nothing in cases such as (50) to require a morphological diacritic in delineating the correct class of special association forms. We need simply assume that the relevant roots are marked for [+ATR] and that this lexically free value associates on stratum 1. We offer no explanation for why cases of this type appear to be restricted to the class 5/6 and 11/10 pairings.

41. The Kinande pattern is also incompatible with the related proposal by Odden (1984).

42. Hyman (1989) suggests that this left-to-right spreading can be equated with a Kinande instantiation of a widespread Bantu rule of height harmony. See Hyman 1989, as well as section 2.3.2 on Haya.

43. To prevent the right-to-left application of General Association from incorrectly assigning [+ATR] to the suffix vowel in such a case, a morpheme-level [+ATR] specification must link at the root level, prior to suffixation. Hyman (1989) interprets such data as an argument for an analysis where [+ATR] specifications are underlyingly linked. Interpreting such an account within the present framework, the ATR/HI Condition would hold of underlying representations, rather than of the process of association. In comparing the association-based approach with such a prelinked approach, two factors are important. First, the prelinked approach requires a distinction between the conditions holding of underlying representations and those holding of stratum 1: a condition on underlying representations no longer holds at stratum 1 (where right-to-left harmony takes place), even though the inventory of F-elements has not changed. Second, the prelinked approach requires a diacritic account of the nouns with free [+ATR] specifications that are incompatible with the root vowels (50). In contrast, the association-based analysis simply requires that association be subject to a grounded path condition that does not hold generally in the language (see section 3.4.1 for more on the domains of grounded path conditions), and it can provide a phonological analysis for all roots including free [ATR] specifications, including the class 5 and 10 cases seen above.

44. As mentioned in note 36, we assume that harmony actually affects low vowels as well as nonlow vowels, but that such harmonic application is salient only in certain contexts. See discussion below in this section.

45. Here we have assumed that low vowels undergo harmony along with high and mid vowels, but that phonetic factors cause the effect to be negated or minimized in certain contexts. Alternatively, one could assume, in contrast to the position taken here, that low vowels are unaffected by the general rule of harmony, but that phonological or phonetic factors cause low vowels to undergo tongue root advancement in certain contexts. These approaches share crucial properties. In particular, both approaches identify low vowels as being resistant to tongue root advancement. Whether this is ultimately the result of phonological or phonetic factors in Kinande, it is entirely consistent with ATR/LO (11) and LO/ATR (8). In addition, both approaches must identify the long, L-toned low vowels of (62) as special. Whether the (more salient) advancement attested in such cases is correctly attributed to phonological spreading or phonetic interpolation (for some discussion of phonetic interpolation, see section 3.4.1.2), there is a plausible phonetic source for the tonal condition. (Thanks to Guy Carden for discussion.) Lowering of the larynx often correlates with the production of a L-tone (Zemlin 1988, Denning 1989). Lowering the larynx is also a way of expanding the pharyngeal cavity, an action that can enhance or even constitute the "[+ATR]" effect (see Lindau 1979, Jacobson 1980, Denning 1989, Meechan 1992). Thus, the presence of a L-tone could serve to enhance the salience of tongue root advancement.

46. Kalenjin (see also section 3.5.3) appears to have the opposite effect: Antell et al. (1973:5) observe, "When a tape is played at half speed, vowels of Set (b) [the [−ATR] vowels] have a noticeable 'creaky' quality. This is especially marked when the vowel occurs on a low tone."

47. See van der Hulst and Smith (1986) for a proposal that in general, transparent vowels result from spreading the F-element that the transparent vowel itself bears, rather than the opposite value, our sympathetic transparency.

48. The rule that derives the raised low vowel [ə] has a gradient effect on the realization of mid vowels as well (Berry 1957, Clements 1981). See discussion in section 3.4.1.2.

49. We would like to thank Kofi Saah for discussion of this section. Our attention here is restricted to the Asante dialect; transcriptions are broad phonemic. Tone has not been indicated because it was not consistently transcribed in our sources.

50. For a somewhat different description, see Dolphyne 1988.

51. As discussed later in the text, there may be a gradient effect nonlocally, but no shift to a fully advanced realization.

52. Thanks to Jennifer Cole for discussion of this possibility.

53. Note that *morpheme-level* does not mean that the feature specifications are independent morphemes. They are not. They are free specifications, assigned to morphemes as opposed to individual moras.

54. Note that no violation of the Locality Condition is proposed here: neither Adjacency nor Precedence can be violated where there is no phonological spreading.

55. Clements (1981) notes two exceptions to this observation: *tene* 'to spread' and *hojo* 'to loosen'.

56. This point suggests that [+ATR] is assigned to the consonant: if [+ATR] were not anchored to the consonant, there would be no explanation for the gradient onset of ATR-ness. Thanks to Pat Shaw for enlightening discussion of this phenomenon. For a process with similar properties, see Turkana (Dimmendaal 1983).

57. As mentioned in section 3.1.2 and note 38, we assume that the appropriate grounded relation between [±ATR] and [±back] is one where {[+ATR], [−back]} and {[−ATR], [+back]} are sympathetic relations, and {[+ATR], [+back]} and {[−ATR], [−back]} are antagonistic relations.

58. For a somewhat different analysis of the vowel system of Wolof, see Ndiaye 1991.

59. The suffixes in (83) are -*Am* 'THIRD PERSON SINGULAR POSSESSIVE', -*At* 'INTENSIVE', -*AndOO* 'COMITATIVE', -*AntE* 'MUTUAL', -*All* 'COMPLETION', and -*AdI* 'DEPRIVING'. The capitalized symbols indicate vowels undistinguished for [ATR].

60. Thanks to Moussa Ndiaye for supplying us with information about and examples of borrowing. He points out one exception to the stated generalization: *naaféq* [naafeq] 'trompeur' (borrowed from Arabic).

61. Thanks to Moussa Ndiaye for providing examples with multiple medial high vowels.

62. If instrumental investigation should provide evidence for retracted high vowels in an appropriate harmonic context, then Wolof could be reanalyzed along the lines of Kinande.

63. In our discussion of Menomini harmony in section 4.7.3, we provide evidence that Menomini requires the same type of analysis as that offered here for Wolof.

64. The suffixes in (92) are -*E* 'INSTRUMENTAL/LOCATIVE', -*lE* 'PARTICIPANT', -*OO* 'RECIPROCAL', -*OOn* 'PAST TENSE', -*Al* 'BENEFACTIVE', and -*AndOO* 'COMITATIVE'. Again, capitals indicate the quality of a vowel in the absence of any [ATR] specifications.

65. The argument that [+ATR] is the active F-element for the [ATR] feature in some cases, but that [−ATR] is the active F-element in others constitutes an argument in favor of [ATR] as a binary feature, rather than as a monovalent F-element ATR. (For a contrary view, see, for

example, Kaye, Lowenstamm, and Vergnaud 1985, van der Hulst 1988, 1989.) Alternatively, cases involving [−ATR] as active might be seen to argue for two monovalent F-elements, ATR and RTR (Goad 1991).

66. Recall from section 2.3.1 that [−high] is the active F-element in Yoruba, not [+high]. Thus, "a high vowel" in Yoruba is one without a [−high] or [+low] F-element.

67. Following Pulleyblank (1988c), we assume that [−high] is active in Yoruba. As a result, it is the positive version of RTR/HI that is relevant (*If [−ATR] then [−high]*). (Were [+high] also present in surface representation, or present in place of [−high], then the negative version of RTR/HI would hold (*If [−ATR] then not [+high]*). For the point being made here, that RTR/HI holds is crucial; that a particular value of [±high] be present is not.)

68. Note that forms such as (100c) are anomalous under the extrametricality account of Yoruba final high vowels offered by Mohanan (1991).

69. A further prediction of the Grounding Conditions is a learning strategy: namely, that the language learner would initially consider RTR/LO to hold of the language. But in Yoruba, there is robust evidence that mid vowels can be [−ATR]: as a result, RTR/LO would be rejected as a condition on the language. However, it remains relevant as a condition on [−ATR] Insertion. See section 3.6.1.1 for more conjecture about learnability.

70. A final point raised by Yoruba has to do with the interpretation of RTR/HI (see note 60 in chapter 2). The features [high] and [low] interact to create a three-way height distinction. When vowels are fully specified for height, [+low] vowels are included in the set of [−high] vowels and [+high] vowels are included in the set of [−low] vowels. The question is whether this same inclusion holds when representations are less than fully specified. Specifically, in Yoruba, RTR/HI restricts [−ATR] to vowels that are [−high]: does "[−high]" include vowels specified as [+low] even if such vowels are not actually specified as [−high]?

Whether [−ATR, +low] (without [−high]) is licensed by RTR/HI depends on whether the condition is given a purely formal interpretation or a fully grounded interpretation. Under a strictly formal interpretation, [−ATR] may occur only in combination with the F-element [−high]. Under the fully grounded interpretation, the combination of [−ATR] with either [+low] or [−high] satisfies the condition.

In order to account for Yoruba [−ATR] harmony, it is essential that the free [−ATR] be able to link to [+low] vowels as well as to [−high] vowels. The fully grounded interpretation of RTR/LO would permit the necessary association while the strictly formal interpretation would require insertion of [−high] on [+low] vowels prior to [−ATR] Association (the latter is the option taken in Archangeli and Pulleyblank 1989).

As noted in note 60 of chapter 2, the two interpretations make testable predictions: unfortunately, at this point we have no data bearing on this issue.

71. As elsewhere, we restrict our attention to the interaction of [ATR] with tongue height. Conditions like ATR/BK also play a role in some of the cases we have looked at, for example, governing Kinande Special Association and possibly the palatalization cases in Akan.

72. With respect to the effect of tongue root movement on F_1, see Pike 1967, Ladefoged 1968, Halle and Stevens 1969, Jacobson 1978, Lindau 1978, 1979, Ladefoged and Maddieson 1990, Khabanyane 1991. Associated with the feature [ATR], there can also be changes in F_2 or F_3, as well as in laryngeal properties; see, for example, Halle and Stevens 1969, Lindau 1979, Denning 1989, Ladefoged and Maddieson 1990, Khabanyane 1991. As elsewhere in this chap-

ter, here we focus on issues involving tongue body height, since this is the phonological factor we examine in the case studies of this book. As a result, we consider F_1 effects.

73. See, for example, Ladefoged and Maddieson 1990.

74. Although our point in this section is that certain surface realizations may be the result of phonetic neutralization (or near-neutralization) of distinct phonological realizations, we are *not* claiming that all cases of surface neutralization result from phonetic interpretation. Neutralization of distinct representations may also result from phonological operations, such as harmony or deletion. See section 4.3.2, especially note 23, for related discussion.

75. Note the discussion of E̲doid in section 3.1.3.1.

76. The precise analysis of low vowels depends, however, on whether there is complete phonetic neutralization (see below) between a derived [+ATR] low vowel and the [+ATR] mid front vowel [e]. Whether or not there is complete neutralization between ą and e, roots cannot have a [+ATR] low vowel if there is a condition prohibiting the association of [+ATR] to low vowels (the more strictly grounded option). Consider the possibility, however, that there is no such condition. Given the free combination of F-elements and a lack of restrictions on the linking of [+ATR], we would predict a stem with a [+low] vowel that triggers [+ATR] harmony, the class that is not attested. This gap could be explained as follows. If a [+low] stem had a free [+ATR] specification, it would induce [+ATR] harmony and suffix vowel deletion. Additionally, as noted in the discussion of the continuous (first person plural inclusive), [+ATR] low vowels are realized at the surface as [e] when not word-final. But there is another source for surface [e], simply a [+ATR] specification. Such a representation would also induce [+ATR] harmony and suffix-initial vowel deletion. Thus, there would be no empirical difference between a [+ATR] stem and a [+low, +ATR] stem: given the absence of any such distinctions, Representational Simplicity would select the formally simpler representation, the one with no linked F-elements and a free [+ATR].

77. Hoffmann (1973) notes that this same glide formation process takes place between verbs and following vowel-initial nouns: if the verb ends with a high vowel, that vowel becomes a glide. If the verb ends with a nonhigh vowel, the verb's vowel deletes.

78. The continuous includes a first person plural inclusive affix in all of (115)–(117).

79. Presumably both vowel deletion and glide formation are syllabically motivated. The precise manner in which these processes are formulated prosodically is orthogonal to the concerns of this section.

80. Calabrese (1988) makes essentially this proposal with respect to Okpẹ, suggesting that the F-element changes are due to repair strategies based on conditions loosely comparable to our path conditions. Calabrese's proposal would not be possible in the model presented here because of the strictly *blocking* effect of path conditions. Archangeli's (1984) principle of Feature Conflict Resolution proposes that one or both offending F-elements could delink: default values for those features would then be inserted (presumably the opposite values from those that were delinked). Calabrese (1988) offers a similar proposal, and allows that the two offending F-elements might be linearly ordered as well.

81. For an analysis of Chukchi in terms of phonologically changing feature values, see Calabrese 1988.

82. The vowel ɪ is the "auxiliary" vowel, usually epenthetic. It typically surfaces as ü when tautosyllabic with p. See Bogoras 1922:656. Also, the vowel ä surfaces in place of the recessive e, when adjacent to q and glottals. See also section 2.7.1 for discussion.

83. Note in this regard that there are no phonological mid vowels in Chukchi. Particularly where there is no high-mid contrast, it would be difficult on purely acoustic/perceptual grounds to determine preanalytically whether a vowel in the [e/ɪ] or [o/ʊ] regions should be considered high or mid. Note the discussion in section 2.8.1.

84. Kenstowicz (1976) reports that Skorik 1961 (which we have not seen) describes Chukchi as having a phonetic distinction between the vowels given here as undergoing neutralization. There is some issue as to whether the differing descriptions correspond to the same dialect or to different dialects. Whichever is the case, according to the account proposed here, the described difference in the pronunciation of advanced low vowels is simply a matter of phonetic detail—broad properties of the phonology of vowel harmony are identical in the two dialects. In contrast, on the assumption that a dialect difference exists (see Calabrese 1988), an account that attributes the phonetic differences to phonological differences requires considerable divergence in the phonological accounts of the two cases in spite of their close relationship.

85. The essence of domains is to delineate the morphological and syntactic sequences within which a particular property holds (e.g., a path condition). See Kiparsky 1982, 1984, 1985, Mohanan 1986, Pulleyblank 1986a, Kaisse and Shaw 1985, among others, for details of the lexical model.

86. At this point, we know of no rules in these languages that would test the hypothesis directly. For example, we know of no rule in Yoruba creating a low vowel from a mid "[+ATR]" vowel. The prediction of Grounding Theory is that such a rule (if not blocked) could apply only to create [−ATR] low vowels, not [+ATR] low vowels. As the data base of languages analyzed in these terms grows, it should be possible to test this prediction.

87. Note that in our view of markedness, it is *not* the case that a grammar with *n* conditions is more marked than a grammar with *m* conditions, where $n > m$.

88. Note also the arguments in the "Akan postlexical [+ATR] harmony" box in section 3.2.3.2 that lexical and postlexical rule applications in Akan are not the result of a single rule.

89. Classes can be defined with respect to both binary features and class nodes. For example, the restriction of laryngeal contrasts to obstruents could be expressed as *If LAR then [−sonorant]*, using a class node; the requirement that rounded vowels be back could be expressed as *If [+round] then [+back]*, two binary features. It is also possible for restrictions to involve prosodic structure (e.g., tones are typically restricted to the mora, whatever its segmental content; see Peng 1992), but we do not examine such restrictions here.

90. Steriade makes this observation during her discussion of Pasiego, not Mongolian, but the point is the same for all such related cases.

91. By this claim, we do not mean to suggest that all rule conditions are path conditions. For example, prosodic conditions are possible, as are certain types of identity conditions. Moreover, the exact relation between syntagmatic contextual conditions and the Grounding Hypothesis has not been examined in any detail (see Mohanan 1988, to appear).

92. Antell et al. (1973:4) remark that the [+ATR] low vowels have an anomalous phonetic realization in Kalenjin: it is "quite markedly backed without … any lip-rounding," while the [−ATR] low vowel "is pronounced very slightly fronted." This fact, combined with the surprising effect of L-tones (see note 46), indicates an intriguing area for further research.

93. Of importance here is the distinction between *marked/unmarked* and *specified/unspecified*. The latter terms refer descriptively to the presence/absence of F-elements in a representation,

while the former terms refer to markedness theory. Under the theory advanced in this chapter, some phonologically specified F- elements are unmarked (e.g., [+low]), while some specified F-elements are marked (e.g., [±ATR]); likewise, some unspecified values are marked (e.g., the absence of [low] in a system), while others are unmarked (e.g., the absence of [ATR] in a system).

Chapter 4

1. Mohanan (to appear) makes the same point, though for a different purpose, and so with a different focus. Mohanan's concern is the characterization of rules that appear in some form in virtually every language. With his focus, the part of the rule that is not manipulated is the part that recurs cross-linguistically.

2. Our study has involved relatively few DELETE/X rules, and we will have little to say about such rules here. For work on deletion rules within a parametric model, see Yip 1988b.

3. There is a class of rules inserting feature content where fusion does not take place. We discuss a case of this type in section 4.5.1, arguing that the lack of fusion is due to a NON-ITERATIVE parameter setting. To be fully explicit, therefore, we should note that the Yoruba case discussed here must have the parameter setting ITERATIVE, the default setting.

4. By Yoruba orthographic convention, [kp] is represented by the symbol *p*.

5. Within graphic approaches to rules, edges for free autosegments are often left undefined, although the view taken here is, we believe, the standard implicit view. With regard to linked features, graphic views typically include a characterization of an edge in each individual rule formulation.

6. For extensive motivation of a H-tone versus ∅ contrast underlyingly in Kinande, see Mutaka 1990. In Kinande transcriptions, H-tone is indicated with an acute accent, and L-tone is indicated by the absence of a diacritic. The data presented in this section reflect forms that would occur in nonfinal position. In phrase-final position, an additional phrasal H-tone would be present (Valinande 1984, Hyman and Valinande 1985, Hyman 1990a, Mutaka 1990).

7. Mutaka (1990) assumes that the root H-tone links via convention to the first root vowel. In the derivations in this section, initial linking has already taken place; given our arguments later in this chapter, we would effect initial association by a left-to-right rule of association, the "default" rule (see section 4.6.6).

8. Jennifer Cole has pointed out to us that this proposal concerning the specification of linked versus free elements in a rule has ramifications for the correct formulation of the principle of geminate inalterability (Hayes 1986, Schein and Steriade 1986). Hayes (1986:331) proposes the Linking Constraint: *Association lines in structural descriptions are interpreted as exhaustive.* Schein and Steriade (1986:727) propose the Uniform Applicability Condition: *Given a node* n, *a set S consisting of all nodes linked to* n *on some tier T, and a rule R that alters the contents of* n: *a condition in the structural description of R on any member of S is a condition on every member of S.* Since the parametric approach to rules does not include association lines to which the Linking Constraint could refer, it would seem incompatible with such a formulation of the constraint that derives inalterability. On the other hand, the Uniform Applicability Condition appears to be perfectly compatible with the parametric approach to rules argued for here.

9. There appears to be no standard way of encoding the *iterative/noniterative* distinction so we simply state this aspect of the two rules even in their graphic expression.

10. Following earlier discussion, we assume that "H-tone" is actually the specification [+upper]. See note 21 in chapter 1.

11. In the few cases involving contextual requirements, they are included under A-Conditions and T-Conditions in the formal expression of rules, since there appears to be some kind of connection between Grounding and such rule contexts.

12. Song (1989) notes that disharmonic roots in Nez Perce may constitute a problem for this hypothesis.

13. For a discussion of the full range of tonal patterns within an autosegmental framework, see Pulleyblank 1986a. For the purposes of discussing directionality, we do not provide the basic motivation for the four underlying tonal classes, [L], [H], [L H], [toneless]. In addition, the tonal patterns illustrated in the text are selective, not exhaustive.

14. Derivational suffixes of the type seen in (20) cannot be L-toned; they can only be H-toned or toneless. Certain pronominal clitics, however, can be underlyingly L (Pulleyblank 1986a).

15. Two complications/exceptions should be noted. First, Pulleyblank (1986a) argues that there is a class of H-toned suffixes that are underlyingly extratonal, this extratonality causing tonal polarity effects. Second, a suffix like *amu̧* 'plural imperative' appears to require the positing of a L-tone on the final, though not initial, vowel to prevent that vowel from participating in the type of tone spreading seen in (20). (Such a suffix might be analyzed as involving final extratonality rather than a final L.)

16. We again abstract away from polarizing prefixes. See note 15.

17. Polarizing prefixes provide additional evidence that tones on a stem do not spread from right to left onto a prefix, even when the tone of such a stem actually has its morphological source in the prefix. See Pulleyblank 1986a for discussion.

18. Maasai is not the only language providing evidence that apparent bidirectionality is necessarily the result of two rules: leftward and rightward spreading of [ATR] in Akan (Schachter and Fromkin 1968, Clements 1981, section 3.2.3.2), in Lango (Woock and Noonan 1979, chapter 5), and in Kinande (Mutaka 1991, section 3.2.3.1) have different properties, as do leftward and rightward spreading of tone in Ewe (Peng 1992).

19. The prefix *E-* 'third person singular' always surfaces as [−ATR]: this phenomenon, reminiscent of initial vowels in Kinande, is discussed in Levergood 1984. It should also be noted that certain other processes such as vowel deletion and prenasalization apply to derive the surface forms presented. These processes are not discussed here; see Levergood 1984.

20. Tone is not consistently marked in Tucker and Mpaayei 1955, so we do not include it here. As the discussion of Kinande in section 3.4.1.2 shows, tone may affect the way [ATR] is pronounced or perceived. We believe that tone does *not* affect the surface distribution/perception of [ATR] in Maasai, because the tone patterns depend on the conjugation and appear to be quite regular in general.

21. The prefix *-tV-* 'past' appears with class I verbs only; the two verb classes are distinguished in that class II verbs are always /I/-initial.

22. Another possibility might be to invoke some kind of morphophonological difference such as the use of different lexical strata (Kiparsky 1982, 1985, Mohanan 1986, etc.) for prefixing and suffixing. This approach suffers from two problems. First, the asymmetrical behavior is not limited to affixes: roots with /a/ also block [+ATR] harmony, yet the lexical model only allows level-ordering of affixes. Second, since both roots and suffixes trigger harmony and if

harmony is bidirectional when suffixes are added, /a/ in suffixes and /a/ in roots should behave identically; yet they do not. To capture the difference, distinct rules or representations are again in order, so the stratal solution reduces to the other two possibilities.

23. The surface result [o] could be derived either phonetically or phonologically. In section 3.3.1, we discuss similar cases where phonologically licensed antagonistic combinations result *phonetically* in compromise realizations. This is a possible analysis of the [a/o] case in Maasai. Alternatively, it could be that after the redundant assignment of a feature like [+back] to a [+low, +ATR] vowel, the [+low] of the combination is removed, resulting in a nonhigh advanced back vowel [o]. This is plausibly the correct analysis of a related set of alternations (a → o → ɔ) in the Nilotic language Turkana (Dimmendaal 1983, Hualde 1984), hence also possible here.

24. It might be proposed that a fourth possibility exists, that of applying neither from left to right nor from right to left. Within the framework proposed here, this cannot be considered a well-formed possibility. It would mean that the Target of a rule is neither to the left nor to the right of the relevant edge, "edge" defined either morphosyntactically or by virtue of a link to the rule's Argument. (For further discussion of edges, see section 4.2.3.) With a different set of assumptions, it has been suggested that this fourth possibility might derive formally bidirectional spreading. See Piggott 1988, Pérez 1991.

25. To be consistent with the Grounding Conditions presented in chapter 3, the restrictions on labializable and palatalizable consonants would have to be grounded. We have not explored grounded path conditions in consonants: cases presented here, like Chaha, indicate directions such exploration might take.

26. Following the conventions of our sources, we assume the following orthographic conventions in our discussion of Chaha: Ç is an ejective consonant; q is a velar ejective, ä is a front low vowel. Also, /b/ regularly surfaces as [β] and /bʷ/ as [w], alternations that are not shown in our data lists.

27. The fact that velars are treated on a par with labials with respect to the labialization rule argues in favor of the convention of Node Generation (chapter 1, (21)): "A rule or convention assigning some F-element α to some anchor β creates a path from α to β." The effect of Node Generation in Chaha is that [+round] associates to the rightmost [+round]-bearing segment, regardless of the node structure of that segment: the absent nodes are automatically created.

The alternative to the Node Generation view would be to preassign dorsal consonants a Labial node, for example, along the lines of the Node Activation Principle of Avery and Rice (1989). Such a Labial node would provide a site on which a morphemic [+round] could dock, in sequences where such a feature is supplied morphologically. Such a proposal appears highly problematical, however. Consider the required representation for labial, coronal, and dorsal consonants under the view that "labializability" and "palatalizability" are to be encoded *representationally*. If one were to assume that palatalization is a Coronal feature, representations of the three place values for consonants would be as follows: Labial; Coronal; Labial-Coronal-Dorsal. If one were to assume that palatalization is a Dorsal feature, then the appropriate representations would be: Labial; Coronal-Dorsal; Labial-Dorsal. Under both possibilities, the class of "labializable" consonants is designated by inclusion of *Labial*. With regard to "palatalizable consonants," the first approach designates the class by *Coronal*, the second by *Dorsal*.

We will mention two problems with such a view. First, such analyses must abandon Sagey's (1986) proposal that articulator nodes are content-bearing nodes. Both versions of the *repre-*

sentational hypothesis posit structures for simple dorsal consonants that involve multiple artic-ulations, either Labial-Coronal-Dorsal or Labial-Dorsal. In the absence of a rounding or palatalizing feature, the nodes other than Dorsal must be disregarded implementationally. Second, the *representational* analysis fails to account for the full range of facts concerning the distribution of labialization and palatalization in Chaha. Both representations postulated for dorsal consonants predict the possibility of palatalized-labialized dorsals. Such segments are in fact disallowed. To rule such cases out, the *representational* theory must postulate supplemen-tary cooccurrence conditions, in conjunction with repair strategies or some other fix-up mecha-nism. Given such supplementary conditions, however, the entire *representational* hypothesis is redundant. For example, a (grounded) condition prohibiting the palatalizing feature from cooccurring with the node Labial would simultaneously rule out both palatalized-labialized segments *and* palatalized labials.

28. As in cases such as Barrow Inupiaq, we assume that the palatalization feature is [−back] (see note 34 in chapter 2). The argument for NONITERATIVE application does not depend in any way on this assumption. Rose (to appear) presents an analysis of Chaha palatalization in terms of Government Phonology (Kaye, Lowenstamm, and Vergnaud 1985), raising certain empirical questions concerning the palatalization of velars and vowels.

29. To complete the argument requires the demonstration that [−ATR] is free in underlying representation and that it associates and spreads from right to left. Both these points are motivated in section 2.3.1; further detail is found in Archangeli and Pulleyblank 1989.

30. An alternative is to posit that the A-Structure condition is the default NONE, rather than FREE as given in (52). One effect of positing NONE is to render formally identical the two rules of Yoruba [−ATR] Insertion and Yoruba [−ATR] Spread. The import of this formal identity is explored in terms of optimization (chapter 5) in Archangeli and Pulleyblank, to appear, and in Akinlabi, Archangeli, and Pulleyblank, in preparation.

31. For this discussion, we abstract away from the fact that long low vowels are always [−ATR] and induce [−ATR] harmony to their right.

32. See also the discussion of Ainu in section 2.3.3.

33. In an appendix, Itô and Mester (1986) suggest that the Lyman's Law effect might be due to the OCP; Ishihara (1989, 1991) develops this idea in detail. We adopt this general approach, although details of theory and implementation vary. In terms of specifics, our analysis is closest to that of Ishihara: he posits a floating [+voiced] specification, while Itô and Mester argue that a skeletal slot linked only to [+voiced] is inserted between the two members of the compound. By positing a floating specification, Ishihara automatically derives Lyman's Law; were the [+voiced] specification linked, then the result would be well formed except in the case of an initial voiced obstruent since the sequences of associated [+voiced] specifications would not be linked to adjacent anchors. See, for example, the discussion of Yoruba in section 4.5.1 as well as the general discussion of adjacency in twin peaks configurations in section 1.5.1. Note that if a *linked* voicing specification were inserted by the Rendaku rule, the correct result could be achieved, but at the cost of adding a rule of deletion/delinking. Interestingly, a deletion or delinking rule is highly marked under the model developed here. This contrasts with the completely unmarked association rule required by an account like ours, in which Rendaku introduces a free [+voiced].

34. Following Itô and Mester, this analysis assumes that [+voiced] is specified on relevant obstruents but elsewhere [voiced] is unspecified (i.e., on sonorants and on voiceless obstruents),

an assumption that is entirely consistent with Combinatorial Specification. We do not assume that [+ voiced] is a privative feature. Phenomena such as Dahl's Law are extremely problematical under the privative view (Davy and Nurse 1982, Pulleyblank 1986b); note Peng 1991.

35. We thank Kazuhiko Fukushima, Junko Itô, and Armin Mester for useful discussion of the material presented in this section.

36. We use quite broad transcriptions in this section for Japanese in order to render the pattern clear. In particular, palatalized coronals are realized as alveopalatals, not coronals with a *y*-glide,—for example, [kašakaša] rather than [kas^{y}akas^{y}a].

37. As in cases like Barrow Inupiaq (section 2.2.2) and Chaha (section 4.4.1), we assume that the palatalization feature is [−back]. Nothing crucial hinges on this decision.

38. Details of the rule formalization given here depend on a particular view of palatalization in Japanese. The status of palatalized consonants in Japanese is a subject of debate, in particular whether they are one consonant or two. (See Vance 1987 for a summary of some of the issues.) The rule given here assumes a "one-consonant" analysis and would have to be appropriately revised under a "two-consonant" analysis.

39. There is one class of coronals that never undergoes palatalization, namely, /r/.

(i) *Rhotic exclusion*

noro-noro	'slow, lazy'	*nor^{y}o-nor^{y}o
goro-goro	'goggle-eyed'	*gor^{y}o-gor^{y}o
zara-zara	'coarse texture'	*zar^{y}a-zar^{y}a
toro-toro	'slow, dumb'	*tor^{y}o-tor^{y}o
horo-horo	'weak'	*hor^{y}o-hor^{y}o

A form like *noro-noro* 'slow, lazy' can be palatalized as *n^{y}oro-n^{y}oro* '(snake's) slow, wriggly movement' (67), but not as **nor^{y}o-nor^{y}o*.

This gap is irrelevant for the characterization of the association process being discussed here. In one way or another, it must be established that the palatalization prosody may not link to /r/; once this is established, by whatever means, right-to-left association skips /r/ and left-to-right/default docking never reaches it. We should mention that it is impossible to determine whether palatalization could noniteratively associate/default dock to an initial /r/, because there simply are none. According to Armin Mester (personal communication), Hamano (1986:22), who surveyed the facts exhaustively, states that there are *no* cases of initial /r/ in bisyllabic mimetic roots, and only two attested cases of initial /r/ in monosyllabic mimetic roots.

(ii) riN-riN   'sound of small bell'
     ruN-ruN   'very excitedly, happily'

Hamano is not convinced that *ruN-ruN* is a mimetic because it does not have the mimetic accent pattern in the preaccenting quotative *-to* context. Mester (personal communication) also notes that the first, *riN-riN*, may well be onomatopoeic.

As pointed out by Mester and Itô (1989), rhotic exclusion does present a potential problem for theories of radical underspecification. They suggest that /r/ is not targeted by mimetic palatalization because it lacks a Coronal node, whereas all other coronals include such a node. They motivate this proposal by appealing to Contrastive Underspecification: there are place contrasts for all consonant types except liquids.

The Contrastive Underspecification approach is problematical on at least two grounds, however. First, it fails to account for certain asymmetries involving coronals that are discussed by Grignon (1984). In addition, it is problematical because there is a contrast between palatalized and nonpalatalized liquids (/r/ vs. /rʸ/) in at least some portions of the vocabulary of Japanese (compare *roku* 'six' with *ryoo* 'quantity'), calling into question the correctness of the generalization on which the Contrastive Underspecification hypothesis is based.

Apart from the above problems of description, which need to be addressed seriously by any model, rhotic exclusion does not appear to present any conceptual problems within Combinatorial Specification. If /rʸ/ is analyzed as a sequence (see note 38), then an implicational condition ruling out monosegmental palatalized rhotics can be imposed generally, holding of mimetics as a subcase; if /rʸ/ is analyzed as a monosegmental, then an implicational condition ruling out palatalized rhotics can be imposed as a T-Condition on the rule of Japanese Mimetics Coronal Palatalization (72).

40. According to Grounding Theory, the condition *If [−back] then Coronal* is an allowable T-Condition only if it is grounded. While this interaction seems plausible, we have not tested it rigorously. Note in this regard that the same condition is one of the two holding of Palatalization in Chaha (section 4.4.1); it also holds of the palatalization rule in Barrow Inupiaq (section 2.2.2).

41. See also Gerfen 1992 for further motivation of this point, based on rules that restrict the nature of the Argument's source, but not the nature of the Target.

42. An immediate result of iterativity as defined here is to derive phoneme-driven association: tokens of the Argument cannot be skipped because skipping would require access to an F-element that is not adjacent to an edge. See, for example, Marantz 1982, McCarthy and Prince 1986.

43. It might be argued that spreading causes a feature to be more robustly recoverable since the domain of the feature is enlarged. Under conditions of "noise" (feature deletion, subsequent changes, etc.), spreading could serve to protect a feature by virtue of making it more salient, by assigning it to a larger domain. While we speculate that such a principle might provide partial motivation for the occurrence of spreading as a process, we suggest that the difference between (i) being free, (ii) being singly linked, and (iii) being multiply linked is such that being free is undesirable enough to overcome the undesirability of forming a contour, while the relative undesirability of being singly linked does not outweigh the undesirability of forming a contour, even though the singly linked configuration is not as desirable as that of being multiply linked.

44. The tones in such melodies are, of course, ordered. Since our assumptions regarding tonal features is that a high tone is [+upper] and a low tone is [−raised] (Yip 1980, Pulleyblank 1986a), we assume that order is represented by postulating Tonal nodes linked to such tonal features in underlying melodies. The postulation of such class nodes is also important for the general rule that associates both L- and H-tones (see below) since the rule must refer to the class of tones, not specifically to either H or L.

45. The data in (83) reflect phrase-medial tonal forms. In final position, H-tones undergo a rule that lowers them to mid. See discussion in section 1.5.1.1.

46. This rule links a free H-tone specification, but does not spread a linked H-tone (where such a linked H-tone would occur as the result of linking). The desired result can be achieved either by selecting NONITERATIVE application, or by imposing the condition A-Structure: FREE

(or both). Once either parameter is appropriately set, the other can receive its default specification. In (86), we arbitrarily select the NONITERATIVE parameter setting.

47. It is intriguing, however, that the LH pattern in Mende exhibits a somewhat similar tendency to associate to the rightmost mora of the domain (see Leben 1978).

48. See Archangeli 1983, 1984, 1991 for discussion of the phonological properties of the suffixes that induce this glottalization and for discussion of the various templates referred to in (87) and elsewhere.

49. The stem-final "obstruent" qualification in this statement is important. If the second consonant is a glottal stop or an underlyingly glottalized sonorant, then no derived glottal stop shows up. We derive this effect by assuming that the rule of association in (93) targets anchors that are already associated to a [+CG] specification as well as anchors that are free of the [+CG] feature. That is, we impose no T-Structure conditions on this rule.

50. See Archangeli 1991 for discussion of what happens when glottalization does not dock on a sonorant consonant, as in (88) and (89).

51. Steve Anderson and Donca Steriade (personal communications) have independently pointed out that the location of glottalized sonorants in Yawelmani may well be a general result deriving from properties of the phonetic realization of glottalized sonorants.

52. The [t, d, t'] series are dental, [ṭ, ḍ, ṭ'] are alveolar, and [c, z, c'] are alveopalatals. The three members of each obstruent series constitute "aspirate," "intermediate," and "glottalized," respectively.

53. As already mentioned in different contexts, according to the Grounding Theory laid out in chapter 3, this means that CG/SON, *If [+ CG] then [+ sonorant]*, ought to be a grounded condition. We do not explore issues involving the appropriate grounding of [constricted glottis] in this book.

54. Hyman and Ngunga (1993) independently reach a comparable conclusion, arguing that tones in Ciyao stray-erase unless linked by any of several language-specific rules of association.

55. Note in this regard Levergood's (1984) arguments that [+ATR] harmony in Maasai is cyclic. Even Halle and Vergnaud's (1987a,b) proposal that cyclic morphology results in separate planes while noncyclic morphology does not would therefore predict separate planes for a case like Maasai.

56. Along with the stipulative representational accounts discussed above, proposals in terms of ad hoc rule properties also exist—for example, stipulating that certain components of the structural description of a rule be "adjacent" (Schein and Steriade 1986, Steriade 1987b) (the default presumably being "nonadjacent"), stipulating a "maximal/minimal" parameter (Archangeli and Pulleyblank 1987), and stipulating that certain nodes of a harmonic domain are pruned (Halle and Vergnaud 1981).

57. This conclusion is supported by four further facts noted by Sharp (1986): (i) nonalternating suffixes have [i] or [u], never [a]; (ii) certain harmonic suffixes may also stand alone, in which case they surface with [a]; (iii) idiosyncratically, certain forms do not undergo harmony, in which case the suffixes surface with [a]; and (iv) a "buffer" [a] surfaces between two harmony domains. See Archangeli 1986 for discussion of the buffer vowel effect in particular.

58. Cases like Barrow Inupiaq and Nyangumarta motivate the substitution of *anchor tier* for *p-bearing tier* in Myers's (1987) definition of Adjacency (see chapter 1, (48)). Unlike reference

to *p-bearing units*, reference to *anchor tier* allows the types of gapped configurations attested in systems where both consonants and vowels are involved in a harmonic process.

59. See section 3.2.3.1 for argumentation. Recall that the initial vowel is outside the lexical harmony domain, and that penultimate length is postlexically assigned.

60. Recall from chapter 1 that (114) does not constitute an OCP violation (because of the intervening anchor) while a representation with a single multiply linked token of [−ATR] would constitute an ill-formed gapped configuration.

61. Note that the necessity for contextual conditions is completely independent of cases of apparent transparency. This is shown by (for example) the rule of Final H Association in Kukuya (section 4.6.4) and the rule of prepalatal [+ATR] Insertion in Akan (section 3.2.3.2).

62. Recall from section 1.5.1 that the adjacency requirement of the OCP is derived from general properties, hence not included in the formulation of the OCP itself: *all* phonological relations are defined over adjacent elements, including a prohibition such as the OCP.

63. Hong (1992) provides a critical review of the "linked feature" account of these effects as well as of the "dependent feature" account (Mester 1986, 1988, Selkirk 1991). Hong also concludes that dependency and linked structure models are inadequate for expressing identity conditions.

64. Thanks to Chip Gerfen for clarifying discussion of this prediction.

65. We do not formalize the Yawelmani Round Harmony rule: [+round] is the Argument, and there is a height identity condition on Argument and Target.

66. A side issue here has to do with the feature Markedness Statements. We assume that the presence of [high] is unmarked, as is the absence of [ATR]. However, in Menomini, [ATR] is crucial: it actively functions in the harmony system, and it distinguishes the two low vowels underlyingly. But once [ATR] is present, representations without [high] are simpler than those with [high]. Representational Simplicity therefore selects representations where [high] is not present. Although we know of no evidence requiring the presence of [±high] in Menomini, if such reference were necessary, then values for [high] could be redundantly determined on the basis of [ATR] specifications, with specifically advanced vowels becoming high.

67. Vowel qualities also vary depending on surrounding consonants and on whether the vowel is in the initial syllable; the variation in [ɪ(:)], [ʊ(:)], and [a̱(:)] discussed in the text is independent of the context. See Bloomfield 1962:3–10.

68. Autosegmental treatments of harmony in Menomini such as Cole and Trigo 1987, 1988, Cole 1987, and Steriade 1987a have treated raising as involving the feature [high]. Several points are important in this regard. Regarding the appropriateness of assigning a "mid vowel" label and specifications to [ɪ] and [ʊ] (the vowels that Bloomfield (1962) transcribes as *e* and *o*), it should be noted that perceptual impressions and/or acoustic information alone are insufficient to establish whether a vowel is phonologically mid or high (see sections 2.8.1 and 3.3.1). In terms of phonological patterns, the evidence comes down clearly in favor of an interpretation of Bloomfield's *e* and *o* as high vowels, not mid, since (as seen in the text) an [ATR] account straightforwardly characterizes both opaque and transparent classes of vowels. The [±high] analysis, in contrast, encounters various problems. It allows no straightforward characterization of the class of opaque vowels. Cole (1987), for example, is forced to assume an ad hoc feature [−tense] to identify the single vowel quality that is opaque, a feature that has no motivation in Menomini independent of harmony. Moreover, a three-way contrast in tense-

ness is required: (i) there is the opaque vowel that is underlyingly [−tense], (ii) there are low vowels that are redundantly assigned [−tense] (such vowels neither block nor participate in harmony), and (iii) other vowels are (redundantly) [+tense], a value that is crucial to Cole's account of harmony since it triggers the parasitic application of harmony to vowels so specified. (Note that the use of [±tense] is not comparable to our use of [ATR] since all nonlow vowels are [+tense].) We will not deal at length with Cole's account, but we note two types of problems. The parasitic harmony proposal must allow the creation of formal gapped configurations—in fact, Cole explicitly argues that harmony of the type seen in Menomini is nonlocal. Under the restrictive Locality proposal made here, with Precedence governing all representations, such an analysis is ruled out. In addition, the parasitic harmony proposal is at best a partial account of Menomini. Although long "[+tense]" vowels undergo harmony, short "[+tense]" vowels are transparent. Parasitic harmony must therefore be supplemented by imposing of conditions on the process of harmonic spreading. But if conditions may be imposed on the rule of Harmony, there is no motivation for parasitic structures.

69. Data are taken from Bloomfield 1962, 1975. Each pair of examples gives, first, a form showing the absence of harmony and, second, a morphologically related form showing the effects of harmony. All data are presented both in terms of the orthographic conventions of Bloomfield 1962 and in terms of the proposed representation in section 4.7.3.1. In addition, as an expository aid, each data list is accompanied by a graphic example where boxes indicate vowels that are Arguments or Targets of harmony, and circles indicate vowels that are transparent. Consonant transcription is quite standard, with the exception of q, which represents a glottal stop.

70. Glosses preceded and followed by ?? are constructed (partially or entirely) rather than provided explicitly in the sources. See for example [wayi:tu:hkatitwaʔ] '??they work together??' in (132).

71. This rule raises very interesting implications for a general characterization of A-Conditions and T-Conditions. Although it appears that the option of invoking contextual conditions should be considered formally marked, Menomini raises the possibility that the grounding of such conditions, as with the grounding of Arguments and Targets themselves, should be considered the unmarked option.

72. For a discussion of related substantive conditions on Argument and Target, see the discussion of Lango in chapter 5.

73. A comparable case is found in Khalkha Mongolian (Poppe 1954, Chinchor 1978–79, Steriade 1979, Rialland and Djamouri 1984), where round high vowels block the propagation of [round] from nonhigh vowel to nonhigh vowel.

74. Spreading would of course violate Precedence since a gapped configuration would be created. But the purpose of this demonstration is to show that whether or not gaps are allowed, the representational approach fails to characterize opacity in Menomini.

75. The model proposed here differs in this respect from parametric proposals such as the pro-drop proposal in syntax (Chomsky 1981, Borer 1986), or the very different parametric proposals in phonology made by Kaye, Lowenstamm, and Vergnaud (1985) and Piggott (1988, 1989), who argue that such parameters are set for the language rather than for particular rules. The type of language-internal variation mentioned in the text argues against the "language-parameter" model.

Chapter 5

1. Prince and Smolensky (1991a,b) provided the initial stimulus for our exploration of optimization, although we differ from their original proposal by arguing for "trade-off" order; our development of these ideas was furthered by discussion with Bruce Hayes and Donca Steriade.

2. Poser (1982) argues that regressive spreading rules in Lango are noniterative, and we analyze progressive spreading as similarly noniterative. It should be noted, however, that with the type of progressive spreading seen here, a single target vowel is available. Spreading is therefore de facto noniterative in such cases, with no evidence apart from the parallelism to regressive spreading making noniterativity appropriate.

3. See the discussions of Kinande, Akan, and Proto-Ẹdoid in chapter 3 for more on ATR/BK.

4. Woock and Noonan (1979) provide no forms with low vowels in the relevant position. Our analysis predicts that an underlying / ... aCu ... / would surface as [... əCu ...].

5. As noted in section 5.2.1, the regressive rules and the progressive rules share another similarity: the regressive rules, too, could be expressed as a single rule through judicious use of angled brackets.

6. Woock and Noonan (1979) show that some affixes have somewhat irregular behavior. For instance, the transitive object suffix [-ɔ/-o] sometimes undergoes harmony and sometimes does not: [àbílɔ̀] 'I tasted it' contrasts with [àlímò] 'I visited it'. We do not address such lexically conditioned application of the harmony rules.

7. The need to posit six rules is not an artifact of the parametric approach to rules: the graphic mode of rule representation would also require six comparable rules, as seen from the graphic expressions of the rules in (3), (6), and (16).

8. Here and elsewhere, we use the × notation in conditions (e.g., $ATR \times HI$, to cover all conditions relating values for [ATR] and values for [high], the ATR/HI, RTR/HI, and HI/ATR Conditions. The specific conditions that may be relevant in any given case are those that have the Argument as their antecedent (see section 3.2.2). In Lango, most rules spread [+ATR], so in general ATR/HI is the relevant condition. One rule also spreads [−ATR]; in that case, RTR/HI is the relevant instantiation of the grounded relation between [±ATR] and [±high]. The HI/ATR Condition can play no role in the rules explored here because [+high] is not an Argument in any of the Lango rules we have studied.

9. See also Trigo 1991 for ranking of a comparable sort. Trigo explores two diminutivization hierarchies in Rengao, a Mon Khmer language: increasing or decreasing the size of an object is indicated by changing the quality of the stem-final vowel, where the vowel quality indicates a relative position on the size scale. Trigo shows first that the more general order of vowels can be expressed by a lexicographic order of the features *[ATR] ≫ [back] ≫ [high] ≫ [round]* (where ≫ corresponds to *is larger than*; the values for each feature are ranked within each step of the scale too: *[+ATR] ≫ [−ATR]*; *[+back] ≫ [−back]*; *[−high] ≫ [+high]*; *[+round] ≫ [−round]*). Trigo goes on to show that there is a less common diminutive paradigm, with a different vowel sequence to indicate the size ranking. The less common paradigm is characterized by reordering the feature scale such that *[back] ≫ [ATR]*; all else remains constant. Steriade (1982:98–99) uses essentially lexicographic order in defining sonority scales.

10. Prince and Smolensky (1991a) demonstrate that a subset of the Lango data can be expressed in terms of a single Lexicographic Optimization, that is, a lexicographic product with a single cutoff. However, an account invoking only Lexicographic Optimization fails when all

six Lango rules are considered: different cutoffs are needed for each set of parametric factors. This failure forces the proposed trade-off between the parametric and grounding scales (see section 5.3.1.3).

11. Note that in this as well as other diagrams that follow, we do not include configurations that are below the cutoff points in a lexicographic product.

12. Again "no conditions" (step 4 in (28)) appears to be "bumped up" when the cutoff is determined: if no grounded conditions hold, as in the leftmost column of (30), the Argument/ Target factor is moot.

13. Note that ATR × HI and ATR × BK distribute over Argument and Target in this case; the Argument is subject to ATR × BK while the Target is subject to ATR × HI. This is only one of several logical possibilities where two conditions hold of two formal elements. For example, the conditions could be distributed in the opposite way (ATR × HI holding of Argument, ATR × BK Holding of Target), or both conditions could hold of either or both Argument and Target. We make no claims here about whether such ambiguous combinations of factors are resolved systematically or idiosyncratically. Note, however, that this is the only case where such ambiguity arises. All other cases in (30) involve one condition mapped onto one or two formal elements, or two conditions mapped onto one formal element—cases where no ambiguity of interpretation exists.

14. The arrangement in these charts was suggested by the analysis of Lardil given in Prince and Smolensky 1991b.

References

Abaglo, P., and D. Archangeli (1989). "Language-Particular Underspecification: Gengbe /e/ and Yoruba /i/." *Linguistic Inquiry* 20, 457–80.

Abraham, R. C. (1940). *A Dictionary of the Tiv Language.* Hertford: Stephen Austin and Sons.

Akinlabi, A. (1984). "Tonal Underspecification and Yoruba Tone." Doctoral dissertation, University of Ibadan.

Akinlabi, A. (1986). "Issues in the Development of Lexical Strata for Yoruba." Paper presented at the 16th Colloquium on African Languages and Linguistics, University of Leiden.

Akinlabi, A. (1991). "Supraglottal Deletion in Yoruba Glides." In *Proceedings of WCCFL* 10, 13–26. Stanford Linguistics Association, Center for the Study of Language and Information, Stanford University.

Akinlabi, A. (1993). "Underspecification and the Phonology of Yoruba /r/." *Linguistic Inquiry* 24, 139–60.

Akinlabi, A., D. Archangeli, and D. Pulleyblank (in preparation). "An Optimal Account of ATR Harmony in Yoruba Dialects." Ms., Rutgers University, University of Arizona, and University of British Columbia.

Akinlabi, A., and F. Oyebade (1987). "Lexical and Postlexical Rule Application: Vowel Deletion in Yoruba." *Journal of West African Languages* 17, 23–42.

Anderson, J. M., and C. Ewen (1987). *Principles of Dependency Phonology.* Cambridge: Cambridge University Press.

Anderson, S. R. (1974). *The Organization of Phonology.* New York: Academic Press.

Anderson, S. R. (1980). "Problems and Perspectives in the Description of Vowel Harmony." In R. M. Vago, ed., *Issues in Vowel Harmony*, 3–48. Amsterdam: John Benjamins.

Anderson, S. R. (1981). "Why Phonology Isn't 'Natural.'" *Linguistic Inquiry* 12, 493–539.

Ann, J. (1990). "Against [Lateral]: Evidence from Chinese Sign Language and American Sign Language." In *Proceedings of Arizona Phonology Conference* 3, 1–13. Department of Linguistics, University of Arizona.

Ann, J. (1991). "Constraining Sign Language Handshapes: Toward a Phonetically Grounded Account of Handshapes in Taiwan Sign Language and American Sign Language." To appear in *Proceedings of 1991 WECOL*.

Antell, S. A., G. K. Cherono, B. L. Hall, R. M. R. Hall, A. Myers, and M. Pam (1973). "Nilo-Saharan Vowel Harmony from the Vantage Point of Kalenjin." *Research Notes from the Department of Linguistics and Nigerian Languages* 6, 1–58. University of Ibadan.

Aoki, K. (1962). "Nez Perce and Northern Sahaptin: A Binary Comparison." *International Journal of American Linguistics* 28, 172–182.

Aoki, K. (1966). "Nez Perce Vowel Harmony and Proto-Sahaptian Vowels." *Language* 42, 759–67.

Archangeli, D. (1983). "The Root CV-Template as a Property of the Affix: Evidence from Yawelmani." *Natural Language & Linguistic Theory* 1, 347–84.

Archangeli, D. (1984). "Underspecification in Yawelmani Phonology and Morphology." Doctoral dissertation, MIT. [Published 1988, Garland, New York.]

Archangeli, D. (1985). "Yokuts Harmony: Evidence for Coplanar Representation in Non-linear Phonology." *Linguistic Inquiry* 16, 335–72.

Archangeli, D. (1986). "The OCP and Nyangumarda Buffer Vowels." In *Proceedings of NELS 16*, 34–46. GLSA, University of Massachusetts, Amherst.

Archangeli, D. (1988). "Aspects of Underspecification Theory." *Phonology* 5, 183–207.

Archangeli, D. (1991). "Syllabification and Prosodic Templates in Yawelmani." *Natural Language & Linguistic Theory* 9, 231–83.

Archangeli, D., and D. Pulleyblank (1987). "Maximal and Minimal Rules: Effects of Tier Scansion." In *Proceedings of NELS 17*, 16–35. GLSA, University of Massachusetts, Amherst.

Archangeli, D., and D. Pulleyblank (1989). "Yoruba Vowel Harmony." *Linguistic Inquiry* 20, 173–217.

Archangeli, D., and D. Pulleyblank (to appear). "Two Rules or One ... or None? [ATR] in Yoruba." In *Proceedings of Berkeley Linguistic Society* 19. Department of Linguistics, University of California, Berkeley.

Arnott, D. W. (1958). "The Classification of Verbs in Tiv." *Bulletin of the School of Oriental and African Studies* 21, 111–33.

Arnott, D. W. (1964). "Downstep in the Tiv Verbal System." *African Language Studies* 5, 34–51.

Avery, P., and K. Rice (1988). "Underspecification Theory and the Coronal Node." In *Toronto Working Papers in Linguistics* 9, 101–19. Department of Linguistics, University of Toronto.

Avery, P., and K. Rice (1989). "Segment Structure and Coronal Underspecification." *Phonology* 6, 179–200.

Awobuluyi, O. (1967). "Vowel and Consonant Harmony in Yoruba." *Journal of African Languages* 6, 1–8.

Awobuluyi, O., and A. Bamgboṣe (1967). "Two Views of Vowel Harmony in Yoruba." *Journal of African Languages* 6, 274–77.

Bagemihl, B. (1987). "The Crossing Constraint and 'Backwards Languages.'" Ms., University of British Columbia.

Bagemihl, B. (1988). "Alternate Phonologies and Morphologies." Doctoral dissertation, University of British Columbia.

Baker, M., K. Johnson, and I. Roberts (1989). "Passive Arguments Raised." *Linguistic Inquiry* 20, 219–51.

Bamgboṣe, A. (1967). "Vowel Harmony in Yoruba." *Journal of African Languages* 6, 268–73.

Bamgboṣe, A. (1986). *Yoruba: A Language in Transition*. J. F. Ọdunjọ Memorial Lecture Series 1. Lagos, Nigeria: Molukom & Co.

Berry, J. (1957). "Vowel Harmony in Twi." *Bulletin of the School of Oriental and African Studies* 19, 124–30.

Besnier, N. (1987). "An Autosegmental Approach to Metathesis in Rotuman." *Lingua* 73, 201–23.

Bessell, N. (1990). "Tongue Root Harmony in Coeur d'Alene." Talk presented at the Canadian Linguistic Association, University of Victoria. [Ms., University of British Columbia.]

Bloomfield, L. (1933). *Language*. London: George Allen and Unwin.

Bloomfield, L. (1962). *The Menomini Language*. New Haven, Conn.: Yale University Press.

Bloomfield, L. (1975). *The Menominee Lexicon*. Ed. by C. F. Hockett. Milwaukee, Wisc.: Milwaukee Public Museum Press.

Bogoras, W. (1922). "Chukchee." In F. Boas, ed., *Handbook of American Indian Languages*, 631–903. Washington, D.C.

Borer, H., ed. (1986). *The Syntax of Pronominal Clitics*. Syntax and Semantics Volume 19. Orlando, Fla.: Academic Press.

Bourgeois, T. (1988). "Underspecification in Barrow Inupiaq." Paper presented at LSA Winter Meeting, December 1988.

Brentari, D. (1990). "Theoretical Foundations of American Sign Language Phonology." Doctoral dissertation, University of Chicago.

Bright, W. (1957). *The Karok Language*. Berkeley and Los Angeles: University of California Press.

Byarushengo, E. (1975). "An Examination of the Segmental Phonology of Haya." Master's thesis, University of Dar es Salaam.

Calabrese, A. (1987). "The Interaction of Phonological Rules and Filters in Salentino." In *Proceedings of NELS 17*, 79–98. GLSA, University of Massachusetts, Amherst.

Calabrese, A. (1988). "Towards a Theory of Phonological Alphabets." Doctoral dissertation, MIT.

Capo, H. B. C. (1985). "On the High Non-expanded Vowels in Yoruboid." *Studies in African Linguistics* 16, 103–21.

Carter, H. (1971). "Morphotonology of Zambian Tonga: Some Developments of Meeussen's System–I." *African Language Studies* 12, 1–30.

Carter, H. (1972). "Morphotonology of Zambian Tonga: Some Developments of Meeussen's System–II." *African Language Studies* 13, 52–87.

Chinchor, N. (1978–79). "On the Treatment of Mongolian Vowel Harmony." In *Proceedings of NELS 9/Cuny Forum Papers in Linguistics 5–6*, 171–86. New York: Queens College Press.

Chomsky, N. (1965). *Aspects of the Theory of Syntax*. Cambridge, Mass.: MIT Press.

Chomsky, N. (1981). *Lectures on Government and Binding*. Dordrecht: Foris.

Chomsky, N. (1982). *Some Concepts and Consequences of the Theory of Government and Binding*. Cambridge, Mass.: MIT Press.

Chomsky, N. (1986). *Barriers*. Cambridge, Mass.: MIT Press.

Chomsky, N., and M. Halle (1968). *The Sound Pattern of English*. New York: Harper and Row.

Christdas, P. (1988). "The Phonology and Morphology of Tamil." Doctoral dissertation, Cornell University.

Churchward, C. M. (1940). *Rotuman Grammar and Dictionary*. Sydney: Methodist Church of Australasia.

Churma, D. (1984). "On Explaining Morpheme Structure." In *Ohio State University Working Papers in Linguistics* 29, 12–29. Department of Linguistics, Ohio State University.

Clark, M. (1985). "Downstep without Floating Tones." Ms., University of New Hampshire.

Clements, G. N. (1981). "Akan Vowel Harmony: A Nonlinear Analysis." In G. N. Clements, ed., *Harvard Studies in Phonology* 2, 108–77. Department of Linguistics, Harvard University.

Clements, G. N. (1982). "A Remark on the Elsewhere Condition." *Linguistic Inquiry* 13, 682–85.

Clements, G. N. (1984). "Vowel Harmony in Akan: A Consideration of Stewart's Word Structure Conditions." *Studies in African Linguistics* 15, 321–37.

Clements, G. N. (1985a). "The Geometry of Phonological Features." *Phonology Yearbook* 2, 225–52.

Clements, G. N. (1985b). "Compensatory Lengthening and Consonant Gemination in LuGanda." In L. Wetzels, and E. Sezer, eds., *Studies in Compensatory Lengthening*, 37–77. Dordrecht: Foris.

Clements, G. N. (1987). "Toward a Substantive Theory of Feature Specification." In *Proceedings of NELS 18*, 79–93. GLSA, University of Massachusetts, Amherst.

Clements, G. N. (1989). "On the Representation of Vowel Height." Ms., Cornell University.

Clements, G. N. (1991a). "Vowel Height Assimilation in Bantu Languages." In *Working Papers of the Cornell Phonetics Laboratory* 5, 37–76. Phonetics Laboratory, Cornell University.

Clements, G. N. (1991b). "Place of Articulation in Consonants and Vowels: A Unified Theory." In *Working Papers of the Cornell Phonetics Laboratory* 5, 77–123. Phonetics Laboratory, Cornell University.

Clements, G. N., and K. Ford (1979). "Kikuyu Tone Shift and Its Synchronic Consequences." *Linguistic Inquiry* 10, 179–210.

Clements, G. N., and K. Ford (1981). "On the Phonological Status of Downstep in Kikuyu." In D. Goyvaerts, ed., *Phonology in the 1980's*. Ghent: Storia Scientia.

Clements, G. N., and J. Goldsmith, eds. (1984). *Autosegmental Studies in Bantu Tone*. Dordrecht: Foris.

Clements, G. N., and S. J. Keyser (1983). *CV Phonology: A Generative Theory of the Syllable*. Cambridge, Mass.: MIT Press.

Clements, G. N., and E. Sezer (1982). "Vowel and Consonant Disharmony in Turkish." In H. van der Hulst and N. Smith, eds., *The Structure of Phonological Representations II*, 213–55. Dordrecht: Foris.

Clements, G. N., and R. Ṣonaiya (1989). "Underlying Feature Specification in Yoruba." Ms., Cornell University and Obafemi Awolowo University.

Cohn, A. (1989). "Phonetic Evidence for Configuration Constraints." In *Proceedings of NELS 19*, 63–77. GLSA, University of Massachusetts, Amherst.

Cohn, A. (1990). *Phonetic and Phonological Rules of Nasalization*. UCLA Working Papers in Phonetics 76. Department of Linguistics, UCLA.

Cole, J. (1987). "Planar Phonology and Morphology." Doctoral dissertation, MIT. [Published 1991, Garland, New York.]

Cole, J. (1990). "Arguing for the Phonological Cycle: A Critical Review." In *Proceedings of Linguistics Society of Mid America* 1, 51–67. Department of Linguistics, University of Wisconsin.

Cole, J., and L. Trigo (1987). "On the Representation of Neutral Segments in Harmony Systems." Ms., MIT.

Cole, J., and L. Trigo (1988). "Parasitic Harmony." In H. van der Hulst and N. Smith, eds., *Features, Segmental Structure, and Harmony Processes II*, 19–38. Dordrecht: Foris.

Coleman, J., and J. Local (1991). "The 'No Crossing Constraint' in Autosegmental Phonology." *Linguistics and Philosophy* 14, 295–338.

Comrie, B. (1981a). *The Languages of the Soviet Union*. Cambridge: Cambridge University Press.

Comrie, B. (1981b). *Language Universals and Linguistic Typology*. Chicago: University of Chicago Press.

Conway, L., K. Denham, B. Fricks, and C. K. Suh (1990). "Vowel Harmony in Djingili." Ms., University of Arizona.

Corina, D. (1990). "Handshape Assimilations in Hierarchical Phonological Representations." In C. Lucas, ed., *Sign Language Research: Theoretical Issues*, 27–49. Washington, D.C.: Gallaudet University Press.

Corina, D., and E. Sagey (1988). "Predictability in ASL Handshape Sequences, with Implications for Features and Feature Geometry." Ms., Salk Institute for Biological Studies and University of California, San Diego.

Courtenay, K. (1968). "A Generative Phonology of Yoruba." Doctoral dissertation, UCLA.

Czaykowska-Higgins, E. (1987). "Characterizing Tongue Root Behaviour." Ms., MIT.

Davy, J. I. M., and D. Nurse (1982). "Synchronic Versions of Dahl's Law: The Multiple Applications of a Phonological Dissimilation Rule." *Journal of African Languages and Linguistics* 4, 157–95.

Denning, K. (1989). "The Diachronic Development of Phonological Voice Quality, with Special Reference to Dinka and the Other Nilotic Languages." Doctoral dissertation, Stanford University.

Dimmendaal, G. J. (1983). *The Turkana Language*. Dordrecht: Foris.

Doak, I. (1992). "Another Look at Coeur d'Alene Harmony." *International Journal of American Linguistics* 58, 1–35.

Dolphyne, F. A. (1988). *The Akan (Twi-Fante) Language: Its Sound Systems and Tonal Structure.* Accra: Ghana Universities Press.

Donegan, P., and D. Stampe (1979). "The Study of Natural Phonology." In D. Dinnsen, ed., *Current Approaches to Phonological Theory*, 126–73. Bloomington, Ind.: Indiana University Press.

Donwa, F. S. (1983). "The Sound System of Isoko." Doctoral dissertation, University of Ibadan.

Dresher, B. E., and A. Johns (1990). "The Law of Double Consonants in Inuktitut." Paper presented at the Canadian Linguistic Association, University of Victoria.

Dudas, K. (1976). "The Phonology and Morphology of Modern Javanese." Doctoral dissertation, University of Illinois.

Elugbe, B. (1982). "The Vowels of Proto-Ẹdoid." *Journal of the Linguistic Association of Nigeria* 1, 107–15.

Ewen, C., and H. van der Hulst (1987). "Single-valued Features and the Distinction between [−F] and [∅F]." In F. Beukema and P. Coopmans, eds., *Linguistics in the Netherlands 1987*, 51–60. Dordrecht: Foris.

Fant, G. (1968). "Analysis and Synthesis of Speech Processes." In B. Malmberg, ed., *Manual of Phonetics*, 173–277. Amsterdam: North-Holland Publishing Co.

Firth, J. R. (1948). "Sounds and Prosodies." *Transactions of the Philological Society*, 127–52.

Fọlarin, A. Y. (1987). "Lexical Phonology of Yoruba Nouns and Verbs." Doctoral dissertation, University of Kansas, Lawrence.

Fresco, E. (1970). *Topics in Yoruba Dialect Phonology, Studies in African Linguistics*, Supplement 1.

Genetti, C. (1989). "Segmental Alternations in the Sunwari Verb Stem: A Case for the Feature [Front]." Ms., University of Oregon.

George (Madugu), I. (1973). "Vowel Harmony: Why So Restricted in Yoruba?" *Research Notes from the Department of Linguistics and Nigerian Languages* 6, 171–88. University of Ibadan.

Gerfen, C. (1991). "Izi Vowel Harmony and Selective Cyclicity." Paper presented at Arizona Phonology Conference 4, University of Arizona.

Gerfen, C. (1992). "Nasal Harmony in Coatzospan Mixtec." Ms., University of Arizona.

Gerfen, C. (to appear). " Trigger Conditions and Nasal Harmony in Terena." In *Proceedings of Berkeley Linguistics Society* 19. Department of Linguistics, University of California, Berkeley.

Goad, H. (1991). "[ATR] and [RTR] are Different Features." In *Proceedings of WCCFL* 10, 163–73. Stanford Linguistics Association, Center for the Study of Language and Information, Stanford University.

Goldsmith, J. (1976). "Autosegmental Phonology." Doctoral dissertation, MIT. [Published 1979, Garland, New York.]

Goldsmith, J. (1982). "Accent Systems." In H. van der Hulst and N. Smith, eds., *The Structure of Phonological Representations I*, 47–63. Dordrecht: Foris.

Goldsmith, J. (1984a). "Tone and Accent in Tonga." In G. N. Clements and J. Goldsmith, eds., *Autosegmental Studies in Bantu Tone*, 19–51. Dordrecht: Foris.

Goldsmith, J. (1984b). "Meeussen's Rule." In M. Aronoff and R. Oehrle, eds., *Language Sound Structure*, 245–59.

Goldsmith, J. (1985). "Vowel Harmony in Khalkha Mongolian, Yaka, Finnish and Hungarian." *Phonology Yearbook* 2, 253–75.

Goldsmith, J. (1989). "Harmonic Phonology: Phonology as an Intelligent System." Talk presented at the Berkeley Workshop on Constraints vs. Rules in Phonology, University of California, Berkeley.

Goldsmith, J. (1990). *Autosegmental and Metrical Phonology*. Oxford: Blackwell.

Goldsmith, J., and G. Larson (to appear). "Local Modeling and Syllabification." In *Papers from the 26th Annual Regional Meeting of the Chicago Linguistic Society, Part Two: Parasession on the Syllable in Phonetics and Phonology*. Chicago Linguistic Society, University of Chicago.

Greenberg, J. H., ed. (1963). *Universals of Language*. Cambridge, Mass.: MIT Press.

Grignon, A. M. (1984). "Phonologie lexicale tridimensionelle du japonais." Doctoral dissertation, Université de Montréal.

de Haas, W. G. (1988). "A Formal Theory of Vowel Coalescence: A Case Study of Ancient Greek." Doctoral dissertation, Katholieke Universiteit te Nijmegen.

Hall, B. L., and R. M. R. Hall (1980). "Nez Perce Vowel Harmony: An Africanist Explanation and Some Theoretical Questions." in R. M. Vago, ed., *Issues in Vowel Harmony*, 201–36. Amsterdam: John Benjamins.

Halle, M. (1962). "Phonology in Generative Grammar." *Word* 18, 54–72.

Halle, M. (1964). "On the Bases of Phonology." In J. A. Fodor and J. J. Katz, eds., *The Structure of Language: Readings in the Philosophy of Language*, 324–33. Englewood Cliffs, N. J.: Prentice-Hall.

Halle, M. (1979). "Formal vs. Functional Considerations in Phonology." In B. Brogyanyi, ed., *Festschrift for Oswald Szemerényi on the Occasion of His 65th Birthday*, 325–41. Amsterdam: John Benjamins.

Halle, M., and K. Stevens (1969). "On the Feature [Advanced Tongue Root]." In *Quarterly Progress Report of the Research Laboratory in Electronics* 94, 209–15. Research Laboratory in Electronics, MIT.

Halle, M., and J.-R. Vergnaud (1981). "Harmony Processes." In W. Klein and W. Levelt, eds., *Crossing the Boundaries in Linguistics: Studies Presented to Manfred Bierwisch*, 1–22. Dordrecht: Reidel.

Halle, M., and J.-R. Vergnaud (1982). "On the Framework of Autosegmental Phonology." In H. van der Hulst and N. Smith, eds., *The Structure of Phonological Representations I*, 65–83. Dordrecht: Foris.

Halle, M., and J.-R. Vergnaud (1987a). *An Essay on Stress*. Cambridge, Mass.: MIT Press.

Halle, M., and J.-R. Vergnaud (1987b). "Stress and the Cycle." *Linguistic Inquiry* 18, 45–84.

Hamano, S. (1986). "The Sound-Symbolic System of Japanese." Doctoral dissertation, University of Florida, Gainesville.

Hammond, M. (1988). "On Deriving the Well-Formedness Condition." *Linguistic Inquiry* 19, 319–25.

Haraguchi, S. (1977). *The Tone Pattern of Japanese: An Autosegmental Theory of Tonology.* Tokyo: Kaitakusha.

Harms, R. T. (1973). "How Abstract Is Nupe?" *Language* 49, 439–46.

Harris, Z. (1951). *Structural Linguistics.* Chicago: University of Chicago Press.

Hayes, B. (1981). "A Metrical Theory of Stress Rules." Doctoral dissertation, MIT. [Distributed by Indiana University Linguistics Club, Bloomington, Ind.]

Hayes, B. (1982). "Extrametricality and English Stress." *Linguistic Inquiry* 13, 227–76.

Hayes, B. (1986). "Inalterability in CV Phonology." *Language* 62, 321–51.

Hayes, B. (1989). "Compensatory Lengthening in Moraic Phonology." *Linguistic Inquiry* 20, 253–307.

Hayes, B. (1990). "Diphthongisation and Coindexing." *Phonology* 7, 31–71.

Hendriks, P. (1989). "Palatalization and Labialization as Morphemes in Chaha." Ms., Yale University.

Hewitt, M., and A. Prince (1989). "OCP, Locality, and Linking: the N. Karanga Verb." In *Proceedings of WCCFL* 8, 176–91. Stanford Linguistics Association, Stanford University.

Hoard, J., and G. O'Grady (1976). "Nyangumarda Phonology: A Preliminary Report." In R. M. W. Dixon, ed., *Grammatical Categories in Australian Languages*, 51–77. Atlantic Highlands, N.J.: Humanities Press.

Hockett, C. F. (1958). *A Course in Modern Linguistics.* New York: Macmillan.

Hoffmann, C. (1963). *A Grammar of the Margi Language.* London: Oxford University Press.

Hoffmann, C. (1973). "The Vowel Harmony System of the Okpẹ Monosyllabic Verb." *Research Notes from the Department of Linguistics and Nigerian Languages* 6, 79–111. University of Ibadan.

Hombert, J. M. (1976). "Perception of Bisyllabic Nouns in Yoruba." In L. Hyman et al., eds., *Papers in African Linguistics in Honor of W. E. Welmers*, 109–22. *Studies in African Linguistics*, Supplement 6.

Hong, S. H. (1991). "Manchu Vowel Harmony." Ms., University of Arizona.

Hong, S. H. (1992). "Parasitic Harmony." Ms., University of Arizona.

Hong, S. H. (in preparation). "Issues in Rounding Harmony." Doctoral dissertation, University of Arizona.

Hoshi, H. (1989). "On Nez Perce Vowel Harmony." Ms., University of Connecticut.

Houis, M. (1963). *Étude descriptive de la langue Susu. Mémoires de l'institut français d'afrique noire* 67, Dakar.

Howard, I. (1972). "A Directional Theory of Rule Application in Phonology." Doctoral dissertation, MIT.

Hualde, J. I. (1984). "Vowel Harmony in Turkana." Ms., University of Southern California.

Hualde, J. I. (1991). "Unspecified and Unmarked Vowels." *Linguistic Inquiry* 22, 205–9.

Hulst, H. G. van der (1988). "The Dual Interpretation of |I|, |U|, |A|." In *Proceedings of NELS 18*, 208–22. GLSA, University of Massachusetts, Amherst.

Hulst, H. G. van der (1989). "Atoms of Segmental Structure: Components, Gestures, and Dependency." *Phonology* 6, 253–84.

Hulst, H. G. van der, and N. Smith (1985). "Vowel Features and Umlaut in Djingili, Nyangumarda and Warlpiri." *Phonology Yearbook* 2, 277–303.

Hulst, H. G. van der, and N. Smith (1986). "On Neutral Vowels." In K. Bogers, H. G. van der Hulst, and M. Mous, eds., *The Phonological Representation of Suprasegmentals*, 233–79. Dordrecht: Foris.

Hyman, L. M. (1970). "How Concrete Is Phonology?" *Language* 46, 58–76.

Hyman, L. M. (1973). "Nupe Three Years Later." *Language* 49, 447–52.

Hyman, L. M. (1982). "The Representation of nasality in Gokana." In H. van der Hulst and N. Smith, eds., *The Structure of Phonological Representations I*, 111–30. Dordrecht: Foris.

Hyman, L. M. (1985). *A Theory of Phonological Weight*. Dordrecht: Foris.

Hyman, L. M. (1987). "Prosodic Domains in Kukuya." *Natural Language & Linguistic Theory* 5, 311–33.

Hyman, L. M. (1989). "Advanced Tongue Root in Kinande." Ms., University of California, Berkeley.

Hyman, L. M. (1990a). "Boundary Tonology and the Prosodic Hierarchy." In S. Inkelas and D. Zec, eds., *The Phonology-Syntax Connection*, 109–25. Chicago: University of Chicago Press.

Hyman, L. M. (1990b). "Structure Preservation and Postlexical Tonology in Dagbani." Ms., University of California, Berkeley.

Hyman, L. M. (1992). "Velar Palatalization in Cibemba: A 'Non-Duplication' Problem." *Linguistique Africaine* 8, 55–71.

Hyman, L. M., and A. Ngunga (1993). "On the Non-Universality of Tonal Association 'Conventions': Evidence from Ciyao." Ms., University of California, Berkeley, and Universidade Eduardo Mondlane, Maputo, Mozambique.

Hyman, L. M. and D. Pulleyblank (1988). "On Feature Copying: Parameters of Tone Rules." In L. M. Hyman and C. N. Li, eds., *Language, Speech and Mind*, 30–48. London: Routledge.

Hyman, L. M., and N. Valinande (1985). "Globality in the Kinande Tone System." In D. L. Goyvaerts, ed., *African Linguistics: Essays in Memory of M. W. K. Semikenke*, 239–60. Amsterdam: John Benjamins.

Inkelas, S. (1989). "Prosodic Constituency in the Lexicon." Doctoral dissertation, Stanford University.

Ishihara, M. (1989). "The Morphemic Plane Hypothesis and Plane Internal Phonological Domains." In *Proceedings of Arizona Phonology Conference* 2, 64–83. Department of Linguistics, University of Arizona.

Ishihara, M. (1991). " The Lexical Prosodic Phonology of Japanese Verbs." Doctoral dissertation, University of Arizona.

Itô, J. (1984). "Melodic Dissimilation in Ainu." *Linguistic Inquiry* 15, 505–13.

Itô, J. (1986). " Syllable Theory in Prosodic Phonology." Doctoral dissertation, University of Massachusetts, Amherst.

Itô, J. (1989). "A Prosodic Theory of Epenthesis." *Natural Language & Linguistic Theory* 7, 217–59.

Itô, J., and R. A. Mester (1986). "The Phonology of Voicing in Japanese: Theoretical Consequences for Morphological Accessibility." *Linguistic Inquiry* 17, 49–73.

Jackson, M. (1988). *Phonetic Theory and Cross-Linguistic Variation in Vowel Articulation.* UCLA Working Papers in Phonetics 71. Department of Linguistics, UCLA.

Jacobson, L. (1978). "DhoLuo Vowel Harmony." In *UCLA Working Papers in Phonetics* 43, 1–121. Department of Linguistics, UCLA.

Jacobson, L. (1980). "Voice-Quality Harmony in Western Nilotic Languages." In R. M. Vago, ed., *Issues in Vowel Harmony*, 183–200. Amsterdam: John Benjamins.

Jaeggli, O. (1986). "Passive." *Linguistic Inquiry* 17, 587–622.

Jakobson, R. (1952). "Langues paléosibériennes." In A. Meillet and M. Cohen, eds. *Les langues du monde*, 403–31. Paris: CNRS.

Jakobson, R., G. Fant, and M. Halle (1963). *Preliminaries to Speech Analysis.* Cambridge, Mass.: MIT Press.

Jensen, J. (1974). "A Constraint on Variables in Phonology." *Language* 50, 675–85.

Jensen, J., and M. Stong-Jensen (1976). "Ordering and Directionality of Iterative Rules." In A. Koutsoudas, ed., *The Application and Ordering of Grammatical Rules*, 104–21. The Hague: Mouton.

Jensen, J., and M. Stong-Jensen (1979). "The Relevancy Condition and Variables in Phonology." *Linguistic Analysis* 5, 125–60.

Johnson, C. D. (1972). *Formal Aspects of Phonological Description.* The Hague: Mouton.

Johnson, C. D. (1975). "Phonological Channels in Chaha." *Afroasiatic Linguistics* 2.2, 1–12.

Ka, O. (1988). "Wolof Phonology and Morphology: A Non-Linear Approach." Doctoral dissertation, University of Illinois at Urbana-Champaign.

Kaisse, E. (1985). *Connected Speech.* Orlando, Fla.: Academic Press.

Kaisse, E. (1990). "Towards a Typology of Postlexical Rules." In S. Inkelas and D. Zec, eds., *The Phonology-Syntax Connection*, 127–43. Chicago: University of Chicago Press.

Kaisse, E., and P. A. Shaw (1985). "On the Theory of Lexical Phonology." *Phonology Yearbook* 2, 1–30.

Kaplan, L. (1981). *Phonological Issues in North Alaskan Inupiaq.* Alaska Native Language Center Research Papers 6. Fairbanks, Alaska: Alaska Native Language Center.

Kaye, J. (1985). "On the Syllable Structure of Certain West African Languages." In D. L. Goyvaerts, ed., *African Linguistics: Essays in Memory of M. W. K. Semikenke*, 285–308. Amsterdam: John Benjamins.

Kaye, J. (1989). *Phonology: A Cognitive View.* Hillsdale, N.J.: Lawrence Erlbaum Associates.

Kaye, J., and J. Lowenstamm (1982). "On the Notion of Concatenation in Phonology." Paper presented at NELS 13, Université du Québec à Montréal.

Kaye, J., and J. Lowenstamm (1984). "De la syllabicité." In F. Dell, D. Hirst, and J.-R. Vergnaud, eds., *Forme sonore du langage*, 123–59. Paris: Hermann.

Kaye, J., J. Lowenstamm, and J.-R. Vergnaud (1985). "The Internal Structure of Phonological Elements: A Theory of Charm and Govemment." *Phonology Yearbook* 2, 305–28.

Kean, M. L. (1975). "The Theory of Markedness in Generative Grammar." Doctoral dissertation, MIT. [Distributed by Indiana University Linguistics Club, Bloomington, Ind.]

Keating, P. (1985). "CV Phonology, Experimental Phonetics, and Coarticulation." *UCLA Working Papers in Phonetics* 62, 1–13. Department of Linguistics, UCLA.

Keating, P. (1988). "Underspecification in Phonetics." *Phonology* 5, 275–92.

Keating, P. (1991). "Phonetic Representation of Palatalization vs. Fronting." Paper presented at The Organization of Phonology: Features and Domains Workshop celebrating the 25th Anniversary of the Department of Linguistics, University of Illinois.

Kenstowicz, M. (1976). "Some Rules of Koryak Phonology." *Studies in the Linguistic Sciences* 6, 22–37.

Kenstowicz, M. (1979). "Chukchee Vowel Harmony and Epenthesis." In *The Elements: A Parasession on Linguistic Units and Levels*, 402–12. Chicago Linguistic Society, University of Chicago.

Kenstowicz, M. (1987). "Tone and Accent in Kizigua—a Bantu Language." In P. M. Bertinetto and M. Loporcaro, eds., *Certamen Phonologicum*, Papers from the 1987 Cortona Phonology Meeting, 177–88. Turin: Rosenberg & Sellier.

Kenstowicz, M., and C. Kisseberth (1977). *Topics in Phonological Theory*. New York: Academic Press.

Khabanyane, K. E. (1991). "The Five Phonemic Vowel Heights of Southern Sotho: An Acoustic and Phonological Analysis." In *Working Papers of the Cornell Phonetics Laboratory* 5, 1–36. Phonetics Laboratory, Cornell University.

Kiparsky, P. (1973). "Phonological Representations." In O. Fujimura, ed., *Three Dimensions in Linguistic Theory*, 2–136. Tokyo: TEC.

Kiparsky, P. (1981). "Vowel Harmony." Ms., MIT.

Kiparsky, P. (1982). "Lexical Morphology and Phonology." In The Linguistic Society of Korea, ed., *Linguistics in the Morning Calm*, 3–91. Seoul: Hanshin.

Kiparsky, P. (1984). "On the Lexical Phonology of Icelandic." In C. C. Elert, I. Johansson, and E. Strangert, eds., *Nordic Prosody III*, 135–64. Stockholm: Almqvist and Wiksell.

Kiparsky, P. (1985). "Some Consequences of Lexical Phonology." *Phonology Yearbook* 2, 85–138.

Kiparsky, P. (1991). "Blocking in Non-Derived Environments." Ms., Stanford University.

Kuroda, S.-Y. (1967). *Yawelmani Phonology*. Cambridge, Mass.: MIT Press.

LaCharité, D. (in preparation). "The Internal Structure of the Affricate." Doctoral dissertation, University of Ottawa.

Ladefoged, P. (1968). *A Phonetic Study of West African Languages*. Cambridge: Cambridge University Press.

Ladefoged, P. (1975). *A Course in Phonetics*. New York: Harcourt Brace Jovanovich.

Ladefoged, P. (1989). *Representing Phonetic Structure*. UCLA Working Papers in Phonetics 73. Department of Linguistics, UCLA.

Ladefoged, P., J. DeClerk, M. Lindau, and G. Papçun (1972). "An Auditory-Motor Theory of Speech Production." *UCLA Working Papers in Phonetics* 22, 48–75. Department of Linguistics, UCLA.

Ladefoged, P., and I. Maddieson (1986). *Some of the Sounds of the World's Languages*. UCLA Working Papers in Phonetics 64. Department of Linguistics, UCLA.

Ladefoged, P., and I. Maddieson (1990). "Vowels of the World's Languages." *Journal of Phonetics* 18, 93–122.

Lakoff, G. (1989). "Cognitive Phonology." Talk presented at the Berkeley Workshop on Constraints vs. Rules in Phonology, University of California, Berkeley.

Laniran, Y. O. (1985). "Vowel Merger and Ẹ̀málhẹ̀ Vowel Harmony." *Journal of the Linguistic Association of Nigeria* 3, 3–11.

Leben, W. (1973). "Suprasegmental Phonology." Doctoral dissertation, MIT. [Distributed by Indiana University Linguistics Club, Bloomington, Ind.]

Leben, W. (1978). "The Representation of Tone." In V. Fromkin, ed., *Tone: A Linguistic Survey*, 177–219. New York: Academic Press.

Levergood, B. (1984). "Rule Governed Vowel Harmony and the Strict Cycle." In *Proceedings of NELS 14*, 275–93. GLSA, University of Massachusetts, Amherst.

Levin, J. (1985). "A Metrical Theory of Syllabicity." Doctoral dissertation, MIT.

Liberman, M., and J. Pierrehumbert (1984). "Intonational Invariance under Changes in Pitch Range and Length." In M. Aronoff and R. Oehrle, eds., *Language Sound Structure*, 157–233. Cambridge, Mass.: MIT Press.

Liberman, M., and A. Prince (1977). "On Stress and Linguistic Rhythm." *Linguistic Inquiry* 8, 249–336.

Lightner, T. (1963). "A Note on the Formulation of Phonological Rules." In *Quarterly Progress Report of the Research Laboratory of Electronics* 68, 187–89. Research Laboratory of Electronics, MIT.

Lightner, T. (1965). "On the Description of Vowel and Consonant Harmony." *Word* 21, 244–50.

Lindau, M. (1978). "Vowel Features." *Language* 54, 541–63.

Lindau, M. (1979). "The Feature Expanded." *Journal of Phonetics* 7, 163–76.

Lindau-Webb, M. (1987). "Acoustic Correlates of TENSE-LAX Vowels and ATR Vowels." Abstract, *Journal of the Acoustical Society of America, Supplement 1*, vol. 82, p. S116.

Lindau, M., and P. Ladefoged (1986). "Variability of Feature Specifications." In J. S. Perkell and D. H. Klatt, eds., *Invariance and Variability in Speech Processes*, 464–79. Hillsdale, N.J.: Lawrence Erlbaum Associates.

Lombardi, L. (1990). "The Nonlinear Organization of the Affricate." *Natural Language & Linguistic Theory* 8, 375–425.

McCarthy, J. (1979). "Formal Problems in Semitic Phonology and Morphology." Doctoral dissertation, MIT.

McCarthy, J. (1981). "A Prosodic Theory of Nonconcatenative Morphology." *Linguistic Inquiry* 12, 373–418.

McCarthy, J. (1983). "Consonantal Morphology in the Chaha Verb." In *Proceedings of WCCFL* 2, 176–88. Stanford Linguistics Association, Stanford University.

McCarthy, J. (1984a). "Theoretical Consequences of Montañes Vowel Harmony." *Linguistic Inquiry* 15, 291–318.

McCarthy, J. (1984b). "Prosodic Organization in Morphology." In M. Aronoff and R. Oehrle, eds., *Language Sound Structure*, 299–317. Cambridge, Mass.: MIT Press.

McCarthy, J. (1986a). "OCP Effects: Gemination and Antigemination." *Linguistic Inquiry* 17, 207–63.

McCarthy, J. (1986b). "Lexical Phonology and Nonconcatenative Morphology in the History of Chaha." *Revue Québécoise de Linguistique* 16, 209–28.

McCarthy, J. (1988). "Feature Geometry and Dependency: A Review." *Phonetica* 43, 84–108.

McCarthy, J. (1989a). "Linear Order in Phonological Representations." *Linguistic Inquiry* 20, 71–99.

McCarthy, J (1989b). "The Phonology of Semitic Pharyngeals." Ms., University of Massachusetts, Amherst.

McCarthy, J., and A. Prince (1986). "Prosodic Morphology." Ms., University of Massachusetts, Amherst, and Brandeis University.

McCarthy, J., and A. Prince (1990). "Foot and Word in Prosodic Morphology: The Arabic Broken Plural." *Natural Language & Linguistic Theory* 8, 209–83.

McCawley, J. (1970). "A Note on Tiv Conjugation." *Studies in African Linguistics* 1, 123–29.

MacKay, I. (1976). "Ultrasonic Investigation of Anterior Pharyngeal Wall (Tongue Root) Position in Syllables Containing Tense and Lax Vowels." Doctoral dissertation, University of Cincinnati.

MacLean, E. A. (1986). *North Slope Iñupiaq Grammar: First Year.* Fairbanks, Alaska: Alaska Native Language Center.

Maddieson, I. (1984). *Patterns of Sounds.* Cambridge: Cambridge University Press.

Marantz, A. (1982). "Re Reduplication." *Linguistic Inquiry* 13, 435–82.

Mascaró, J. (1976). Catalan Phonology and the Phonological Cycle. Doctoral dissertation, MIT. [Distributed by Indiana University Linguistics Club, Bloomington, Ind.]

Meechan, M. (1992). "Register in Khmer: The Laryngeal Specification of Pharyngeal Expansion." Master's thesis, University of Ottawa.

Meeussen, A. E. (1963). "Morphotonology of the Tonga Verb." *Journal of African Linguistics* 2, Part I, 72–92.

Mester, R. A. (1986). "Studies in Tier Structure." Doctoral dissertation, University of Massachusetts, Amherst.

Mester, R. A. (1988). "Dependent Tier Ordering and the OCP." In H. van der Hulst and N. Smith, eds., *Features, Segmental Structure, and Harmony Processes II*, 127–44. Dordrecht: Foris.

Mester, R. A., and J. Itô (1989). "Feature Predictability and Underspecification: Palatal Prosody in Japanese Mimetics." *Language* 65, 258–93.

Miura, I., and R. F. Sasaki (1965). *The Zen Koan*. New York: Harcourt, Brace & World.

Mohanan, K. P. (1986). *The Theory of Lexical Phonology*. Dordrecht: Reidel.

Mohanan, K. P. (1988). "Universals in Phonological Alternation." Ms., Stanford University.

Mohanan, K. P. (1991). "On the Bases of Underspecification." *Natural Language & Linguistic Theory* 9, 285–325.

Mohanan, K. P. (to appear). "Fields of Attraction in Phonology." In J. Goldsmith, ed., *The Last Phonological Rule*. Chicago: University of Chicago Press.

Mohanan, K. P., and T. Mohanan (1984). "Lexical Phonology of the Consonant System of Malayalam." *Linguistic Inquiry* 15, 575–602.

Mutaka, M. N. (1990). "The Lexical Tonology of Kinande." Doctoral dissertation, University of Southern California. [To appear, De Gruyter, Berlin.]

Mutaka, N. M. (1991). "Vowel Harmony in Kinande." Ms., University of Southern California.

Mutaka, N. M. (n.d.). "The Augment in Kinande." Ms., University of Southern California.

Myers, J. (1990). "Rule Ordering in Mandarin Segmental Phonology." Ms., University of Arizona.

Myers, S. (1987). "Tone and the Structure of Words in Shona." Doctoral dissertation, University of Massachusetts, Amherst.

Myers, S. (1991). "Persistent Rules," *Linguistic Inquiry* 22, 315–44.

Ndiaye, M. D. (1991). "Quel système vocalique pour le Wolof?" Ms., University of Ottawa.

Nespor, M., and I. Vogel (1982). "Prosodic Domains of External Sandhi Rules." In H. van der Hulst and N. Smith, eds., *The Structure of Phonological Representations I*, 225–55. Dordrecht: Foris.

Nespor, M., and I. Vogel (1986). *Prosodic Phonology*. Dordrecht: Foris.

Newman, S. (1944). *The Yokuts Language of California*. The Viking Fund Publications in Anthropology 2. New York: The Viking Fund.

Nishikawa, M. (1987). "Japanese Lexical Phonology and Morphology." Doctoral dissertation, University of Southern California.

Odden, D. (1977). "Overspecification and Variables in Phonology." *Linguistic Analysis* 3, 177–96.

Odden, D. (1980). "The Irrelevancy of the Relevancy Condition: Evidence for the Feature Specification Constraint." *Linguistic Analysis* 6, 261–304.

Odden, D. (1984). "Stem Tone Assignment in Shona." In G. N. Clements and J. Goldsmith, eds., *Autosegmental Studies in Bantu Tone*, 255–80. Dordrecht: Foris.

Odden, D. (1986). "On the Role of the Obligatory Contour Principle in Phonological Theory." *Language* 62, 353–83.

Odden, D. (1988). "Anti Antigemination and the OCP." *Linguistic Inquiry* 19, 451–75.

Odden, D. (1989). "Vowel Geometry." Ms., Ohio State University.

O'Grady, G. (1964). *Nyangumata Grammar*. Oceania Linguistic Monographs. University of Sydney, Australia.

Ohala, J. J. (1975). "Phonetic Explanations for Nasal Sound Patterns." In C. A. Ferguson, L. M. Hyman, and J. J. Ohala, eds., *Nasalfest: Papers from a Symposium on Nasals and Nasalization*, 289–316. Language Universals Project, Stanford University.

Ọla, Ọ. (1992). "Yoruba Vowel Harmony." Master's thesis, School of Oriental and African Studies, University of London.

Omamor, A. (1973). "Uvwiẹ: A Case of Vowels Merging." In *Research Notes from the Department of Linguistics and Nigerian Languages* 6, 113–43, University of Ibadan.

Omamor, A. (1988). "Okpẹ and Uvwiẹ: A Case of Vowel Harmony Galore." *Journal of West African Languages* 18, 47–64.

Owolabi, D. K. O. (1981). "A Pedagogical Description of Derived Nouns in Yoruba." Ms., University of Ibadan.

Owomoyela, O. (1988). *A Kì í: Yorùbá Proscriptive and Prescriptive Proverbs*. Lanham, Md.: University Press of America.

Oyelaran, Ọ. (1971). "Yoruba Phonology." Doctoral dissertation, Stanford University.

Oyelaran, Ọ. (1973). "Yoruba Vowel Co-occurrence Restrictions." *Studies in African Linguistics* 4, 155–82.

Padden, C., and D. Perlmutter (1987). "American Sign Language and the Architecture of Phonological Theory." *Natural Language & Linguistic Theory* 5, 335–75.

Painter, C. (1973). "Cineradiographic Data on the Feature 'Covered' in Twi Vowel Harmony." *Phonetica* 28, 97–120.

Painter, C. (1976). "Pitch Control and Pharynx Width in Twi: An Electromyographic Study." *Phonetica* 33, 334–52.

Palmer, F. R. (1970). *Prosodic Analysis*. London: Oxford University Press.

Paradis, C. (1986). "Phonologie et morphologie lexicales: Les classes nominales en pulaar (Fula)." Doctoral dissertation, University of Montreal. [Revised and published in English as *Lexical Phonology and Morphology: The Nominal Classes in Fula*, Garland, New York (1992).]

Paradis, C. (1988). "On Constraints and Repair Strategies." *The Linguistic Review* 6, 71–97.

Paradis, C., and J.-F. Prunet (1991). *The Special Status of Coronals: Internal and External Evidence*. San Diego, Calif.: Academic Press.

Patrie, J. (1982). *The Genetic Relationship of the Ainu Language*. Honolulu, Hawaii: The University Press of Hawaii.

Paulian, C. (1974). *Le Kukuya: Langue teke du Congo*. Paris: S.E.L.A.F.

Peng, L. (1990). "Banning Constraint Violations: Kikuyu Evidence." Paper presented at WECOL 20.

Peng, L. (1991). "A Phonological Argument against Privative Voicing." Paper presented at WCCFL X, Arizona State University, Tempe.

Peng, L. (1992). "Toward a Unified Theory of Tone and Voice." Doctoral dissertation, University of Arizona.

Pérez, P. (1991). "Navajo Strident Assimilation: Another Perspective." Ms., University of Arizona.

Perkell, J. S. (1971). "Physiology of Speech Production: A Preliminary Study of Two Suggested Revisions of the Features Specifying Vowels." In *Quarterly Progress Report of the Research Laboratory of Electronics* 102, 123–39. Research Laboratory of Electronics, MIT.

Peterson, G. E., and H. L. Barney (1952). "Control Methods Used in a Study of the Vowels." *Journal of the Acoustical Society of America* 24, 175–84. [Reproduced in D. B. Fry, ed. (1976). *Acoustic Phonetics: A Course of Basic Readings*, 104–22. Cambridge: Cambridge University Press.]

Pierrehumbert, J., and M. Beckman (1988). *Japanese Tone Structure*. Cambridge, Mass.: MIT Press.

Piggott, G. L. (1971). "Some Implications of Algonquian Palatalization." In J. D. Kaye, G. L. Piggott, and K. Tokaichi, eds., *Odawa Language Project, First Report*, 11–38. Anthropological Series no. 9, Department of Anthropology, University of Toronto.

Piggott, G. (1988). "The Parameters of Nasalization." Ms., McGill University.

Piggott, G. (1989). "Variability in Feature Dependency: The Case of Nasality." Ms., McGill University.

Piggott, G., and R. Singh (1985). "The Phonology of Epenthetic Segments." *The Canadian Journal of Linguistics* 30, 415–51.

Pike, K. L. (1967). "Tongue-Root Position in Practical Phonetics." Phonetica 17, 129–40.

Poppe, N. (1954). *Grammar of Written Mongolian*. Porta Linguarum Orientalium, Neue Serie I.

Poser, W. J. (1982). "Phonological Representation and Action-at-a-Distance." In H. van der Hulst and N. Smith, eds., *The Structure of Phonological Representations II*, 121–58. Dordrecht: Foris.

Poser, W. J. (1984). "The Phonetics and Phonology of Tone and Intonation in Japanese." Doctoral dissertation, MIT.

Prince, A. (1983). "Relating to the Grid." *Linguistic Inquiry* 14, 19–100.

Prince, A. (1990). "Quantitative Consequences of Rhythmic Organization." Ms., Brandeis University.

Prince, A., and P. Smolensky (1991a). "Optimality." Paper presented at the Arizona Phonology Conference 4, University of Arizona.

Prince, A., and P. Smolensky (1991b). "Harmonic Phonology." Cognitive Science Workshop, University of Arizona.

Pulleyblank, D. (1985). "A Lexical Treatment of Tone in Tiv." In D. L. Goyvaerts, ed., *African Linguistics: Essays in Memory of M. W. K. Semikenke*, 421–76. Amsterdam: John Benjamins.

Pulleyblank, D. (1986a). *Tone in Lexical Phonology*. Dordrecht: Reidel.

Pulleyblank, D. (1986b). "Rule Application on a Non-cyclic Stratum." *Linguistic Inquiry* 17, 573–80.

Pulleyblank, D. (1986c). "Underspecification and Low Vowel Harmony in Okpe." *Studies in African Linguistics* 17, 119–53.

Pulleyblank, D. (1988a). "Underspecification, the Feature Hierarchy and Tiv Vowels." *Phonology* 5, 299–326.

Pulleyblank, D. (1988b). "Tone and the Morphemic Tier Hypothesis." In M. Hammond and M. Noonan, eds., *Theoretical Morphology*, 353-70. Orlando, Fla.: Academic Press.

Pulleyblank, D. (1988c). "Vocalic Underspecification in Yoruba." *Linguistic Inquiry* 19, 233–70.

Pulleyblank, D. (1988d). "Vowel Deletion in Yoruba." *Journal of African Languages and Linguistics* 10, 117–36.

Pulleyblank, D. (1989). "Patterns of Feature Cooccurrence: The Case of Nasality." In *Proceedings of Arizona Phonology Conference 2/Coyote Papers* 9, 98–115. Department of Linguistics, University of Arizona.

Pulleyblank, E. (1989a). "The Role of Coronal in Articulator Based Features." In *Papers from the 25th Regional Meeting of the Chicago Linguistic Society*, 379–94. Chicago Linguistic Society, University of Chicago.

Pulleyblank, E. (1989b). "Articulator Based Features of Vowels and Consonants." Ms., University of British Columbia.

Purcell, K. (1989). "Palatalization and Labialization in Nupe." Ms., University of Ottawa.

Rialland, A., and R. Djamouri (1984). "Harmonie vocalique, consonantique et structures de dépendance dans le mot en Mongol Khalkha." *Bulletin de la Société de Linguistique de Paris* 79, 333–83.

Rice, K. (1987). "The Function of Structure Preservation: Derived Environments." In *Proceedings of NELS 17*, 501–19. GLSA, University of Massachusetts, Amherst.

Rice, K. (1990). "Predicting Rule Domains in the Phrasal Phonology." In S. Inkelas and D. Zec, eds., *The Phonology-Syntax Connection*, 289–312. Chicago: University of Chicago Press.

Ringen, C. (1975). "Vowel Harmony: Theoretical Implications." Doctoral dissertation, Indiana University.

Ringen, C. (1988). "Transparency in Hungarian Vowel Harmony." *Phonology* 5, 327–42.

Rose, S. (to appear). "Locality Conditions in Chaha Palatalization." In *Proceedings of the 1992 Annual Conference of the Canadian Linguistic Association*. Department of Linguistics, University of Toronto.

Sagey, E. (1986). "The Representation of Features and Relations in Nonlinear Phonology." Doctoral dissertation, MIT.

Sagey, E. (1988). "On the Ill-Formedness of Crossing Association Lines." *Linguistic Inquiry* 19, 109–18.

Saito, M. (1981). "An Autosegmental Approach to Metathesis in Rotuman." Ms., MIT.

Salami, A. (1972). "Vowel and Consonant Harmony and Vowel Restrictions in Assimilated English Loan Words in Yoruba." *African Language Studies* 13, 162–81.

Sandler, W. (1990). *The Phonological Representation of the Sign: Linearity and Nonlinearity in American Sign Language*. Dordrecht: Foris.

Saussure, F. de (1916). *Cours de linguistique générale*. Paris: Payot.

Schachter, P., and V. Fromkin (1968). *A Phonology of Akan: Akuapem, Asante, and Fante*. Working Papers in Phonetics. Department of Linguistics, UCLA.

Schane, S. (1984). "The Fundamentals of Particle Phonology." *Phonology Yearbook* 1, 129–55.

Schein, B., and D. Steriade (1986). "On Geminates." *Linguistic Inquiry* 17, 691–744.

Schlindwein, D. (1987). "P-bearing Units: A Study of Kinande Vowel Harmony." In *Proceedings of NELS 17*, 551–67. GLSA, University of Massachusetts, Amherst.

Schlindwein, D. (1988). "The Phonological Geometry of Morpheme Concatenation." Doctoral dissertation, University of Southern California.

Schlindwein, D. (1989). "Context Sensitive Fill-in Rules and Underspecification Theory." *Linguistic Analysis* 19, 77–98.

Schlindwein, D. (1990). "Absolute Neutralization in a Feature-Based Theory of Underspecification." Ms., University of Southern California and University of Georgia.

Seki, M. (1986). "The Augment in Kinande." Ms., University of Southern California.

Selkirk, E. (1984). *Phonology and Syntax: The Relation between Sound and Structure.* Cambridge, Mass.: MIT Press.

Selkirk, E. (1988). "A Two-Root Theory of Length." Paper presented at NELS 19; published 1991 in *University of Massachusetts Occasional Papers in Linguistics* 16, 123–70. GLSA, University of Massachusetts, Amherst.

Selkirk, E. (1991). "Major Place in the Vowel Space: Vowel Height Features." Ms., University of Massachusetts, Amherst.

Sharp, J. (1986). "Spreading in Nyangumarta: A Nonlinear Analysis." Ms., University of Arizona.

Shaw, P. (1991a). "Consonant Harmony Systems: The Special Status of Coronal Harmony." in C. Paradis and J.-F. Prunet, eds., *The Special Status of Coronals: Internal and External Evidence*, 125–57. San Diego, Calif.: Academic Press.

Shaw, P. (1991b). "Syllable Structure in Northwest Coast Languages: Melodic Skipping in Nisgha." Paper presented at the Conference on Linguistic Research, University of British Columbia, October 1991.

Singh, R. (1987). "Well-formedness Conditions and Phonological Theory." In W. Dressler et al., eds., *Phonologica 1984*, 273–85. Cambridge: Cambridge University Press.

Skorik, P. (1961). *Grammatika Chukotskogo Jazyka.* Moscow: Akademia Nauk.

Smolensky, P. (1986). "Information Processing in Dynamical Systems: Foundations of Harmony Theory." In D. Rumelhart, J. McClelland, and the PDP Research Group, eds., *Parallel Distributed Processing: Explorations in the Microstructure of Cognition*, vol. 1, 194–281. Cambridge, Mass.: MIT Press.

Smolensky, P. (1988). "On the Proper Treatment of Connectionism." *Behavioral and Brain Sciences* 11, 1–74.

Song, J.-S. (1989). "Vowel Harmony in Nez Perce and Korean." Master's thesis, University of Ottawa.

Stampe, D. (1979). *A Dissertation on Natural Phonology.* Bloomington, Ind.: Indiana University Linguistics Club.

Stanley, R. (1967). "Redundancy Rules in Phonology." *Language* 43, 393–436.

Steriade, D. (1979). "Vowel Harmony in Khalkha Mongolian." In *MIT Working Papers in Linguistics* 1, 25–50. Department of Linguistics and Philosophy, MIT.

Steriade, D. (1981). "Parameters of Metrical Harmony Rules." Ms., MIT.

Steriade, D. (1982). "Greek Prosodies and the Nature of Syllabification." Doctoral dissertation, MIT.

Steriade, D. (1986a). "Yokuts and the Vowel Plane." *Linguistic Inquiry* 17, 129–46.

Steriade, D. (1986b). "Vowel Tiers and Geminate Blockage." Paper presented at the LSA Winter Meeting.

Steriade, D. (1987a). "Redundant Values." In *Parasession on Autosegmental and Metrical Phonology* 339–62. (Papers from the 23rd Regional Meeting of the Chicago Linguistic Society, Part 2.). Chicago Linguistic Society, University of Chicago.

Steriade, D. (1987b). "Locality Conditions and Feature Geometry." In *Proceedings of NELS 17*, 595–617. GLSA, University of Massachusetts, Amherst.

Steriade, D. (1990). "Closure, Release, and Nasal Contours." Paper presented at Arizona Phonology Conference 3, University of Arizona.

Steriade, D. (1991). "Aperture Positions and Syllable Structure." Paper presented at The Organization of Phonology: Features and Domains Workshop celebrating the 25th Anniversary of the Department of Linguistics, University of Illinois.

Stevens, K., and S. J. Keyser (1989). "Primary Features and Their Enhancement in Consonants." *Language* 65, 81–106.

Stevens, K. N., S. J. Keyser, and H. Kawasaki (1986). "Toward a Phonetic and Phonological Theory of Redundant Features." In J. S. Perkell and D. H. Klatt, eds., *Symposium on Invariance and Variability of Speech Processes*, 426–49. Hillsdale, N.J.: Lawrence Erlbaum Associates.

Stewart, J. M. (1967). "Tongue Root Position in Akan Vowel Harmony." *Phonetica* 16, 185–204.

Stewart, J. M. (1983). "Akan Vowel Harmony: The Word Structure Conditions and the Floating Vowels." *Studies in African Linguistics* 14, 111–39.

Thomas, J. M. C. (1963). *Le parler Ngbaka de Bokanga: Phonologie, morphologie, syntaxe.* Paris: Mouton.

Tranel, B. (1990). "Tone Sandhi and Vowel Deletion in Margi." Ms., University of California, Irvine.

Travis, L. (1984). "Parameters and Effects of Word Order Variation." Doctoral dissertation, MIT.

Trigo, L. (1991). "Scales and Diminutivization." *Linguistic Inquiry* 22, 578–83.

Trubetzkoy, N. S. (1969). *Principles of Phonology.* Berkeley and Los Angeles: University of California Press.

Tucker, A. N., and M. A. Mpaayei (1955). *Linguistic Analyses: The Non-Bantu Languages of North-Eastern Africa.* London: Oxford University Press.

Vago, R. M. (1988). "Underspecification in the Height Harmony System of Pasiego." *Phonology* 5, 343–62.

Valinande, N. (1984). "The Structure of Kinande." Doctoral dissertation, Georgetown University.

Vance, T. (1987). *An Introduction to Japanese Phonology*. Albany, N.Y.: State University of New York Press.

Welmers, W. E. (1973). *African Language Structures*. Berkeley and Los Angeles: University of California Press.

Wescott, R. W. (1965). *Review of J. M. C. Thomas, Le parler Ngbaka de Bokanga: Phonologie, morphologie, syntaxe. Language* 41, 346–47.

Wilbur, R. (1987). *American Sign Language: Linguistic and Applied Dimensions*. 2d ed. Boston: Little, Brown.

Williams, E. S. (1976). "Underlying Tone in Margi and Igbo." *Linguistic Inquiry* 7, 463–84.

Wiswall, W. (1991a)."Tunica Partial Vowel Harmony as Evidence for a Height Node." Paper presented at Arizona Phonology Conference 4, University of Arizona.

Wiswall, W. (1991b). "Partial Vowel Harmonies as Evidence for a Height Node." Doctoral dissertation, University of Arizona.

Woock, E. B., and M. Noonan (1979). "Vowel Harmony in Lango." In *Papers from the 15th Regional Meeting, Chicago Linguistic Society*, 20–29. Chicago Linguistic Society, University of Chicago.

Yip, M. (1980). "The Tonal Phonology of Chinese." Doctoral dissertation, MIT.

Yip, M. (1988a). "Template Morphology and the Direction of Association." *Natural Language & Linguistic Theory* 6, 551–77.

Yip, M. (1988b). "The Obligatory Contour Principle and Phonological Rules: A Loss of Identity." *Linguistic Inquiry* 19, 65–100.

Yip, M. (1989a). "Cantonese Morpheme Structure and Linear Ordering." In *Proceedings of WCCFL* 8, 445–56. Stanford Linguistics Association, Stanford University.

Yip, M. (1989b). "Feature Geometry and Cooccurrence Restrictions." *Phonology* 6, 349–74.

Zemlin, W. R. (1988). *Speech and Hearing Science: Anatomy and Physiology*. Englewood Cliffs, N.J.: Prentice-Hall.

Index